Ius Gentium: Comparative Perspectives on Law and Justice

Volume 74

More information about this series at http://www.springer.com/series/7888

Sabine Gless · Thomas Richter
Editors

Do Exclusionary Rules Ensure a Fair Trial?

A Comparative Perspective on Evidentiary Rules

Springer Open

Editors
Sabine Gless
Juristische Fakultät der Universität Basel
Basel, Switzerland

Thomas Richter
Freiburg im Breisgau, Germany

ISSN 1534-6781 ISSN 2214-9902 (electronic)
Ius Gentium: Comparative Perspectives on Law and Justice
ISBN 978-3-030-12519-6 ISBN 978-3-030-12520-2 (eBook)
https://doi.org/10.1007/978-3-030-12520-2

Library of Congress Control Number: 2019930360

This Springer imprint is published by the registered company Springer Nature Switzerland AG
The registered company address is: Gewerbestrasse 11, 6330 Cham, Switzerland

Acknowledgements

We are grateful to all contributors or their work, commitment, and passion for this project. We studied how exclusionary rules are established in the respective procedural codes and how they are applied in practice, with a focus on case law, and conducted interviews in almost all relevant jurisdictions. We explored the potential of alternative and supplementary means of compelling law enforcement to respect human rights, including criminal sanctions, disciplinary action, and civil liability. Throughout the project, we learned a great deal from each other.

National issues and legal solutions, as well as comparative issues and basic principles, were discussed at two workshops and conferences. The first meeting took place in March 2016 in Taipei, Taiwan, and was co-organized by the Taiwan Ministry of Justice. We are especially grateful to Pauline Tsai for her exceptional support. The second meeting occurred in May 2017 in Basel, Switzerland, and received remarkable financial support from the Sino-Swiss Science and Technology Cooperation Program of the Swiss National Research Foundation.

Major financial funds for this project, including the publication of its results, have been provided by the Swiss National Research Foundation and without it, the project could never have been realized. We are very grateful for the Foundation's generous assistance and enduring support.

Last but not least, we wish to thank MLaw Laura Macula for her meticulous planning and monitoring throughout the project and all her precious advice, stud. iur. Lia Börlin for the time and energy she dedicated to checking references and material, and Claudine Abt for her support in finalizing all the papers for publication.

Basel, Switzerland
November 2018

Sabine Gless
Thomas Richter

Contents

Part II Exclusionary Rules—Quo Vadis

Editors and Contributors

About the Editors

Sabine Gless teaches criminal law, criminal procedure, and international criminal law at the University of Basel, Switzerland. Her research includes comparative work in evidence law and international cooperation with a focus on human rights issues and exclusionary rules.

Thomas Richter served as the Head of the East Asian Department of the Max Planck Institute for Foreign and International Law in Freiburg, Germany. In this capacity, he analyzed the criminal law and criminal procedure law of the People's Republic of China and co-directed a comparative study on non-prosecution policies in Germany and the People's Republic of China. In cooperation with the German Institute for Human Rights (DIMR), he evaluated the Human Rights Dialogue between the People's Republic of China and Switzerland (2006/2007). Most recently, Thomas Richter assessed the Rule of Law Programme for Asia instituted by the Konrad Adenauer Foundation (2013). His research interests include criminal law, human rights law, and environmental law in East and Southeast Asia, especially in China.

Contributors

Chung-Yen Chen University of Tübingen, Tübingen, Germany

Sabine Gless Faculty of Law, University of Basel, Basel, Switzerland

Hock Lai Ho Faculty of Law, National University of Singapore (NUS), Singapore, Singapore

Na Jiang College for Criminal Law Science, Beijing Normal University (BNU 北京师范大学), Beijing, China

Susanne Knickmeier Department of Criminology, Max Planck Institute for Foreign and International Criminal Law, Freiburg, Germany

Rongjie Lan Law School, Southwestern University of Finance and Economics, Chengdu, China

Yu-Hsiung Lin National Taiwan University, Taipei, Taiwan

Laura Macula MLaw, Faculty of Law, University of Basel, Basel, Switzerland

Thomas Richter Freiburg im Breisgau, Germany

Chiou-Ming Tsai Department of International and Cross-Strait Legal Affairs, Ministry of Justice, Taipei, Taiwan

Tsai-Chen Tsai Shihlin District Court, Taipei, Taiwan

Jenia Iontcheva Turner SMU Dedman School of Law, Dallas, USA

Shih-Fan Wang National Taipei University, New Taipei City, Taiwan

Thomas Weigend Faculty of Law, University of Cologne, Cologne, Germany

Weimin Zuo Law School, Sichuan University, Chengdu, China

Abbreviations

ACHR	African Charter of Human Rights of 1981
AG	Aktiengesellschaft (=stock corporation)
AGC	Attorney-General's Chambers
art./arts.	Article/articles
ASEAN	Association of Southeast Asian Nations
ATCom	Committee against Torture
BGE	Bundesgerichtsentscheid (=Decision of the Swiss Supreme Court)
BGer	Bundesgericht (=Swiss Supreme Court)
BGG	Bundesgesetz über das Bundesgericht (=Federal Court Act of 17 June 2005, SR 173.110)
BGH	Bundesgerichtshof (=German Federal Court of Justice)
BGHSt	Entscheidungen des Bundesgerichtshofs in Strafsachen (=Decisions of the German Federal Court of Justice in criminal matters)
BPCs	Basic Peoples' Courts (China)
BVerfG	Bundesverfassungsgericht (=German Federal Constitutional Court)
BVerfGE	Bundesverfassungsgerichtsentscheid (=Decision of the German Federal Constitutional Court)
CAT	UN Convention against Torture and Other Cruel, Inhuman or Degrading Treatment or Punishment of 10 December 1984
CCMS	Criminal Case Management System
CCP	Code of Criminal Procedure
CCR	Criminal Case Resolution
CCRC	Criminal Code of the Republic of China
cf.	Compare
Ch/CH	Swiss/Switzerland
CID	Criminal Investigation Department
cir.	Circle
CL	Criminal Law of 1979, revised in 1997 (China)

co.	Company
col./cols.	Column/columns
consid.	Consideration
CPC	Criminal Procedure Code/Communist Party of China
CPIB	Corruption Practices Investigation Bureau
CPL	Criminal Procedure Law of 1979, revised 1996 and 2012 (China)
CRC	Constitution of the Republic of China
CRC	Convention on the Rights of the Child of 20 November 1989
CSSA	Communication Security and Surveillance Act of 2018
CTDR	Central Task Force of Deepening Reforms
de/DE	German
DNA	Deoxyribonucleic acid
e.g./eg	For example
EA	Evidence Act (Singapore)
ECHR	European Convention on Human Rights of 1950
ECJ	European Court of Justice
ECtHR	European Court of Human Rights
ed./eds.	Editor/editors
EHRR	European Human Rights Reports
et al.	And others
et seq.	And the following
EU	European Union
GC	Grand Chamber
Ger./Germ	Germany
GSSt	Grosser Senat in Strafsachen (Germany)
HPC	High Peoples' Court (China)
HRCom	Human Rights Committee
i.e.	That is
ibid.	In the same place
ICCPR	International Covenant on Civil and Political Rights of 16 December 1966
id.	Same
IPC	Intermediate People's Court
JA	Judge of Appeal
JR	Joint regulation
JYI	Judicial Yuan Interpretations
LAC	Legislative Affairs Commission of the Standing Committee of the National People's Congress
Ltd	Private Limited Company
MOJ	Ministry of Justice
MOPS	Ministry of Public Security

MPs	Members of Parliament
MPS	Ministry of Public Security
MSS	Ministry of State Security
MURUAH	Singapore Human Rights NGO
n.	Note
NGO	Non-governmental organization
NJW	Neue Juristische Wochenschrift (German journal)
no.	Number
NStZ	Neue Zeitschrift für Strafrecht (German journal)
NY	New York
NZZ	Neue Zücher Zeitung (Swiss newspaper)
PACE	Police and Criminal Evidence Act of 1984
para.	Paragraph
PFA	Police Force Act of 2004, revised 2006
PP	Public Prosecutor
PPL	People's Police Law
PPs	People's Procuratorates
PRC	People's Republic of China
ret.	Retired
ROC	Republic of China
ROC	Republik of China (Taiwan)
s./ss.	Section/sections
SC	Supreme Court
SCHR	Swiss Centre of Expertise in Human Rights
SCL	State Compensation Law
sec./secs.	Section
sent.	Sentence
Sing	Singapore
SPC	Supreme People's Court (China)
SPF	Singapore Police Force
SPP	Supreme People's Procuratorate
SR	Systematische Rechtssammlung (=classified compilation of swiss law; https://www.admin.ch/gov/en/start/federal-law/classified-compilation.html)
SSC	Swiss Supreme Court
StPO	Strafprozessordnung (Swiss Criminal Procedure Code of 5 October 2007 (Status as of 1 October 2016), SR 312.0/German Code of Criminal Procedure of 7 April 1987 (Status as of 17 August 2017))
StV	Strafverteidiger (german journal)
Taiw/TW	Taiwan
tbl.	Table
U.S./ US/USA	United States of America
UDHR	Universal Declaration of Human Rights of 1948
UK	United Kingdom

UN	United Nations
UPR	Universal Periodic Review
USC	United States Code
v./vs.	Versus
vol.	Volume

Keywords

Criminal procedure · Comparative criminal law · Exclusionary rules · Fair trial · Torture · Right to silence · Right against self-incrimination · Evidence law · Defense rights

Introduction

Sabine Gless and Thomas Richter

Abstract Criminal justice systems are barometers of social development. This claim, put forward by German criminal law scholars, alludes to the fact that inherent in the criminal justice process are conflicting interests between the need to ensure comprehensive fact-finding on the one hand, and the wish to safeguard individual rights, especially those of defendants, on the other hand. In all criminal justice systems, there exists a strong public interest in determining the truth due to the assertion that a determination of innocence or guilt is based upon "true" facts. This pursuit of "the truth" has led to procedural rules that expose both suspects and witnesses to coercive measures that often interfere with individual rights.

In recent decades, human rights have come to the forefront in criminal justice systems around the world, but at the same time more and more jurisdictions have adopted exclusionary rules. Country reports on Germany, Switzerland, P.R. China, Taiwan, Singapore, and the U.S., along with contributions discussing the rationales behind exclusionary rules, legal practices, or potential alternatives, all address the question of whether, and under what circumstances, the use of exclusionary rules can be an effective means for protecting human rights in criminal proceedings.

1 Criminal Justice as a Barometer of Social Developments

Criminal justice systems are barometers of social development. This claim, put forward by German criminal law scholars,[1] alludes to the fact that inherent in the criminal justice process are conflicting interests between the need to ensure com-

[1] Roxin, 2014 at 9.

S. Gless (✉)
Faculty of Law, University of Basel, Basel, Switzerland
e-mail: Sabine.Gless@unibas.ch

T. Richter
Attorney-at-Law, Freiburg im Breisgau, Germany
e-mail: info@sinojus.eu

S. Gless and T. Richter (eds.), *Do Exclusionary Rules Ensure a Fair Trial?*
Ius Gentium: Comparative Perspectives on Law and Justice 74,
https://doi.org/10.1007/978-3-030-12520-2_1

prehensive fact-finding on the one hand, and the wish to safeguard individual rights, especially those of defendants, on the other hand. In all criminal justice systems, there exists a strong public interest in determining the truth due to the assertion that a determination of innocence or guilt is based upon "true" facts. This pursuit of "the truth" has led to procedural rules that expose both suspects and witnesses to coercive measures that often interfere with individual rights.

Modern day criminal justice systems are designed to not only ensure comprehensive fact-finding, but also protect the human rights of defendants, victims, and witnesses. Individual rights applicable to criminal proceedings include the right to have one's dignity respected, protection from physical force and torture, the right against self-incrimination, and the right to privacy of person and property. Because these rights run counter to authorities' fact finding, they are regularly at risk of being disregarded. As such, preventing human rights violations remains a challenge within criminal procedure law worldwide and the means to do so are limited. A promising method of reducing human rights violations is the exclusion of illegally obtained evidence from trial. The rationale behind these so-called exclusionary rules is the expectation that law enforcement officers will refrain from engaging in unlawful evidence-gathering techniques if they are aware that the physical or testimonial evidence produced will be inadmissible at trial.

Based on the hypothesis that excluding unlawfully obtained evidence is an effective tool for safeguarding human rights in criminal proceedings, the core question of this comparative project is twofold: How can criminal procedure law ensure respect for human rights and what role does the exclusion of illegally obtained evidence actually play in this regard? In order to answer this question in a global context, we investigated three European jurisdictions (Switzerland, Germany, England), three Asian jurisdictions (People's Republic of China [PRC], Taiwan/Republic of China [ROC], Singapore), and the United States. The aim of the study was not to find a single universally applicable model of human rights protection, but to determine features that are conducive to enhancing respect for individual rights in different criminal justice systems.

2 Criminal Trials and Human Rights

In recent decades, human rights have become more prominent in criminal justice systems around the world. This was especially the case following the end of World War II, and, more recently, the Cold War, which essentially divided the world into The East and The West. The right to preserve one's dignity and privacy, to be free from physical coercion and torture, and the right to avoid self-incrimination are paramount in the criminal process. At the same time, these human rights are especially vulnerable to abuse because they tend to conflict with law enforcement's primary goal of obtaining information about potential crimes and because the source of such information is primarily human (suspects, victims, and witnesses). For that reason, human rights require special protection in criminal proceedings.

The current project starts with the hypothesis that a potentially promising way of providing human rights protections is the exclusion of evidence obtained through violation of a procedural right. This hypothesis is tested by analyzing exclusionary rules and, as far as possible, their practical application in different legal and cultural contexts. It is our goal to determine whether the existence and application of exclusionary rules are an effective means to safeguard human rights in the criminal process and, if so, under what circumstances. In order to test our hypothesis, we considered several aspects of criminal procedure: Under what conditions does a given legal system recognize exclusionary rules? What additional or alternative ways does a system provide to hold authorities accountable? Who may challenge the admission of evidence, and, at what stage of the proceedings? The role of defense attorneys is also addressed, along with the extent and means by which a system separates judicial and executive powers in the context of criminal proceedings.

Starting with the adoption of the "*Déclaration des droits de l'homme et du citoyen*" by the leaders of the French Revolution at the end of the 18th century, the concept of human rights has continued to be a part of the identity of European countries.[2] In North America, libertarian ideals and the notion of inherent human rights led to the independence movement, culminating with the adoption of the United States Constitution and its first ten amendments (The Bill of Rights). Based on the philosophical views of the Enlightenment and the idealism of the early 19th century, the Western concept of human rights emphasized the applicability of such rights to every human being regardless of the law in the person's state of residence. The promise of human rights, the propagation of the rule of law, and progress in the area of civil liberties is a recurring theme in modern criminal justice systems.

That said, East Asian and Western states have not yet developed a similar understanding of what basic individual human rights entails. Based, amongst other things, on Confucian traditions of thinking, the emphasis in Asian states has been on the collective (family and state) rather than the autonomy and rights of the individual. In the past, Chinese politicians have denounced the Western concept of protecting human rights as an ideological tool for justifying intervention in the internal affairs of East Asian states.[3] In the People's Republic of China (PRC), the traditional priority of collective interests was reinforced by the influence of Marxist political thought, which simultaneously minimized the importance of individual interests relative to those of the collective.[4] Recent research suggests that the

[2]The European Court of Justice (ECJ) has referred to human rights as the value system common to all EU member states, ECJ judgment of 13 December 1979, Hauer v Land Rheinland-Pfalz, C-44/79, § 15.

[3]For the implications on the understanding of human rights in criminal proceedings, *see*, for example, Jiang, 2013 at 745 et seq.

[4]Information Office of the State or China's Cabinet, White Paper on Progress in China's Human Rights in 2012, Beijing May 2013 <http://news.xinhuanet.com/english/china/2013-05/14/c_132380706.htm>, accessed 19 November 2018; Freeman/Geeraerts, BICCS at 7 et seq.

Chinese public still holds this view.[5] Similarly, in Singapore, former Prime Minister Lee Kuan Yew emphasized the importance of Asian values, including the notion that the individual cannot claim individual rights separate from the family, which is considered to be an integral part of the society.[6]

This difference between the East and the West in the understanding of individual rights, and in particular human rights, has long been observed by legal scholars.[7] In recent years, however, there has been a distinct trend toward a universalization of certain human rights as well as globally recognized standards for the protection of human rights.[8]

Many Asian states, including the PRC, have joined major international human rights treaties, such as the International Covenant on Civil and Political Rights (ICCPR) which grants specific procedural rights in criminal proceedings. Additionally, the Member States of The Association of Southeast Asian Nations (ASEAN) executed a regional human rights instrument in 2012.[9] As a consequence of the growing prominence of human rights, the domestic laws of some jurisdictions, including Vietnam[10] and the Republic of China (ROC),[11] have been amended to expressly guarantee such rights. Despite this trend, while the PRC signed the ICCPR, it has neither ratified the Covenant nor incorporated it into national law. After a long debate, Art. 33 para. 3 of the PRC Constitution was amended in 2004 to read that "the State respects and protects human rights." In 2012, a similar reference to the "respect and protection of human rights" was inserted in Art. 2 of the PRC Criminal Procedure Code (PRC-CPC) and described to be one of several reasons for the newly revised Code. Although these changes to written law may not have a discernible effect upon daily law enforcement in the PRC, they represent a major shift towards official recognition of individual human rights. They may also signify a move away from the strict adherence to Eastern values, which, historically, have afforded limited protections for individuals.

[5]Freeman/Geeraerts, 2011 at 25–26.

[6]See Zakaria, Fareed, *A Conversation with Lee Kuan Yew*, Foreign Affairs March/April 1994. *See also* Elgin, 2010 at 138.

[7]*See*, for example, Steiner/Alston/Goodman, 2008.

[8]*See* Parlett, 2011; Klabbers/Peters/Ulfstein, 2012; Peters, 2006.

[9]The ASEAN Human Rights Declaration was adopted by Brunei, Cambodia, Indonesia, Laos, Malaysia, Myanmar, the Philippines, Singapore, Thailand and Vietnam on 18 November 2012; <https://asean.org/asean-human-rights-declaration/>, accessed 19 November 2018.

[10]For Vietnam, *see* Nguyen, 2009 at 1 et seq.

[11]Human rights law in Taiwan is primarily domestic law because the United Nations has decided to recognize the representatives of the Government of the PRC as "the only lawful representatives of China to the UN" (UN Resolution 2758 (XXVI) of 1971) and have thus excluded the ROC from official participation in UN organizations.

3 Exclusionary Rules as Safeguards

Inherent in criminal procedure is the conflict between the state's interest in determining the facts relevant to a suspect's guilt (and potential sentence) and the interests of the other parties (i.e. the accused, witnesses, victims). The state's pursuit of "the truth" has led to the adoption of procedural rules that expose suspects and witnesses to coercive measures. In some jurisdictions this takes the form of a legal obligation to tell the truth when questioned. The recognition of human rights for suspects and witnesses, particularly the right to remain silent, clearly conflicts with the state's interest in fact finding. Therefore, the potential for state agents to disregard individual human rights in pursuit of "the truth" is a real risk. Preventing human rights violations in the context of criminal procedure thus remains an ongoing challenge and the means available for preventing such violations are limited. Legal prohibitions on torture and other human rights violations, as well as the threat of criminal sanctions and disciplinary measures, may help but are often ineffective due to issues of evidentiary proof and enforcement. The same problem is true where civil damages are offered as a potential remedy.

A more promising means of preventing human rights violations is the exclusion of illegally obtained evidence at trial. If, for example, a police officer has unlawfully coerced a suspect's confession, the confession and, if *the fruit of the poisonous tree* doctrine is followed, subsequent evidence found on the basis of this confession, all become inadmissible at trial. The rationale behind this rule is the expectation that law enforcement will refrain from engaging in such methods if they know that the resulting physical and testimonial evidence will be excluded. The effectiveness of this incentive-based approach has been challenged on the basis of limited applicability. For example, in cases where a defendant pleads to a charge and is convicted without a trial, as is the case in many jurisdictions, the opportunity to exclude illegally obtained evidence may be limited. Moreover, using the exclusion of evidence as a remedy for human rights violations raises other important questions. Is it acceptable to release an offender who would otherwise be convicted because a police officer has violated a procedural rule? What about the interests of the community and, in particular, of the victim(s)? Should the exclusionary rule also be applied where there was a violation, but the officer acted in good faith? And what should the rule be if illegally obtained evidence, such as a confession obtained under the threat of torture, leads to crucial evidence, like the body of a victim? All of these questions are difficult to answer, particularly where the underlying rationale of the exclusionary rule is not clear: Is the exclusion of evidence meant to discipline police and prosecutors? Is it a means of protecting the integrity of court proceedings? Does exclusion ensure that the trial court does not consider inherently unreliable evidence? Or is the purpose to protect human rights?

In spite of these controversial issues, many Western legal systems have followed the United States and adopted a variant of the exclusionary rule with the hope of curbing procedural violations intended to protect individual human rights. Some

East Asian jurisdictions have also followed suit and enacted legislation requiring courts to reject evidence obtained through torture or other illicit means.

4 Comparative Perspectives on Exclusionary Rules

The first part of this project entails a comparison of exclusionary rules and their application in three Asian jurisdictions (PRC, JIANG Na, see also ZUO Weimin/ LAN Rongjie; Taiwan, LIN Yu-Hsiung/WANG Shih-Fan/CHEN Chung-Yen/ TSAI Tsai-Chen/TSAI Chiou-Ming; Singapore, HO Hock Lai) and three Western jurisdictions (Switzerland, Laura MACULA; Germany, Thomas WEIGEND; U.S. Jenia Iontcheva TURNER). The jurisdictions tend to diverge, not along geographical lines, but rather by legal heritage. There is the common law tradition of the adversarial system (e.g., Singapore, the U.S., England and Wales), the European continental "inquisitorial" system (e.g., Germany, Switzerland, and France), and "mixed systems" (PRC, ROC) all represented in our sample. The project covers a broad selection of legal systems where we can see exclusionary rules at work, and from which we can learn about the possibilities of alternative mechanisms for ensuring compliance with legal rules.

The six country reports cover the relevant legal framework. While each legal system provides for the exclusion of evidence obtained in violation of certain rules, each has its own distinct approach. The two continental European jurisdictions differ in legislative technique: *Switzerland* has adopted a blanket statute calling for the exclusion of some (but not all) illegally obtained evidence in a single stand-alone provision.[12] By contrast, *Germany*'s procedural code contains few explicit rules, which leaves the decision of exclusion to be made on a case-by-case basis, and primarily by the courts.[13] While *England* has adopted a statute governing

---

[12]The Swiss Criminal Procedure Code outlaws torture in Art. 140 para 1 and requires all authorities to treat fairly everyone involved in criminal proceedings (Art. 3 para 2). Art. 141 CH-CPC declares in absolute terms that any evidence acquired through torture or other undue coercion is inadmissible, but grants the trial court discretion when other procedural rules have been violated.

[13]German criminal procedural law recognizes the right to a fair trial and prohibits the use of torture and coercion in any interrogation of a suspect or witness (§§ 136a, 69 sec. 3 Code of Criminal Procedure, DE-CCP). There is no general rule prohibiting the use of illegally obtained evidence, but statements made after prohibited means of interrogation have been used cannot be used as evidence (§ 136a sec. Art. 3 DE-CCP). With respect to most other violations of procedural rules or human rights, the DE-CCP does not explicitly provide for exclusion and courts follow a case-by-case approach. In recent years, the Federal Constitutional Court has shown an increased readiness to exclude illegally obtained evidence, especially where law enforcement authorities had intentionally violated the suspect's rights or applicable procedural rules. See, for example, German *Bundesverfassungsgericht* of 12/04/2005–2 BvR 1027/02, 113 Entscheidungen des Bundesverfassungsgerichts 29 (2005).

the exclusion of certain evidence, it is not comprehensive.[14] The assumption across European states is that every legal system seeks to protect human rights in criminal proceedings. It is this common attitude that is the reason there has not been an in-depth analysis of the impact of these legislative differences to date.[15]

The Criminal Procedure Code of the PRC (PRC-CPC, 中华人民共和国刑事诉讼法) dates back to 1979 but underwent a major reform in 1996. After proclamation of the People's Republic in 1949 and rejection of all former legislation of the Republic of China (founded in 1911), it was the first code of criminal procedure in its history. The original version of the Code emphasized strict enforcement of the law and the language alluded to a strong stance against crime. Confronted with frequent international and domestic criticism of illegally coerced confessions and torture in criminal proceedings,[16] the Supreme People's Court, the Supreme People's Procuratorate, and the Ministry of Public Security adopted the Rules Concerning Questions about Exclusion of Illegal Evidence in Handling Criminal Cases (2010 Exclusionary Rules).[17] A thorough revision of the PRC-CPC culminated in an amended version of the Code, which was passed in 2012. This updated version of the Code was intended to better protect the human rights of defendants. For example, Art. 50 PRC-CPC grants the right against self-incrimination and Art. 54 PRC-CPC provides for the exclusion of statements obtained by illegal means, particularly by torture. However, the PRC-CPC does not acknowledge the *fruit of the poisonous tree* doctrine and, as a result, secondary evidence obtained through torture or other illegal means remains admissible at trial.[18] The breadth of this exclusionary rule as interpreted by Chinese prosecutors and courts has yet to be seen.

Taiwan's Code of Criminal Procedure (TW-CCP, 刑事訴訟法)[19] dates back to a statute of the Republic of China (ROC) adopted in 1928 and has been revised many

[14]Torture is implicitly barred by Code of Practice C for the *Detention, Treatment and Questioning of Persons by Police Officers* made under s. 66 *Police and Criminal Evidence Act* 1984 (PACE), which sets minimum standards of treatment and specifies procedural and welfare rights. Under s. 76(2)(a) PACE, the court must exclude a confession if the defendant asserts that it was obtained by oppression and the prosecution fails to demonstrate that this was not the case. Oppression is partially defined as including "torture or inhuman or degrading treatment". Although the English courts are tolerant of the enhanced psychological pressure experienced by a suspect under interrogation (*Holgate-Mohammed* v *Duke* [1984] A.C. 437; *Fulling* [1987] 2 All E.R. 65; *Heaton* [1993] Crim L.R. 593), extensive hectoring or bullying of a suspect will be treated as oppression (*Paris, Abdullahi, Miller*) [1992], 97 Cr.App.R. 99). Additionally, under s. 78 PACE, the court has discretionary power to exclude any prosecution evidence where, having regard to the circumstances in which the evidence was obtained, the admission of the evidence would have an adverse effect on the fairness of the trial.

[15]Thaman, 2013; Jackson/Summers, 2012.

[16]*See* He/He, 2013 at 73 et seq.

[17]Rosenzweig et al., 2013 at 466–467.

[18]Jiang, 2013 at 746.

[19]For an English translation (dating from 2007) see: <http://law.moj.gov.tw/Eng/LawClass/LawContent.aspx?PCODE=C0010001>, accessed 19 November 2018.

times.[20] In 2003, a number of Western ideas were integrated into Taiwanese criminal procedure[21] and an increase in awareness of human rights has shaped the rules around evidence gathering. For example, section 156 para. 1 TW-CCP[22] stipulates that only confessions "of an accused not extracted by violence, threat, inducement, fraud, exhausting interrogation, unlawful detention or other improper means and consistent with facts may be admitted as evidence." The protection against involuntary self-incrimination is guaranteed through provisions on the admissibility of confessions.[23] In 2009, Taiwan incorporated the ICCPR into domestic law,[24] thus requiring all law enforcement personnel to adhere to international standards. Some new rules, such as the rules on exclusion of evidence,[25] mirror those found in continental Europe.[26]

By contrast, in Singapore there is no explicit constitutional prohibition of torture, nor is there a constitutional provision on the exclusion of illegally obtained evidence. However, Section 258(3) of the Criminal Procedure Code, read together with Explanation 1, renders inadmissible any statement by an accused obtained through "inducement, threat or promise" or by oppression. Section 258(3) does not cover all cases of illegally obtained evidence and it does not apply where the evidence is anything other than a statement (i.e. physical evidence). Whether the judicial power of exclusion extends beyond cases covered by Section 258(3) remains a contentious matter. However, in recent years the Singapore courts have narrowed the scope of exclusionary discretion,[27] thus sacrificing the protection of individual liberties for the state's interest in convicting wrongdoers.

[20]*See* He, 2011 at 172 et seq.

[21]*See* Lin, 2003 at 224 et seq.

[22]*See* Lin, 2013 at 190–195.

[23]*See*, for example, § 156 para 3–4 TW-CCP.

[24]*See* Liao, 2009 at 223 et seq.

[25]§§ 156, 158–2, 158–4 TW-CCP.

[26]*See* Art. 141 CH-CCP.

[27]In 1964, the majority in Cheng Swee Tiang v PP acknowledged the existence of a broad and general discretion to exclude unlawfully obtained evidence. This discretion was to be exercised on a case-by-case basis by balancing "the interest of the individual to be protected from illegal invasions of his liberties" against "the interest of the State to secure evidence bearing upon the commission of crime and necessary to enable justice to be done shall not be withheld from the courts on any merely technical ground". The existence of this exclusionary power was put in doubt by the decision in the 2007 case of Law Society of Singapore v Tan Guat Neo Phyllis. In Muhammad bin Kadar v PP, the Court clarified that a general discretion does exist but held that the discretion was available only where the prejudicial effect of the wrongfully obtained evidence exceeds its probative value.

5 Core Issues Surrounding the Effectiveness of Exclusionary Rules

The reports included in this publication address the question whether, and under what circumstances, the use of exclusionary rules is an effective means for protecting human rights in criminal proceedings. We started with the hypothesis that the exclusion of illegally obtained evidence could potentially be an effective tool for ensuring that certain human rights are respected in criminal proceedings. Given that the starting point for any legal comparison is the law itself,[28] an analysis of the existing legal rules in the selected jurisdictions was needed to test our hypothesis, which was done via individual country reports.

In the interest of comprehensiveness, our study sought to look beyond the law to its application. If the primary goal is the protection of human rights, states need not only establish the corresponding legal framework, but also incentivize law enforcement to abide by such provisions. Cultural values appear to heavily influence a number of criminal justice systems, particularly those that place a strong emphasis on confessions, presumably as a result of the societal belief in the importance of admitting wrongdoing and experiencing regret. In such systems, the desire to extract a suspect's confession may override any concern that the confession could later be deemed inadmissible.[29] Importantly, the efficiency of criminal justice systems is affected by aspects outside the law, including tolerance of abuse by state authorities and support of state authority over civil rights. In the current study an effort was made to consider relevant cultural norms, as well as the social roles of the police, prosecutors, and the courts.

One defining feature of our project is its emphasis on social and inter-cultural discourse, which are directly linked to the overarching debate of whether human rights are universal or culturally-relative. By studying human rights protections in criminal procedure within selected European, American, and Asian jurisdictions, we sought to highlight the extent to which the effective protection of suspect and witnesses' rights has been recognized as a necessity in both the East and the West, and how it is linked to the implementation of exclusionary rules. This analysis is covered in five topical chapters: *The Purposes and Functions of Exclusionary Rules: A Comparative Overview* (Jenia Iontcheva TURNER and Thomas WEIGEND), *Exclusionary Rule of Illegal Evidence in China: Observation from Historical and Empirical Perspectives* (ZUO Weimin and LAN Rongjie), *The Fair Trial Rationale for Excluding Wrongfully Obtained Evidence* (HO Hock Lai), *Securing a fair trial through exclusionary rules: Do theory and practice form a well-balance whole?* (Susanne KNICKMEIER) and *Exclusionary Rules—Is it Time for Change?* (Sabine GLESS and Laura MACULA).

[28] *See*, for example, Ellis, 2011 at 971.

[29] *See* He/He, 2013 at 73 et seq.

References

Books

Jackson, John D. / Summers, Sarah J., *The Internationalisation of Criminal Evidence, Beyond the Common Law and Civil Law Traditions*, Cambridge 2012. [Jackson/Summers, 2012]

Klabbers, Jan / Peters, Anne / Ulfstein, Geir, *The Constitutionalization of International Law*, Oxford 2012. [Klabbers/Peters/Ulfstein, 2012]

Lin, Yu-Hsiung (林鈺雄), *刑事訴訟法上冊* (*Criminal Procedure Law (I)*) 7th edition, Taipei 2013. [Lin, 2013]

Parlett, Kate, *The Individual in the International Legal System: Continuity and Change in International Law*, Cambridge 2011. [Parlett, 2011]

Roxin, Claus/Schünemann, Bernd, *Strafverfahrensrecht*, 28. Aufl., München 2014. [Roxin, 2014]

Steiner, Henry J. / Alston, Philip / Goodman, Ryan, *International Human Rights in Context: Law, Politics, Morals*, 3rd ed., Oxford 2008. [Steiner/Alston/Goodman, 2008]

Journal Articles

Elgin, Molly, 'Asian Values: A New Model for Development?', (2010) *Southeast Asia*, 135–145 [Elgin, 2010]

Freeman, Duncan / Geeraerts, Gustaaf, 'Europe, China and Expectations for Human Rights', (2011) 4 *The Chinese Journal of International Politics*, 179–203 [Freeman/Geeraerts, 2011]

Freeman, Duncan / Geeraerts, Gustaaf, 'Europe, China and the expectations for human rights', Brussels Institute of Contemporary China Studies (BICCS) *Asia Paper Vol.* 5 (1), 7–31. [Freeman/Geeraerts, BICCS]

He, Lai-Jier (何賴傑), 論刑事訴訟法之傳承與變革–從我國與德國晚近刑事訴訟法修法談起 ('Continuity and Reform in Criminal Procedure–Discussion about recent revisions of Criminal Procedure Law in Taiwan and Germany'), (2011) 100 *Taiwan Jurist*, 172–183. [He, 2011]

Jiang, Na 'The Presumption of Innocence and Illegally Obtained Evidence: Lessons from Wrongful Convictions in China?', (2013) 43 *Hong Kong Law Journal*, 745–769. [Jiang, 2013]

Peters, Anne, 'Compensatory Constitutionalism. The Function and Potential of Fundamental International Norms and Structures' (2006) 19 *Leiden Journal of International Law*, 579–610. [Peters, 2006]

Contributions to Edited Volumes and Annotated Law

Ellis, Jaye, 'General Principles and Comparative Law', (2011) 20 *European Journal of International Law*, 949–971. [Ellis, 2011]

He, Jiahong / He, Ran, 'Wrongful Convictions and Tortured Confessions: Empirical Studies in Mainland China', in: McConville, M. / Pils E. (eds.), *Comparative Perspectives on Criminal Justice in China*, Cheltenham 2013, 73–90. [He/He, 2013]

Liao, Fu-Te (廖福特), 批准聯合國兩個人權公約及制訂施行法之評論 ('Comments on the Two Ratified United Nations Covenants on Human Rights and the Enforcement Act'), (2009) 174 *The Taiwan Law Review*, 223–229. [Liao, 2009]

Lin, Yu-Hsiung (林鈺雄), 鳥瞰2003年1月刑事訴訟法之修法, ('A Summary about the Code of Criminal Procedure Amendment in January 2003'), (2003) 45 *Taiwan Law Journal* (*台灣法學雜誌*), 224–246. [Lin, 2003]

Nguyen, Thi Thuy, 'Criminal Justice Reform in Viet Nam. Achievement and Lesson' in: (2009) ASEAN Law Association 10th General Assembly, 1–5. [Nguyen, 2009]

Rosenzweig, Joshua / Sapio, Flora / Jiang, Jue / Teng, Biao / Pils, Eva 'The 2012 Revision of the Chinese Criminal Procedure Law: (Mostly) Old Wine in New Bottles', in: McConville, M. / Pils E. (eds.), *Comparative Perspectives on Criminal Justice in China*, Cheltenham 2013, 405–503. [Rosenzweig et al., 2013]

Thaman, Stephen C., 'Balancing Truth Against Human Rights: A Theory of Modern Exclusionary Rules', in: Thaman, St. C. (ed.), *Exclusionary Rules in Comparative Law*, Heidelberg 2013, 403–443. [Thaman, 2013]

Sabine Gless holds a chair for criminal law, criminal procedure, and international criminal law at the University of Basel, Switzerland. Her research includes comparative work in evidence law and international cooperation with a focus on human rights issues, procedural safeguards, and in particular exclusionary rules.

Thomas Richter served as the Head of the East Asian Department of the Max Planck Institute for Foreign and International Law in Freiburg, Germany. In this capacity, he analyzed the criminal law and criminal procedure law of the People's Republic of China and co-directed a comparative study on non-prosecution policies in Germany and the People's Republic of China. In cooperation with the German Institute for Human Rights (DIMR), he evaluated the Human Rights Dialogue between the People's Republic of China and Switzerland (2006/2007). Most recently, Thomas Richter assessed the Rule of Law Programme for Asia instituted by the Konrad Adenauer Foundation (2013). His research interests include criminal law, human rights law, and environmental law in East and South-East Asia, especially in China.

Part I
Comparative Perspectives

The Potential to Secure a Fair Trial Through Evidence Exclusion: A Swiss Perspective

Laura Macula

Abstract Swiss criminal procedure has a strong inquisitorial tradition and its primary purpose is the search for the "material truth." However, authorities are neither obliged nor allowed to search for this truth at any cost and are limited by procedural rules, which also serve to protect a defendant from the authorities. One possible means of enforcing such procedural rules is the exclusion of improperly obtained evidence. In Switzerland, the legislature established explicit provisions around the collection of evidence and its admissibility in criminal proceedings by adopting art. 139–141 of the Criminal Procedure Code in 2011. This is a comprehensive statutory regulation that is unique in Europe. Nevertheless, the Swiss Supreme Court continues to find ways to preserve its own power over the admission of evidence and often errs on the side of admitting evidence. With a focus on this tension between the legal framework and the jurisprudence of the Supreme Court, the Swiss country report describes the relevant legal framework, phases of the criminal process, and the relevant parties to criminal proceedings. Also discussed in detail are the current regulations as well as the Supreme Court's case law on exclusionary rules. An assessment of the potential for such rules to safeguard individual rights and prevent improper evidence acquisition is a focus of the paper.

1 Introduction

It was not until 2011 that a unified Swiss criminal procedure code amalgamated the legal framework for criminal trials in the 26 cantons of Switzerland. Bringing together different legal traditions of continental Europe, Swiss criminal procedure is characterized by legal scholars as inquisitorial. This assessment corresponds with a traditional focus on searching for the "material truth" (or, what actually happened)[1]

[1]Schmid, 2017 at § 1 no. 7.

L. Macula (✉)
MLaw, University of Basel, Basel, Switzerland
e-mail: Laura.Macula@unibas.ch

S. Gless and T. Richter (eds.), *Do Exclusionary Rules Ensure a Fair Trial?*
Ius Gentium: Comparative Perspectives on Law and Justice 74,
https://doi.org/10.1007/978-3-030-12520-2_2

as the primary aim of criminal proceedings.[2] Today, however, the search for truth is neither an absolute goal in the Swiss criminal justice system nor do police, prosecutors, or courts have unlimited powers.[3] Rather, present-day legislation acknowledges the competing interests of the State and the individuals involved and appreciates a need for them to be balanced on a case-by-case basis via legislation and, more specifically, law enforcement authorities and courts. Accordingly, Swiss criminal proceedings are characterised by formal requirements that seek to ensure a fair trial while also safeguarding individual rights and preventing abuses of power by the authorities.[4] According to the theory espoused in legal texts, exclusionary rules play an important role in establishing this balance by banning the use of illegally obtained evidence and enforcing limitations in criminal proceedings.[5] However, the exclusion of evidence also poses a constraint on the establishment of the material truth.[6] Thus, by defining formal requirements and individual rights in criminal procedure, the legislature determines the cost of finding the material truth[7]—at least in theory.

The first Swiss Criminal Procedure Code (CPC)[8] explicitly stipulates exclusionary rules in art. 141, which establishes a far-reaching and relatively comprehensive legal regime.[9] These largely clear-cut rules represent a new approach since they have significantly reduced the amount of judicial discretion allowed relative to the prior cantonal regime. Before the advent of the CPC, the Swiss Supreme Court (SSC) made decisions around the admissibility of evidence by balancing competing interests on a case-by-case basis[10] and often admitted illegally obtained evidence in pursuit of the material truth.[11] In a 2007 case (prior to the implementation of the CPC), the Court rejected *strict* exclusion of indirect evidence on the ground that the acquittal of an obviously guilty defendant would be "disturbing" ("stossend").[12]

---

[2] *See e.g.*, Gless/Martin, 2015 at 164 with further references.

[3] Wohlers in Donatsch et al., 2014 at art. 6 no. 2 with further references.

[4] Keller, 2011 at 231.

[5] Oberholzer, 2012 at no. 695.

[6] Wohlers in Donatsch et al., 2014 at art. 6 no. 2.

[7] Keller, 2011 at 231 et seq.

[8] Schweizerische Strafprozessordnung (StPO), officially translated as Swiss Criminal Procedure Code (CPC) of 5 October 2007 (Status as of 1 October 2016), SR 312.0, available online at <https://www.admin.ch/opc/en/classified-compilation/20052319/index.html>, accessed 22 November 2018.

[9] With exceptions, *see* below 3.1.3.

[10] Wohlers/Bläsi, 2015 at 160.

[11] Keller, 2011 at 234 with further references; *see also* below 3.1.3 and 3.2.5.2.

[12] Entscheidungen des Schweizerischen Bundesgerichts (BGE) 133 IV 329, consideration (consid.) 4.5; the decisions of the Swiss Supreme Court are available online at <http://www.bger.ch/index/juridiction/jurisdiction-inherit-template/jurisdiction-recht.htm>, accessed 22 November 2018.

Even after the CPC was put into place, the Supreme Court has continued to rule in favor of admitting illegally obtained evidence.[13]

With a focus on this tension between the legal framework in the CPC and the jurisprudence of the Swiss Supreme Court, this report seeks to:

- explain the fundamental principles, stages, and actors in Swiss criminal proceedings;
- detail the present regulation in the CPC as well as the Swiss Supreme Court's case law on exclusionary rules;
- assess the potential of those exclusionary rules to safeguard individual rights and to prevent torture and improper compulsion in particular.

2 Establishing Facts in Swiss Criminal Proceedings

2.1 Legal Framework and Relevant Actors

2.1.1 General Rules

Until 2011, Switzerland, a country of approximately eight million inhabitants, had 26 diverse[14] cantonal criminal procedure codes, three federal codes of military law,[15] laws around administrative criminal procedure,[16] and laws around federal criminal procedure.[17] The different cantonal codes, as well as the Swiss legal system in general, were significantly influenced by the German and the French legal systems due to the various German-speaking and Francophone parts of the country. The Swiss cantonal codes thus embodied diverse components of continental European legal traditions.[18]

This fragmented regulation of criminal procedure necessitated the criminal justice system be flexible enough to accommodate the various legal regimes. The cantonal and federal legislature assured this flexibility by leaving considerable discretion to law enforcement authorities.[19] The Federal CPC, which came into

[13]Schweizerisches Bundesgericht (Swiss Supreme Court, BGer) 6B_684/2012 of 15 May 2013; BGE 138 IV 169; Wohlers/Bläsi, 2015 at 169.

[14]Ruckstuhl et al., 2011 at no. 59.

[15]Militärstrafgesetz of 13 June 1927 (Status as of 1 January 2017), SR 321.0, available online at <https://www.admin.ch/opc/de/classified-compilation/19270018/index.html>, accessed 22 November 2018.

[16]Bundesgesetz über die Bundesstrafrechtspflege of 15 June 1934, SR 312.0, invalidated.

[17]Bundesgesetz über das Verwaltungsstrafrecht of 22 March 1974 (Status as of 1 Oktober 2016), SR 313.0, available online at <https://www.admin.ch/opc/de/classified-compilation/19740066/index.html>; accessed 22 November 2018.

[18]Gless/Martin, 2015 at 160.

[19]Gless/Martin, 2015 at 160.

effect in January 2011, represents the effort to unify and harmonize all of the different cantonal criminal procedure codes. Its primary goal is not to accommodate different regional traditions, rather it is to create nation-wide consistency in criminal law and procedure, and promote uniform and efficient enforcement of those laws.[20] Accordingly, the CPC of 2011 established a stricter legal framework compared to the former cantonal procedure codes, and particularly so for exclusionary rules.[21] Currently, a further reform of selected articles of the CPC is being planned.[22]

2.1.1.1 Duties in Criminal Investigations

Swiss criminal procedure is rooted in the inquisitorial tradition with the primary purpose of searching for the material truth. At least in theory, the proceedings aim to create a "precise reproduction of the historical incidents"[23] and convict and punish defendants only for the acts or omissions for which he or she is responsible.[24] The inquisitorial principle, explicitly laid out in art. 6 CPC, commits all prosecution authorities (police, public prosecution),[25] as well as the courts[26] to establish all relevant facts in the assessment of an alleged criminal offense in addition to an evaluation of the accused's personal situation. Different from adversarial systems, authorities in Swiss criminal proceedings act *ex officio*—regardless of the parties' conduct and requests.[27] As art. 6 (2) CPC stipulates, the authorities must investigate all circumstances—exculpatory and incriminatory—with equal care, requiring them to keep an open mind throughout the investigation.

If prosecution authorities fail to comply with art. 6 CPC, the relevant evidence must be "re-taken" and presented to the appellate court where possible. If this is not feasible, the failure to do so cannot be interpreted to the detriment of the defendant.[28] On the contrary, the presumption of innocence (art. 10 (1) CPC) and the principle *in dubio pro reo* ("when in doubt, for the accused," art. 10 (3) CPC) impose the burden of proof on the prosecution. It is their duty not only to investigate, but to *prove* all circumstances creating criminal liability. This duty is limited by art. 139 (2) CPC, which states that "no evidence shall be led on matters that are irrelevant, obvious, known to the criminal justice authority or already adequately

[20] Keller, 2011 at 230.

[21] Gless/Martin, 2015 at 161.

[22] <https://www.bj.admin.ch/bj/de/home/sicherheit/gesetzgebung/aenderungstpo.html>, accessed 22 November 2018.

[23] Keller, 2011 at 230.

[24] Schmid, 2017 at § 1 no. 7.

[25] Spelled out in detail in art. 306 et seq. and 308 et seq. CPC; *see* below 2.1.3.1 and 2.1.4.

[26] Spelled out in detail in art. 343 CPC; *see* below 2.1.3.1 and 2.1.4.

[27] Art. 6 (1) CPC; Schmid, 2017 at § 9 no. 154.

[28] Wohlers in Donatsch et al., 2014 at art. 6 no. 10 et seq.

proven in law."[29] Where this evidentiary duty cannot be fulfilled or insurmountable doubts as to the defendant's guilt persist, the court must base its decision on the circumstances that are most favorable to the defendant and, where necessary, acquit.[30] The court, however, has wide discretion in this regard; art. 10 (2) CPC provides that the court shall assess all available evidence in accordance with the opinions it has formed throughout the entire course of the proceedings. Consequently, in Swiss criminal proceedings, there is no ranking order for evidence; as long as all evidence is gathered lawfully, each piece can be relevant. The weight of any one piece of evidence depends on how persuasive the court finds it to be.[31] Importantly, the court's decision, including the assessment of evidence, has to be objective, transparent and comprehensible.[32] Indeed, the aim of art. 10 (2) CPC is to avoid the arbitrary assessment of evidence while simultaneously fulfilling the principles of the inquisitorial system. The rationale behind this provision is that judgments are more likely to be based on the material truth if the court is not bound by rigid evidentiary rules and is free to form an opinion based on the entire proceeding.[33]

2.1.1.2 Securing a Fair Trial

The general principle of a fair trial, both in Swiss law and elsewhere, finds its origin in a variety of legal principles. Firstly, it is binding as a general principle of international law imposed by art. 6 (1) of the European Convention on Human Rights (ECHR)[34] and art. 10 and 14 (1) of the International Covenant on Civil and Political Rights, Part II[35] (ICCPR II).[36] Second, it has been expressly codified in Swiss law in art. 29 (1) of the new Federal Constitution of 1999[37] and in art. 3 (2) lit. c of the new CPC.[38] Article 3 (2) lit. c CPC explicitly stipulates that all persons involved in criminal proceedings should be treated equally and fairly and should be granted the right to be heard.

---

[29]Gless in Niggli et al., 2014 at art. 139 no. 31; *see* below 2.1.4.

[30]Pieth, 2016 at 55 et seq.; *also* BGE 124 IV 88 consid. 2.a.

[31]Schmid, 2017 at § 13 no. 229; Pieth, 2016 at 186.

[32]Pieth, 2016 at 186 with further references.

[33]Schmid, 2017 at § 13 no. 225.

[34]European Convention for the Protection of Human Rights and Fundamental Freedoms of 4 November 1950, available online at <http://www.echr.coe.int/Documents/Convention_ENG.pdf>, accessed 22 November 2018.

[35]Second Optional Protocol to the International Covenant on Civil and Political Rights of 16 December 1966, available online at <http://www.ohchr.org/Documents/ProfessionalInterest/ccpr.pdf>, accessed 22 November 2018.

[36]Brun, 2015 at 55 with further references.

[37]Swiss Federal Constitution of 18 April 1999 (Status as of 12 February 2017), SR 101, available online at <https://www.admin.ch/opc/de/classified-compilation/19995395/index.html>, accessed 22 November 2018.

[38]Schmid, 2017 at § 6 no. 95.

The principle of a fair trial does not ensure that the outcome of the proceedings reflects what actually happened (i.e. the material truth), but it attempts to safeguard the fairness of the procedure itself. Although this may result in the finding of the material truth, that is not always the case.[39] The concept of a "fair trial" is broad and, as a result, its core meaning can be difficult to grasp.[40] In practice, however, the principle of a fair trial encompasses a number of specific objectives. It addresses compliance with procedural rules[41] (which is of particular importance in criminal proceedings)[42] and requires that the parties to the proceedings be treated as "subjects rather than objects." In other words, the right to a fair trial guarantees that the parties be given the opportunity to influence the proceedings (and, therefore, the outcome), and to be able to effectively exercise their individual rights. The principle can be understood more concretely through the individual procedural rights of the parties, although it represents more than just a summation of those rights.[43]

The individual rights and procedural guarantees that comprise the general principle of a fair trial are detailed in different provisions of the CPC, namely the right to an independent and impartial tribunal (cf. art. 4 CPC), the right to be heard (cf. art. 107 CPC and 109 et seq. CPC), formal requirements for criminal proceedings (cf. art. 2 CPC), the right to a public (cf. art. 69 (1) CPC) and expeditious proceeding (cf. art. 5 CPC), the presumption of innocence (cf. art. 10 (1) CPC), the right against self-incrimination (art. 113 (1) CPC), the right to be present and participate in the proceedings (cf. art. 147 CPC), and the right to defense counsel (cf. art. 127 et seq., particularly art. 132 et seq. CPC). The CPC also explicitly prohibits the obtainment of evidence through torture and other methods that violate human dignity (cf. art. 3 (2) lit. d and art. 140 CPC).[44] Other aspects of a fair trial include the requirement that the authorities inform parties to the proceeding of their rights (cf. for instance art. 107 (2) and 143 (1) lit. c CPC) and the authorities' duty of care. The duty of care seeks to prevent scenarios where parties lose their rights simply because they are unfamiliar with the law, or are otherwise in a compromised position (see, for instance, the protective measures in art. 149–156 CPC).[45] Furthermore, art. 6 (2) CPC obliges the prosecution authorities to investigate *ex officio*, and with equal care, both incriminating and exculpating circumstances related to the criminal act and the accused. The provision itself specifies the principle of a fair trial with regard to the establishment of facts.[46] The principle of a fair

[39]Demko, 2007 at 356 et seq.

[40]Demko, 2007 at 359.

[41]Thommen, 2013 at 301.

[42]Vetterli, 2012 at 451.

[43]Demko, 2007 at 360 et seq. with further references.

[44]Wohlers in Donatsch et al., 2014 at art. 3 no. 22; *see* in detail 2.1.1.2, 2.1.3.1, 2.1.4., 2.2.2., 3.2.1., 3.2.2.

[45]Schmid, 2017 at § 6 no. 102; *also* Wohlers in Donatsch et al., 2014 at art. 3 no. 22 and BGE 124 I 185 consid. 3.

[46]Schmid, 2017 at § 6 no. 99.

trial is also closely related to the so-called "principle of equality of arms," which states that the defense and the prosecution should have equal means at their disposal to pursue and safeguard their respective interests.[47] That said, absolute equality is generally not feasible in criminal proceedings, which is why the defendant's opportunity to influence the proceedings is of the utmost importance.[48]

2.1.1.3 Balancing Fact-Finding and Individual Rights

A court must strive to establish the truth to give a just and correct judgment.[49] This belief has been a cornerstone of the inquisitorial model and is a primary reason that Swiss criminal proceedings place a strong emphasis on the search for the material truth. However, according to current law, authorities are neither obliged nor allowed to search for the truth at any cost. Instead, there are limitations created through procedural rules designed to protect a defendant from the authorities while also preventing abuse of power, arbitrariness, and legal inequality[50] in an environment that still promotes efficient law enforcement.[51] Not surprisingly, Swiss scholars argue that criminal proceedings today are only required to lead to the *forensic truth*.[52] The forensic truth is the result of a truth-seeking process in which the authorities abide by the formal rules of criminal procedure and seek what may be, depending on the circumstances, a limited version of the material truth.[53] Thus, a fair criminal judgment is not necessarily based on the material truth, but is the outcome of fair and lawful proceedings.[54] Nevertheless, it is important to keep in mind that the formal procedural rules are not an end in and of themselves and that complying with them is not a reason to lose sight of the main objective to find the material truth and arrive at a fair and just decision.[55]

Despite the importance of the search for the material truth (reflected in art. 6 CPC), the Swiss legal framework prioritizes the forensic truth in many ways, especially in its efforts to ensure fair trials. According to art. 159 CPC, for instance, an accused can briefly consult a defense attorney before the first police interrogation. The defense attorney is also allowed to attend the interrogations.[56] This is a big step forward in the protection of procedural rights in criminal trials for

[47]Schmid, 2017 at § 6 no. 97.

[48]Wohlers in Donatsch et al., 2014 at art. 3 no. 24.

[49]Keller, 2011 at 231.

[50]Keller, 2011 at 231 et seq.

[51]Keller, 2011 at 232.

[52]Wohlers in Donatsch et al., 2014 at art. 6 no. 2 with further references.

[53]Keller, 2011 at 231 et seq.

[54]*See* to the tension between material truth and justice Fornito, 2000 at 40 et seq.; Trechsel, 2000 at 6 et seq.

[55]Demko, 2007 at 352 et seq. with further references.

[56]In detail however, there are some enforcement problems, Pieth, 2016 at 96 et seq.

Switzerland; prior to the adoption of the CPC, only a few cantons allowed an accused such rights.[57] On the other hand, these procedural protections introduce the possibility that an accused will be advised by his or her counsel to remain silent or deny the truth, and may even be coached as to what to say. Naturally, this can hinder the search for the material truth.[58]

It is also the case that the establishment of numerous strict exclusionary rules have placed greater emphasis on the forensic truth.[59] For example, evidence is to be excluded in cases of incomplete or omitted warnings to the accused informing them of the proceedings against them and their legal rights (similar to the *Miranda* warning in the US),[60] denial of an essential defense,[61] procurement of evidence without regard for all parties' participation rights,[62] use of coercion to obtain evidence,[63] or indirect evidence gathered as a result of previously tainted evidence.[64] Art. 141 (2) CPC addresses evidence obtained through a criminal offense or the violation of so-called "regulations on admissibility" and does not establish a strict exclusionary rule, but stipulates a discretionary approach where the search for evidence and the infringement of the defendant's rights are balanced.[65] The new CPC has formalized the police's investigative procedures and provides for a right to appeal actions by the police and prosecution.[66] Additionally, regulations around the use of compulsory measures[67] (i.e. those that give coercive power to the authorities and restrict individuals' personal freedom in order to secure the establishment of the material truth) still require that the interest in finding the truth is balanced with the individual rights at risk. To achieve this balance, the CPC implemented the use of the proportionality principle,[68] which requires that a sufficient, respectively strong, suspicion for wrongdoing must exist.[69] Taken together, all of these aspects of the CPC place limitations on the search for the material, objective truth to safeguard the defendant's right to a fair trial.

Changes to the commitment to searching for the material truth are also related to efficiency.[70] Resource management and cost saving were of great importance to the

[57] Jackson/Summers, 2013 at 127; Bundesblatt 2006 at 1193.

[58] Keller, 2011 at 237.

[59] Keller, 2011 at 246.

[60] Art. 158 (2) CPC; Keller, 2011 at 239.

[61] Art. 131 (3) CPC; Keller, 2011 at 241 et seq.

[62] Art. 147 (4) CPC; Keller, 2011 at 243.

[63] Art. 140 (1) and 141 (1) CPC, *see* in detail below 3.2.4.

[64] Art. 141 (4) CPC, *see* in detail below 3.2.5.

[65] *See* below 3.1.2.3.

[66] Keller, 2011 at 247 et seq.; art. 393 (1) lit. a CPC.

[67] Art. 196 et seq. CPC.

[68] Spelled out for instance by art. 197 (1) lit. c CPC (principle of necessity), and art. 221 (1) CPC (exclusion of custody for minor offences), Pieth, 2016 at 132.

[69] Pieth, 2016 at 132 et seq.

[70] in detail Thommen, 2013 at 249 et seq.

drafters of the CPC.[71] The underlying rationale of the legislation is that not every investigation can be conducted with the same degree of effort and penal authorities must comply with the demands of efficiency in law enforcement, including the need for quick and effective methods that are also economical.[72] As a consequence, in modern Swiss criminal procedure there is a strong tendency to utilize summary proceedings.[73] In fact today, 90–99% of all cases that go forward conclude with a *summary penalty order* ("Strafbefehl"),[74] a decision taken by the public prosecutor in a special procedure. Such penalty orders can be issued without prior criminal investigation, including without even interviewing an accused, and can thus be based on insufficient evidence.[75] However, in theory, art. 352 (1) CPC requires a confession or an otherwise sufficient establishment of the facts for a summary penalty order to be appropriate. If a defendant does not agree with the "offered" order, he or she has the right to object (or "reject") within ten days.[76] That said, defendants rarely object, often out of a lack of awareness of their right to do so.[77] Taken together, all of these issues can make summary penalty orders susceptible to error. This was confirmed by a study on miscarriages of justice,[78] although it should be noted that a large portion of summary penalty orders involve petty offenses with minor penalties.[79]

Another way in which the law places limitations on the establishment of the material truth in order to promote efficiency is through *accelerated proceedings* ("abgekürztes Verfahren").[80] In these proceedings—arising, for instance, in a complicated financial crime case where facts are difficult to establish—the defendant is allowed to contest the facts and the penalty. The truth then becomes a matter

---

[71]Brun, 2015 at 105.

[72]Keller, 2011 at 232.

[73]Brun, 2015 at 98 et seq.

[74]Pieth, 2016 at 249 and 251 with further references; *also* Gilliéron/Killias, 2007 at 381 who speak of 76% according to a study from 2002 and Schweizer, 2013 at 1388 who speaks of 95%.

[75]Keller, 2011 at 249; *also* Gilliéron/Killias, 2007 at 389. However, recent reform efforts plan to introduce the mandatory interrogation of the defendant in some cases, e.g. before issuing a penalty order for over 4 months of imprisonment, see art. 352a of the preliminary draft regarding a reform of the CPC submitted by the Swiss Federal Council in December 2017, available online at <https://www.bj.admin.ch/dam/data/bj/sicherheit/gesetzgebung/aenderungstpo/vorentw-d.pdf>, accessed 22 November 2018.

[76]However, recent reform efforts plan to extend this period to 20 days in cases where the prosecution did not hand over the penalty order personally, see art. 354 (1ter) of the preliminary draft regarding a reform of the CPC submitted by the Swiss Federal Council in December 2017, available online at <https://www.bj.admin.ch/dam/data/bj/sicherheit/gesetzgebung/aenderungstpo/vorentw-d.pdf>, accessed 22 November 2018.

[77]Art. 354 et seq. CPC; Gilliéron/Killias, 2007 at 390 et seq.

[78]67.5 % of all discovered miscarriages of justice between 1995 and 2004 concerned wrong summary penalty orders, *see* Gilliéron/Killias, 2007 at 378 et seq.

[79]Gilliéron/Killias, 2007 at 388 et seq.

[80]Art. 358 et seq. CPC; Keller, 2011 at 254.

of negotiation.[81] Summary proceedings have, therefore, been criticized as adversely affecting the establishment of the material truth and, in turn, legal equality.[82] Some scholars have even claimed that the quest to establish the material truth becomes an illusion in summary proceedings[83] and this should be compensated for to justify a proscribed penalty.[84] The CPC, however, significantly *limits* procedural safeguards in summary proceedings.[85]

2.1.2 Establishing the Facts, Procedural Rules, and Stages

Criminal proceedings are typically initiated by the police at the instruction of the public prosecutor or following observations made by police officers and other authorities.[86] Preliminary investigations (i.e. securing the crime scene; searching for evidence; interviewing witnesses; stopping, arresting or searching for suspects, etc.) fall within the scope of police duties.[87]

Art. 139 CPC enumerates potential types of evidence:

- testimony provided by witnesses or *persons providing information* ("Auskunftspersonen");
- reports by experts;
- statements by an accused;
- documents and (judicial) inspections.[88]

Although the police handle preliminary investigations, the public prosecutor may provide instructions because such investigations are part of the preliminary proceedings, which fall under the direction of the prosecution.[89] After the preliminary investigations conclude, the public prosecutor must assess the evidence and make a decision to either investigate further, file charges, make an offer for a summary penalty order, or stop the proceedings altogether. For each of those decisions, the public prosecutor must have sufficient evidence to establish the necessary facts.[90]

---

[81]Brun, 2015 at 100 et seq. with further references; dissenting as far as fact bargaining is concerned Schwarzenegger in Donatsch et al., 2014 at art. 358 no. 6 et seq. with further references.

[82]Brun, 2015 at 107 et seq.

[83]Thommen, 2013 at 250, 309.

[84]Thommen, 2013 at 292 et seq., which the CPC neglects to do, Thommen, 2013 at 81 (as to the summary penalty order).

[85]Thommen, 2013 at 224 et seq.

[86]Art. 306 (1) CPC.

[87]Art. 306 (2) CPC.

[88]Pieth, 2016 at 187 et seq. with further explanations to the question of whether means of evidence other than those mentioned in the CPC are admissible or not.

[89]Art. 307 (2) CPC.

[90]Schmid, 2017 at § 2 no. 15; art. 308 et seq. CPC.

Traditionally, public prosecutors in inquisitorial systems choose to either prosecute a case (and go to trial) or dismiss it altogether. They are required to give written notice of the decision to the parties involved and provide a deadline for the submission of a request for further investigation,[91] which supposedly satisfies an accused's right to participation (and thus, a fair trial). Today, however, most cases that could be prosecuted (half of which are traffic offences),[92] conclude with the prosecution issuing a summary penalty order.[93] These decisions are made without a public hearing[94] and often without even interviewing the defendant (who, most likely, is not represented by defense counsel).[95] This does not satisfy the four-eye principle (or its equivalent)[96] and in most cases evidence will never be presented to a court for evaluation and a formal judgement. Only where a party raises an objection to the summary penalty order does an action for additional fact-finding begin.[97] Where the summary penalty order is accepted, it becomes binding as a final judgment.[98]

Even where a public prosecutor decides to take a case to trial, the deciding judges may not hear all relevant evidence in the main hearing because the principle of immediacy is quite flexible under the CPC.[99] During public main hearings, which are the centerpiece of the main proceedings,[100] the court ideally takes and *directly* examines all evidence relevant to the case (e.g., statements of the parties, documents etc.) to form an opinion. The CPC, however, leaves it to the discretion of the court to decide if direct knowledge of the evidence is necessary to reach a decision.[101] Apart from direct evidence, the court can make a decision based on an accused's criminal file, which is circulated to all judges involved.[102] As the CPC states, the court shall only take directly *new* evidence, *supplemental* evidence that was previously incomplete, and re-take evidence that was *improperly obtained* during the preliminary proceedings.[103] Nevertheless, during the main public

---

[91]Art. 318 (1) CPC.

[92]Riklin, 2016 at 477.

[93]*See* above 2.1.2.

[94]Pieth, 2016 at 218; critical Brun, 2015 at 98 et seq.; Riklin, 2016 at 493 et seq.

[95]Gilliéron/Killias, 2007 at 394 et seq. However, recent reform efforts plan to introduce the mandatory interrogation of the defendant in some cases, e.g. before issuing a penalty order for over 4 months of imprisonment, see art. 352a of the preliminary draft regarding a reform of the CPC submitted by the Swiss Federal Council in December 2017, available online at <https://www.bj.admin.ch/dam/data/bj/sicherheit/gesetzgebung/aenderungstpo/vorentw-d.pdf>, accessed 22 November 2018.

[96]Riklin, 2016 at 495 who is critical of the fact that the prosecution is the sole issuing authority, acting without participation of an independent court. As to the problems concerning the supervision of the prosecution, *see* below 2.1.3.2.

[97]Art. 355 CPC.

[98]Art. 354 (3) CPC.

[99]Art. 343 CPC.

[100]Schmid, 2017 at § 2 no. 18.

[101]Critical Pieth, 2016 at 51 et seq.; art. 343 (3) CPC.

[102]Art. 330 (2) CPC; critical Pieth, 2016 at 51 et seq.

[103]Art. 343 (1 and 2) CPC.

hearing the accused is always questioned directly by the judge overseeing the proceedings.[104]

After the main hearing and the presentation of all relevant evidence before the court, the evidence is considered in accordance with the opinions the court has formed throughout the entire course of the proceedings[105] and a decision to either convict or acquit the accused is made. The judgment is first pronounced orally to the parties with a short explanation (unless the parties waive their right to have the judgment issued publicly) and is later handed down in writing.[106] Where an appeal is filed against the court of first instance, the appellate court generally bases its decision on the evidence already documented in the criminal file. As a result, the appellate court does not directly take evidence.[107]

In all procedural stages, exclusionary rules are formally binding on authorities.[108] However, according to the jurisprudence of the Swiss Supreme Court, it is the *judge of fact* who has the power to enforce exclusionary rules, and who also decides the outcome of a case.[109]

2.1.3 Establishing the Facts: Actors and Accountability

2.1.3.1 Primary Actors

The main actors involved in establishing the facts of a criminal case are the police, prosecution and judges. The accused and his or her defense counsel have a limited role in influencing the fact-finding process. Those that do play a role in fact-finding have different interests and views around what the search for truth should look like. On the one hand, police and prosecutors aim to establish the material truth. Their actions must be efficient and consistent with the principles of urgency, economy and effectiveness.[110] To them, extensive formal requirements around evidence gathering, participation rights, and exclusionary rules are a hindrance to the search for the material truth.[111] The Supreme Court also appears to fall on the side of pursuing the material truth, particularly in cases where it clearly went to great lengths to admit and consider illegally obtained evidence.[112] On the other hand, the defense is typically in favor of rigid, formal rules around the taking of evidence, as well as extensive participation rights, and strict exclusionary rules in case of violations. They do not

[104]Art. 241 (3) CPC.

[105]Art. 10 (2) CPC.

[106]Art. 351 (3) and art. 84 (1–3) CPC.

[107]Schmid, 2017 at § 16 no. 308; *also* art. 389 (1) CPC.

[108]Gless in Niggli et al., 2014 at art. 141 no. 35.

[109]*See* below 3.1.4.

[110]Keller, 2011 at 232.

[111]Keller, 2011 at 233 et seq.

[112]Keller, 2011 at 234, *see also* below 3.1.3, 3.2.4.2, 3.2.5.2.

necessarily have an incentive to find the material truth and instead tend to look for a version of the facts that is the most favorable to the defendant.[113]

In some cantonal procedure codes, the police were traditionally tasked with making only the first (and urgent) inquiries autonomously. In practice, however, they did much more.[114] The new Swiss CPC explicitly states that the police are to establish facts relevant to the criminal offense in question.[115] The police can autonomously take any evidence; search for, observe, and arrest suspects; and, in emergency cases, search persons and seize property.[116] Only in the case of severe criminal offenses and other serious matters are the police obliged to immediately inform the prosecution.[117] Typically, they procure all necessary evidence independently and prepare the entire criminal file (thereby concluding the preliminary investigation) for the prosecution.[118] Additionally, summary penalty orders and potential judgments are often based entirely on police reports.[119] Thus, the police play a significant role during preliminary proceedings. This can lead to problems, as individual procedural rights may be circumvented at this less formalized stage of the proceedings,[120] a stage where the defendant is rarely interviewed or represented by counsel.[121]

The prosecution occupies a powerful place in criminal proceedings in both statutory text and practical application. The new CPC conferred a number of duties and powers upon the prosecution; they are tasked with consistently applying the duty to prosecute, conducting the preliminary proceedings, pursuing criminal offenses within the scope of an investigation, bringing charges, and obtaining favorable plea agreements.[122] Furthermore, the prosecution can also discontinue criminal proceedings[123] or chose to issue a summary penalty order, which carries up to six months' imprisonment.[124] These powers, in addition to others, lead to a concentration of authority within the prosecution, who, in fact, act as lead investigator, judge, and

---

[113]Keller, 2011 at 233.

[114]Pieth, 2016 at 67 et seq.

[115]Art. 306 (1 and 2) CPC.

[116]Pieth, 2016 at 68 et seq.

[117]Art. 307 (1) CPC.

[118]Art. 307 (3) CPC.

[119]Gilliéron/Killias, 2007 at 383 with further references. However, recent reform efforts plan to introduce the mandatory interrogation of the defendant in some cases, e.g. before issuing a penalty order for over 4 months of imprisonment, see art. 352a of the preliminary draft regarding a reform of the CPC submitted by the Swiss Federal Council in December 2017, available online at <https://www.bj.admin.ch/dam/data/bj/sicherheit/gesetzgebung/aenderungstpo/vorentw-d.pdf>, accessed 22 November 2018.

[120]Pieth, 2016 at 68.

[121]Gilliéron/Killias, 2007 at 394 et seq.

[122]Art. 16 (1 and 2) CPC.

[123]Art. 310, 319 et seq. CPC.

[124]Art. 352 (1) CPC.

prosecutor. While this may be efficient, it can compromise the accused's right to an impartial judgment.[125]

Despite the powerful positions occupied by the police and prosecution in criminal investigations, the CPC does set limits in an effort to protect individual rights that fall within the scope of art. 5 (3) ECHR and art. 6 ECHR, including the right to an impartial judgment. The CPC also reserves certain powers for judicial authorities. For example, compulsory measures affecting the personal freedoms of a defendant or third party in a serious way (e.g., custody, preventive detention, bank account monitoring, mass DNA tests, surveillance of post and telecommunications, surveillance using technical devices and undercover investigations) cannot be applied without consent of a special "*compulsory measures court*" (Zwangsmassnahmengericht).[126] Furthermore, in all matters that exceed the authority of the prosecution to issue summary penalty orders, the prosecution merely provides the charges while the courts of first instance and the appellate courts decide the substantive issues of the case.[127] It remains, however, that where summary penalty orders can be issued, a defendant retains the right to object and to ask for a court trial reviewing the punishment order.[128]

The CPC grants full participation rights to the accused with particular attention paid to the right to be heard, including the right to counsel prior to the first police interrogation, the right to access the case file, and the right to request that evidence be taken.[129] These rights are unfortunately not strictly enforced in practice,[130] which weakens the role of the accused and the ability of the defense to influence the proceedings. If the defense seeks to exclude a piece of evidence, he or she must submit a removal request to the person overseeing the proceedings.[131] This is also the case in proceedings before the *compulsory measures court*. Where the request is rejected, the defense can file an appeal with the court of second instance and, if necessary, the Swiss Supreme Court.[132]

2.1.3.2 Supervision of Judicial Authorities and Legal Remedies

Swiss law only partially regulates the supervision of prosecution authorities; it is, therefore, up to the cantons to decide how to "guard the guardians." Supervision of

---

[125]Pieth, 2016 at 70 et seq.

[126]Custody, preventive detention and bank account monitoring can only be ordered by the court; the other measures simply need an approval by the court; Pieth, 2016 at 73 with further references.

[127]Schmid, 2017 at § 3 no. 18 et seq.

[128]Art. 354 et seq. CPC.

[129]Pieth, 2016 at 57 et seq.

[130]*See* below 2.1.4.

[131]"Verfahrensleitung", in the official English translation of the CPC the "director of the proceedings".

[132]*See* generally Wohlers/Bläsi, 2015 at 173 et seq.

police in routine operations is also under the auspices of cantonal law.[133] Cases of alleged police misconduct can be reported to the supervisory authority[134] and, where the suspicion that a crime occurred can be substantiated, police will be prosecuted.

The prosecution also exercises control over the police when conducting criminal investigations. It may instruct the police in a particular way or take control of the proceedings at any time.[135] Nevertheless, in practice it is difficult for prosecutorial authorities to adequately supervise police work because the CPC does not provide efficient tools to do so.[136] It is clear, however, that if prosecution authorities observe a police officer improperly eliciting a confession, the officer must be reported to the appropriate authorities.[137] In order to enable the prosecution and the courts to consider whether evidence has been obtained improperly, the police are obliged to continually record their findings and the means by which they have gathered evidence in a written report provided to the prosecution.[138] If evidence has been obtained improperly, the public prosecutor will re-take it personally or instruct the police to do so.[139] The defendant may also submit an application requesting that the official(s) in question be recused from future proceedings.[140] If the case goes to court, the judges must examine whether the evidence was obtained improperly. Where the court decides to exclude certain evidence, it must re-take it.[141] Theoretically, in doing this, the courts control not only the final result of the investigation, but also the police and the prosecution.

The supervision of the prosecution is regulated by cantonal law and varies widely across Switzerland. Many questions remain unanswered due to the fragmentary character of the cantonal regulations.[142] The supervision of judicial authorities, like the prosecution, is difficult because the supervisory body is generally not authorized to intervene in cases; rather its role is limited to administrative and technical supervision. There is one exception in the case of significant violations of the law,[143] such as police abuse or the improper use of compulsory measures. Additionally, certain cantons have a Chief Public Prosecutor's Office that has the authority to issue instructions on a case-by-case basis.[144] Supervisory bodies

---

[133]Depending on the canton, the supervisory authority is the superordinate department or the cantonal governing council; *see* Künzli et al., 2014 at 26.

[134]*See* Künzli et al., 2014 at 26 et seq.

[135]Art. 307 (2), 312 CPC.

[136]Ruckstuhl et al., 2011 at no. 62; as to the possible legal remedies for misconduct by police *see* Künzli et al., 2014 at 19 et seq. in detail.

[137]Pursuant to art. 302 CPC, Committee Against Torture (CAT) Report, 2016 at 2.

[138]Art. 307 (3) CPC.

[139]Art. 308 (1), art. 311 (1), art. 312 (1) CPC.

[140]Art. 56 et seq. CPC; CAT Report, 2016 at 1.

[141]BGer 6B_690/2015 of 25 November 2015, consid. 3.4.; art. 343 (2) CPC.

[142]Schweizer, 2013 at 1381 et seq.

[143]Schweizer, 2013 at 1381.

[144]Schweizer, 2013 at 1381.

can also initiate an administrative investigation into alleged misconduct of individual officials and determine the appropriateness of disciplinary measures where necessary.[145] Overall, there is a risk that prosecutorial authorities will remain largely unsupervised, especially in cantons where the supervision is conducted by executive authorities with limited judicial expertise.[146]

The courts, as judicial authorities, also have supervisory powers, but they are limited to administrative and technical aspects unless there is a severe violation of the law. Aside from that, the errors of judicial authorities can only be challenged through legal remedies.[147] Accordingly, a defendant has the right to appeal decisions, lodge complaints against the police and the prosecution,[148] and appeal final judgments.[149] Where the cantonal remedies have been exhausted, a defendant may appeal to the Swiss Supreme Court.[150] However, according to the case law on this matter, it is not possible for a defendant to ask that his or her request for an assessment of allegedly illegally obtained evidence (and its potential exclusion) be completed *before* the court has received the evidence.[151] This is particularly problematic as the court deciding the admissibility of the evidence will have already seen it and is also the court deciding the substantive matters of the case.

2.1.3.3 Liability of the State and Legal Officials for Improper Compulsion in Criminal Investigations

Apart from accountability in a disciplinary proceeding, an official that has improperly used compulsory measures against a defendant (for example, during an interrogation) is also subject to criminal liability. In such a case, the defendant may report the offense directly to the prosecution.[152] He or she may also request compensation for damages, including mental suffering. Such claims following alleged misconduct by officials are subject to cantonal law. That said, all cantons have adopted the concept of *exclusive* state liability for such claims. Accordingly, they

145 Schweizer, 2013 at 1383 with further references; as to disciplinary measures against police officers in particular, *see* Künzli et al., 2014 at 57 et seq.; *see also* CAT Report, 2016 at 3.

146 Schweizer, 2013 at 1389.

147 Schweizer, 2013 at 1384.

148 Art. 393 (1) lit. a CPC. However, this possibility is of little practical relevance so far; Künzli et al., 2014 at 65 et seq.; *see also* Gless in Niggli et al., 2014 at art. 140 no. 74.

149 Art. 398 (1) CPC.

150 Art. 80 (1) Bundesgesetz über das Bundesgericht (BGG) of 17 June 2005 (Status as of 1 January 2017), SR 173.110, available online at <https://www.admin.ch/opc/de/classified-compilation/20010204/index.html>, accessed 22 November 2018.

151 *See* below 3.1.4.

152 Pursuant to art. 301 CPC; CAT Report, 2016 at 1 et seq.; as to criminal liability of police officers in detail *see* Künzli et al., 2014 at 32 et seq.

may only be brought against the state, not the individual official.[153] Along the same lines, several cantons have created specific procedures for dealing with cases of criminal complaints alleging police misconduct. This involves a hearing conducted exclusively by representatives of the prosecution, police officers from outside the unit in question, or officers from a special police corps addressing such matters.[154] In addition to these procedures, many cantons and respective municipalities provide for alternative mechanisms of dispute resolution, such as a mediator bureau and/or ombudsman.[155]

2.1.4 Establishing the Facts: Institutional Safeguards

In Swiss criminal investigations various institutional safeguards are in place to ensure the objectivity of investigative authorities and the transparency of proceedings. First, art. 6 (2) CPC[156] stipulates that authorities must investigate all circumstances—exculpatory and incriminatory—with equal care. Second, art. 3 (2) lit. c and 107 CPC codify the right to be heard, which preserves important participation rights such as access to the criminal file, the opportunity to take part in procedural activities, the right to counsel, the right to comment on the facts and proceedings, and the right to request that further evidence be taken.[157] The right to be heard also includes the right to be informed about the charge(s) as well as one's own rights.[158] All of these aspects are institutional safeguards that allow the parties to influence the fact-finding process through participation should they wish to do so.[159] Hence, the "truth" is not only constructed by the prosecution authorities, but also the defense, each of whom enter into this "open process" with their own biases. In an effort to promote objectivity, art. 141 (5) CPC mandates that authorities keep an open, unbiased view of the case even where illegally obtained evidence incriminating the defendant exists. The provision states that records of inadmissible evidence shall be removed from the criminal files, kept separately until a final judgment has been reached, and then destroyed.

In addition to the principles and rights explicitly granted in the CPC, the code also provides for some degree of flexibility in certain provisions, which has led to a more lenient application of the legal framework around individual rights. Using the example of participation rights, the following three issues have arisen: First,

---

[153]Künzli et al., 2014 at 70 et seq. Thus, those claims cannot be asserted directly in the criminal proceedings against the official either which is incorrectly stated in CAT Report, 2016 at 3.

[154]Zürich, Vaud, Basel-Stadt, Basel-Land, Zug, Bern, Luzern, Sankt-Gallen, Rapperswil-Jona, Wallisellen, Winterthur; *see* CAT Report, 2016 at 2.

[155]CAT Report, 2016 at 2; *also* Künzli et al., 2014 at 28 et seq.

[156]*See* above 2.1.1.1.

[157]Art. 107 (1) CPC. All of these rights are spelled out in detail in other provisions of the CPC.

[158]Pieth, 2016 at 57 et seq.

[159]Demko, 2007 at 360.

according to the Supreme Court's jurisprudence, the prosecution and the court hearing the case may reject the defense's request that further evidence be taken (*Beweisantrag*) by providing a brief reasoning as soon as the competent body is convinced that no further evidence is needed to decide the case (subject to a review for arbitrariness).[160] The defendant has no formal remedy, but can submit a new request for additional evidence during the preparation of the main hearing and again during the main hearing.[161] Second, the defense's access to the file can be suspended until the first interrogation of the accused has taken place and other important evidence has been taken.[162] Therefore, up to that point, the case file is built upon facts only from the police perspective. Third, in cases of summary penalty orders, the defendant often does not participate in the proceedings at all[163]; instead he or she receives a sentencing offer by mail without a hearing and without the assistance of a defense lawyer.[164] The prosecution's "offer" frequently is difficult for a layperson to understand[165] and only in a few specific cases does it provide a rationale (albeit brief) for the decision.[166] The summary penalty order is thus criticized as problematic for many reasons[167] and is deemed compatible with art. 6 ECHR only because a defendant theoretically[168] has the option to reject the "offer" and request a trial.[169]

---

[160] This is called "anticipated assessment of evidence" (*antizipierte Beweiswürdigung*), BGE 134 I 140, consid. 5.3. et seq. with further references; *also* art. 139 (2) and art. 318 (2) CPC as well as Bundesblatt 2006 at 1182; critical Pieth, 2016 at 44, 108 et seq. and 188 et seq. with further references; *see also* Gless in Niggli et al., 2014 at art. 139 no. 48 et seq., stating that apart from art. 318 (2) CPC requests for additional evidence cannot be rejected due to anticipated assessment of evidence.

[161] Art. 318 (2) CPC; art. 331 (2 and 3) CPC.

[162] Art. 101 (1) CPC; critical Pieth, 2016 at 93 et seq.

[163] Schweizer, 2013 at 1388.

[164] Gilliéron/Killias, 2007 at 394 et seq. However, recent reform efforts plan to introduce the mandatory interrogation of the defendant in some cases, e.g. before issuing a penalty order for over 4 months of imprisonment, see art. 352a of the preliminary draft regarding a reform of the CPC submitted by the Swiss Federal Council in December 2017, available online at <https://www.bj.admin.ch/dam/data/bj/sicherheit/gesetzgebung/aenderungstpo/vorentw-d.pdf>, accessed 22 November 2018.

[165] And thus, only rarely "rejected", Riklin, 2016 at 486 et seq.; Gilliéron/Killias, 2007 at 390 et seq.

[166] Riklin, 2016 at 485; Thommen, 2013 at 94 et seq.

[167] *See* the enumeration in Riklin, 2016 at 495 et seq.; *see also* the references on critical scholars in Schweizer, 2013 at 1387 fn. 84.

[168] Only in 5 % of the cases does the summary penalty order not become a legally binding judgment, but the case will go to court, *see* Schweizer, 2013 at 1380.

[169] Gilliéron/Killias, 2007 at 383 et seq. and 390 et seq.; critical Riklin, 2016 at 485.

2.2 *Relevance of the Truth and Individual Rights in Criminal Trials*

2.2.1 Public Interest in Determining the Truth

In continental Europe, the public traditionally expects the truth to be established following a criminal trial. Due to widespread interest in criminal proceedings, prosecution authorities are under considerable public pressure to establish the truth[170] and prosecute, particularly in high-profile cases. In contrast, the idea that the alleged perpetrator has human rights that could potentially restrict the search for truth receives little public support.[171] This is also reflected in the skeptical, and sometimes disapproving, portrayal of criminal procedures in the media, especially where relevant evidence is excluded. This can be observed in even the most well-reputed Swiss newspapers, such as the NZZ (Neue Zürcher Zeitung). For example, in a case where a defendant was acquitted after illegally obtained evidence was excluded, the NZZ reported that the accused was "profiting" from faulty procedure.[172] The public emphasis on the importance of finding the truth is also illustrated by the growing discontent with public prosecutors "acting like judges" and routinely issuing summary penalty orders without the scrutiny of a formal, transparent procedure. The same goes for accelerated proceedings (a form of negotiated justice[173]) which carry with them an elevated risk of a miscarriage of justice given that a defendant might confess solely to ensure a particular outcome.[174]

2.2.2 Presenting the "Truth" to the Public

In Switzerland, the fact-finding process prior to a trial is not public[175] and the investigative work and its results are not officially published by the authorities. Instead, information is published by the media, which tend to be motivated by sensationalist news and are often inadequately informed.

---

[170]Thommen/Samadi, 2016 at 84.

[171]Vetterli, 2012 at 450.

[172]NZZ online 5 August 2002, Ausschlaggebender Beweis darf nicht verwertet werden. Freispruch für Polizisten trotz Tatverdacht, available online at <https://www.nzz.ch/article8BGKE-1.414015>, accessed 22 November 2018.

[173]For both NZZ online 19 April 2013, Immer mehr Strafbefehle. Der Staatsanwalt als Richter, available online at <https://www.nzz.ch/zuerich/der-staatsanwalt-als-richter-1.18067194?reduced=true>, accessed 22 November 2018; *also* Brun, 2015 at 99 et seq. with further references.

[174]NZZ 29 March 2016 at 9, Deals in Strafverfahren häufen sich. Kritiker befürchten, dass Beschuldigte unter Druck falsche Geständnisse ablegen.

[175]Art. 69 (3) lit. a CPC; Schmid, 2017 at § 15 no. 265.

With few exceptions, the main hearings and the presentation of evidence before courts of first instance[176] (and the Swiss Supreme Court[177]) are public. Court proceedings on compulsory measures, such as rulings on search warrants, preventative detention, or remand are not public.[178] However, judgments rendered by the courts of first and second instance,[179] as well as the Supreme Court,[180] are open to the public. Since April 2016, the Supreme Court has also made publicly available short video recordings of select proceedings.[181]

2.2.3 Miscarriages of Justice

A study on miscarriages of justice in Switzerland found that during the period between 1995 and 2004, 237 judgments had been set aside by cantonal courts in retrial proceedings. At first sight, this does not seem to be a large number when compared to the tens of thousands of judgments handed down each year but, given that the requirements for a retrial are very strict, the actual number of miscarriages of justice is likely several times higher.[182] In almost all of these cases, the contested judgment was decided in favor of the defendant.[183] It is also noteworthy that 67.5% of those cases concerned summary penalty orders which, as previously mentioned, are particularly prone to error.[184] This is due to the fact that summary penalty orders are issued after only a cursory examination of the facts.[185] Given the nature of this

---

[176] Art. 69 (1) CPC; art. 30 (3) Swiss Federal Constitution; art. 6 (1) ECHR and art. 14 (1) ICCPR II. The exceptions (for example for the proceedings of second instance and in case of prevailing interest in secrecy) are mentioned in art. 69 (3) and art. 70 CPC as well as in other particular provisions, Schmid, 2017 at § 15 no. 260 et seq.

[177] Art. 59 (1 and 2) BGG.

[178] Art. 69 (3) lit. b CPC.

[179] Art. 69 (1) CPC; Schmid, 2017 at § 15 no. 261. In case the defendant waived the right to the public pronouncement of the judgment or in case of a summary penalty order, the decisions are open for public inspection.

[180] Art. 27 (1) BGG; art. 59 (3) BGG.

[181] Media Release of the Swiss Supreme Court: „Filmaufnahmen zu öffentlichen Urteilsberatungen" of 27 April 2016, available online at <https://www.bger.ch/files/live/sites/bger/files/pdf/de/11.5.2_15.0.0.3_01_2016_yyyy_mm_dd_T_d_14_41_15.pdf>, accessed 22 November 2018.

[182] Gilliéron/Killias, 2007 at 387.

[183] Gilliéron/Killias, 2007 at 388.

[184] *See* Gilliéron/Killias, 2007 at 388 et seq.

[185] Gilliéron/Killias, 2007 at 389; *see* above 2.2. However, recent reform efforts plan to introduce the mandatory interrogation of the defendant in some cases, e.g. before issuing a penalty order for over 4 months of imprisonment, see art. 352a of the preliminary draft regarding a reform of the CPC submitted by the Swiss Federal Council in December 2017, available online at <https://www.bj.admin.ch/dam/data/bj/sicherheit/gesetzgebung/aenderungstpo/vorentw-d.pdf>, accessed 22 November 2018.

approach, it is also likely that exclusionary rules are applied perfunctorily and the reliability of the evidence is, therefore, diminished.

3 Limitations of Fact-Finding with Exclusionary Rules in Switzerland

3.1 Exclusionary Rules in Swiss Criminal Proceedings

3.1.1 Rationale

As the primary aim of criminal proceedings is to establish the truth, exclusionary rules require special justification.[186] The rationale behind exclusionary rules[187] is not clearly established in Swiss legal literature and case law. Three primary justifications have been proffered: to safeguard procedural rules (including individual rights), to establish the material truth, and to discipline prosecution authorities.

Some see the primary rationale behind exclusionary rules as a guarantee that criminal procedure conforms with the rule of law and that authorities do not infringe upon individual rights, which are more important than the search for the truth.[188] This is of particular significance in criminal proceedings due to the gravity of the possible sentences.[189] The exclusion of illegally obtained evidence is thus understood as a safeguard for the accused's rights and a means of preserving the presumption of innocence.[190] Indeed, the Supreme Court has stated that the accused's right to a fair trial includes the exclusion of unlawfully collected evidence.[191] In a 1994 decision, the Supreme Court emphasized that *after* evidence has been illegally collected, the only way to honor the human rights of the accused is to ensure that such evidence is not used against him or her.[192]

The justification for the argument that exclusionary rules ensure the reliability of evidence primarily refers to evidence obtained through torture or other improper force. Because such evidence is deemed unreliable due to coercion, exclusionary rules are seen as necessary to protect the fact-finding process. Therefore, it is argued that the establishment and enforcement of exclusionary rules can optimize the ascertainment of truth in criminal proceedings.[193] In cases where the witness or

---

[186]Gless in Niggli et al., 2014 at art. 139 no. 23.

[187]*See* in detail Fornito, 2000 at 51 et seq.

[188]For more on this double purpose, *see* Wohlers/Bläsi, 2015 at 159 with further references.

[189]Groner, 2011 at 135.

[190]Gless/Martin, 2015 at 163.

[191]BGE 131 I 272, consid. 3.2.1; *also* Gless/Martin, 2015 at 162 et seq. with further references.

[192]BGE 120 Ia 314, consid. 2.c.

[193]In detail Ruckstuhl, 2006 at 20 et seq.; *also* Gless/Martin, 2015 at 163; Gless in Niggli et al., 2014 at art. 141 no. 6.

suspect has not been under duress, the exclusion of evidence is more likely to hinder the search for the material truth.[194]

The disciplinary component of exclusionary rules refers to the potential deterrent effect they have upon misconduct by prosecution authorities, and in particular, police officers. While in the United States this is considered to be the primary goal of exclusionary rules, the same rationale is subject to controversial debate in Switzerland.[195] Some Swiss scholars reject the general applicability of this approach because the concept of disciplining prosecution authorities does not fit into the inquisitorial Swiss system where the prosecution authorities are legally obliged to gather both incriminatory and exculpatory evidence[196] and are not a party to the criminal proceedings.[197] However, the dominant opinion in Swiss scholarship maintains that one of the primary purposes of exclusionary rules is to render human rights violations by law enforcement unnecessary since the resulting evidence cannot be used. Thus, according to this line of reasoning, exclusionary rules also have the secondary effect of disciplining prosecution authorities.[198] Since this view emphasizes the preventive rather than punitive element of exclusionary rules, its proponents argue that it is compatible with the inquisitorial Swiss criminal procedure system.[199] In fact, this aspect of exclusionary rules (disciplinary measures for prosecution authorities) is one reason they are said to safeguard human rights. Therefore, one could argue that, at least with respect to the use of torture and the use of unauthorized compulsory techniques by prosecution authorities, exclusionary rules can help to (1) enforce human rights by discouraging authorities from violating human rights or by removing from trial any evidence gained in violation of human rights, and (2) establish the material truth.

3.1.2 The CPC's System of Exclusionary Rules

As noted above, exclusionary rules place procedural limitations on the fact-finding process.[200] In Switzerland, the legislature established comprehensive, explicit provisions on the taking of evidence and its admissibility in criminal proceedings

---

[194]Schlauri, 2003 at 100; but *see* Ruckstuhl, 2006 at 20, who claims that all influence exerted during the taking of evidence might change the content of the evidence.

[195]Wohlers/Bläsi, 2015 at 159.

[196]Art. 6 (2) CPC.

[197]Fornito, 2000 at 59; Gless/Martin, 2015 at 164; Häring, 2009 at 238.

[198]Gless, 2016 at 130; Gless in Niggli et al., 2014 at art. 141 no. 6; Gless/Martin, 2015 at 163 et seq.; *also* Fornito, 2000 at 59; Groner, 2011 at 135; Häring, 2009 at 238; Thommen/Samadi, 2016 at 81 et seq., 84; Vest/Eicker, 2005 at 891; Vetterli, 2012 at 456; *see also* the discussion in the National Council in: Official Bulletin of the National Council, Summer Session 2007 at 955 et seq.

[199]Gless/Martin, 2015 at 164 et seq. with further references. However, also the sanctioning aspect is mentioned, Vetterli, 2012 at 456 with further references.

[200]*See* above 2.1.1.3.

through art. 139–141 CPC. This regulation, which is unique in Europe, is an important step towards upholding the rule of law.[201] However, art. 141 CPC leaves some unanswered questions regarding evidence exclusion.[202]

Prior to the adoption of art. 139–141 CPC, evidence exclusion was regulated very differently across cantons.[203] When the federal legislature drafted art. 141 CPC, it adopted principles that were developed based upon an overview of the various cantonal provisions and the requirements of federal law.[204] However, in contrast to the previous discussion of case law on the matter,[205] the legislature intended that the admission of unlawfully obtained evidence be the exception rather than the rule.[206] The new core provisions of the CPC on the exclusion of evidence are found in art. 140 and 141 CPC. Article 140 (1) CPC addresses prohibited methods of obtaining evidence, stating that "*the use of coercion, violence, threats, promises, deception and [other] methods that may compromise the ability of the person concerned to think or decide freely are prohibited when taking evidence.*" Article 140 (2) CPC adds that "*such methods remain unlawful even if the person concerned consents to their use.*"[207]

As to the legal framework on evidence exclusion, art. 141 CPC constitutes a blanket exclusionary rule and contains 5 sections. It reads:

(1) *Evidence obtained in violation of Article 140 is not admissible under any circumstances. The foregoing also applies where this Code declares evidence to be inadmissible.*
(2) *Evidence that criminal justice authorities have obtained by criminal methods or by violating regulations on admissibility is inadmissible unless it is essential that it be admitted in order to secure a conviction for a serious offence.*
(3) *Evidence that has been obtained in violation of administrative regulations is admissible.*
(4) *Where evidence that is inadmissible under paragraph 2 has made it possible to obtain additional evidence, such evidence is not admissible if it would have been impossible to obtain had the previous evidence not been obtained.*[208]

---

[201] Gless, 2016 at 128 et seq.; Gless in Niggli et al., 2014 at art. 141 no. 1; Gless, 2012 at 136.

[202] *See* in detail Häring, 2009 at 118 et seq.; Gless, 2016 at 134.

[203] *See* the examples in Gless in Niggli et al., 2014 at art. 141 no. 5.

[204] Gless in Niggli et al., 2014 at art. 141 no. 2. *See* in detail to the legislative process Gless, 2007 at 401 et seq.; Hersch, 2012 at 359, 363, 367, 371 et seq. however, explains in detail various differences between art. 141 (2) CPC and the Supreme Court's case law.

[205] *See* below 3.1.3.

[206] Vetterli, 2012 at 462 referring to Official Bulletin of the National Council, Summer Session 2007 at 955 et seq.

[207] *See* generally Gless, 2010 at 149 et seq.

[208] Recent reform efforts plan to amend art. 141 (4) CPC by extending its scope of application also to evidence inadmissible under paragraph 1 of art. 141 CPC, see art. 141 (4) of the preliminary draft regarding a reform of the CPC submitted by the Swiss Federal Council in December 2017, available online at <https://www.bj.admin.ch/dam/data/bj/sicherheit/gesetzgebung/aenderungstpo/vorentw-d.pdf>, accessed 22 November 2018.

(5) *Records relating to inadmissible evidence shall be removed from the case documents, held in safekeeping until a final judgment has concluded the proceedings, and then destroyed.*

Article 141 CPC does not prescribe the general exclusion of all evidence gathered in violation of the law. Rather, it differentiates between absolute exclusionary rules, relative exclusionary rules, and violations of administrative regulations.[209]

Article 141 (1) CPC establishes the absolute exclusionary rule, which does not allow the use of judicial discretion[210]: If evidence falls under the auspices of art. 141 (1) CPC, its exclusion is mandatory.[211] Such evidence includes that which is obtained through explicitly prohibited methods, including coercion, violence, threats, promises, deception and other methods that may compromise the ability of the person concerned to think or decide freely, as well as evidence excluded pursuant to other provisions of the CPC.[212] The latter includes, for instance, the exclusionary rules found in art. 158 (2) CPC (statements made prior to the accused being informed of the proceedings against them and their legal rights)[213] and in art. 289 (6) CPC (unauthorized undercover investigations).[214]

Alternatively, art. 141 (2) CPC provides a so-called "relative" exclusionary rule, which gives courts some discretion in deciding the admissibility of evidence.[215] The exclusionary rule of art. 141 (2) CPC is termed relative because it only excludes evidence in principle. The admission of the same evidence remains possible under art. 141 (2) CPC if it is essential to establish the facts of a serious offence.[216] This provision applies to evidence gathered through criminal means that do not require exclusion under art. 141 (1) CPC[217] or evidence gathered in violation of *regulations on admissibility* (Gültigkeitsvorschriften). Regulations on admissibility are legal provisions deemed so crucial to the safeguarding of individual rights that their objective can only be achieved if their violation results in the invalidity of any subsequent action(s) and the exclusion of evidence garnered.[218] In contrast, the violation of administrative regulations[219] does not require the exclusion of evidence

[209]Oberholzer, 2012 at no. 702.

[210]Gless/Martin, 2015 at 167.

[211]Pieth, 2016 at 192; Schmid, 2017 at § 58 no. 793.

[212]*See* the enumeration in Gless in Niggli et al., 2014 at art. 141 no. 48 et seq.

[213]Pieth, 2016 at 193.

[214]Gless/Martin, 2015 at 167 et seq.

[215]Gless/Martin, 2015 at 168 et seq.; Pieth, 2016 at 194 et seq.

[216]Oberholzer, 2012 at no. 705.

[217]*See* in detail Hersch, 2012 at 366 et seq.; *also* Gless in Niggli et al., 2014 at art. 141 no. 65 as well as the example in Thommen/Samadi, 2016 at 69 et seq. with further references; *see also* BGE 141 IV 417, consid. 2.

[218]Bundesblatt, 2006 at 1183 et seq.; BGE 139 IV 128, consid. 1.6.

[219]"Designed to guarantee the smooth administration of criminal proceedings", Thommen/Samadi, 2016 at 71; *also* Vest/Eicker, 2005 at 890.

obtained thereafter (as art. 141 (3) CPC states). It may, however, lead to disciplinary sanctions.[220]

Article 141 (2) CPC is criticized on several fronts. First, it can be difficult to apply as a result of vague verbiage, which has led to numerous attempts at defining the terms "serious offence"[221] and "essential."[222] The differentiation between regulations on admissibility and administrative regulations has also been critiqued.[223] As regulations on admissibility have the primary aim of safeguarding individual rights, it should follow that their violation *always* results in the evidence being excluded without any exceptions.[224] However, the exception for serious offences found in Art. 141 (2) CPC negates this rationale and more or less implies that the severity of the crime committed can justify the violation of procedural rules (or even crimes) by the police and may even encourage such misconduct.[225] This idea has been summed up in the legal literature using the phrase: "The bigger the crime, the smaller the chance of a fair trial."[226] It is undeniable that defendants accused of serious offenses are in greater need of procedural safeguards yet it is in this very context that a defendant's rights are most often compromised.[227] To minimize the problems raised by art. 141 (2) CPC, the admission of illegally obtained evidence should only be considered if other interests such as the accused's individual rights do not disproportionately outweigh the public interest in fighting crime.[228]

Ultimately, it is problematic to give courts the discretion to balance competing interests when it comes to the exclusion of evidence. Additionally, it is much more difficult for a court to knowingly acquit a guilty defendant by excluding evidence than it is for the legislature to set procedural limitations to the search for truth in order to secure fair trials.[229] As such, a more definitive rule would be preferable. On the other hand, exclusionary rules that are too strict and do not provide the courts with any discretion can also lead to judges finding ways to reassert their authority

---

[220]Thommen/Samadi, 2016 at 71.

[221]Gless in Niggli et al., 2014 at art. 141 no. 72; Hersch, 2012 at 368 et seq.; Ruckstuhl et al., 2011 at no. 556; Wohlers/Bläsi, 2015 at 164 et seq., all with further references.

[222]It is particularly disputed whether a balancing approach is still possible under the terms of art. 141 (2) CPC; *see* Hersch, 2012 at 369 et seq. with further references; *see also* below at 3.3.; Ruckstuhl et al., 2011 at no. 557, however, state that the term "essential" has no independent significance.

[223]Donatsch/Cavegn, 2008 at 165 et seq. with further critical points; *also* Fornito, 2000 at 239 et seq.; Gless in Niggli et al., 2014 at art. 141 no. 74; Häring, 2009 at 239 et seq.; Keller, 2011 at 245; Vest/Höhener, 2009 at 102; Vetterli, 2012 at 463.

[224]Vetterli, 2012 at 463.

[225]Thommen/Samadi, 2016 at 84 et seq.; Vest/Eicker, 2005 at 891; Vest/Höhener, 2009 at 103.

[226]Thommen/Samadi, 2016 at 85 et seq.

[227]Gless, 2010 at 157; Gless, 2012 at 140; Oberholzer, 2012 at no. 706; Fornito, 2000 at 250; Vest/Eicker, 2005 at 891; also Vest/Höhener, 2009 at 103; Vetterli, 2012 at 457; Thommen/Samadi, 2016 at 84.

[228]Gless/Martin, 2015 at 169.

[229]Vetterli, 2012 at 458 et seq.

by creatively interpreting the provisions and potentially encouraging their nonenforcement.[230]

A distinct provision of the Swiss CPC is art. 141 (4), which excludes indirect (or derivative) evidence that would have been impossible to obtain without the use of evidence deemed inadmissible under art. 141 (2) CPC.[231] This is unique because the fruit of the poisonous tree doctrine, while typical of adversarial systems, is rarely found in inquisitorial criminal justice systems.

3.1.3 Jurisprudence of the Supreme Court

The Swiss CPC established a legal framework of fairly strict exclusionary rules. This led to conflicts in their application because, among other things, Swiss courts had formerly enjoyed wide discretion in the application of their respective cantonal codes.[232] The Swiss Supreme Court was previously using a balancing approach to evidence exclusion in criminal proceedings. Under this approach, the question of whether or not a piece of evidence was admissible at trial was determined by the court after balancing the varying interests of the particular case.[233] While this allowed for a thorough consideration of all aspects of the particular case, it included with it the risk that courts would justify purely subjective decisions.[234] It also had the potential of leading to inconsistent decisions across cases, as is highlighted by the Supreme Court's case law on exclusionary rules.[235]

Today, the strict exclusionary rules of the CPC grant little discretional power to the courts.[236] Courts are allowed to return to a balancing approach only where the CPC fails to give an answer about the admissibility of a particular piece of evidence. This is the case for the exclusion of evidence resulting from principles based on so-called *autonomous exclusionary rules* ("selbständige Beweisverwertungsverbote"), or the taking of evidence through private individuals, and the exclusion of exonerating

[230]Gless/Martin, 2015 at 179 et seq.

[231]However, recent reform efforts plan to amend art. 141 (4) CPC by extending its scope of application also to evidence inadmissible under paragraph 1 of art. 141 CPC, see art. 141 (4) of the preliminary draft regarding a reform of the CPC submitted by the Swiss Federal Council in December 2017, available online at <https://www.bj.admin.ch/dam/data/bj/sicherheit/gesetzgebung/aenderungstpo/vorentw-d.pdf>, accessed 22 November 2018.

[232]Gless/Martin, 2015 at 160 et seq.

[233]BGE 130 I 126, consid. 3.2.; BGE 120 Ia 314, consid. 2.d.

[234]Wohlers/Bläsi, 2015 at 160; *also* Fornito, 2000 at 248 et seq.; Häring, 2009 at 245 et seq.; Vest/Eicker, 2005 at 890 et seq.

[235]Vest/Höhener, 2009 at 102 et seq.

[236]Gless/Martin, 2015 at 171.

evidence.[237] However, the restriction of discretion through art. 141 CPC should not be overestimated either given that the legislature sought to codify the current jurisdiction of the Supreme Court with this provision.[238] Despite this rationale, there are some deviations. Section 2 of art. 141 CPC, in particular, differs from the Supreme Court's earlier case law.[239] Specifically, the provision only allows evidence obtained by illegal means or in violation of *regulations on admissibility* to be admitted if it is essential to the resolution of a serious offense. The statute does not mention the additional balancing criteria the Supreme Court had been relying upon in the case law up to that point, including the determination of whether the evidence could have been obtained legally[240] and the application of the principle of a fair trial.[241] The continued applicability of such criteria under the terms of art. 141 (2) CPC is disputed in the legal literature.[242]

In addition to the aforementioned changes, the legislature has emphasized that the exclusion of evidence under the terms of art. 141 (2) CPC (which does leave some discretion to the courts) should be the rule and that the admission of evidence gathered by violation of regulations on admissibility or a criminal offense must be the exception.[243] Before the CPC was enacted, the Supreme Court made the exclusion of evidence the exception rather than the rule by applying the balancing approach.[244] Under this approach an increasing number of minor offenses were classified as "serious offence" for the purposes of evidence admission.[245] However, in a more recent judgement (still under cantonal law) the Supreme Court stated that offenses punishable by imprisonment up to three years or a fine ("Vergehen")[246] represent relatively

[237]*See* in detail Häring, 2009 at 118 et seq.; *also* BGE 133 IV 329 consid. 4.4., referring to exclusionary rules explicitly mentioned in a special law. Autonomous exclusionary rules provide for the exclusion of *legally* obtained evidence in case that other interests outweigh the interest in using the evidence, Gless in Niggli et al., 2014 at art. 141 no. 9 et seq.; Vest/Höhener, 2009 at 98 et seq.; Wohlers/Bläsi, 2015 at 160 and 161 et seq.

[238]*See* above 3.1.2.

[239]*See* Hersch, 2012 at 363, 367, 371 et seq.

[240]BGE 130 I 126, consid. 3.2; BGE 103 Ia 206 consid. 9.b.; BGE 96 I 437, consid. 3.b.; Vest/Eicker, 2005 at 889, 892; Vest/Höhener, 2009 at 105 et seq.

[241]BGE 137 I 224; BGE 131 I 272 consid. 3.2.3.5 et seq.; Vest/Höhener, 2009 at 103; Vetterli, 2012 at 460 et seq.

[242]Answering in the negative Hersch, 2012 at 361, 367 et seq., 372 with further references; *also* Wohlers/Bläsi, 2015 at 164 et seq.; Häring, 2009 at 243 et seq. on the other hand, points out that the legislator wanted to establish a balancing approach, however limited.

[243]The discussion in the National Council in: Official Bulletin of the National Council, Summer Session 2007 at 955 et seq.; *also* Vetterli, 2012 at 462; Hersch, 2012 at 367 et seq.; Vest/Höhener, 2009 at 107.

[244]*See* in detail Vest/Höhener, 2009 at 95 et seq.; *also* Hersch, 2012 at 358; Keller, 2011 at 234; Vetterli, 2012 at 458.

[245]Vetterli, 2012 at 458 et seq. with further references.

[246]Art. 10 (3) Swiss Criminal Code (SCC) of 21 December 1937 (Status as of 1 January 2017), available online at <https://www.admin.ch/opc/en/classified-compilation/19370083/index.html>, accessed 22 November 2018.

grave, but not *very serious* offenses, thereby ruling in favor of excluding illegally obtained evidence in these cases.[247] This judgment was commended by legal scholars and said to mark an important change in the Court's jurisprudence.[248]

Despite some changes, the Swiss Supreme Court has generally continued to try to find ways to preserve its balancing power since the CPC was enacted.[249] This is especially the case in its restrictive application of the absolute exclusionary rule (cf. art. 141 (1) CPC) and the fruit of the poisonous tree doctrine (cf. art. 141 (4) CPC).[250] Since the Supreme Court did not elaborate on clear criteria for the distinction between *regulations on admissibility* (cf. art. 141 (2) CPC) or mere *administrative regulations,* there has been a tendency for evidence to be admitted.[251] At the same time, it has also categorized several important provisions (e.g. the search of a person without a warrant) as *administrative regulations,*[252] thereby allowing the admission of evidence obtained through their violation.[253] This practice has rightfully been criticized by legal scholars.[254] It is not the case, however, that the Supreme Court categorically admits evidence wherever possible; there have been other situations where it has decided to exclude evidence.[255]

3.1.4 Enforcement of Exclusionary Rules

Violations of procedural rules and individual rights by the prosecution authorities cannot be undone. The negative consequences for the defendant, however, can be eliminated effectively through exclusionary rules where any tainted (incriminating) evidence is removed in its entirety from the file and not considered in the judgment.[256] The Code endorses this idea in Art. 141 (5) CPC which stipulates that all records relating to excluded evidence must be removed from the criminal files and kept separately until the final judgment, after which they are to be destroyed. Therefore, the excluded evidence should not be available to the prosecuting

---

[247] BGE 137 I 218, consid. 2.3.5.2.; the recent cantonal decision of the Kantonsgericht Schwyz, Strafkammer, of 20 June 2017, STK 2017 1, consid. 4.b.

[248] Vetterli, 2012 at 461.

[249] Gless/Martin, 2015 at 178 (referring to BGE 138 IV 169), 179 et seq., with further references.

[250] Wohlers/Bläsi, 2015 at 169; regarding the jurisprudence on the exclusion of indirect evidence, *see* below 3.2.5.2.

[251] Wohlers/Bläsi, 2015 at 164; *also* Gless, 2010 at 156; Gless, 2012 at 139; Gless in Niggli et al., 2014 at art. 141 no. 74; Vest/Höhener, 2009 at 102.

[252] *See, for instance,* BGE 141 IV 423, consid. 3 regarding the legal instruction of judicial experts.

[253] BGE 139 IV 128, consid. 1.7.; *see also* the examples in Gless in Niggli et al., 2014 at art. 141 no. 74.

[254] Thommen/Samadi, 2016 at 71; Wohlers/Bläsi, 2015 at 166.

[255] *For instance,* BGer 6B_1025/2016 of 24 October 2017, consid. 1; BGer 6B_656/2015 of 16 December 2016, consid. 1; BGE 141 IV 220, consid. 5.

[256] Vetterli, 2012 at 455 et seq.

authorities at any point in time during the investigation or court proceedings.[257] At first sight, art. 141 (5) CPC seems to specify clear rules, but in practice its application has led to problems, particularly where the excluded evidence relates to more than one defendant or is (also) potentially exonerating.[258]

Another issue with the CPC is that it does not contain any provisions addressing the way in which the exclusionary rules are to be enforced.[259] Specifically, the CPC does not outline which authority (judge(s) of fact, judges within the appellate body, or another authority) should decide the admissibility of evidence and at which stage of the proceedings. Typically, the *judge(s) of fact* decide[260] all substantive questions based on the complete criminal file, generally in the form of a conviction or an acquittal. The *court of appeal* is then tasked with examining only specifically contested procedural steps based on excerpts from the case file and providing an opinion in the form of an interim decision.[261]

The Swiss Supreme Court holds that the judges of fact have the authority to determine whether or not to exclude evidence from the main trial,[262] although there are some exceptions, for example, where the law[263] explicitly stipulates the immediate restitution or destruction of illegally obtained evidence.[264] There, the prosecution is required to exclude the evidence during the preliminary investigation.[265] With respect to illegally obtained confessions, the Supreme Court held that judges of fact should not have access to the confession for fear that they may consider it in the final judgment despite its exclusion.[266] Unfortunately, the Supreme Court has not elaborated on this last exception. In fact, it has made inconsistent statements on the matter, commenting that it is not in and of itself a problem that judges of fact have knowledge of illegally obtained evidence because they can be expected to refrain from considering it in their decisions.[267]

---

[257]Donatsch/Schwarzenegger/Wohlers, 2014 at 122.

[258]Donatsch/Schwarzenegger/Wohlers, 2014 at 122.

[259]Geisselhardt, 2014 at 300.

[260]Depending on the canton, the instance and the case, the court can consist of a single judge, three or five judges, Oberholzer, 2012 at no. 99 et seq.; art. 19 (2) CPC, art. 395 CPC.

[261]*See* generally Geisselhardt, 2014 at 300 et seq.

[262]BGE 141 IV 289, consid. 1.2.; BGer 1B-179/2012 of 13 April 2012, consid. 2.4.; *also* BGE 120 Ia 314, consid. 2.c. et seq., saying that evidence *may* be excluded in the trial. In BGE 122 I 182, consid. 4.c. (a decision dating from 1996 on evidence obtained by telephone tapping), however, the SSC emphasized that in certain cases the exclusion of evidence *by a court* may be necessary even during the preliminary proceedings.

[263]*See e.g*, art. 277 CPC (on the monitoring of post and telecommunications) or art. 289 (6) CPC (on undercover investigations).

[264]BGE 141 IV 284, consid. 2.3.; BGE 141 IV 289, consid. 1.3.

[265]Hansjakob in Donatsch et al., 2014 at art. 277 no. 10, regarding art. 277 CPC on the findings of unauthorized surveillence.

[266]BGer 1B_445/2013 of 14 February 2014, consid. 1.2 et seq.; *also* BGer 1B_124/2014 of 21 May 2014, consid. 1.2.3.; *also* BGE 122 I 182, consid. 4.c).

[267]BGE 141 IV 289, consid. 1.2.; *also* BGer 1B_124/2014 of 21 May 2014, consid. 1.2.4.

The jurisdiction of the judge(s) of fact remains disputed by legal scholars. Some agree with the Supreme Court's view because art. 343 (2) CPC stipulates that judges of fact are competent to re-take improperly obtained evidence during preliminary proceedings.[268] This is related to the idea that judges of fact should have unrestricted access to all available evidence[269] because only then can they fully evaluate the interests of all parties involved and make a determination as to whether the proceedings as a whole are fair.[270] Other scholars, however, have made convincing arguments criticizing the jurisdiction of judges of fact based upon the premise that the subsequent removal of evidence from the files does not erase the judges' knowledge of it. As a result, it is likely that they will still consider excluded evidence in their decisions,[271] which significantly reduces the effectiveness of exclusionary rules. This is even more problematic when crucial incriminating evidence is involved because judges seem to have difficulty in acquitting a defendant that is apparently guilty.[272] Furthermore, because exclusionary rules are binding at all stages of the judicial process, they must be considered in every procedural decision—and always with the same standards.[273] This is particularly important given the fact that, practically speaking, the police exert significant influence over the fact-finding process.[274] They should, therefore, also investigate exonerating evidence and potentially even implement exclusionary rules in order to effectively secure a fair trial. Thus, it seems preferable to grant defendants the right to request that evidence be excluded (and the right to appeal a denial of this request)

[268]Geisselhardt, 2014 at 301, 304, with exceptions at 305; *also* Groner, 2011 at 142; Oberholzer, 2012 at no. 714. However, art. 343 (2) CPC only stipulates that the court should re-take evidence in case it was improperly obtained in the preliminary proceedings, but it does not prohibit another authority to decide on the exclusion of the improperly obtained evidence.

[269]Geisselhardt, 2014 at 301, 302, 304; *also* Oberholzer, 2012 at no. 714. Gless in Niggli et al., 2014 at art. 139 no. 15, however, argues that only lawfully obtained evidence may be the basis for the free assessment of evidence.

[270]Geisselhardt, 2014 at 302 et seq., 304; differing, however Wohlers/Bläsi, 2015 at 171.

[271]Wohlers, 2016 at 430 et seq.; Wohlers/Bläsi, 2015 at 169 et seq.; *also* the illustration of this problem in Gless, 2013 at 346; the same argument in BGE 122 I 182, consid. 4.c. on evidence obtained by telephone tapping: "*Zudem besteht stets die Gefahr, dass der einmal zur Kenntnis genommene Inhalt von Schriftstücken auch bei förmlicher Entfernung aus den Akten haften bleibt und Entscheidungen mitbeeinflussen kann. Aus Gründen eines wirksamen Grundrechtsschutzes ist es daher nach Art. 36 Abs. 4 BV geboten, dass auf entsprechenden Antrag hin die Zulässigkeit der Telefonabhörung von Gesprächspartnern des Beschuldigten und Mitbenützern des überwachten Telefonanschlusses bereits im Untersuchungsstadium geprüft wird.*" Differing, however, BGE 141 IV 289, consid. 1.2. "*Von diesem [dem Sachrichter] kann erwartet werden, dass er in der Lage ist, die unzulässigen Beweise von den zulässigen zu unterscheiden und sich bei der Würdigung ausschliesslich auf Letztere zu stützen.*" As well as BGer 1B_124/2014 of 21 May 2014, consid. 1.2.2., differentiating, however, in consid. 1.2.3., referring to BGer 1B_445/2013 of 14 February 2014, consid. 1.2 et seq.

[272]Vetterli, 2012 at 457 et seq.

[273]Gless in Niggli et al., 2014 at art. 141 no. 35.

[274]*See* above 2.1.3.1.

during preliminary proceedings.[275] However, the authority that judges of fact have over the application of exclusionary rules does not equate to sole control over exclusionary rules. Rather, it should be the duty of the acting authority at each stage of the proceedings (police, public prosecution, judges) to examine whether evidence must be excluded—even if in the end judges of fact view it anyway.

Under Swiss law, if a party to criminal proceedings (particularly an accused) wants to make a motion for the exclusion of evidence, he or she can submit a request to the person in charge of the proceedings.[276] This is possible during both the pre-trial proceedings[277] or the main hearing.[278] It is recommended that the request be submitted as soon as practicably possible—in fact, if the exclusionary rule is not invoked until the appeal proceedings, the defendant might be considered to be capitalizing on the situation and his or her request denied as a result.[279] Depending on the stage of the proceedings, the prosecution or the court determines whether to exclude evidence in an interim decision.[280] The Supreme Court has held that until such a decision is made, the evidence in question may still be used for intermediate decisions and to support further investigation, unless it is *a priori* inadmissible.[281] In order to estimate whether unauthorized compulsory techniques have been used, the courts rely on the continual documentation and recording of the evidence collected.[282]

According to the jurisprudence of the Supreme Court, where the request to exclude evidence is denied, there is no right to object[283] except where mentioned above. Under these exceptions, the defendant has the opportunity to appeal the interim decision not to exclude evidence to an appellate court and, if necessary, the Swiss Supreme Court. For cases that do not fall under one of the exceptions, the aggrieved party is free to repeat the request for exclusion[284] or, alternatively, appeal the final decision[285] if based upon the contested evidence.[286] The court of appeals

---

275 *Also* Wohlers/Bläsi, 2015 at 174.

276 Wohlers in Donatsch et al., 2014 at art. 141 no. 10a.

277 Donatsch/Schwarzenegger/Wohlers, 2014 at 122.

278 Art. 339 (1) lit. d CPC; Oberholzer, 2012 at no. 714.

279 Oberholzer, 2012 at no. 716 and BGE 138 I 97, consid. 4.2.4.; dissenting Bürge, 2017 at 324. In BGE 129 I 85, consid. 4.4., however, the SSC stated that the right to request the exclusion of improperly obtained evidence can also be asserted in appeal proceedings.

280 *See*, amongst others, BGE 141 IV 289, consid. 1.1.

281 BGer 1B_2/2013 of 5 June 2013, consid. 1.2.; BGer 1B_179/2012 of 13 April 2012, consid. 2.4.; differing Wohlers in Donatsch et al., 2014 at art. 141 no. 1 with further references.

282 Gless in Niggli et al., 2014 at art. 140 no. 75; *also* art. 76 et seq. CPC; Oberholzer, 2012 at no. 699.

283 BGer 1B_414/2012 of 20 September 2012, consid. 1.2.; BGer 1B_584/2011 of 12 December 2011, consid. 3.2.

284 BGE 141 IV 289, consid. 2.7.

285 Art. 398 CPC; BGE 141 IV 289, consid. 1.2.; Wohlers in Donatsch et al., 2014 at art. 141 no. 10b.

286 Groner, 2011 at 143; BGer 6P.124/2002 of 6 October 2003, consid. 5.

will then evaluate the lower court's consideration of the evidence, including the issue of admissibility.[287] After all cantonal legal remedies are exhausted, a defendant may appeal to the Swiss Supreme Court.[288] If, at any point during the process, a court holds that evidence has been obtained improperly and, therefore, must be excluded, the evidence may not be considered in the final judgment.[289] The court must then re-take the evidence,[290] but only within the scope of art. 141 (4) CPC.[291]

3.2 *Exclusion of Illegally Obtained Evidence Following Improper Compulsory Techniques*

3.2.1 The Right Against Self-Incrimination and Improper Compulsory Measures

The legal authority for the right against self-incrimination can be found in both domestic and international law. First, it is expressly codified in art. 113 CPC, which states, "*The accused may not be compelled to incriminate him or herself. In particular, the accused is entitled to refuse to make a statement or to cooperate in the criminal proceedings. He or she must however submit to the compulsory measures provided for by the law.*" At the international level, the right against self-incrimination is considered by the European Court of Human Rights (ECtHR) to be one of the most important components of a fair trial and is guaranteed by art. 6 (1) of the ECHR.[292] It is also explicitly mentioned in art. 14 (3) lit. g of the ICCPR II.

The right against self-incrimination hypothetically grants a defendant the right to refuse to collaborate whatsoever at any point during criminal proceedings.[293] As a result, prosecution authorities are not allowed to improperly compel[294] a defendant

---

[287]Oberholzer, 2012 at no. 714.

[288]Gless in Niggli et al., 2014 at art. 141 no. 121; BGE 141 IV 289, consid. 1.2.; Wohlers/Bläsi, 2015 at 174 argue that already the interim decision on the exclusion of evidence should be contestable.

[289]Groner, 2011 at 141.

[290]BGer 6B_690/2015 of 25 November 2015, consid. 3.4.; art. 343 (2) CPC.

[291]Häring, 2009 at 253; *see also* above 3.1.4.

[292]European Court of Human Rights (ECtHR), *Saunders* v. *United Kingdom*, case no. 19187/91, Judgment (Grand Chamber) of 17 December 1996, § 68.

[293]Lieber in Donatsch et al., 2014 at art. 113 no. 1.

[294]ECtHR, *Saunders* v. *United Kingdom*, case no. 19187/91, Judgment (Grand Chamber) of 17 December 1996, § 68; *see also* BGE 131 IV 36, consid. 3.1.

to collaborate.[295] Whilst the authorities are permitted to use compulsory measures under certain circumstances,[296] including searching people and their property[297] and tapping their phones,[298] art. 140 (1) states that "*the use of coercion, violence, threats, promises, deception and* [other] *methods that may compromise the ability of the person concerned to think or decide freely are prohibited when taking evidence.*"[299] Accordingly, coercing a defendant is improper and violates the right against self-incrimination where it aims to influence or break the will of a defendant.[300] Article 140 (1) CPC applies to any point during which time evidence is taken, although traditionally it referred solely to the interrogation of an accused.[301]

3.2.2 Torture and Inhuman or Degrading Treatment

Law enforcement authorities are limited by all individuals' inherent and inalienable right to dignity, which is absolute and cannot be outweighed by other interests.[302] As a consequence, art. 3 and 15 (2) ECHR, art. 7 and 4 (2) ICCPR II, art. 10 (3) BV, as well as art. 3 (2) lit. d CPC strictly prohibit gathering evidence in any manner that violates human dignity, including the use of torture and degrading treatment. The classification of any technique depends on the specific circumstances of the case, such as the duration and consequences, as well as the age, sex, and current state of health of the affected person.[303] According to art. 1 (1) UN Convention Against Torture (CAT),[304] *torture* includes "any act by which severe pain or suffering, whether physical or mental, is intentionally inflicted on a person." However, this high threshold required for an act to constitute torture has been lowered in recent years.[305] Additionally, *inhuman treatment* is defined as that which causes injuries or intense physical or psychological pain[306] while *degrading*

[295]Lieber in Donatsch et al., 2014 at art. 113 no. 37. In detail, however, it is quite controversial what is meant by "improper compulsion", *see e.g.*, Macula, 2016 at. 24 et seq. with further references.

[296]As art. 113 (1) CPC explicitly states.

[297]Art. 249 et seq. CPC.

[298]Art. 269 et seq. CPC.

[299]For a detailed definition of those methods, *see* Gless in Niggli et al., 2014 at art. 140 no. 32 et seq.; Wohlers, in Donatsch et al., 2014 at art. 140 no. 3 et seq.

[300]Lieber in Donatsch et al. 2014 at art. 113 no. 44 with further references.

[301]Gless in Niggli et al., 2014 at art. 140 no. 21 et seq.

[302]Wohlers, in Donatsch et al., 2014 at art. 3 no. 5 with further references.

[303]Wohlers, in Donatsch et al., 2014 at art. 3 no. 47 et seq. and 50 with further references.

[304]Of 10 December 1984, available online at <www.ohchr.org/Documents/ProfessionalInterest/cat.pdf>, accessed 22 November 2018.

[305]Wohlers, in Donatsch et al., 2014 at art. 3 no. 48 with further references.

[306]Wohlers, in Donatsch et al., 2014 at art. 3 no. 49 with further references.

treatment involves the causing of pain or degradation, for example through corporal punishment or the threat of torture.[307]

3.2.3 Institutional Bans on Torture and the Right to Remain Silent

Swiss law provides several institutional measures banning torture and preserving the right to remain silent, which are included in the discussion of remedies (supervision, disciplinary, and criminal liability) above, although their enforcement is problematic due to a fragmented statutory code and restricted legal practice.[308] Other legal remedies also exist[309] and a large majority of the cantons have introduced a duty for doctors to report any violations of a patient's physical or mental well-being observable to them in their medical practice.[310] Within this system of safeguarding individual rights, exclusionary rules are of the utmost importance—at least in theory.

3.2.4 Exclusionary Rules Applicable to Illegally Obtained Evidence

3.2.4.1 Legal Framework

Evidence obtained through torture or other improper compulsory techniques violates art. 140 (1) CPC (prohibited methods of taking evidence) and triggers the absolute exclusionary rule of art. 141 (1) CPC. The exclusion of such evidence is mandatory, without exception, and is not subject to judicial discretion.[311]

The CPC does not outline a standard procedure to determine whether improper compulsory procedures have been used in an investigation. However, some cantons have established specific protocols in cases of criminal complaints alleging police abuse.[312] A study by the Swiss Centre of Expertise in Human Rights (SCHR) found numerous media reports on alleged abuse by police in Switzerland,[313] but none of the cases studied involved violations with the specific intent of obtaining evidence from an accused. If a defendant alleges that evidence—a confession for instance—has been obtained in violation of the CPC, but cannot prove it, the reliability and significance of such evidence is at the discretion of the court due to the principle of

[307]Wohlers, in Donatsch et al., 2014 at art. 3 no. 50 with further references. As to the threat of torture, *see* ECtHR, *Gäfgen* v. *Germany*, case no. 22978/05, Judgment (Grand Chamber) of 1 June 2010, § 65, 69.

[308]*See* above 3.1.2 et seq. and below 3.2.4 et seq.

[309]*See* above 2.1.3.2 et seq.

[310]In the other cantons, the doctor must previously seek to be released from his or her duty to maintain secrecy; *see* CAT Report, 2016 at 2 et seq.

[311]Pieth, 2016 at 192; Schmid, 2017 at § 58 no. 793.

[312]*See* below 2.1.3.3.

[313]Künzli et al., 2014 at 6 et seq. with further references.

unrestricted access to evidence.[314] However, recent reform efforts plan to amend the CPC by adding a new art. 78a CPC on the recording of interviews with technical devices (such as videotaping). Such recording techniques provide an important tool to monitor interviews and to ensure that police and prosecutors adhere to procedural rules.[315]

3.2.4.2 Jurisprudence of the Supreme Court

As mentioned above, the mandatory exclusionary rule of art. 141 (1) CPC leaves no discretion to the courts.[316] However, art. 140 (1) CPC leaves some room for the courts to specify "methods that may compromise the ability of the person concerned to think or decide freely." Swiss Supreme Court case law on this issue indicates that prohibited methods under this section include inducing intoxication with alcohol,[317] using a lie detector,[318] and using narcoanalysis ("truth serum").[319] By contrast, the Supreme Court tends to find evidence admissible that has been obtained through cooperation duties of administrative law.[320]

The use of torture in criminal proceedings does not appear to be a major problem in Switzerland. Cases decided by the Supreme Court have primarily addressed issues around conditions of detention and imprisonment,[321] not compulsory techniques in evidence gathering.

3.2.5 Admissibility of Fruit of Poisonous Tree in Cases of Torture and Improper Compulsory Techniques

3.2.5.1 Legal Framework

Article 141 (4) CPC creates a limited version of the fruit of the poisonous tree doctrine (i.e. the exclusion of indirect evidence). As previously mentioned, such provisions are uncommon in inquisitorial criminal procedure systems as they stem from adversarial criminal justice systems. As a result, there can be problems with

---

[314]Art. 10 (3) CPC, *see* above 2.1.1.1.

[315]*See* art. 78a of the preliminary draft regarding a reform of the CPC submitted by the Swiss Federal Council in December 2017, available online at <https://www.bj.admin.ch/dam/data/bj/sicherheit/gesetzgebung/aenderungstpo/vorentw-d.pdf>, accessed 22 November 2018.

[316]*See* above, 3.1.2.

[317]BGE 90 I 29, consid. 5.b.

[318]BGE 109 Ia 273, consid. 7.

[319]BGE 118 Ia 28, consid. 1.c.

[320]Macula, 2016 at 51 et seq.; *see also*, for instance, BGE 142 IV 207, consid. 8 et seq.; BGE 140 II 384, consid. 3.

[321]BGE 141 I 141; BGE 141 IV 423; BGE 140 I 246, consid. 2.4.2.; BGE 139 IV 41.

applying the doctrine.[322] Article 141 (4) CPC codifies the Swiss Supreme Court's case law since 2007[323] on indirect evidence.[324] The provision states that such evidence "shall not be used, if it would not have been possible to obtain it, without relying on the previously obtained evidence."[325] Thus, the legislature opted to create a statute that excluded some, but not all indirect evidence.[326]

Specifically, Art. 141 (4) CPC excludes only evidence that would not have been possible to obtain without relying on evidence deemed inadmissible under art. 141 (2) CPC. Thus, the legal text of section 4 paradoxically does not explicitly exclude indirect evidence based on primary evidence obtained by torture and other illegal compulsory techniques. The legislature did, however, require the *strict* exclusion of *any* evidence in these cases, which implicitly includes also indirect evidence.[327] Legal scholars agree that evidence excluded under the terms of the more stringent art. 141 (1) CPC must *a fortiori* include exclusion of subsequent, indirect evidence,[328] but they do not agree on the details. Whilst the prevailing theory advocates for the *strict* exclusion of indirect evidence obtained following a violation of art. 141 (1) CPC,[329] other scholars argue for the application of the *limited* exclusionary rule stipulated in art. 141 (4) CPC.[330] As a consequence of these debates, recent reform efforts plan to amend art. 141 (4) CPC by extending its scope of application explicitly to evidence inadmissible under paragraph 1 and 2 of art. 141 CPC.[331]

The exclusion of indirect evidence should also be considered where authorities seek to re-take improperly obtained evidence. In light of art. 141 (4) CPC, not only is the illegally gathered evidence tainted, but so is the knowledge acquired through

---

[322]Gless/Martin, 2015 at 161 with further references.

[323]BGer 6B_211/2009 of 22 June 2009, consid. 1.4.2.; BGE 134 IV 266, consid. 5.3.; BGE 133 IV 329, consid. 4.5.

[324]Wohlers/Bläsi, 2015 at 167.

[325]*See* the English translation of art. 141 (4) in Wohlers in Donatsch et al., 2014 at 703.

[326]Keller, 2011 at 246.

[327]The discussion in the Council of States, in: Official Bulletin of Council of States, Winter Session 2006 at 1014: „*Une preuve indirecte est également inexploitable si la première preuve a été obtenue par la violation de prescriptions qui la rend inexploitable. Il y a une exception qui découle de la dernière partie de l'alinéa 2 qui dit que la première preuve est exploitable à certaines conditions*"; *also* Pieth, 2016 at 199 and Vetterli, 2012 at 466 both with further references.

[328]Gless in Niggli et al., 2014 at art. 141 no. 90; Ruckstuhl et al., 2011 at no. 565; Pieth, 2016 at 199; Wohlers in Donatsch et al., 2014 at art. 141 no. 14, all with further references.

[329]Gless, 2010 at 159; Gless, 2012 at 142; Häring, 2009 at 251; Pieth, 2016 at 199 with further references; Wohlers/Bläsi, 2015 at. 166 et seq.

[330]Since the unlimited exclusion would be exaggerated, *see* Vetterli, 2012 at 466.

[331]*See* art. 141 (4) of the preliminary draft regarding a reform of the CPC submitted by the Swiss Federal Council in December 2017, available online at <https://www.bj.admin.ch/dam/data/bj/sicherheit/gesetzgebung/aenderungstpo/vorentw-d.pdf>, accessed 22 November 2018.

it. Therefore, the re-taking of such evidence should only be possible where it conforms to the limitations set forth in art. 141 (4) CPC.[332]

3.2.5.2 Jurisprudence of the Supreme Court

Until quite recently, the question of whether evidence deemed fruit of the poisonous tree should be admissible was not clearly answered by Swiss law or jurisprudence.[333] Finally, in October 2007, the Supreme Court ruled on the issue. After considering the varying arguments by legal scholars,[334] the Supreme Court held that whilst the admission of indirect evidence may undermine the rules of evidence, its exclusion would hinder the search for the truth. It went on to say that the most appropriate solution is to exclude indirect evidence, but only where it could not have been obtained without the initial, direct evidence.[335] This ruling was subsequently codified in art. 141 (4) CPC.

On its face, the Supreme Court's holding was clear. However, the question of whether or not indirect evidence could have been obtained without the initial, illegally obtained, evidence introduces ambiguity.[336] To make matters worse, in the 2007 ruling the Court emphasized the importance of balancing the relevant interests in determining whether or not to exclude fruit of the poisonous tree.[337] Since the codification of the fruit of the poisonous tree doctrine in Article 141 Abs. 4 CPC, however, there is no longer any room to balance competing interests because the statute does not explicitly grant the courts discretion to do so. In such situations, the court has very little leeway in determining the mere factual question of whether the indirect evidence could have been obtained without the initial unlawfully procured evidence.[338]

Since the 2007 decision, the Supreme Court has interpreted the newly adopted fruit of the poisonous tree doctrine quite narrowly, repeatedly arguing in favor of admitting evidence based on speculative and hypothetical clean path analyses.[339] It even went as far to state that the acquittal of an obviously guilty defendant under on the fruit of the poisonous tree doctrine would be "disturbing" ("stossend").[340] This argument is in stark contrast to the underlying rationale of safeguarding human rights by placing clear-cut limitations on law enforcement's search for the truth and the state's interest in obtaining convictions. If the impending acquittal of a guilty

---

[332]Häring, 2009 at 253.

[333]BGE 109 Ia 244, consid. 2.b.; BGE 132 IV 70, consid. 2.6.

[334]*See* the references in BGE 133 IV 329, consid. 4.5.

[335]BGE 133 IV 329, consid. 4.5.

[336]*Also* BGE 133 IV 329, consid. 3.3.1.

[337]BGE 138 IV 169, consid. 3.3.2.

[338]Gless/Martin, 2015 at 169 et seq.

[339]BGE 133 IV 329, consid. 4.6; Ruckstuhl et al., 2011 at no. 569; Wohlers/Bläsi, 2015 at 167.

[340]BGE 133 IV 329, consid. 4.5.

person is perceived as unacceptable and as a reason for admitting evidence, exclusionary rules become meaningless. Additionally, acquitting a defendant due to a lack of admissible evidence does not nullify the pursuit of the truth, but is a necessary consequence of setting boundaries and limitations in criminal proceedings.[341]

After being criticized by a number of legal scholars,[342] the Supreme Court redefined the hypothetical clean path analysis more clearly and held that the theoretical possibility that evidence was obtained legally is insufficient; rather, a strong probability that the indirect evidence would have been obtained without relying on the illegally gathered evidence is required.[343] Notwithstanding this clarification, the Supreme Court still seems to be lenient in its decisions on what constitutes "a strong probability."[344] Notably, in the same case where it clarified the clear path analysis, the Court subsequently admitted indirect evidence based on a less-than convincing hypothetical clean path. In that case, a drug trafficker passed the Swiss border in possession of drugs hidden in a fire extinguisher and the Swiss prosecution authorities had knowledge about his involvement due to an illegal wiretap in Slovenia. Consequently, the border patrol stopped him, searched his car, and located a large quantity of drugs.[345] The Swiss Supreme Court held that the drugs were admissible because, despite the abolition of systematic border controls in the Schengen Area, the defendant was likely to be stopped and searched at the Swiss border because of his nervous demeanor.[346]

This holding is problematic because it is based upon hindsight analyses using all the facts, including the illegally obtained evidence.[347] From this perspective it is very easy to construct a hypothetical clean path to admit the evidence in question, even if it is highly speculative. Therefore, some scholars correctly advocate for admitting indirect evidence only in cases where—from an ex ante point of view—its obtainment without the tainted direct evidence constitutes a "*probability bordering on certainty*".[348] Although it is likely that such cases will be rare,[349] it should be noted that the Swiss Supreme Court's jurisprudence is not entirely

---

[341]Vetterli, 2012 at 457.

[342]Gless, 2010 at 154 et seq.; Gless in Niggli et al., 2014 at art. 141 no. 97; Pieth, 2016 at 199 et seq.; Ruckstuhl et al., 2011 at no. 569 et seq.; Wohlers in Donatsch et. al, 2014 at art. 141 no. 15.

[343]BGE 138 IV 169, consid. 333.

[344]Gless, 2016 at 136; Wohlers/Bläsi, 2015 at 168, both with further references.

[345]BGE 138 IV 169, consid. 3.4.1. and 3.4.3.

[346]BGE 138 IV 169, consid. 3.4.3.; critical Vetterli, 2012 at 468; Wohlers/Bläsi, 2015 at 168. Another case where the SSC admitted indirect tainted evidence: BGer 6B_684/2012 of 15 May 2013, consid. 3.3.2.

[347]Häring, 2009 at 252 et seq.; Ruckstuhl et al., 2011 at no. 570; Wohlers/Bläsi, 2015 at 168.

[348]Gless, 2010 at 155, 159; Gless, 2012 at 141, 143; Häring, 2009 at 253; Pieth, 2016 at 199 with further references; Vetterli, 2012 at 467 et seq.; Wohlers in Donatsch et al., 2014 at art. 141 no. 15.

[349]Vetterli, 2012 at 467.

one-sided. It excluded indirect evidence based on art. 141 (4) CPC in a case where the defendant confessed, but only after the prosecution authorities showed him an illegally recorded video containing information they could not have known otherwise.[350] However, upon closer inspection, the issue is not related to fruit of the poisonous tree because presentation of illegally obtained evidence constitutes deceptive police tactics and the obtained confession was required to be excluded directly under the terms of art. 141 (1) CPC.[351]

Overall, the case law of the Swiss Supreme Court illustrates how the effectiveness of exclusionary rules is completely dependent upon the local practice and jurisprudence. It should also be kept in mind, however, that the Swiss legislature chose not to establish a stricter fruit of the poisonous tree doctrine,[352] and instead codified the Supreme Court's case law through art. 141 (4) CPC.[353] Furthermore, the Supreme Court's narrow interpretation of the statute up until now is limited to cases where evidence was obtained by unauthorized searches or surveillance. It is thus unclear how it will decide if and when confronted with a case of torture or the use of improper compulsory measures. If the Court elects to *strictly* exclude evidence in such cases, defendants will be afforded comprehensive protection. However, even if it decides to apply the *limited* exclusionary rule of art. 141 (4) CPC, it is still unlikely that it will admit tainted evidence as freely as it has in the past.

3.2.6 The Effect of International Human Rights Law

It is the prevailing opinion that evidentiary rules in criminal procedure are the prerogative of the national legislature. As such, only a few (and rather vague)[354] international guidelines on exclusionary rules exist.[355] Nevertheless, international law and jurisprudence do still influence national evidentiary law and are of particular importance when defining concepts such as torture and inhuman treatment.[356] Article 15 of the UNCAT implies the absolute exclusion of evidence obtained through torture and degrading treatment.[357] The ECtHR has also set clear limitations on evidence taking in recent cases and has held that the admission of evidence obtained through torture is strictly prohibited as violative of art.

[350]BGE 137 I 218, consid. 2.4.2; *see also* the detailed analysis of this case in Vetterli, 2012 at 447 et seq.

[351]Vetterli, 2012 at 469.

[352]*Also* the examples on admissible and inadmissible indirect evidence in Bundesblatt 2006 at 1184.

[353]*See* above 3.2.5.1.

[354]Gless in Niggli et al., 2014 at art. 139 no. 12.

[355]Gless in Niggli et al., 2014 at art. 141 no. 19.

[356]Gless in Niggli et al., 2014 at art. 140 no. 35; *see* above 3.2.2.

[357]Gless in Niggli et al., 2014 at art. 141 no. 15.

3 ECHR.[358] However, the ECtHR has not taken a similar path with respect to the exclusion of evidence gathered by inhuman treatment[359] or indirect evidence acquired through torture.[360] In these cases, the ECtHR appears to be more likely to exclude evidence where the offense in question constitutes a less serious, victimless crime, such as a drug offense.[361] Additionally, according to the ECHR, the violation of rights ensuring a fair trial such as the right against self-incrimination[362] may, but do not require, that the evidence in question be excluded.[363] On the contrary, the ECtHR generally limits itself to examine "whether the proceedings as a whole, including the way in which the evidence was obtained, were fair" [364] and if they conformed with art. 6 ECHR. The result is that many decisions by the ECtHR are not strictly followed by the national courts,[365] thereby weakening the rights enshrined in the ECHR.

4 Statistics

There is, unfortunately, very little empirical data evaluating the importance of fair trial principles in Swiss criminal procedure.[366] This is particularly the case with regard to the practical impact of exclusionary rules. That said, a trial observation project was recently finished and included the evaluation of criminal proceedings in first instance courts in four Swiss cantons over the course of two years. The project investigated how often defense rights were asserted and how the courts dealt with those requests.[367] The study was based on the observation of 439 randomly chosen[368] court hearings and subsequent interviews with the parties involved

[358]For example, ECtHR, *Gäfgen* v. *Germany,* case no. 22978/05, Judgment (Grand Chamber) of 1 June 2010, § 131 et seq. and 167; Gless, in Niggli et al., 2014 at art. 141 no. 22; Thommen/Samadi, 2016 at 76.

[359]ECtHR, *Jalloh* v. *Germany,* case no. 54810/00, Judgment (Grand Chamber) of 11 July 2006, § 83 and 103 et seq.; Thommen/Samadi, 2016 at 77.

[360]ECtHR, *Gäfgen* v. *Germany,* case no. 22978/05, Judgment (Grand Chamber) of 1 June 2010, § 169 et seq.; *also* Gless in Niggli et al., 2014 at art. 140 no. 14 with further references.

[361]Oberholzer, 2012 at no. 700 et seq.

[362]*See* Macula, 2016 at 28 et seq., 56 et seq.; Vest/Eicker, 2005 at 886.

[363]Thommen/Samadi, 2016 at 77 et seq. with further references.

[364]*See*, among others, ECtHR, *Bykov* v. *Russia,* case no. 4378/02, Judgment (Grand Chamber) of 10 March 2009, § 89 with further references; ECtHR, *Schenk* v. *Switzerland,* case no. 10862/84, Judgment of 12 July 1988, § 46.

[365]Gless in Niggli et al., 2014 at art. 139 no. 12. As to the problem of the reception of Strasbourg case law on criminal evidence, *see also* Jackson/Summers, 2013 at 114 et seq.

[366]Summer/Studer, 2016 at 45 et seq.

[367]Summer/Studer, 2016 at 46.

[368]Summer/Studer, 2016 at 54.

(defendant, prosecution, defense counsel).[369] During the project, infringements on the right to a fair trial were qualified as *initiated by a party to the proceedings*, *initiated by the court*, or *exclusively observed by the project members*.[370] The results of this study showed that, out of 714 infringements on the right to a fair trial (initiated or observed), only 35 were related to infringements on the right against self-incrimination. Furthermore, 15 infringements were related to otherwise illegally obtained evidence that do not fall under the scope of art. 6 (1) ECHR (evidence obtained in violation of art. 3 or art. 8 ECHR). However, the infringement on rights related to other aspects of a fair trial, including the right to summon and question witnesses (113), the right to have an interpreter (104), the presumption of innocence (102) and the right to a speedy trial (98), were much more often discussed and observed.[371] Furthermore, the project found that most infringements on defendant rights observed by the project members did not lead to a complaint by the defendant or the defense counsel.[372] Although this data does not provide a basis for a definitive assessment, it does indicate that, in the end, the exclusion of evidence obtained in breach of the right against self-incrimination and of the prohibition on torture is of less practical importance in Switzerland than would be suggested by the level of importance given to this issue in literature.

5 Conclusion

Swiss exclusionary rules look very promising as law on the books. In 2011, a far-reaching, concise statute established what appeared to be clear-cut guidelines to safeguard individual rights in criminal proceedings in Switzerland. The harmonization of the law and the clarification of exclusionary rules in a few specific cases has triggered a lively discussion among courts, defense lawyers, academics, and occasionally even the public.

Practically speaking, however, the Swiss statutes face several hurdles impairing the efficiency of exclusionary rules in the Swiss criminal justice system. First, art. 141 CPC leaves open several important questions, including means of enforcing exclusionary rules and the admissibility of indirect evidence obtained following a violation of art. 141 (1) CPC. Furthermore, the wording of art. 141 CPC is vague,

---

[369]Summer/Studer, 2016 at 51 et seq.

[370]Summer/Studer, 2016 at 60.

[371]The charts in Summer/Studer, 2016 at 60 et seq. The numbers in brackets indicate the numbers of incidents brought up or observed.

[372]Such omission might be due to lack of information on the side of the defence, especially if a defendant is not represented by a lawyer. Furthermore, formally claiming a violation of rights might not lead to a clear advantage and the defendant may even be afraid to rebuff the judges by claiming the authorities violated procedural rights. Some rights might even be law on the books only, poorly implemented in practice, which might eventually lead to a largely accepted "custom" of non-compliance. Summers/Studer, 2016 at 62 et seq. and 72.

including terms such as "serious offence," and "essential [...] to secure a conviction." Statutory concepts are also unclear at times, such as the distinction between "regulations on admissibility" and "administrative regulations," as well as the hypothetical clean path analysis. These ambiguities confer a great deal of discretion upon the courts. Finally, art. 141 (2) CPC allows, under certain circumstances, the use of evidence obtained in violation of regulations on admissibility. Such regulations are of considerable importance for safeguarding individual rights and limited exclusion of evidence obtained in their violation does not provide effective protection of those rights.

The problems of art. 141 CPC stem from the fact that the statute is essentially a codification of the Supreme Court's case law. Accordingly, issues continue with the Court closing the legal loopholes and defining the vague legal terms through a longstanding and heavy emphasis on the importance of establishing the truth and prosecuting crimes. Thus, on the one hand, the Supreme Court is quite restrictive in its classification of provisions as regulations on admissibility. On the other hand, it is very quick to define an offense as "serious" or to construct a speculative (and hypothetical) clean path. The case law assigning authority to decide the admissibility of evidence to the same judge who later determines the guilt or innocence of a defendant further reduces the efficacy of art. 141 CPC.

As a result, the initially promising exclusionary rules in the new Swiss CPC lose a great deal of practical impact in their ability to safeguard individual rights in criminal proceedings. Article 141 CPC and the Supreme Court's case law are also criticized by legal scholars. Nevertheless, exclusionary rules are the only possible way to ensure that an irreversible violation of the law does not pose any further detriment to a defendant. Other measures, such as disciplinary or criminal proceedings against a guilty law enforcement official, may be useful as supporting measures, but are not viable *alternatives* to exclusionary rules. As such, it is particularly important to ensure effective exclusionary rules and to limit the amount of judicial interpretation that can be used to narrow their scope. To achieve this, it is important that the legislature drafts clear statutes. With respect to art. 141 CPC, clearer definitions of vague terms, a critical assessment of the balancing approach in cases of violations of regulations of admissibility, as well as the explicit and *strict* exclusion of indirect evidence stemming from evidence obtained through torture and other improper compulsion would be helpful. Moreover, a clear stipulation addressing means of enforcement by an authority other than the judge of fact would be preferable to ensure objectivity. Unfortunately, the recent reform efforts regarding exclusionary rules are limited to an amendment of art. 141 (4) CPC, extending its scope of application explicitly to "evidence inadmissible under paragraph 1 and 2" of art. 141 CPC.[373]

[373] *See* art. 141 (4) of the preliminary draft regarding a reform of the CPC submitted by the Swiss Federal Council in December 2017, available online at <https://www.bj.admin.ch/dam/data/bj/sicherheit/gesetzgebung/aenderungstpo/vorentw-d.pdf>, accessed 22 November 2018.

Pursuant to the wording of this preliminary draft, a violation of art. 140 (1) CPC, however, would not lead to the strict but to a rather limited exclusion of indirect evidence: Such evidence would remain admissible if it could have been obtained without the direct evidence. It is unclear whether the Federal Counsil intended this consequence or whether he just had in mind to clarify that a violation of art. 141 (1) CPC should also entail the exclusion of indirect evidence.[374]

References

Books

Brun, Marcel, *Staatsanwaltschaft und Fehlurteilsrisiken im Vorverfahren,* Diss. Basel 2015. [Brun, 2015]

Fornito, Roberto, *Beweisverbote im Schweizerischen Strafprozess,* Diss. St. Gallen 2000. [Fornito, 2000]

Donatsch, Andreas/Schwarzenegger, Christian/Wohlers, Wolfgang, *Strafprozessrecht* 2nd ed., Zürich 2014. [Donatsch/Schwarzenegger/Wohlers, 2014]

Macula, Laura, *Verwaltungs(aufsichts)rechtliche Mitwirkungspflichten und strafprozessuale Selbstbelastungsfreiheit,* Zürich 2016. [Macula, 2016]

Oberholzer, Niklaus, *Grundzüge des Strafprozessrechts* 3rd ed., Bern 2012. [Oberholzer, 2012]

Pieth, Mark, *Schweizerisches Strafprozessrecht. Grundriss für Studium und Praxis* 3rd ed., Basel 2016. [Pieth, 2016]

Ruckstuhl, Niklaus/Dittmann, Volker/Arnold, Jörg, *Strafprozessrecht unter Einschluss der forensischen Psychiatrie und Rechtsmedizin sowie des kriminaltechnischen und naturwissenschaftlichen Gutachtens,* Zürich 2011. [Ruckstuhl et al., 2011]

Schlauri, Regula, *Das Verbot des Selbstbelastungszwangs im Strafverfahren: Konkretisierung eines Grundrechts durch Rechtsvergleichung*, Zürich 2003. [Schlauri, 2003]

Schmid, Niklaus, *Handbuch des schweizerischen Strafprozessrechts* 3rd ed., Zürich/St. Gallen 2017. [Schmid, 2017]

Thommen, Marc, *Kurzer Prozess - fairer Prozess? Strafbefehls- und abgekürzte Verfahren zwischen Effizienz und Gerechtigkeit*, Habil. Bern 2013. [Thommen, 2013]

Groner, Roger, *Beweisrecht. Beweise und Beweisverfahren im Zivil- und Strafrecht*, Bern 2011. [Groner, 2011]

Journal Articles

Bürge, Lukas, 'Die Unverwertbarkeit von Beweisen – ein Überblick', (2017) *Anwaltsrevue*, 322–24. [Bürge, 2017]

Donatsch, Andreas/Cavegn, Claudine, 'Ausgewählte Fragen zum Beweisrecht nach der schweizerischen Strafprozessordnung', (2008) 126 *Schweizerische Zeitschrift für Strafrecht*, 158–73. [Donatsch/Cavegn, 2008]

374*See* Swiss Federal Council, Erläuternder Bericht zur Änderung der Strafprozessordnung of December 2017, at 25, available online at <https://www.bj.admin.ch/dam/data/bj/sicherheit/gesetzgebung/aenderungstpo/vn-ber-d.pdf>, accessed 22 November 2018.

Geisselhardt, Angela, 'Zuständigkeit bei Beweisverboten im Strafverfahren', (2014) 7 *forumpoenale*, 300–06. [Geisselhardt, 2014]

Gless, Sabine, 'Beweisverbote und Fernwirkung', (2010) 128 *Schweizerische Zeitschrift für Strafrecht*, 146–60. [Gless, 2010]

Gless, Sabine, 'Urteilsbesprechung Obergericht Zürich, III. Strafkammer, Beschluss vom 24. April 2013 i.S. X. gegen Staatsanwaltschaft Zürich-Sihl - UH120368', (2013) 6 *forumpoenale*, 343–47. [Gless, 2013]

Häring, Daniel, 'Verwertbarkeit rechtswidrig erlangter Beweise gemäss Schweizerischer Strafprozessordnung – alte Zöpfe oder substanzielle Neuerungen?', (2009) 127 *Schweizerische Zeitschrift für Strafrecht*, 225–57. [Häring, 2009]

Hersch, Gabriel, 'Die Verwertbarkeit rechtswidrig erlangter Beweise gemäss Art. 141 Abs. 2 StPO: Kodifizierung der Rechtsprechung des Bundesgerichts?', (2012) 130 *Schweizerische Zeitschrift für Strafrecht*, 352–72. [Hersch, 2012]

Jackson, John/Summers, Sarah, 'Confrontation with Strasbourg: UK and Swiss approaches to criminal evidence', (2013) 60 *Criminal Law Review*, 114–30. [Jackson/Summers, 2013]

Keller, Andreas J., 'Die neue schweizerische StPO: Formalisierung und Effizienz – bleibt die materielle Wahrheit auf der Strecke?', (2011) 129 *Schweizerische Zeitschrift für Strafrecht*, 229–57. [Keller, 2011]

Riklin, Franz, 'Strafbefehlsverfahren – Effizienz auf Kosten der Rechtsstaatlichkeit?', (2016) 152 *Zeitschrift des Bernischen Juristenvereins*, 475–99. [Riklin, 2016]

Ruckstuhl, Niklaus, 'Rechtswidrige Beweise erlaubt', (2006) 23 *plädoyer*, 15–22. [Ruckstuhl, 2006]

Schweizer, Rainer J., 'Die Aufsicht über die Staatsanwaltschaften', (2013) 26 *Aktuelle Juristische Praxis*, 1378–89. [Schweizer, 2013]

Summers, Sarah/Studer, David, 'Fairness im Strafverfahren? Eine empirische Untersuchung', (2016) 134 *Schweizerische Zeitschrift für Strafrecht*, 45–72. [Summers/Studer, 2016]

Thommen, Marc/Samadi, Mojan, 'The Bigger the Crime, the Smaller the Chance of a Fair Trial? Evidence Exclusion in Serious Crime Cases Under Swiss, Dutch and European Human Rights Law', (2016) 24 *European Journal of Crime, Criminal Law and Criminal Justice*, 65–86. [Thommen/Samadi, 2016]

Trechsel, Stefan, 'Gerechtigkeit im Fehlurteil' (2000) 118 *Schweizerische Zeitschrift für Strafrecht*, 1–18. [Trechsel, 2000]

Vest, Hans/Eicker, Andreas, 'Aussageverweigerungsrecht und Beweisverwertungsverbot. Zugleich eine Besprechung von BGE 130 I 126', (2005) 14 *Aktuelle Juristische Praxis*, 883–92. [Vest/Eicker, 2005]

Vest, Hans/Höhener, Andrea, 'Beweisverwertungsverbote – quo vadis Bundesgericht?', (2009) 127 *Schweizerische Zeitschrift für Strafrecht*, 95–108. [Vest/Höhener, 2009]

Vetterli, Luzia, 'Kehrtwende in der bundesgerichtlichen Praxis zu den Verwertungsverboten', (2012) 130 *Schweizerische Zeitschrift für Strafrecht*, 447–70. [Vetterli, 2012]

Wohlers, Wolfgang/Bläsi, Linda, 'Dogmatik und praktische Relevanz der Beweisverwertungsverbote im Strafprozessrecht der Schweiz' (2015) 134 *recht*, 158–75. [Wohlers/Bläsi, 2015]

Contributions to Edited Volumes and Annotated Law

Demko, Daniela, 'Das „(Un-)Gerechte" am Fair-Trial-Grundsatz nach Art. 6 Abs. 1 EMRK im Strafverfahren', in: Niggli, Marcel Alexander/Hurtado Pozo, José/Queloz, Nicolas (eds.), *Festschrift für Franz Riklin. Zur Emeritierung und zugleich dem 67. Geburtstag*, Zürich 2007, 351–64. [Demko, 2007]

Donatsch, Andreas/Hansjakob, Thomas/Lieber, Viktor (eds.), *Kommentar zur Schweizerischen Strafprozessordnung (StPO)* 2nd ed., Zürich 2014. [Author in Donatsch et al., 2014]

Gilliéron, Gwlady/Killias, Martin, 'Strafbefehl und Justizirrtum: Franz Riklin hatte Recht!', in: Niggli, Marcel Alexander/Hurtado Pozo, José/Queloz, Nicolas (eds.), *Festschrift für Franz Riklin. Zur Emeritierung und zugleich dem 67. Geburtstag*, Zürich 2007, 379–98. [Gilliéron/Killias, 2007]

Gless, Sabine, 'Heiligt der Zweck die Mittel? Beweisverbote im vereinheitlichten eidgenössischen Strafprozess', in: Niggli, Marcel Alexander/Pozo, José Hurtado/Queloz, Nicolas (eds.), *Festschrift für Franz Riklin. Zur Emeritierung und zugleich dem 67. Geburtstag*, Zürich 2007, 399–14. [Gless, 2007]

Gless, Sabine, 'Verwertungsverbote im Schweizer Strafprozess', in: Degener, Wilhelm/Heghmanns, Michael (eds.), *Festschrift für Friedrich Dencker zum 70. Geburtstag*, Tübingen 2012, 135–45. [Gless, 2012]

Gless Sabine/Martin, Jeannine, 'Water Always Finds Its Way – Discretion and the Concept of Exclusionary Rules in the Swiss Criminal Procedure Code', in: Caianiello, Michele/Hodgson, Jacqueline S. (eds.), *Discretionary Criminal Justice in a Comparative Context*, Durham, North Carolina 2015, 159–84. [Gless/Martin, 2015]

Gless, Sabine, 'Gesetzliche Regelung von Beweisverwertungsverboten – die Schweiz als Vorreiter?', in: Gropp, Walter/Hecker, Bernd/Kreuzer, Arthur/Ringelmann, Christoph/Witteck, Lars/Wolfslast, Gabriele (eds.), *Strafrecht als ultima ratio. Giessener Gedächtnisschrift für Günter Heine*, Tübingen 2016, 127–41. [Gless, 2016]

Niggli, Marcel Alexander/Heer, Marianne/Wiprächtiger, Hans (eds.), *Basler Kommentar. Schweizerische Strafprozessordnung/Jugendstrafprozessordnung (StPO/JStPO)* 2nd ed., Basel 2014. [Author in Niggli et al., 2014]

Wohlers, Wolfgang, 'Verwertungs-, Verwendungs- und/oder Belastungsverbote – die Rechtsfolgenseite der Lehre von den Beweisverwertungsverboten', in: Herzog, Felix/Schlothauer, Reinhold/Wohlers, Wolfgang (eds.), *Rechtsstaatlicher Strafprozess und Bürgerrechte. Gedächtnisschrift für Edda Weßlau*, Berlin 2016, 427–44. [Wohlers, 2016]

Reports, Legislative History

Swiss Federal Council, Erläuternder Bericht zur Änderung der Strafprozessordnung of December 2017 <https://www.bj.admin.ch/dam/data/bj/sicherheit/gesetzgebung/aenderungstpo/vn-ber-d.pdf>, accessed 22 November 2018.

Swiss Federal Council, Vorentwurf zur Änderung der Strafprozessordnung of December 2017 <https://www.bj.admin.ch/dam/data/bj/sicherheit/gesetzgebung/aenderungstpo/vorentw-d.pdf>, accessed 22 November 2018.

Swiss Federal Department of Justice and Police, 'Examen du septième rapport périodique de la Suisse par le Comité contre la torture. Prise de position de la Suisse suite à l'adoption des observations finales par le CAT, le 13 août 2015', (6 July 2016). [CAT Report, 2016] <https://www.google.com/url?sa=t&rct=j&q=&esrc=s&source=web&cd=4&ved=2ahUKEwiCm7Wj24bgAhVKLVAKHcspApcQFjADegQIABAB&url=https%3A%2F%2Ftbinternet.ohchr.org%2FTreaties%2FCAT%2FShared%2520Documents%2FCHE%2FINT_CAT_FCO_CHE_22382_F.pdf&usg=AOvVaw1yCr3fN0Na3Tbo9L4amFYA>, accessed 22 November 2018.

Swiss Centre of Expertise in Human Rights (SCHR), Künzli, Jörg/Sturm, Evelyne/Veerakatty, Vijitha, 'Rechtsschutz gegen polizeiliche Übergriffe. Eine Darstellung der Beschwerdemechanismen in der Schweiz', (21 February 2014). [Künzli et al., 2014] <http://www.skmr.ch/de/themenbereiche/justiz/publikationen/missbraeuchliche-polizeigewalt.html?zur=106>, accessed 22 November 2018.

Swiss Federal Council, Botschaft zur Vereinheitlichung des Strafprozessrechts of 21 December 2005, 05.092, Bundesblatt no. 6 (2006) 1085. [Bundesblatt, 2006] <https://www.admin.ch/opc/de/federal-gazette/2006/index_5.html>, accessed 22 November 2018.

Swiss National Council, Official Bulletin of the National Council, Summer Session 2007. [Official Bulletin of the National Council, Summer Session 2007] <https://www.parlament.ch/en/ratsbetrieb/amtliches-bulletin>, accessed 22 November 2018.

Council of States, Official Bulletin of Council of States, Winter Session 2006. [Official Bulletin of Council of States, Winter Session 2006] <https://www.parlament.ch/centers/documents/de/SR_06_12.pdf>, accessed 22 November 2018.

Laura Macula holds a Master's degree in law (summa cum laude). Her master's thesis discusses possible conflicts between the right against self-incrimination and information duties under the Swiss financial market regulation. It was published in 2016. Her doctoral theses analyzes exclusionary rules from a comparative perspective with a particular focus on the exclusion of exonerating evidence.

The Potential to Secure a Fair Trial Through Evidence Exclusion: A German Perspective

Thomas Weigend

Abstract German criminal procedure law places great emphasis upon judgements made pursuant to the "substantive truth." Therefore, exclusion of evidence tends to be an anomaly as it compels the trial court to disregard certain evidence, which implies that the court must base its judgement on something less than the whole truth. German law does provide for the exclusion of evidence in some situations, but its effect is limited to preventing the trial court from explicitly relying on the inadmissible evidence as a basis for the judgement. That said, in most cases the judges nevertheless remain aware of the excluded evidence. Under German law there is absolute protection of conversations between individuals in intimate relationships as a result of the protection of core privacy. If such conversations are captured and stored during surveillance they cannot be used unless related to past or future crimes. If evidence is obtained by violating this law, the approach of most German courts is to weigh the individual privacy interests against the interests of the justice system in having access to all available information. If the violation was intentional, however, the evidence is typically excluded. Section 136a of the German Code of Criminal Procedure provides that statements obtained through the use of prohibited means of interrogation, such as force, threats, and illicit promises, cannot be used as evidence.

1 Introduction

Exclusion of evidence creates a dilemma. On the one hand, there exists a great systemic interest in basing the judgement in criminal cases on true and complete facts; a finding of guilt or innocence should not be made on the basis of inaccurate factual assumptions.[1] This fundamental interest in determining the relevant facts

[1] *See* Stuckenberg, 2016 at 695 et seq., with further references.

T. Weigend (✉)
Faculty of Law, University of Cologne, Cologne, Germany
e-mail: Thomas.Weigend@uni-koeln.de

S. Gless and T. Richter (eds.), *Do Exclusionary Rules Ensure a Fair Trial?*
Ius Gentium: Comparative Perspectives on Law and Justice 74,
https://doi.org/10.1007/978-3-030-12520-2_3

leads to an intensive search for the truth, first by the agents of criminal law enforcement, then by the trial court. The goal, in all legal systems, is to assemble all relevant evidence and to enable the factfinders to base their judgement on information that is as complete as possible.

On the other hand, there are instances in which the use of individual pieces of evidence in court appears to be unfair or even counterproductive. A piece of evidence may in fact impede the goal of truth-finding, e.g., when a document has been forged or a confession has been brought about by torture. More frequently, the goal of finding the truth competes with other interests, most importantly the interest in conducting fair proceedings. The ideal of a fair trial requires that the agents of the state comply with all rules designed to protect the suspect's procedural rights, such as his right to remain silent and his right to be free from arbitrary searches and seizures. If the suspect's rights have not been respected, it appears unfair to employ, for proving his guilt, an item that the agents of the state should not have obtained at all, or should not have obtained under the particular circumstances. In that situation, there exists a conflict between the goal of a fair trial and the judicial system's interest in collecting and using all relevant information for the sake of finding the truth.

The German response to such conflicts is determined, to a large extent, by the German legal system's traditional reliance on the inquisitorial system, which places on the trial court the responsibility for collecting and evaluating the evidence as well as for finding the facts relevant to the judgement. According to § 244 sec. 2 German Code of Criminal Procedure (CCP), the trial court, in particular the presiding judge, is responsible for deciding what evidence will be presented at the trial. The prosecution as well as the defense may propose additional pieces of evidence, but the court decides on the relevance and admissibility of the proposed evidence (§ 244 secs. 3–6 CCP). The court is in any event free to introduce evidence that neither party has proposed.

2 General Framework for Establishing Facts in Criminal Proceedings

The German procedural system places great emphasis on the determination of the "substantive truth" as a basis for a just and fair outcome of any criminal case.[2] The criminal process is conceived as a sequence of two independent efforts to find the truth; first by the prosecutor and the police, then by the trial court. As soon as the suspicion of a criminal offense becomes known to him, the prosecutor is obliged to investigate the matter (§ 160 sec. 1 CCP). The police are likewise mandated with investigating criminal offenses and with taking all measures necessary to avoid the loss of evidence (§ 163 sec. 1 CCP). When an indictment has been filed, it is the

[2]*See* Kühne, 2010 at 195–6; Roxin/Schünemann, 2014 at 85–87.

trial judge who must collect all evidence necessary for establishing the facts relevant for the determination of guilt or innocence (§ 244 sec. 2 CCP). In order to prevent the court's truth-finding process from being predetermined by the prosecutor's investigation, the court may base its judgement only on what has been said and done at the public trial (§ 261 CCP, so-called principle of immediacy); moreover, live witness testimony must not be replaced by the introduction of protocols of prior interrogations of the witness or by similar documents at the trial (§ 250 CCP).

2.1 Legal Framework and Relevant Actors

2.1.1 General Rules

2.1.1.1 Law Determining Duties in Criminal Investigations

Although the Code of Criminal Procedure does not explicitly mention the "search for truth" as a goal of the process, it contains several provisions which confer obligations on prosecutors and judges to collect relevant evidence (see 2 above). Importantly, the Federal Constitutional Court has declared that the criminal process has the purpose of making certain that no punishment is imposed without a determination of the defendant's guilt, and that it is therefore necessary for the trial court to determine the true facts before it may convict a person.[3] According to this decision, the principle of truth-finding is an element of German constitutional law, ultimately linked to the protection of the dignity of the person (Art. 1 Basic Law).

The Code of Criminal Procedure does not explicitly state that a conviction requires proof of the defendant's guilt beyond reasonable doubt. Instead, § 261 CCP provides that the court renders the judgement in accordance with its free conviction, based on the evidence presented at the trial. This legal rule is in line with the inquisitorial principle, according to which no "party" in the criminal process bears a burden of proof. But there can be no doubt that the court's conviction must be based on a rational evaluation of the available evidence, and that the defendant must not be convicted if the judge entertains a reasonable doubt of his guilt.[4] § 244 sec. 2 and § 261 CCP presuppose that the trial court has pursued all reasonable avenues of inquiry before it renders the judgement. As mentioned above, the trial court must, according to the inquisitorial principle, take the initiative in investigating the relevant facts and must hear all relevant evidence.

On the other hand, the principle that the judgement is to be based on the "free" conviction of the court (§ 261 CCP) implies that there exist no formal rules that

---

[3]BVerfG, Judgement of 19 March 2013 – 2 BvR 2628/10, 2 BvR 2883/10, 2 BvR 2155/11 (=Entscheidungen des Bundesverfassungsgerichts (BVerfGE) 133, 168, 199).

[4]*See* Sander in Löwe/Rosenberg, 2007 at § 261 notes 103 et seq., with further references.

would oblige the court to hear a certain type or amount of evidence. For example, the court may rely on the testimony of a single witness if that testimony is convincing and is not put into serious doubt by a plausible statement of the defendant. German law does not have a corroboration rule; hence a single witness's testimony can be sufficient for convicting the defendant. The "free conviction" principle also applies to statements of the defendant: if the defendant makes a statement in open court,[5] explaining in detail how he committed the offense, the court may determine that this statement is sufficient for finding the defendant guilty, and may dispense with calling witnesses or hearing other evidence. The fact that the court is free to base its judgement on a single piece of evidence has led to the practice of "confession bargaining", which the legislature in 2009 has introduced into the Code of Criminal Procedure (§ 257c CCP). According to that practice, the trial judges and the defense can negotiate a lenient sentence in exchange for the defendant making a confession in open court to the crime charged. Although the law provides that the court still retains the obligation to diligently search for the truth,[6] trial courts often accept the defendant's confession as a sufficient basis for finding him guilty and for sentencing him to a penalty previously agreed upon.

2.1.1.2 Law Securing a Fair Trial

The Code of Criminal Procedure, which dates from 1877, does not explicitly mention the guarantee of a fair trial. The right to a fair trial is nevertheless safeguarded under German law. The European Convention on Human Rights (ECHR) has in 1952 been transformed into (sub-constitutional) statutory domestic law.[7] The right to a fair hearing guaranteed in Art. 6 (1) ECHR is thus applicable in Germany, and German courts are obliged to take the relevant jurisprudence of the European Court of Human Rights (ECtHR) into consideration when applying domestic law.[8] Moreover, the Federal Constitutional Court has repeatedly declared that the right to a fair trial is part of the constitutional concept of *Rechtsstaat* (a state based on the rule of law) as guaranteed in Articles 20 sec. 3 and 28 sec. 1 Basic Law[9]; the right to a fair trial thus has constitutional status. It is an open question, however, to what extent specific rights beyond those conferred by statutory law can be directly

[5]According to § 243 sec. 5 deutsche Strafprozessordnung (StPO), officially translated as German Code of Criminal Procedure (CCP) of 7 April 1987 (Status as of 17 August 2017), available online at <https://www.gesetze-im-internet.de/stpo/BJNR006290950.html>, accessed 1 November 2018, at the beginning of the trial the defendant is invited to respond to the accusation. The defendant, of course, retains the right to remain silent.

[6]§ 257c sec. 1, 2nd sent. in connection with § 244 sec. 2 CCP.

[7]Bundesgesetzblatt II 1952 at 685.

[8]BVerfG, Decision of 14 October 2004 - 2 BvR 1481/04 (=BVerfGE 111, 307).

[9]BVerfG, Decision of 3 June 1969 - 1 BvL 7/68 (=BVerfGE 26, 66, 71); Decision of 8 October 1974 - 2 BvR 747/73 (=38, 105, 111); Decision of 26 May 1981 - 2 BvR 215/81 (=57, 250, 274).

deduced from the fair trial principle.[10] For example, the rights of a suspect to remain silent, to confront adverse witnesses, to have access to counsel even during the first stages of an investigation, and to be free from entrapment by state agents have been based on the right to a fair trial.[11]

The Code of Criminal Procedure also contains specific rights commonly associated with the general right to a fair trial. For example, according to § 136 sec. 1 CCP anyone questioned as a suspect has the right to remain silent and to be informed of that right before the start of an interrogation; he also has the right to consult with a lawyer and to have the lawyer present during the interrogation (§§ 163a sec. 4, 168c sec. 1 CCP). § 148 CCP guarantees suspects the right of unsupervised contacts with a defense lawyer even if they are held in pretrial detention.

The presumption of innocence is enshrined in Art. 6 sec. 2 ECHR and has been transformed into domestic law through adoption of the ECHR in 1952. There has been some debate as to the consequences of the presumption of innocence for procedural law, specifically whether the "beyond a reasonable doubt" standard for conviction is part of the presumption of innocence and whether the reach of the presumption extends beyond the criminal process.[12]

2.1.1.3 Other Individual Rights with Relevance for the Criminal Process

The Constitution (Basic Law) provides for several individual (basic) rights which can have an impact on the criminal process. For example, Art. 104 Basic Law guarantees the freedom of movement, which may be restricted only by decision of a judge. As a consequence, a person may be held by the police without a judicial warrant only until the end of the day following arrest, and pretrial detention requires a judicial order (Art. 104 sec. 2 and 3 Basic Law, §§ 112, 128 CCP).

Art. 10 sec. 1 Basic Law states that the secrecy of the mail and of telecommunications is inviolable. This constitutional guarantee is subject to restriction by specific statutory law, but the general constitutional protection limits the state's authority to implement wiretaps and mail inspections. Consequently, wiretaps may be installed only for the purpose of investigating certain serious criminal offenses, and may be ordered only by a judge (§§ 100a and 100e sec. 1 CCP). Similarly, the constitutional protection of the home (Art. 13 Basic Law) restricts the possibility of conducting searches as well as of audio and video surveillance of homes for the purposes of a criminal investigation. Art. 13 sec. 3 Basic Law provides that technical devices for the audio surveillance of a home may be installed only upon judicial warrant and only with respect to serious crime. § 100c and § 100e CCP

[10]Rzepka, 2000; Beulke, 2016 at 33–34.

[11]BGH, Decision of 27 February 1992 - 5 StR 190/91(=BGHSt 38, 214, 220); Judgement of 18 November 1999 - 1 StR 221/99 (=45, 321, 335); Judgement of 25 July 2000 - 1 StR 169/00 (=46, 93, 100).

[12]For a brief discussion, *see* Weigend, 2014; for an extensive treatment, *see* Stuckenberg, 1998.

have transformed this general authority into a specific regulation concerning audio surveillance of homes. Since the Constitution does not mention the possibility of video surveillance of homes, such surveillance is impermissible for investigation purposes.[13]

Art. 1 sec. 1 Basic Law declares that the dignity of the person is inviolable and that the state must respect and protect human dignity. Courts have drawn several conclusions from this general principle for the criminal procedure context. For example, examinations of a person's body, which are generally permissible for investigation purposes (§ 81a CCP), must not be conducted in a way that violates human dignity; the forced induction of vomiting in order to produce evidence of drug dealing is therefore constitutionally impermissible.[14] Another consequence of the supreme value of human dignity in the German legal system is the far-reaching guarantee of a right to privacy. This right has been developed by the Federal Constitutional Court from a combination of the protection of human dignity and the right to develop one's personality, as guaranteed in Art. 2 sec. 1 CCP.[15] Importantly, the Federal Constitutional Court recognizes a core sphere of privacy which the state must not enter. One aspect of this sphere is the communication between spouses and persons in a similar intimate relationship, unless their conversation concerns the past or future commission of criminal offenses.[16] The absolute protection of the core sphere of privacy limits the state's authority to conduct wiretaps and audio surveillance of homes; if protected communication has been captured by legitimate surveillance measures, this communication must not be used as evidence (§ 100d CCP).[17] This may apply, for example, to a suspect's soliloquy recorded through use of a hidden microphone,[18] or to a diary that a suspect has kept.[19]

---

[13]*See* Meyer-Goßner/Schmitt, 2016 at § 100c note 2.

[14]*See* BGH, Judgement of 29 April 2010 - 5 StR 18/10 (=BGHSt 55, 121, 135); Judgement of 20 June 2012 - 5 StR 536/11 (=NJW 2012, 2453); *see also* ECtHR, *Jalloh* v. *Germany*, case no. 54810/00, Judgement of 11 July 2006.

[15]*See, e.g.*, BVerfG, Judgement of 16 January 1957 - 1 BvR 253 56 (=BVerfGE 6, 32, 41); Decision of 8 March 1972 - 2 BvR 28/71 (=32, 373, 378–79); Decision of 31 January 1973 - 2 BvR 454/71 (=34, 238, 245); Decision of 26 April 1994 - 1 BvR 1689/88 (=90, 255, 260 et seq.); Judgement of 3 March 2004 - 1 BvR 2378/98 u. 1 BvR 1084/99 (=109, 279, 313); Judgement of 27 July 2005 - 1 BvR 668/04 (=113, 348, 390–91). For an overview, *see* Roxin/Schünemann, 2014 at 184–85.

[16]*See* BVerfG Judgement of 3 March 2004 - 1 BvR 2378/98 u. 1 BvR 1084/99 (=BVerfGE 109, 279, 323–333).

[17]A similar exclusionary rule applies to communications between the suspect and his defense lawyer (§ 160a sec. 1 2nd sent. CCP). In this instance, it is not the right to privacy but the protection of the integrity of the defense that prompts the exclusion.

[18]BGH, Judgement of 10 August 2005 - 1 StR 140/05 (=BGHSt 50, 206); Judgement of 22 December 2011 - 2 StR 509/10 (=NStZ 2012, 277).

[19]BVerfG Decision of 14 September 1989 - 2 BvR 1062/87 (=BVerfGE 80, 367).

2.1.1.4 Law Balancing the Search for Evidence and Infringements of Individual Rights

German law does not have any general rule for the resolution of conflicts between the protection of individual rights and the search for the truth. As has been pointed out above, there are some instances in which statutory law provides for the exclusion of evidence obtained in violation of privacy rights. In another area, § 136a sec. 3 CCP demands the exclusion of statements of suspects and witnesses if these statements have been obtained through the use of prohibited methods of interrogation (see below). But, given the importance of truth-finding in Germany's inquisitorial system, German law remains reluctant to dispense with relevant information because of the way in which this information has been obtained. For the same reason, factual doubts about the legality of state agents' conduct in obtaining evidence will not necessarily be resolved in favour of the suspect; on the contrary, there is an unwritten presumption that state agents abide by the law; and the courts will base their decisions on that presumption unless they have clear evidence to the contrary.[20]

2.1.2 Establishing Facts—Stages and Rules

The criminal process can roughly be divided into four stages. At the investigation stage, the prosecutor's office, with the assistance of the police, seeks to determine whether an initial suspicion of criminal wrongdoing is well-founded, and collects evidence as a basis for the decision whether to bring charges against one or more individuals (§ 160 secs. 1 and 2 CCP). When the prosecution has filed a formal accusation (*Anklage*) with the trial court, the case enters into the second stage, the so-called intermediary procedure (*Zwischenverfahren*). These proceedings are normally conducted in writing, but the court may hold a hearing (§ 202a CCP) and take evidence (§ 202 CCP).[21] The trial court then determines, on the basis of the prosecutor's findings and possibly of its own (limited) investigation, whether there exists sufficient evidence for holding a public trial of the person(s) named in the accusation (see §§ 199–211 CCP). The court also examines the legal correctness of the charges raised in the indictment and may change the legal appreciation of the facts charged (§§ 206, 207 sec. 2 CCP).

If the trial court finds that there is sufficient suspicion that the defendant has committed a crime, it holds a public trial in the presence of the defendant (§§ 226–275 CCP). At the end of the trial and after deliberations of the judges, the presiding judge announces the court's judgement. If the defendant has been convicted, the

---

[20]BGH, Judgement of 28 June 1961 - 2 StR 154/61 (=BGHSt 16, 164); OLG Hamburg, Decision of 14 June 2005 - IV-1/04 (=NJW 2005, 2326). For criticism of this rule, *see* Gless in Löwe/ Rosenberg 2007 at § 136a note 78. *See* below for a discussion with respect to allegations of torture.

[21]In practice, this option is very rarely used.

judge also pronounces the sentence. When the judgement has been rendered, the case may enter into the appeals stage. In Germany, both the defendant and the prosecutor can appeal a judgement that goes against their interests. The appeal against the judgement of a local court (*Amtsgericht*) can lead to a new trial (*Berufung*; §§ 312–331 CCP); if the trial was held in district court, the losing party may file an appeal on the law (*Revision*). This appeal is successful if the trial court misapplied the relevant substantive law and/or committed a procedural fault that could have had an impact on the outcome of the case (conviction or sentence) (§§ 337, 338 CCP).

2.1.3 Establishing Facts—Actors and Accountability

At the pretrial stage, the responsibility for fact-finding is divided between the prosecutor's office and the police. The prosecutor is charged with investigating the matter once an initial suspicion has arisen (§ 160 CCP). The prosecutor has the authority to undertake investigatory measures of any kind (§ 161 sec. 1 CCP), in particular to summon and interrogate witnesses and experts (§ 161a CCP). However, with respect to certain investigatory acts that infringe upon basic individual rights (e.g., searches and seizures), authorization by a judge is required. The police have a dual function in the pretrial investigation: on the one hand, they are obliged to carry out investigatory acts upon request of the prosecutor (§ 161 sec. 1, 3rd sent. CCP); on the other hand, they are authorized to investigate criminal offenses and to take all measures immediately necessary to avoid the loss of evidence (§ 163 sec. 1 CCP). According to the law, the police are obliged to transmit their findings to the prosecutor "without delay" (§ 163 sec. 2, 1st sent. CCP). But in practice this requirement is not observed strictly: police often complete the investigation of routine matters on their own and send the file to the prosecutor's office only when they deem the case cleared.

As soon as the court has accepted a case for trial, the legal responsibility for fact-finding moves from the prosecutor to the court, in particular the presiding judge. It is the presiding judge who is in charge of summoning the defendant and witnesses as well as of obtaining other evidence to be presented at the trial (§§ 214, 216, 221 CCP), and he is ultimately responsible for the completeness of the fact-finding process (§ 244 sec. 2 CCP). The defendant (and his lawyer) as well as the prosecutor have the right to demand the taking of further evidence by making a formal motion naming the witness or other item of evidence and the facts expected to be proved (*Beweisantrag*).[22] With respect to witnesses, the court may reject such a motion only if the proposed testimony would be redundant or evidently irrelevant (§ 244 sec. 3 CCP). As mentioned above, the prosecution does not carry a formal

[22]For details, *see* § 244 sec. 3 – 6 CCP. The victim of an offense has the same right to move for taking additional evidence if the victim has joined the accusation as an auxiliary prosecutor (*Nebenkläger*) (§ 397 3rd sent. CCP).

burden of proof; but in practice, the prosecutor will make sure that the court has available all the evidence the prosecutor deems necessary for proper fact-finding. The defendant and his lawyer may also summon witnesses and may introduce them at the trial (§ 220 CCP); but the court can refuse to hear these witnesses if their testimony would be redundant or evidently irrelevant (§ 245 sec. 1 CCP). Importantly, the defendant, his lawyer, and the prosecutor have the right to ask questions of any witness or expert witness after the presiding judge and the other judges have concluded their interrogation (§ 240 sec. 2 CCP). The presiding judge may reject individual questions only if they are irrelevant or impermissible (§ 241 sec. 2 CCP), but he cannot generally curtail the parties' right to ask questions unless the party clearly abuses that right.[23]

In sum, fact-finding at the trial is a collective effort dominated by the presiding judge. The interests of the persons involved do not always concur, however. Whereas the court and the prosecutor seek to establish the truth, the defendant may have a strong interest in hiding the truth. The German procedural system tolerates that countervailing interest to the extent that the defendant is not penalized for telling lies in court. But the defendant must not forge documents or induce witnesses to give false testimony.

2.1.4 Establishing Facts—Institutional Safeguards

The pretrial investigation is conducted unilaterally by the prosecutor and the police. The investigation can be conducted in secret, without the knowledge of the suspect; there is no formal announcement to the suspect that he has become the object of a criminal investigation. The prosecutor is obliged to provide the suspect with the opportunity to present his side of the case only before the *conclusion* of the investigation (§ 163a sec. 1 CCP); The investigation should not be partisan, however. According to § 160 sec. 2 CCP, the public prosecutor shall investigate not only circumstances incriminating the suspect but also those possibly exonerating him. At least in the early phase of a criminal investigation, the prosecutor and the police are likely to abide by this rule, because they have no interest in filing an accusation that will not hold up at trial.

Irrespective of the inquisitorial structure of the pretrial process, the defense has (limited) participation rights. For example, the suspect may request the prosecutor to take exonerating evidence; yet, the prosecutor must honour that request only if he thinks that the evidence suggested by the suspect is of relevance (§ 163a sec. 2 CCP).[24] The defense lawyer has a right to attend (and to ask questions at) any interrogation of the suspect by a judge, a prosecutor, or the police (§§ 168c sec. 1,

[23]Meyer-Goßner/Schmitt, 2016 at § 241 note 6.

[24]The prosecutor's decision not to take the requested evidence is not subject to judicial review; *see* Kölbel in Münchener Kommentar, 2016 at § 163a note 48.

163a sec. 3, 4 CCP). If a judge interrogates a witness,[25] both the suspect and the defense lawyer have a right to be present and ask questions (§ 168c sec. 2 CCP). The suspect and the defense lawyer are free to conduct their own investigation and to collect evidence to be offered at the trial; however, they cannot oblige any witness or other person to make a statement or otherwise cooperate with them. If the defense lawyer wishes, for example, that premises be searched he must file a request with the prosecutor, who in turn would have to seek a judicial search warrant if he agrees with the defense lawyer's request.

Although the prosecutorial investigation is not public, the defense lawyer has a general right to inspect the prosecutor's file. According to § 147 CCP, defense counsel may request to inspect the prosecution file at any time; the prosecutor may, however, withhold disclosure of certain sensitive parts of the file until the investigation has been concluded.[26] There is no reciprocal duty on the part of the defense to grant the prosecutor access to the results of their own investigation.

2.2 Social Relevance of Truth and Individual Rights in Criminal Trials

2.2.1 Relevance of Determining the Truth

The great importance of determining the truth for the German system of criminal procedure has been described in the Introduction (above). "Determining the truth" is not exclusively focused on obtaining confessions, however. Given the fact that scientific or documentary evidence in combination with witness and expert testimony is often sufficient to establish the relevant facts, the German system is not dependent on making the suspect confess. Procedure law clearly respects the suspect's right to remain silent (cf. § 136 sec. 1 CCP), and the courts have made certain that no adverse inferences may be drawn from a suspect's decision not to make a statement.[27] Moreover, the suspect must specifically be informed of his right to remain silent; if that information was not given, any statement the suspect makes cannot be used as evidence without his consent.[28]

[25]The prosecutor may request a judge to interrogate individual suspects and witnesses or conduct other acts of investigation in the course of pretrial proceedings (§ 162 CCP). The results of judicial interrogations can be introduced as evidence at the trial under less restrictive conditions than the protocols of police or prosecutorial interrogations (§§ 251, 254 CCP).

[26]For details, *see* § 147 sec. 2, 3 and 6 CCP.

[27]*See, e.g.*, BGH, Decision of 29 August 1974 - 4 StR 171/74 (=BGHSt 25, 365, 368); Judgement of 26 October 1983 - 3 StR 251/83 (=32, 140, 144). For details, *see* Gless in Löwe/Rosenberg, 2007 at § 136 note 36.

[28]BGH, Decision of 27 February 1992 - 5 StR 190/91 (=BGHSt 38, 214, 220).

There is no general information available on the satisfaction of the German public with the functioning of the criminal justice system, especially with respect to the relationship between truth-determination and the protection of individual rights. Print media reporting on criminal trials frequently mention the fact that the defendant has chosen to remain silent, but they normally do so without negative comment.

2.2.2 Presentation of "Facts" Respectively "Fact-Finding" And/Or "Truth" to the Public

Although the pretrial investigation is not public, media reporting before trial is not prohibited.[29] Ethical rules for the press discourage the media from disclosing the full name of a suspect or defendant unless he is a publicly known person, and media also should not portray a person as "guilty" before the court has rendered the verdict. But such limitations apart, the media are free to report on crime and on the criminal process, and they often do so. Reporters receive their information mainly from press releases or press conferences of the prosecutor's office and possibly of the defense lawyer. The question whether a suspect in a spectacular case has made a confession to the police or prosecutor will normally be communicated to the media and will promptly be reported.

Trials of adults are open to the public and the media, except that the public can be excluded for certain parts of the trial in order to protect the privacy of witnesses, victims or defendants (§§ 171b, 172 *Gerichtsverfassungsgesetz* (Court Organisation Act)). Sound and video recordings as well as live reporting from criminal trials are prohibited (§ 169 2nd sent. *Gerichtsverfassungsgesetz*).

2.2.3 Public Discussion of Miscarriages of Justice

Miscarriages of justice are relatively rarely discussed in Germany. The Code of Criminal Procedure provides for a special procedure to re-try terminated cases if new evidence is presented that casts doubt on the correctness of the judgement (*Wiederaufnahme*, §§ 359-373a CCP). Such re-trials are not frequent. There have been a number of spectacular cases in which persons convicted of murder were later found to be innocent,[30] but these cases have not indicated systemic problems concerning the process of truth-finding.

[29] For a brief discussion of media publicity (and many further references), *see* Roxin/Schünemann, 2014 at 109–11.

[30] *See, e.g.*, Oberlandesgericht Frankfurt am Main, Decision of 4 December 1995 – 1 Ws 160/95, (1996) 16 Strafverteidiger, 138–41; Schwenn, 2010.

3 Limitations of Fact-Finding in Criminal Proceedings

3.1 General Rules on Taking Evidence (Admissibility of Evidence)

3.1.1 Legal Framework

3.1.1.1 Legal Framework for Taking Evidence and Admissibility of Evidence

The Code of Criminal Procedure does not contain a systematic set of rules on evidence law. There are few general provisions regulating the acquisition of evidence at the pretrial stage. According to §§ 160 sec. 1 and 163 sec. 1 CCP, the prosecutor and the police may conduct investigations of any kind, subject to specific statutory restrictions. Such restrictions are mostly geared toward the protection of the constitutional basic rights of persons subject to an investigation. For example, the Code of Criminal Procedure provides for testimonial privileges aiming at protecting family relationships (§ 52 CCP) and the confidentiality of professional communications with, e.g., lawyers and physicians (§ 53 CCP). Restrictions apply on the search of a building or a person (§§ 102–107 CCP), secret surveillance of communications (§§ 99–101 CCP), and on obtaining information through the use of undercover police agents (§§ 110a–110c CCP). In many of these instances, there exist substantive limitations (e.g., a measure may be taken only for the investigation of certain serious offenses) as well as procedural requirements (e.g., a judicial warrant is needed). This area, which is characterized by the tension between the interest in an efficient search for the truth and the need to protect various individual interests, seems to be in constant flux. Sometimes changes in the law are triggered by technological developments,[31] sometimes they reflect a change in the normative balance between the interests involved.[32]

At the trial, only four types of evidence are available for the proof of a person's guilt: witness testimony, expert testimony, documents, and real evidence. The trial court is free to choose among available items of evidence, except that the testimony of a witness must not be replaced by using as documentary evidence the protocol of his interrogation before trial (§ 250 2nd sent. CCP). The general guideline for the taking of evidence at the trial is the court's responsibility for determining the truth: according to § 244 sec. 2 CCP, the court shall extend the taking of evidence to all facts and items of evidence that are necessary for the court's decision. This rule

---

[31]*See, e.g.*, § 100i CCP, introduced in 2002, regulating the determination of the identification number and location of a mobile phone.

[32]For example, the possibility of installing hidden microphones in private homes for surveillance purposes was severely restricted in 2005, following a ruling of the Federal Constitutional Court (BVerfG, Judgement of 3 March 2004 - 1 BvR 2378/98 u. 1 BvR 1084/99 (=BVerfGE 109, 279)) that the prior version of the law had neglected the necessary protection of core privacy.

shows the inquisitorial heritage of German law, and it has been in the Code of Criminal Procedure since its adoption in 1877.

In the German inquisitorial system, exclusion of evidence appears as an anomaly because it prevents the trial court from establishing the facts on which its judgement is to be based. Since the German system is, at least theoretically, not party oriented, the loss of a piece of incriminating evidence does not hurt the prosecutor or the police but affects the court's truth-finding process. If evidence is excluded, the judges, who are responsible for determining the truth, have to bear the consequences of another actor's procedural fault. No wonder, then, that both the German legislature and the courts are reluctant to accept broad rules of excluding illegally obtained evidence. The Federal Constitutional Court has indeed argued that it is an important element of the system of criminal justice to find the truth and that therefore exclusion of relevant evidence must remain an exception.[33]

The first legal provision explicitly demanding the exclusion of illegally obtained evidence (§ 136a sec. 3 CCP; see below at 3.2) was introduced in 1950. Its adoption was a reaction to the abuses, including torture, prevalent in interrogations during the National-Socialist era. The exclusion of evidence obtained through physical force, threats and other forbidden methods was introduced not so much because of the unreliability of statements resulting from such methods but in order to protect the dignity of the persons interrogated and the general principle of a state based on the rule of law (*Rechtsstaat*).[34] Other explicit exclusionary rules were introduced after 2000 in order to protect core privacy rights in connection with the surveillance of conversations and telecommunications (§ 100e CCP) as well as the confidential relationship between a suspect and his lawyer (§ 160a sec. 1, 2nd sent. CCP). These rules provide for the mandatory exclusion of "core private" evidence obtained, although the measure (wiretap, surveillance of live conversations) as such was perfectly legal.

There is no statutory rule demanding the exclusion of evidence derived from inadmissible statements or communications.

3.1.1.2 Practice and Jurisprudence

With regard to the exclusion of tainted evidence, German courts do not accept the principle that unlawfully obtained evidence is inadmissible. Rather, the illegal source of evidence is said to create a conflict between the need to vindicate the rights of the affected individual (which favors excluding the evidence) and the interest of criminal justice in determining the truth and rendering decisions based on broad information (which favors admitting the evidence).[35] The courts balance

[33]BVerfG, Decision of 9 November 2010 - 2 BvR 2101/09 (=NJW 2011, 2417, 2418-19).

[34]Gless in Löwe/Rosenberg, 2007 at § 136a note 1.

[35]BVerfG (1. Kammer des Zweiten Senats), Decision of 9 November 2010 - 2 BvR 2101/09 (=NJW 2011, 2417, 2418); BGH, Decision of 21 January 1958 - GSSt 4/57 (=BGHSt 11, 213,

these competing interests in each individual case and thus determine whether the evidence should be admitted in spite of the unlawful way in which it was obtained.[36] Factors relevant in the weighing process are, among others, the purpose of the rule that had been violated,[37] the gravity of the violation, in particular the question whether the state agent knowingly violated a procedural rule, the seriousness of the crime charged, and the importance of the evidence for finding the truth.[38] Many academics are critical of the courts' pragmatic and unpredictable case law. But even those who favor a more exclusion-friendly approach would require that the procedural fault had an impact on the availability of the piece of evidence in question; for that reason, many authors have proposed to borrow the United States Supreme Court's "hypothetical clean path" doctrine,[39] permitting the use of evidence if it would have (or: could have) become available even without the procedural fault.[40]

German courts do not normally discuss the "justification" of exclusionary rules, except by indicating that they enhance the respect for the individual rights that had been violated in obtaining the evidence. It is for that reason that the Federal Court of Justice as well as the Federal Constitutional Court favor exclusion of illegally obtained evidence if the procedural rule that had been violated is meant to safeguard the basis of the defendant's procedural position.[41]

3.1.1.3 Consequences of a Violation of Exclusionary Rules

If a statute declares that certain evidence must not be used ("*verwertet*"),[42] neither the prosecutor nor the court are permitted to rely on that evidence in their decision-making; in particular, the court's judgement must not refer to this

214); Decision of 27 February 1992 - 5 StR 190/91 (=38, 214, 219); Kudlich in Münchener Kommentar, 2014 at Einleitung notes 454–55; Meyer-Goßner/Schmitt, 2016 at Einleitung note 55.

[36]*See* BGH, Decision of 27 February 1992 - 5 StR 190/91 (=BGHSt 38, 214, 219).

[37]For example, § 81a sec. 1, 2nd sent. CCP provides that certain intrusive examinations of a person's body may only be performed by a licensed physician. The purpose of this rule is to protect the examinee's health. It would therefore make little sense to exclude the result of an examination conducted by a nurse, since its relevance for the criminal process is in no way affected by the violation of the "licensed physician" rule. *See* BGH, Decision of 17 March 1971 - 3 StR 189/70 (=BGHSt 24, 125, 128).

[38]For an overview of relevant factors and various academic theories on the subject *see* Kudlich in Münchener Kommentar, 2014 at Einleitung notes 449–94.

[39]*See Nix* v. *Williams*, 467 US 431 (1984).

[40]*See* Beulke, 1991 at 666–71; Wohlers, 2013 at 1190–91; Rogall in Systematischer Kommentar, 2016 at § 136a notes 115–22, with further references in n. 763. For a similar argument, *see* BGH, Judgement of 24 August 1983 - 3 StR 136/83 (=BGHSt 32, 68, 71).

[41]BGH, Decision of 27 February 1992 - 5 StR 190/91 (=BGHSt 38, 214, 220); BVerfG, Decision of 16 March 2006 - 2 BvR 954/02 (=NJW 2006, 2684).

[42]This is the term used in § 136a sec. 3, 2nd sent. CCP and in § 100d sec. 2 CCP (concerning "core" private conversations).

evidence.[43] The evidence must not be introduced at the trial in any way; for example, an expert witness is precluded from referring to that evidence in his statement. But a prohibition of "using" the item as evidence does not rule out that an investigator takes clues from the item for further investigation.[44] For example, if a suspect makes a coerced statement in which he refers to other persons who allegedly committed the offense together with him, the "exclusion" of the statement by § 136a sec. 3 CCP does not block further police investigation into the identity of these persons, and the police may also interrogate them.[45] A more comprehensive prohibition is indicated by the term "*verwendet*"[46] (meaning: employed): If the item in question must not be "*verwendet*" by law enforcement, any use is prohibited, including basing further investigative measures on the information the item contains.[47]

A prohibition of using a piece of evidence does not normally mean that the members of the trial court (which consists of a single professional judge or a mixed panel of professional and lay judges) do not become aware of the evidence in question. If the relevant evidence (for example, a statement of the suspect or of a witness) is included in the prosecutor's case file, the professional judges see this item before trial because the prosecutor sends them his file along with the formal accusation.[48] If evidence is introduced at trial and is subsequently determined to be inadmissible, even the lay judges will have seen or heard the statement in question. "Exclusion" thus means only that the court must not base its judgement on the evidence in question. Judges are, in other words, supposed by law to "forget about" inadmissible evidence when deliberating on the judgement and when giving their (oral and written) reasons for the verdict and sentence. It is an open question to what extent judges (and especially lay judges) are capable of performing that psychological acrobatics.

If the trial court has admitted evidence that should have been excluded, the convicted defendant may base an appeal on legal grounds (*Revision*, § 337 CCP) on this fault. The appeal will be successful if it is possible that the judgement would have been different if the court had disregarded the evidence in question. In the memorandum supporting the appeal, the defendant must explain that his lawyer had objected to the introduction of the evidence at the trial.[49]

[43]Kudlich in Münchener Kommentar, 2014 at Einleitung note 449.

[44]Roxin/Schünemann, 2014 at 187.

[45]BGH, Judgement of 24 August 1983 - 3 StR 136/83 (=BGHSt 32, 68, 70).

[46]*See, e.g.*, § 160a sec. 1, 2nd sent. CCP (concerning conversations between the suspect or defendant and his lawyer).

[47]Kölbel in Münchener Kommentar, 2016 at § 160a note 14.

[48]The lay judges do not see the prosecutor's file.

[49]BGH, Decision of 27 February 1992 - 5 StR 190/91 (=BGHSt 38, 214, 225-26); BGH, Decision of 11 September 2007 - 1 StR 273/07 (=NJW 2007, 3587).

3.1.2 Debate on Exclusionary Rules

There is presently no public debate on this issue.

3.1.3 Institutional Arrangements Securing Individual Rights

In many instances, the Code of Criminal Procedure provides that suspects, defendants and witnesses shall be informed about their rights. As has been mentioned before, this applies to the suspect's right to remain silent and to obtain the assistance of a lawyer (§ 136 sec. 1, 2nd sent. CCP). Other examples are a suspect's rights after he has been detained (§ 114b CCP) and a witness's right not to incriminate himself (§ 55 sec. 2 CCP). Detained persons can also demand to be examined by a physician (§ 114b sec. 2 no. 5 CCP). Generally, these rights are protected by judicial surveillance, either by a right to appeal directly to a judge (as with detained suspects, § 119a CCP) or by basing a motion for reviewing the judgement (*Revision*) on the alleged procedural fault.

3.2 Evidence Obtained by Torture

In the German procedural system, the use of torture, force and threats is strictly prohibited. § 136a Code of Criminal Procedure (CCP) explicitly protects the suspect's (and any witness's[50]) autonomy with regard to making or not making statements to the court, the prosecutor, or the police. § 136a sec. 1 CCP lists certain means that may not be used in any interrogation, namely

- physical abuse
- psychological torment
- invasive measures
- mind-altering medication, drugs or hypnosis
- illegal constraint
- deprivation of rest or sleep
- threats with impermissible measures
- promises of improper benefits
- deceit.

These means are prohibited because they tend to overbear the individual's will, but they are prohibited regardless of whether they actually have this effect in the individual case. The means listed must not be applied even with the consent of the interrogated person.

[50] § 69 sec. 3 declares that § 136a CCP is applicable as well to the interrogation of any witness.

The prohibition of the means listed relates only to "interrogations". The Federal Court of Justice has defined an interrogation as a situation where an agent of the state openly confronts a person and requests information.[51] The legal protection of a person's free will in connection with an "interrogation" thus does not apply to spontaneous utterances, even to a police officer,[52] or to conversations among acquaintances.[53] According to the courts, there exists no "interrogation" if an undercover agent or a police informer seeks to elicit information from a suspect without disclosing his police affiliation.[54] Yet the prohibition of the methods listed in § 136a CCP has been extended to these persons if their activity had been initiated by a police officer or other state agent.[55]

3.2.1 Definitions of Torture and Inhuman Treatment

§ 136a CCP does not employ the term "torture" (*Folter*) among the forbidden means of interrogation. But any case of physical torture is necessarily included in the broader term "physical abuse" (*Misshandlung*), which has been held to include any significant impairment of a person's physical well-being, such as bodily injury, beatings, excessive noise or light, and frequent interruption of sleep.[56]

Art. 104 sec. 1, 2nd sent. of the German Constitution of 1949 provides that persons in (state) custody must not be subjected to mental or physical abuse (*Misshandlung*). Again, the constitution does not use the term "torture" but employs a rather extensive concept of abuse, which has been interpreted broadly by courts and writers.[57]

---

[51]BGH, Decision of 13 May 1996 - GSSt 1/96 (=BGHSt 42, 139, 145).

[52]BGH, Decision of 9 June 2009 - 4 StR 170/09 (=NJW 2009, 3589). But *see* BGH, Judgement of 27 June 2013 – 3 StR 435/12 (=BGHSt 58, 301, 305-08): Suspect's spontaneous utterance after he had unsuccessfully asked to speak to a lawyer triggered further judicial questioning; use of the suspect's ensuing statement was held to violate the privilege against self-incrimination and the right to counsel.

[53]Most writers support an analogous application of § 136a CCP to egregious violations of human rights by private persons conducting an „interrogation"; *see, e.g.* Roxin/Schünemann, 2014 at 188; Schuhr in Münchener Kommentar, 2014 at § 136a notes 83–84.

[54]BGH, Decision of 13 May 1996 - GSSt 1/96 (= BGHSt 42, 139, 145-48).

[55]*See* BGH, Judgement of 26 July 2007 - 3 StR 104/07 (=BGHSt 52, 11, 18-21); Decision of 18 May 2010 - 5 StR 51/10 (=55, 138); Gless in Löwe/Rosenberg, 2007 at § 136a note 4; Meyer-Goßner/Schmitt, 2016 at § 110c note 3, § 136a note 3.

[56]*See* Gless in Löwe/Rosenberg, 2007 at § 136a note 22; Meyer-Goßner/Schmitt, 2016 at § 136a note 7. Psychological torture is covered by the prohibition of *Quälerei* (psychological torment).

[57]*See* BGH, Judgement of 3 May 1960 - 1 StR 131/60 (=BGHSt 14, 269, 271); Schulze-Fielitz in Dreier, 2013 at Art. 104 note 61.

Since Germany has ratified the European Convention on Human Rights and has transformed it into domestic law,[58] the prohibition of torture and inhuman and degrading treatment in Art. 3 ECHR is directly applicable in Germany. German courts generally follow the definition that these terms have been given by the European Court of Human Rights (ECtHR). According to the ECtHR, torture is a more serious infringement of the victim's bodily integrity than inhuman treatment. It depends on the individual case whether maltreatment has reached the level of torture; relevant factors are the nature and context of the maltreatment, its duration, its physical and mental effect on the victim, and also the age, gender and physical condition of the victim.[59] In a judgement concerning the application of international criminal law, the German Federal Court of Justice (*Bundesgerichtshof*) has defined torture in the sense of the 4th Geneva Convention as any intentional infliction of severe physical or mental pain by organs of the state or with their acquiescence.[60]

In connection with the case of *Gäfgen*,[61] German jurists in the early 2000s engaged in a debate on possible limits of the prohibition of torture, especially whether torture could be used as a means to save innocent lives. The majority of authors and courts have maintained the absolute ban on torture, arguing that the dignity of the person protected by Art. 1 Basic Law could not be infringed even where human lives are at stake.[62]

3.2.2 Definition of Privilege Against Self-incrimination

German statutory law neither defines nor explicitly protects a suspect's right to remain silent. The Code of Criminal Procedure mentions this right only indirectly by requiring that a suspect, at his first interrogation, shall be informed of the fact that "according to the law"[63] he is free to respond to the allegation of guilt or not to say anything with regard to the subject matter (§ 136 sec. 1, 2nd sent. CCP).

---

[58] *See* the notification of 15 December 1953 (Bundesgesetzblatt 1954 II 14). Germany has also ratified the European Convention against Torture and Inhuman and Degrading Treatment of 1987 (Bundesgesetzblatt 1989 II 946).

[59] ECtHR, *Ireland* v. *UK*, case no. 5310/71, Judgement of 18 January 1978, § 162; *Asalya* v. *Turkey*, case no. 43875/09, Judgement of 15 April 2014, § 47.

[60] BGH, Judgement of 21 February 2001 - 3 StR 372/00 (=BGHSt 46, 292, 302-303).

[61] *See* ECtHR, *Gäfgen* v. *Germany*, case no. 22978/05, Judgement of 30 June 2008; Judgement (Grand Chamber) of 1 June 2010, §§ 165-166. For a comment, *see* Weigend, 2011 at 325. *See also* ECtHR, *Harutyunyan* v. *Armenia*, case no. 36549/03, Judgement of 28 June 2007, § 63; *Cesnieks* v. *Latvia*, case no. 9278/06, Judgement of 11 February 2014, § 65.

[62] *See, e.g.*, LG Frankfurt am Main, Decision of 9 April 2003 – 5/22 Ks 3490 Js 230118/02, (2003) 23 Strafverteidiger, 325-27; Hamm, 2003; Wittreck, 2003; Hilgendorf, 2004; Saliger, 2004; Erb, 2005; *but see also* Brugger, 2000; Herzberg, 2005.

[63] Curiously, § 136 sec. 1 CCP refers to a written law (*Gesetz*) which, as such, does not exist. Germany did however ratify the International Covenant on Civil and Political Rights, which protects the privilege in Art. 14 (3) (g).

Similarly, a witness may decline to respond to any question if the answer would lead to the risk that he or one of his relatives could be prosecuted for a criminal offense or an administrative infraction (§ 55 sec. 1 CCP). The privilege implies that a suspect's (or his relative's) silence must not be used as evidence of his guilt.[64]

These provisions of statutory law implicitly show that Germany recognizes any person's right to decline any active contribution to his or her own prosecution. The Federal Constitutional Court has held that the privilege against self-incrimination follows from the constitutional principle that Germany is a state based on the rule of law (*Rechtsstaatsprinzip*; see Art. 20 sec. 3 and Art. 28 sec. 1 Basic Law).[65] The exact constitutional basis of the privilege against self-incrimination is difficult to identify; the Federal Constitutional Court and many authors regard the principle as based on the dignity of the person as protected in Art. 1 Basic Law.[66]

According to German case law and doctrine, the privilege against self-incrimination is not limited to verbal statements but extends to any form of activity, including participation in psychological or physical tests and providing handwriting samples, even just blowing into a breathalyzer.[67] It is not quite clear against what kind of official inducements to speak or cooperate the privilege protects. Without doubt, agents of the state must not use force or threats of force in order to make a person actively incriminate himself.[68] But according to the majority view, deceit is a permissible method of obtaining a person's active cooperation.[69]

Suspects, defendants and witnesses must be informed of the privilege as it applies to them (§§ 55 sec. 2, 136 sec. 1, 2nd sent., 243 sec. 5 CCP). It is irrelevant

[64]BGH, Decision of 29 August 1974 - 4 StR 171/74 (=BGHSt 25, 365, 368); Judgement of 2 April 1987 - 4 StR 46/87 (=34, 324, 326); Judgement of 26 May 1992 - 5 StR 122/92 (=38, 302, 305). If the suspect makes a statement but declines to respond to further questions, this fact may be used with respect to the credibility of his statements; *see* BGH, Judgement of 3 December 1965 - 4 StR 573/65 (=BGHSt 20, 298); Meyer-Goßner/Schmitt, 2016 at § 261 note 17.

[65]BVerfG, Decision of 8 October 1974 - 2 BvR 747/73 (=BVerfGE 38, 105, 113); Decision of 13 January 1981 - 1 BvR 116/77 (=56, 37, 43); Judgement of 3 March 2004 - 1 BvR 2378/98 u. 1 BvR 1084/99 (=109, 279, 324).

[66]BVerfG, Decision of 13 January 1981 - 1 BvR 116/77 (=BVerfGE 56, 37, 43); for further references *see* Bosch, 1998; Schuhr in Münchener Kommentar, 2014 before § 133 notes 74–76.

[67]BGH, Judgement of 9 April 1986 - 3 StR 551/85 (=BGHSt 34, 39, 46); Judgement of 24 February 1994 - 4 StR 317/93 (=40, 66, 71-72); Judgement of 21 January 2004 - 1 StR 364/03 (=BGHSt 49, 56); Roxin, 1995 at 466; Rogall in Systematischer Kommentar, 2016 before §133 notes 73, 146–50. For a critical assessment, *see* Verrel, 2001.

[68]BGH, Judgement of 26 July 2007 - 3 StR 104/07 (=BGHSt 52, 11, 17-18); Rogall in Systematischer Kommentar, 2016 before §133 notes 79–81.

[69]BGH, Decision of 13 May 1996 - GSSt 1/96 (=BGHSt 42, 139, 153); Decision of 31 March 2011 - 3 StR 400/10 (=NStZ 2011, 596). *But see,* contra, Wolfslast, 1987 at 104; Ransiek, 1990 at 54-58; Roxin, 1997. In BGH, Judgement of 26 July 2007 - 3 StR 104/07 (=BGHSt 52, 11, 18), the Federal Court of Justice in 2007 explicitly left open whether it will continue its restrictive interpretation of the privilege against self-incrimination.

whether the suspect or witness already is aware of his right to remain silent.[70] According to the Federal Court of Justice, an undercover police agent talking with a suspect in order to elicit information need not tell the suspect that he has a right to remain silent, because that would undermine the usefulness of undercover police investigations.[71]

3.2.3 Exclusionary Rules for Evidence Obtained by Torture

3.2.3.1 Procedure

There are no special rules in German criminal procedure with respect to weeding out before trial evidence that has been obtained by torture. In theory at least, the public prosecutor's office conducts the pretrial proceedings (§§ 160 sec. 1, 161 sec. 1 CCP). If the police use torture and this becomes known to the prosecutor, he must refrain from using any statement obtained through torture for the further investigation (§ 136a Sec. 3 CCP; see below). In fact, however, prosecutors rarely participate actively in the investigation but leave it largely to the police. Prosecutors typically review the police file only when the police consider the investigation terminated, with the case ready for dismissal or for indictment. The prosecutor may then send the case back to the police, however, for further investigation if he thinks that not all relevant facts have been elucidated or that critical evidence would be inadmissible in court.

When the prosecutor has filed a formal accusation, the trial court—sitting without lay judges—reviews the file of the investigation and decides whether there is sufficient evidence available to make the accused stand trial on the charges (§ 199 CCP; see above). At this stage of the proceedings, the trial court will also consider whether evidence proposed by the prosecution is admissible at trial. If critical evidence (e.g., a confession of the accused) is inadmissible, the court may decide that the remaining evidence will probably not be sufficient for conviction, and may on that ground refuse to open trial proceedings. Although German law does not provide for a hearing on the admissibility of evidence, such issues can be discussed either during the intermediary phase or at a special hearing held by the court before trial (§ 212 CCP). As has been noted above, the trial court is solely responsible for deciding what evidence is to be presented at trial (§ 244 sec. 2 CCP).

If evidence (e.g., a witness statement) has been presented at the trial, according to the Federal Court of Justice it will be presumed that the defense consents to its

[70]BGH, Decision of 27 February 1992 - 5 StR 190/91 (=BGHSt 38, 214, 224). *See also* Judgement of 12 October 1993 - 1 StR 475/93 (=BGHSt 39, 349) (if suspect, due to mental incapacity, was unable to understand the information, his statement may be used only with his consent).

[71]BGH, Decision of 13 May 1996 - GSSt 1/96 (=BGHSt 42, 139, 145). *See* the criticism of Roxin, 1995 at 466.

use unless the defendant's lawyer[72] explicitly objects as soon as the evidence has been introduced.[73] This means that defense counsel must immediately raise any doubts he may have as to the admissibility of any evidence.

3.2.3.2 Exclusionary Rules in Public Debate

Cases of police torture are not at the center of public debate in Germany. It is unknown to what extent non-lawyers are aware of the rules on inadmissibility of statements obtained by torture. In the *Gäfgen* case, opinions were divided on whether the relatively mild threat of applying painful force to the suspect was justified in order to save the victim's life.[74] In any event, the public was less than enthusiastic about the fact that Mr. Gäfgen received a substantial sum of money for pain and suffering in that context.[75]

3.2.4 Institutional Arrangements Securing the Ban on Torture

One means to prevent torture is the presence of a defense lawyer in torture-prone situations, especially during police interrogations. § 137 CCP provides that anyone may avail himself of the assistance of a lawyer at all stages of criminal proceedings. Since 2017, the defense lawyer has the right to be present at any interrogation of the suspect (§ 163a sec. 3 and 4 in connection with § 168c sec. 1 CCP). Yet, the suspect must normally pay his lawyer's fee, and if he is too poor the state will not necessarily appoint a free lawyer for him.[76]

There are no special procedures available for bringing cases of torture to the attention of courts. Anyone may file a criminal complaint (for assault—§ 223 Penal Code—or for coercing testimony—§ 343 Penal Code) or a civil suit for damages (§§ 823, 839 Civil Code) against the offending officer. The issue may also be raised

[72]Or the defendant himself, if he has no lawyer and had been specifically informed by the judge that he must object to the use of the evidence.

[73]BGH, Decision of 27 February 1992 - 5 StR 190/91 (= BGHSt 38, 214, 226); Judgement of 12 January 1996 - 5 StR 756/94 (=BGHSt 42, 15, 22); *see also* BVerfG, Decision of 7 December 2011 - 2 BvR 2500/09 (=NJW 2012, 907, 911) (holding this decision constitutional). For criticism, *see* Fezer, 1997 at 58; Heinrich, 2000, 398.

[74]*See* the compromise judgement of *Landgericht* Frankfurt in the criminal case against the police officer who had uttered the threat of torture (convicting the defendant of coercion but imposing an extremely lenient sentence), LG Frankfurt am Main, Decision of 9 April 2003 – 5/22 Ks 3490 Js 230118/02, (2003) 23 Strafverteidiger, 325-27.

[75]*See* the comments under <http://www.focus.de/panorama/welt/verurteilter-kindsmoerder-neues-verfahren-wegen-entschaedigung-fuer-gaefgen_aid_808457.html>, accessed 1 November 2018.

[76]§ 140 CCP describes the situations when a lawyer has to be provided for a suspect or defendant. One such situation exists when the suspect has been taken into pretrial custody (§ 140 sec. 1 no. 4 CCP). Pretrial custody however requires a judicial order and is to be distinguished from mere provisional arrest, which does not trigger the right to have a lawyer appointed.

in the context of the criminal proceedings against the tortured person as an objection to the use of evidence under § 136a sec. 3 CCP.

Germany has installed a national agency for the prevention of torture, as demanded by Arts. 17–23 of the Optional Protocol of 2002 to the U.N. Convention against Torture and Other Cruel, Inhuman or Degrading Treatment or Punishment.[77] The independent national agency for the prevention of torture consists of sub-agencies with competence for Federal and State institutions. Its ten members have the right to visit closed institutions, and they prepare annual reports for the Federal and State governments and parliaments. Germany has not so far installed independent institutions to which individual complaints of torture and degrading treatment can be directed; the Federal government deems it sufficient that inmates can send petitions to the Federal or State legislatures.[78]

3.2.5 Exclusion of Evidence and Other Remedies Following a Breach of the Ban on Torture

There has been some debate as to whether the use of torture so vitiates a criminal proceeding that it must be terminated without a conviction.[79] The courts have, however, rejected that proposition, arguing that a dismissal of the case might infringe upon the protection of third parties; moreover, dismissal might hurt the important constitutional interest in prosecuting and convicting criminal offenders,[80] failing to provide satisfaction through punishment.[81]

With regard to torture, § 136a sec. 3, 2nd sent. CCP clearly provides that statements elicited from a suspect or witness by the forbidden means listed in § 136a secs. 1 and 2 CCP (see above) are inadmissible as evidence.[82] Such statements

---

[77]Resolution of the UN General Assembly on the Optional Protocol to the Convention against Torture and Other Cruel, Inhuman or Degrading Treatment or Punishment, UN Doc A/RES/57/199 of 9 January 2003.

[78]*See* <http://www.institut-fuer-menschenrechte.de/fileadmin/user_upload/PDF-Dateien/Europarat_Dokumente/Bericht_Menschenrechtskommissar_Deutschland_2015_Kommentar_Bundesregierung_de.pdf> accessed 1 November 2018.

[79]For an overview and discussion *see* Julius in Heidelberger Kommentar, 2012 at § 206a notes 8–15.

[80]The Federal Constitutional Court has held this interest to be part of the principle of *Rechtsstaatlichkeit* (a state based on the rule of law); *see* BVerfG, Decision of 15 January 2009 - 2 BvR 2044/07 (=BVerfGE 122, 248, 273); Judgement of 19 March 2013 – 2 BvR 2628/10, 2 BvR 2883/10, 2 BvR 2155/11 (=133, 168, 200-201); BVerfG, Decision of 18 December 2014 – 2 BvR 209, 240, 262/14 (=StV 2015, 413, 415).

[81]*See* BGH, Judgement of 18 November 1999 - 1 StR 221/99 (=BGHSt 45, 321, 333-34); Judgement of 11 December 2013 - 5 StR 240/13 (=NStZ 2014, 277, 280).

[82]It is a matter of controversy whether the inadmissibility of coerced statements also applies to evidence that favors the defense; *see* Gless in Löwe/Rosenberg, 2007 at § 136a note 71; Roxin, 2009 at 113; Wohlers, 2012 at 391; Diemer in Karlsruher Kommentar, 2013 at § 136a note 37; Roxin/Schünemann, 2014 at 173.

have to be excluded even if the declarant consents to their use (§ 136a sec. 3, 2nd sent. CCP).[83] If an illicit method of interrogation as listed in § 136a secs. 1 and 2 CCP was used, it will normally be assumed (and does not require proof) that the statement was actually caused by employing the forbidden method; exclusion does therefore not require a positive showing that the statement was in fact involuntary or was brought about by the illicit means.[84]

Tainted statements must not be introduced even in an indirect way, for example, by asking a witness of the interrogation what the person had said; nor is it permissible for an expert witness to base his expert opinion on a coerced statement.[85]

According to the Federal Court of Justice, violations of Art. 136a CCP can be proved and disproved by any means.[86] There is no technical burden of proof either on the defendant or on the prosecutor. But the courts presume the "regularity of the criminal process". This means that evidence will not be excluded if the court cannot determine whether or not a violation of § 136a CCP occurred.[87] While it is true that the principle *in dubio pro reo* is not directly applicable here, because the question of whether a violation of § 136a CCP occurred is not directly related to the defendant's guilt, the majority of commentators reject the view that it is in fact the defendant who has to prove that he had been maltreated. They claim that the burden of proving that there was no violation of § 136a CCP shifts to the state as soon as the defendant has made a plausible initial showing that a violation may have occurred.[88]

There is broad agreement that the exclusion of evidence in this situation not only serves the truth-finding process by eliminating evidence of inherently doubtful reliability,[89] but that the rule of exclusion is rooted in the Constitution. Opinions differ, however, as to the exact constitutional principle that is applicable. Some authors regard the exclusion of evidence obtained through torture as a corollary of the protection of human dignity[90]: others emphasize the integrity of judicial

---

[83]This rule does, of course, not preclude the declarant from making the same statement again in court. Such a statement is admissible if the declarant had been informed that his prior statement is inadmissible.

[84]BGH, Judgement of 24 March 1959 - 5 StR 27/59 (=BGHSt 13, 60, 61).

[85]BGH, Judgement of 4 March 1958 - 5 StR 7/58 (=BGHSt 11, 211). *See further* Meyer-Goßner/Schmitt, 2016 at § 136a note 29; Schuhr in Münchener Kommentar, 2014 at § 136a note 96.

[86]BGH, Judgement of 28 June 1961 - 2 StR 154/61 (=BGHSt 16, 164, 166-67); Judgement of 21 July 1994 - 1 StR 83/94 (=NJW 1994, 2904, 2905); but *see contra* Gless in Löwe/Rosenberg, 2007 at § 136a note 77; Eisenberg, 2015 at note 707.

[87]BGH, Judgement of 28 June 1961 - 2 StR 154/61 (=BGHSt 16, 164, 167); Decision of 7 June 1983 - 5 StR 409/81 (=BGHSt 31, 395); Rogall in Systematischer Kommentar, 2016 at § 136a note 101.

[88]*See, e.g.*, Gless in Löwe/Rosenberg, 2007 at § 136a note 78; Kühne, 2010 at note 966; Volk, 2010 at 178–79; Roxin/Schünemann, 2014 at 394; Eisenberg, 2015 at notes 708–709.

[89]BGH, Judgement of 14 June 1960 - 1 StR 683/59 (=BGHSt 14, 358); Judgement of 21 February 1964 - 4 StR 519/63 (=19, 325, 329-30); Krack, 2002 at 124.

[90]*See* BVerfG, Decision of 14 December 2004 - 2 BvR 1249/04 (=NJW 2005, 656); Merten, 2003 at 406; Meyer-Goßner/Schmitt, 2016 at § 136a note 1.

proceedings that would be compromised if such evidence were employed by the court.[91] German doctrine places little weight on the deterrent effect that exclusion of coerced evidence may have on illegal police practices[92]; but the Federal Court of Justice has emphasized that exclusion is to make certain that police do not intentionally neglect the legal requirements.[93]

The ECtHR likewise demands exclusion of any evidence produced by torture.[94] It has found violations of Art. 3 ECHR where the results of torture or inhuman treatment were the sole or decisive evidence on which the judgement was based.[95]

3.2.6 Admissibility of Indirect Evidence ("Fruits of the Poisonous Tree") in Cases of Torture

It is unclear whether the use of torture precludes not only the admission of statements made by the tortured person but also the use of evidence discovered as a result of such statements.[96] The general German debate on how to deal with "fruits of the poisonous tree" resonates here. German courts do not categorically exclude evidence derived from violations of individual procedural rights.[97] As noted above, The Federal Constitutional Court has argued that exclusion of relevant evidence must remain an exception.[98] Moreover, it has been said that exclusion of any derivative evidence would have the effect that one procedural fault could entirely disrupt the criminal process.[99] Some authors think, however, that a violation of § 136a CCP should invariably foreclose the admission of any evidence derived from the statement made by the declarant.[100] An argument in favor of this view is that § 136a CCP sec. 3, 2nd sent. CCP declares that "statements" (*Aussagen*) that have been brought about by forbidden means must not be "used"—and it is one way of

---

[91]*See* Neuhaus, 1997 at 314–315; Rogall in Systematischer Kommentar, 2016 at § 136a note 4; Eisenberg, 2015 at note 330.

[92]See Beulke, 1990 at 180; Amelung, 1999 at 181; Eisenberg, 2015 at note 368; Paul, 2013 at 494; Roxin/Schünemann, 2014 at 172–173 (arguing that the function of „disciplining" police is misplaced in an inquisitorial procedual system); Ransiek, 2015 at 950–51.

[93]BGH, Judgement of 18 April 2007 - 5 StR 546/06 (=BGHSt 51, 285, 296).

[94]ECtHR, *Harutyunyan* v. *Armenia*, case no. 36549/03, Judgement of 28 June 2007, § 63; *Gäfgen* v. *Germany*, case no. 22978/05, Judgement (Grand Chamber) of 1 June 2010, §§ 165-166; *Cesnieks* v. *Latvia*, case no. 9278/06, Judgement of 11 February 2014, § 65.

[95]ECtHR, *Jalloh* v. *Germany*, case no. 54810/00, Judgement of 11 July 2006, § 107; *Gäfgen* v. *Germany*, case no. 22978/05; Judgement (Grand Chamber) of 1 June 2010, § 178; *El Haski* v. *Belgium*, case no. 649/08, Judgement of 25 September 2012, § 85.

[96]For a detailed analysis, *see* Rogall in Systematischer Kommentar, 2016 at § 136a notes 108-126.

[97]*See* BGH, Judgement of 28 April 1987 - 5 StR 666/86 (=BGHSt 34, 362, 364).

[98]BVerfG, Decision of 9 November 2010 - 2 BvR 2101/09 (=NJW 2011, 2417, 2418-19).

[99]BGH, Judgement of 22 February 1978 - 2 StR 334/77 (=BGHSt 27, 355, 358); Judgement of 24 August 1983 - 3 StR 136/83 (=32, 68, 70-71).

[100]See, e.g., Neuhaus, 1990 at 1221; Müssig, 1999 at 136–37; Hüls, 2009 at 167–68; Kühne, 2010 at 558; Eisenberg, 2015 at note 408.

"using" such statements for law enforcement to base further inquiries on them.[101] Moreover, limiting inadmissibility to the coerced statement itself would virtually invite the police to apply forbidden means in the hope of obtaining further leads which then could be used as evidence. The German courts, by contrast, extend their general skepticism about excluding derivative evidence to the situation of a violation of § 136a CCP. They make admissibility depend on a weighing of the conflicting interests of law enforcement on the one side and individual rights on the other (see above).[102]

According to the ECtHR judgement in *Gäfgen v. Germany*, use of evidence derived from torture or degrading treatment as a rule violates Art. 3 ECHR.[103]

3.3 *Exclusion of Illegally Obtained Evidence—Cases of Undue Coercion*

§ 136a CCP does not distinguish between cases of torture and of other undue physical or mental coercion. What has been said above about the procedural consequences of torture therefore applies as well to other (lesser) forms of physical abuse or mental torment.

3.3.1 Institutional Arrangements Securing the Right to Remain Silent

Procedural safeguards for the protection of the right to remain silent are similar to those protecting against torture: suspects have a general right to consult with a lawyer before they submit to questioning by the police or other law enforcement personnel. Suspects must explicitly be informed of the right to consult with a lawyer prior to any interrogation, and they must be assisted in obtaining access to a lawyer (§ 136 sec. 1, 2nd and 3rd sent. CCP).[104] The defense lawyer has the right to be present during any interrogation of a suspect and can advise his client of the proper use of his right to remain silent (§§ 168c sec. 1, 163a sec. 3, 2nd sent., sec. 4 3rd sent. CCP).

---

[101]Ransiek, 2015, at 957–958. *See*, however, above as to the distinction between use (*Verwertung*) and employment (*Verwendung*) of evidence in German law and doctrine.

[102]BGH, Judgement of 22 February 1978 - 2 StR 334/77 (=BGHSt 27, 355, 358); Judgement of 18 April 1980 - 2 StR 731/79 (=29, 244, 249) (concerning illicit wiretapping); Judgement of 24 August 1983 - 3 StR 136/83 (=32, 68, 71); Judgement of 28 April 1987 - 5 StR 666/86 (=34, 362, 364); Decision of 7 March 2006 - 1 StR 316/05 (=51, 1, 8). *Accord*, Gless in Löwe/Rosenberg, 2007 at § 136a notes 75–76; Rogall in Systematischer Kommentar, 2016 at § 136a notes 1112–13.

[103]ECtHR, *Gäfgen* v. *Germany*, case no. 22978/05, Judgement (Grand Chamber) of 1 June 2010, § 178.

[104]If the information was not given, any statement of the suspect is inadmissible as evidence; BGH, Judgement of 22 November 2001 - 1 StR 220/01 (=BGHSt 47, 172).

3.3.2 Exclusionary Rules for Evidence Obtained in Violation of the Privilege Against Self-incrimination

If the requisite information on the right not to incriminate oneself (§§ 55 sec. 2, 136 sec. 1, 2nd sent. CCP) was not provided, the declarant's statement cannot be used as evidence against him.[105] In a case concerning the admissibility of unwarned self-incriminating statements, the Federal Court of Justice has affirmed the principle that the court should seek the truth, but should not do so at any cost.[106] The Court held that any (even unintentional) omission of the required information about the right to silence jeopardizes the suspect's ability to intelligently decide whether to remain silent; the suspect's statements therefore are presumed to be involuntary.[107] Yet the Court recognized an exception if it can be proved that the suspect was in fact aware of his right to remain silent.[108] Furthermore, the defendant can consent to the use of his prior unwarned statement at trial, thus rendering it admissible.[109]

If the information about the privilege was not provided, the suspect may nevertheless be interrogated again at a later date, either by the same interrogator or by a different person. In order for any statement made at this latter date to be admissible as evidence, the suspect needs to be told (a) that he is free to speak or to remain silent, and (b) that his prior (unwarned) statement cannot be used as evidence.[110] It is not clear, however, whether a statement made in the second interrogation may be used if the second part of the warning was not given. Some authors think that, without the complete warning, the second statement is inadmissible because the interrogated person is likely to think that the earlier statement is good evidence and that it therefore does not matter whether he repeats it.[111] The Federal Court of Justice, on the other hand, favors a "weighing" solution: the trial court is to decide whether the importance of the statement for finding the truth outweighs the seriousness of the violation of the suspect's rights. The latter is unlikely to be the case

[105]BGH, Decision of 27 February 1992 - 5 StR 190/91 (=BGHSt 38, 214) (concerning defendant); Oberlandesgericht Celle of 7 February 2001 - 32 Ss 101/00 (=NStZ 2002, 386). According to a controversial decision of the Federal Court of Justice, the self-incriminating statement of an unwarned *witness* can be used as evidence against the defendant (but not against the witness); BGH, Decision of 21 January 1958 - GSSt 4/57 (=BGHSt 11, 213).

[106]BGH, Decision of 27 February 1992 - 5 StR 190/91 (=BGHSt 38, 214).

[107]BGH, Decision of 27 February 1992 - 5 StR 190/91 (=BGHSt 38, 214, 220-22).

[108]BGH, Decision of 27 February 1992 - 5 StR 190/91 (=BGHSt 38, 214, 224-25); Judgement of 12 January 1996 - 5 StR 756/94 (=BGHSt 42, 15, 22). The Court explained that knowledge of the right to remain silent can be assumed when the suspect makes a statement in the presence of counsel, but that knowledge cannot be inferred from the fact that the suspect had previously been prosecuted or convicted.

[109]Gless in Löwe/Rosenberg, 2007 at § 136 note 81.

[110]BGH, Judgement of 18 December 2008 - 4 StR 455/08 (=BGHSt 53, 112) (overruling Judgement of 31 May 1990 - 4 StR 112/90 (=BGHSt 37, 48, 53)).

[111]*See, e.g.*, Gleß/Wennekers, 2009 at 383; Jahn, 2009 at 468; Beulke, 2016 at note 119.

where the second interrogator *intentionally* omitted to provide the requisite information.[112]

With regard to evidence *derived* from unwarned statements, the Federal Court of Justice is likely to admit such evidence given its general reluctance to exclude "fruits of the poisoned tree".[113] In conformity with its treatment of other violations of the defendant's procedural rights, the Federal Court of Justice can be expected to prefer the so-called sentencing solution, i.e. denying any impact on the process but granting the convicted defendant a reduction of the deserved sentence as a compensation for the violation of his rights.[114]

3.3.3 Remedies Following Violations of Exclusionary Rules

As with violations of § 136a CCP, the principle *in dubio pro reo* is said not to apply to the question whether the suspect's right to silence had been observed at all times. If the trial court is not convinced that a violation occurred, it will admit the evidence in question.

As for the evidentiary consequences of undue coercion, see supra on § 136a CCP.

4 Statistics

Statistical evidence on the application of exclusionary rules is not available.

5 Conclusion

In summary, one can say that Germany still pursues the ideal of finding the truth in the criminal process and places great emphasis on this goal. Although the protection of human rights is seen as part of the constitutional principle of *Rechtsstaatlichkeit*, and although human dignity has been accorded the highest rank in the German constitutional hierarchy, the exclusion of evidence is regarded as an anomaly. There are only few instances of mandatory exclusion. Some of them concern the protection of core privacy (§§ 100a sec. 4 and 100c sec. 5 CCP), and some are to safeguard the integrity of interrogations (especially § 136a sec. 3 CCP, but also

[112]BGH, Judgement of 3 July 2007 - 1 StR 3/07 (=StV 2007, 450, 452); Judgement of 18 December 2008 - 4 StR 455/08 (=BGHSt 53, 112, 114).

[113]BGH, Judgement of 28 April 1987 - 5 StR 666/86 (=BGHSt 34, 362, 369).

[114]*See, e.g.*, BGH, Judgement of 18 November 1999 - 1 StR 221/99 (=BGHSt 45, 321, 339) (for a case of entrapment).

judge-made rules such as the exclusion of a suspect's statements if information on the right to remain silent and the right to a lawyer had not been provided[115]). In most other instances of the violation of individual rights, German courts engage in a balancing process, excluding relevant evidence only if there is no overriding interest in using the evidence for determining the truth. Moreover, exclusion of evidence generally covers only evidence that has been directly obtained through a violation of procedural rules; derivative evidence is generally accepted, with few exceptions.

Institutional mechanisms for ensuring respect for human rights in the context of the criminal process are limited. The most important tools are the obligation of interrogators to inform suspects and witnesses of their respective rights, and a suspect's right to have the assistance of a lawyer.[116] Yet, it should be noted that not every suspect can receive the services of a lawyer free of charge (cf. § 140 CCP).

With regard to the balance between truth-finding and protection of human rights, the trend in Germany is toward cautiously extending the scope of exclusionary rules, especially in cases where a state agent intentionally or arbitrarily violated a procedural rule protecting the rights of the suspect. This trend has been initiated and fuelled by the jurisprudence of the ECtHR and the German Federal Constitutional Court, sometimes against the persistent opposition of the criminal courts.

It is an open question whether exclusion of tainted evidence is actually effective in discouraging rule violations. It is difficult to find out to what extent and in what areas police and prosecutors may tend to disregard the restrictions on collecting evidence that procedural law provides. From the published case law, it appears that searches and examinations of the body are more susceptible to rule violations than interrogations; but there may exist a dark figure of unknown size in either area. Given the remoteness of police activities in investigating crime from actual trials, and the relative scarcity of trials (in relation to written procedures and consensual dispositions), it is unlikely that exclusion of evidence has a strong educative or deterrent effect on individual police officers who may have committed a procedural fault in the early stages of an investigation. On the other hand, the inquisitorial tradition is still strong in Germany, and that tradition is inimical to any effort of purposely manipulating the factual basis of the court's judgement.

Alternative ways of curbing disregard of individual procedural rights by police and prosecutors are limited to the usual mechanisms of imposing individual responsibility through disciplinary and (depending on the factual situation) criminal law. There is a functioning disciplinary system of police forces in place, but it seems that it is more geared toward combating police violence and corruption than toward suppressing the use of illicit investigatory measures.

Academic writers as well as the defense bar tend to support increased reliance on the exclusion of evidence and a general strengthening of tools for guaranteeing

---

[115]BGH, Decision of 27 February 1992 - 5 StR 190/91 (=BGHSt 38, 214); Judgement of 22 November 2001 - 1 StR 220/01 (=BGHSt 47, 172).

[116]Witnesses also have a right to have a lawyer present during their interrogation (§ 68b CCP).

respect for human rights. But the influence of both groups on law reform is very limited. At this time, the emphasis of official "reform" measures is on increasing the speed, economy, and "efficiency" of the criminal process.[117] Exclusion of evidence does not seem to be a welcome instrument for achieving these goals.

References

Books

Beulke, Werner, *Strafprozessrecht* 13th ed., Heidelberg 2016. [Beulke, 2016]
Bosch, Nikolaus, *Aspekte des nemo-tenetur-Prinzips aus verfassungsrechtlicher und strafprozessualer Sicht*, Berlin 1998. [Bosch, 1998]
Eisenberg, Ulrich, *Beweisrecht der StPO* 9th ed., München 2015. [Eisenberg, 2015]
Kühne, Hans-Heiner, *Strafprozessrecht. Eine systematische Darstellung des deutschen und europäischen Strafverfahrensrechts* 8th ed., Heidelberg 2010. [Kühne, 2010]
Ransiek, Andreas, *Die Rechte des Beschuldigten in der Polizeivernehmung*, Heidelberg 1990. [Ransiek, 1990]
Roxin, Claus/Schünemann, Bernd, *Strafverfahrensrecht* 28th ed., München 2014. [Roxin/ Schünemann, 2014]
Rzepka, Dorothea, *Zur Fairness im deutschen Strafverfahren*, Frankfurt am Main 2000. [Rzepka, 2000]
Stuckenberg, Carl-Friedrich, *Untersuchungen zur Unschuldsvermutung*, Berlin 1998. [Stuckenberg, 1998]
Verrel, Thorsten, *Die Selbstbelastungsfreiheit im Strafverfahren*, München 2001. [Verrel, 2001]
Volk, Klaus, *Grundkurs StPO* 7th ed., München 2010. [Volk, 2010]

Journal Articles

Amelung, Knut, 'Die Verwertbarkeit rechtswidrig gewonnener Beweismittel zugunsten des Angeklagten und deren Grenzen', (1999) 14 *StrafverteidigerForum*, 181–86. [Amelung, 1999]
Beulke, Werner, 'Die Vernehmung des Beschuldigten – Einige Anmerkungen aus der Sicht der Prozeßrechtswissenschaft', (1990) 10 *Strafverteidiger*, 180–84. [Beulke, 1990]
Beulke, Werner, 'Hypothetische Kausalverläufe im Strafverfahren bei rechtswidrigem Vorgehen von Ermittlungsorganen', (1991) 103 *Zeitschrift für die gesamte Strafrechtswissenschaft*, 657–80. [Beulke, 1991]
Brugger, Winfried, 'Vom unbedingten Verbot der Folter zum bedingten Recht auf Folter?', (2000) 55 *Juristenzeitung*, 165–72; [Brugger, 2000]

[117] *See* the 2017 amendments to the Code of Criminal Procedure enacted through the Law for the more efficient and practical organisation of the criminal process (*Gesetz zur effektiveren und praxistauglicheren Ausgestaltung des Strafverfahrens*) of 17 August 2017, Bundesgesetzblatt 2017 I, 3202.

Erb, Volker, 'Notwehr als Menschenrecht - Zugleich eine Kritik der Entscheidung des LG Frankfurt am Main im Fall Daschner', (2005) 25 *Neue Zeitschrift für Strafrecht*, 593–602; [Erb, 2005]

Fezer, Gerhard, 'Anmerkung zu BGH, Beschluß vom 20.12.1995 – 5 StR 445/95. Fortwirkungen des Einsatzes verbotener Vernehmungsmethoden, Anforderungen an Revisionsbegründung', (1997) 17 *Strafverteidiger*, 57–59. [Fezer, 1997]

Gless, Sabine/Wennekers, Jan, 'Anmerkung zu BGH, Urt. v. 18.12.2008 – 4 StR 455/08. Zu den Voraussetzungen einer qualifizierten Belehrung und eines darauf gründenden Verwertungsverbotes', (2009) 2009 *Juristische Rundschau*, 380–85. [Gless/Wennekers, 2009]

Hamm, Rainer, 'Schluss der Debatte über Ausnahmen vom Folterverbot', (2003) 56 *Neue Juristische Wochenschrift*, 946-47. [Hamm, 2003]

Heinrich, Bernd, 'Rügepflichten in der Hauptverhandlung und Disponibilität strafverfahrensrechtlicher Vorschriften', (2000) 112 *Zeitschrift für die gesamte Strafrechtswissenschaft*, 398–428. [Heinrich, 2000]

Herzberg, Rolf Dietrich, 'Folter und Menschenwürde', (2005) 60 *Juristenzeitung*, 321–27. [Herzberg, 2005]

Hilgendorf, Eric, 'Folter im Rechtsstaat?', (2004) 59 *Juristenzeitung*, 331–39. [Hilgendorf, 2004]

Hüls, Silke, 'Der Richtervorbehalt – seine Bedeutung für das Strafverfahren und die Folgen von Verstößen', (2009) 4 *Zeitschrift für internationale Strafrechtsdogmatik*, 160–69. [Hüls, 2009]

Jahn, Matthias, 'Anmerkung zu BGH, Urteil vom 18. 12. 2008 - 4 StR 455/08. Beweisverbot und qualifizierte' Belehrung', (2009) 49 *Juristische Schulung*, 468–70. [Jahn, 2009]

Krack, Ralf, 'Der Normzweck des § 136a StPO', (2002) 22 *Neue Zeitschrift für Strafrecht*, 120–24. [Krack, 2002]

Merten, Jan O., 'Folterverbot und Grundrechtsdogmatik. Zugleich ein Beitrag zur aktuellen Diskussion um die Menschenwürde', (2003) 2003 *Juristische Rundschau*, 404–08. [Merten, 2003]

Müssig, Bernd, 'Beweisverbote im Legitimationszusammenhang von Strafrechtstheorie und Strafverfahren', (1999) 146 *Goltdammer's Archiv für Strafrecht*, 119–42. [Müssig, 1999]

Neuhaus, Ralf, 'Zur Fernwirkung von Beweisverwertungsverboten', (1990) 43 *Neue Juristische Wochenschrift*, 1221–22. [Neuhaus, 1990]

Neuhaus, Ralf, 'Zur Notwendigkeit der qualifizierten Beschuldigtenbelehrung. Zugleich Anmerkung zu LG Dortmund NStZ 1997, 356', (1997) 17 *Neue Zeitschrift für Strafrecht*, 312–16. [Neuhaus, 1997]

Paul, Tobias, 'Unselbständige Beweisverwertungsverbote in der Rechtsprechung', (2013) 33 *Neue Zeitschrift für Strafrecht*, 489–97. [Paul, 2013]

Roxin, Claus, 'Anmerkung zu BGH, Beschl. v. 5.8.2008 – 3 StR 45/08. Verwertung einer einem Beweisverbot unterliegenden Aussage mit Zustimmung des Betroffenen', (2009) 29 *Strafverteidiger*, 113–15. [Roxin, 2009]

Roxin, Claus, 'Nemo tenetur: die Rechtsprechung am Scheideweg', (1995) 15 *Neue Zeitschrift für Strafrecht*, 465–69. [Roxin, 1995]

Roxin, Claus, ‚Zum Hörfallen-Beschluß des Großen Senats für Strafsachen' (1997) 17 *Neue Zeitschrift für Strafrecht*, 18–21 [Roxin, 1997]

Saliger, Frank, 'Absolutes im Strafprozess? Über das Folterverbot, seine Verletzung und die Folgen seiner Verletzung', (2004) 116 *Zeitschrift für die gesamte Strafrechtswissenschaft*, 35–65. [Saliger, 2004]

Schwenn, Johann, 'Fehlurteile und ihre Ursachen – die Wiederaufnahme im Verfahren wegen sexuellen Missbrauchs', (2010) 30 *Strafverteidiger*, 705–11. [Schwenn, 2010]

Stuckenberg, Carl-Friedrich, 'Schuldprinzip und Wahrheitserforschung: Bemerkungen zum Verhältnis von materiellem Recht und Prozessrecht', (2016) 163 *Goltdammer's Archiv für Strafrecht*, 689–701. [Stuckenberg, 2016]

Weigend, Thomas, 'Assuming that the Defendant Is Not Guilty: The Presumption of Innocence in the German System of Criminal Justice', (2014) 8 *Criminal Law and Philosophy*, 285–99. [Weigend, 2014]

Weigend, Thomas, 'Folterverbot im Strafverfahren', (2011) 31 *Strafverteidiger*, 325–29. [Weigend, 2011]

Wittreck, Fabian, 'Menschenwürde und Folterverbot – Zum Dogma von der ausnahmslosen Unabwägbarkeit des Art. 1 Abs. 1 GG', (2003) 56 *Die Öffentliche Verwaltung*, 873–83. [Wittreck, 2003]

Wohlers, Wolfgang, 'BGH v. 22. 12. 2011 – 2 StR 509/10. Verwertbarkeit eines in einem Kraftfahrzeug mittels akustischer Überwachung aufgezeichneten Selbstgesprächs', (2012) 2012 *Juristische Rundschau*, 386–91. [Wohlers, 2012]

Wolfslast, Gabriele, 'Beweisführung durch heimliche Tonbandaufzeichnung - Besprechung des BGH-Urteils vom 9. 4. 1986 - 3 StR 551/85', (1987) 7 *Neue Zeitschrift für Strafrecht*, 103–6. [Wolfslast, 1987]

Contributions to Edited Volumes and Annotated Law

Dreier, Horst (ed.), *Grundgesetz Kommentar* 3rd ed., Tübingen 2013. [*Author* in Dreier, 2013]

Erb, Volker et al. (eds.), *Löwe/Rosenberg. Die Strafprozessordnung und das Gerichtsverfassungsgesetz. StPO Band 4: §§ 112-150* 26th ed., Berlin 2007; *Band 6/2: §§ 256-295,* 26th ed., Berlin 2013 [*Author* in Löwe/Rosenberg, 2007/2013]

Gercke, Björn et al. (eds.), *Heidelberger Kommentar. Strafprozessordnung* 5th ed., Heidelberg 2012. [*Author* in Heidelberger Kommentar, 2012]

Hannich, Rolf (ed.), *Karlsruher Kommentar. Strafprozessordnung* 7th ed., München 2013. [*Author* in Karlsruher Kommentar, 2013]

Kudlich, Hans (ed.), *Münchener Kommentar. Strafprozessordnung. StPO Band 1: §§ 1-150 StPO*, München 2014. [*Author* in Münchener Kommentar, 2014]

Meyer-Goßner, Lutz/ Schmitt, Bertram, *Strafprozessordnung (StPO), Kommentar. Gerichtsverfassungsgesetz, Nebengesetze und ergänzende Bestimmungen* 59th ed., München 2016. [Meyer-Goßner/Schmitt, 2016]

Ransiek, Andreas, 'Rechtswidrige Ermittlungen und die Fernwirkung von Beweisverwertungsverboten', in: Fahl, Christian et al. (eds.), *Ein menschengerechtes Strafrecht als Lebensaufgabe. Festschrift für Werner Beulke zum 70. Geburtstag*, Heidelberg 2015, 949–61. [Ransiek, 2015]

Schneider, Hartmut (ed.), *Münchener Kommentar. Strafprozessordnung. StPO Band 2: §§ 151-332 StPO*, München 2016. [*Author* in Münchener Kommentar, 2016]

Wohlers, Wolfgang, 'Fernwirkung - zur normativen Begrenzung der sachlichen Reichweite von Verwertungsverboten', in: Zöller, Mark A. et al. (eds.), *Gesamte Strafrechtswissenschaft in internationaler Dimension. Festschrift für Jürgen Wolter*, Berlin 2013, 1181–1201. [Wohlers, 2013]

Wolter, Jürgen (ed.), *Systematischer Kommentar. Strafprozessordnung. StPO Band 2: §§ 94-136a StPO* 5th ed., Köln 2016. [*Author* in Systematischer Kommentar, 2016]

Thomas Weigend taught criminal law and criminal procedure at the University of Cologne (Germany). He also served as a visiting professor at Peking University and the University of Political Science and Law in Beijing. He retired from teaching in 2016. His research is primarily dedicated to comparative criminal procedure and international criminal law.

Regulating Interrogations and Excluding Confessions in the United States: Balancing Individual Rights and the Search for the Truth

Jenia Iontcheva Turner

Abstract This chapter discusses U.S. constitutional law surrounding the admissibility of confessions and the contexts in which the law demands exclusion and those in which a cost-benefit analysis by the court results in its inclusion. Justifications and practical effects of exclusionary rules and the public debates surrounding their use are explained. In the U.S., rights that are expressly protected by the Constitution—such as the right to remain silent, the right to be free from an unreasonable search or seizure, and the right to counsel—are weighed more heavily than the state's need to fully explore the facts in a criminal case. The values of fairness, dignity, privacy, and liberty embodied in these rights frequently outweigh the need for reliable fact finding. In deciding how to enforce these constitutional rights, however, U.S. courts are well aware of competing interests throughout the criminal justice system.

1 Introduction

Like other criminal justice systems, the U.S. system must balance, on the one hand, enforcing the criminal law and, on the other, protecting individual rights in the process. Reliable fact-finding is a prerequisite to the effective enforcement of criminal law and to just outcomes. Protection of individual rights often promotes reliable fact-finding, as when a ban on involuntary confessions prevents the introduction of unreliable testimony at trial. On occasion, however, the commitment to accurate fact-finding may conflict with individual rights in a particular case. One of the clearest examples of such a conflict occurs when a court must decide whether to admit reliable and probative evidence obtained in violation of constitutional rights.

In the United States, rights that are expressly protected by the Constitution—such as the right to remain silent, the right to be free from unreasonable search or

J. I. Turner (✉)
SMU Dedman School of Law, Dallas, USA
e-mail: Jenia@mail.smu.edu

S. Gless and T. Richter (eds.), *Do Exclusionary Rules Ensure a Fair Trial?*
Ius Gentium: Comparative Perspectives on Law and Justice 74,
https://doi.org/10.1007/978-3-030-12520-2_4

seizure, and the right to counsel—are given more weight in the balance than the state's need to explore fully the facts in a criminal case. The values of fairness, dignity, privacy, and liberty embodied in these rights frequently outweigh the concern for reliable factfinding. But in deciding how to enforce these constitutional rights, U.S. courts have recognized the relevance of competing interests in the criminal justice system, such as the interest in truthseeking. In deciding whether to exclude evidence, for example, courts have considered whether exclusion is expressly required by the Constitution and whether the benefits of exclusion, such as deterring police misconduct, outweigh its costs to truthseeking.

This report examines U.S. constitutional law on admissibility of confessions and discusses the contexts in which the law demands exclusion and contexts in which a cost-benefit analysis has led courts to reject exclusion. The report further explains the justifications and practical effects of exclusionary rules and the public debates surrounding their use.

2 Fact-Finding Procedure: Stages, Rules, and Actors

Before examining the law that regulates the search for truth and the protection of individual rights in criminal cases, it is useful to review the stages and rules of the factfinding process and the actors involved in it. A brief overview of the structure and institutions of criminal justice helps illustrate more clearly how legal rules apply in practice.

2.1 Stages and Rules

In the U.S. criminal justice system, the investigative and trial stages of the criminal process are not as strictly delineated as they are in some inquisitorial systems. The investigation frequently continues after formal charges are filed and, in some cases, even after the trial has begun. Yet the actors who investigate—the police or other government agents—do so independently and without supervision from prosecutors.[1] As a practical matter, police officers may end a case by choosing not to investigate further or not to arrest a suspect.[2] In serious cases, however, police officers typically are held accountable by political pressure to maintain a high clearance rate.

[1] At the state level, police are generally not supervised by prosecutors during their investigations. While in some specialized units and in some larger urban counties, police may run applications for a warrant by a prosecutor, this is the exception rather than the rule. By contrast, at the federal level, prosecutors routinely review warrant applications and other key investigative decisions with agents.

[2] *See* Saltzburg/Capra, 2014 at 958–59.

When police officers do identify a suspect and bring forward evidence to support a complaint, prosecutors decide whether and what charges to file with the court. In some jurisdictions, in felony cases, prosecutors must obtain an indictment through a grand jury composed of ordinary citizens.[3] The grand jury has an investigative as well as a screening function. It can subpoena witnesses and documents to aid the investigation, and it must decide whether the evidence provides probable cause to confirm an indictment. A little over half of U.S. states rely on a different mechanism —a preliminary hearing to evaluate whether probable cause supports the charges brought by the prosecutor. Unlike the grand jury, the preliminary hearing is adversarial in nature and allows both the prosecution and the defense to present evidence to a neutral magistrate. Defendants may and frequently do waive preliminary hearings, and the case then proceeds directly to the trial court. Regardless of whether the case proceeds via a preliminary hearing or via a grand jury indictment, the prosecutor retains broad discretion over charging decisions.[4]

The next step in the process is frequently a plea hearing before the trial court, as the overwhelming majority of U.S. state and federal cases are resolved through guilty pleas rather than trials. Guilty pleas typically result from negotiations between the defense and the prosecution. The negotiations may occur at any point before or during trial, although the vast majority of cases are resolved before trial. A major advantage of the guilty plea, from the perspective of the prosecution, is that it abbreviates the investigation and dispenses with a trial, saving precious resources. In some cases, plea bargaining also induces defendants to reveal valuable information about other cases, thus contributing to the search for truth.

Yet the abbreviated process also increases the risk of inaccurate or unfair judgments. Recognizing this risk, state and federal rules require that, before accepting a guilty plea, the court must examine the record and the defendant to determine that the guilty plea is voluntary, knowing, and factually based.[5] In practice, however, the plea hearing is typically perfunctory and courts rarely challenge the version of the facts negotiated by the parties and presented summarily at the hearing.

If the case is not resolved by a guilty plea, the defendant has the right to a jury trial.[6] Evidence rules that apply at trial generally attempt to increase the accuracy

---

[3]Saltzburg/Capra, 2014 at 987 (noting that "slightly less than half" the states require the use of a grand jury for felonies).

[4]A judge or a grand jury may reject charges filed by a prosecutor, but the prosecutor retains the ultimate discretion to decline charges, even where a grand jury chooses to indict. Furthermore, as long as the evidence supports a charge, neither the grand jury nor the judge can question the prosecutor's choice about which of several possible charges the prosecutor chooses to file. Overlapping statutes frequently give prosecutors several choices of charges to pick from, often with different sentencing consequences.

[5]*See*, *e.g.*, Federal Rules of Criminal Procedure (Rule 11 of 1 December 2016 as amended).

[6]Some defendants waive this right and opt for a bench trial. Note that, in some jurisdictions, the prosecution has to consent to the waiver of a jury trial. *See Singer* v. *United States*, 380 US 24, 36 (1965).

and fairness of the process by preventing the jury from seeing certain overly prejudicial or potentially unreliable evidence.[7] The trial is public, and a verbatim transcript is produced. The transcript can be used as needed for purposes of challenging and reviewing the verdict on appeal. Some jurisdictions also allow for the broadcasting of criminal proceedings, as discussed below in Sect. 3.4.2.

Unlike in inquisitorial systems, sentencing is a separate stage of the criminal process in the United States. It follows different, typically more relaxed rules of evidence and procedure from those at trial. For example, the Fourth Amendment exclusionary rule has been held not to apply at sentencing.[8] The Privilege against Self-Incrimination, however, continues to apply at sentencing as it does at trial, and so does the rule requiring exclusion of coerced confessions.[9]

2.2 Actors and Accountability

At the state level, American police officers conduct investigations. Prosecutors are typically not involved in the investigations and do not have supervisory power over police officers, although they rely on the evidence collected by officers to support the charges they choose to file.[10] At the federal level, prosecutors are more likely to take part in the investigation, particularly in more complex cases, such as those concerning white-collar crimes.[11] Even at the federal level, however, prosecutors have no authority to discipline investigative agents, so their "supervision" is generally informal and limited to correcting errors as the investigation unfolds.[12]

Because prosecutors depend on police officers to obtain convictions in their cases, however, they often refrain from looking too closely for gaps and flaws in police investigations.[13] More importantly, prosecutors typically lack the time and resources to adequately review police investigations in a thorough fashion.[14] Finally, chief prosecutors at the state level are typically chosen in popular elections, and support by police unions is important for electoral success. Political calculations therefore further discourage critical oversight of police actions by prosecutors.

---

[7] *See, e.g.*, Federal Rules of Evidence (Rules 403, 801, 802 of 1 December 2015 as amended).

[8] *See United States* v. *Tejada*, 956 F2d 1256, 1262–63 (2nd Cir. 1992).

[9] *See Mitchell* v. *United States*, 526 US 314, 325–27 (1999).

[10] Luna/Wade, 2010 at 1467–68; *see also* Geller, 1975 at 721 ("Historically, the American police department has been independent of the prosecutor's office: that is, neither police nor prosecutor directly gives or takes orders from the other. As a result, the prosecutor … is unable to command police officers to conduct their searches within constitutional bounds.").

[11] *See generally* Richman, 1999 at 780; Richman, 2003 at 756–794.

[12] Richman, 2003 at 756–794.

[13] *See, e.g.*, Luna/Wade, 2010 at 1467–68; Laurin, 2014 at 817 (noting some recent departures from the traditional practice under which prosecutors do not oversee police investigations).

[14] *See, e.g.*, Gershowitz/ Killinger, 2011 at 261.

Courts provide a level of oversight over police conduct. With respect to searches and seizures, magistrate judges review warrant applications to ensure that these are based on probable cause. Magistrates reject warrant applications extremely rarely, however, causing some to argue that they are mere "rubber stamps for law enforcement."[15] On the other hand, the requirement to submit a warrant application may serve a valuable function on its own, causing police departments to invest in training their officers in constitutional criminal procedure and encouraging officers to consider the facts and the law more carefully before applying for a warrant.

In most arrests and searches, officers are not required to obtain a warrant. But even where no warrant is required before an arrest, magistrates must review the decision to detain a suspect within 48 hours of the arrest. Likewise, even where no warrant is required for a search, the defendant may challenge the legality of the search through a pretrial motion to suppress evidence obtained as a result of an unlawful search or seizure. Defendants may also move the court to exclude a confession that is involuntary or unreliable, or was obtained in violation of *Miranda* or the pretrial right to counsel. The exclusion of evidence continues to be regarded by most commentators as the most effective mechanism for holding police accountable for their investigative actions. As Sect. 3.3 discusses, however, the Supreme Court has become more skeptical of the usefulness of the exclusionary rule and has gradually restricted its scope.[16] Indeed, the Court has limited the application of the rule in part because of a concern that in many cases, it interferes with the search for truth.

Beyond examining the legality of searches, arrests, and interrogations, judges could theoretically probe more deeply into the accuracy and completeness of investigations when they review charges at a preliminary hearing or on a defendant's motion to dismiss the indictment. Judges could also scrutinize the quality of the investigation when they examine whether a guilty plea is based on sufficient facts. In practice, however, judges have little information at their disposal about how an investigation has been conducted because they do not have access to an "investigative file." As a consequence, their ability to review the investigation for accuracy and completeness is limited in practice. Separation of powers principles further discourage judges from inquiring into investigative or charging decisions.[17]

When it comes to police misconduct during an investigation, a few other methods of accountability are potentially available. If police officers violate a person's constitutional rights, the person may bring a civil action requesting

---

[15]Saltzburg/Capra, 2014 at 108 (quoting Labaton, 'Before the Explosion, Official Saw Little Risk for Building in Oklahoma City', *New York Times*, 2 May 1995, A19).

[16]*See below* Sect. 3.3.

[17]*United States* v. *Janis*, 428 US 433, 458–59 (1976) (noting that separation of powers principles limit judicial supervision of police misconduct); *Rizzo* v. *Goode*, 423 US 362 (1976) (same); *Payner* v. *United States*, 447 US 774, 737–38 (1980) (Chief Justice Burger, concurring); *see also Bordenkircher* v. *Hayes*, 434 US 357, 364–65 (1978) (noting the breadth of prosecutorial charging discretion).

monetary compensation for damages. Civil actions have not proven very effective in disciplining police, however, for several reasons. First, officers are entitled to qualified immunity for their actions done in the course of performing official duties, so they can be held liable only if their conduct violates clearly established constitutional rules, a standard that is difficult to meet.[18] Second, damages for an unlawful search are generally nominal, which discourages citizens from pursuing a lawsuit. Third, even where damages may be more substantial, plaintiffs have difficulty collecting the judgment, because individual officers are typically unable to pay, and governmental entities employing the officers are only liable where the injury resulted from the entity's custom or policy.[19] Finally, civil actions typically concern violations of privacy or the use of excessive force, so they do little to improve reliable factfinding by police.

Officers may also be subject to discipline by external oversight mechanisms (citizen review boards) or internal ones (internal affairs investigators). Over a hundred departments around the country are at least partially supervised by review boards or commissions staffed by ordinary citizens, and these have increased the transparency and legitimacy of police work.[20] Yet statistics from citizen review boards suggests that they are "more reluctant to second-guess officers than are officers themselves."[21] Moreover, they focus on resolving citizen complaints about police misconduct, which typically relate to excessive force, discourtesy, or invasions of privacy, rather than on unreliable factfinding.

Compared to citizen review boards, internal affairs divisions are more willing to impose discipline for officer misconduct.[22] Unfortunately, scholars have not yet examined what makes internal affairs divisions effective, or the extent to which they have improved police accountability since the 1960s.[23] Nor is it clear whether internal discipline, without an exclusionary rule as a backstop, could be effective on its own to deter misconduct. A study from California, where state constitutional law prohibits warrantless searches of trash placed on the curbside, but where exclusion for violations of this rule was abandoned in 1982, suggests that without exclusion, compliance with the underlying law suffers significantly.[24] More empirical research is needed to examine whether internal discipline can operate effectively in the absence of judicial remedies such as exclusion.

Furthermore, internal disciplinary mechanisms have focused on limiting the use of force, improving police-citizen interactions, and preventing unwarranted

[18]*See, e.g.*, Sklansky, 2008 at 572.

[19]Saltzburg/Capra, 2014 at 558 (citing *Monell* v. *Department of Social Services*, 436 US 658 (1978)).

[20]Finn, 2001 at 7–12; Sklansky, 2008 at 573.

[21]Sklansky, 2008 at 573.

[22]*Ibid.*

[23]*Ibid.*; *see also* Schwartz, 2012 at 870 ("[N]o outside reviewer has 'found the operations of internal affairs divisions in any of the major US cities satisfactory.'").

[24]Sklansky, 2008 at 580–81.

invasions of privacy.[25] They have not directly addressed the problems of incomplete or inaccurate investigations. An important obstacle to accuracy in investigations is the increased emphasis on efficiency as a goal of police departments. An emphasis on arrests and clearance rates encourages officers to clear cases quickly and discourages them from investigating more thoroughly and from following up on potentially exculpatory evidence.[26] Of particular relevance to this report, officers have a strong incentive to obtain confessions so as to save the significant resources needed to investigate the case independently.[27] Examination of wrongful conviction cases shows that once officers have obtained a confession, they rarely investigate further.[28] This increases the risk that a wrongful confession remains uncorrected.

3 General Framework for Fact-Finding in Criminal Proceedings

3.1 Law Relating to the Search for Truth

In the United States, neither the Constitution nor criminal procedure codes expressly require investigators, prosecutors, or courts to seek truth.[29] Yet U.S. courts and policymakers have recognized that accurate factfinding helps ensure the legitimacy of the verdict and the effective enforcement of criminal law. Numerous court decisions mention the search for truth as a guiding principle in criminal cases.[30]

In pursuit of this goal, jurisdictions have adopted a range of evidence rules that aim to sort reliable from unreliable evidence. Accurate factfinding is often stated as an overarching goal of evidence rules. For example, the Federal Rules of Evidence are supposed to "be construed so as to administer every proceeding fairly, eliminate

---

[25]*See, e.g.*, Schwartz, 2012 at 870.

[26]Fisher, 1993 at 20–21.

[27]Fisher/Rosen-Zvi, 2008 at 878–79.

[28]*Ibid.* at 879; *see also* Garrett, 2012 at 35.

[29]For example, the Federal Criminal Procedure Rules suggest that the following principles should guide interpretation: "These rules are to be interpreted to provide for the just determination of every criminal proceeding, to secure simplicity in procedure and fairness in administration, and to eliminate unjustifiable expense and delay." Federal Rules of Criminal Procedure (Rule 2 of 1 December 2016 as amended).

[30]For example, in *Tehan* v. *United States*, the US Supreme Court stated that "[t]he basic purpose of a trial is the determination of the truth." 383 US 406, 416 (1966); *see also United States* v. *Havens*, 446 US 620, 626 (1980) ("arriving at the truth is a fundamental goal of our legal system"); *Colorado* v. *Connelly*, 479 US 157, 166 (1986) ("[T]he central purpose of a criminal trial is to decide the factual question of the defendant's guilt or innocence," *Delaware* v. *Van Arsdall*, 475 US 673, 681 (1986), "and while we have previously held that exclusion of evidence may be necessary to protect constitutional guarantees, both the necessity for the collateral inquiry and the exclusion of evidence deflect a criminal trial from its basic purpose.").

unjustifiable expense and delay, and promote the development of evidence law, *to the end of ascertaining the truth and securing a just determination*."[31] U.S. jurisdictions have also adopted special evidentiary safeguards to ensure the reliability of confessions admitted at trial. Some states require prosecutors to offer evidence corroborating the confessions before they can obtain a conviction[32]; other states and the federal system require judges to examine the trustworthiness of the confession and admit the confession only if it is found to be reliable by preponderance of the evidence.[33]

The commitment to an accurate determination of the facts is not absolute, however, and at times bends to other goals of the criminal justice system. The pursuit of efficiency, for example, has resulted in speedier resolutions of cases and less thorough and careful examination of the underlying facts. Over 95% of convictions in the United States today result from guilty pleas, which substitute consensual disposition of the case for an objective and thorough inquiry into the facts. Although judges must evaluate whether guilty pleas are voluntary, informed, and factually based, the "factual basis" requirement is very permissive. Under the pressure of heavy caseloads, judges typically conduct merely a cursory review of the facts, requiring little more than the defendant's confirmation that the allegations in the indictment are correct.[34] In practice, courts and prosecutors frequently compromise the commitment to comprehensive fact-finding in order to obtain the efficiency benefits of guilty pleas.

Of greater relevance to this report, factfinding may also be constrained to some degree by protections of individual rights. The Privilege against Self-Incrimination, the ban on double jeopardy, rules for excluding unlawfully obtained evidence, and unreviewable jury acquittals may impair the search for truth. This interference with truthseeking is justified by reference to fundamental values, such as liberty, privacy, dignity, and fairness, which are expressly or implicitly incorporated in constitutional provisions.

In addition, the constraint on factfinding imposed by some of these constitutional provisions—notably, the Privilege against Self-Incrimination—may be justified by an underlying commitment to minimize particular types of erroneous outcomes—namely, wrongful convictions. In other words, following the Blackstone maxim that "it is better that ten guilty persons escape, than that one innocent suffer," the Privilege against Self-Incrimination may be read to be specially concerned with avoiding one type of inaccuracy—wrongful convictions—even at the expense of an overall increase in erroneous outcomes.[35]

---

[31] Federal Rules of Evidence (Rule 102 of 1 December 2015 as amended).

[32] *See, e.g.*, Arkansas Code § 16-89-111(d); Fisher/Rosen-Zvi, 2008 at 885.

[33] *See, e.g.*, Fisher/Rosen-Zvi, 2008 at 886; *see also Opper* v. *United States*, 348 US 84, 90-93 (1954) (requiring substantial corroboration of confession).

[34] Brown, 2005 at 1611; Turner, 2006 at 212–23.

[35] For a more thorough discussion of this concern with error allocation, see, for example, Stacy, 1991, at 1406–09.

Section 3.2 discusses these constitutional provisions in greater detail, and Sect. 3.3 examines how courts have balanced the need to protect individual rights against the interest in uncovering the truth and ensuring the effective enforcement of the criminal law.

3.2 Law Protecting Individual Rights

The Fourth, Fifth, and Sixth Amendments of the U.S. Constitution contain key provisions safeguarding individual rights in the criminal process. This part of the report focuses on aspects of the amendments that could give rise to exclusion of evidence and therefore may potentially conflict with the search for truth.

The Fourth Amendment protects "the people" from unreasonable searches and seizures. The Amendment also regulates the conditions on which warrants must be issued—they must be approved by a neutral magistrate, be based on probable cause, and particularly describe the place to be searched and the evidence to be seized. The Court has held that searches of houses and non-public arrests of individuals are presumed to be unreasonable unless they are conducted pursuant to a warrant.[36] When it comes to searches of persons, cars, and other effects, courts have carved out exceptions to the warrant requirement, although the reasonableness requirement still applies.[37]

Two other important provisions protecting individual rights in the criminal process are the Fifth Amendment's Privilege against Self-Incrimination and the Fourteenth Amendment's Due Process Clause. The former provides that no person should be compelled to be a witness against himself in a criminal case. The latter guarantees that no one shall be deprived of life, liberty, or property without due process of law. Due process is held to require a fair opportunity for a suspect to test the prosecution's case and to prohibit "inquisitorial" methods of investigation.[38] Courts have relied on these provisions to regulate the methods by which police can obtain confessions and to exclude confessions obtained through torture or coercion.[39]

---

[36]*See, e.g.*, *Kyllo* v. *United States*, 533 US 27, 40 (2001); *Payton* v. *New York*, 445 US 573, 586–88 (1980).

[37]*See, e.g.*, *California* v. *Carney*, 471 US 386, 392–93 (1985) (warrantless search of car); *United States* v. *Robinson*, 414 US 218, 224 (1973) (warrantless search of person incident to arrest); *Terry* v. *Ohio*, 392 US 1, 20 (1968) (warrantless stop & frisk); *Arizona* v. *Gant*, 556 US 332, 343 (2009) (warrantless search of car incident to arrest); *United States* v. *Watson*, 423 US 411, 423 (1976) (warrantless arrest of person in public); *Schneckloth* v. *Bustamonte*, 412 US 218, 219 (1973) (warrantless consent search).

[38]*Gallegos* v. *Colorado*, 370 US 49, 50–51 (1962); *Chambers* v. *Florida*, 309 US 227, 237 (1940); *Watts* v. *Indiana*, 338 US 49, 54–55 (1949).

[39]*See below* Part 4.1.

Both the Due Process Clause and the Privilege against Self-Incrimination prohibit methods of interrogation that overwhelm the will of the accused. To determine what methods violate these provisions, courts use a totality of circumstances approach, which focuses above all on the coerciveness of police tactics, but also takes into account the characteristics of the accused and features of the environment in which the interrogation took place. More recent cases have clarified that personal characteristics of the suspect do not on their own render a confession invalid, absent some proof of police coercion.[40]

While an important concern about coerced confessions—from the common law rule preventing involuntary confessions until today—has been that they may be unreliable, police coercion appears to be the preeminent reason for suppressing involuntary confessions under contemporary constitutional doctrine. The Supreme Court has clarified that coercion may lead to exclusion even in situations where no question about the reliability of the confession exists: "The abhorrence of society to the use of involuntary confessions does not turn alone on their inherent untrustworthiness. It also turns on the deep-rooted feeling that the police must obey the law while enforcing the law."[41] Conversely, in the absence of police coercion, lack of reliability would be addressed under state or federal rules of evidence (potentially also leading to exclusion), rather than under the Constitution.[42]

The Fifth Amendment's Privilege against Self-Incrimination also prohibits lesser compulsion of a person, but only in the context of official proceedings. The privilege protects individuals from answering questions in any official process, including civil, legislative, or administrative proceedings, if the answers might harm the persons in *future* criminal proceedings.[43] The level of compulsion needed to trigger this protection under the privilege is lower than that which renders a confession coerced in the context of police interrogations. While the threat of imprisonment or being held in contempt of court is the classic type of compulsion prohibited under the privilege, lesser compulsion may also suffice. For example, the threat of imposing economic sanctions for invoking the privilege is often enough. Economic sanctions may include the denial of government contracts[44]; disbarment[45]; or dismissal from employment.[46] Somewhat more controversially, the Supreme Court has also held that a comment, by the prosecutor or the court, on the defendant's invocation of the privilege also constitutes official compulsion that violates the privilege.

---

[40]*Colorado* v. *Connelly*, 479 US 157, 163 (1986). Thus, where a defendant confesses because he suffers from command hallucinations telling him to confess, or where a private party coerces the defendant to give a statement, this does not render the statement involuntary under the Due Process Clause.

[41]*Spano* v. *New York*, 360 US 315, 320 (1959).

[42]*Colorado* v. *Connelly*, 479 US 157, 159 (1986).

[43]*See, e.g., Lefkowitz* v. *Turley*, 414 US 70, 77 (1973).

[44]*Lefkowitz* v. *Turley*, 414 US 70, 82–83 (1973).

[45]*Spevack* v. *Klein*, 385 US 511, 516 (1967).

[46]*Garrity* v. *New Jersey*, 385 US 493, 500 (1967).

In its famous ruling in *Miranda v. Arizona*, the U.S. Supreme Court extended the reach of the privilege further and held that the coercive environment of pretrial custodial interrogations constitutes the type of compulsion that has the potential to overwhelm the will of the accused. To dispel this coercive effect, before interrogation, officers must warn detained suspects of their right not to make a statement, of the risk that any statement can be used as evidence against them, of the right to consult a lawyer, and of the right to have an attorney appointed for them, if they cannot afford to retain one. After receiving the warnings, suspects may choose to waive their rights to remain silent and to have a lawyer present during the interrogation. The waiver must, however, be intelligent, knowing, and voluntary.

After a suspect has been formally charged, the Sixth Amendment right to an attorney attaches and governs interactions between the accused and government agents. Police may not deliberately elicit statements from an indicted defendant without providing the requisite warnings of the right to remain silent and to consult an attorney and then obtaining a valid waiver.[47] The Sixth Amendment applies to undercover investigations as well, prohibiting the surreptitious elicitation of statements from an accused.

To enforce these rules contained in the Fourth, Fifth, and Sixth Amendments, courts frequently rely on evidentiary exclusion. Exclusion is justified on somewhat different grounds and has a different scope depending on which underlying rule is violated. It is automatic for statements taken in violation of the Due Process Clause or the Privilege against Self-Incrimination. When a statement is coerced under these provisions, it cannot be introduced at trial for any purpose, and even fruits of the statement are generally suppressed. Exclusion is not automatic, however, for violations of the Fourth Amendment, of the rules announced in *Miranda v. Arizona*, and of the ban on deliberate elicitation under the Sixth Amendment. The constitutional text does not expressly mandate exclusion as a remedy in these cases, and the Court has held that there are typically no reliability concerns for the evidence at issue.

Evidentiary exclusion was originally adopted because it was seen as necessary to effectuate constitutional guarantees inscribed in the Fourth, Fifth, and Sixth Amendments. Without exclusion, the Court held in an early Fourth Amendment case, provisions that protect fundamental rights would be reduced to "a form of words"[48] such that they "might as well be stricken from the Constitution."[49]

Most of the time, however, the Court has justified exclusion on the grounds that it helps discourage misconduct by police officers. Under this view, the "[exclusionary] rule is calculated to prevent, not to repair. Its purpose is to deter—to compel respect for the constitutional guaranty in the only effectively available

---

[47] *Massiah* v. *United States*, 377 US 201, 205 (1964); *Montejo* v. *Louisiana*, 556 US 778, 786–87 (2009).

[48] *Silverthorne Lumber Co.* v. *United States*, 251 US 385, 392 (1920).

[49] *Weeks* v. *United States*, 232 US 383, 393 (1914). In the early days of the exclusionary rule, the Court also put forward judicial integrity as a reason for exclusion. Under this view, excluding unlawfully obtained evidence is necessary to protect the court from the taint of official illegality.

way—by removing the incentive to disregard it."[50] More recently, the Court has extrapolated from this focus on deterrence that the exclusionary rule should be used *only* when it would effectively dissuade law enforcement officials from violating the law in the future.[51] If the deterrence potential of the rule is too negligible or if it is vastly outweighed by the costs of the exclusionary rule, then exclusion should not be imposed.[52]

3.3 Law Balancing the Search for Truth and Individual Rights Protections

While U.S. courts mandate exclusion with respect to conduct that violates the Due Process Clause or the Privilege against Self-Incrimination, this is not always the case with respect to other constitutional violations in the investigative process. U.S. courts balance the costs and benefits of excluding evidence in certain cases involving Fourth Amendment violations, violations of *Miranda v. Arizona*, and violations of the Sixth Amendment pretrial right to counsel. The balancing process is not done on a case-by-case basis, but is rather done on a category-by-category basis. In other words, if the costs of exclusion for certain categories of evidence of for certain uses of the evidence outweigh the benefits, then exclusion is never imposed for that type or that use of evidence.

In the Fourth Amendment context, the conflict between truth-seeking and individual rights is expressly acknowledged in exclusionary rule decisions. In deciding whether to mandate exclusion for certain categories of evidence, the Supreme Court balances the benefits of exclusion—deterrence of police misconduct and protection of individual rights, against the costs of exclusion—interference with truthfinding and with the enforcement of criminal law.[53] For example, the Court has held that at certain preliminary or non-criminal proceedings, such as grand jury, sentencing, deportation, or habeas, the likelihood of deterring police misconduct is too negligible to warrant exclusion of reliable evidence obtained in violation of the Fourth Amendment.[54] As the Court has explained in the context of grand jury proceedings, "[a]ny incremental deterrent effect which might be achieved by extending the [exclusionary] rule to grand jury proceedings is uncertain at best. … Such an extension would deter only police investigation consciously directed toward the discovery of evidence solely for use in a grand jury investigation."[55]

[50]*Elkins* v. *United States*, 364 US 206, 217 (1960).

[51]*United States* v. *Leon*, 468 US 897, 918 (1984); *Hudson* v. *Michigan*, 547 US 586, 591 (2006); *Herring* v. *United States*, 555 US 135 (2009).

[52]*See, e.g., Herring* v. *United States*, 555 US 135, 141, 144 (2009).

[53]*United States* v. *Leon*, 468 US 897, 907 (1984); *Hudson* v. *Michigan*, 547 US 586, 591, 599 (2006); *Herring* v. *United States*, 555 US 135, 141 (2009).

[54]*See, e.g., United States* v. *Calandra*, 414 US 338, 347 (1974).

[55]*Ibid.* at 351.

Applying the exclusionary rule in the grand jury and non-criminal contexts would achieve a merely "speculative and undoubtedly minimal advance in the deterrence of police misconduct," and yet it would come at the expense of the ability of the grand jury or civil factfinders to uncover the truth.[56] Therefore, balancing the costs and benefits has led the Court to deny Fourth Amendment exclusion in these contexts.

A similar balancing exercise has led the Court to allow the introduction of unlawfully obtained evidence to impeach the defendant's credibility. The incremental deterrent benefit in such cases is said to be small: "[T]he deterrent function of the rules excluding unconstitutionally obtained evidence is sufficiently served by denying its use to the government on its direct case."[57] The minimal incremental benefit served by forbidding the use of unlawfully obtained evidence to impeach the defendant is outweighed by the costs of allowing perjured testimony to stand uncorrected and impairing the integrity of the factfinding process.[58] Accordingly, evidence obtained in violation of the Fourth Amendment, *Miranda*, or Sixth Amendment can be admitted for purposes of impeaching the defendant's credibility.[59]

Additionally, the Court has limited the group of people who can invoke the Fourth Amendment exclusionary rule. Only those whose Fourth Amendment rights have been violated can ask for exclusion of evidence; the rule cannot be asserted vicariously. The Court justified this limitation in large part by pointing to the significant costs of excluding evidence:

> Each time the exclusionary rule is applied it exacts a substantial social cost for the vindication of Fourth Amendment rights. Relevant and reliable evidence is kept from the trier of fact and the search for truth at trial is deflected […]. Since our cases generally have held that one whose Fourth Amendment rights are violated may successfully suppress evidence obtained in the course of an illegal search and seizure, misgivings as to the benefit of enlarging the class of persons who may invoke that rule are properly considered when deciding whether to expand standing to assert Fourth Amendment violations.[60]

As subsequent sections elaborate, similar standing limitations on exclusion likely apply with respect to other constitutional violations as well, including violations of the Fifth Amendment and the Due Process Clause.

Although the Court has generally extended the Fourth Amendment exclusionary rule to "fruits" of the original violation, it has also placed some limits on how far the "fruit of the poisonous tree" doctrine extends. For example, if the connection

---

[56] *Ibid.* at 351–52.

[57] *United States* v. *Havens*, 446 US 620, 626 (1980).

[58] *Ibid.* at 627.

[59] *Ibid.*; *Harris* v. *New York*, 401 US 222, 225–26 (1971); *Kansas* v. *Ventris*, 556 US 586, 593–94 (2009).

[60] *Rakas* v. *Illinois*, 439 US 128, 137–38 (1978).

between the original violation and the derivative evidence is too attenuated (e.g., if an event has broken the chain of causation between the original illegality and the derivative evidence), then the derivative evidence can be admitted.[61] Furthermore, if the police would inevitably have discovered the evidence, even absent the constitutional violation, then the exclusionary rule does not apply.[62] Once again, the Court has justified these restrictions on the exclusionary rule by pointing to the high costs of excluding probative evidence and the limited deterrent effect of excluding evidence that either has been or would have been discovered independently by lawful means.[63] As discussed in more detail later in the report, these limitations on the fruit of the poisonous tree doctrine likely apply to violations of the Fifth Amendment, Due Process Clause, and the Sixth Amendment.[64]

In more recent Fourth Amendment exclusion cases, the Supreme Court has also considered the availability of alternative sanctions, which may be able to discipline officers at a lesser cost to the administration of justice.[65] To the extent that such alternative sanctions are viable, exclusion is less likely to be ordered. The Court also examines whether police misconduct is an isolated occurrence or part of a pattern, under the theory that systemic abuses are in greater need of deterrence.[66] Finally, the Court considers officers' state of mind in committing a violation and reserves discipline only for reckless or deliberate breaches of the law.[67] Therefore, officers' reasonable, good faith reliance on a warrant, a statute, or a court decision will not give rise to exclusion, even where the warrant is subsequently found to be defective or mistakenly entered into a database after expungement,[68] the statute is held unconstitutional,[69] or the court decision is overruled.[70] On the other hand,

---

[61] *Brown* v. *Illinois*, 422 US 590, 603–04 (1975); *Murray* v. *United States*, 487 US 533, 537 (1988).

[62] *Nix* v. *Williams*, 467 US 431, 444 (1984).

[63] "If the prosecution can establish by a preponderance of the evidence that the information ultimately or inevitably would have been discovered by lawful means — here the volunteers' search — then the deterrence rationale has so little basis that the evidence should be received. The requirement that the prosecution must prove the absence of bad faith … wholly fails to take into account the enormous societal cost of excluding truth in the search for truth in the administration of justice." *Nix* v. *Williams*, 467 US 431, 444–45 (1984).

[64] When it comes to *Miranda* violations, evidence derived from the original violation is almost never excluded, for reasons discussed *below* Part 4.3.

[65] *Hudson* v. *Michigan*, 547 US 586, 591, 599 (2006).

[66] *Herring* v. *United States*, 555 US 135, 144 (2009).

[67] *Ibid.* at 144.

[68] *United States* v. *Leon*, 468 US 897 (1984); *Herring* v. *United States*, 555 US 135, 142 (2009).

[69] *Illinois* v. *Krull*, 480 US 340, 349–50 (1987).

[70] *Davis* v. *United States*, 564 US 229, 241 (2011).

good faith has not been used to limit exclusion of statements obtained in violation of the Fifth and Sixth Amendment or the Due Process Clause,[71] but it has limited exclusion under *Miranda* to some degree.[72]

In general, the exclusionary rule has been weakest and most likely to be subordinated to the interest in truthseeking when it comes to statements obtained in violation of *Miranda* safeguards. The Court has justified restrictions on exclusion in this setting by noting that *Miranda* sets out a broad prophylactic rule that sweeps more broadly than the Privilege against Self-Incrimination itself.[73] *Miranda*-defective statements are therefore not presumed to be unreliable.[74] And unlike the admission of coerced statements, the admission of *Miranda*-defective statements at trial is not considered to be compulsion of a person in direct violation of the Constitution. Furthermore, the Court has held that the benefits of deterring police violation of *Miranda* are frequently outweighed by the cost of excluding reliable evidence—for example, when *Miranda*-defective statements are introduced for impeachment, when fruits of *Miranda* violation are at issue, and when an officer fails to give *Miranda* warnings based on a reasonable belief that public safety requires him or her to dispense with the warnings. The scope of the *Miranda* exclusionary rule is considered in greater detail in Sect. 4.3 below.

In brief, the Supreme Court has considered the tradeoff between truthseeking and evidentiary exclusion in a number of cases. In cases where the Constitution does not expressly mandate exclusion, the Court has done a category-by-category analysis of the costs and benefits of the exclusionary rule in deciding whether to impose it. This has created a patchwork of rules that apply differently depending on the rule that is violated, the nature of the evidence being considered, and the use to which the evidence would be put at trial.

3.4 Social Relevance of Truth and Individual Rights in Criminal Trials

3.4.1 Relevance of Determining the Truth

As discussed in Sect. 3.1, the goal of seeking truth in criminal cases is not expressly mentioned in the U.S. Constitution or criminal procedure codes. Nonetheless, numerous court decisions mention it as a guiding principle. The search for truth is considered important for the effective enforcement of the criminal law and for the

[71] *See below* Parts 4.1–4.2.

[72] *See below* Part 4.3 (discussing public safety exception to *Miranda*, as well as the relevance of good faith to exclusion of statements derived from earlier *Miranda*-defective statements).

[73] *See, e.g., United States* v. *Patane*, 542 US 630, 639 (2004).

[74] *See, e.g., Mincey* v. *Arizona*, 437 US 385, 397–98 (1978) (involuntary confession cannot be used even for impeachment purposes as it is more likely to be unreliable and the police action in question is more outrageous and therefore in greater need of discipline).

pursuit of justice more generally. As DNA testing has revealed a high incidence of wrongful convictions, reliable factfinding has become a topic of public discussion and concern. There is growing recognition that the public legitimacy of the criminal justice system depends at least in part on the ability of the system to attain accurate outcomes.

3.4.2 Presentation of Factfinding to the Public

To increase the transparency and reliability of factfinding, a number of U.S. jurisdictions have recently taken measures to record critical stages of the criminal process. Police departments are increasingly recording police-citizen interactions on the street, custodial interrogations, and identification procedures. Some courts are in turn allowing the recording and even broadcasting of trial proceedings. Beyond improving reliability, such recording is regarded as helping to improve the fairness and public legitimacy of the proceedings.

Recording of interrogations is seen as particularly useful in preventing involuntary and false confessions. It is said to reduce the risk that police would use coercive tactics to obtain statements, to provide a more transparent record for courts to evaluate the voluntariness and reliability of confessions, and to offer a more accurate and thorough transcription of the defendant's statements for use at trial.[75] For all these reasons, a growing number of U.S. jurisdictions now require the recording of interrogations.[76]

While police officers were initially concerned that taping would reduce suspects' willingness to confess, early evidence from jurisdictions that have adopted taping policies suggests that the risk of lost confessions is not significant. While one early study reported that suspects were less willing to talk when they knew they were being recorded,[77] more recent research has found no decrease in confessions that can be attributed to the taping of interrogations.[78] Even the study that found a small drop in confessions also reported incidental benefits of recording, such as "better preparation by detectives and better monitoring of detectives' work by supervisors."[79]

Police-citizen interactions outside the police station are also increasingly being recorded on body or dashboard cameras employed by police officers.[80] Public discussion has emphasized how recording of these interactions can help reduce police violence, as well as unwarranted complaints against police. Recording also helps preserve evidence for use in subsequent prosecution and thus contributes to the search for truth. On the other hand, without careful regulation, recording may

[75]Fisher/Rosen-Zvi, 2008 at 888.

[76]Taslitz, 2012 at 409 (acknowledging trend but adding that "the vast majority of police departments still do not record" interrogations).

[77]*Ibid.*

[78]Leo, 2008 at 303.

[79]Miller/Wright, 2007 at 643 (citing Geller, 1993).

[80]Miller et al., 2014.

interfere with the privacy interests of citizens captured on camera. The cost of recording, storing, and reviewing the massive amounts of data is also a serious concern weighing against the broad use of body cameras.[81]

When it comes to the recording and broadcasting of trials, rules vary significantly from jurisdiction to jurisdiction. Some U.S. jurisdictions categorically ban televising trials, others expressly permit it, while yet others have no specific rules and leave the decision to the discretion of the court. For example, Federal Rule of Criminal Procedure 53 prohibits the broadcasting of judicial proceedings in criminal cases. Courts have upheld the constitutionality of the rule against First Amendment challenges.[82] Florida permits the broadcasting of all trials, including criminal trials, under guidelines to ensure the fair administration of justice.[83] In Texas, no specific rule governs the broadcasting of criminal trials, but trial courts have occasionally permitted such broadcasting based on their own discretion to control the conduct of the proceedings.[84] The propriety of the judge's orders is then analysed for its consistency with the Due Process Clause.

The televising of trials affects a number of interests, which may at times be in conflict with one another: the fair trial of the defendant, witness rights, First Amendment rights of the media, and the interests in judicial integrity and efficiency. The U.S. Supreme Court, in *Chandler v. Florida*, held that broadcasting of criminal trials might in some circumstances violate the Due Process Clause but that it does not inherently do so. To mount a successful Due Process challenge, a defendant must show that broadcasting in his specific case is likely to adversely impact the fairness of his trial. The defendant may succeed in his challenge if he demonstrates that coverage would compromise the ability of the jury to judge him fairly or would adversely affect the participants in his trial to such a degree as to constitute a denial of due process.

Some state rules also attempt to address other concerns raised by televising trials. For example, California rules on televising trials lay out certain requirements concerning the type of equipment to be used to minimize disruption of the proceedings.[85] California courts also often prohibit the broadcasting of witness testimony to prevent concerns about the safety of witnesses and their willingness to testify.[86] Other rules balance such interests against First Amendment rights to broadcast trials of public significance.[87]

---

[81]*Ibid.*

[82]*See, e.g.*, *United States* v. *Moussaoui*, 205 FRD 183, 185 (2002); *United States* v. *Edwards*, 785 F 2d 1293, 1295–96 (5th Cir. 1986).

[83]Florida Rules of Judicial Administration, Rule 2.450. Broadcasting was first regulated by the Florida Supreme Court in In re *Petition of Post-Newsweek Stations Fla., Inc.*, 370 So 2d 764 (Fla. 1979) (laying out standards for broadcasting of criminal trials).

[84]*See, e.g.*, *Wright* v. *State*, 374 SW 3d 564 (Tex.App.—Houston [14 Dist.], 2012).

[85]2013 California Rules of Court Rule 1.150 (e)(8).

[86]*See, e.g.*, *KFMB-TV Channel 8* v. *Municipal Court*, 221 Cal App 3d 1362, 1364 (Cal. App. 4 Dist. 1990); Judicial Council of California, Administrative Office of the Courts, 2007 at 2–3.

[87]In re *Petition of Post-Newsweek Stations Fla., Inc.*, 370 So 2d 764 (Fla. 1979).

In summary, while recording of interrogations and police-citizen interactions is broadly advocated and increasingly adopted by U.S. states and localities, televising trials is not regarded as critical to improving the accuracy and fairness of the criminal process. Indeed, it is sometimes said to conflict with these goals, as when a witness is discouraged from testifying truthfully or when broadcasting prejudices or distracts the jury. Accordingly, policymakers and commentators have been less ardent about introducing the broadcasting of trials than about the recording of interrogations and other citizen-police interactions.

3.4.3 Public Discussion of Miscarriages of Justice

In the 1990s, DNA testing became more broadly available and led to the first exonerations of wrongfully convicted individuals. The Innocence Project, founded initially at Cardozo Law School, helped numerous defendants obtain DNA testing and prove their innocence. Over the years, the Innocence Project transformed into a nationwide movement, which included Innocence clinics at law schools across the country, Conviction Integrity Units within prosecutor's offices, and Innocence Review Commissions. The work of the Innocence Movement has given rise to broad public discussion of miscarriages of justice, and the problem of wrongful convictions has been highlighted in popular culture, TV shows, movies, and books.[88]

Most relevant to this report, the Innocence Movement has shed light on the problem of unreliable confessions. The Innocence Project has reported that 27% of the first 325 wrongful convictions were based at least in part on a false confession. Another study of wrongful convictions, by Brandon Garrett, found that forty of the first 250 people exonerated through DNA (16%) made a false confession.[89] Garrett closely examined the features of the false confessions in these cases and found several common elements. First, almost all of these confessions were quite detailed and contained information about the crime that only the true suspect and the investigating officers could have known.[90] Given the subsequent exoneration of the defendants, the only plausible explanation for these confessions is that the police, whether intentionally or accidentally, fed information about the crime to the suspect. Moreover, psychological coercion, including trickery, was brought to bear on the suspects to force them to confess to a crime they did not commit. Notably, a high number of the innocent defendants who confessed were mentally retarded, mentally ill, or juveniles, making them particularly susceptible to psychological

[88]Garrett, 2012 at 6.

[89]*Ibid.* at 18.

[90]*Ibid.* at 19–20.

pressure.[91] Another remarkable fact is that in the majority of the false confession cases, the interrogations were partially recorded, whether by audio or video.[92] But the recordings typically included only the final confession, not what came before.[93] Finally, in a number of the cases, police stopped investigating once they obtained a confession, which meant that they failed to unearth critical inconsistencies in the evidence.[94]

Public discussion of the sources of wrongful convictions, including contaminated and coerced confessions, has led to calls for reform across the country. Most notably, as discussed in the previous Section, it has encouraged a number of jurisdictions to introduce mandatory recording of interrogations in order to reduce the risk of unreliable confessions.[95]

4 Constitutional Limitations on the Admissibility of Confessions in Criminal Proceedings

4.1 Fifth and Fourteenth Amendment Limits on Admissibility of Confessions

Confessions in the United States were originally regulated exclusively by common law. Under the common law, two principles prohibited the admission of coerced confessions. The "nemo tenetur" principle prohibited the use of torture and coercion by government agents to force individuals to incriminate themselves.[96] The voluntariness doctrine prohibited the use of involuntary confessions because such confessions were presumed to be unreliable.[97]

In 1897, the Supreme Court for the first time relied on the Constitution to exclude a statement in *Bram v. United States*. It held that the common-law rule banning the admission of involuntary confessions was "embedded in the Fifth Amendment" Privilege against Self-Incrimination and that the privilege thus precluded the admission of compelled statements.[98] This new constitutional rule applied only in federal court, however, as the Supreme Court had not yet applied the Fifth Amendment to the states.[99] As a result, for a long time, the Fifth

[91] *Ibid.* at 21.

[92] *Ibid.* at 32.

[93] *Ibid.*

[94] *Ibid.* at 35.

[95] *See above* Part 3.4.2.

[96] Tomkovicz, 2011 at 64; Godsey, 2005 at 479–80.

[97] *Hopt* v. *Utah*, 110 US 574 (1884); Tomkovicz, 2011 at 64; Godsey, 2005 at 482.

[98] *Bram* v. *United States*, 168 US 532, 548 (1897).

[99] *Twining* v. *New Jersey*, 211 US 78 (1908). The Fifth Amendment was first applied to the states in *Malloy* v. *Hogan*, 378 US 1 (1964).

Amendment rule did not have a broad impact, as the vast majority of criminal cases were brought at the state level.

The first time that the Supreme Court held that a confession obtained by state officials was unconstitutional was in 1936, in *Brown v. Mississippi*.[100] The use of physical violence to extract confessions was "widespread throughout the country" at the time.[101] In *Brown*, the confessions were obtained through particularly heinous and brutal acts—repeated mock lynching, beatings, and other degrading treatment. The Court held that the methods used to obtain confessions were "revolting to the sense of justice."[102] Accordingly, using the coerced confessions as evidence at trial was "a clear denial of due process" and a violation of the Constitution.[103]

In the following three decades, the Court continued to rely on the Due Process Clause to evaluate the admissibility of confessions obtained through coercive methods. In 1964, the Court explained that the Fifth Amendment Privilege against Self-Incrimination likewise prohibited coerced confessions and that the standards for evaluating extrajudicial confessions under the Due Process Clause and the privilege were identical.[104] In deciding whether a confession is coerced under these provisions, the Court applies a totality of circumstances test to determine whether the confession was voluntarily given. The Court examines the personal characteristics of the accused (education level, age, mental state, etc.),[105] as well as physical or psychological coercion applied by the authorities.[106] Physical coercion includes violence as well as food or sleep deprivation,[107] while psychological pressure includes threats, humiliation, isolation, trickery, and prolonged interrogation.[108] The critical question is whether official pressure has overborne the will of the suspect, preventing him from making a rational decision whether to confess.

In the early cases suppressing involuntary confessions, the Court emphasized the need to condemn the coercion at issue and the concern that coerced confession are unreliable. It further held that the admission of coerced confessions violated the U.S. criminal justice system's commitment to "fair state-individual balance [that requires] the government to leave the individual alone … [and] to shoulder the entire load."[109]

---

[100]297 US 278 (1936).

[101]National Comm'n on Law Observance and Enforcement, 'Report on Lawlessness in Law-Enforcement' 1931, 3, *cited in* Miller/Wright, 2007 at 518.

[102]*Brown* v. *Mississippi*, 297 US 278, 286 (1936).

[103]*Ibid.*

[104]*Murphy* v. *Waterfront Comm'n of New York Harbor*, 378 US 52, 79–80 (1964).

[105]*E.g.*, *Payne* v. *Arkansas*, 356 US 560, 567 (1958); *Culombe* v. *Connecticut*, 367 US 568, 620 (1961).

[106]*E.g.*, *Payne* v. *Arkansas*, 356 US 560, 567 (1958); *Ashcraft* v. *Tennessee*, 322 US 143, 153–54 (1944); *Spano* v. *New York*, 360 US 315, 323 (1959).

[107]*E.g.*, *Payne* v. *Arkansas*, 356 US 560, 567 (1958); *Ashcraft* v. *Tennessee*, 322 US 143, 167 (1944).

[108]*E.g.*, *Spano* v. *New York*, 360 US 315, 322–23 (1959); *Arizona* v. *Fulminante*, 499 US 279, 288 (1991).

[109]*Murphy* v. *Waterfront Comm'n of New York Harbor*, 378 US 52, 55 (1964).

Over time, disapproval of offensive police tactics, rather than reliability, became the dominant reason for excluding coerced confessions.[110] In 1959, the Court stated that "[t]he abhorrence of society to the use of involuntary confessions does not turn alone on their inherent untrustworthiness. It also turns on the deep-rooted feeling that the police must obey the law while enforcing the law."[111] By 1986, the Court held that the existence of police coercion is a prerequisite for a finding that a confession is constitutionally invalid.[112] Thus a confession cannot be considered coerced in violation of the Due Process Clause or the privilege where a suspect faces absolutely no government influence and responds to his own "command hallucinations."[113] Likewise, coercion by a private party does not violate the Constitution: "If a relative of a crime victim were to torture a person until he admitted his guilt, neither constitutional guarantee would bar that confession [although an evidentiary rule focused on reliability might]." Suppression under the Fifth and Fourteenth Amendment is therefore justified primarily as necessary to condemn and deter future police conduct. Concerns about the reliability of the evidence are resolved by state evidentiary rules, not through constitutional interpretation.[114]

By 1967, physical brutality had largely vanished from interrogation rooms. This was in part the result of judicial scrutiny of confessions, in part a product of the increasing professionalization of police, and in part a response to broad public outrage at revelations of third-degree tactics.[115] Yet while physical violence during interrogations was a rare occurrence by the late 1960s, the police applied other types of pressure to extract confessions: denial of food or sleep, protracted interrogations, isolation, and various psychological ploys, including trickery.[116]

Some commentators have criticized the voluntariness test for failing to address adequately these more subtle, yet nonetheless coercive tactics. Part of the difficulty is that judges have to resolve, without a reliable record, competing claims of what

---

[110] Kamisar, 1995 at 939.

[111] *Spano* v. *New York,* 360 US 315, 320 (1959).

[112] *Colorado* v. *Connelly*, 479 US 157, 167 (1986).

[113] *Ibid.* at 161, 167.

[114] *Ibid.* at 159.

[115] Miller/Wright, 2007 at 521–22; Cassell, 1996 at 474–75.

[116] *Miranda* v. *Arizona*, 384 US 436, 447, 448 (1966). Interviews with two Texas defense attorneys and two prosecutors suggest that although physical coercion is a thing of the past, psychological tactics—especially lying to suspects about the evidence in the case—continue to be commonly used. As the defense attorneys interviewed suggested, such tactics, particularly when used with vulnerable (e.g., young or cognitively impaired) suspects, can result in false confessions. Interview with Texas Prosecutor #1, by Jenia I. Turner, July 20, 2016, Dallas, Texas; Interview with Texas Prosecutor #2, by Jenia I. Turner, July 27, 2016, Dallas, Texas; Interview with Texas Defense Attorney #1, by Jenia I. Turner, August 8, 2016, Dallas, Texas; Interview with Texas Defense Attorney #2, by Jenia I. Turner, September 20, 2016, Dallas, Texas.

transpired in the interrogation room. Although the state bears the burden of proof to show admissibility, in practice, courts frequently credit police accounts of the interrogation over inconsistent accounts by the defendant.[117] In addition, the voluntariness test has been criticized as too malleable and unpredictable, as it relies on many different factors to determine whether a confession was involuntary.[118]

While courts and commentators have debated the voluntariness test and its effectiveness, the exclusion of statements found to be involuntary has not been contested. Courts have maintained a robust exclusionary rule, which applies to the coerced confession and to evidence derived from it. Coerced statements cannot be used by the prosecution for any purpose at trial—not even to impeach the defendant's credibility. Nor can coerced statements be admitted under a good-faith or public safety exception.[119] This means that even a "ticking bomb" scenario, under which a government agent coerces a suspect to obtain evidence that he believes would save many lives, would not permit the subsequent admission of statements coerced from a suspect.

Fruits of a coerced confession are also generally excluded, under the theory that such exclusion is necessary to deter police misconduct more effectively.[120] But there are some limits on the fruits doctrine with respect to coerced statements. The prosecution may be able to introduce evidence derived from coerced confession if the government can show that it obtained the same evidence through an independent source, or that it would have inevitably obtained it from an independent source.[121] Additionally, the prosecution may be able to introduce fruits of the initial involuntary statement if it can show that the taint of the initial violation was attenuated.[122] In other words, as time passes and circumstances change, the effect of the initial coercion may dissipate to the point that a subsequent statement or other evidence can no longer be considered to be tainted by the coercion.[123]

Finally, if the prosecution can show that the coerced confession is reliable, it may be able to introduce the confession itself in evidence against a third party who

---

[117]*See, e.g.*, Pepson/Sharifi, 2010 at 1228–29.

[118]*See, e.g.*, Saltzburg/Capra, 2014 at 717–18.

[119]*Mincey* v. *Arizona*, 437 US 385, 397–98 (1978); *New York* v. *Quarles*, 467 US 649, 654 (1984) (clarifying that "we have before us no claim that respondent's statements were actually compelled by police conduct which overcame his will to resist").

[120]Cammack, 2013 at 23.

[121]*See, e.g.*, *Kastigar* v. *United States*, 406 US 441, 460 (1972); *Nix* v. *Williams*, 467 US 431 (1984).

[122]*See, e.g.*, Broun, 2013 § 159 at 875; *Oregon* v. *Elstad*, 470 US 298, 310 (1985).

[123]Tomkovicz, 2011 at 89.

was not subject to coercion.[124] Both the Due Process and Fifth Amendment privilege are considered personal rights, so a third party would not have "standing" to challenge the coercion of another person.[125]

4.2 *Sixth Amendment Limits on Admissibility of Confessions*

Because of concerns about the effectiveness of the voluntariness test, in 1964, the Supreme Court began relying on the Sixth Amendment right to counsel as a safeguard against coerced confessions. In *Massiah v. United States*, the Court invalidated a confession obtained by a government informant after the defendant had been charged and obtained counsel.[126] It held that once a person is formally charged, he is entitled to the assistance of counsel whenever government agents deliberately elicit any incriminating statements from him.[127] The Court suggested that if an indicted defendant is denied counsel during pretrial proceedings, he is effectively denied "effective representation by counsel at the only stage when legal aid and advice would help him."[128] In a more recent case, the Supreme Court explained that the right to counsel is extended to pretrial "deliberate elicitations" to ensure that the trial right to counsel is not "render[ed] … entirely impotent" by the pretrial interrogation.[129] If the government breaches the right to counsel by eliciting statements from an indicted defendant, any statements obtained in the process will be excluded from evidence at trial.[130]

The extension of the Sixth Amendment right to counsel to the pretrial stage, and the use of exclusion to enforce it, generated heated debate among the Justices in *Massiah*. The dissenters were concerned about the barring of "relevant, reliable and highly probative" evidence.[131] As the dissenting Justices noted, "Without the evidence, the quest for truth may be seriously impeded and in many cases the trial court, although aware of proof showing defendant's guilt, must nevertheless release him because the crucial evidence is deemed inadmissible."[132] Because Massiah's statements were not coerced and communications between counsel and client were

---

[124]*See Fisher* v. *United States*, 425 US 391, 397–98 (1976); *see also People* v. *Badgett*, 10 Cal 4th 330, 343, 895 P 2d 877 (1995).

[125]*Fisher* v. *United States*, 425 US 391, 397–98 (1976); Tomkovicz, 2011 at 94–95.

[126]377 US 201 (1964).

[127]*Ibid.* at 206.

[128]*Ibid.* at 204 (quoting *Spano* v. *New York*, 360 US 315, 326 (1959) (Justice Douglas, concurring)).

[129]*Kansas* v. *Ventris*, 556 US 586, 591 (2009).

[130]*Massiah* v. *United States*, 377 US 201, 207 (1964).

[131]*Ibid.* at 208 (Justice White, dissenting).

[132]*Ibid.*

in no way disturbed, the extension of the exclusionary rule to statements elicited by government agents after formal charges appeared unwarranted to the dissent.[133]

More recently, a majority of Supreme Court justices have revived the idea that the Sixth Amendment ban on deliberate elicitations and the exclusionary rule that enforce it sweep too broadly. The Court has made it easier for defendants to waive their pretrial right to counsel[134] and has carved out exceptions to the Sixth Amendment exclusionary rule.[135] In *Kansas v. Ventris*, the Court held that statements obtained in violation of the pretrial right to counsel may be used to impeach the defendant's credibility if he testifies at trial in a manner inconsistent with those statements.[136] The Court reasoned that the exclusionary rule in this context protects the core Sixth Amendment right—to have counsel's assistance *at trial*—only indirectly. Exclusion is not expressly mandated by the Constitution. Moreover, the rule's purpose is primarily deterrent—to prevent future violations, rather than to remedy a violation that has already occurred at the pretrial stage and cannot be undone.[137] Conducting a balancing analysis, the Court concluded that any deterrent benefit served by extending the exclusionary rule to cover the use of evidence for impeachment purposes is outweighed by the interest in protecting the integrity of the trial against false statements. Following a similar cost-benefit analysis, some lower courts have further limited the Sixth Amendment exclusionary rule and admitted the fruits of statements obtained in violation of the Sixth Amendment.[138]

The Supreme Court has yet to clarify the precise scope of the Sixth Amendment exclusionary rule. Given the cost-benefit analysis the Court used in *Ventris*, however, we are likely to see a further narrowing of this exclusionary rule, as we have seen with the Fourth Amendment and the *Miranda* exclusionary rule (the subject of the next Section). Like evidence obtained in violation of the Fourth Amendment and *Miranda*, but unlike confessions coerced in violation of the Due Process Clause and the Privilege against Self-Incrimination, statements elicited in contravention of the Sixth Amendment are presumed to be reliable and probative evidence; "[t]he fact that an accused lacked legal assistance when he made inculpatory statements in response to noncoercive official inducements does not raise serious questions about the accuracy of those statements."[139] Because exclusion of such statements is not expressly mandated by the Constitution and stands in the way of accurate factfinding, it is likely to be imposed more sparingly by the current Supreme Court,

---

[133] *Ibid.* at 208–10.

[134] *Montejo* v. *Louisiana,* 556 US 778, 786 (2009).

[135] *Nix* v. *Williams*, 467 US 431 (1984); *Michigan* v. *Harvey*, 494 US 344 (1990); *Kansas* v. *Ventris*, 556 US 586 (2009).

[136] 556 US 586, 593–94 (2009).

[137] *Ibid.* at 593.

[138] *See, e.g., United States* v. *Fellers*, 397 F 3d 1090 (8th Cir. 2005).

[139] Tomkovicz, 2012 at 48 ("There is nothing about the governmental conduct that is the concern of *Massiah*–deliberate elicitation of admissions from an uncounseled defendant–that casts doubt upon the reliability of statements made or the fruits of those statements.").

which is both more textualist in its interpretation of the Constitution and more hostile to remedies that impede the search for truth in criminal cases.[140]

4.3 *The* Miranda *Safeguards Against Coerced Confessions*

Sixth Amendment protections are limited to citizen-police interactions that occur after the filing of formal charges. As a result, the Sixth Amendment does not apply to most police interrogations, which occur earlier in the process.[141] This helps explain why, even after the Supreme Court had decided *Massiah* and established Sixth Amendment protections during certain pretrial encounters between police and suspects, it remained concerned that police interrogations were not sufficiently regulated. A majority of the Justices believed that pretrial interrogations—as a result of their isolated and non-transparent setting—harbored the risk that police would use physical or psychological pressure to compel suspects to confess.

To minimize this risk of compelled statements, in 1966, in *Miranda v. Arizona*, the Court established new safeguards for custodial interrogations. It held that whenever police interrogate a suspect who is in custody, they must warn him that he has the right to remain silent, that anything he says may be used in evidence against him, that he has the right to the presence of an attorney, and that if he cannot afford an attorney, one will be appointed for him. If the suspect asserts his right to remain silent, the police must honor that right and cease questioning, although they can resume questioning after a "cooling off" period and after taking measures (such as providing a new set of *Miranda* warnings) to ensure that the subsequent interrogation is free of coercion.[142]

When a suspect invokes his right to counsel, police must again stop interrogation and are forbidden from initiating any further questioning.[143] As the Court explained in *Edwards v. Arizona*, "additional safeguards are necessary when the accused asks for counsel [as opposed to invoking only the right to remain silent]."[144] This is because the request for counsel indicates that the suspect does not feel capable to face the pressures of interrogations on his own, so the need for protection appears stronger.

While police must stop questioning once the suspect has asked for an attorney, they do not need to provide an attorney to him at the stationhouse. Indigent suspects typically have a lawyer appointed for them—and meet their lawyer for the first time—at their initial arraignment before a magistrate, which must occur within 48 hours of arrest.

---

[140]*Ibid.* at 48–49.

[141]*Moran* v. *Burbine*, 475 US 412, 428–32 (1986).

[142]*Michigan* v. *Mosley*, 423 US 96, 106–07 (1975).

[143]*Edwards* v. *Arizona*, 451 US 477, 484–85 (1981). A sufficiently long break in custody, however, allows the police to reapproach the subject and attempt to interrogate him anew, after giving a fresh set of Miranda warnings. *Maryland* v. *Shatzer*, 559 US 98, 104 (2010). Likewise, the suspect may himself reinitiate contact with the authorities, in which case they may resume the interrogation and obtain a valid waiver of Miranda rights.

[144]*Edwards* v. *Arizona*, 451 US 477, 484 (1981).

Miranda therefore assures them that suspects would not be further interrogated by the police until they have an attorney present with them—not that counsel will be made available to them immediately upon request (in practice, once an attorney is present, she advises her client not to say anything in response to police questioning, so police do not in fact conduct further interrogations of the suspect once counsel is present).

If the police fail to follow the *Miranda* rules, any resulting statement will be excluded from trial.[145] Moreover, the prosecution is prohibited from commenting to the jury about the silence of the defendant during a custodial interrogation, or about the defendant's decision to invoke his *Miranda* rights.[146]

The suspect may waive his right to remain silent and his right to the presence of an attorney. The government must prove that the suspect did so knowingly, voluntarily, and intelligently.[147] Statements made after a waiver are admissible into evidence. However, the suspect can reassert his right to remain silent or his right to an attorney at any point during the interrogation, and the police must honor that invocation.[148] The Court's ruling on waivers has been criticized by many, including the dissenters in *Miranda*. Critics note that police officers who might coerce a confession might similarly coerce a waiver, and the warnings do little to reduce that likelihood.[149]

When *Miranda* was decided, it was greeted with hostility by many in law enforcement and in Congress. In fact, just two years after the decision was handed down, Congress passed a statute that re-imposed the totality-of-circumstances voluntariness test for evaluating confessions in federal court; under that standard, *Miranda* warnings were optional.[150] Federal prosecutors ignored the statute, however, as they doubted its constitutionality. When the law was finally challenged in the courts in 2000, the Supreme Court struck it down as incompatible with *Miranda*.[151]

Some critics of *Miranda* have complained that it has stifled efforts to reform the law governing confessions in the United States:

> The *Miranda* decision has petrified the law of pre-trial interrogation for the past twenty years, foreclosing the possibility of developing and implementing alternatives that would be of greater effectiveness both in protecting the public from crime and in ensuring fair treatment of persons suspected of crime. ... Nothing is likely to change in the future as long as *Miranda* remains in effect and perpetuates a perceived risk of invalidation for any alternative system that departs from it.[152]

---

[145]As subsequent discussion elaborates, the statement may be used to impeach the defendant, if he testifies at trial.

[146]*See, e.g., Miranda* v. *Arizona*, 384 US 436, 468 n. 37 (1966).

[147]*Ibid.* at 444–45.

[148]*Ibid.*

[149]*See, e.g., ibid.* at 505 (Justice Harlan, dissenting) ("The new rules are not designed to guard against police brutality or other unmistakably banned forms of coercion. Those who use third-degree tactics and deny them in court are equally able and destined to lie as skillfully about warnings and waivers.").

[150]18 USC § 3501.

[151]*Dickerson* v. *United States*, 530 US 428, 443 (2000).

[152]Cassell, 1996 at 498 (citing Office of Legal Policy, 1989 at 437).

Contrary to this prediction, however, recent years have seen a steady increase in jurisdictions that have adopted policies and laws requiring audio- or video-recording of interrogations.[153] Such recording is mandated in addition to, rather than as an alternative to, *Miranda* warnings, and is therefore consistent with federal constitutional requirements.

While legislative efforts have largely focused on supplementing *Miranda* rules, the Supreme Court has itself gradually reduced the scope of *Miranda* protections. The first way in which this weakening has occurred is the definition of custody. *Miranda* only applies to defendants who are in custody, because the Court has held that it is only then that the police-dominated atmosphere and isolation leads to the type of compulsion that the Fifth Amendment prohibits. But over time, the Court has explained that not every interrogation at a police station is necessarily custodial. For example, a suspect is not in custody if he comes to the station voluntarily and is told that he is free to leave.[154] Likewise, an ordinary traffic stop is not considered custodial for purposes of *Miranda* protections.[155]

Over time, the Court has also made it more difficult for suspects to invoke their *Miranda* rights and easier to waive those rights. While *Miranda* suggested that the government bears a "heavy burden" to show that a suspect has knowingly, voluntarily, and intelligently waived his rights, more recent cases have suggested that the burden is not that difficult to meet. For example, the suspect need not be told of the scope of investigation and need not be told that an attorney was trying to reach him.[156] Essentially, for a waiver to be knowing, all that the suspect must understand is the meaning of the *Miranda* warnings themselves. Recent cases have further expanded the ability of suspects to provide implied—and therefore potentially unintentional—waivers. Thus a suspect who remained silent in the face of prolonged questioning was found to have waived his rights because he spoke English, showed no signs of mental disability, and ultimately, after several hours of questioning by the police, provided answers to a few questions.[157]

At the same time that it has loosened the standard for valid *Miranda* waivers, the Court has tightened the requirements for invoking *Miranda* rights. It has held that for *Miranda* protections to attach, the suspect must invoke his rights in a clear and

[153]For example, of statutory regulation, see 725 Illinois Compiled Statutes 5, Section 103-2.1; Texas Code of Criminal Procedure article 38.22. For example, of judicial regulation, see *Stephan* v. *State*, 711 P 2d 1156 (Alaska 1985); *State* v. *Scales*, 518 NW 2d 587, 592 (Minnesota 1994). The Innocence Project reports that "24 states, from North Carolina to Massachusetts to Illinois, require the recording of custodial interrogations through law or court action. More than a thousand additional law enforcement agencies voluntarily record interrogations." Innocence Project, 2017; *see also* Sullivan, 2014. The Department of Justice has also announced a policy that establishes a presumption in favor of recording of custodial interrogations. Memorandum from James M. Cole, 2014 at 2.

[154]*California* v. *Beheler*, 463 US 1121, 1123–24 (1983); *Oregon* v. *Mathiason*, 429 US 492, 495 (1977).

[155]*Berkemer* v. *McCarty*, 468 US 420, 439–41 (1984).

[156]*Moran* v. *Burbine*, 475 US 412, 422–23 (1986).

[157]*Berghuis* v. *Thompkins*, 560 US 370, 385–86 (2010).

unequivocal fashion. If the assertion is ambiguous or hesitant at all, police are free to proceed with their questions.[158] Under this jurisprudence, only the confident or legally well-educated suspects can properly invoke their *Miranda* rights.

The Supreme Court has also gradually shrunk the scope of *Miranda*'s exclusionary rule. The *Miranda* decision itself did not spend much time justifying the need to exclude evidence to remedy *Miranda* violations. Because a violation of *Miranda* was presumed to be a violation of the Privilege against Self-Incrimination, the admission of *Miranda*-defective statements into evidence was thought to be itself a compulsion banned by the Fifth Amendment.[159]

Just five years later, however, in *Harris v. New York*, the Court held that the prosecution may introduce *Miranda*-defective statements at trial to impeach the credibility of the defendant if he testifies in a manner inconsistent with those statements.[160] The Court justified this exception in part by noting the importance of impeachment as a "traditional truth-testing device[] of the adversary process."[161] It further stated that exclusion of *Miranda*-defective statements is not always required because a violation of *Miranda* is not necessarily a violation of the Fifth Amendment.[162] The Court suggested that exclusion under *Miranda* should be examined separately from the underlying Fifth Amendment right and should be imposed only when it is necessary to deter police misconduct in obtaining confessions.[163]

In several subsequent cases, the Court reaffirmed the idea that *Miranda* is a "mere" prophylactic device that sweeps more broadly than the Privilege against Self-Incrimination itself. Because of this, *Miranda* exclusion is generally limited only to those cases where the need to deter police misconduct is greatest and outweighs the interest in admitting probative statements into evidence. Accordingly, while *Miranda*-defective statements themselves must be suppressed from trial, evidence derived from these statements can generally be used.[164]

For similar reasons, the Court has also carved out a public safety exception to the *Miranda* exclusionary rule. A statement obtained without proper warnings may nonetheless be admissible if police reasonably believed that a threat to public safety

---

[158] *Davis* v. *United States*, 512 US 452, 459 (1994); *Berghuis* v. *Thompkins*, 560 US 370, 381 (2010).

[159] *See, e.g.*, *Miranda* v. *Arizona*, 384 US 436, 439, 461–62, 479, 490–91 (1966).

[160] 401 US 222, 225–26 (1971).

[161] *Ibid.* at 225.

[162] *Ibid.* at 224. The Court points out that "[p]etitioner makes no claim that the statements made to the police were coerced or involuntary" and then later suggests that interrogations that violate *Miranda* may nonetheless produce trustworthy statements.

[163] *See ibid.* at 225 ("Assuming that the exclusionary rule has a deterrent effect on proscribed police conduct, sufficient deterrence flows when the evidence in question is made unavailable to the prosecution in its case in chief.").

[164] *Michigan* v. *Tucker*, 417 US 433, 449 (1974); *United States* v. *Patane*, 542 US 630, 643–44 (2004). The one situation in which the fruits of a *Miranda* violation may be inadmissible is when a suspect first provides a statement in the absence of *Miranda* warnings and then makes a subsequent confession after warnings are properly given. The second confession may be inadmissible, particularly if officers act in bad faith. *Missouri* v. *Seibert*, 542 US 600, 615–17 (2004).

required them to interrogate the suspect swiftly and without giving *Miranda* warnings.[165] Therefore, if police need to quickly obtain information about a hidden weapon, an explosive device, or a dangerous associate of the suspect who is on the loose, they may be permitted to question the suspect about those subjects without first giving *Miranda* warnings.[166]

At bottom, the narrowing of the *Miranda* exclusionary rule has been motivated by a belief that *Miranda* protections are not expressly required by the Constitution, that *Miranda*-defective statements are reliable, and that the *Miranda* exclusionary rule interferes too greatly with the search for truth and the effective enforcement of criminal law.

4.4 Exclusion of Evidence Obtained by Torture or Undue Coercion

U.S. law criminalizes torture and mandates exclusion for evidence obtained in violation of this prohibition. The United States is a party to the Convention Against Torture (CAT), and the U.S. Congress passed the Torture Act, which criminalizes torture under federal law, to comply with its obligations under CAT.[167] The Act defines torture as "an act committed by a person acting under the color of law specifically intended to inflict severe physical or mental pain or suffering (other than

[165]*New York* v. *Quarles*, 467 US 649, 655–56 (1984).

[166]*See* Wright, 2011.

[167]18 USC §2340. The Act provides that "whoever outside the United States commits or attempts to commit torture shall be fined… or imprisoned not more than 20 years, or both, and if death results … shall be punished by death or imprisoned for any term of years or for life." The federal courts have jurisdiction if "the alleged offender is a national of the United States, or if the alleged offender is present in the United States, irrespective of the nationality of the victim or alleged offender." The Act narrows the scope of mental pain or suffering and limits it to severe mental pain or suffering caused by threats of death, torture, or drugging the victim or third party. The UN Committee Against Torture has requested that the US "ensure that acts of psychological torture were not limited to prolonged mental harm but constituted a wider category of acts, which caused severe mental suffering, irrespective of duration." Luban et al., 2014 at 1162. Torture is already criminalized under US law (for example, torture could be prosecuted as assault and murder under state law), so Section 2340A is meant to apply to torture outside the country. But the UN Committee Against Torture has expressed concern that state prohibitions typically carry lower sentences than the Torture and War Crimes Statutes. *Ibid.* at 1165–66.

When ratifying CAT, the US Senate added an understanding that the phrase "cruel, inhuman or degrading treatment" means only the kind of treatment forbidden by US constitutional prohibitions on cruel and unusual punishment and on violations of due process law. The Supreme Court has held that government conduct violates due process when it "shocks the conscience." Because the "shock the conscience" test is a sliding scale, lawyers in the Bush administration had argued that certain methods of "enhanced interrogation" used to interrogate suspected terrorists after September 11 would not shock the conscience and were therefore not prohibited by the Torture Act. Luban, 2014 at 122.

pain or suffering incidental to lawful sanctions) upon another person within his custody or physical control."[168]

While the Torture Act applies to acts committed outside the United States, other state and federal statutes prohibit the use of excessive force by government officials.[169] These have occasionally given rise to criminal prosecutions.[170] Civil remedies provide another mechanism of enforcing the ban against torture.[171]

American courts have also aimed to deter police brutality and limit its effects by excluding evidence obtained by torture. As discussed in Sect. 4.1, coerced confessions (i.e., confessions obtained through either coercion or torture) were excluded initially under the common law and subsequently under the Privilege against Self-Incrimination and the Due Process Clause. Under a voluntariness analysis, evidence obtained by any coercion that overwhelms the will of the accused—which is certain to include torture—is inadmissible.

As a preventive matter, safeguards such as *Miranda* warnings, access to a lawyer (including appointed lawyer when the detainee cannot afford one), and access to medical staff in jail all help prevent undue coercion and torture of detainees. Torture and physical coercion by officers are therefore almost unheard of in civilian settings in the United States today.[172]

4.5 Debate on Exclusionary Rules

Debates on exclusionary rules have focused primarily on the exclusion of physical evidence obtained in violation of the Fourth Amendment and statements obtained in violation of *Miranda*. While commentators have argued about the contours of the law defining coerced statements under the Due Process Clause and the Privilege against Self-Incrimination, exclusion of coerced statements has not been controversial.[173] This Section therefore focuses on the debates about the *Miranda* exclusionary rule, which has garnered significant attention from the law enforcement community, lawyers, academic commentators, and the public at large.

---

[168]18 USC § 2340.

[169]*See, e.g.*, 18 USC § 113 (criminalizing assaults within special maritime and territorial jurisdiction of the United States, such as federal land); *United States* v. *Parker*, CR-H-83-66 (S.D. Texas 1983), *aff'd sub. nom. United States* v. *Lee*, 744 F 2d 1124 (5th Cir. 1984).

[170]*See, e.g.*, *United States* v. *Parker*, CR-H-83-66 (S.D. Texas 1983).

[171]Individuals can bring claims for violations of civil rights against state officials under 14 USC § 1983, and for negligence and intentional torts of federal officials under the Federal Tort Claims Act, 22 USC § 2671. In addition, the Torture Victims' Protection Act provides US national with a cause of action for torture committed under color of foreign law, and the Alien Tort Claims Act provides a similar cause of action to foreigners. 28 USC § 1350.

[172]This report does not discuss allegations of torture by US agents in military settings after 9/11. For a review of these allegations, *see* Senate Select Committee on Intelligence, 2014.

[173]*See, e.g.*, Alschuler, 1997; Godsey, 2005; Primus, 2015.

Some commentators have praised *Miranda* for reducing the coerciveness of interrogations by forcing officers to remember and state the suspects' rights before each interrogation.[174] Some have also argued that *Miranda* has been easier to administer, as it provides brighter and more predictable rules for the legality of confessions than the voluntariness test.[175] *Miranda* has also been lauded for educating individuals about their rights to remain silent and to consult a lawyer. As the Supreme Court has noted, *Miranda* has "become part of our national culture" and is thus well-known by a broad segment of the population.[176]

Yet *Miranda* has also been subject to scrutiny and criticism from the very beginning. When it was first decided, most law enforcement officers were skeptical and resistant.[177] (Not long afterward, however, empirical studies found that departments complied with "the letter, though not always the spirit" of *Miranda* rules.)[178]

Some law enforcement officers and scholars have expressed concerns that *Miranda* has reduced the number of confessions that police have obtained and has thus reduced the crime clearance rate and hurt victims of crime, innocent suspects, and the public at large.[179] Indeed, several studies have found that *Miranda* has reduced the number of confessions obtained by police.[180] A couple have reported a 15–18% drop in the success rate of obtaining incriminating statements after *Miranda*; others have found a less significant reduction.[181] Yet even if *Miranda* has limited law enforcement's ability to obtain confessions, this has not led to an appreciable loss of convictions, because prosecutors have been able to obtain convictions based on other sources of evidence.[182]

---

[174]Some have argued that it has made law enforcement officers "more professional" in their interrogations. Brief of Griffin B. Bell, et al. as Amici Curiae in Support of Petitioner, *Dickerson* v. *United States*, 530 US 428 (2000) (No. 99-5525), *cited in* Weisselberg, 2008 at 1595; *see also* Leo, 2001 at 1010 ("[S]ome researchers have argued that *Miranda* eradicated the last vestiges of third degree interrogation present in the mid-1960s, increased the level of professionalism among interrogators, and raised public awareness of constitutional rights"). Others, however, have argued that "*Miranda* is … virtually worthless as a safeguard against specific interrogation practices that were characterized as abusive in the *Miranda* decision …." (OLP Report, *cited in* Cassell, 1996 at 477).

[175]Brief of Griffin B. Bell, et al. as Amici Curiae in Support of Petitioner, *Dickerson* v. *United States*, 530 US 428 (2000) (No. 99-5525), *cited in* Weisselberg, 2008 at 1595.

[176]*Dickerson* v. *United States*, 530 US 428, 443 (200).

[177]Leo, 2001 at 1002–03.

[178]*Ibid.* at 1003.

[179]*E.g.*, Cassell, 1996 at 115.

[180]Cassell/Hayman, 1996 at 871 (finding a drop from 55–60% pre-*Miranda* to 42.2% post-*Miranda* in the success rate of obtaining confessions); Seeburger/Wettick, 1967 at 12 tbl. 2 (finding that confessions dropped from 48.5% pre-*Miranda* to 32.3% after *Miranda*); Witt, 1973 at 320.

[181]For a summary of the studies, some of which conflict in their findings, see Leo, *above* note 174, at 1004–06.

[182]Leo, 2001 at 1004–06.

Critics of *Miranda* have argued, however, that the total societal cost of *Miranda* is higher, as it includes cases that never result in charges being filed (and are therefore not even calculated as "convictions lost"), sentence discounts given during plea bargains to account for possible *Miranda* violations and for failure to obtain incriminating statements,[183] and the costs to the judicial system of litigating *Miranda* issues. Others have disputed these conclusions, as well as the methodology underlying the studies that produced them.[184] After reviewing the empirical research on *Miranda*, one scholar argued that "for all practical purposes, *Miranda*'s empirically detectable net damage to law enforcement is zero."[185]

In short, thc question whether *Miranda* has resulted in an appreciable number of lost confessions or lost convictions continues to be debated. There is, however, broad consensus among scholars that 80–90% of suspects today waive their *Miranda* rights and make statements to the police, most of which are incriminating or otherwise helpful to the prosecution.[186] In addition, even when *Miranda* violations are raised with courts, these claims are only rarely successful (less than 10% of the time), at least in part because of the numerous exceptions to the *Miranda* exclusionary rule that the Court has carved out.[187] This helps explain why police officers have learned that they can "live" with *Miranda*.[188]

The high rate of *Miranda* waivers and the rarity of suppression of *Miranda*-defective statements provide the basis for a different critique of *Miranda* safeguards —that they are too ineffectual in preventing coerced and false confessions. Critics point to the 80% waiver figure to argue that in too many cases, suspects waive their rights, and officers are free to proceed with coercive psychological tactics to procure a confession. Other critics have also pointed out that *Miranda* has distracted courts from examining the voluntariness of confessions. Once judges see that warnings have been given, they rarely inquire further into the voluntariness of the ensuing confession.[189] On this view, the warnings regime by *Miranda* has done little to reduce the psychological pressure that officers place on suspects to confess.[190]

---

[183]Cassell, 1996 at 439–46.

[184]*See, e.g.*, Leo/Ofshe, 1998 at 557 n. 2; Schulhofer, (1996) 91 at 280; Weisselberg, 1998 at 173–74.

[185]Schulhofer, (1996) 90 at 547.

[186]Cassell, 1996; Leo, 2001 at 1009.

[187]Nardulli, 1983 at 593, 595 tbl. 2, 596, 597 tbl. 7 (finding that motions to suppress confessions were filed in 6.6% of all cases and that only 2.5% of these motions were successful); Valdes, 2005 at 1729 (finding that motions to suppress confessions on the basis of *Miranda* were made in 3.97% of cases and succeeded 9.86% of the time).

[188]*See, e.g.*, Leo, 2001 at 1012.

[189]*Ibid.* at 1025–26.

[190]Interviews with two Texas defense attorneys and two prosecutors suggest that although physical coercion is a thing of the past, psychological tactics—especially lying to suspects about the evidence in the case—continue to be commonly used. As the defense attorneys interviewed suggested, such tactics, particularly when used with vulnerable (e.g., young or cognitively impaired) suspects, can result in false confessions. *See above* note 116.

The problem is said to be particularly acute with respect to certain more vulnerable suspects, such as juveniles, non-native speakers, and mentally disabled suspects, who are most likely to confess falsely as a result of psychological pressure and are least likely to comprehend the *Miranda* warnings.[191]

Finally, some critics argue that, over time, Supreme Court jurisprudence has weakened the *Miranda* safeguards to such a point that whatever effectiveness the rule might have had when originally adopted has now been undermined.[192] Some have accordingly called for a rethinking and strengthening of the voluntariness analysis as an alternative to *Miranda*, because it is regarded as the only doctrine left to regulate pretrial interrogations in a meaningful way.[193] Others have called for videotaping—imposed via legislative or judicial means—as the most effective supplement to *Miranda* in ensuring the voluntariness of confessions.[194] Finally, another preventive measure that scholars have increasingly proposed to minimize false confessions is the training of police officers in less manipulative interrogation techniques, particularly when interrogating vulnerable suspects.[195]

5 Conclusion

Although U.S. law does not expressly impose a duty to search for truth in criminal cases, courts recognize the importance of accurate factfinding to just outcomes and the effective enforcement of criminal law. Yet truthseeking at times must give way to protections of individual rights. The conflict between the search for truth and the protection of rights arises when courts decide whether to exclude unlawfully obtained evidence. When the Constitution does not expressly require exclusion as a remedy, U.S. courts have openly considered the costs of exclusion to the search for truth and have tried to limit those costs. Courts have therefore admitted *Miranda*-defective confessions for purposes of impeachment, *Miranda*-defective statements obtained to protect public safety, as well as most fruits of *Miranda*-defective statements. At the same time, courts always exclude coerced confessions, in part because the Constitution requires such exclusion, in part because of concerns about the confessions' reliability, and in part because of the greater need to deter the police misconduct at issue.

On their own, U.S. exclusionary rules for tainted confessions have not succeeded in eliminating involuntary confessions. Recent DNA exonerations have revealed that false confessions continue to occur and are a leading contributing factor to

[191]Weisselberg, 2008 at 1565–68 (discussing studies); *see also* Garrett, 2012 at 38.

[192]*E.g.*, Weisselberg, 2008.

[193]Primus, 2015.

[194]Interviewees also suggested that videotaping has been very important in reducing coerced confessions in Texas. *See above* note 116.

[195]See, e.g., Kassin et al., 2010 at 3–38.

wrongful convictions. Accordingly, policymakers and commentators have looked for additional safeguards to prevent the occurrence of such confessions. The main reform being proposed and implemented in this regard is the audio- or video-recording of interrogations.[196] An increasing number of cities and states are adopting policies and laws requiring such recording. As evidence about the operation of recording becomes available, law enforcement is becoming more receptive to the practice.

Additionally, scholars and police departments are increasingly recognizing the importance of training officers in special techniques for interrogating vulnerable suspects[197] Such techniques, focused on open-ended questioning rather than psychological manipulation, are expected to minimize the risk of false confessions.[198]

Whatever additional reforms of interrogation practice are adopted, *Miranda* safeguards and the exclusion of coerced confessions provide an important backstop for regulating police conduct. While imposing some burdens on the search for truth, these procedures encourage police compliance with the Constitution and educate suspects (as well as the population) about their rights.

References

Books

Broun, Kenneth S. (ed.), *McCormick on Evidence* 7th ed., St. Paul 2013. [Broun, 2013]

Garrett, Brandon L., *Convicting the Innocent: Where Criminal Prosecutions Go Wrong,* Cambridge/Massachusetts/U.S.A. 2012. [Garrett, 2012]

Leo, Richard A., *Police Interrogation and American Justice,* Cambridge/Massachusetts/U.S.A. 2008. [Leo, 2008]

Luban, David, et al., *International and Transnational Criminal Law* 2nd ed., July 2014. [Luban et al., 2014]

Luban, David, *Torture, Power, and Law*, October 2014. [Luban, 2014]

Miller, Marc L./Wright, Ronald F., *Criminal Procedures: The Police,* July 2007. [Miller/Wright, 2007]

Saltzburg, Stephen A./Capra, Daniel J., *American Criminal Procedure: Cases and Commentary* 10th ed., May 2014. [Saltzburg/Capra, 2014]

Tomkovicz, James J., *Constitutional Exclusion,* New York 2011. [Tomkovicz, 2011]

---

[196] *See above* Part 3.4.2; *see also* Cassell, 1997 at 1132 (noting that "there seems to be virtual unanimity among those who have reviewed the problem that videotaping interrogations is an effective solution to the false confession problem"). Other proposed reforms include replacing police interrogations with questioning by a neutral magistrate (Amar/Lettow, 1995), reinforced corroboration rules, including mandatory DNA testing (Drizin/Leo, 2004 at 1006), and training police officers about the causes of false confessions (*Ibid.*).

[197] *See, e.g.*, Cleary/Warner, 2016 at 282; Kassin et al., 2010 at 3–38.

[198] For a comparative review of interrogation policies and training, see, for example, Dixon, 2019.

Journal Articles

Alschuler, Albert W., 'Constraint and Confession', (1997) 74 *Denver University Law Review*, 957–978. [Alschuler, 1997]

Amar, Akhil/Lettow, Renee Lerner, 'Fifth Amendment First Principle: The Self-Incrimination Clause', (1995) 93 *Michigan Law Review*, 857–928 [Amar/Lettow, 1995]

Brown, Darryl K., 'The Decline of Defense Counsel and the Rise of Accuracy in Criminal Adjudication', (2005) 93 *California Law Review*, 1585–1646. [Brown, 2005]

Cassell, Paul/Hayman, Bret, 'Police Interrogation in the 1990s: An Empirical Study of the Effects of Miranda', (1996) 43 UCLA Law Review, 839–931. [Cassell/Hayman, 1996]

Cassell, Paul G., 'Balanced Approaches to the False Confession Problem: A Brief Comment on Ofshe, Leo, and Alschuler', (1997) 74 *Denver University Law Review*, 1123–1133. [Cassell, 1997]

Cassell, Paul G., 'Miranda's Social Costs: An Empirical Reassessment', (1996) 90 *Northwestern University Law Review*, 387–499. [Cassell, 1996]

Cleary, Hayley M. D./Warner, Todd C., 'Police Training in Interviewing and Interrogation Methods: A Comparison of Techniques Used with Adult and Juvenile Suspects', (2016) 40 *Law & Human Behavior*, 270–284. [Cleary/Warner, 2016]

Drizin, Steven A./Leo, Richard A., 'The Problem of False Confessions in the Post-DNA World', (2004) 82 *North Carolina Law Review*, 891–1004 [Drizin/Leo, 2004]

Fisher, Stanley Z., '"Just the Facts, Ma'am": Lying and the Omission of Exculpatory Evidence in Police Reports', (1993) 28 *New England Law Review*, 1–62. [Fisher, 1993]

Fisher, Talia/Rosen-Zvi, Issachar, 'The Confessional Penalty', (2008) 30 *Cardozo Law Review*, 871–916. [Fisher/Rosen-Zvi, 2008]

Geller, William, 'Enforcing the Fourth Amendment: The Exclusionary Rule and Its Alternatives', (1975) 1975 *Washington University Law Quarterly*, 621–722. [Geller, 1975]

Gershowitz, Adam/Killinger, Laura R., 'The State (Never) Rests: How Excessive Prosecutorial Caseloads Harm Criminal Defendants', (2011) 105 *Northwestern University Law Review*, 261–301. [Gershowitz, 2011]

Godsey, Mark A., 'Rethinking the Involuntary Confession Rule: Toward a Workable Test for Identifying Compelled Self-Incrimination', (2005) 93 *California Law Review*, 465–540. [Godsey, 2005]

Kamisar, Yale, 'On the 'Fruits' of Miranda Violations, Coerced Confessions, and Compelled Testimony', (1995) 93 *Michigan Law Review*, 929–1010. [Kamisar, 1995]

Kassin, Saul M., et al., 'Police-induced Confessions: Risk Factors and Recommendations', (2010) 34 *Law and Human Behavior*, 3–38. [Kassin et al., 2010]

Laurin, Jennifer E., 'Quasi-Inquisitorialism: Accounting for Deference in Pretrial Criminal Procedure', (2014) 90 *Notre Dame Law Review*, 783–846. [Laurin, 2014]

Leo, Richard A./Ofshe, Richard J., 'Using the Innocent to Scapegoat *Miranda*: Another Reply to Paul Cassell', (1998) 88 *Journal of Criminal Law & Criminology*, 557–577. [Leo/Ofshe, 1998]

Leo, Richard A., 'Questioning the Relevance of *Miranda* in the Twenty-First Century', (2001) 99 *Michigan Law Review*, 1000–1029. [Leo, 2001]

Luna, Erik/Wade, Marianne, 'Prosecutors as Judges', (2010) 67 *Washington and Lee Law Review*, 1413–1532. [Luna/Wade, 2010]

Nardulli, Peter F., 'The Societal Cost of the Exclusionary Rule: An Empirical Assessment', (1983) 1983 *American Bar Foundation Research Journal*, 585–609. [Nardulli, 1983]

Pepson, Michael D./Sharifi, John N., 'Lego v. Twomey: The Improbable Relationship Between an Obscure Supreme Court Decision and Wrongful Convictions', (2010) 47 *American Criminal Law Review*, 1185–1250. [Pepson/Sharifi, 2010]

Primus, Eve Brensike, 'The Future of Confession Law: Toward Rules for the Voluntariness Test', (2015) 114 *Michigan Law Review*, 1–56. [Primus, 2015]

Richman, Daniel C., 'Federal Criminal Law, Congressional Delegation, and Enforcement Discretion', (1999) 46 *UCLA Law Review*, 757–814. [Richman, 1999]

Richman, Daniel C., 'Prosecutors and Their Agents, Agents and Their Prosecutors', (2003) 103 *Columbia Law Review*, 749–832. [Richman, 2003]

Schulhofer, Stephen J., '*Miranda* and Clearance Rates', (1996) 91 *Northwestern University Law Review*, 278–294. [Schulhofer, (1996) 91]

Schulhofer, Stephen J., '*Miranda*'s Practical Effect: Substantial Benefits and Vanishingly Small Social Costs', (1996) 90 *Northwestern University Law Review*, 500–563. [Schulhofer, (1996) 90]

Schwartz, Joanna C., 'What Police Learn from Lawsuits', (2012) 33 *Cardozo Law Review* 841–894. [Schwartz, 2012]

Seeburger, Richard/Wettick, Stanton, '*Miranda* in Pittsburgh—A Statistical Study', (1967) 29 *University of Pittsburgh Law Review*, 1–26. [Seeburger/Wettick, 1967]

Sklansky, David Alan, 'Is the Exclusionary Rule Obsolete?', (2008) 5 *Ohio State Journal of Criminal Law*, 567–584. [Sklansky, 2008]

Stacy, Tom, 'The Search for the Truth in Constitutional Criminal Procedure', (1991) 91 *Columbia Law Review* 1369–1451. [Stacy, 1991]

Taslitz, Andrew E., 'High Expectations and Some Wounded Hopes: The Policy and Politics of A Uniform Statute on Videotaping Custodial Interrogations', (2012) 7 *Northwestern Journal of Law & Social Policy*, 400–454. [Taslitz, 2012]

Tomkovicz, James J., 'Sacrificing *Massiah*: Confusion over Exclusion and Erosion of the Right to Counsel', (2012) 16 *Lewis & Clark Law Review*, 1–67. [Tomkovicz, 2012]

Turner, Jenia Iontcheva, 'Judicial Participation in Plea Negotiation: A Comparative View', (2006) 54 *American Journal of Comparative Law*, 199–267. [Turner, 2006]

Valdes, Stephen G., 'Frequency and Success: An Empirical Study of Criminal Law Defenses, Federal Constitutional Evidentiary Claims, and Plea Negotiations', (2005) 153 *University of Pennsylvania Law Review*, 1709–1814. [Valdes, 2005]

Weisselberg, Charles D., 'Mourning *Miranda*', (2008) 96 *California Law Review*, 1519–1602. [Weisselberg, 2008]

Weisselberg, Charles D., 'Saving *Miranda*', (1998) 84 *Cornell Law Review*, 109–192. [Weisselberg, 1998]

Witt, James, 'Non-Coercive Interrogation and the Administration of Criminal Justice: The Impact of *Miranda* on Police Effectuality', (1973) 64 *Journal of Criminal Law & Criminology*, 320–332. [Witt, 1973]

Wright, Joanna, 'Mirandizing Terrorists? An Empirical Analysis of the Public Safety Exception', (2011) 111 *Columbia Law Review*, 1296–1331. [Wright, 2011]

Contributions to Edited Volumes and Annotated Law

Cammack, Mark E., 'The United States: The Rise and Fall of the Constitutional Exclusionary Rule', in: S. C. Thaman (ed.), *Exclusionary Rules in Comparative Law*, New York 2013, 3–32. [Cammack, 2013]

David Dixon, 'Interrogation Law and Practice in Common Law Jurisdictions', in: D. Brown et al. (eds.), *Oxford Handbook of Criminal Process*, forthcoming 2019. [Dixon, 2019]

Reports, Legislative History

Finn, Peter, 'Citizen Review of Police: Approaches and Implementation', (National Institute of Justice 2001). [Finn, 2001] <https://www.ncjrs.gov/pdffiles1/nij/184430.pdf>, accessed 1 November 2018.

Geller, William, 'Videotaping Interrogations and Confessions: National Institute of Justice Research in Brief' (National Institute of Justice 1993). [Geller, 1993]

Innocence Project, 'The Causes: False Confessions or Admissions', (2017). [Innocence Project, 2017] <https://www.innocenceproject.org/causes/false-confessions-admissions>, accessed 1 November 2018.

Judicial Council of California, Administrative Office of the Courts, 'Fact Sheet: Cameras in the California Courts, (Feb. 2007). [Judicial Council of California, Administrative Office of the Courts, 2007] <http://www.courts.ca.gov/documents/camerasc.pdf>, accessed 1 November 2018.

'Memorandum from James M. Cole, Deputy Att'y Gen., to Assoc. Att'y Gen. et al.', (12 May 2014). [Memorandum from James M. Cole, 2014] <http://s3.documentcloud.org/documents/1165406/recording-policy.pdf>, accessed 1 November 2018.

Miller, Lindsay et al., 'Implementing a Body-Worn Camera Program: Recommendations and Lessons Learned', (2014). [Miller et al., 2014] <http://www.justice.gov/iso/opa/resources/472014912134715246869.pdf>, accessed 1 November 2018.

Office of Legal Policy, U.S. Dep't of Justice, 'Report to the Attorney General on The Law of Pre-Trial Interrogation', (1986) 99, *reprinted in* (1989) 22 *University of Michigan Journal of Law Reform*, 437–572. [Office of Legal Policy, 1989]

Senate Select Committee on Intelligence, 'Committee Study of the Central Intelligence Agency's Detention and Interrogation Program, Findings and Conclusions', (2014). [Senate Select Committee on Intelligence, 2014] <http://www.intelligence.senate.gov/sites/default/files/press/findings-and-conclusions.pdf>, accessed 1 November 2018.

Sullivan, Thomas P., Nat'l Ass'n of Criminal Def. Lawyers, 'Compendium: Electronic Recording of Custodial Interrogations', (2014). [Sullivan, 2014] <https://www.nacdl.org/WorkArea/DownloadAsset.aspx?id=33287&libID=33256>, accessed 1 November 2018.

Jenia Iontcheva Turner is the Amy Abboud Ware Centennial Professor in Criminal Law at SMU Dedman School of Law, where she teaches criminal procedure, comparative criminal procedure, criminal procedure in the digital age, international criminal law, and international law. She is the author of "Plea Bargaining Across Borders" (2009) and co-editor of "The Oxford Handbook of Criminal Process" (forthcoming 2019) and "Criminal Procedures: Cases, Statutes, and Executive Materials" (as of the 6th ed. 2019).

The Potential to Secure a Fair Trial Through Evidence Exclusion: A Taiwanese Perspective

Yu-Hsiung Lin, Shih-Fan Wang, Chung-Yen Chen, Tsai-Chen Tsai and Chiou-Ming Tsai

Abstract Taiwan, as one of the jurisdictions comprising the so-called "fourth wave of democratization," fundamentally altered its criminal justice system over the course of just decades. This was particularly true with respect to the rule of law and the procedural law around the exclusion of evidence. For example, although illegally obtained, or "tainted" evidence may be crucial in the search for the truth, it is to be excluded if it was obtained under certain circumstances, including torture or coercion. The legal theory behind this area of Taiwanese law is grounded in the common law criminal justice system, although Taiwan has developed its own procedures and remedies. How illegally obtained evidence is excluded in Taiwanese criminal procedure is discussed, as is the melding of the Thai approach with its theoretical basis in Anglo-US criminal procedure. Both practical and theoretical perspectives are explored and the gaps between the formation of legislation and its enactment into judicial practice are addressed.

Y.-H. Lin (✉)
National Taiwan University, Taipei, Taiwan
e-mail: yslmy41@yahoo.com.tw

S.-F. Wang
National Taipei University, New Taipei City, Taiwan
e-mail: shihfan.wang@gmail.com

C.-Y. Chen
University of Tübingen, Tübingen, Germany
e-mail: thechosenjoe@gmail.com

T.-C. Tsai
Shihlin District Court, Taipei, Taiwan
e-mail: alberts@mail.moj.gov.tw

C.-M. Tsai
Department of International and Cross-Strait Legal Affairs, Ministry of Justice, Taipei, Taiwan
e-mail: grace@mail.judicial.gov.tw

S. Gless and T. Richter (eds.), *Do Exclusionary Rules Ensure a Fair Trial?*
Ius Gentium: Comparative Perspectives on Law and Justice 74,
https://doi.org/10.1007/978-3-030-12520-2_5

1 Introduction

Taiwan's legal system is committed to the rule of law as well as to respect for human rights. It bridges the legacy of Chinese law from the penultimate century with modern legal rules. With regard to the criminal justice system, and more particularly with regard to fact-finding in criminal proceedings, Taiwan's Code of Criminal Procedure (CCP: 刑事訴訟法[1]) obliges the authorities to search for the truth, while protecting human rights at the same time.[2] These principles also translate into the making of exclusionary rules: While all authorities are bound to search for the truth in a criminal investigation (Art. 2 of the CCP[3]), they must not put the search for truth above all other considerations.[4] The Taiwanese criminal justice system sets clear limits with the provisions of the CCP.[5] Therefore, criminal proceedings may not be initiated and punishment may not be imposed other than in conformity with the procedure specified in this Code or in other laws.

If evidence is obtained in violation of procedural rules, the question thus arises as to whether such evidence can be excluded from the fact-finding process.[6] From the point of view of courts, according to Taiwanese law exclusionary rules serve different purposes: (a) protecting human dignity of the defendant and his status as a party, (b) safeguarding the liberty of mental decision and mental activities of the defendant, and (c) deterring illegal investigatory activity based on the principle of due process.[7] The lawmaker has not addressed this problem with one general provision, but provided several key statutes (Arts. 156 para. 1,[8] 158-2[9] and 158-4[10] of the CCP) that provide for an exclusion of certain evidence, which is obtained in

---

[1]Available online at <http://law.moj.gov.tw/LawClass/LawAll.aspx?PCode=C0010001>, officially translated as The Code of Criminal Procedure of 28 July 1928 (Status as of 12 December 2007), available online at <http://law.moj.gov.tw/Eng/LawClass/LawAll.aspx?PCode=C0010001>, accessed 21 November 2018.

[2]LIN Yu-Hsiung, 2013 (I) at 7–10; ZHU Shi-Yan, 2015 at 8.

[3]*See* Annex.

[4]"Keine Wahrheit um jeden Preis. "In Taiwanese practice this is a general consensus, e.g. the interpretation No. 130 of the Judicial Yuan (22 December 1995) states: Although the state has the goal of finding out the truth in criminal justice proceedings, it does not mean that the state can attain this goal by whatever means available (國家爲達成刑事司法究明案件真象之目的, 非謂即可訴諸任何手段).

[5]Art. 1 of the CCP clearly states that all criminal investigations and criminal prosecutions are bound by the rule of law.

[6]E.g. Supreme Court precedent 93 taishangzih No. 664 (最高法院 94 年台上字第 664 號判例) and Supreme Court decision 94 taishangzih No. 275 (最高法院 94 年度台上字第 275 號判決); WANG Jaw-Perng, 2011 at 8–10.

[7]*See below* 3.2.

[8]*See* Annex.

[9]*See* Annex.

[10]*See* Annex.

violation of a legal requirement. These specific provisions often balance the interests of criminal justice and the need for coherent fact-finding with the protection of individual rights.[11]

2 General Framework for Establishing Facts in Criminal Proceedings

Taiwan's CCP was enacted in 1928.[12] At first, it was published and implemented in mainland China as first Code of Criminal Procedure in the Republic of China (ROC). After World War II and further struggle with the Communist Party of China, the government of the Republic of China relocated to the island of Taiwan which, at that moment, was not longer colonized by Japan. The Republic of China brought its legal system to Taiwan, including the CCP, whereas all former laws were abolished in mainland China after proclamation of the People's Republic of China (PRC).

2.1 Legal Framework and Relevant Actors

2.1.1 General Rules

The commitment that criminal proceedings primarily serve the ascertainment of truth is reflected in various provisions of the CCP: First of all Art. 2 para. 1 of the CCP obligates public officials investigating a criminal case to give equal attention to circumstances both favorable and unfavorable to a defendant. This means that the investigation is conducted open-mindedly and authorities are bound to objectivity, in order to discover the truth and thus not wronging innocent individuals or

[11]In the law-materials the following factors are formulated: (a) the circumstances of the violation of the procedure prescribed by the law: must be taken into account of whether there were difficulties in collecting evidence lawfully; (b) the subjective intentions of the official: referring to whether the official knows that his conduct is unlawful; (c) the nature and the severity of the right that was infringed: referring to the circumstances of the infringement; (d) the risk and harm of the crime: referring to the nature of the crime and its circumstances; (e) the deterrence effect of excluding such evidence; (f) whether it is unavoidable that officials will discover such evidence using procedure prescribed by law: the standard may be loosened if such evidence can be acquired through normal proceedings; and (g) the effect of the unlawful evidence has on the defense of the accused. *See also*: LIN Yu-Hsiung, 2013 (I) at 593 et seq.

[12]About the detailed development *see* CHEN Yu-Jie, 2011 at 713–28; WANG Jaw-Perng, 2011 at 19–21.

condoning offenders.[13] In that respect, Taiwan's Criminal justice system is more based on the inquisitorial model, as found in Continental Europe, than the adversarial system, as found in England or the United States.

2.1.1.1 Law Determining Duties in Criminal Investigations

In Taiwan, prosecutors and police officers act as investigating authorities. As soon as an investigative authority learns about an alleged crime, it can *ex officio* start investigating. Investigating authorities are obligated to actively investigate the facts of an alleged crime that comes to their knowledge as a result of a complaint, report, voluntary surrender or other reason.[14] Finally, if a case is prosecuted, the court must actively—*ex officio*—investigate all the circumstances relevant to the assessment of the criminal act and the defendant.[15] For the court, there is not only an *ex officio* obligation to discover the solid truth, but also, by legal requirements, to prove that the defendant indeed committed a crime if it is to bring in a guilty verdict. Guilt is proven if the evidence presented before a court[16] shows that the defendant is guilty beyond a reasonable doubt.[17]

Although confessions of defendants are regarded as evidence in Taiwan's criminal procedure, the law specifically stipulates that confessions cannot be the only reference for a guilty verdict. As stipulated in Art. 156 para. 2 of the CCP: a "[c]onfession of a defendant, or a co-offender, shall not be used as the sole basis of conviction and other necessary evidence shall still be investigated to see if the confession is consistent with facts." The statute shall prevent the prosecution authorities from overly relying on confessions of defendants or accomplices.[18]

In fact, Taiwan's CCP has seen many strict regulations on the use of confessions, which shows a certain caution in this respect.[19] Under the heavy judiciary burden of recent years, however, Taiwan's criminal justice system had no other choice but to introduce plea-bargaining in 2004.[20] But it refrained from fact bargaining: The court

[13]Nonetheless, in 2004 we have introduced the bargaining process, which is regulated from Arts. 455-2 to 455-11 in the CCP. The expert criticize that establishment of plea-bargaining does not base on truth, but on the admitted facts, *see e.g.* LIN Yu-Hsiung, 2013 (II) at 289–90.

[14]*See* Arts. 228 para. 1, 230 para. 2, 231 para. 2 of the CCP.

[15]Art. 163 para. 2 of the CCP.

[16]The exception is so-called Summary Procedure in Arts. 449 of the CCP (簡易程序): If a defendant's confession in the investigation process or other existing evidence is sufficient for the court of first instance to determine a defendant's offense, a sentence may be pronounced through summary judgment without common trial procedure upon request by the prosecutor; provided that the defendant shall be questioned before sentencing if necessary.

[17]*See* Arts. 154 para. 2, 163 para. 2 of the CCP.

[18]ZHU Shi-Yan, 2015 at 179.

[19]*See* with more details in 3 Limitations of Fact-Finding in Criminal Proceedings.

[20]Arts. 455-2 to 455-11 of the CCP. *See* LIN Yu-Hsiung, 2013 (II) at 254–55; ZHU Shi-Yan, 2015 at 577–79.

may not pronounce a bargaining judgment, when facts established by the court are different from the facts agreed on during the bargaining process. Nonetheless, inevitably questions about "confessions for bargaining" or "fact trading" have been raised. Scholars fear that justice will be for sale ("*Handel mit Gerechtigkeit*").[21]

2.1.1.2 Laws Securing a Fair Trial

Despite the fact that prosecution authorities have the obligation to search for the truth and to investigate all circumstances of a case, both unfavorable and favorable for the defendant, it is naturally difficult for a prosecutor to always stay impartial and detached while collecting evidence. Therefore, the defendant and the defense counsel have rights of their own in order to ensure a fair trial. Taiwan's CCP grants defendants various procedural rights, placing an overall limitation on the powers at the disposal of the investigating authorities.

In particular, the defendant enjoys the following procedural rights, any violation of which may result in an exclusionary effect according Arts. 158-2 or 158-4 of the CCP:

- The right to counsel according to Art. 27 para. 1 and Art. 34 para. 1 of the CCP
- The right of the defendant to be properly informed according to Art. 95 para. 1 of the CCP
- Audio and, eventually, video recording of the interrogation of the defendant must be in its entirety according to Art. 100-1 para. 1 of the CCP.

2.1.1.3 Laws Balancing the Search for the Truth and Infringements of Individual Rights

If the rights of a defendant were violated during criminal proceedings, the defendant may ask for the exclusion of evidence based on Art. 158-4 of the CCP. But the question of the burden of proof in such an instance remains unresolved. There is no general provision setting out the burden of proof in the event of an authorities' violation of rules. Only in the particular case of a defendant pleading that a confession was coerced is burden on the authorities to prove that the confession was in fact made voluntarily.[22] If the defendant claims that a confession was extracted by improper means, the confession shall be investigated prior other evidence being investigated by the court that decides on the merit of the (public) trial. If such a confession is presented by the public prosecutor, the court shall order the public prosecutor to indicate the method of proving that the confession has been given voluntarily (see. Art. 156 para. 3 of the CCP[23]). It is noteworthy (a) that the

---

[21]LIN Yu-Hsiung, 2013 (II) at 287.

[22]Supreme Court decision 94 taishangzih No. 275 (最高法院 94 年度台上字第 275 號判決).

[23]*See* Annex.

evidence that is possibly to be excluded is then made public and (b) that in court practice, the responsibility to prove whether the legal procedures are violated or not has always been bestowed on the state institutions. If the state institution is not able to prove that the defendant's rights are not damaged, the Supreme Court (最高法院) clearly pointed out that the defendant's right will be seen as damaged and the confession must be excluded.[24]

Additionally, in order to document that a defendant's interrogation is conducted according to the rules and a possible confession is based on free-will, Art. 100-1[25] of the CCP provides that the whole proceeding of examining the defendant shall be recorded without interruption in audio, and also, if necessary, in video. The effect of a violation is then provided for in Art. 100-1 para. 2. If there is an inconsistency between the content of the record and that of the audio or video record regarding the statements made by the defendant, any such portion of the statement shall not be used as evidence. Of course, if the criminal investigation authority informally talks to the defendant about the case and press for a confession of the crime prior to the "official" recording, the purposes of all these specific measures for the interrogation are rendered void and the safeguards can be circumvented.

2.1.2 Establishing Facts—Stages and Rules

The handing of a case in the Taiwanese criminal procedure can be divided into four stages: the police investigation stage, the prosecutor investigation stage, the court trial stage and, if a guilty verdict is rendered, the enforcement of a judgment.

The police and prosecutors' investigations are so called pre-trial investigations. According to the Taiwanese model, prosecutors are in charge of supervising the police, who do the main body of work during investigations.[26] After the police have finished their investigations, the case is handed over to the prosecution service. The competent prosecutor decides whether the requirements for an indictment are met or not. If a case is prosecuted, it will be referred to the court and, until this stage, the potential for evidence to be excluded plays a role. Generally, a criminal case is run by the normal three-tiered judicial system, i.e. prosecuted at a District Court in first instance, the High Court, and the Supreme Court. If a conviction is final, the prosecutor of the competent court shall perform the execution of the judgement.

Furthermore, due to the requirement for courts to seek the truth (see Art. 163 para. 2 of the CCP), people often state that, "judges are doing God's work." (法

[24]*See* Supreme Court decision 94 taishangzih No. 275 (最高法院 94 年度台上字第 275 號判決). The literature consistently stands for the decision, e.g. LIN Yu-Hsiung, 2013 (I) at 202; ZHU Shi-Yan, 2015 at 178.

[25]*See* Annex.

[26]*See* Art. 230 para. 1 of the CCP.

官在做神的工作).[27] Prior to amendments on February 8, 2002, Art. 163 of the CCP stipulated that due to the necessity of truth finding, courts "shall" *ex officio* investigate evidence. Although subsequently influenced by the adversarial system of US-American criminal procedure, the code still states "[t]he court may, for the purpose of discovering the truth, *ex officio* investigat[e] evidence" (Art. 163 para. 2 of the CCP). The stipulation that "for the purpose of maintaining justice or discovering facts that are critical to the interest of the defendant, the court shall ex officio investigate evidence" reflects the importance of fact-finding in Taiwan's criminal justice system.

2.1.3 Establishing Facts—Actors and Accountability

In Taiwan's CCP, during the stage of investigation the prosecutor is in charge of fact-finding. If a member of the prosecution does not fulfill the duty and eventually causes a wrongful sentence, the person will not be subject to a special procedure, but—in theory—faces a prosecution for "Abuse of Prosecution" ("濫權追訴罪"), according to Art. 125 of the Criminal Code of the Republic of China (CCRC).[28]

Defendants are considered to be a subject rather than an object of criminal procedure in the Taiwanese criminal justice system. Among other entitlements, defendants are protected by the presumption of innocence[29] and the privilege against self-incrimination (Art. 95 para. 1 CCP; Art. 14 para. 3 (g) of ICCPR).

Furthermore, defendants have a right to assistance by a defense attorney (see Arts. 27 and 34 of the CCP). A defense attorney, in theory, plays an important role in Taiwan's CCP and should, in a situation of equality of arms, make use of defense rights to safeguard the defendant's interests. In practice, however, compared to the power of the prosecution authorities, there still appears to be a lot of room for improvement to empower defense lawyers in Taiwan[30] if the goal is ultimately to reach an equality of arms.

---

[27]Supreme Court decision 104 taikangzih No. 766 (最高法院 104 年度台抗字第 766 號裁定): "the judge is also a person, not God, of course he inevitably does something wrong." (法官也是人, 不是神, 當然難免絕對無錯).

[28]*See* Annex. The text is available online at <http://law.moj.gov.tw/LawClass/LawContent.aspx?PCODE=C0000001>, officially translated as Criminal Code of the Republic of China of 1 January 1925 (Status as of 13 June 2018), available online at <http://law.moj.gov.tw/Eng/LawClass/LawContent.aspx?PCODE=C0000001>, accessed 21 November 2018.

[29]*See* Art. 154 para. 1 of the CCP.

[30]*See* WANG Jaw-Perng, 2011 at 15–18, especially at 17, who states: "Unfortunately, in some police stations, the accused's right to counsel means nothing more than the attorney may be present during interrogations. Even if the accused's attorney appears at the police station, some do not allow the attorney to speak with the accused. They sometimes ask the attorney to sit far behind the table at which they conduct interrogations. The major function of an attorney at the police station is not to consult the accused, but rather to watch for torture or other improper actions by the police."

2.2 *Social Relevance of Truth and Individual Rights in Criminal Trials*

2.2.1 Relevance of Determining the Truth

In criminal proceedings, striking a balance between the search for truth and the protection of civil liberties (particularly those of the defendant) has been a long-standing and difficult issue. From the perspective of the Taiwanese CCP, discovering the truth has always been an extremely important value. Fortunately, during the last decades, compliance with the legal requirements for obtaining evidence has generally improved in Taiwan, which could make for balance, at least on the surface; if a violation of such procedural requirements takes place, criminal defense attorneys today advocate for the exclusion of illegally evidence.[31] However, such pursuits by defense lawyers still occasionally draw public criticism, since the search for truth is held in much higher regard than the protection of individual rights (particularly those of the defendant).

Due to tradition, in the eyes of the public a confession by a defendant is still one of the most important proofs of guilt. Aside from very few exceptions, in practice, if a defendant confesses a crime, judges will not be open-minded, but handle proceedings with prejudice against the defendant. The existence of a confession directly affects how proceedings are conducted (such as whether to start a cross-examination or a more onerous investigation for evidence, etc.) and how they ought to be concluded (such as whether to proceed with plea bargaining procedures and quickly terminate legal proceedings).

2.2.2 Presentation of "Facts", "Fact-Finding" and/or "Truth" to the Public

Taiwan's public has considerable interest in criminal cases, which are featured in daily press and other media on a regular basis.

However, to ensure authenticity, while at the same time protecting the rights of the defendant and other stakeholders, Art. 245 para. 1 of the CCP[32] states that the investigation shall not be public. Para. 3 of that provision[33] makes further specifications. The provisions delineated in Art. 132 para. in CCRC provide the legal basis for the penal sanctioning of any investigators for willful or negligent

[31]WANG Jaw-Perng, 2011 at 19–21.

[32]*See* Annex.

[33]*See* Annex.

misconduct leading to the leaking of investigation secrets. Persons restricted from coming into contact with or having knowledge of investigation secrets include not only any members of the public, but also the defendants themselves as well as the legal representatives of the defendant. According to Art. 33 of the CCP, the preceding parties are prohibited from examining the investigation case files or exhibits and making copies or taking photographs of the investigation case files or exhibits.[34] The above applies regardless of whether the defendant has been placed under detention at the time of the investigation.[35]

Nevertheless, even when taking into account the strictness of the aforementioned rules on investigation conduct, and the understandable difficulties which lie in the preservation of investigation secrets due to media involvement, the majority of reported violations against Taiwanese prosecutors' offices are for misconduct resulting in the leakage of investigation secrets.[36] The reasons for such violations are generally divided into two categories: the first being the result of investigators catering to bureaucratic pressure. High-level political figures therefore gain favorable information. Investigators may also have better chances of promotion as a result of providing investigative secrets.[37]

The second category of violation is the leaking of investigation secrets by investigators for media exposure. These types of violations primarily occur due to the poor practice of evaluating the performance of investigators by the amount of media exposure their prosecuting cases receive. This tendency is especially evident in publicly witnessed cases, such as when the accused parties reveal their actions to the public, or voluntarily accept media attention. Due to the intense amount of attention given to publicly witnessed cases by the Taiwanese media, and the broadcasting of the confessions of the defendant (possibly through interviews by anonymous investigators or the media raises questions during the transfer of the defendant), public opinion on the guilt of the defendant is often formed without consideration of the due process of law (public judgment). Such public opinion often only recognizes subjective evidence, while disregarding objective evidence showing inconsistencies between motive and legality. Although the implementation of legal restrictions on the disclosure of evidence through confessions by accused parties through the media have yet been established, if the court holding a specific

[34]In practice, during the investigation process in Taiwan, considerations are made to ensure smooth proceedings or prosecution, resulting in the tipping off or leaking of investigation secrets to trial participants. To some extent, such an approach is necessary for finding the truth.

[35]Whether the restriction on the right of the defendant to view investigation case files or exhibits is unconstitutional, is currently being deliberated over by the Justices of the Constitutional Court of the Judicial Yuan.

[36]For example, Judicial Reform Foundation has set up a project on this, available online at <https://www.jrf.org.tw/articles/300>, accessed 21 November 2018.

[37]The Control Yuan has produced a review report, available online at <www.cy.gov.tw/dl.asp?fileName=011261063171.pdf>, accessed 21 November 2018.

trial finds the defendant not guilty based on evidence unrelated to the public confession of the defendant (see Art. 156 paras. 1, 2 of the CCP), then the court judgment naturally comes into conflict with the opinion of the public.

2.2.3 Public Discussion of Miscarriages of Justice

As in the case in Taiwan, high profile criminal cases are a focal point of front pages of newspapers and, ever increasingly, on social media. Even at the early stages of an investigation, sometimes even before prosecutors begin their investigation, criminal cases are the focus of public discussion and speculation. After a case is brought to court, all the way along to the stage of enforcing the judgment, the proceedings are repeatedly discussed in the media. In more conservative newspapers, the focus is mainly on the various cases that heavily influence the political situation or directly influence people's lives. In addition, new electronic newspapers and real-time news, which are not bound by space restrictions, keep a close eye on news of interesting cases and include information of various kinds relevant to the criminal case. Moreover, readers interactively comment, deepening the discussion on these criminal cases. Such information policy is two-edged: While it informs the public, albeit, once a specific atmosphere has been created (possibly helping to convincing the public that the defendant is guilty), it sometimes does not aid in finding the truth, but actually does the opposite.

Newly-emerged social media (such as Facebook, Line, Twitter, etc.) combined with the widespread use of smartphones and other electronic devices have drastically increased media coverage of criminal cases in terms of range, depth and speed. Due to the preference for text-based narration, the content quality of traditional media is substantially higher than that of electronic media. However, there are not many readers who like long in-depth reports. Fast-paced reading habits limit the ability to reflect deeply and decrease the desire to explore the truth. Also, the division between the opposing views of the social community reduces opportunities for exchange. The desire and possibility for dismissing preconceived ideas and exploring the truth is therefore also limited.

As for case decisions in criminal justice practice, there is relatively little discussion in the legal world on whether or not they are influenced, to a certain degree, by the media described above and little discussion on corresponding legal regulations. How to ensure that erroneous information among the many opinions does not influence judicial decisions and follows the principles of oral trial and direct trial, and ensure that the prosecutors and judges pass judgment, in accordance with the principles of law and evidence rather than deliberately following or opposing public opinion, is an important issue which needs to be urgently solved in Taiwan's current criminal justice system.

3 Limitations of Fact-Finding in Criminal Proceedings

As of 2015, Taiwan's CCP has more than thirty amendments. Evidence exclusion laws have also been modified over the years. Originally only one provision, Art. 156 para. 1 of the CCP,[38] aimed at preventing the coercion of confessions and this protected human rights. Later more provisions were adopted, like Arts. 158-2 and 158-4 of the CCP in 2003.[39] There is also specific law that may lead to the exclusion of evidence. For instance, Taiwan's "Communication Security and Surveillance Act" (CSSA: 通訊保障及監察法),[40] which may even be stricter than the evidence exclusionary laws of the CCP.[41]

Even before exclusionary rules were adopted in 2003, the Supreme Court had already made it clear that "if authorities in a criminal proceeding present wiretap transcripts as evidence, the transcripts shall be excluded if the wiretapping fails to meet the legal requirements and gravely breaches privacy and/or the freedom of correspondence as protected by Art. 12 of the CRC; in order to deter unlawful investigative methods, it would be inappropriate to use such information as evidence."[42] This decision is one of the rare cases in which a court discusses the admissibility of evidence; according to this decision the exclusion of evidence depends on a balance of the severity of the breach of legal rules when collecting the evidence and the probative value, with a proportionality test eventually deciding on the exclusion of such evidence.

This case law followed the adoption of a balancing approach in 1999, when the Supreme court held that "when deciding whether a piece of evidence that was collected illegally should be excluded, the court must first consider whether the admission of such evidence would jeopardize fairness and justice. A comprehensive assessment that includes consideration of the spirit of the Constitution, the severity of the violation of procedural rules and the damages caused by the crime shall determine whether such evidence must be excluded in order to conform with fairness and justice."[43] In 2003, the newly amended Art. 158-4 of the CCP followed the rationale of this case law, which sets the current legal framework for the exclusion of evidence.

---

[38]About the introduction for Art. 156 para. 1 of the CCP, *see below* 3.2.

[39]WANG Jaw-Perng, 2011 at 19–20.

[40]Available online at <http://law.moj.gov.tw/LawClass/LawAll.aspx?PCode=K0060044>, officially translated as The Communication Security and Surveillance Act of 14 July 1999 (Status as of 23 May 2018), available online at <http://law.moj.gov.tw/Eng/LawClass/LawContent.aspx?PCODE=K0060044>, accessed 21 November 2018.

[41]Art. 18-1 para. 3 of the CSSA.

[42]Supreme Court decision 87 taishangzih No. 4025 (最高法院 102 年度台上字第 3254 號判決). In that case, the telephone record was excluded.

[43]Supreme Court decision 88 taishangzih No. 233 (最高法院 88 年度台上字第 233 號判決).

3.1 General Rules of Evidence Taking (Admissibility of Evidence)

As has been pointed out above, all information relevant for fact-finding in a criminal case is admitted as evidence in a criminal trial in Taiwan. Nevertheless, the CCP also provides explicitly for the exclusion of evidence. An important feature of Taiwan's framework for the exclusion of evidence is thus its stipulation by a legal rule, rather than by case law.

Its origin lies with the Judicial Yuan (司法院)[44]: In 2003 the Judicial Yuan proposed a revision of the CCP to the Legislative Yuan (立法院).[45] The new law stipulates certain circumstances for mandatory exclusion of evidence obtained illegally, e.g. Art. 158-2 of the CCP. Furthermore, the law sets a general rule—Art. 158-4 of the CCP—for a case-by-case decision in certain situations, including when the evidence was "obtained in violation of the procedure prescribed by the law by an official in execution of criminal procedure", balancing human rights protection and public interest. These exclusionary rules were adopted in September 2003.

According to the current law, when the procedural rules are violated, two forms of evidence exclusion rules exist: Specific (obligatory) exclusionary rules (Arts. 156 para. 1, 158-2 of the CCP) and general (relative) exclusionary rules (Arts. 158-2, 158-4 of the CCP). The following is an introduction of the evidence exclusion rules of the CCP. It will be separated into these two parts.

3.1.1 Specific Exclusionary Rules of the CCP

This specific set of rules, Arts. 156 para. 1, 158-2 of the CCP, focuses on oral testimony. It needs special regulation, because the admissibility of oral testimony depends on the voluntariness of the person giving the testimony. The voluntariness of giving such evidence may be often questioned because of certain coercive measures, especially if there is a violation of the investigative procedure. As a result, to promote procedural justice, the CCP mandates that oral testimony

---

[44]The Judicial Yuan is one of the five branches of government in the Republic of China as stipulated by the Constitution of the Republic of China. The Judicial Yuan is vested with the power of interpretation, adjudication, discipline, and judicial administration; more information available online at <http://www.judicial.gov.tw/aboutus/aboutus00/english.pdf>, accessed 21 November 2018.

[45]The Executive Yuan is the executive branch of the government in Taiwan, headed by the premier. The premier is directly appointed by the president, while other members of the Executive Yuan Council, or Cabinet are appointed by the President of the Republic upon the recommendation of the Premier. In addition to supervising the subordinate organs of the Executive Yuan, the Premier explains administrative policies and reports to the Legislative Yuan (Legislature) and responds to the interpellations of legislators; more information available online at <http://english.ey.gov.tw/cp.aspx?n=0B5424E21E6FF0A5>, accessed 1 November 2018.

evidence collected by methods that amount to grave breaches of investigative procedure will be considered to lack voluntariness and thus lead to obligatory exclusion.[46]

3.1.1.1 Confessions Collected During Specific Periods of Time Mandated by Law or at Night (Art. 158-2 Para. 1 of the CCP)

The lawmaker appears to especially mistrust confessions obtained during the night or while a defendant is in jail. It is against this backdrop that one must read the different provisions regulating the exclusion of confessions, especially specific constitutional law and the key provision of the CCP: Art. 158-2.

According to Art. 8 para. 2 of the Constitution of the Republic of China (CRC),[47] when a person is arrested or detained on suspicion of having committed a crime, the organ making the arrest or detention shall, within 24 h, turn him over to a competent court for trial. The 24 h limitation refers to the actual time that can be used for investigation. Art. 93-1 of the CCP[48] provides reasons of delay that shall not be counted in the 24 h time limitation. These reasons include: the time used for transferring the defendant, the time used to wait for bonds to be presented or for the acceptance of custody, the time when being examined by the court, unavoidable delay caused by traffic or force majeure, examination not being possible due to health related emergency suffered by the defendant, the examination not going ahead due to no defense attorney, an assisting person authorized by law or an interpreter being present. To respect human rights and to ensure the legality of these procedures, there shall be no examination or interrogation conducted should these circumstances prevail and at night. Otherwise the testimony collected is, in principle, inadmissible.

The key provision is Art. 158-2 para. 1 of the CCP. This provision, however, allows for exceptions which are combined with the good-faith-doctrine[49] and voluntary doctrine, according to Art. 158-2 para. 1: "provided that a lack of bad faith in such violations and the voluntariness of the confession or statement has been proven, the preceding section shall not apply."

Applying Art. 158-2 para. 1 of the CCP, the Supreme Court held that unless a defendant consents (according to Art. 100-3 para. 1 of the CCP[50]), no interrogation may take place at night. The burden to prove an exception is on the

---

[46] *See* LIN Yu-Hsiung, 2013 (I) at 190–91.

[47] *See* Annex.

[48] *See* Annex.

[49] *See* references to the (US-American) good-faith-doctrine exception *United States* v. *Leon*, 468 US 897 (1984). *See* ZHU Shi-Yan, 2015 at 161.

[50] It states that the interrogation of a defendant by police shall, in principle, not proceed at night; exceptions are (1) express consent by the person being interrogated, (2) identity check of the person arrested with or without a warrant at night, (3) permission by a public prosecutor or judge, or (4) in case of emergency, see Annex.

prosecutor.[51] However, only if night-time interrogation amounts to coercion prohibited by Art. 156 para. 1 of the CCP[52] is the oral testimony inadmissible, regardless of whether consent has been acquired.[53]

3.1.1.2 Right to Remain Silent and Access to a Defense Attorney (Art. 158-2 Para. 2 of the CCP)

Taiwanese law grants the defendant the right to remain silent and the right to have a defense lawyer.

Authorities must inform the defendant of his or her rights: Art. 95 para. 1 cll. 2 and 3 of the CCP provides for the duty to inform the defendant, among other things, about the right to remain silent and the right to access a defense attorney. This rule is important because the defendant may not be familiar with his legal rights or how to exercise his rights. In order to ensure that police officers and other investigative officials follow the rule, Art. 158-2 para. 2 of the CCP provides that the oral testimony acquired without complying with the duty to inform is inadmissible.[54] However, the good-faith-doctrine and voluntary doctrine[55] applies here also.[56]

The fact that the Taiwanese judiciary will not tolerate violations of the duty to caution a defendant also becomes clear when looking at the interpretation of Art. 158-2 para. 2 of the CCP: The Supreme Court held that after an arrest, the suspect must be read his rights by police, irrespective of whether a subsequent questioning takes place in form of a (formal) interrogation or an informal chat. Only such an interpretation of Art. 158-2 para. 2 of the CCP is in conformity with the spirit of Art. 9 cl. 2 of the International Covenant on Civil and Political Rights.[57]

3.1.2 Specific Exclusionary Rules of the Communication Security and Surveillance Act

Specific rules also apply when investigations take place in secret:

Art. 18-1 of the Communication Security and Surveillance Act (CSSA: 通訊保障及監察法) provides that any content acquired through communications surveillance enforced in accordance with Arts. 5, 6 or 7, or any evidence derived

[51]Supreme Court decision 100 taishangzih No. 4577 (最高法院 100 年度台上字第 4577 號判決).

[52]The introduction for Art. 156 para. 1 of the CCP, *see below* 3.2.

[53]Supreme Court decision 98 taishangzih No. 6024 (最高法院 98 年度台上字第 6024 號判決).

[54]E.g. Supreme Court decision 104 taishangzih No. 3936 (最高法院 104 年度台上字第 3936 號判決).

[55]*Above* 3.1.1.1.

[56]Supreme Court decision 100 taishangzih No. 4163 (最高法院 100 年度台上字第 4163 號判決).

[57]Supreme Court decision 99 taishangzih No. 1893 (最高法院 99 年度台上字第 1893 號判決).

from such surveillance that is not related to the purpose of the surveillance, shall not be used as evidence or for any other purpose in any judicial investigation, judgment or other proceeding.

Before January 2014, Arts. 5 and 6 of the CSSA adopted a relative exclusionary model,[58] the law provided that if the surveillance amounts to a grave breach of the rules, the acquired content and the derived evidence shall not be admitted as evidence. According to these rules, the Supreme Court ruled that if a state official responsible for a criminal investigation fails to acquire an interceptive warrant, then the conduct is not only an arbitrary misconduct that violates the "warrant requirement" of the law, but is also a severe infringement of people's freedom of private communications and privacy. The admissibility of the content acquired shall be decided according to the Communication Security and Surveillance Act.[59] However, following the amendment of Art. 18-1 in the CSSA in January 2014, the law now mandates that the acquired content shall not be admissible if the surveillance was conducted illegally or if the content is not related to the purpose of the surveillance. The new law adopts an obligatory exclusionary model.[60]

This specific exclusionary rule thus does not only prevent the use of information that was acquired illegally, but also excludes information subsequently obtained, based on tainted evidence. It is noteworthy that this provision is the only law that recognizes a fruit of poisonous tree doctrine in Taiwan's criminal justice system. The CCP does not acknowledge such a rule for other violations of procedural rules, nor did courts elsewhere recognize such a doctrine in the past. The Supreme Court once ruled that "when officials in execution of criminal procedure collect evidence illegally and use that piece of evidence to acquire derived evidence, irrespective of the causal relationship of the original evidence and the derived evidence, as long as the derived evidence is acquired lawfully and the investigation process is independent from the previous action, it shall not be excluded by the CCP. However, if the procedure of the previous unlawful evidence collection is not independent from the subsequent evidence collection and the previous evidence contaminated the investigation and collection of the derived evidence, only then may the court apply the evidence exclusionary rules from the CCP to exclude the derived evidence."[61]

3.1.3 General Exclusionary Rules of the CCP

Besides specific exclusionary rules explained in the previous paragraphs, Taiwanese law provides a general rule, Art. 158-4 of the CCP. This article provides

---

[58]According to the current law, when the procedural rules are violated, two forms of evidence exclusionary rules exist: obligatory exclusionary rules and relative exclusionary rules. *See above* 3.1.

[59]Supreme Court decision 98 taishangzih No. 1495 (最高法院 98 年度台上字第 1495 號判決).

[60]ZHU Shi-Yan, 2015 at 158.

[61]Supreme Court decision 102 taishangzih No. 3254 (最高法院 102 年度台上字第 3254 號判決).

that "the admissibility of the evidence obtained in violation of the procedure prescribed by the law by an official in execution of criminal procedure shall be determined by balancing the protection of human rights and the preservation of public interests, unless otherwise provided by law."

This article provides that, except for the obligatory exclusion rules, the admissibility of other unlawfully collected evidence shall be determined on a case-by-case basis, by balancing human rights protection and public the interest. The court shall consider things such as due process of law, right to a fair trial, the integrity of the judicial system and proportionality. The goal is to reach a balancing point between human rights and protection of the public interest, two seemingly contradictory ideas. The legislative note provided a list of factors that should be taken into account of the balancing test[62]: (a) The circumstances of the violation of the procedure prescribed by the law take into account whether there were difficulties in collecting evidence lawfully; (b) The subjective intentions of the official, i.e. whether the official knows his conduct is unlawful; (c) The nature and the severity of the right that was infringed, i.e. the circumstances of the infringement; (d) The risk and harm of the crime, i.e. the nature of the crime and its circumstances; (e) The deterrence effect of excluding such evidence; (f) Whether it is unavoidable that officials will discover such evidence using the procedure prescribed by law (the standard may be relaxed if such evidence can be acquired through normal proceedings); (g) The effect the unlawful evidence has on the defense of the defendant. In sum, the law authorizes the court to have discretion according to the specific circumstances of the case.[63]

After the enactment of Art. 158-4 of the CCP, the Supreme Court re-emphasized the legislative note through a precedent. The Court ruled in Supreme Court precedent 93[64] that "referring to evidence collected by unlawful search, in order to take into account of both procedural justice and the obligation to seek the truth, courts shall decide objectively on the protection of human rights and the preservation of social security on a case-by-case basis, and in accordance with proportionality and the interest balancing principle." The Court also provided guidance regarding the factors to be considered. These factors are generally the same as the factors in the legislative note, except "the circumstances of the violation of the procedure prescribed by the law" was replaced by the "severity of the violation of the procedure prescribed by the law" and "the conditions of the violation of the procedure prescribed by the law when it happened."

---

[62]"人權保障及公共利益之均衡維護, 如何求其平衡, 因各國國情不同, 學說亦是理論紛歧, 依實務所見, 一般而言, 違背法定程序取得證據之情形, 常因個案之型態、情節、方法而有差異, 法官於個案權衡時, 允宜斟酌 (1) 違背法定程序之情節。(2) 違背法定程序時之主觀意圖。(3) 侵害犯罪嫌疑人或被告權益之種類及輕重。(4) 犯罪所生之危險或實害。(5) 禁止使用證據對於預防將來違法取得證據之效果。(6) 偵審人員如依法定程序有無發現該證據之必然性及 (7) 證據取得之違法對被告訴訟上防禦不利益之程度等各種情形, 以爲認定證據能力有無之標準, 俾能兼顧理論與實際, 而應需要。".

[63]LIN Yu-Hsiung, 2013 (I) at 616–17; ZHU Shi-Yan, 2015 at 166–67.

[64]Supreme Court decision 93 taishangzih No. 664 (最高法院 93 年台上字第 664 號判例).

3.2 *Exclusion of Evidence Obtained by Torture and Undue Coercion*

The information obtained by applying torture or coercing the defendant is to be mandatorily excluded and is, accordingly, inadmissible as evidence in criminal trials in Taiwan (see Art. 156 para. 1 of the CCP).

3.2.1 Definitions of Torture, Undue Coercion and Degrading Punishment

The Taiwanese criminal justice system clearly rejects torture (see. Art. 98 of the CCP, Art. 125 of the CCRC). However, one cannot find a clear-cut definition of torture or undue coercion in the CCP or in the Criminal Code of the Republic of China. Art. 8 of the Constitution of the Republic of China does enshrine personal liberty as being one of the most fundamental rights against undue physical harm or improper detention. However, the wording of the Constitution article is extremely concise.

At the level of legislation, Art. 125 para. 1 cl. 2 of the CCRC threatens investigators with criminal punishment in the case of torture.[65] The corresponding statute provision on this issue in the CCP is Art. 98.[66]

3.2.2 Definitions of Right to Remain Silent/Privilege Against Self-incrimination

The CCP expressly accords the defendant the right to silence and the privilege against self-incrimination in Art. 95 para. 1 cl. 2.[67]

On 22 April 2009, the Legislature in Taiwan adopted the "Act to Implement the International Covenant on Civil and Political Rights and the International Covenant on Economic, Social and Cultural Rights".[68] The law came into effect on 10 December (Human Rights Day) the same year. Art. 2 of this Act stipulates: "Human rights protection provisions in the two Covenants have domestic legal status".[69] The ICCPR became part of national law in Taiwan from as of that day.[70]

---

[65] *See* Annex.

[66] *See* Annex.

[67] *See* Annex.

[68] 公民與政治權利國際公約及經濟社會文化權利國際公約施行法. The text is available online at <http://law.moj.gov.tw/Law/LawSearchResult.aspx?p=A&k1=%E5%85%AC%E7%B4%84%E6%96%BD%E8%A1%8C%E6%B3%95&t=E1F1A1&TPage=1>, official English translation at <http://law.moj.gov.tw/Eng/LawClass/LawContent.aspx?PCODE=I0020028>, accessed 21 November 2018.

[69] "兩公約所揭示保障人權之規定, 具有國內法律之效力".

[70] For more information, *see below* 3.2.7.

3.2.3 Exclusionary Rules for Evidence (Possibly) Obtained by Torture and Undue Coercion

As in most criminal justice systems, Taiwan has special rules for evidence obtained by torture or undue coercion.

3.2.3.1 Legal Framework

Art. 156 para. 1 of the CCP was introduced for the purpose of assuring the applicability of the aforementioned Art. 98 of the CCP.[71] The word "violence" refers to Art. 98 of the CCP and can be interpreted as "torture" in a general sense[72]; the other five items provided as examples of improper means of extracting incriminating statements are seen as undue coercion.[73]

3.2.3.2 Practice; (High Court) Jurisprudence

The law excluding involuntary statements made by the defendant has basically been set by the Taiwanese judiciary—including district courts, high courts and the Supreme Court. The legal reasoning of Taiwanese courts is generally extremely short and simple, maybe due to the tradition of conciseness in Chinese literature. But in some cases the Supreme Court explained specific issues more detailed. Following are three explanations given for a possible exclusion of evidence. This reasoning also highlights the rationale behind exclusionary rules—from the point of view of the courts.

Protecting Human Dignity of the Defendant and His Status as a Party

The judgment refers to the safeguarding of the human dignity of the defendant and his status as a party to the trial proceedings as the rationale for the exclusion of confessions retrieved from an interrogation that lasted too long and become oppressive to the interrogated person. Accordingly, such a confession is absolutely inadmissible without exception and subject to no discretion by the trial court.[74]

---

[71] *See* Annex.

[72] ZHU Shi-Yan, 2015 at 175.

[73] LIN Yu-Hsiung, 2013 (I) at 191.

[74] Supreme Court decision 104 taishangzih No. 3052 (最高法院 104 年度台上字第 3052 號判決).

Safeguarding the Liberty of Decision Making and Mental Activities of the Defendant

In an extraordinary appeal[75] case, the Supreme Court held: "The combination of Art. 98 and Art. 156 para. 1 of the CCP constitutes a complete exclusionary rule on involuntary confession. With this ruling the court aims to secure the voluntariness of statements, liberty of decision making and mental activities of the defendant."[76]

Deterrence from Illegal Investigatory Activity Based on the Principle of the Due Process of Law

The Supreme Court expressed in another case involving illegal search activities that exclusionary rules are based on constitutional requirements and are intended to have a deterrent effect: By excluding evidence illegally obtained by law-enforcement agencies due process will be upheld and the police will be deterred from illegal activities in collecting evidence.[77] This explanation can be seen as a general statement, an effort to underpin the application of all exclusionary rules (not only those related to illegal searches).

3.2.4 Institutional Arrangements Securing the Ban on Torture Undue Coercion

The Supreme Court confirmed the Art. 156 para. 3 of the CCP[78] requirement that demands a prioritized investigation while citing an earlier case: "As long as the defendant claims his previous confession was made involuntarily, the court should investigate this claim before other matters. The court should instruct the prosecutor to introduce the means by which the defendant gave his confession and that this was voluntary. The means for establishing the voluntariness may include an audio-record of video-record of, or witness to the whole proceeding of the interrogation in question."[79] In addition, "if the defendant's confession of the offense was extracted by violence, threat, inducement, fraud, exhausting interrogation, unlawful detention or other improper means, the law-enforcement officers are likely to bear administrative or

[75]The extraordinary appeal, according to Chapter VI of the CCP, is a special relief litigation procedure filed with the Supreme Court by the Prosecutor General of the Supreme Prosecutors Office for a conclusive criminal judgment on the grounds that the judgment in question was made contrary to the law. Thus the object of an extraordinary appeal is to obtain a conclusive criminal judgment or an arbitral award which has substantially the same effect as a sentence of inflicting punishment, provided that the judgment or litigation procedure is against the law. More information available online at the homepage of the Supreme Prosecutors Office <http://www.tps.moj.gov.tw/ct.asp?xItem=31768&CtNode=12112&mp=096>, accessed 21 November 2018.

[76]Supreme Court decision 104 taifeizih No. 212 (最高法院 104 年度台非字第 212 號判決).

[77]Supreme Court decision 99 taishangzih No. 3168 (最高法院 99 年度台上字第 3168 號判決).

[78]*See above* 2.1.1.3.

[79]Supreme Court decision 91 taishangzih No. 2908 (最高法院 91 年度台上字第 2908 號判決).

criminal liability. Under such circumstances, one cannot reasonably expect the officers in charge to tell the truth while taking the stand as a witness. Thus when the defendant raised a claim alleging that his confession was extracted involuntarily, the court should have undertaken an in-depth investigation into such claims. It is not supposed to dismiss the defendant's claim only on the ground that the officers responsible for the interrogation testified that the confession had been given voluntarily."[80]

3.2.5 Exclusion of Evidence or Other Remedies Following a Breach of the Ban on Torture and Undue Coercion

Apart from the exclusion of the improperly obtained evidence,[81] the victims of torture or similar improper means of investigation which violate Art. 98 of the CCP[82] are entitled to financial compensation for the injury or damage they suffered or the loss of freedom caused accordingly, following the State Compensation Law (國家賠償法[83]) or the Law of Compensation for Wrongful Detentions and Executions (刑事補償法[84]). The policemen, investigators, or prosecutors who are liable for such wrongdoing may be prosecuted. They may be sued—also by the State—and asked to reimburse the payment already made by the Government to the victim. In addition, the liable law-enforcement officers and/or prosecutors may also face administrative disciplinary measures.

3.2.6 Admissibility of Indirect Evidence ("Fruits of Poisonous Tree") in Cases of Torture and Undue Coercion

3.2.6.1 Legal Framework

As pointed out at the beginning of this paper, both the Taiwanese courts and public attach great importance to coherent fact-finding: The search for the truth is important. Therefore, one finds only few exclusionary rules and one cannot or will not find a statutory rule acknowledging the fruit of poisonous tree doctrine and generally banning the admission of evidence deriving from tainted evidence, for instance, an involuntary confession or an illegal search without warrant. However,

---

[80]Supreme Court decision 100 taishangzih No. 4430 (最高法院 100 年度台上字第 4430 號判決).

[81]*See above* 3.2.1.

[82]With reference to Art. 98 of the CCP, *see above* 3.2.1 and 3.2.3.1.

[83]Officially translated as State Compensation Law of 2 July 1980 (Status as of 2 July 1980), available online at <http://law.moj.gov.tw/Eng/LawClass/LawContent.aspx?PCODE=I0020004>, accessed 21 November 2018.

[84]Officially translated as Law of Compensation for Wrongful Detentions and Executions of 11 June 1959 (Status as of 11 July 2007), available online at <http://law.moj.gov.tw/Eng/LawClass/LawContent.aspx?PCODE=C0010009>, accessed 21 November 2018.

Art. 18-1 of the Communication Security and Surveillance Act provide for exclusion of evidence if a secret surveillance investigation gravely violated procedural rules. Then neither the information gained nor any "derived evidence" shall be admitted in court. The parliament adopted this statute after it had been victim to a bugging scandal.[85]

3.2.6.2 Practice; (High Court) Jurisprudence

Based on a principle of judicial interest balance that underlines Art. 158-4 of the CCP, the Supreme Court adopted a discretionary exclusionary standard for dealing with the evidence generally known as the fruit of poisonous tree doctrine. Thus is held that "unlike the American practice that excludes tainted evidence derived from previous illegally obtained evidence, a different approach is taken in this country. Namely, while the secondary evidence derived from the previous improperly obtained evidence should be excluded, the evidence acquired by an independent legitimate investigation shall not be suppressed."[86] It appears that, as the Court tried hard to draw a distinction from the American fruit of poisonous tree doctrine, the previous ruling in fact makes differs little from the local ruling because the American fruit of poisonous tree doctrine also bears certain exceptions and renders itself far from a mandatory rule of exclusion.

3.2.7 Effect of International Human Rights

International human rights do have an impact on the Taiwanese criminal justice system, especially when exclusionary rules are applied:

For instance, when weighing the "defendant's rights" and the "public interest in criminal prosecution" (Art. 158-4 of the CCP), the protection of human rights by international human rights covenants should also be taken into consideration, especially the "International Covenant on Civil and Political Rights" (ICCPR).[87] For geopolitical reasons, Taiwan is no longer a member of the United Nations (UN), it has, however, adopted the ICCPR, although it could not deposit the documents accordingly with the UN. In order to demonstrate its conformity with international human rights, Taiwan passed the "Act to Implement the International Covenant on Civil and Political Rights and the International Covenant on Economic, Social and Cultural Rights" in 2009. Art. 2 of this instrument states that "[h]uman rights protection provisions in the two Covenants have domestic legal status". The ICCPR has become the human rights law that Taiwan's prosecution personnel must respect,

---

[85]YANG Yun-Hua, 2014–7 at 3–4.

[86]Supreme Court decision 102 taishangzih No. 4177 (最高法院 102 年度台上字第 4177 號判決).

[87]LIN Yu-Hsiung, 2013 (I) at 25–26; ZHU Shi-Yan, 2015 at 645.

especially the fair trial-clause in Art. 14 of the ICCPR. Thus in when deciding on possible exclusion of evidence, the authorities (i.e. all levels of governmental institutions and agencies)[88] have to consider these international human rights. Taiwan is no longer confined to its original provisions on human rights.[89]

Despite Taiwan's solitude in a geopolitical and diplomatic context, the national laws and legislation have been heavily influenced by the most well-known international instruments on human rights, such as United States Declaration of Independence, the Declaration of Human Rights of the French Revolution, the ICCPR adopted by the United Nations General Assembly, and the European Convention for the Protection of Human Rights and Fundamental Freedoms. They can often be found in the prologues, grounds and justifications of relative laws, and the Judicial Yuan Interpretations (JYI: 司法院大法官解釋).[90]

4 Statistics

Empirical research on crime and statistical criminal information have both always been neglected areas in Taiwanese criminal law. These are not only relevant topics for academic research or studies of interest; even the judicial statistics of the authorities[91] and statistical reports created by the Judicial Yuan[92] put special emphasis on items such as the number of criminal cases received and finalized. Therefore, exclusion of evidence or evidence material are both lacking as specific research topics or statistical items.

The contents of Taiwanese criminal judgments (not including prosecution investigation documents, such as indictments or non-prosecutorial dispositions), apart from specific documents prohibited from disclosure, can in principle be found on the Judicial Yuan's Law and Regulations Retrieving System[93] or private judicial databases such as Lex Data.[94] Using the words "exclusion of evidence" (including "not to be used as evidence", but also eliminated especially because of the hearsay principle) as a query, there are many results. If we just take the Supreme Court as an example, there are already more than three thousand query results. In District

---

[88]*See* Art. 4 of the Act to Implement the International Covenant on Civil and Political Rights and the International Covenant on Economic, Social and Cultural Rights.

[89]LIN Yu-Hsiung, 2013 (I) at 26.

[90]E.g. Interpretation Nos. 392 (The "court" provided in Article 8 of the Constitution does not include the "prosecutor's office", hence not empower the prosecutor to detain a person beyond the 24-h period as authorized by said Article for the court.), 582 (the relevant precedents holding that a statement made by a criminal co-defendant against another co-defendant may be admissible are unconstitutional.).

[91]<https://www.moj.gov.tw/mp-001.html>, accessed 21 November 2018.

[92]<http://www.judicial.gov.tw>, accessed 21 November 2018.

[93]<http://jirs.judicial.gov.tw/Index.htm>, accessed 21 November 2018.

[94]<http://fyjud.lawbank.com.tw/index.aspx>, accessed 21 November 2018.

Courts, there are a number of times more. Therefore, more detailed and accurate proof and statistical information of evidence exclusion can only be found if exclusion of evidence becomes a subject for empirical research or research projects. Only when criminal judgments are extensively collected, analyzed, concluded and dealt with can there be a way.

After the adoption of evidence rules, the Supreme Court frequently discussed issues arising from the difficult question of when evidence should actually be excluded in a specific case. This is an indicator of the importance attached to these rules. According to standing case law the admissibility of evidence shall be decided on the basis of factors including due process of law, the integrity of the judicial system and the deterrence effect for unlawful collection of evidence. Ultimately the exclusion of illegally obtained evidence is decided case-by-case, based on a balancing test, albeit a "relative exclusionary model". Only if the law explicitly mandates the exclusion of evidence, there is no space for balancing. A search of the Judicial Yuan's decision database gives the following result: From February 2003, when Art. 158-4 of the CCP was enacted until December 2015, the Supreme Court assessed 258 cases on possible exclusion of evidence using the balancing test. Among these cases, 155 cases were remanded because the lower court had failed to apply the balancing test in its decision. A total of 103 cases were upheld and in 95 cases the Court held that the evidence at stake was admissible and in only in 8 cases it opted for inadmissibility.

5 Conclusion

The Taiwanese criminal justice system is still struggling to find the appropriate balance between truth finding and protection of individual rights when investigating crime and prosecuting a case. On the one hand, in order to find substantive truth, all relevant evidence appears to be needed, even if it is obtained as a result of the investigating authorities infringing human rights. On the other hand, not only the people, but also the government is bound by law and thus the rule of law is a principle to be followed by all official authorities. Each country handles this issue differently. The Taiwanese CCP provides defendants with various entitlements, including the right to counsel, the right to information, the right to an audio/video recording of any interrogation, the right to remain silent and exclusionary rules ensuring that the relevant individual rights in the criminal process are protected. Whether or, rather, how these rights are granted in practice is yet another question, as is the question of what remedies an individual has in cases of violation of these rights.

The CCP's exclusionary rules, adopted in 2003, were meant to safeguard the rule of law and judicial integrity. The lawmaker acted in the firm belief that an exclusion of evidence obtained through torture, undue coercion or other misconduct of the authorities will send a message—to the public and investigating authorities alike—that courts will condemn any lawless acts.

Today, the Taiwanese CCP adopts a multitrack approach to the exclusion of evidence. In some cases, for example, the information obtained by applying torture or undue coercion to a defendant is to be mandatorily excluded and thus inadmissible as evidence in criminal trials (Art. 156 para. 1 of the CCP). In some other cases, the court is to balance the interest in finding truth and individual rights. The catch-all clause is prescribed in Art. 158-4 of the CCP to allow the court to exclude evidence illegally obtained after considerations.

More than a decade after adopting exclusionary rules as part of the procedural law it appears that the rules are still a work in progress and pose, in fact, a challenge to the various stakeholders in the criminal justice system. It seems to be too early to decide whether exclusionary rules have proven to be effective tools in safeguarding human rights, while at the same time securing the search for the truth in a criminal case.

I. Code of Criminal Procedure (CCP: 刑事訴訟法)

Chinese	English
第 2 條第 1 項 實施刑事訴訟程序之公務員, 就該管案件, 應於被告有利及不利之情形, 一律注意。	Art. 2 para. 1 A public official who conducts proceedings in a criminal case shall give equal attention to circumstances both favorable and unfavorable to an accused
第 27 條 I. 被告得隨時選任辯護人。犯罪嫌疑人受司法警察官或司法警察調查者, 亦同。 II. 被告或犯罪嫌疑人之法定代理人、配偶、直系或三親等內旁系血親或家長、家屬, 得獨立爲被告或犯罪嫌疑人選任辯護人。 III. 被告或犯罪嫌疑人因精神障礙或其他心智缺陷無法爲完全之陳述者, 應通知前項之人得爲被告或犯罪嫌疑人選任辯護人。但不能通知者, 不在此限。	Art. 27 I. An accused may at any time retain defense attorneys. The same rule shall apply to a suspect being interrogated by judicial police officers or judicial policemen II. A statutory agent, spouse, lineal blood relative, collateral blood relative within the third degree of kinship, family head, or family member may independently retain defense attorneys for the accused or suspect III. In case an accused or a suspect is unable to make a complete statement due to unsound mind, the persons listed in the preceding section shall be notified of the same, provided that the said notification is not required if it can not be made practically
第 34 條第 1 項 辯護人得接見羈押之被告, 並互通書信。非有事證足認其有湮滅、偽造、變造證據或勾串共犯或證人者, 不得限制之。	Art. 34 para. 1 A defense attorney may interview and correspond with a suspect or an accused under detention, provided that if facts exist sufficient to justify an apprehension that such defense attorney may destroy, fabricate, or alter evidence or form a conspiracy with a co-offender or witness, such interviews or correspondence may be limited

(continued)

(continued)

Chinese	English
第 35 條 被告或犯罪嫌疑人因精神障礙或其他心智缺陷無法爲完全之陳述者，應有第一項得爲輔佐人之人或其委任之人或主管機關、相關社福機構指派之社工人員或其他專業人員爲輔佐人陪同在場。但經合法通知無正當理由不到場者，不在此限。	Art. 35 In cases an accused or a suspect is unable to make a complete statement due to unsound mind, he shall be accompanied by one of the qualified assistant, under the first section of this article, or his authorized agent, or a social worker appointed by a governmental agency in charge thereof; provided that if, upon being properly served, the persons who shall accompany the accused or suspect fail to appear without good reason, the provision of this section shall not apply
第 91 條 I. 第 91 條及前條第 2 項所定之 24 小時，有下列情形之一者，其經過之時間不予計入。但不得有不必要之遲延: 一、因交通障礙或其他不可抗力事由所生不得已之遲滯。 二、在途解送時間。 三、依第 100 條之 3 第 1 項規定不得爲詢問者。 四、因被告或犯罪嫌疑人身體健康突發之事由，事實上不能訊問者。 五、被告或犯罪嫌疑人因表示選任辯護人之意思，而等候辯護人到場致未予訊問者。但等候時間不得逾 4 小時。其等候第 31 條第5項律師到場致未予訊問或因精神障礙或其他心智缺陷無法爲完全之陳述，因等候第 35 條第 3 項經通知陪同在場之人到場致未予訊問者，亦同。 六、被告或犯罪嫌疑人須由通譯傳譯，因等候其通譯到場致未予訊問者。但等候時間不得逾 6 小時。 七、經檢察官命具保或責付之被告，在候保或候責付中者。但候保或候責付時間不得逾四小時。 八、犯罪嫌疑人經法院提審之期間。 II. 前項各款情形之經過時間內不得訊問。 III. 因第1項之法定障礙事由致 24 小時內無法移送該管法院者，檢察官聲請羈押時，並應釋明其事由。	Art. 91 I. Time spent in one of the following circumstances shall not be counted against the twenty-four hour limitation in Article 91 and the second section of the preceding article, provided that there is no unnecessary delay: (1) unavoidable delay caused by traffic obstruction or force majeure; (2) in the transfer of arrestee; (3) interrogation cannot be made according to the first section of Article 100-3; (4) examination cannot be made due to health emergency of the accused or suspect; (5) examination is not made because of waiting for the presence of a defense attorney when the accused or suspect has made the presentation that a defense attorney has been retained. The said waiting time allowed shall not exceed four hours. The same rule applies to the case while waiting for the presence of the persons named in the third section of Article 35 if the accused or the suspect is unable to make a clear and complete statement due to unsound mind; (6) examination is not made because of waiting for the presence of the interpreter if there is a need for having an interpreter for the accused or suspect, provided that the waiting time shall not exceed six hours; (7) if the public prosecutor orders the release of the arrestee on bail or to the custody of another, while waiting for bonds to be presented or for the acceptance of custody, provided that the waiting time allowed shall not exceed four hours; or

(continued)

(continued)

Chinese	English
	(8) the time when the suspect was examined by the court according to the Habeas Corpus Act II. No examination shall be made in the above period of time described in the preceding section III. If the accused cannot be sent to a court with jurisdiction within twenty-four hours due to the existence of one of the reasons specified in the first section of this article, the public prosecutor shall specify the reason in his application of detention order
第 95 條第 1 項 I. 訊問被告應先告知下列事項: 一、犯罪嫌疑及所犯所有罪名。罪名經告知後, 認爲應變更者, 應再告知。 二、得保持緘默, 無須違背自己之意思而爲陳述。 三、得選任辯護人。如爲低收入戶、中低收入戶、原住民或其他依法令得請求法律扶助者, 得請求之。 四、得請求調查有利之證據。	Art. 95 para. 1 I. In an examination, an accused shall be informed of the following: (1) that he is suspected of committing an offense and all of the offenses charged. If the charge is changed after an accused has been informed of the offense charged, he shall be informed of such change; (2) that he may remain silent and does not have to make a statement against his own will; (3) that he may retain defense attorney; and (4) that he may request the investigation of evidence favorable to him
第 98 條 訊問被告應出以懇切之態度, 不得用強暴、脅迫、利誘、詐欺、疲勞訊問或其他不正之方法。	Art. 98 Violence, threat, inducement, fraud, exhausting examination or other improper means may not be applied during the interrogation of the defendant
第 100 條之 1 第 1 項 訊問被告, 應全程連續錄音; 必要時, 並應全程連續錄影。但有急迫情況且經記明筆錄者, 不在此限。	Art. 100-1 para. 1 The whole proceeding of examining the accused shall be recorded without interruption in audio, and also, if necessary, in video, provided that in case of an emergency, after clearly stated in the record, the said rule may not be followed
第 100 條之 3 第 1 項 司法警察官或司法警察詢問犯罪嫌疑人, 不得於夜間行之。但有左列情形之一者, 不在此限: 一、經受詢問人明示同意者。 二、於夜間經拘提或逮捕到場而查驗其人有無錯誤者。 三、經檢察官或法官許可者。 四、有急迫之情形者。	Art. 100-3 para. 1 The interrogation of criminal suspects by judicial police officer or judicial policeman shall not proceed at night, except for the following circumstances: (1) express consent by the person being interrogated; (2) identity check of the person arrested with or without a warrant at night;

(continued)

(continued)

Chinese	English
	(3) permission by a public prosecutor or judge; or (4) in case of emergency
第 154 條第 1 項 被告未經審判證明有罪確定前, 推定其爲無罪。	Art. 154 para. 1 Prior to a final conviction through trial, an accused is presumed to be innocent
第 156 條第 1 項 被告之自白, 非出於強暴、脅迫、利誘、詐欺、疲勞訊問、違法羈押或其他不正之方法, 且與事實相符者, 得爲證據。	Art. 156 para. 1 Confession of an accused not extracted by violence, threat, inducement, fraud, exhausting interrogation, unlawful detention or other improper means and consistent with facts may be admitted as evidence
第 156 條第 3 項 被告陳述其自白係出於不正之方法者, 應先於其他事證而爲調查。該自白如係經檢察官提出者, 法院應命檢察官就自白之出於自由意志, 指出證明之方法。	Art. 156 para. 3 If the accused states that his confession was extracted by improper means, his confession shall be investigated prior to investigating other evidences; if the said confession is presented by the public prosecutor, the court shall order the public prosecutor to indicate the method to prove that the confession is obtained under the free will of the accused
第 158 條之 2 I. 違背第 93 條之 1 第 2 項、第 100 條之 3 第 1 項之規定, 所取得被告或犯罪嫌疑人之自白及其他不利之陳述, 不得作爲證據。但經證明其違背非出於惡意, 且該自白或陳述係出於自由意志者, 不在此限。 II. 檢察事務官、司法警察官或司法警察詢問受拘提、逮捕之被告或犯罪嫌疑人時, 違反第 95 第 2 款、第 3 款之規定者, 準用前項規定。	Art. 158-2 I. Any confession or other unfavorable statements obtained from the accused or suspect in violation of the provisions of section II of Article 93-1 or section I of Article 100-3 shall not be admitted as evidence, provided that if lack of bad faith in such violation and the voluntariness of the confession or statement has been proven, the preceding section shall not apply II. The provision of the preceding section shall apply mutatis mutandis to the case where the public prosecuting affairs official, judicial police officer, or judicial policeman violates the provisions of Items II and III of Article 95 in interrogating an accused or suspect arrested with or without a warrant
第 158 條之 4 除法律另有規定外, 實施刑事訴訟程序之公務員因違背法定程序取得之證據, 其有無證據能力之認定, 應審酌人權保障及公共利益之均衡維護。	Art. 158-4 The admissibility of the evidence, obtained in violation of the procedure prescribed by the law by an official in execution of criminal procedure, shall be determined by balancing the protection of human rights and the preservation of public interests, unless otherwise provided by law

(continued)

(continued)

Chinese	English
第 163 條第 2 項 法院爲發見真實，得依職權調查證據。但於公平正義之維護或對被告之利益有重大關係事項，法院應依職權調查之。	Art. 163 para. 2 The court may, for the purpose of discovering the truth, ex officio investigating evidence; in case for the purpose of maintaining justice or discovering facts that are critical to the interest of the accused, the court shall ex officio investigate evidence
第 228 條第 1 項 檢察官因告訴、告發、自首或其他情事知有犯罪嫌疑者，應即開始偵查。	Art. 228 para. 1 If a public prosecutor, because of complaint, report, voluntary surrender, or other reason, knows there is a suspicion of an offense having been committed, he shall immediately begin an investigation
第 230 條第 2 項 前項司法警察官知有犯罪嫌疑者，應即開始調查，並將調查之情形報告該管檢察官及前條之司法警察官。	Art. 230 para. 2 The judicial police officer specified in the preceding section who suspects that an offense has been committed shall initiate an investigation immediately and report the results thereof to the competent public prosecutor and the judicial police officer referred to in the preceding article
第 231條第 2 項 司法警察知有犯罪嫌疑者，應即開始調查，並將調查之情形報告該管檢察官及司法警察官。	Art. 231 para. 2 A judicial policeman who suspects that an offense has been committed shall initiate an investigation immediately and report the results thereof to the competent public prosecutor and judicial police officer
第 245 條第 1 項 偵查，不公開之。	Art. 245 para. 1 An investigation shall not be public
第 245 條第 3 項 檢察官、檢察事務官、司法警察官、司法警察、辯護人、告訴代理人或其他於偵查程序依法執行職務之人員，除依法令或爲維護公共利益或保護合法權益有必要者外，偵查中因執行職務知悉之事項，員 敬啓 不得公開或揭露予執行法定職務必要範圍以外之人員	Art. 245 para. 3 The public prosecutor, public prosecution affairs official, judicial police officer or any other person performing their legally mandated duty during an investigation shall not in any way disclose the information acquired in their conduct of the investigation, unless otherwise permitted by law, or if necessary for the protection of public or legal interests

II. Criminal Code (CCRC: 刑法)

Chinese	English
第 57 條第 10 款	Art. 57 clause 10 Sentencing shall base on the liability of the offender and take into account all the

(continued)

(continued)

Chinese	English
科刑時應以行爲人之責任爲基礎, 並審酌一切情狀, 尤應注意下列事項, 爲科刑輕重之標準: 十、犯罪後之態度。	circumstances, and special attention shall be given to the following items: (10) The offender's attitude after committing the offense
第 125 條第1項 有追訴或處罰犯罪職務之公務員, 爲左列行爲之一者, 處一年以上七年以下有期徒刑: 一、濫用職權爲逮捕或羈押者。 二、意圖取供而施強暴脅迫者。 三、明知爲無罪之人, 而使其受追訴或處罰, 或明知爲有罪之人, 而無故不使其受追訴或處罰者。	Art. 125 para. 1 A public official charged with the duty of investigation or bringing offenders to justice who commits one of the following offenses shall be sentenced to imprisonment for not less than one year but not more than seven years: (1) Abusing his authority in arresting or detaining a person (2) Using threat or violence with purpose to extract confession (3) Knowingly causing an innocent person to be prosecuted or punished or causing a guilty person not be prosecuted or punished

III. Constitution (CRC: 憲法)

Chinese	English
第 8 條第 2 項 人民因犯罪嫌疑被逮捕拘禁時, 其逮捕拘禁機關應將逮捕拘禁原因, 以書面告知本人及其本人指定之親友, 並至遲於 24 小時內移送該管法院審問。本人或他人亦得聲請該管法院, 於 24 小時內向逮捕之機關提審。	Art. 8 para. 2 When a person is arrested or detained on suspicion of having committed a crime, the organ making the arrest or detention shall in writing inform the said person, and his designated relative or friend, of the grounds for his arrest or detention, and shall, within 24 hours, turn him over to a competent court for trial. The said person, or any other person, may petition the competent court that a writ be served within 24 hours on the organ making the arrest for the surrender of the said person for trial

IV. Communication Security and Surveillance Act (CSSA: 通訊保障及監察法)

Chinese	English
第 18 條第 3 項 違反第 5 條、第 6 條或第7條規定進行監聽行爲所取得之內容或所衍生之證據, 於司法偵查、審判或其他程序中, 均不得採	Art. 18-1 para. 3 Any content acquired through interception that is in violation of Communication Security and Surveillance Act or any

(continued)

(continued)

Chinese	English
爲證據或其他用途, 並依第 17 條第 2 項規定予以銷燬。	evidence deriving therefrom shall not be used as evidence or used for any other purpose in any judicial investigation, judgment or other proceeding

V. Act to Implement the International Covenant on Civil and Political Rights and the International Covenant on Economic, Social and Cultural Rights (公民與政治權利國際公約及經濟社會文化權利國際公約施行法)

Chinese	English
第 4 條 各級政府機關行使其職權, 應符合兩公約有關人權保障之規定, 避免侵害人權, 保護人民不受他人侵害, 並應積極促進各項人權之實現。	Art. 4 Whenever exercise their functions all levels of governmental institutions and agencies should confirm to human rights protection provisions in the two Covenants; avoid violating human rights; protect the people from infringement by others; positively promote realization of human rights

References

林鈺雄 (LIN Yu-Hsiung): 刑事訴訟法上冊 *(Criminal Procedure Law (I))* 7nd edition, Taipei 2013. [LIN Yu-Hsiung, 2013 (I)].

林鈺雄 (LIN Yu-Hsiung): 刑事訴訟法下冊 *(Criminal Procedure Law (II))* 7nd edition, Taipei 2013. [LIN Yu-Hsiung, 2013 (II)].

朱石炎 (ZHU Shi-Yan): 刑事訴訟法論 *(Criminal Procedure)* 5nd edition, Taipei 2015. [ZHU Shi-Yan, 2015].

CHEN Yu-Jie (陳玉潔), 'One Problem, Two Paths: A Taiwanese Perspective on the Exclusionary Rule in China', (2011) 43 Journal of International Law and Politics NYU, 713–28. [CHEN Yu-Jie, 2011].

楊雲驊 (YANG Yun-Hua): 失衡的天平—評新修正通訊保障及監察法第18條之1 (An unbalanced balance—Comment on new Art. 18-1 of the Communication Security and Surveillance Act), 2014-7 檢察新論 *(Taiwan Prosecutor Review)*, 3-24. [YANG Yun-Hua, 2014-7].

WANG Jaw-Perng (王兆鵬), 'The Evolution and Revolution of Taiwan's Criminal Justice', (2011) 3 Taiwan in Comparative Perspective, 8–29. [WANG Jaw-Perng, 2011].

Yu-Hsiung Lin is a professor of law at National Taiwan University, where he teaches criminal law and criminal procedure. He holds a Ph.D. from University of Munich (Germany) based on his thesis "Richtervorbehalt und Rechtsschutz gegen strafprozessuale Grundrechtseingriffe", which addresses remedies for court-ordered and non-court-ordered violations of constitutional rights in the criminal procedure. His main research interests lie in the field of criminal procedure and human rights law. This includes analyzes especially evidence, coercive measures and the human rights standards applied with a comparative view. He has published textbooks of criminal law and criminal procedure and edited several books on the issue of transnational judicial practice, including four volumes of essays published in 2007–2012 deal with ECHR cases suitable to providing guidance for future practice of Taiwan.

Shih-Fan Wang holds Ph.D. from University of Munich (Germany) and LL.M. from National Chengchi University (Taiwan). His research include comparative criminal procedure law and european and international criminal law. He teaches criminal procedure law and european and international criminal law at the National Taipei University, Taiwan.

Chung-Yen Chen is a lawer and also a Ph.D. candidate at the University of Tübingen (Germany) and hold an LL.M. from Fu Jen Catholic University (Taiwan). He used to serve as the prosecutor of the Taipei District Prosecutors Office. His research includes criminal law, criminal procedure law and criminal enforcement law, and mainly engaged in such cases. He also teaches criminal law at the National Tsing Hua University in Taiwan.

Tsai-Chen Tsai holds her Master degree from Finance college of Management in National Taiwan University. The topic of her Master thesis is empirical research of sentencing in respect of homicide. She served as a criminal division judge in the Supreme Court (1995–2014). After that, she became the director of Criminal Department of Judicial Yuan, R.O.C. (2014–2016). During her tenure, she was in charge of drafting and amending the criminal procedure law and criminal law, which is also related to her research topics. And recently, her researches are focusing on the evidence rules and standards of proof in criminal proceedings.

Chiou-Ming Tsai Director General, Department of International and Cross-Strait Legal Affair, Ministry of Justice, Taiwan. He had been working as prosecutor in Taiwan for more than 26 years before he was appointed as the Department head. As an amateur scholar, his interests of research range from intellectual property right, criminal evidence and comparative study of criminal procedure, to asset recovery, and international judicial cooperation in criminal matters.

The Potential to Secure a Fair Trial Through Evidence Exclusion: A Chinese Perspective

Na Jiang

Abstract This chapter addresses the People's Republic of China's aim to engage in comprehensive fact-finding before handing down punishments to wrongdoers. In 2012 exclusionary rules were added to the Chinese Criminal Procedure Law. In doing so, lawmakers restricted the pool of information accessible to the courts when deciding guilt or innocence of defendants. This change may also make it more difficult to establish the truth in criminal trials. On the other hand, the justification for excluding certain evidence was the discovery of ongoing torture occurring during criminal investigations, which eventually led to many miscarriages of justice. The initial legislation was initiated in 2010 by the Supreme People's Court. Efforts by the Supreme People's Procuratorate, together with three separate Ministries led to the modification of the Criminal Procedure Law. The exclusionary rules seek to make it more difficult to introduce illegally obtained evidence into a criminal trial, and particularly material acquired through torture. Nevertheless, the pressure upon judicial authorities to find perpetrators of crimes quickly remains. Thus, the drive to get confessions from suspects also continues.

1 Introduction

Many justice systems grabble with the conflict between determining what really happened when an alleged crime took place and ensuring that investigative methods do not violate the rights of the accused. This is true also for the Chinese justice system that in recent years has been accused of neither achieving either objective in social media. Especially cases in which violations of the rights of the accused lead to wrongful convictions have been exposed. The protection of human rights and the need to exclude improperly-obtained evidence is recognized by Chinese law. In practice, however, news reports suggest that suspects in Chinese criminal cases

N. Jiang (✉)
College for Criminal Law Science, Beijing Normal University (BNU 北京师范大学), Beijing, China
e-mail: na.jiang@bnu.edu.cn

S. Gless and T. Richter (eds.), *Do Exclusionary Rules Ensure a Fair Trial?*
Ius Gentium: Comparative Perspectives on Law and Justice 74,
https://doi.org/10.1007/978-3-030-12520-2_6

have been convicted based on false confessions, which have been extracted through torture. It is yet to determine whether these violations of human rights are the result of excessive zeal to obtain the truth, or caused by institutional structures that encourage authorities to obtain a conviction at all costs.

In a nutshell, Chinese law currently provides specific provisions for the exclusion of illegally-obtained evidence. In 2010, the *Rules Concerning Questions about Exclusion of Illegally-Obtained Evidence in Handling Criminal Cases* (*Rules*) were created by the Supreme People's Court (SPC), the Supreme People's Procuratorate (SPP), the Ministry of Public Security (MOPS), the Ministry of State Security (MOSS) and the Ministry of Justice (MOJ). The *Rules* were the first to set down ways in which illegally-obtained evidence should be excluded from use at criminal trials, but they regrettably failed to prevent wrongful convictions that were caused by the use of tainted evidence. In an attempt to succeed where the *Rules* failed, China's top legislature, the Standing Committee of National People's Congress, adopted a revised *Criminal Procedural Law* in 2012 (*2012CPL*), which became effective in 2013. The *2012 CPL* entrench the above exclusionary rules in formal law. Official reports claimed that the *2012 CPL* would be a significant step towards the rule of law and the protection of human rights in China.[1]

Without anticipating the final findings of this report, but looking at discussion during the last decade, one may have doubts whether the legal rules have so far been effective.[2] SPC Judges have admitted that 'almost all of recently identified wrongful convictions resulted from forced confessions', but 'judges still have many difficulties in excluding illegally-obtained evidence by law'.[3] Judges fail to enforce laws because doing so is rational under the institutional arrangement in which judges are embedded. Currently, defence lawyers are placed in a very weak position, making it difficult for them to press for the exclusion of evidence.[4] Also, judges are often 'unwilling, afraid or unable to exclude' evidence in practice.[5] Even after People's Courts successfully exclude evidence extorted through torture in rare cases, the use of indirect evidence derived from extorted confessions is still permitted by law and in practice. Tolerating the "fruits of the poisonous tree" cannot make the exclusion of extorted confessions essentially influence final judgements or prevent wrongful convictions. In fact, People's Courts generally accept the prosecution's evidence material without cautious examination. Often, decisions rely on circular logic: judges do not examine case procedures, so cases must have been

[1] *See* Elaine Duan, 'Highlights of Criminal Procedure Law revision', *China.org.cn*, 12 March 2012, available online at <http://www.china.org.cn/china/NPC_CPPCC_2012/2012-03/12/content_24876541.htm>, accessed 31 October 2018.

[2] *See* WU Hongyao, 2014 at 121–130; WANG Chao, 2013 at 100–108; DU Yusu, 2013 at 184–189.

[3] 廉颖婷 (LIAN Yingting): 非法证据排除规则实施五年效果几何 (How is the Implementation Effect of the Exclusionary Rule for Five Years), *Legal daily*, 12 May 2015, available online at <http://law.southcn.com/c/2015-05/12/content_124074146.htm>, accessed 31 October 2018.

[4] *See* NING Ping, 2015.

[5] ZUO Weimin, 2015b.

conducted properly, which means judges do not need to examine them. Unless the traditional institutional constraints change, the use of tainted evidence to obtain convictions will continue.[6] Thus, the transformation of China's criminal justice institutions is necessary to prevent the use of illegally-obtained evidence. One of the most important reforms that could be made would be to strengthen the ability of defence counsel to seek the exclusionary remedy.

2 General Framework for Fact-Finding in Criminal Proceedings

In Chinese legal framework for fact-finding, the major principle can be found in Art. 51 of the *2012 CPL* as a general order to search for find the truth. In all criminal justice system, search for truth comes first, which is followed by individual rights later. The *Constitution of the PRC* (*Constitution*) and the *2012 CPL* contain a series of explicit provisions pertaining to protecting individual rights, including those of suspects, the accused, witnesses and so on. Art. 37 of the *Constitution* generally prohibits unlawful detention of citizens or restriction of their personal liberty without mentioning fair trial or evidence exclusion. Art. 37 states that "[F]reedom of the person of citizens of the People's Republic of China is inviolable", "[N]o citizen may be arrested except with the approval or by decision of a People's Procuratorate or by decision of a People's Court, and arrests must be made by a public security organ", and that "[U]nlawful detention or deprivation or restriction of citizens' freedom of the person by other means is prohibited, and unlawful search of the person of citizens is prohibited." Articles 39 and 40 also relate to prohibiting illegally obtained evidence. But other Chinese legislation specifically punishes the extortion of confession by torture or the use of force. The main provisions relating to the protection of rights include: Arts. 247, 248, 254 of the *Criminal Law of the PRC (1997 CL)*, Arts. 14 and 22 of the *Prison Law*, Art. 22 of the *People's Police Law*, Art. 33 of the *Procuratorate Law*, and Art. 30 of the *Judge's Law, of the PRC*. Even so, the actual implementation of the provisions is still poor. Police investigators and even the public have a high tolerance for confessions extorted through torture, particularly for the purpose of maintaining public order or efficiently solving cases.[7] Official assertions and data purporting to show a sharp decrease of cases involving torture have been challenged.[8]

---

[6]*See* Nolan, 2009 at 95.

[7]*See* KONG Yi, 2001; LIN Lihong/YU Tao/ZHANG Chao, 2006; DONG Xiaowei, 2004; LIN Lihong/YU Tao/ZHANG Chao, 2009.

[8]*See* 宋识径 (SONG Shijing): 刑讯逼供案件去年下降 87% (The Cases of Inquisition by Torture decreased by 87% in the Last Year), *The Beijing News*, 27 June 2013, available online at <http://epaper.bjnews.com.cn/html/2013-06/27/content_443457.htm?div=-1>, accessed 31 October 2018; CHEN Ruchao, 2015.

2.1 Legal Framework and Relevant Actors

Concerning the duty to ascertain the truth, the *2012 CPL* provides for the People's Court's duty to judge cases based on facts that 'are proved with evidence' 'beyond reasonable doubt' in Arts. 51, 53, 54 and 118. The duty is balanced with a series of rights enshrined mainly in Arts. 50 to 63 of the *2012 CPL*. Among them, the right not to self-incriminate, the right to apply for the exclusion of illegally obtained evidence and the right not to be tortured or ill-treated are designed to protect suspects, the accused or witnesses from abuses of power during the criminal process.

Chinese courts include the Supreme People's Court, local People's Courts and special courts. The local People's Courts are divided into basic People's Courts, intermediate People's Courts and higher People's Courts, respectively at the level of counties, cities and provinces. Chinese courts independently exercise judicial power according to law, and shall not be subject to interference by any administrative organs, public organizations or individuals. That follows that Chinese People's Courts may not be independent from People's Procuratorates, or that People's Courts at lower levels depend on instructions from those at higher levels. Meanwhile, most of Chinese judges are appointed by leaders and the presidents or chief judges of Chinese courts are selected by people's congress. Even in law, there is no independence of judges, and courts' independence is limited, differing from judicial independence in the west.

Courts also have the duty to ensure the right to a fair trial. This duty is upheld by granting the accused the following specific rights: the right to equal treatment before the law, the right to a fair and public hearing, the right not to be found guilty except by a courts' judgement according to law, the right to criminal defence, the right to legal assistance, the right to be tried without undue delay, the right to be present during his or her trial, the right to cross-examine witnesses; the right to have the assistance of an interpreter; the right to appeal, the right to apply for compensation if wrongfully convicted or imprisoned.

Accordingly one could assume that the legislative preconceptions require courts to pay equal attention to both: a most comprehensive fact-finding, leading to the punishment of crime, and the safeguarding of individual rights of those affected by criminal investigation, especially the defendant. By law, courts must therefore strictly examine evidence and ensure that the fact-finding process does not violate the rights of any relevant party. Also, based on legal provisions, courts should exclude illegally obtained evidence from use in conviction to ensure justice based on facts and evidence, rather than cooperate with other justice agencies or follow leaders' instructions to wrongly convict the accused. In fact, courts often use the aim of crime control to justify any investigative method.[9] Recommended reform will be outlined in conclusions or Chinese international human rights duties.

[9]More details will be further explained in 3.1.1.2, 3.2.3.2 and 3.3.2.2.

2.1.1 General Rules

2.1.1.1 Law Determining a Duty to Search for the Truth

There are no constitutional rules that directly set out a search for the truth. However, some provisions in the *2012 CPL* explicitly set out such a duty from diverse perspectives in several major aspects, as follows:

Firstly, some provisions set out the importance of searching for the truth. As Art. 51 of the *2012 CPL* specifies, all "documents of a public security organ authorising arrest, all bills of prosecution of a People's Procuratorate and all judgments of a People's Court, must truly rest on facts." Accordingly, only facts and not confessions can become the basis of conviction or sentence in any court judgements. Also, Art. 51 explicitly imposes on the above three institutions the duties to prohibit "intentionally concealing facts" and to punish those doing so by law. If they do so against the accused, it could lead to self-incrimination in a broad sense.

Secondly, some provisions relate to the significance of confessions. As Art. 53 of the *2012 CPL* provides, "emphasis must be placed on evidence, investigation and analysis, "… and [courts] shall not readily rely on confessions" when deciding cases. Accordingly, courts cannot by law reach verdicts based on confessions alone. Specifically, the law states that "the accused shall not be found guilty or imposed a criminal penalty" with only his/her confession, rather than other evidence", but, by law, "may be convicted or imposed a criminal penalty based on reliable and sufficient evidence" even "without his or her confessions at all".

Thirdly, some provisions prescribe the means by which the authorities can obtain confessions from suspects. Art. 54 of the *2012 CPL* imposes on judges the duty to exclude the use of suspects' or the accused's confessions if they were obtained through torture, extortion or other illegal methods, apart from the obtained illegally witness testimony and victim statements. Also, Art. 54 requires the authorities to exclude physical or documentary evidence from use if it was collected contrary to legal procedures and could potentially seriously prejudice justice. However, such evidence can be included in the admissible scope if the evidence can be corrected or supplemented by investigators, or if a reasonable explanation be provided for its errors. Fourthly, some provisions dealt with how authorities may interrogate suspects. Art. 118 of the *2012 CPL* requires investigators to begin interrogating suspects by asking "whether he or she has committed a crime or not, so as to let him/her state details of the crime or explain his/her innocence", and "then ask other questions". In order to efficiently search for the truth, investigators are required to "inform criminal suspects of such legal provisions that they may receive lenient treatment after honest confessions" in Art. 118. This article is against the general principles of prohibiting extorted confessions in *1997 Criminal Law* and in Art. 60 of the *2012 CPL*. This promise of leniency in Art. 118 may lead suspects to confess during interrogation or leave much room for investigators to misjudge or punish the silent innocent[10] on the basis that they refuse to "truthfully" answer the questions that are put to them.

Additionally, there is no statutory or constitutional rule that formally recognizes acceptance of plea-bargaining in Chinese legislation. However, compulsory provisions on the imposition of lenient treatment in exchange for honest confessions may allow for a sort of plea-bargaining or indicate its implicit acceptance in practice. The cautious use of leniency in exchange for a confession is intended to promote efficiency and achieve justice.

2.1.1.2 Law Securing a Fair Trial and/or Individual Rights

Constitutional Rules

In China, the *Constitution of the PRC* (*Constitution*), adopted in 1982, is supreme over all other laws. It establishes essential national institutions, and sets out the basic rights and obligations of citizens, all of which embody primary policies or guidelines. In 2004, 'human rights' were newly enshrined as a principle in Art. 33 of the *Amendment IV to the Constitution* (*2004 Constitution*), without mentioning such basic rights as the right to a fair trial. The limited constitutional coverage of human rights appears to indicate the lack of importance that China attaches to the rights of the accused. Even so, there is no constitutional court at all in China. Also, the role that the *2004 Constitution* plays in any court is often symbolic, because it is officially deemed as a national fundamental law, but cannot be used as substantive laws in application.

Statutory Rules

In order to implement human rights principle set down in the *2004 Constitution*, the *2012 CPL* both enshrines respect for and protection of human rights as its major task, and further improves the rights of suspects or the accused in the criminal process. Apart from the right not to self-incriminate oneself is introduced in Art. 50 of the *2012 CPL* as new progress; other rights can be divided into three categories in light of their nature or function.

(a) The first category contains the right to defence and the right to legal aid.

Under Art. 125 of the *2004 Constitution* that states that the accused has the right to defence, the *2012 CPL* sets out the range of different aspects with which the defence system deals. The first aspect relates to the duty of justice authorities to inform criminal suspects of their rights. Art. 33 of the *2012 CPL* provides for the investigation organ's duty to inform suspects of their right.

The second aspect is on the right to appoint or have defence counsel. The third aspect relates to the legal duties and rights of defense lawyers in the criminal

[10] *See* CHEN Ruihua, 2012 at 46.

process. Their duties are "to provide materials and opinions proving suspects' or the accused's innocence or the limited seriousness of the crime, showing the mitigating circumstances of the case or grounds for exempting the accused from criminal liability, and protecting their procedural rights and other legal rights and interests" based on facts and the law.[11] During investigations, defence counsel have the right to provide legal advice, the right to file petitions and accusations on behalf of their clients, the right to apply the modification of a compulsory measure, the right to learn details about the charges and case information from investigative authorities, and the right to offer opinions to judges.[12] When examining the case of the prosecution, defence lawyers can consult, extract and duplicate materials, or meet and correspond with suspects in custody.[13] Also, they can collect case materials from witnesses or others if permitted, and apply to People's Procuratorates or courts to request collection of evidence.[14] As Art. 41(1) states, "[A] defense lawyer may gather information regarding a case from a witness or any other relevant entity or individual with the consent thereof, and may also apply to the People's Procuratorate or People's Court for gathering or submission of evidence or apply to the People's Court for notifying a witness to testify before court." Chinese counsels do need permission from witnesses or others. If the collection of evidence by counsel is forbidden by witnesses or other relevant institution or individuals, counsel have to ask for the relevant court's help to notify witnesses of testifying in court or to permit victims to offer counsels evidence.

A revision of the *2012 CPL* grants a suspect access to legal counsel after the initial interrogation or upon the imposition of a coercive measure, so as to resolve inconsistencies. The changes stress the significant role that lawyers play in defending suspects during investigation, and augment the inequality of defense and prosecution (see Arts. 33-36 of the *2012 CPL*). The reform furthermore provides lawyers with further guarantees 'to overcome difficulties in meeting suspects or defendants, accessing case material or obtaining evidence through investigation'.[15] Along with expanding the scope of legal aid to all stages of the process, the new changes also clarify lawyers' role in the final review of death sentences in order to enhance the rights guaranteed by Arts. 120, 222, 239 or 240 of the *2012 CPL*.

However, the current law limits the right to defence in certain ways. Chinese law, i.e., Art. 40 of the *2012 CPL*, still does not fully meet the requirements of Art. 14(3)(b) and 3(e) of the International Covenant on Civil and Political Rights (ICCPR). One deficiency is that defence lawyers still face difficulties when collecting information from the victim, their relatives, and witnesses provided by the

[11]Art. 35 of the *2012 CPL*.

[12]Art. 36 of the *2012 CPL*.

[13]Arts. 37 and 38 of the *2012 CPL*.

[14]Art. 41(1) of the *2012 CPL*.

[15]Information Office of the State Council of the PRC, 'Judicial reform in China' (October 2012), available online at <http://www.chinadaily.com.cn/kindle/2012-10/10/content_15806147.htm>, accessed 31 October 2018.

victim. The difficulty is created by the fact that both the consent and the permission of the People's Procuratorates or People's Courts are prerequisites to collecting information. But a lack of specific applicable conditions for granting permission leaves much room for the authorities to refuse applications for investigating evidence or asking witnesses to testify in court. The abuse of procuratorial power and judicial power hampers the ability of defence lawyers to collect evidence necessary for the defence of their client required to fully protect the right to defence.

Another limitation relates to obstacles defence lawyers face when trying to meet with some suspects. According to Art. 37 of the *2012 CPL*, for instance, defence counsel who plan to meet 'a suspect of an offence that involves a crime endangering state security, a crime of terrorism or the particularly serious bribery crime' during investigation, 'should seek permission from the investigating authority'. As officially recognized in 2012, the bribery crime should involve the suspected amount of bribery no more than RMB 500,000, serious criminal circumstances, significant social impacts, or major national interests. The authority has the opportunity to refuse to allow such a meeting, and defence counsel have no remedy for such a refusal. The obstacle arises when defence counsel wish to meet with suspects under residential surveillance. It is hard for counsel to actually protect the above suspects, given the opportunity for the authorities to abuse their powers.

In the overall light of real politics, the worst limitation that defence lawyers face in practice is that the use of certain defence tactics may jeopardize their ability to practice law. Particularly combined with Art. 306 of the *1997 Criminal Law* (*CL*), which is the current criminal law code of the PRC, the Art. 42 of the *2012 CPL* obliges defence lawyers not to conceal, destroy or falsify evidence or modify witness testimonies. Article 306 *CL* is called as the 'Big Stick' hanging over lawyers' head in criminal defence,[16] due to criminalizing defenders and *agent ad litem* who destroy evidence, falsify evidence, or interfere with witnesses' testifying. The authorities can use these provisions to punish defence counsel who present evidence that contradicts the prosecution's theory of the case. The threat of such a penalty often leads counsel to refrain from zealously upholding their clients' rights.

Moreover, the efficiency of exclusionary rules is highly influenced by inadequate defence. The *2012 CPL* does not safeguard the right to prompt legal assistance following arrest or detention, but leaves the detained suspects subject to an initial interrogation without the presence of counsel or access to legal advice. Thus, counsel have no opportunity to collect direct evidence on the use of illegal means like torture to extort confessions from suspects or accused. The legal duty of suspects to tell the truth, combined with inadequate methods for excluding illegally-obtained evidence provides investigators with the ability and the motive for forcing suspects to confess. The law has not yet enshrined the right to silence or abolished the duty to provide investigators with the facts, not to mention guaranteeing the presumption of innocence. Given these shortfalls, most accused are still likely to be presumed to be guilty in reality, in spite of the aforementioned reforms.

---

[16]YU Ping, 2002 at 857.

(b) The second category of legal rights are those that allow suspects to request that justice bodies examine, change or withdraw disadvantageous conduct, decisions or judgements made by others. As well as the right to appeal or present a petition against conviction or sentencing, the convicted enjoy the legal 'right to file charges against judges, prosecutors and investigators' for violating their procedural rights or subjecting them to indignities.[17]

Defendants or their legal representatives 'have the right to appeal [first-instance judgements] in writing or orally' to the court 'at the next higher level'.[18] Defence counsel and relatives of the defendant may only file an appeal 'with the consent of the defendant'.[19] Appeals resolve around the convictions or sentences of defendants, which is designed to protect their right to appeal from being violated in the criminal process.

It is worthy of note that, in principle, no appeal from a defendant can result in additional criminal punishments. The use of the principle against stricter punishment following an appeal from the defence is designed to encourage defendants to appeal without having to worry about increased punishment, so as to better protect their rights and achieve greater justice. However, the prosecution is also able to appeal and request a stricter sentence, and sometimes both parties' appeals are heard concurrently.

(c) The last, but not the least, group of rights includes procedural rights that arise from the legitimate duties of judges, prosecutors and investigators. Such rights mainly involve the right of suspects or the accused to equality before the law,[20] their right not to be convicted without a court verdict according to the law,[21] their right to a public and independent trial,[22] the right of *ne bis in idem*[23] and of *nulla poena sine lege*.[24]

International Human Rights Law

China is bound by international laws that affect how its trials are conducted, but has not yet ratified the *ICCPR* after signing it in 1998 and actually deviates from international standards to a large degree. Primary international human rights instruments contain the right to a fair trial, though they do not provide a definition of what exactly that means. The right might be customarily subsumed in 'judicial guarantees'. A series of human rights standards pertaining to the right to a fair trial,

[17]Art. 14 of the *2012 CPL*.

[18]Art. 216(1) of the *2012 CPL*.

[19]*Ibid*.

[20]Art. 6 of the *2012 CPL*.

[21]Art. 12 of the *2012 CPL*.

[22]Art. 5 of the *2012 CPL*.

[23]Art. 10 of the *2012 CPL*.

[24]Art. 12 of the *2012 CPL*.

i.e., Arts. 6(2), 14(1) of the *ICCPR*, Arts. 2(1), 6 of the *ECHR* and Arts. 4(2), 8 of the *ACHR*, require State parties to observe related standards. Major resolutions of the United Nations Economic and Social Council also deal with a fair trial. These resolutions act as "soft laws" that urge all States to respect the right to a fair trial.[25] The "fair trial" mandated in Art. 14 of the *ICCPR* is further incorporated into Art. 6 of that instrument, which cannot be suspended in emergency, which makes the right non-derogable in all criminal cases.[26] Fair trial appears in the *2012 CPL* only and not in practice. Among minimum guarantees of fair trial, the *2012 CPL* partly protects the rights to be informed of charges, to be tried without undue delay, to defence, to call and examine witnesses, and to appeal, but never mentions the presumption of innocence. In practice, no minimum guarantee can be ensured totally.

Moreover, Art. 14(1) of the *ICCPR* indicates that 'a competent, independent and impartial' trial by law on the basis of equality 'before the courts and tribunals' is the requirement for a fair trial. Arts. 14(2)-(7) of the *ICCPR* require States to offer all accused persons the minimum rights guarantees established by law that define and guarantee rights at trial. *General Comment No. 06* also stresses that 'procedural guarantees therein prescribed must be observed, including the right to a fair hearing by an independent tribunal, the presumption of innocence, the minimum guarantees for the defense, and the right to review by a higher tribunal.'[27] These procedural guarantees contribute to a fair trial and apply universally to all trials.

The right to 'be equal before the courts and tribunals' contained in Art. 14(1) of the *ICCPR* clarifies the general principle of equality in Art. 26 of the *ICCPR*. The right to a fair and public hearing pursuant to Art. 14(1) of the *ICCPR* is the core of due process. All provisions in Art. 14(2) to (7) and Art. 15 of the *ICCPR* specify this right. Aside from institutional guarantees, Art. 14(1) of the *ICCPR* requires the establishment of a competent, independent and impartial tribunal by law to determine criminal charges in a fair and public hearing and to pronounce them publicly.

The *ICCPR* provides minimum guarantees to the accused, including the presumption of innocence, the right to be informed of charges, the right to be tried without undue delay, the right to defence, the right to call and examine witnesses, and the right to appeal. Art. 14(2) of the *ICCPR* provides the right to be presumed innocent for everyone who is charged with criminal offences 'until proved guilty according to law'. Judges have the duty not to convict an accused unless on the

[25]Economic and Social Council, 'Safeguards Guaranteeing Protection of the Rights of Those Facing the Death Penalty. 45th plenary meeting (23 July 1996)' E/RES/1996/15 (1996), available online at <http://www.un.org/documents/ecosoc/res/1996/eres1996-15.htm>, accessed 31 October 2018.

[26]United Nations Human Rights Committee, 'CCPR General Comment No. 6 Art. 6 (Right to Life). Sixteenth Session (30 April 1982)' (1982), available online at <http://www.refworld.org/docid/45388400a.html>, 31 October 2018.

[27]See footnote 28.

basis of reasonable grounds of guilt, in order to 'refrain from prejudging the outcome of a trial', as stressed by the Human Rights Committee.[28] Art. 14(3)(a) of the *ICCPR* contains the right of an accused to 'be informed promptly and in detail in a language which he understands of the nature and cause of the charge against him', thus imposing obligations on the State. The duty to inform requires that information must be sufficient to allow him or her to prepare for a defence, as per Art. 14(3)(b) of the *ICCPR*. In criminal hearings, the authority has the duty to supply translation services under Art. 14(3)(f) of the *ICCPR*.

Art. l4(3) (c) of the *ICCPR* stipulates that any person charged with a criminal offence has the right '[T]o be tried without undue delay', implicit in Art. 9(2) and (3) of the *ICCPR*. This claim relates to the pronouncement of definitive judgements[29] and overlaps with the guarantee in Art. 9(3) of the *ICCPR* on the pre-trial detention. Art. 14(3)(d) of the *ICCPR* specifies the right to a defence as comprising five categories of individual rights. They are: the right to be tried in one's presence; the right to defend oneself in person; the right to choose one's own counsel; the right to be informed of the right to counsel; and the right to receive free legal assistance. Such legal representation must be available at all stages of criminal proceedings. Art. 14(3)(b) of the *ICCPR* involves the right of accused persons to 'have adequate time and facilities for the preparation of his defence'. What constitutes "adequate time" generally depends on the circumstances and complexity of particular cases. The word 'facilities' grant the accused or his defence counsel the right to access the documents necessary for trial preparation. Art. 14(3)(b) also contains the accused's right 'to communicate with counsel of his own choosing'. This right is solely directed to the preparation of the defence, especially when the accused is held in pre-trial detention.

Under Art. 14(3)(e) of the *ICCPR*, the right to 'obtain the attendance and examination of witnesses' 'under the same conditions' as the prosecutor is an essential element of a fair trial. It guarantees that the accused parties are treated equally on the interrogation of witnesses and the introduction of evidence. The right of the accused to 'obtain the attendance' is restricted 'under the same conditions as witnesses against him'. Art. l4(5) of the *ICCPR* safeguards that everyone 'convicted of a crime shall have the right to his conviction and sentence being reviewed by a higher tribunal according to law'. This general formulation recognises the right of convicts to appeal.

[28]United Nations Human Rights Committee, 'CCPR General Comment No. 13: Art. 14 (Administration of Justice), Equality before the Courts and the Right to a Fair and Public Hearing by an Independent Court Established by Law. Twenty-first Session (13 April 1984)' (1984), available online at <http://www.refworld.org/docid/453883f90.html>, accessed 31 October 2018.

[29]*Ibid.*

2.1.1.3 Law Balancing a Duty to Determine the Truth and Infringements on Individual Rights

Concerning the balance between a duty to tell the truth and infringements on the right not to self-incriminate themselves, the *2012 CPL* imposes the duty on all suspects to "answer the questions of the investigatory personnel truthfully" in Art. 118, but it also provides suspects with the right not to "be forced to prove his or her own guilt" in Art. 50. The importance of confession is highly stressed, so the right to silence has not yet been established in China. There is a great need for the introduction of legislation to protect the right to silence.

Art. 118 of the *2012 CPL* implies that suspects have no right to remain silent when being questioned. The provision is especially important to investigators, given their dependence on confessions in clearing up criminal cases. But from the perspective of the better protection of the rights of suspects or accused under the principle of human rights, one possible interpretation of Art. 118 is that the law allows them remain silent, but requires them to tell the truth if they waive that right.[30] In other words, there might be the right to silence, but no right to lie. The institutions of the Chinese justice system do not yet recognize the right to silence as "possible interpretation" that Art. 118 set out above and this deficiency needs to be rectified. In the systemic context of the law, it is necessary to adopt an interpretation that preserves the right to silence.

Meanwhile, it is worthy of note that no article in the *2012 CPL* explicitly articulates criminal suspects' right to silence, including Art. 50, which comes closest to doing so. Therefore, many legal scholars in China do not consider this right to be fully established. Even if Chinese law has already established an implied right to silence, there is still a long way to go before the ideal system is transformed into a real one. First, the legislature and judiciary should clarify the right of suspects and the accused to remain silent under interrogation when they implement the interpretative regulations of the *2012 CPL*. Second, the judiciary should further improve the exclusionary rules on illegal evidence and specify the circumstances in which evidence obtained illegally should be excluded. Furthermore, investigators should be fully recorded when interrogating suspects to protect the human rights of the accused, who are innocent until proven otherwise. Prosecutors should also adhere to the principle of handling cases by law. In a nutshell, it is necessary to make the Chinese right to silence worthy of the name.

In order to balance a duty to determine the truth and infringements on individual rights, the *2012 CPL* requires the authorities not to seek the truth at any costs, but to protect from abuse the human rights of suspects, the accused and witnesses. Particularly, they should exclude illegally obtained evidence from use, and should also not force anyone to confess or testify by torture or undue coercion.

---

[30] *See* 何家弘 (HE Jiahong): 从新刑诉法看中国已确立沉默权制度 (In View of the New Criminal Procedure Law China Establishes the Right to Remain Silent), *Renmin Fayuan Bao*, 1 August 2012, available online at <http://www.chinacourt.org/article/detail/2012/08/id/538703.shtml>, accessed 31 October 2018.

Accordingly, the right of suspects not to self-incriminate themselves, the right of suspects or witnesses not to be tortured or ill-treated, and the right to apply for excluding illegally-obtained evidence should be fully protected throughout the criminal process.

Specifically, the law is concerned with the significance of confessions or other statements, as well as the legality of collecting and using such statements as evidence. As provided in Art. 50 of the *2012 CPL*, confessions in any form can be used for conviction or acquittal if the authorities collect them according to legal procedures. For protecting the right not to self-incriminate and the right not to be forced to prove one's innocence, it is strictly prohibited to extort confessions by unlawful means, including threats, inducement or deceit. When torture or undue coercion are employed, coerced confessions, witness testimony and victim statements should be excluded from use, as required by Art. 54 of the *2012 CPL*.

However, there is no explicit provision in the *2012 CPL* on a standard procedure to test whether or not torture was applied to a suspect. The procedure for excluding illegally obtained evidence may involve examination of evidence extorted through torture to a certain degree, which can be addressed in detail as follows:

There are two main approaches for initiating the procedure for testing whether torture has occurred, which are based on the legal procedure for excluding evidence. One approach is initiated by judges. After noticing the potential that torture was used in the course of evidence collection, they should take the initiative to exercise their legal power during court hearings to investigate the manner in which evidence was collected. The other approach is based on an application by a party in the trial to the relevant court. As provided in Art. 56 of the *2012 CPL*, the parties, defence counsel or representatives of the accused have the legal right to apply to the People's Court for the exclusion of evidence obtained by illegal means like torture. The first and foremost issue that courts should examine when deciding whether to exclude evidence is whether torture was used to collect it.

Furthermore, potential difficulties in taking the second approach are implied in Arts. 56-57 of the *2012 CPL*, and Arts. 97, 101 of its *Interpretation* as well. At first, applicants should provide a court with information and materials on the persons involved with the alleged torture, the time and place when it allegedly occurred, and the means by which it was allegedly conducted in their application for excluding illegally-obtained evidence. Next, it is at the discretion of the court to decide whether to investigate torture in a hearing. If the court initiates a hearing, prosecutors should present evidence to prove the legality of evidence or the fact that torture was not used, i.e., by playing a video or audio recording. Given courts' great discretion when investigating torture, as well as all justice officers' tolerance of torture, the procedure does not actually provide much assistance in revealing whether or not torture was actually used.

2.1.2 Fact-Finding Procedure—Stages and Rules

In China's criminal justice system, there are several primary stages, with diverse rules applying at each stage. This is particularly the case for the legal structure governing procedures for fact-finding.

Specifically, the ordinary fact-finding procedures that are universally applicable to all cases basically involve each stage of the criminal process. During investigation, the police[31] "conduct preliminary interrogation and verify the evidentiary materials" "where there is evidence of the existence of facts of a crime", as per the *2012 CPL*. During interrogation, investigators must inform suspects of legal provisions regarding "lenient treatment for their honest confessions". Investigators must also make an "entire and complete record" of the interrogations of suspects facing life imprisonment or the death penalty. When questioning a witness, investigators are also required by law to inform him or her "that evidence or testimony provided by him or her shall be based on facts".

For initiation of public prosecutions, the People's Procuratorate should ascertain whether or not the criminal facts or details are clear, whether evidence is reliable or sufficient, whether the nature or charge of crime is correctly determined, and whether the investigative acts used to gather evidence were legal. In examining case facts, the People's Procuratorate by law should also interrogate suspects and listen to the opinions of both, the accused and the People's Procuratorate. If the People's Procuratorate believes the fact to be clear and the evidence to be reliable and sufficient, a decision should be made to initiate a prosecution.

Where the prosecution can clearly set out facts underlying a given criminal charge, the court must hold an open hearing. After a prosecutor has read out particulars of the charge at trial, the accused and victims may state the alleged crime, and then the procurator may interrogate the accused. If witnesses should testify in court but fail to do so, the court may compel them to testify. By law, only after the facts and evidence are debated and witnesses have been examined can the court decide a case law. If case facts are clear and evidence is reliable and sufficient, the court should convict the accused and impose an appropriate sentence. Otherwise, the accused should be acquitted.

Apart from aforementioned three basic steps to a criminal trial, fact-finding procedures applying to special cases may involve four more stages, namely, appeal, death penalty review, trial supervision and execution. Either the defendant's appeal or the People's Procuratorate's protest can initiate the appeal procedure. Appeal courts should completely review the facts found and the law applied in the original judgements in order to correct errors in convictions or sentences. After a complete

[31]In this context, police mean investigatary organs, mainly including public security authoritiesand national security authorities.The formeris responsible for criminal investigation, detention, execution of arrest warrants, and interrogation in criminal cases, and the later handles criminal cases regarding compromising national security and performs the same functions as those of public security authorities by law.

revision, the courts may affirm an initial decision, revise judgements, or return cases for retrial by a new collegial panel.

Chinese law mandates that death sentences should be reviewed by the Supreme People's Court (SPC). During the review of death sentences, the SPC should interrogate the person on whom the sentence has been imposed and should hear arguments from his or her defence lawyers' opinion upon the lawyers' request. The SPP may advise the judges of the SPC of its opinions on the sentences and the SPC should, in turn inform the SPP of its final decision, apart from informing the accused whose sentence is being reviewed.

The court should open a new trial if the party's petition satisfies one of the following conditions: Firstly, if the petition introduces new evidence that proves that the determination of facts in the original judgments or orders was clearly wrong, and that it is likely to affect conviction and sentencing. Secondly, if the petition shows that evidence used when deciding the case or during sentencing is unreliable or insufficient, should have been excluded by law, or that major evidence regarding case facts is conflicting. Thirdly, if the petition can demonstrate that the judges applied the wrong law. Fourthly, if the petition can demonstrate that violations of legal procedures during the initial trial may have impaired its fairness. Fifthly, if it can be demonstrated that the trial judge was engaged in embezzlement, or the acceptance of bribes, the practice of nepotism, or that he or she was influenced to "bend" the laws when making his or her judgement.

In addition, fact-finding procedure is also found in enforcing criminal penalties. By legislation, those instructing execution or enforcement should verify the identity of criminals.

Differing from the above requirements in legislation, death penalty reviews are conducted without transparency, so the SPC actually dominates the review process. Generally the person whose sentence is being reviewed must passively wait for the SPC's decision. In practice, the ability of defence counsel to effectively participate in the process or to bring new facts to the attention of the SPC limits the ability of the procedure to correct errors. The death penalty review procedure does not meet the requirements set down by the minimum guarantees of due process.

2.1.3 Fact-Finding Procedure—Actors and Accountability

As important actors in the fact-finding procedure, People's Courts, People's Procuratorates and the police (the "three justice authorities")[32] should use facts as the basis of handling a criminal case. Parties to the case, mainly including victims, private prosecutors, suspects and the accused, also play an essential role in seeking the truth, albeit they do so when trying to protect their own rights and interests.

[32]People's Courts are "ren min fayuan" in Chinese pinyin, People's Procuratorates are "ren min jiancha yuan" and the police are "gong anji guan" in general. The three of them are called "san ji guan" in Chinese pinyin.

Other actors, i.e., legal representatives, *agents ad litem*, defenders, witnesses, experts or interpreters, assist their clients or the authorities to efficiently ascertain the facts.

Among these actors, both the People's Procuratorates, as the public prosecution organs, and private prosecutors are placed in the position of the accusing party, respectively in the cases of public and private prosecutions. Both public and private prosecutors not only should collect or present evidence to prove the facts of the case or their claims favourable to prosecution in court, but also should bear the burden of proof by law, so as to face adverse consequences for their failure to proving facts or claims. In this point, the police and courts differ from the People's Procuratorates because they do not bear the responsibility for proving facts at trial.

The three justice authorities have diverse legal powers and duties relating to fact-finding. Among them, the police mainly exercise investigative powers to find facts or collect evidence in order to assist People's Procuratorates to prepare for prosecution. The People's Procuratorates must further examine the facts and evidence provided by the police before presenting them to courts. After hearings, the courts should independently and impartially judge which party's claims are well-established. Apart from fulfilling their own responsibilities, the three should coordinate and check with each other to correctly and promptly determine the facts of guilt or innocence by law.

Unlike the prosecution, the accused or suspects should in principle not bear the burden of proving the facts or demonstrating their own guilt or innocence. Together with the accused's legal duty to truthfully answer questions, a lack of the right to silence suggests that they might be forced to confess during interrogation. Also, there are a few exceptions to the above principle in law. For instance, suspects and the accused are legally required to include relevant information or materials relating to illegally obtained evidence in applications to exclude such evidence from use.

As non-parties, representatives, *agents ad litem*, witnesses, expert witnesses or interpreters have no direct interest in the outcome of the cases with which they are involved, but they still play an essential role in fact-finding. For example, legal representatives can directly represent the relevant party, helping him or her exercise rights or complete his or her duties perform duties. Even without the right to state case facts or testify in court on behalf of the party, legal representatives can request the People's Procuratorate to lodge a protest against judgments due to errors in the facts of a case. Their general rights or powers are based on legal safeguards, rather than judicial decisions or approval, in order to effectively help the party with no or a limited capacity to actually attend proceedings.

Once entrusted, *agents ad litem* can protect their clients' rights and interests by participating in fact-finding within a commission scope on behalf of victims. Defenders and *agents ad litem* who help to conceal, destroy or falsify evidence, who threaten or induce witnesses to alter testimony, or who perjure or had commit other acts to interfere with judicial activities, are held legally accountable for their offences.

Witnesses who have knowledge of case details have the duty to provide evidence or testimony based on the truth.[33] Those who intentionally give false testimony or conceal evidence of guilt are legally accountable. Assigned or hired experts and translators are involved in fact-finding. Expert witnesses can use expertise or skills to give written examination advice on special problems in order to assist judges to find the facts. Those who deliberately provide false examination results are legally accountable. Additionally, translators should faithfully provide clients with translation services.

2.2 *Social Relevance of the Truth and Individual Rights in Criminal Trials*

2.2.1 Relevance of Determining the Truth

The relevance of determining the truth is highly stressed in the Chinese criminal justice system. The *2012 CPL* suggests the significance of obtaining a confession from suspects or the accused. For example, Art. 118(2) of the *2012 CPL* explicitly requires the accused or other suspects to answer the relevant "investigators' questions truthfully" during interrogations. Certainly in this context, the questions that suspects have to truthfully answer indeed include those on case facts, e.g., whether or not he or she committed crime. Thus, the clause fails to constitute the prohibition of self-incrimination, not to mention protecting his or her right to silence.

The diverse possible interpretations of the *2012 CPL* regarding the right to silence leave much room for the authorities to abuse their powers. If suspects rely on Arts. 50(2) and 118(2) of the *2012 CPL* to make full use of their right to refuse to answer questions irrelevant to the case, investigators could resort to Art. 118(2) to ask them to perform their duty to truthfully answer questions. Also, it is not difficult for investigators to find some relevance of their questions to the case, i.e. they might need an oral confession to assist with further investigations. Under this interpretation, investigators can justify the potential relevance of their questions by any means, suspects lose their right to silence and have to confess their guilt. If this interpretation prevails, the legal principle of prohibiting self-criminalization in Art. 50(2) of the *2012 CPL* would likely become a rule on paper, rather than in practice.

Like any employees trying to meet managerial targets, some investigators often take advantage of loopholes. In the criminal justice context, such loopholes include the extortion of false confessions by means fair or foul, including torture. In order to reach the rigid target for solving cases, the authorities may resort to falsifying guilt,

[33]Art. 123 of the *2012 CPL* states that "[W]hen a witness is interviewed, the witness shall be informed of the requirement of truthfully providing evidence and testimony and the legal liability for perjury or concealing criminal evidence.

possibly by extracting a false confession from the first suspect to be arrested. As long as such a confession is obtained, a case is considered to be solved for the purpose of meeting the target. For example, Shanghai and Beijing, where nearly 99 and 99.16% of cases were solved in 2013, achieved the highest rates of solved homicide cases in China.[34] The managerial system can cause injustices. Identified wrongful convictions also demonstrate a high risk that tortured confessions will first be used at trial.

On the other hand, the *2012 CPL* improves evidentiary rules to further emphasize the significance of making confessions public during trial. Art. 121 of the law requires investigators to make a complete audio or visual record of the entire interrogation process in cases in which suspected criminals may be punished by life imprisonment or the death penalty. In theory, if recordings are played back and made public, that would make cases of tortured confessions easy to identify, but recordings are often not complete with lawyer's absence in the course of interrogation. Given the legal incentive of leniency when punishing those who confess and the widespread use of torture, almost all suspects confess under the pressure of torture. Combined with a possibility of playing the record to examine confessions at trial as required by Art. 80 of the *Interpretation* on the *2012 CPL*, transparency of investigation can be increased to make them public, thus reducing confession reached through torture.

In court hearings, confessions regarding case facts or evidence should be investigated and debated, so that judges can examine whether it is true or false and decide whether or not to use it as evidence. False confessions cannot be used to support a conviction. Also, judges should examine whether the collection of a confession was contrary to law. By Art. 54 of the *2012 CPL*, confessions extorted by torture should be excluded from use. According to the *Interpretation* of the law, Art. 81 also prohibits the use of confession without confirmation in transcripts, or from the deaf, dumb or those unfamiliar with local languages, unless they were provided with assistance regarding translation. Accordingly, at trial making the record of confessions public can help courts examine all material evidence to exclude false or coerced confession in facts-finding. In order to promote publicity help this, there is a great need for judges to abandon privately reviewing evidence of torture in practice.

The *Decision*, made by the third Plenary Session of meeting of the Communist Party of China (CPC) in 2013, also requires that strict prohibitions be placed on extorting confessions by torture, particularly through applying exclusionary rules to

[34]For example, *see* 北京警方年度工作报告出炉命案破案率达 99.16% (The Beijing Police Annual Report Was Released to Show that the Detection Rate of Murder Cases Rose up to 99.16%), *Zhongguo Net*, 24 January 2014, available online at <http://www.china.com.cn/news/2014-01/24/content_31289621.htm>, accessed 31 October 2018; *also see* 潘高峰 (PAN Gaofeng): 去年上海命案破案率近百分之九十九 (The Shanghai Detection Rate of Murder Cases Being Nearly 99% in the Last Year), *Dayang Net*, 12 January 2014, available online at <http://roll.sohu.com/20140112/n393370187.shtml>, accessed 31 October 2018.

illegally obtained evidence. Under political guidance, the SPC released the *Directive* to stress the implementation of exclusionary rules and the trial-centered doctrine in 2013. Following the acquittal of NIANB in, who was convicted of murder four times in the past ten years and was finally exonerated of all crime in 2014, Procurator-General CAO Jianming urged prosecutors to break away from their excessive reliance on confessions.[35] The discovery of NIAN's innocence raised public outcry for the proper implementation of laws, which in part contributed to CAO's pledge.

However, legislation does not clarify lawyers' role in interrogation so that they have no legal way to protect their clients' rights from power abuses. In the NIAN Bin case, for instance, lawyers could not obtain a copy of the recording until it was played back at trial. Even then, their applications for excluding illegally obtained evidence were repeatedly rejected by courts. Worse than that, prosecutorial supervision over interrogations and investigations has actually tolerated tortured confessions in practice. Given the lack of an effective remedy for rights breaches and the closed environment of interrogation, police investigators often select a part of interrogation for recording favourable to the interests of the investigation. Thus, the recording system becomes a legal cover for illegal interrogation.

2.2.2 Presentation of "Fact-Finding" and/or "Truth" to the Public

2.2.2.1 Publicity of Fact-Finding Before a Judgment

Publicity of fact-finding including confessions before judgments may help the public better understand case facts and also urge judges to cautiously exercise judicial power. As Art. 11 of the *2012 CPL* requires, courts shall hear cases in open trial, except as otherwise provided by this Law. Accordingly, open trial is courts' legal duty, during which confessions will be publicized for public supervision over the judiciary.

In practice, courts selectively allow substantive trial information, i.e., confessions or facts in doubt, to be open to the public. In hearing high-profile cases, courts should arrange a suitable place for the trial according to the number of the parties' close relatives, media reporters and the public in audience, but often set obstacles to their attendance by providing a small place. Courts also should give priority to the media's and their relatives' needs, but actually limit some media's attendance and publicity.

---

[35] Mark Godsey, 'China's Top Prosecutor Vows to Fight to Prevent Wrongful Convictions', *ShanghaiDaily.com*, 8 September 2014, available online at <https://wrongfulconvictionsblog.org/2014/09/08/chinas-top-prosecutor-vows-to-fight-to-prevent-wrongful-convictions/>, accessed 31 October 2018.

2.2.2.2 Existence of Court TV

Some of court trials can be broadcasted live, as a permissible way to publicize confessions in fact-finding. The SPC's *Six Provisions on Judicial Transparency* issued in 2009 requires courts to meet the needs of the public and the media in understanding live trials by the means of court trial video, live video or others. The SPC's *2013 Pilot Programs on Promoting Three Platforms for Judicial Transparency* requires courts to make public the hearing process in the ways of video, audio, graphics and micro-blog.

Through broadcast live, details on cross-examination and debates at trial are open to the public so that they can understand controversies between two sides in order to supervise and evaluate court trial. Thus, everyone can fully know and judge whether there is illegal means for collecting evidence in interrogations, and whether courts should exclude such evidence from use. For example, how the prosecution answer questions on the documented evidence that suggests defendants' tortured confessions, and how courts examine it for decision-making will be live through micro-blog. Once the public knows flaws in evidence, it will be hard for any court to tolerate them.[36]

Moreover, broadcast or webcast live only makes trial and not decision-making public, both of which are separate from each other in reality. Whether to publicize the truth also depends on superiors' or leaders' willingness. Courts mainly focus on assessments on their work achievements, rather than enhance judicial transparency.[37]

2.2.3 Public Discussion of Miscarriages of Justice

In social media or print media, the public share the opinion that factual, legal or procedural errors in fact-finding may constitute or lead to more miscarriages of justice. A number of wrongful convictions were caused by coerced and false confessions obtained through torture against law and justice. It is generally accepted by the public, officials and scholars at home and abroad that illegally obtained evidence is the main cause of almost all known wrongful convictions in China.[38] Some of official commentators or top leaders have admitted that illegal methods have been used to gather, examine and exclude evidence in various cases in recent decades.

In fact, the term 'miscarriage of justice', (a translation of cuòàn, lit. 'wrong cases'), is short of a universal definition, as is indicated in the relevant judicial interpretation issued by the SPP, local (non-national) regulation enacted by the local People's Congress and various instruments adopted by police and judicial organs at

[36]ZHOU Changjun, 2014.
[37]XIE Peng, 2012 at 65–75.
[38]HE Jiahong, 2012.

the basic level. The concept has been broadly applied by Chinese courts to any criminal proceeding 'where there was human error in the basic facts, underlying evidence or applicable laws, caused by police, procuratorates, courts [and/or state security organs]'.[39,40] These bodies do not limit miscarriages of justice to cases of proven or factual innocence, but include those with procedural errors as well as unfair or partial trials which render criminal convictions factually unreliable even without fresh evidence. Thus, such convictions in China can be both re-opened and quashed on the grounds of proven innocence, or of substantive or procedural unfairness. Proper fact-finding can ensure justice at trial.

Despite the inertia and corruption of Chinese criminal justice system, the scope of what constitutes a miscarriage of justice should further expand in order to properly and effectively prevent wrongful convictions, as a part of ongoing reforms to China's judicial system. It is worthy to note that a system of accountability for miscarriages of justice, which is one of the SPC's judicial reform tasks, is intended to strengthen supervision over and decrease the number of illegal trials or other miscarriages of justice in criminal cases, albeit excluding the differences in legal recognition among judges, as revealed by the senior ones from the SPC.[41]

Furthermore, the issue of what constitutes wrongful convictions in China remains to be clarified. While any level of courts can declare that a miscarriage of justice has occurred, sometimes expressly describing particular cases in such terms, there are profound lessons to learn from high profile or long standing convictions that have been overturned on the basis of fresh evidence.[42] In practice, the official media generally support the opinions of politicians or senior judges so as to shield them from criticism. More attention is paid to the vulnerability of current justice systems, whereas not all of those wrongfully convicted in the view of media would be necessarily acquitted or fully exonerated by courts, e.g., certain controversial illegal money-raising case.[43] Increasingly in contemporary society, the recognition of innocence and exoneration has been sharply defined and universally acknowledged to be 'a political, social and scientific process that is not fully supported by the criminal justice system'.[44] Neither the wrongly convicted SHE Xianglin nor

---

[39]ZHANG Jun, 1990 at 3.

[40]In China, the People's Procuratorates (PPs) are agencies that combine the functions of prosecutors, investigators, court supervisors and penal officials.

[41]孙莹 (SUN Ying): 最高法: 132 项司法体制改革任务完成 103 项 (The SPC: 103 judicial Reform tasks have been finished in the total of 132), *Renmin Net*, 20 March 2012, available online at <http://legal.people.com.cn/GB/188502/17441465.html>, accessed 31 October 2018.

[42]*See* 命案必破, 疯人顶罪? (Homicide must be detected, the insane being scapegoats?), *Nanfang Net*, 6 May2010, available online at <http://view.news.qq.com/a/20100511/000014.htm>, accessed 31 October 2018; *See also* 'Judicial reform in Henan gets public support (2)', *People's Daily Online*, 12 December 2011, available online at <http://english.peopledaily.com.cn/102774/7674038.html>, accessed 31 October 2018.

[43]*See* 'Wu Ying case underlines need for private financing reform', *Xinhua Net*, 21 April 2012, available online at <http://news.xinhuanet.com/english/china/2012-04/21/c_131541731.htm>, accessed 31 October 2018.

[44]*See* Roach, 2009; Sherrin, 2010.

ZHAO Zuohai's factual innocence could be officially recognized until judicial exonerations, followed with their DNA testing and other legal procedures, even if there was a remarkable consensus on serious doubts retained before convicting them.[45]

3 Limitations of Fact-Finding in Criminal Proceedings

3.1 General Rules of Evidence Taking (Admissibility of Evidence)

3.1.1 Legal Framework

3.1.1.1 Legal Framework for Evidence Taking/Admissibility of Evidence

Legal Framework and Its Context on the Books

Within the legal framework for evidence taking in China, the relevant evidence rules in the *Criminal Procedure Law of the PRC*, the *Constitution of the PRC*, the *Convention against Torture*, and judicial interpretations contribute to regulating the use of evidence. In the *Constitution of the PRC*, Art. 37 provides that Chinese citizens' personal freedom is inviolable. Also, Art. 39 requires that their home is inviolable, and Art. 40 provides that their freedom and privacy are protected by law.

Among the above framework, the *2012 Criminal Procedure Law of the PRC* is a main source of evidence rules in the criminal process.

Concerning judicial interpretations, the Supreme People's Court's *Interpretation on Several Issues regarding Enforcement* provides in Art. 61 that "it shall be prohibited to collect evidence by illegal means" and that "no witness testimony, victims' statements or confessions of the accused that are verified to be obtained by the use of torture or threat, enticement, cheating and other illegal methods, can be used as the basis for deciding cases".

Similarly, the SPPs Criminal Procedure Rules of People's Procuratorates which bind both people's and special procuratorates, also stipulate exclusionary rules, as showed in more articles. First, Art. 140 tells that "… it shall be prohibited to obtain confessions by using torture and threats, enticement, deceit or taking other unlawful methods". Next, Art. 160 states that "… it shall be prohibited to obtain testimony by the means of custody, torture, threats, enticement, deceit or other illegal methods." Then, Art. 265 states that it shall be prohibited to obtain evidence by illegal means and that no suspects' confessions, victims' statements or witness testimony

[45]李柏涛 (LI Botao): 赵作海冤案疑点明显公检法均失职致一错再错 (Obvious Doubts in Misjudged Case ZHAO Zuohai, Errors of the Police, Procuratorates and Courts Leading to More Errors), *Xinhua Net*, 11 May 2010, available online at <http://china.huanqiu.com/roll/2010-05/809896.html>, accessed 31 October 2018.

that had been collected by torture or threat, enticement or other illegal methods can be used as the basis of bringing a charge.

The historical contexts of that law in its changes and reforms are as follows: The *Convention against Torture and Other Cruel, Inhuman or Degrading Treatment or Punishment* that China joined in September 1988 provides in Art. 12 that "[E]ach State Party shall ensure that its competent authorities proceed to a prompt and impartial investigation, wherever there is reasonable ground to believe that an act of torture has been committed in any territory under its jurisdiction". Accordingly, any Party State to the above *Convention*, including China that has ratified it, must promptly investigate any allegation of torture.

In the *1996 CPL*, there was an article on evidence, which also stated that it shall be strictly forbidden to collect evidence by the means of tortured confessions, threat, enticement, cheating or by other unlawful means. Since this article was too general without a supporting system, it is just a principled regulation without practical functions. The SPC's 1998 *Interpretation on Several Issues in Enforcing the Criminal Procedure Law of the PRC* also provided in Art. 61 that it shall be strictly prohibited to collect evidence by illegal means and that no witness testimony, victims' statement or defendants' statements that had been actually verified to use tortured confession or take threat, enticement, deceit or other unlawful means can be used as the basis for deciding cases. The *People's Procuratorate's Criminal Procedure Rules* also regulated that it should be strictly prohibited to collect evidence by illegal means. The above two judicial interpretations had make more progress than the *1996 Criminal Procedure Law of the PRC*, but did not mention how to and when to exclude illegally obtained evidence.

As above demonstrated, the Chinese criminal legislation on the effect of illegally obtained evidence was very simple then. There was no provision on illegally obtained material evidence, and regulations on illegally obtained oral evidence were also diverse among the police, national security organs,[46] the People's Procuratorates and courts. Thus, the legislative situation brought law enforcement departments many problems, and in the actual operation process of nowhere, with too much discretionary power, led to the departure from each department. In recent years, confessions extorted through torture have led to frequent occurrences of wrongful convictions, detrimental to public confidence with the justice system.

In order to prevent tortured confessions and curb torture as serious injustices in justice practice, SPC, SPP, MOPS, MOSS and MOJ promulgated the *Regulation on Several Problems of Excluding Illegally Obtained Evidence in Handling Criminal Cases* on June 13, 2010. Its main contents focus on detailed provisions of the illegally obtained evidence, in order to establish exclusionary rules. The *2012 CPL* has established legal rules on the exclusion of illegally obtained evidence, as the first act excluding the evidence. The act includes the scope of excluding the

[46]They are different from the police. National security authorities handle criminal cases regarding compromising national security and performs the same functions as those of public security authorities by law, whereas the police are responsible for criminal investigation, detention, execution of arrest warrants, and interrogation in criminal cases.

evidence, court examination and legal supervision. Later, relevant judicial interpretations on the Law further define the meaning of tortured confession. The SPC's *2013 Opinions on Establishing Sound Working Mechanisms for Preventing Wrongful Convictions* also specify detailed circumstances where to exclude the evidence. Thus, China's criminal evidence system on preventing tortured confessions has basically taken in shape.

The Development and Reforms of Chinese Rules on Evidence Exclusion

In the set-up of rules excluding evidence in Chinese criminal justice system, such rules were first introduced as a principled article of the SPC's *1998 Interpretation on Several Issues in Enforcing the Criminal Procedure Law of the PRC*. Since then, such rules have been subject to further reforms again and again. The *2010 Regulation on Several Issues of Excluding Illegally Obtained Evidence in Handling Criminal Cases* delineates the exclusion of the illegally obtained evidence, so as to establish exclusionary rules. Also, the *2012 CPL* further improves the rules, both in the form of legislation and for the first time.

The Impact of Exclusionary Rules on the Actors Within Criminal Proceedings

When first introduced in Art. 61 of the SPC's *1998 Interpretation on Several Issues in Enforcing the Criminal Procedure Law of the PRC*, the exclusionary rule had no actual impact on actors in the criminal process. Art. 61 defined the meaning of illegally obtained evidence, clarified its scope and legal consequences, but did not mention specific procedures for excluding it. In practice, Art. 61 cannot be applied as expected, but actually became "law in the paper".

When introduced as an explicit rule in the *2010 Regulation on Several Issues of Excluding Illegally Obtained Evidence in Handling Criminal Cases*, the rule details procedures for excluding it, the burden of proof and investigators' presence in court. It signals that the exclusionary rule has been officially established. More importantly than that, the rule can be used by the relevant justice authorities as legal bases in practice. For instance, it imposed the police, prosecutor and courts duties to examine and to exclude illegally obtained evidence at diverse stages of the criminal process. Also, the accused and defence can exercise the right to produce that confession was illegally obtained. Many points on evidence exclusion introduced in the *Evidence Rules of 2010* as departmental regulations are later used in the *2012 CPL* as a basic law of all criminal procedures and the accused's rights.

When introduced as a legal rule in the first time, the exclusionary rule in the *2012 CPL* further recognizes the People's Procuratorates' burden of proof to prove the legitimacy of evidence collection in principle. This rule also establishes the prosecution's standard of proof, such that facts are clear and evidence is reliable and sufficient. Also, the rule includes more actors in the process of applying for excluding illegally obtained evidence. Thus, the party and their defenders or litigation representatives can enjoy the legal right to apply to courts for its exclusion.

Such legal improvements on its exclusion have promoted the procedural judgement system' gradual formation, with more actors involved in initiating modes, preliminary examination, formal investigation, burden or standard of proof, and remedy means.

The Justification of Exclusionary Rules in Paper Law

According to the law on the books, justifications of exclusionary rules mainly involve restraints on state power, protection on human rights and procedural justice. The main objectives of the *2012 CPL* are to punish criminals and to respect and protect human rights. Rights remedy can effectively curb power abuses.

The legal duties of the police, prosecutors and courts to exclude illegally obtained evidence at their respective stage of the criminal process can help find errors sooner, in order to improve the quality of solved cases and to protect suspects' legal rights.[47] In law, the three institutions should check and restrict each other in the process for the purpose of properly enforcing laws, while cooperating to punish or control crime. In this sense, mutual restraints can promote them to well exclude the evidence from use. Similarly, procedures for the second instance aim to correct errors in the first instance procedures and procedures for the death penalty review aim to mend the flaw made by the former procedures. If the justice system works well, the evidence can be excluded.

The Mandatory or Discretionary Feature of Exclusionary Rules

There are three kinds of exclusionary rules in China's criminal evidence system. They are respectively mandatory exclusionary rule applicable to illegally obtained oral evidence, discretionary exclusionary rule used for excluding illegally obtained material evidence and correctable exclusionary rule used for tainted evidence as well.

No Acknowledgment of the "Fruit of the Poisonous Tree" Doctrine

There is no acknowledgment of the "fruit of the poisonous tree" doctrine in China's criminal justice system. One dangerous use of an illegally extracted confession would be to legally allow police to gather leads in finding additional admissible evidence, witnesses, or suspects. The failure to ban derivative evidence can contribute to wrongful convictions. For example, after learning that an accused counterfeiter "may have been beaten before confessing" during his detention, "one Jiangsu prosecutor investigated and decided that the evidence should be excluded" but that a later confession could be used in the trial.[48] Without "inquiry into the independent voluntariness of a second confession", "there is little to stop further

[47]LANG Sheng (ed.), 2012 at 11.

[48]Daum, 2011.

interrogation from becoming a backdoor for admitting illegal confessions".[49] Those who confess once under torture may likely make subsequent false confessions and these confessions will be admitted on the basis that they were not obtained through torture.

The Significance of International Human Rights Law in the Chinese Context

Notably, international human right law is of significance to human rights progress and justice practice in the Chinese context. As an international citizen, China should abide by all of treaty obligations that it has accepted, i.e., preventing torture or excluding tortured confessions as a party to the *Convention against Torture*. The prohibition of torture and degrading punishment is also customary. Such obligations universally bind all States, including China that is not a persistent objector. It is obliged not to engage in patterns of gross and flagrant violations of human rights.

But many of rights safeguards are seriously abused in China. They include the right to presumption of innocence, to defence, to legal aid, to a fair trial, to humane treatment, to equality before the law and the principle of *ne bis in idem*. In practice, the right to a public, independent, and impartial trial, or to appeal is often abused.

3.1.1.2 Practice; (High Court) Jurisprudence

On the Judicial Acceptance of a General "Exclusionary Rule"

Chinese (High Court) jurisprudence does recognize a general "exclusionary rule" in practice. As many wrongful convictions that were judicially rectified in recent years, local courts have used the exclusionary rule to achieve justice, by law or regulations.

On the Judicial Acceptance of the Duty to Find the Truth

Chinese (High Court) jurisprudence also acknowledges the duty to find the truth in the name of an effective administration of justice, so as to overrule explicit or implied exclusionary rules. Particularly based on case studies, Chinese courts hardly exclude the illegally obtained evidence by law in most circumstances of recent five years.[50] In practice, the so-called "illegally obtained evidence" that has been excluded at trial is actually such the evidence that has an illegal form, rather than the evidence that was collected by means against defendants' legal rights. The former evidence usually means that the evidence does not meet the formal elements of legal requirements. But in fact, the most fundamental feature of collecting evidence by illegal means is the violation of the accused's legitimate rights i.e., liberty or property rights protected by the *Constitution of the PRC* and the *CPL*. Thus, the

[49] *Ibid.*

[50] GAO Jie, 2016 at 32.

evidence that was collected by means against the accused's legal rights should be excluded from use as a priority.[51]

The Justifications of Exclusionary Rules and Their Application in Specific Cases

The justification(s) of exclusionary rules include the legality of evidence collection and justice in each case, whereas in particular cases their application is often limited to accurate and sufficient evidence of tortured confession during interrogations. For example, evidence can be excluded only in cases where recordings show investigators' making interrogation transcripts or audio-video recordings not in the actual trial time, and also prosecutors failed to prove the means of collecting evidence legitimate, and the relevant investigator cannot make a reasonable explanation on them.

For instance, in what was called the first case of excluding illegally-obtained evidence in China, legal commentators have noted that differences between the decision at the initial trial and the decision at appeal of the bribery case of ZHANG Guoxi revolve around critical issues. These issues are the distinction between illegal and defective evidence, the "range" of exclusionary rules, what constitutes "other illegal means of evidence collection" and the degree of proof necessary to demonstrate that evidence was obtained illegally. After the initial trial in 2011, the prosecution lodged a protest against the trial judgment, which excluded evidence on a guilty plea provided by the prosecution. Based on new evidence from new witnesses provided by the prosecution, the decision to exclude the confession and the evidence of other witnesses was reversed on appeal in July 2012. The final judgment stated that ZHANG Guoxi's "confession of guilt was not made under inquisition by torture" and that the prosecution "sufficiently proved the legitimacy of his confession obtained by investigative organs", so that "his pre-trial confession of guilt can be admissible as evidence".[52]

3.1.1.3 Consequences of a Violation of Exclusionary Rules

In the *2012 CPL*, remedies for violating the exclusionary rules are absent. In practice, the most needed remedies for consequences of breaching the rules appear in three main situations: (1) When the defence is dissatisfied with the ultimate non-initiation of the procedure for excluding illegal evidence, after providing the evidentiary material required for starting the procedure and reaching the degree under which another rational judge would have "reasonable doubts" as to the

---

[51]YANG Yuguan, 2015 at 395.

[52]祝优优陈佳玮 (ZHU Youyou/CHEN Jiawei): "中国非法证据排除第一案" 终审遭遇大逆转 (The Final Trial of the First Case of 'Excluding Illegal Evidence in China' Suffered from A Big Reversal), *Fenghuang Net*, 25 July 2012, available online at <http://news.ifeng.com/mainland/detail_2012_07/25/16269272_0.shtml>, accessed 31 October 2018.

legitimacy of evidence; (2) When the defence continues to refuse to accept the court's decision not to exclude evidence after the court's final review; (3) When the prosecutor refuses to accept the court's decision to exclude potentially illegal evidence in court. The absence of effective remedies demonstrates how the institutions of Chinese criminal justice system are set against the accused.

3.1.2 Debate on Exclusionary Rules (in Civil Society, etc.)

3.1.2.1 The Public Debate on Exclusionary Rules

There are many public debates on chances, impactor(in) effectiveness of exclusionary rules in Chinese criminal justice system. Debates continue as to the effects of exclusion. For example, relevant laws or regulations clearly state that illegal oral evidence cannot be the basis of conviction, for approving arrest or for indictment,[53] but it remains unclear whether it can be used for other purposes, such as at sentencing.

Some critics hold that there is an obvious shortcoming because while coerced oral statements cannot be used at trials, physical and documentary evidence derived from such statements can be used as evidence. The definition of illegally obtained testimony only refers to "statements by criminal suspects or defendants obtained through illegal means such as forced confessions as well as witness testimony or victim statements obtained through illegal means such as the use of violence or threats".[54] This law has been interpreted, contrary to the intent and plain meaning of Art. 43 in the *2012 CPL*, so that evidence collected by enticement, deceit and some other illegal means is not excluded.[55]

Also, the above debates appear even in individual cases. For instance, the first controversy in case ZHANG Guoxi revolved around a distinction between illegal and defective evidence, particularly in the original judgment. Illegal evidence is evidence collected via serious violations of human rights. Defective evidence, on the other hand, is evidence that is collected in a manner that, while not in complete accordance with proper forms or procedures, does not involve human rights violations. ZHANG Guoxi's lawyers claimed that investigators' extended inquiry into ZHANG Guoxi's corruption during the preliminary investigation, before criminal proceedings commenced, constituted illegal detention that seriously violated the basic human rights of the accused.[56] The judgment at trial agreed with this reasoning and excluded ZHANG Guoxi's confession of guilt. This decision was

[53] Art. 2 of the *Rules*.

[54] Art. 1 of the *Rules*.

[55] Art. 43 of the *CPL*.

[56] 姚培硕 (YAO Peishuo): 刑法非法证据排除条款困境: 侦查人员自证清白 (The dilemma of Exclusionary Clauses on Illegal Evidence in Criminal Law: Investigators Testifying Own Innocence), *The Beijing News*, 2 August 2012, available online at <http://www.chinanews.com/fz/2012/08-02/4077216.shtml>, accessed 31 October 2018.

reversed on appeal because new evidence was introduced by the prosecution which demonstrated that ZHANG Guoxi's confession had not been extracted via torture.[57] In this sense, the detention was found not to be a serious violation of human rights, so the confession was merely defective evidence, not illegal evidence.

The second controversy in case ZHANG Guoxi was about the effective "range" of exclusionary rules, that is, whether evidence collected during preliminary investigations can be illegal evidence. The trial court excluded the use of his pre-trial confessions as the basis for convictions,[58] suggesting that the "range" of evidence to exclude should not be limited to the investigation stage, even if the acquisition of illegal evidence occurred before the investigation and ended when the criminal trial began. Exclusionary rules should be applied broadly to all cases where there is a causal relationship between the conduct of illegal collection and the evidence. In fact, the interrogation transcripts, key evidence in the case, did not result from interrogation after taking criminal compulsory measures, but from prior intensive interrogation by investigative organs. One ground on which the trial court's decision was reversed on appeal was that the *Rules* do not explicitly provide for the exclusion of evidence collected during preliminary investigations. This regulatory silence can only lead to miscarriages of justice based on faulty evidence. If evidence is collected illegally, it should be excluded as illegal evidence no matter when it was collected.

The third issue in case ZHANG Guoxi revolved around what the *Rules* mean when they refer to "other illegal means". Confessions made by suspects who have been deprived of sleep, food or other essentials should be excluded along with the typical confessions extorted under torture. Regrettably, when the defence party argued for the exclusion of evidence obtained by means of forced confessions, sleep deprivation, threats, enticements, deceit or other underhanded means used to obtain confessions of guilt, only the first was adopted as a reason to exclude evidence. The other methods were "strategically" declined by the court.[59] Continuous ill treatment, however, can be similar to torture because the accused's spirit is broken along with the accused's body. Methods like sleep deprivation are inhumane procedures are serious violations of citizens' basic human rights. Since the *CPL* stipulates that a "summons term", that is, the length of time a witness can be held at the pleasure of an investigatory body, shall not exceed 12 h,[60] overtime questioning of an accused should be regarded as ill treatment or an "oppressive atmosphere", particularly

[57]祝优优陈佳玮 (ZHU Youyou/Zhu & CHEN Jiawei): "中国非法证据排除第一案" 终审遭遇大逆转 (The Final Trial of the First Case of 'Excluding Illegal Evidence in China' Suffered from A Big Reversal), *Fenghuang Net*, 25 July 2012, available online at <http://news.ifeng.com/mainland/detail_2012_07/25/16269272_0.shtml>, accessed 31 October 2018.

[58]孔令泉 (KONG Lingquan): 国内非法证据排除第一案 (The 'First Case' of Excluding Illegal Evidence in China), *Democracy and Legal System Times*, 25 April 2012, available online at <http://news.ifeng.com/opinion/special/xieyalongfanan/detail_2012_04/25/14152917_0.shtml>, accessed 31 October 2018.

[59]*Ibid.*

[60]Art. 126 of *2012 CPL.*

when "necessary diet and rest time" like three meals and continuous rest of no less than six hours within a 24-h are also denied.[61] China should adopt rules similar to those of countries like Canada, where confessions extracted in "oppressive atmospheres" are excluded and also define the crime of torture as a matter of priority in accordance with Art. 1 of *CAT*, with penalties commensurate with the gravity of torture.[62]

Concerning the fourth issue, the burden of proof, the prosecution should bear the burden of proving the legitimacy of evidence. In other words, the prosecution should adduce evidence to prove that a confession was not collected illegally to the level of "beyond a reasonable doubt". Where the prosecution cannot satisfy this degree of proof, with significant doubts remaining about the possibility that illegal methods were used to obtain evidence, illegal evidence should be recognized and excluded under the principle that it is doubtful evidence. In case ZHANG, the trial court upheld this principle, to the benefit of the accused, but the appeal court overturned the trial court's judgment, ruling that the prosecution "sufficiently proved the legitimacy of his coerced confession" such that the trial judge should have included the "pre-trial confession of guilt … as evidence",[63] without considering whether the confession was not obtained through torture "beyond a reasonable doubt". This disregard for the "reasonable doubt" standard implies that 'abuse of discretion' by a court leaves much room for the inclusion of evidence obtained illegally.

In critical commentaries, almost all legal professionals have agreed that China's exclusionary rules have "not been strictly implemented".[64] ZHANG Jun, the Vice-President of the SPC, criticized defence lawyers because, as of early 2011, he was unable to find any cases in which a lawyer had successfully excluded DNA evidence on the grounds that it had not been properly collected.[65] Lawyers claim that this situation derives from their long practice "in a system emphasizing substantive over procedural justice", in which they focus "predominately on factual arguments".[66] As indicated by a recent survey, approximately only 20% of defence

[61]United Nations Commission on Human Rights, 'Report of the Special Rapporteur on torture and other cruel, inhuman or degrading treatment or punishment, Manfred Nowak. Sixty-second session (10 March 2006)' E/CN.4/2006/6/Add.6 (2006), available online at <http://www.refworld.org/docid/45377b160.html>, accessed 31 October 2018.

[62]*See* footnote 61.

[63]聚焦 "非法证据排除" 第一案: 疲劳审讯算不算逼供 (The Focus of 'First Case of Excluding Illegal Evidence in China': Whether Fatigue in Investigation is Torture or not), *China Youth*, 3 September 2011, available online at <http://news.xinhuanet.com/legal/2011-09/03/c_121958850.htm>, accessed 31 October 2018.

[64]任芳 (REN Fang): 非法证据排除原则未严格执行亟待律师激活避免冤错案 (The Principle of Evidence Exclusion Has Not Been Strictly Implemented), *cnr.cn*, 10 January 2011, available online at <http://www.cnr.cn/china/newszh/yaowen/201101/t20110110_507564061.html>, accessed 31 October 2018.

[65]Daum, 2011.

[66]TIAN Wenchang.

attorneys had attempted to invoke the *Rules*,[67] even though mounting a procedural defence is legally "an obligation performed by lawyers to protect judicial fairness".[68] Moreover, the lawyers who most frequently attempt to invoke the *Rules* are often frustrated by judges' lack luster responses to their advocacy, such as ignoring their request, contrary to Art. 5 of the *Rules*, for the examination of allegations of illegal evidence.[69] Lawyers also found that judges were often unwilling to debate whether evidence was collected illegally, even if inquiries into the propriety of evidence were initiated following written motions.[70] The failure of the *Rules* is best exemplified by Case FAN Qihang. In that case, the *Rules* were not invoked in Mr. FAN's favour until the SPC reviewed his death sentence, even though Mr. FAN and his lawyers had repeatedly protested that his confessions were false and had been extracted under torture. His lawyer 'publicly released and submitted to the court clandestine videotapes of Mr. FAN discussing his treatment and displaying scars on his arms', but the SPC, the court of final appeal for death sentences, never permitted the defence to use this video. The SPC conducted the trial behind closed doors, and the only way that Mr. FAN was able to participate in the process was by being executed for his "crime".[71]

3.1.2.2 The Role of the International Monitoring Bodies' Report on the Debate

The reports of the international monitoring bodies have played an essential role in Chinese debates to a certain degree. For instance, the Committee Against Torture is the body that monitors implementation of the *Convention against Torture and Other Cruel, Inhuman or Degrading Treatment or Punishment (CAT)*, and the Human Rights Committee monitors implementation of the *ICCPR*. China as a party to CAT and to the ICCPR is obliged to submit regular reports on implementation of them. Treaty bodies examine each report and address concerns and recommendations in the form of "concluding observations".

The expansive protection of the accused from torture in China has been greatly inspired by the definition of "torture" in CAT. Particularly in the context of the current *2012 CPL*, illegally collecting evidence by the means of torture or other illegal acts refers to the use of corporal punishments, disguised corporal punishments or other physical or mental suffering in a physically or mentally painful way in order to force the accused to confess against his or her willingness. Accordingly, "torture" was not a mere label any more, but has physical pains or mental suffering

---

[67]YANG/ZHANG, 2010.

[68]*See* footnote 66.

[69]*Ibid.*

[70]*Ibid.*

[71]*Ibid.*

as the standards for determining which illegal acts constitute "torture" in the context of CAT, and also has forcing the accused to confess against willingness as the essence of torture.[72]

3.1.3 Institutional Arrangements Securing Exclusionary Rules

1. There are many institutional arrangements on securing individual rights in China's criminal justice system. They mainly include cautioning or informing the accused of his or her rights, access to his or her lawyer and application for medical surveillance, as mentioned in the current *2012 CPL.*
2. Unfortunately, it is still short of an effective remedy for appeals on the ground of a violation of an exclusionary rule in law. Thus, those facing the risk of rights violations can hardly find a way to remedy or correct the above violation in practice.
3. Only law enforcement authorities including the police, prosecutors and courts actually control whether to respect limitations of fact-finding. Benefit like promotion or awards can be obtained from extorted confession through torture or guilty plea.
4. In law or practice, there is no essential interest of such actors in limiting fact-finding. They often seek substantive justice and not procedural justice in order to achieve the goal of crime control and even a very-high or almost-full conviction rate.

3.2 Exclusion of Evidence Obtained by Torture

3.2.1 Definitions of Torture and Degrading Punishment

One of major differences between Chinese legislation and international standards are related to the definition of torture. The *1997 CL* punishes those torturing suspects and the accused in the criminal process only, whereas in the definition of CAT, torture applies to any process.

In legislation, the *1982 Constitution, Law on Prisons adopted in 1994, Law on State Compensation adopted in 1994, People's Police Law adopted in 1995 (1995 PPL),*[73] *Judges Law adopted in 1995, and* the *2012 CPL effective 2013*, and the *1997 CL*, are primary legal safeguards against torture as 'a criminal act'.[74]

---

[72]CHEN Ruihua, 2015.

[73]Its Art. 33 stipulates: '[A] people's policeman has the right to refuse to carry out any directive that exceeds the mandate of the people's police as defined by laws and regulations and, at the same time, has the right to report such a breach to a higher authority.' This appears to effectively 'prevent anyone from citing a superior's order as a pretext for using torture'.

[74]CAT Report, 1996a at paras. 6 and 7.

Moreover, the *1997 CL* attaches importance to the prohibition of the crime of torture. It includes retention 'of the crime of extorting confessions by torture and the crime of physically abusing prisoners' and 'introduction of the crime of the use of force by judicial personnel to extract testimony'.[75] It explicitly stipulates 'that those who extort confessions by torture, extract testimony from witnesses by force or physically abuse prisoners shall be punished more severely'; and those 'who cause injury, disability or death through the above three crimes shall be sentenced to death, life imprisonment or fixed-term imprisonment of not less than 10 years.'[76]

More importantly, the *1997 CL* introduced the crime of extracting testimony by force and amended 'the punishment given to those who cause death through extortion of confessions by torture', 'the provisions on the applicable charges and punishment for persons who cause injury, disability or death through unlawful detention' and 'on the applicable charges and punishment for abuses of prisoners that cause injury, disability or death'.[77] This appears to aggravate relevant punishments to prohibit torture.

3.2.2 Definitions of Right to Remain Silent/Privilege Against Self-incrimination

In China, there is no statutory rule or constitutional rule on the right to remain silent, but are statutory rules on privilege against self-incrimination only. But China needs to enshrine the right in its legislation in order to better protect human rights. The *ICCPR* addresses both the right to remain silent and privilege against self-incrimination, as a major international human rights treaty that China has signed but not yet a State party.

Art. 118 of the *2012 CPL* retains the provisions that require suspects to truthfully answer investigators' questions, implying that suspects have no right to remain silent when being questioned. These provisions are especially important to prosecutors, given investigators' dependence on confessions. But since legislators have retained these provisions in the systemic context of the Amendment, it is necessary to adopt an interpretation that preserves the right to silence. One possible interpretation is that the law allows the accused to remain silent but requires them to tell the truth if they waive that right. In other words, in the *2012 CPL* there might be the right to silence, but no right to lie. The institutions of the Chinese justice system do not yet recognize the right to silence and this deficiency needs to be rectified.

It is worthy of note that no article in the *2012 CPL* explicitly articulates criminal suspects' right to silence, including the closest Art. 50, and thus many legal scholars in China do not consider this right to be fully established. Even if Chinese law has

[75] *Ibid.* at para. 8.

[76] *Ibid.* at para. 8.

[77] *Ibid.* at para. 14.

already established an implied right to silence, there is still a long way to go before the ideal system is transformed into the real one.

First, the legislature and judiciary should clarify the right of suspects and the accused to remain silent under interrogation when they implement the interpretative regulations of the 2012 *CPL*.

Second, any later amendment to the *CPL* should remove the requirement that suspects and the accused should truthfully answer police questions. While proper interpretation can reconcile Art. 118 with the presumption of innocence, it is still too open to misinterpretation. Art. 118 should be revised by removing the provision that suspects should truthfully answer questions from investigators, so as to fully embody the principle of the presumption of innocence.

In this case, the current *CPL* could be modified as follows: "[A]ny person should be presumed innocent before proved guilty by the People's Court in accordance with the law". These few words would clarify a principle that is already essentially embodied in the *CPL* and would immediately improve China's international image and status. If the words are faithfully followed to counteract institutional obstacles, they would constitute one of the greatest advances in the promotion of justice and in the adoption of the rule of law in China's history. Given China's population and global influence, they would also constitute a significant advance in the struggle for international human rights recognition.

3.2.3 Exclusionary Rules for Evidence (Possibly) Obtained by Torture

3.2.3.1 Legal Framework

1. As a part of the legal framework governing the exclusion of evidence in the case of (possible) torture or degrading treatment, the *2012 CPL* improves the exclusionary rules for illegally obtained evidence and also requires recording of certain interrogations.

Concerning direct prohibitions on torture or degrading treatment, the *2012 CPL* explicitly barred "extorting confession[s] by torture, or gather[ing] evidence by threat, enticement, deceit or other illegal means, or to force anyone to commit self-incrimination" in Art. 50. The *2012 CPL* codified a specific exclusionary rule for confessions obtained by torture or other illegal means, i.e., in Art. 54. Moreover, it explicitly requires the exclusion of confessions from suspects and accused that have been extracted by torture or other illegal methods. They also exclude witness testimony and victims' statements collected by means of violence, threats and other illegal methods, as well as physical and documentary evidence that is collected against the law and that seriously affect trial fairness.

In the *2012 CPL*, Art. 121 specifically requires an audio or visual record of an interrogation be kept in any cases involving those facing life imprisonments or the death penalty. Different from mandatory exclusion, Art. 121 also authorizes and not requires investigators to do so in other cases. There is also a new basic interrogation rule in Art. 116. Art. 116 further requires investigators of the People's Procuratorate or the public security authority to conduct an interrogation of criminal suspects and also provides that such interrogation should be done in a jail after a suspect has been transferred to a jail.

But in fact, the *2012 CPL* still imposes the legal duty to objectively and fully provide evidence on those involving in or having information of a case. Accordingly, such citizens or suspects might be required to assist investigation even by any means.

Furthermore, some regulations also constitute a major part of the above framework. For example, the SPC's 2013 *Notice on Establishing and Improving Working Mechanisms for the Prevention of Miscarriages of Justice in Criminal Cases* simply excludes confessions obtained through torture or other illegal methods. Accordingly, Chinese courts should not convict the accused based on confessions alone, but should exclude the use of confessions collected by the means of torture or other illegal methods, i.e., cold, hunger, bright light, heat, fatigue of the accused. Except in cases of emergency when on-site interrogation must be adopted, courts should exclude the use of confessions, made outside the required place, confessions, not wholly audio-video recorded by law or confessions, obtained by measures without being excluded the possible use of illegal methods during interrogation.

2. Both Chinese legislation and regulations address special procedures for screening investigations conducted by torture or other illegal means. Among them, the *2012 CPL* stipulates the obligation of the PPs, courts and the police to exclude illegally obtained evidence, along with the procedure of investigation for its exclusion in court hearings. In the trial process, the relevant PPs shall prove at trial or in appeal that all evidence was collected legally. Courts will be able to command investigators or other personnel to appear in court and explain how they collected evidence in interrogation. By the law, upon notice, investigators will also have to appear in court to justify their methods. Indeed, some investigators are already proactively demonstrating the legality of the evidence that they have collected before it is challenged.

Moreover, the SPP mentions the special procedures in its *Notice on Issuing the Guiding Opinions of the SPP on the Application of the Provisions on Several Issues concerning the Examination and Judgment of Evidence in Death Penalty Cases and the Provisions on Several Issues concerning the Exclusion of Illegal Evidence in Criminal Case*. Art. 7 of the *Notice* requires procuratorial organs to strictly implement the synchronized recording system in the whole process of interrogation of duty-related criminal suspects. Art. 7 further states the accountability system that when "any adverse consequence is caused due to any failure to strictly implement the relevant provisions or falsehood in the implementation, the major liable persons shall be investigated and punished according to the relevant provisions".[78]

Discretionary audio or video recording of interrogations, i.e., in cases without involving the punishment of life imprisonment or the death penalty, as an essential adjunct to transcripts of interrogations in procedure can be found in more regulations. For example, the SPC, the SPP, MOPS, MOSS, MOJ, and LAC (the Legislative Affairs Commission of the Standing Committee of the National People's Congress) jointly issued their *Provisions of Several Issues on the Implementation of the Criminal Procedure Law* following the adoption of the *2012 CPL*. The *Provisions* explicitly include the procedural requirement, such that "where investigators keep an audio or visual record of the interrogation process, it shall be indicated in interrogation transcripts".[79]

Similarly, the MPS'2014 *Notice on Working Rules of Public Security Organs on Audio-visual Recording of Interrogation of Suspects* requires mandatory recording of interrogations applicable to several kinds of serious criminal cases in Art. 4. They are potentially capital cases, cases of "serious injury or death, serious harm to public safety or serious violation of civil rights", or involving organised crime, serious drug crimes, and of "other intentional crimes that can be sentenced to ten years in prison by law".

The MOPS'2014 *Notice* also specify special procedures for and the mandatory scope of interrogation recordings in Art. 3. Accordingly, they "shall include the whole process of each interrogation and be uninterrupted, to maintain the integrity and shall not be selectively recorded, edited or deleted". In this context, "interrogation" broadly involves interrogating the accused in law enforcement facilities, at detention houses or at suspects' homes when they are not detained. The mandatory scope of such recordings is even expanded to "on the scene" questioning in an emergency. In addition, Art. 16 of the above *Notice* also provides that individuals other than interrogators are responsible for maintaining custody of the recordings.

The *Notice* also details pre-recording checks of the equipment, when recording should start, the frame coverage and camera angle, in Art. 9, and the identification on the record of evidence in Art. 11. It further requires such details as "time, place, modus operandi, tool of criminal purpose, state of victim(s), subjective state of mind and other key facts involved with the crime" be transcribed exactly as showed in the confession recording, in its Art. 13.

---

[78]Notice of the SPP on Issuing the Guiding Opinions of the SPP on the Application of the Provisions on Several Issues concerning the Examination and Judgment of Evidence in Death Penalty Cases and the Provisions on Several Issues concerning the Exclusion of Illegal Evidence in Criminal Cases, No. 13 [2010] (30 December 2010), available online at <http://www.lawinfochina.com/display.aspx?lib=law&id=8745&CGid=>, accessed 31 October 2018.

[79]Para. 19 of the Provisions of the SPC, the SPP, the MOPS, the MOSS, the MOJ, and the LAC on Several Issues concerning the Implementation of the Criminal Procedure Law, (26 December 2012), available online at <http://www.lawinfochina.com/display.aspx?lib=law&id=13295&CGid=>, accessed 31 October 2018.

3. According to the law on books, the justifications for the exclusionary rules mainly include respecting and safeguarding human rights, ensuring justice in each criminal case and the reliability of tortured confessions as well.
4. The above exclusion rules are mandatory in principle as indicated in Arts. 50, 54-57 of the *2012 CPL*, but appear to be discretionary in the cases of collecting material or document evidence by illegal means as exceptions in Art. 54 of the law. Specifically, Art. 50(2) of the law requires strictly prohibiting investigators from extorting confessions by torture and from collecting evidence by threat, enticement, deceit or other unlawful means. The provision implies that any form of evidence collected by the illegal means should be excluded from use in principle. Art. 54(1) of the law further states that "[C]onfessions of the criminal suspect or defendant extorted by torture or other illegal means, testimonies of the witness and statements of the victim collected by violence, threat or other illegal methods shall be excluded." So, the above rules are mandatory in principle, particularly in the case of such confession.

Art. 54(1) of the *2012 CPL* also states that "[W]here the material evidence or documentary evidence is obtained against the legally prescribed procedure, which may severely impair the judicial impartiality or justice, supplements and corrections, or reasonable explanations shall be made; if the above-mentioned measures cannot be taken, the said evidence shall be excluded." Thus, not all of material evidence or documentary evidence collected by illegal means like torture can be excluded by law. Only if such evidence may severely impair justice and also no supplement, correction or reasonable explanation on its illegal means is available, the mandatory scope of the exclusionary rules should include the evidence. Otherwise, exclusion is discretionary.

3.2.3.2 Practice; (High Court) Jurisprudence

In practice, Chinese courts recognize a general "exclusionary rule" in the cases of possible torture, in order to safeguard human rights or seek for justice. Particularly given unreliability of a confession or other statement, many courts have begun to initiate the procedure for excluding illegally obtained evidence by law in recent years.

Also, the courts often read the duty to find the truth into a specific rule in order to overrule any explicit or implied exclusionary rules in China's justice practice. According to Art. 118 of the *2012 CPL*, the accused should "answer investigators' questions truthfully" and also they should inform him or her that confessing truthfully may be treated mercifully, so that confession is encouraged to find the truth in law. On the one hand, the difficulty of changing the traditional idea of "confession first", leaving facts and evidence as the second against both law and justice, partly results from the usual policy of leniency for those who confess his or her guilt. As early as in the *SPP's 2010 Notice*, the SPP urges courts to make wholesale changes on confession in their traditional judicial attitude. Courts "shall attach great importance to evidence and investigation and research, practically change the idea of 'confessions first'", and "to the examination and use of physical evidence. If there is no other evidence except for the accused's confession, no defendant can be found guilty".[80]

On the other hand, the *2012 CPL* allows interrogators to remind suspects of their legal duty to "answer investigators' questions truthfully" and of the benefit from their truthful confession in order to seek the truth at the cost of justice and human rights. Only with the legal duty as an incentive to find the truth, Chinese courts and judges would usually exercise their discretion to overrule the exclusionary rules in practice in order to control crime and maintain social stability in the name of substantive justice.

3.2.3.3 Exclusionary Rules in Public Debate

The *2012 CPL* have once again made the use of illegally obtained evidence a point of controversy amongst domestic and foreign legal experts. Supporters of the new law claim that it is a revolutionary step towards the elimination of the use of illegally obtained evidence,[81] while critics of the law argue that it will not lead to any substantial change but could even make the situation worse.[82] Almost daily, some pundit decries the high human cost of wrongful convictions while another pundit intones about the dangers of allowing dangerous criminals to go free due to evidentiary technicalities. Both sides impugn the wisdom of the legislature, alternatively excoriating its harshness and its leniency. The resulting law is a complex mosaic of political compromises.

3.2.4 Institutional Arrangements Securing the Ban on Torture

In China, institutional arrangements appear to respect for prohibiting torture, particularly given that the relevant law can protect the accused's access to lawyers or appeals on the ground of tortured confession.

Specifically, the *2010 State Compensation Law* (*2010 SCL*) imposes a duty on detention facilities to demonstrate no mistreatment on a wrongfully convicted

---

[80]Notice of the SPP on Issuing the Guiding Opinions of the SPP on the Application of the Provisions on Several Issues concerning the Examination and Judgment of Evidence in Death Penalty Cases and the Provisions on Several Issues concerning the Exclusion of Illegal Evidence in Criminal Cases, (30 December 2010), available online at <http://www.lawinfochina.com/display.aspx?lib=law&id=8745&CGid=>, accessed 31 October 2018.

[81]*See* Time, 2012 at 144.

[82]*See* Joshua Rosenzweig, Flora Sapio, Jiang Jue, Teng Biao and Eva Pils, 'The 2012 Revision of the Chinese Criminal Procedure Law: (Mostly) Old Wine in New Bottles', *CRJ Occasional Paper*, 17 May 2012, available online at <https://papers.ssrn.com/sol3/papers.cfm?abstract_id=2462686>, accessed 31 October 2018.

prisoner. This reform is intended to discourage authorities from torturing or otherwise mistreating suspects and would help to curb torture and ill-treatment in detention.

Concerning preventing torture of suspects, the *2012 CPL* has made clear that confessions extorted through illegal means, such as torture, and witness testimony and depositions of victims obtained illegally, such as by violence or threats, should be excluded from use. To institutionally prevent extortion of confession by torture, it has regulated that suspects be sent to a detention facility for custody after being detained or arrested and be interrogated there, apart from the audio or video-taped process of interrogation. Revisions on ruling out illegal evidence and strictly regulating the procedure of collecting evidence are designed to effectively curb torture.

Furthermore, the new procedure allowing courts to call investigators to explain the legality of evidence (amended Art. 56), to call on prosecutors to provide evidence of the legality of evidence (amended Art. 55), and to require a witness statement to be examined and verified in court before it can serve as the basis for deciding a case (amended Art. 59), is intended to safeguard the right of a defendant and his or her lawyers to apply to the court for excluding evidence illegally gathered as they allege, in amended Art. 56. Both evidence provisions and exclusionary rules have been regarded as instrumental in changing a situation from that 'the confession is king' (证据为王 *Zhengjuwei Wang*), to the proper relation between material evidence and oral statements, of which the latter should be completely relied on.

In 2006, the SPP issued "*Directives to Eliminate Interrogation through Torture*", which requires that People's 'Procuratorates throughout China begin audio and video taping police interrogations in some cases to prevent coerced confessions'.[83]

Concerning appeals, the Chinese criminal justice system, in practice, does not appear to effectively protect an accused, even if he or she is persistent in claiming his or her factual innocence.

But the law enforcement authorities usually seeking for crime control by any means are legally endowed the power to control whether limitations of fact-finding are respected. Such limitations are often against the authorities' common goal of crime control. Also, they often benefit a lot from the high rate of conviction based on confession and have no real interests to limit fact-finding in handing criminal cases. If the detection or punishment rate is low in ranking, crime control authorities would be punished by less financial support, fewer human resources or no promotion of leaders. On the contrary, high or almost-full rates often bring more benefits in many aspects. It is not only a question of honour, but also means more funds, promotion or awards.

The *2012 CPL* contain some loopholes and other defects which will frustrate their intent and damage the exclusion of illegally obtained evidence. A major defect

[83]*See* Bureau of Democracy, Human Rights, and Labor, 'Country Report on Human Rights: China (includes Tibet, Hong Kong, and Macau)' (11 March 2008), available online at <http://www.state.gov/j/drl/rls/hrrpt/2007/100518.htm>, accessed 31 October 2018.

is on unfair burdens of proof, frequently imposed on the accused. The law imposes an onus on the prosecution to demonstrate that evidence was not collected through torture. This recognizes that it would be very difficult for the accused to show that he or she was tortured, but the provision is nonetheless flawed because the prosecution often has no better knowledge of what occurred during interrogation, which is in most cases was not conducted by the prosecution but by the police. This again points to the need for institutional reforms to ensure that the police who conduct interrogations are present and can answer for their conduct at trial.

Who bears the burden of proof in practice in China is not uniform. Sometimes it is borne by the PPs, sometimes by the PCs and, in the worst cases, simply by defence.[84] The common law voluntariness rule is more protective of the accused in those countries. Consistent with the presumption of innocence, it requires the prosecutor to prove beyond a reasonable doubt that the statement was voluntary.

Hence, the following institutional improvements are necessary. First, existing legal and judicial interpretations only provide for "strictly prohibiting extorted confessions by torture and collecting evidence by illegal means of threat, enticement, deceit or other methods". This narrow approach leaves many loopholes through which injustice can pass. To close these loopholes, further clarification of such concepts as "extorted confessions by torture", "threat", "lure" and "deceit" is necessary, and what constitutes "other methods" should be further defined in order to enhance the operability of the provision. Second, regarding the procedure for exclusion of illegal evidence, exclusionary rules should be considered as a right of criminal suspects and defendants. Such rights should limit investigative powers and protect the right of the accused to a fair trial. Where the defence applies for the review process but the court refuses to start it, or where the defence is dissatisfied with the outcome made by the court after the process, the defence and prosecution parties should be entitled to express objections as a relief right. On this basis, if the accused refuses to accept court judgements or the prosecution believes definite errors exist in the first-instance court's decision on illegally obtained evidence, either party could object them at appeal. Appeal courts should review the defence's appeal and the prosecution's protest.[85] Only in this way can the procedural rights of both parties can be effectively protected.

---

[84]刘梦月、杜晓 (LIU Mengyue/DU Xiao): 乐至原交通局长受贿 "大闹" 公堂 (Former Lezhi County Head of Transportation Ministry, Accused of Accepting Bribes, and Creates Spectacle in Court), People *Net*, 20 January 2011, available online at <http://fanfu.people.com.cn/GB/13777390.html>, accessed 31 October 2018.

[85]Art. 218 of the 2012 CPL states that "[A]gainst a sentence of a local people's court at any level as a court of first instance, a victim or his or her legal representative shall, within five days after receiving a written sentence, have the right to request that the People's Procuratorate file an appeal. The People's Procuratorate shall, within five days after receiving the request of the victim or his or her legal representative, make a decision on whether to file an appeal and make a reply to the requesting party."

Its Art. 222 also states that "[T]he people's court of second instance shall conduct a comprehensive review of the facts found and application of law in the sentence of the people's court of first instance, without limitations to the extent of appeal.".

3.2.5 Admissibility of Indirect Evidence ("Fruits of Poisonous Tree") in Cases of Torture

3.2.5.1 Legal Framework

China's criminal justice system does address the problem of *indirect evidence gained from torture*, but not acknowledge a "fruit of the poisonous tree" doctrine in statutory rules. In practice, there is no way to apply such rules that have no legal basis and clearly go against the law enforcement authorities' common goal of crime control.

3.2.5.2 Practice; (High Court) Jurisprudence

Justifications for the non-application of "*fruit of the poisonous tree*" in China include both very complex situation of evidence collection and many difficulties of excluding typical involuntary confession in the current judicial environment of the PRC.[86]

3.2.6 Effect of International Law (Human Rights)

Both CAT and the ICCPR as major international human rights treaties have an impact with regard to the ban on "torture evidence", as detailed above.[87] After ratifying CAT, China has taken diverse measures to reform the evidence system of prohibiting or preventing torture. Following ratifying the ICCPR, China further improves its human rights protection in procedure. All of efforts to revisions on Chinese criminal law and criminal procedures are mainly based on such international standards as the effect of international law on China.

3.2.7 Remedies Following Violations of Exclusionary Rules

There are special procedures for initiating the application for excluding with regard to a possible violation of the ban on torture, and no remedy for a violation of exclusionary rules safeguarding the ban on torture in the PRC.

In PRC's criminal justice system, there is a standard procedure for testing confessions or other statements for "torture stains" or trace.[88] As showed in Arts.

---

[86]*See* GAO Jie, 2016 at 32; LIN Guoqiang, 2013 at 182, 183.

[87]*See* above 2.1.1.2 (3) and 3.1.1.1.

[88]In the 2012 CPL, Art. 55 states that "[A]fter receiving a report, accusation, or tip on any illegal obtainment of evidence by criminal investigators or after discovering any illegal obtainment of evidence by criminal investigators, a People's Procuratorate shall conduct investigation and verification. If it is confirmed that evidence has been illegally obtained, the People's Procuratorate shall provide an opinion on correction; if any crime is committed, criminal liability shall be investigated in accordance with law." Art. 56 states that "[W]here, in a court session, a judge believes that there may

55-58, the procedure for excluding the evidence involves five steps: the first is to initiate the procedure in court examination; the second is courts' preliminary examination; the third is the prosecution's testifying in court; the fourth is cross-examination of both the accused and the prosecution; the fifth is courts' decision-making on the evidence.

Prosecutors also have the burden to prove whether torture has been used when a confession or other statement was obtained, apart from the police and courts.

3.3 Exclusion of Illegally Obtained Evidence—Cases of Undue Coercion

3.3.1 Right to Remain Silent/Privilege Against Self-incrimination and Undue Coercion

In PRC's criminal justice system, there is the "red line" drawn when fact-finding is deemed invasive with regard to individual rights, and not clear definition of undue coercion. In fact, the accused have no legal right to remain silent during interviews or interrogations in the criminal process, and only have the legal privilege against self-incrimination at a very basic level, as implied in Art. 50 of the *2012 CPL.*

3.3.2 Exclusionary Rules for Illegally Gathered Evidence in Cases of Undue Coercion (Other Than Torture)

3.3.2.1 Legal Framework

There are some statutory rules governing the exclusion process of evidence in the case of (possible) undue coercion. Justifications for the exclusionary rules according to the law on the books are diverse. They are mainly safeguarding the respect for human rights and justice.

be any illegal obtainment of evidence as described in Art. 54 of this Law, the judge shall conduct an investigation in court regarding the legality of obtainment of evidence. A party or the defender or litigation representative thereof shall have the right to apply to a people's court for excluding illegally obtained evidence. Relevant clues or materials shall be provided for an application for excluding illegally obtained evidence." Art. 57 states that "[D]uring the investigation in court regarding the legality of obtainment of evidence, a People's Procuratorate shall prove the legality of obtainment of evidence. If the existing evidentiary materials cannot prove the legality of obtainment of evidence, the People's Procuratorate may request the people's court to notify relevant investigators or other persons to appear before court to explain; and the people's court may notify relevant investigators or other persons to appear before court to explain. The relevant investigators or other persons may also file a request for appearing before court to explain. The relevant persons notified by the people's court shall appear before court." Art. 58 states that "[W] here, at trial, any illegal obtainment of evidence as described in Art. 54 of this Law is confirmed or cannot be ruled out, the relevant evidence shall be excluded.".

The exclusion of witness testimony collected by illegal means is mandatory in the cases of undue coercion and the exclusion of material or documentary evidence collected by such means is discretionary, as showed in Art. 40 of the *2012 CPL*. By the law, there are also some exceptions to the above principle of mandatory exclusion.

3.3.2.2 Practice; (High Court) Jurisprudence

In practice, courts hardly recognize the general "exclusionary rule" in cases of undue coercion in order to control crime. But they often read the duty to find the truth into specific rules, so as to overrule explicit or implied exclusionary rules against law.

3.3.3 Institutional Arrangements Securing the Right to Remain Silent

There is no institutional arrangement safeguarding the right to silence. Given the common goal of crime control, the authorities have no interest in limiting fact-finding.

3.3.4 Admissibility of Indirect Evidence ("Fruits of Poisonous Tree") in Cases of Undue Coercion

3.3.4.1 Legal Framework

China's criminal justice system does address the problem of indirect *evidence gained through evidence obtained by undue coercion*, but not acknowledge a "fruit of the poisonous tree" doctrine in any statutory rules. Hence, there is no legal framework on admissibility of indirect evidence in cases of undue correction.

3.3.4.2 Practice; (High Court) Jurisprudence

Also, there is no clear justification for the exclusion of indirect evidence in China's law or practice. So far, no court practices such exclusion in any cases of undue correction.

3.3.5 Remedies Following Violations of Exclusionary Rules

There are remedy procedures with regard to a possible use of undue coercion, as showed in Arts. 55 to 57 of the *2012 CPL* in China, but no such procedures to remedy the right to silence. In China's criminal justice system, these articles also provide for a standard procedure for testing statements for the use of undue coercion according to the law. In law, the law enforcement authorities have the burden to prove whether or not undue coercion has been used when a confession or other statement was obtained. In practice, the actual situation on the burden of proof is quite diverse.

4 Statistics

There are limited statistics on the implementation of exclusionary rules available in Mainland China. They include official data on new progress in implementation of exclusionary rules and academic findings on problems in the actual implementation.

On the one hand, academic research based on data cannot show significant progress after evidence reforms. For instance, the Criminal Procedure Law Institution of China University of Political Science and Law developed a pilot project on exclusionary rules in 2009 at three Basic Peoples' Courts (BPCs) out of nine BPC sin Yancheng City of Jiangsu Province. The three ones received 34 cases involving the application for illegally obtained evidence for a period of six months, from May 28 to November 28, 2010. The rate of applications was 5.2% in the three, higher than 0.6% as the rate in other six BPCs located in the same City during the same period of time. Also, the rate of cases with lawyers involved was 47.8% in the three pilots during the above period, higher than 33.9% as the rate in other six BPCs during the same period, and 30.7% as the rate in the three pilots during six months before the pilot period.[89] With more lawyers to help apply for excluding the evidence, defendants' expectation from lawyers was increasing, but their initiative application was reported to be rare.[90]

Another example is an academic survey on the actual implementation of the *2010 Evidence Regulations* among judges responsible for criminal trials in a court located in Guangzhou City of Guangdong Province.[91] In about 25% of cases that interviewed judges here, the defence argued that pre-trial confessions were illegally obtained before the implementation, whereas after that the defence did so in about 30% of the cases. Although the defence can provide clues or evidence sources in 55% of the 30% part, courts only identify 5% of the 55% as cases involving illegally obtained evidence.

Also, the cases involving torture was found to be about 10% of all cases in the survey and only 1% of those involving torture had been officially identified as those with tortured confession. About 10% of the cases were found to include technical flaws, of which 85% can be used as the basis of deciding cases after "corrections or reasonable explanations". Although about 5% of interrogation transcripts were not

---

[89]GUO Xinyang, 2012.

[90]*Ibid.*

[91]HE Jiahong, 2013.

checked, confirmed, signed or fingerprinted by suspects, almost all or exactly about 90% of the flawed were still used for deciding cases. In the surveyed cases, about 50% of material or documentary evidence was from suspects' confession or identification. Among the half, about 5% of it involves tortured confession and another 10% or so involves threats, enticement and deceit. Even so, about 80% of the flawed half was still used as the basis of deciding cases. Among the material or documentary evidence that the police provided to the court, approximately 15% involves technical flaws, of which about 80% have been "corrected or reasonably explained" for being used as the bases of deciding cases. Before the implementation, in cases involving requests of proving the course of collecting evidence to be legal, about 85% of all cases involve the approach of official seals in explanatory materials, whereas 80% of the cases after the implementation.[92] There is no significant change on the new reforms in practice.

Another empirical study of the early implementation of the new *CPL* also showed problems in implementation.[93] A survey of recording practices by prosecutors in Fujian Province from January to October 2013 has shown some prosecutors or leaders cannot fully recognise the important role of synchronised recording in preventing torture and excluding tortured confession.[94] Also, local people's Procuratorates' investment in recording technology was far from insufficient to meet the actual needs of providing dedicated interrogation rooms and other recording equipments.[95] This survey found that among the 96 Procuratorial agencies in the same province, two thirds (67%) only had one employee to record interrogations, and 61% of such agencies merely have part-time employees to do so. The serious lack of recording employees reveals the fact that interrogators often or at least sometimes conduct recordings. Clearly, this practice fails to separate sections in conducting recording from those in interrogating suspects during investigation, detrimental to justice.[96]

In fact, prosecutors showed no interest in recording requirements or concern about allegations of torture in interrogations before or after the implementation of the *2012 CPL*. Another survey was conducted among 642 participants as prosecutors, judges, police officers or lawyers of a Chinese province, in order to examine their attitudes towards torture during investigation.[97] The finding is that 79.7% of lawyers reported that prosecutors had no response to the allegation of torture in interrogations, and that 45.7% of the prosecutors agreed that they would not address the allegation.[98]

---

[92]Art. 7(3) of Exclusionary Rules states that explanation documents provided by prosecutors with stamps on, cannot be admitted as evidence to prove the legitimacy of collecting evidence, unless the relevant investigators signed their names on or annexed their seals to the documents.

[93]LI Mingrong//TENG Zhong/Zhang Min, 2014 at 40.

[94]*Ibid.*

[95]*Ibid.*

[96]*Ibid.* at 41.

[97]LIANG Bin/HE Ni Phil/LU Hong, 2014 at 591.

[98]*Ibid.* at 594.

5 Conclusion

In Chinese law on the books, the interest in finding the truth should be balanced with suspects' or the accused's rights. Particularly since the adoption of the *2012 CPL* effective from 2013, more and more evidence illegally obtained has been successfully excluded from use at trial. In a sharp contrast with numerous rejections in such cases, successful exclusion is very rare in practice. These facts have suggested that reforms to PRC's criminal justice system are intended to promote, but actually fail to ensure, respect for relevant human rights in the criminal process due to institutional obstacles. The above imbalance between the interest and rights has persisted for many decades.

The implementation of excluding tortured confession in China has not been used to promote human rights, ensure justice or increase the reliability of evidence collected by interrogation. Given a combination of selective exclusion or recording at the discretion and institutional hurdles to challenging admissibility of a confession as evidence, recordings are often abused as a tool for hiding torture or coercion in interrogations. The actual operation of the exclusionary rules in China is not satisfying without better protection of the accused from torture or coercion within the current institutional environment.

Hence, China's institutions of criminal justice must change and become more truly adversarial for exclusion of evidence to better prevent torture. In order to better find the truth and properly enforcing People's Courts, prosecutors and the police must pay better attention to due process, human rights and material evidence. By empowering defence lawyers to seek the exclusion of improperly-obtained evidence, China could better protect human rights and enhance the ability of courts to find the truth.

References

Books

Nolan, James L., Legal Accents, *Legal Borrowing: The International Problem-Solving Court Movement,* Princeton 2009. [Nolan, 2009]

郎胜 (LANG Sheng (ed.)): 中华人民共和国刑事诉讼法释义 *(最新修订版) (Explanations of Criminal Procedure Law in the People's Republic of China)* new edition, Beijing 2012. [LANG Sheng (ed.), 2012]

张军 (ZHANG Jun): 刑事错案追究 *(Research on Criminal Wrongful Conviction)*, Beijing 1990. [ZHANG Jun, 1990]

Journal Articles

Daum, Jeremy, 'Tortuous Progress: Early Cases Under China's New Procedures for Excluding Evidence in Criminal Cases', (2011) 43 *New York University's Journal of International Law and Politics*, 699–711. [Daum, 2011]

LIANG Bin/HE Ni Phil/LU Hong, 'The Deep Divide in China's Criminal Justice System: Contrasting Perceptions of Lawyers and the Iron Triangle', (2014) 62 *Crime, Law and Social Change*, 585–601. [LIANG Bin/HE Ni Phil/LU Hong, 2014]

Roach, Kent, 'Exonerating the Wrongfully Convicted: Do We Need Innocence Hearings', in: Margaret E. Beare (eds.), *Honouring Social Justice: Honouring Dianne Martin*, Toronto 2009, 55–84. [Roach, 2009]

Sherrin, Christopher, 'Declarations of Innocence', (2010) 35 *Queen's Law Journal*, 437–492. [Sherrin, 2010]

Time, Victoria M., 'Evidence Gathering: The Exclusionary Rule in China', (2012) 1 *International Law Research*, 144–148. [Time, 2012]

YU Ping, 'Glittery Promise vs. Dismal Reality: The Role of a Criminal Lawyer in the People's Republic of China after the 1996 Revision of the Criminal Procedure Law', (2002) 35 *Vanderbilt Journal of Transnational Law*, 827–864. [YU Ping, 2002]

陈如超 (CHEN Ruchao): 刑讯逼供的中国治理 (The Chinese Rectification of Inquisition by Torture), 甘肃政法学院学报 *(Gansu Zhengzhi Xueyuan Xuebao)* 2015-1, 1–17. [CHEN Ruchao, 2015]

陈瑞华 (CHEN Ruihua): 论被告人口供规则 (On the Rules about the Confession of the Accused), 法学杂志 *(Faxue Zazhi)* 2012-6, 46–55. [CHEN Ruihua, 2012]

陈瑞华 (CHEN Ruihua): 非法证据排除规则的适用对象 (The Exclusive Object of Illegal Evidence Exclusion Rule: An Analysis of Involuntary Confession), 当代法学 *(Dangdai Faxue)* 2015-1, 37–48. [CHEN Ruihua, 2015]

董晓伟 (DONG Xiaowei): 十年刑讯逼供致人死亡案件的回顾与反思 (Retrospection and Rethink of the Cases With Death Consequence because of the Inquisition by Torture in the Last Ten Years), *(公安学刊〉一浙江公安专科学校学报 (Gongan Xuekan) – Zhejiang Gongan Zhuanke Xuexiao Xuebao)* 2004-1, 5–7. [DONG Xiaowei, 2004]

杜豫苏 (DU Yusu): 非法证据排除审理程序的困境与完善 (The Dilemma of the Trial Process about the Exclusionary Rule and its Improvement), 法律科学 *(Falü Kexue)* 2013-6, 184–189. [DU Yusu, 2013]

高洁 (GAO Jie): 非法证据排除规则适用的实证研究——从 "中国裁判文书网" 的100份裁判文书谈起 (An Empirical Study on the Exclusionary Rule of Illegally Obtained Evidences), 江苏警官学院学报 *(Jiangsu Jingguan Xueyuan Xuebao)* 2016-1, 31–35. [GAO Jie, 2016]

郭欣阳 (GUO Xinyang): 检察改革视域中的非法证据排除规则 (The Exclusionary Rule in Light of Procuratorial Reform), 国家检察官学院学报 *(Guojia Jianchaguan Xueyuan Xuebao)* 2012-5, 9–16. [GUO Xinyang, 2012]

何家弘 (HE Jiahong): 刑事诉讼中证据调查的实证研究 (Empirical Research on Evidence Investigation in Criminal Litigation), 中外法学 (*Zhongwai Faxue*) 2012-1, 173–189. [HE Jiahong, 2012]

何家弘 (HE Jiahong): 适用非法证据排除规则需要司法判例 (Judicial Precedents are Needed in the Application of Exclusionary Rule), 法学家 *(Faxue Jia)* 2013-2, 106–118. [HE Jiahong, 2013]

孔一 (KONG Yi): 刑讯逼供调查 (Survey of the Inquisition by Torture), 青少年犯罪研究 *(Qingshaonian Fanzui Yanjiu)* 2001-2, 11–15. [KONG Yi, 2001]

李明蓉、滕忠、张旻 (LI Mingrong/TENG Zhong/Zhang Min): 福建检察机关刑诉法实施情况调研报告 (Research Report on the Procuratorates' Implementation of the Criminal Procedure Law in Fujian Province), 国家检察官学院学报 (Guojia Jianchaguan Xueyuan Xuebao) 2014-5, 40–54. [LI Mingrong/TENG Zhong/Zhang Min, 2014]

林国强 (LIN Guoqiang): 论毒树之果在我国刑事诉讼法中的适用空间 (On the Application of the Fruits of Poisonous Tree in Chinese Criminal Procedure Law), 河北法学 *(Hebei Faxue)* 2013-10,182–187. [LIN Guoqiang, 2013]

林莉红、余涛、张超 (LIN Lihong/YU Tao/ZHANG Chao): 刑讯逼供社会认知状况调查报告 (监狱服刑人员卷) (Survey of the Cognition About the Inquisition by Torture (Part: Prisoner)), 法学评论 *(Faxue Pinglun)* 2009-3, 119–129. [LIN Lihong/YU Tao/ZHANG Chao, 2009]

林莉红、余涛、张超 (LIN Lihong/YU Tao/ZHANG Chao): 刑讯逼供社会认知状况调查报告 (下篇·警察卷) (Survey of the Cognition About the Inquisition by Torture (Part Two: Police)), 法学评论 *(Faxue Pinglun)* 2006-5, 123–140. [LIN Lihong/YU Tao/ZHANG Chao, 2006]

宁平 (NING Ping): 我国 "抗辩式" 侦查讯问模式构建的必要性及可行性探究 (Research on the Necessity and Feasibility of the Establishment of an Adversarial Investigative Interrogation Model in China), 犯罪研究 *(Fanzui Yanjiu)* 2015-4. 39–46. [NING Ping, 2015]

田文昌 [TIAN Wenchang]: 刑事辩护不能放纵非法证据 (Criminal Defense Cannot Abide Illegal Evidence), 法制周末 *(Fazhi Zhoumo),* 11 January 2011, available online at <http://opinion.hexun.com/2011-01-11/126731224.html>, accessed 31 October 2018. [TIAN Wenchang]

王超 (WANG Chao): 非法证据排除规则的虚置化隐忧与优化改革(The Hidden Worry of an Empty Shell in Regard of the Exclusionary Rule and the Optimum Reform of This Rule), 法学杂志 *(Faxue Zazhi)* 2013-12, 100–108. [WANG Chao, 2013]

吴宏耀 (WU Hongyao): 非法证据排除的规则与实效——兼论我国非法证据排除规则的完善进路 (The Exclusionary Rule, its Actual Effect and the Approach of Improvement on the Exclusionary Rule in People's Republic of China), 现代法学 *(Xiandai Faxue)* 2014-4, 121–130. [WU Hongyao, 2014]

谢澍 (XIE Peng): 刑事审判公开的信息化转型 (The Transformation of Informatisation in the Criminal Public Trial), 中国刑事法杂志 *(Zhongguo Xingshifa Zazhi)* 2012-12, 65–75. [XIE Peng, 2012]

闫召华 (YAN Zhaohua): "名禁实允" 与 "虽令不行": 非法证据排除难研究 (Forbid Nominally, but Allow Actually and Despite Decree, but not Execute: Research on the Difficulties of the Exclusionary Rule), 法制与社会发展 *(Fazhi Yu Shehuifazhan)* 2014-2, 181–192. [YAN Zhaohua, 2014]

杨明、张海林 [YANG Ming/ZHANG Hailin]: 非法证据排除规则施行 4 月律师称新规作用有限 (Evidence Exclusion off to a Shaky Start), 瞭望东方周刊(Liaowang Dongfang Zhoukan), 29 November 2010, available online at <http://news.sohu.com/20101129/n277987689.shtml>, accessed 31 October 2018. [YANG/ZHANG, 2010]

杨宇冠 (YANG Yuguan): 论法治视野下的非法证据排除规则 (On the rule of excluding illegal evidence under the rule of law), 证据科学 *(Zhengju Kexue)* 2015-4, 389–399. [YANG Yuguan, 2015]

周长军 (ZHOU Changjun): 微博直播庭审对侦查法治化的可能意义 (The Possible Importance of the Trial Live Broadcasting by Weibo-Software to the Rule by Law during the Investigation), 法学论坛 *(Faxue Luntan)* 2014-1. 90–99. [ZHOU Changjun, 2014]

左卫民 (ZUO Weimin): "热" 与 "冷" 非法证据排除规则适用的实证研究 (The Favourite and the Underdog in the Empirical Research on the Exclusionary Rule), 法商研究 *(Fashang Yanjiu)* 2015-3,151–160. [ZUO Weimin, 2015a]

左卫民 (ZUO Weimin): 中国《刑事诉讼法》第三次修改前瞻 (Prospect of the Third Reform of the Chinese Criminal Procedure Code), 现代法学 *(Xiandai Faxue)* 2015-4. 3–11. [ZUO Weimin, 2015b]

Internet Links for UN-Documents

United Nations Committee Against Torture, 'Second Periodic Reports of States Parties Due in 1993: China. (15 February 1996)' CAT/C/20/Add.5 (1996), available online at <http://

tbinternet.ohchr.org/_layouts/treatybodyexternal/Download.aspx?symbolno=CAT%2fC%2f20%2fAdd.5&Lang=zh>, accessed 31 October 2018. [CAT Report, 1996a]

Case List

Case FAN Qihang
Case NIAN Bin
Case SHE Xianglin
Case ZHAO Zuohai
Case ZHANG Guoxi

Professor Na Jiang holds a Ph.D. from Durham University (UK) where she successfully completed her thesis titled "China and international human rights: Capital punishment and detention for re-education in the context of the International Covenant on Civil and Political Rights." Professor Jiang's research interests include comparative law, international human rights law, criminal law and procedure, and exclusionary rules in the Chinese criminal justice system. She joined Beijing Normal University in 2008 where she has been a professor of law since 2015. She has published numerous articles and books in English and Chinese in the areas of criminal law, criminal procedure, and international human rights law in the Western world and China.

Criminal Justice and the Exclusion of Incriminating Statements in Singapore

Hock Lai Ho

Abstract There is inevitably tension in any criminal justice system between the state's interest in securing the evidence necessary to convict a guilty party and the need to respect individual rights, uphold the rule of law and protect the legitimacy of criminal convictions. This tension is examined in the context of the criminal justice system in Singapore. A general overview is given of the criminal process, including its social and international dimensions. Focus is placed upon the law on the exclusion of incriminating statements obtained wrongfully from the accused person. The principal features of this law are the voluntariness test for the admissibility of such evidence, the oppression doctrine and the discretion to exclude incriminating statements where their prejudicial effect if admitted at the trial is likely to outweigh their probative value. In defending the operation and scope of these exclusionary rules, and the weakening of certain rights such as the right of silence and the right to counsel, local conditions and values are often invoked in official discourse. One theme that emerges is the influence of crime control ideology in shaping the criminal process.

1 Introduction

A tension is often said to exist in the criminal process between the interest in finding the truth and respect for the rights of persons suspected or accused of having committed a crime. The interest in the truth has two dimensions: one is the interest in finding the accused guilty when he is in fact guilty and the other is the interest in acquitting the accused when he is in fact innocent. A type 1 error occurs when a factually innocent person is convicted and a type 2 error occurs when a factually

Faculty of Law, National University of Singapore. I am grateful to my students Chan Kah Wai Kenneth, Loo Tze Ding Dorothy Ann and Ng Wei Jie Benjamin for their research assistance.

H. L. Ho (✉)
Faculty of Law, National University of Singapore (NUS), Singapore, Singapore
e-mail: lawhohl@nus.edu.sg

S. Gless and T. Richter (eds.), *Do Exclusionary Rules Ensure a Fair Trial?*
Ius Gentium: Comparative Perspectives on Law and Justice 74,
https://doi.org/10.1007/978-3-030-12520-2_7

guilty person is acquitted. Upholding of the rights of suspects or accused persons is sometimes motivated by the interest in protecting an innocent person from a type 1 error (that is, wrongful conviction), and this is consistent with the second aspect of the interest in determining the truth. In diluting or weakening such rights, it is the first dimension of the interest in determining the truth (avoiding a type 2 error of acquitting a factually guilty person) that is often invoked. On the standard argument, rights of individuals have sometimes to give way to the social interest in crime control.[1] It is from this perspective that there is a supposed conflict between determining the truth and respect for individual rights.

This supposed conflict will be examined in relation to evidence of a confession or an incriminating statement taken from the accused person by police officers in Singapore. The principal sources of law that govern the obtaining and admissibility of such statements are the Criminal Procedure Code ('CPC'),[2] the Evidence Act ('EA')[3] and, to some extent, the common law. The goal of ascertaining the truth is not explicitly declared in the CPC or the EA. However, as we shall see, it underpins various aspects of the criminal process (such as the presumption of innocence, pre-trial criminal case disclosure and judicial scrutiny of the factual basis for a guilty plea), and actors in the criminal process are expected to respect the truth in discharging their respective duties. At the same time, it is recognized that the search for the truth needs to be balanced against other countervailing interests. In the 1976 case of *Cheng Swee Tiang v PP*, the majority of the High Court judges formulated the competing considerations thus in the context of excluding illegally obtained evidence[4]:

> …two important interests come into conflict when considering the question of admissibility of … evidence [that the police had improperly] obtained. On the one hand there is the interest of the individual to be protected from illegal invasions of his liberties by the authorities and on the other hand the interest of the State to secure that evidence bearing upon the commission of crime and necessary to enable justice to be done shall not be withheld from the courts on any merely technical ground.

Local conditions are taken into account in deciding how the balance is to be struck. In the 2008 case of *Law Society of Singapore v Tan Guat Neo Phyllis*, in which issues were raised relating to the admissibility of evidence obtained in an alleged entrapment, the High Court (sitting as a bench of three judges) cautioned against uncritical following of decisions from Australia, Canada and England. It stressed that 'the legal and social environments in these jurisdictions are not the same, and that the courts in each jurisdiction must take into account the values and objectives of the criminal justice system which they wish to promote.'[5]

---

[1]Packer, 1968 at Part II.

[2]Cap 68, 2012 rev. ed.

[3]Cap 97, 1997 rev. ed.

[4]*Cheng Swee Tiang* v. *PP* (1964) 30 MLJ 291 at 293.

[5]*Law Society of Singapore* v. *Tan Guat Neo Phyllis* [2008] 2 SLR(R) 239 at [58]. For a critique, *see* Ho, 2012. Similar sentiments were expressed by the High Court a year earlier in the different

This chapter will proceed as follows. Part 2 provides background information. It gives an overview of the stages of the criminal process and the duties and accountability of the actors involved in the process, and discusses the main constitutional rights that exist in the context of administering criminal justice. Part 3 explores the social dimension. It discusses the extent to which the state of criminal justice has received public attention and drawn public debate. Part 4 summarizes the legal rules governing police questioning, the admissibility of statements obtained from the suspect, and the drawing of adverse inferences from omissions to mention material facts. This is followed by a study of the exclusion of incriminating statements obtained by torture in Part 5 and by other forms of undue pressure in Part 6. Part 7 addresses briefly the admissibility and effect of derivative evidence. The influence of international law on human rights is considered in Part 8 and the availability of safeguards in Part 9. Part 10 relay such little statistics as are available. Part 11 concludes with some general observations.

2 Overview of Criminal Proceedings

This Part provides background information by way of an overview of the administration of criminal justice in Singapore and the relevant constitutional rights.

2.1 Stages

2.1.1 Investigation, Decision to Prosecute, Procedural Preliminaries

Typically, criminal investigations begin when a first information report is filed with the police[6] alleging the commission of an offence.[7] The law vests the police with an array of investigative powers such as the power of arrest, entry, and search and seizure. Most pertinent for present purposes is the power to question and take statements from the suspect or accused person. This is considered in detail later.

When a person is arrested and detained in custody, the police officer must bring him before a Magistrate within 48 hours.[8] The magistrate may order that he be further detained if investigation is on-going. It is not difficult to persuade the court

context of sentencing: *PP* v. *Law Aik Meng* [2007] 2 SLR(R) 814 at [19]. *See also Yuan Suan Piau Steven* v. *PP* [2013] 1 SLR 809 at [31].

[6]The Police Force is the main investigative agency. There are other specialised law enforcement agencies such as the Corrupt Practices Investigation Bureau and the Central Narcotics Bureau. This chapter concentrates on the Police.

[7]s. 14 CPC.

[8]s. 68 CPC; Art. 9(4) Constitution of the Republic of Singapore.

to grant such extensions of detention.[9] Upon completion of investigation, the matter will be referred to the Attorney-General's Chambers which will make an assessment of the sufficiency of admissible evidence to support a criminal conviction.[10] The power to institute, conduct and discontinue criminal proceedings lies with the Attorney-General.[11] Should the decision be taken to commence prosecution against the person, different court procedures will apply depending on whether the case is tried in the High Court or the State Courts.

In cases before the State Courts, the case will begin with the 'first mention' where the charge will be read and explained to him[12] after which he will be asked whether he wishes to claim trial or plead guilty to the charge. Alternatively, the court may grant an adjournment without the plea being taken.[13] For more serious cases which are triable only in the High Court, the accused will first be produced before a Magistrate's Court and the charge will be explained to him. Usually this will be followed by committal proceedings where a magistrate will decide whether there are sufficient grounds for committing the accused for trial before the High Court.[14] If there are not sufficient grounds, the magistrate will discharge the accused and if there are sufficient grounds, he will commit the accused for trial before the High Court.[15]

2.1.2 Plea-Negotiation

In 2004, the Attorney-General's Chambers introduced the Criminal Case Management System (CCMS). This is an arrangement that brings the prosecution and the defence together to discuss the merits of and issues in the case and to engage in plea negotiation.[16] The judge is not involved in this process. If the case is

---

[9]Concerns over the ease with which extensions are obtained have been raised in Parliament. *See, eg*, 'Parliamentary Debates Singapore: Official Report', vol. 69 (1 June 1998) at cols. 77 (Mr J B Jeyaretnam): 'Once a person is picked up and is taken into police custody, there is, under the Constitution, a maximum limit of 48 hours that the police may hold anyone in custody before they produce them in the courts. But, unfortunately, this protection of not being kept in police custody too long is eroded by the readiness of the courts to grant such custody'.

[10]*See* generally Walter Woon, 'The public prosecutor, politics and the rule of law', *The Straits Times*, 29 September 2017.

[11]Art. 35(8), Constitution of the Republic of Singapore.

[12]s. 158(a) CPC.

[13]s. 158(b) CPC.

[14]For certain types of offences, the case may be transmitted directly to the High Court for trial: s. 175(3) and s. 210 CPC. After a recent amendment, this transmission procedure now applies to all offences: see the Addendum at the end of this chapter.

[15]s. 187, CPC.

[16]The CCMS was launched in 2013 as part of a Code of Practice for the Conduct of Criminal Proceedings by the Prosecution and the Defence (discussed further below). *See* guidelines 10 and 11 of this Code which is available online at <https://www.agc.gov.sg/docs/default-source/newsroom-doucments/media-releases/2013/code-of-practice-for-the-conduct-of-criminal-proceedings—final.pdf?sfvrsn=2>, accessed 31 October 2018.

unresolved at this stage, there is a further opportunity for resolution in the State Courts. After the trial date is set, and before the trial, the parties may agree to have the case referred for 'Criminal Case Resolution' (CCR).[17] The purpose is 'to ascertain whether there are alternative options to trial that may not have been fully and adequately explored' and 'not to reduce the number of trials by actively encouraging pleas of guilty.'[18] The CCR process is facilitated by a judge who will not be the one presiding at the trial should the case remain unresolved. Plea-negotiation in Singapore at present remains largely an informal practice.[19] Representations made in the course of plea-negotiation are privileged.[20] 'There is a long-established practice or convention… that such representations are made "without prejudice" and that the [Public Prosecutor] will not seek to admit them in evidence against the accused should the representations be rejected.'[21]

2.1.3 Pre-trial

Prior to the trial, a criminal case disclosure conference will be held for the purpose of settling the following matters: (a) the filing of the Case for the Prosecution and the Case for the Defence; (b) any issues of fact or law which are to be tried by the trial judge at the trial proper; (c) the list of witnesses to be called by the parties to the trial; (d) the statements, documents or exhibits which are intended by the parties

---

[17]This was introduced via Subordinate Courts Registrar's Circular No. 4 of 2011. *See* Soh, 2011 and See, 2013.

[18]*See* See, 2013 at 78.

[19]*See Chua Qwee Teck* v. *PP* [1990] 2 SLR(R) 571 at [19] ('"plea bargaining", in the sense of the court bargaining with the accused as to sentence, is not part of the administration of justice in Singapore') and at [20] ('no such thing as "plea bargaining" with the judge'). In a speech delivered at the Criminal Law Conference on 16 January 2014, the Minister of Law announced that the government was working on a formalised framework on plea bargaining: <https://www.mlaw.gov.sg/news/speeches/speech-by-min-at-criminal-law-conference-2014.html>, accessed 31 October 2018. It has since been reported that the government has decided not to implement any major changes: 'Plea Bargaining, Singapore-style', *The Straits Times*, 15 March 2017. According to this same report, 810 of the 851 convictions in the first two months of 2017 resulted from pleading guilty 'after some sort of talks between the prosecution and defence'. *PP* v. *Knight Glenn Jeyasingam* [1999] 1 SLR(R) 1165 at [15] where the prosecutor cited statistics revealing that only 2.3% of persons charged in 1997 made representations (both plea and non-plea bargaining) to the AGC.

[20]*PP* v. *Knight Glenn Jeyasingam* [1999] 1 SLR(R) 1165. *See also Azman bin Jamaluddin* v. *PP* [2012] 1 SLR 615 at [50] and *Ng Chye Huay* v. *PP* [2006] 1 SLR(R) 157 (letters of representation made to the police are similarly inadmissible provided certain conditions are satisfied, namely 'the letter must refer specifically to the investigation or charge faced by the accused', it 'must have been written with the object of reducing the charge or halting investigations' and 'contain a statement that the author of the letter understands the consequence of making a false statement under s 182 of the Penal Code.' *PP* v. *Khartik Jasudass* [2015] SGHC 199 at [103]-[104].

[21]*Law Society of Singapore* v. *Tan Guat Neo Phyllis* [2008] 2 SLR(R) 239 at [118].

to the case to be admitted at the trial; and (e) the trial date.[22] The filing obligations referred to in item (a) arise from a new regime of criminal pre-trial discovery, known as 'criminal case disclosure', which came into effect in 2011.[23] This statutory regime of criminal case disclosure is augmented by a common law duty of disclosure.[24] According to the Court of Appeal in *PP v Li Weiming*,[25] pre-trial criminal case disclosure serves the objective of finding the truth[26]:

> The interest of the Prosecution in a criminal trial is not to obtain a conviction at any costs, and a procedure whereby the Prosecution first lays its cards on the table is an acknowledgment that it is the duty of the Prosecution to prove its case beyond reasonable doubt and to assist the court by placing before it all relevant facts and evidence so that the truth may be ascertained... From the perspective of the accused, an early disclosure of the Prosecution's case enables him to make preparations for his defence, and although the mutual exchanges of information makes a limited incursion into the accused's right to silence, it ensures that relevant facts are not concealed from the trial judge. Reciprocal discovery, *if properly implemented*, therefore enhances the reliability and transparency of the criminal justice process in searching for the truth.

2.1.4 Trial

At the commencement of the trial, the charge will be read and explained to the accused and his plea will be taken.[27] Judges are conscious of their duty to ascertain the truth even in cases where the accused elects to plead guilty. The court must be satisfied, before recording his plea, that his choice is free and informed,[28] in particular, that the accused 'understands the nature and consequences of his plea' and 'intends to admit to the offence without qualification'.[29] Where the accused is charged with an offence punishable with death, the High Court will not record a guilty plea unless the accused has been committed to stand trial and evidence is led by the prosecution to prove its case.[30]

---

[22]*See* ss. 160(1), 192(2), and 212(1) CPC.

[23]*See* Division 2 of Part IX and Division 2 of Part X of the CPC. This procedure applies to cases to be tried before the High Court and a significant number of cases to be tried in the District Court. Where this procedure does not apply, a pre-trial conference will be held to settle any administrative matter in relation to the trial: s. 171 CPC. For detailed discussion, *see* Wong, 2013.

[24]*Muhammad bin Kadar* v. *PP* [2011] 3 SLR 791 and *Muhammad bin Kadar* v. *PP* [2011] 3 SLR 1205. *See* Wong, 2013 at [14]. *See also* Code of Practice for the Conduct of Criminal Proceedings by the Prosecution and the Defence, above note 16, Section 4, Guidelines 40 and 41(containing non-binding guidelines on prosecutorial disclosure).

[25]*PP* v. *Li Weiming* [2014] 2 SLR 393.

[26]*Ibid* at [26], citing Chng, 2011 at [38].

[27]s. 230(1)(a) CPC.

[28]*Yunani bin Abdul Hamid* v. *PP* [2008] 3 SLR(R) 383 at [57].

[29]s. 227(2) CPC.

[30]s. 227(3) CPC.

In practice, 'before a plea of guilty by the accused is accepted by the court, a statement of facts setting out the circumstances in which the offence is alleged to have been committed is read to the accused by the Prosecution and the accused is required to admit such statement.'[31] The trial judge has a legal duty to record the statement of facts and to scrutinise it to ensure that all the elements of the charge are made out on those facts.[32] This is to enable the judge to ascertain that the accused understands the nature of his guilty plea and intends to admit without qualification the offence alleged against him,[33] and also to assist the judge to determine the appropriate sentence.[34]

Where the accused refuses to plead or does not plead or claims trial, the court will proceed to hear the case.[35] Trials are of an adversarial nature. Parties are responsible for presenting their respective cases and evidence. There is no jury system; the judge acts as the fact-finder. For non-capital offences, the Law Society's Criminal Legal Aid Scheme provides legal assistance to accused persons who cannot afford to hire a lawyer and meet certain criteria.[36] All persons facing capital charges are eligible for free legal representation under the Legal Assistance Scheme for Capital Offences which is administered by the Supreme Court.[37]

At the commencement of the trial, the prosecutor will present an opening address in which he will state shortly the nature of the offence and the evidence he proposes to adduce.[38] Following the opening address, the prosecutor will proceed to present the evidence. After the prosecutor has examined a witness, the defence will have the opportunity to cross-examine him, and this may be followed by re-examination of the witness by the prosecutor.[39] After the prosecutor has concluded its case, it is open to the defence to apply to dismiss the case on the ground that there is no case to answer.[40] The court will then have to decide whether the prosecution has succeeded in producing 'some evidence which is not inherently incredible and which

[31] *Chota bin Abdul Razak* v. *PP* [1991] 1 SLR(R) 501 at [11]. *See also Mok Swee Kok* v. *PP* [1994] 3 SLR(R) 134. A statement of agreed facts could also be tendered as a formal admission of guilt by the accused: *PP* v. *Mohamad Noor bin Abdullah* [2017] 3 SLR 478.

[32] *Mok Swee Kok* v. *PP* [1994] 3 SLR(R) 134 at [14].

[33] *Chota bin Abdul Razak* v. *PP* [1991] 1 SLR(R) 501 at [16].

[34] *Mok Swee Kok* v. *PP* [1994] 3 SLR(R) 134 at [14]; *Biplob Hossain Younus Akan* v. *PP* [2011] 3 SLR 217 at [9].

[35] s. 230(1)(c) CPC.

[36] This scheme, which began in 1985, has been enhanced with direct government funding since January 2015. *See* Thio, 2015. It is reported that 2433 persons were helped under the enhanced scheme in 2015, a five-fold increase from the number in 2014: 'Criminal Legal Aid Scheme helping more accused people', *The Straits Times*, 29 February 2016.

[37] Information is available from the website of the Supreme Court. *See* <http://www.supremecourt.gov.sg/rules/court-processes/criminal-proceedings/legal-assistance-scheme-for-capital-offences-(lasco)>, accessed 31 October 2018.

[38] s. 230(1)(d) CPC.

[39] s. 230(1)(e) CPC.

[40] s. 230(1)(f) CPC.

satisfies each and every element of the charge'[41]; if the court forms the view that such evidence exists, it will call on the accused to give his defence.[42] At this point, the court will have to inform the accused of the following options[43]:

> First, if you elect to give evidence you must give it from the witness box, on oath or affirmation, and be liable to cross-examination. Second, if you elect not to give evidence in the witness box, that is to say, remain silent, then I must tell you that the court in deciding whether you are guilty or not, may draw such inferences as appear proper from your refusal to give evidence, including inferences that may be adverse to you.

When the court calls upon the accused to give his defence, he may either plead guilty or choose to enter his defence.[44] Should the latter option be taken, the defence will proceed to open its case and call its witnesses.[45] The accused cannot be compelled to give evidence.[46] However, if he chooses not to give evidence at his trial, the court may draw adverse inferences against him as appear proper.[47] If the accused elects to take the witness stand, his evidence must be given on oath or affirmation and he is liable to cross-examination. After the defence has presented its evidence, it will give a closing address to which the prosecution will have the final right of reply.[48]

Thereafter the court will deliberate and give its judgment. If the court finds the accused guilty as charged, it will proceed to hear submissions by the prosecution and the plea in mitigation by the defence prior to deciding on the sentence.[49]

2.1.5 Post-trial

The prosecution may appeal against the acquittal of the accused and the sentence delivered by the trial court. Similarly, the accused may appeal against his conviction and against his sentence.[50] There is also the possibility of petitioning to the High Court for criminal revision in respect of criminal proceedings and matters in the State Courts.[51] This power is 'exercised sparingly' and 'the possible existence

[41]This is a low evidential threshold. At this stage, the court is not to decide whether the prosecution has proved its case beyond reasonable doubt.

[42]s. 230(1)(j) CPC.

[43]s. 230(1)(m) CPC.

[44]s. 230(1)(n) CPC.

[45]s. 230(1)(o), (p) CPC.

[46]s. 122(3) EA; s. 291(4) CPC.

[47]s. 291(3) CPC.

[48]s. 230(1)(u), (v) CPC.

[49]s. 228 CPC.

[50]*See* ss. 374(3) and (4) CPC respectively. *See* generally, Part XX of the CPC for the appeal procedure.

[51]s. 23 Supreme Court of Judicature Act, Cap 322, 2007 rev. ed.

of a serious injustice must be present' before the High Court will act.[52] The option of petitioning for criminal revision is important to an accused person whose conviction was on a guilty plea. This is because once a guilty plea is entered, the accused loses the right to appeal on the conviction.[53] 'In such a situation, an application by way of criminal revision would be the only means by which the accused could have a wrongful conviction set aside.'[54] An appropriate situation for the exercise of this revisionary power is where 'additional evidence before the reviewing court casts serious doubts as to the guilt of the accused'.[55]

2.2 *Actors: Duties and Accountability*

2.2.1 Police Officers

An important function of the police is crime detection. The law confers on the police an array of powers to perform this function. Most pertinent for our purposes is the power to detain and question suspects.[56] The Police Force Act (PFA)[57] contains provisions on 'duties and discipline of police officers'.[58] Under section 28 PFA, senior police officers may be disciplined under the authority of the Public Service Commission. Disciplinary proceedings against senior police officers are regulated by the Public Service (Disciplinary Proceedings) Regulations. For officers below the rank of inspector, disciplinary proceedings are provided for in the Police Regulations. The Internal Affairs Office is an investigation entity within the Singapore Police Force which is tasked to conduct investigations into disciplinary offences and crimes committed by police officers.[59] Police improprieties in the course of conducting investigation, including interrogation of suspects, are referred to the Internal Affairs Office for investigation. Such improprieties may constitute a disciplinary offence under section 40 of the Police Force Act as well as a criminal offence.[60]

[52] *Yunani bin Abdul Hamid* v. *PP* [2008] 3 SLR(R) 383 at [56].

[53] s. 375(1) CPC. The accused may appeal only against the extent or legality of the sentence.

[54] *Yunani bin Abdul Hamid* v. *PP* [2008] 3 SLR(R) 383 at [43].

[55] *Yunani bin Abdul Hamid* v. *PP* [2008] 3 SLR(R) 383 at [56].

[56] *See* Part IV of the CPC.

[57] Cap 235, 2006 rev. ed.

[58] *See* Part III Division 1 and Division 2 of the PFA. Sections 117-119 of the PFA empowers the Commissioner to make Police Regulations, General, Force and Standing Orders.

[59] 'Parliamentary Debates Singapore: Official Report', vol. 63 (25 August 1994) at cols. 381-2 (calls to make the Internal Investigation Section (now Internal Affairs Office) independent of the police force were rejected).

[60] The officer may be prosecuted for an offence under the Penal Code, Cap 224, 2008 rev. ed., or under other legislation such as the Prevent of Corruption Act, Cap 241, 1993 rev. ed. (*see*, *eg*, *PP* v. *Peter Benedict Lim Sin Pang* [2013] SGDC 192). Voluntarily causing hurt or grievous hurt to extort a confession is criminalised under s. 330 and s. 331 of the Penal Code respectively; *cf. PP* v. *GBZ* [2017] SGDC 271 (involving a private citizen causing hurt to another in order obtain a confession).

While criminal prosecution[61] of, and civil claims against,[62] police officers do occur, more often than not the matter is dealt with as a disciplinary offence.[63]

2.2.2 Prosecutors

Under the Legal Profession (Professional Conduct) Rules 2015,[64] the prosecutor 'must present the evidence against an accused person fairly and impartially, and without malice, fear or favour'[65] and 'must comply with the constitutional, evidential and procedural rules which operate in a criminal trial'.[66] As a general principle, the prosecutor 'is under a fundamental duty to assist in the administration of justice'[67] and 'must assist the court... by drawing the court's attention to any apparent error..., any apparent omission of fact, and any procedural irregularity, which...ought to be corrected.'[68] The Supreme Court has jurisdiction to discipline public prosecutors for professional misconduct under section 82A of the Legal Profession Act.[69] In a speech by a judge of the Supreme Court, who was

---

[61]*See, eg*, 'Cop beat up suspect at police post', *The Straits Times*, 5 July 2002; *Chua Yong Khiang Melvin* v. *PP* [1999] 2 SLR(R) 1108; *Mohd Shahrin bin Shwi* v. *PP* [1996] 3 SLR(R) 174; *Vance John Doray* v. *PP* [2001] SGMC 43.

[62]In *Zainal bin Kuning* v. *Chan Sin Mian Michael* [1996] 2 SLR(R) 858, the plaintiffs brought a civil action against a police inspector for false imprisonment and malicious prosecution, alleging that false incriminating statements had been obtained from them by subjecting them to assault and other forms of ill treatment: *ibid* at [18]-[20]. The Court of Appeal upheld the decision of the trial court to dismiss the plaintiffs' action with costs. It seems that this was one of the cases that prompted a member of Parliament to propose the setting up of a commission of inquiry to look into the state of criminal justice in Singapore: *see* 'Parliamentary Debates Singapore: Official Report', vol. 69 (1 June 1998) at cols. 75-108, especially col. 92.

[63]*See* s. 40 PFA. The disciplinary offences set out in the Schedule to this Act include 'conduct to the prejudice of good order and discipline' (item 3) and 'excess of duty resulting in loss or injury to any other person' (item 12). *See, eg, Leong Kum Fatt* v. *AG* [1985-1986] SLR(R) 165: a police inspector was dismissed after a disciplinary hearing for assaulting two suspects and failed in his application for judicial review of the disciplinary decision.

[64]S.706/2015.

[65]Rule 15(2).

[66]Rule 15(1)(b).

[67]Rule 15(1)(a).

[68]Rule 15(6).

[69]Cap 161, 2009 rev. ed. *See Re Nalpon Zero Geraldo Mario* [2012] 3 SLR 440 (High Court), unsuccessful application made by defence counsel under this section. Subsequently the Attorney-General filed a complaint against the defence counsel to the Law Society for, among other things, making and disseminating to various third parties offensive remarks, including remarks that would undermine the integrity of the office of the Attorney-General. The defence counsel was eventually censured by the Court. *See Law Gazette*, June 2014, 'Findings and Determination of the Disciplinary Tribunal, *In the matter of Zero Geraldo Mario Nalpon, an Advocate and Solicitor*', available online at <http://v1.lawgazette.com.sg/2014-06/>, accessed 31 October 2018.

formerly the Attorney-General, the following was said of the ethical duties of prosecutors[70]:

> The goal of the prosecution is *not* to secure a conviction at all costs….[71] Because the decision to charge an accused is made after a process of careful consideration, the Prosecutor would be expected to pursue the case with vigour to secure the conviction of one whom he sincerely believes to be guilty. Yet, the point is that the desire to secure a conviction *flows from his basic commitment to justice*: the Prosecutor desires to convict the guilty only because that is what justice demands. The fact that the Prosecutor's ultimate duty is to justice also means that the Prosecutor has a duty to withdraw a charge or, even, to apply for a criminal revision if clear evidence emerges to disprove the guilt of the accused.

The same emphasis on fairness was stressed recently in a speech delivered by the Attorney-General at the Opening of Legal Year 2016 where he stated[72]:

> There is no point in securing convictions if the public is not confident that the process is fair and the convictions are safe…. [P]rosecutors have a special responsibility to uphold the integrity of the criminal justice system. We share a responsibility with the court for ensuring that prosecution is carried out fairly and the process is one in which the public can have confidence. Fulfilling this responsibility is a big part of a prosecutor's role.

2.2.3 Defence Counsel

Defence counsel is 'under a fundamental duty to assist in the administration of justice.'[73] He 'must pursue every reasonable defence, and raise every favourable factor, on behalf of the accused person in accordance with the law'[74] and must not be influenced by his 'personal opinion as to whether the accused person is guilty'.[75] Where the accused person confesses to the defence counsel, the latter may continue to represent him but 'must not adduce any evidence or make any submission which is inconsistent with the confession'.[76]As the judge in the same speech noted above puts it, 'the goal of criminal defence is not to secure an acquittal at all costs.' 'The duty of the Defence Counsel is to ensure that no conviction is entered *unless* it is

---

[70]Chong, 2015 at [9].

[71]*See Muhammad bin Kadar and another* v. *PP* [2011] 3 SLR 1205 at [200]: 'the duty of the Prosecution is not to secure a conviction at all costs. Rather, the Prosecution owes a duty to the court and to the wider public to ensure that only the guilty are convicted, and that all relevant material is placed before the court to assist it in its determination of the truth.'

[72]Speech delivered by the Attorney-General, Mr V K Rajah, SC, at the Opening of the Legal Year 2016 on 11 January 2016, at [14], available online at <https://www.agc.gov.sg/docs/default-source/speeches/2016/ag's-oly-speech-2016-(as-delivered)-(4).pdf?sfvrsn=2>, accessed on 31 October 2018.

[73]Rule 14(1), Principle (a) of the Legal Profession (Professional Conduct) Rules 2015.

[74]*Ibid*, rule 14(2).

[75]*Ibid*, rule 14(3)(b).

[76]*Ibid*, rule 14(4).

done: (a) by a competent Court; and (b) upon legal evidence sufficient to support a conviction.'[77]

In May 2013, a Code of Practice for the Conduct of Criminal Proceedings was jointly issued by the Attorney-General's Chambers and the Law Society of Singapore.[78] This Code does not have the force of law.[79] It merely sets out 'best practices guidelines in the conduct of criminal proceedings' by the Prosecution and the Defence.[80] The guidelines are aspirational and non-binding. One of them stresses that both prosecutors and defence counsel must 'respect the fundamental rights of suspects and the right of the accused person to a fair trial'.[81]

2.2.4 Judges

The trial judge's role is to make findings of fact on the basis of admissible evidence that the parties have adduced before the court.[82] In *XP v PP*,[83] the Singapore High Court viewed the presumption of innocence and the prosecution's burden to prove guilt beyond reasonable doubt as a reflection of the judicial duty to search for the truth. The trial judge has a duty to assess the evidence with care. He is required 'to apply his mind to the evidence; to carefully sift and reason through the evidence to ensure and affirm that his finding of guilt or innocence is grounded entirely in logic and fact.'[84] In *Thong Ah Fat v PP*,[85] the Court of Appeal held that there was an inherent duty at common law for judges to give reasons for their decisions, including decisions on matters of fact.[86]

Given the adversarial nature of the trial, the presentation of evidence is generally controlled by the parties. However, this is qualified by section 167(1) EA. This provision gives the trial judge wide powers to intervene in the proceedings by directly asking questions of witnesses and parties and to order the production of any evidence. However, the courts have exercised self-restraint in using this power.[87] In an adversarial system, the trial judge is to take a relatively passive role and must not 'descend into the arena'.[88]

---

[77]Chong, 2015 at [11].

[78]*See* above note 16.

[79]*Ibid*, guideline 2.

[80]*Ibid*, guideline 1.

[81]*Ibid*, guideline 7(d).

[82]*See* s. 167(2) EA which states: 'The judgment must be based upon facts declared by this Act to be relevant and duly proved.'

[83]*XP* v. *PP* [2008] 4 SLR(R) 686 at [98].

[84]*Jagatheesan s/o Krishnasamy* v. *PP* [2006] 4 SLR(R) 45 at [61].

[85]*Thong Ah Fat* v. *PP* [2012] 1 SLR 676.

[86]*See also Lai Wee Lian* v. *Singapore Bus Service (1978) Ltd.* [1983-1984] SLR(R) 388.

[87]*See, eg, Yap Chwee Khim* v. *American Home Assurance Co* [2001] 1 SLR(R) 638 at [25].

[88]*Mohammed Ali bin Johari* v. *PP* [2008] 4 SLR(R) 1058 at [154].

Judicial findings of fact at the trial level is subject to appellate control. Although appellate courts are conscious that the trial judge is generally better placed to assess evidence, especially oral evidence of witnesses, they will intervene in appropriate circumstances.[89]

2.3 *Constitutional Rights in the Criminal Process*

Article 9 of the Singapore Constitution provides for a limited number of rights in relation to the administration of criminal justice. They are the right not to be deprived of life or personal liberty 'save in accordance with law', the right to counsel, and the right to be brought before the magistrate within 48 hours of his arrest.

2.3.1 Right to Counsel

The right to be defended by a lawyer at the trial is also to be found in section 236 CPC.[90] However, the present discussion is on the right to counsel prior to the trial while the person is being investigated and in police custody. While Article 9(3) of the Constitution provides that '[w]here a person is arrested, he … shall be allowed to consult… a legal practitioner of his choice', this right has failed to receive as strong a vindication as in other jurisdictions. First, it has been held that the police do not have to inform the arrestee of his right to counsel. The judiciary has declined to read this 'further right' into article 9(3).[91] Neither has the arrested person any right to contact family members or friends.[92] Secondly, the Courts have held that article 9(3) does not require the police to give the accused access to legal advice immediately upon arrest. The police do not have to wait for him to receive legal advice before they start to question and take statements from him, and the lawyer is not and does not need to be present during the questioning.[93] It is not uncommon to deny access to counsel until the investigation is completed and the police have

[89]*See, eg, PP* v. *Muhammad Farid bin Mohd Yusop* [2015] 3 SLR 15 at [54].

[90]It states: 'Every accused person before any court may of right be defended by an advocate.'

[91]*Rajeevan Edakalavan* v. *PP* [1998] 1 SLR(R) 10 at [19]-[21]; *Sun Hongyu* v. *PP* [2005] 2 SLR (R) 750 at [34].

[92]*Sun Hongyu* v. *PP* [2005] 2 SLR(R) 750; criticized by Thio, 2012 at [12.088], [12.089].

[93]*See Muhammad bin Kadar* v. *PP* [2011] 3 SLR 1205 at [57]: 'Even after the accused engages counsel (assuming he does), there is no legal rule requiring the police to let counsel be present during subsequent interviews with the accused while investigations are being carried out.' But the situation appears to be different after the investigation has been completed. In *Azman bin Mohamed Sanwan* v. *PP* [2012] 2 SLR 733 (CA), the investigating officer visited the accused at the Queenstown Remand Prison after investigation had apparently been completed and he took further statements from the accused. These visits were made without informing, and in the absence of, counsel appointed by the accused. The Court of Appeal and the Deputy Public Prosecutor himself were of the view that the conduct of the investigating officer was improper.

taken all the statements that they want from the suspect.[94] As judicially construed, article 9(3) is satisfied so long as the person is allowed to consult a lawyer 'within a reasonable time after his arrest'.[95] In *James Raj s/o Arokiasamy v PP*,[96] the Court of Appeal highlighted the need to balance 'the arrested person's undoubted right to legal representation' and 'the public interest in enabling the police to discharge their duty and carry out investigations effectively and expeditiously'.[97] The inability to get early access to their clients has long been a major source of concern for the criminal bar.[98]

2.3.2 Right not to Deprived of Life or Personal Liberty Save in Accordance with Law

Article 9(1) is the closest provision that one can find in the Constitution relating to the right to a fair trial. It states that no one shall be deprived of life or personal liberty save in accordance with 'law'. In *Ong Ah Chuan v PP*,[99] the constitutionality of a statutory provision which created a rebuttable legal presumption was challenged. This case is not immediately related to the present project but it is noteworthy for interpreting 'law' for the purposes of article 9(1) as including fundamental rules of natural justice. In *Yong Vui Kong v AG*,[100] the Court of Appeal interpreted *Ong Ah Chuan* as endorsing the view that:

> ...[the Singapore] criminal justice system contains the following fundamental elements: (a) the accused can be convicted of the offence charged only if the ingredients of the offence have been proved by the Prosecution according to the standard of proof applicable to criminal proceedings (i.e., the standard of beyond reasonable doubt); (b) the tribunal trying

---

[94]'Lawyers can seek earlier access to accused persons', *The Straits Times*, 27 April 2007 (pilot scheme which allows lawyers to request to see their clients towards the end of their remand period provided it does not interfere with investigations).

[95]*Lee Mau Seng* v. *Minister for Home Affairs* [1971–1973] SLR(R) 135 at [12]; *Jasbir Singh* v. *PP* [1994] 1 SLR(R) 782; *James Raj s/o Arokiasamy* v. *PP* [2014] 3 SLR 750.

[96]*James Raj s/o Arokiasamy* v. *PP* [2014] 3 SLR 750 at [31].

[97]*See also* 'Parliamentary Debates Singapore: Official Report', vol. 69 (1 June 1998) at col. 99 (Minister of State for Home Affairs, Assoc Prof Ho Peng Kee): 'In Singapore, we see it right to balance the rights of an accused to be given a fair trial with the right of the State to devise rules to ensure that those who are guilty will not take advantage of the law and get away scot-free. Hence, under our approach, a suspect has no inherent right to have his lawyer present when the Police questions him.'

[98]This concern has been aired many times and most recently in the speech of the President of the Law Society delivered at the Opening of the Legal Year 2016 on 11 January 2016, at [14]-[15]. Available online at <https://www.lawsociety.org.sg/Portals/0/MediaAndResourceCentre/Speeches/President's%20OLY%202016%20speech%20(as%20of%201%20Jan%2016%203%2011pm).pdf>, accessed 31 October 2018. This speech received media attention: *see* 'LawSoc repeats call for accused to have early access to lawyers', *Today*, 12 January 2016.

[99]*Ong Ah Chuan* v. *PP* [1979-1980] SLR(R) 710.

[100]*Yong Vui Kong* v. *AG* [2011] 2 SLR 1189 at [107].

> the accused must be independent and unbiased; and (c) the accused must be heard on his defence to the offence charged. Accordingly, legislation that abrogates any of these fundamental elements may be open to challenge on the ground of inconsistency with Art 9(1).

The Court of Appeal has held that the right of silence, discussed below, is not a fundamental rule of natural justice protected under Article 9(1).[101] This Article was relied upon unsuccessfully in a number of cases to challenge the constitutionality of the statutory power to draw an adverse inference from the accused's silence or omission to mention material facts in his statement to the police.[102]

3 Social Interest in Criminal Justice

3.1 Media Publicity and Public Comments

Criminal trials are held in open court. They are not televised.[103] In 1987, a number of persons were arrested and detained without trial under the Internal Security Act over an alleged Marxist plot to overthrow the government. Confessions by these persons were aired publicly on television. Allegations that these persons were tortured into confessing were rejected by the Government.[104]

Criminal cases regularly receive press and other media coverage. This is allowed by the law but is subject to the doctrine of *sub judice* contempt. Under that doctrine, publication of views that carry a real risk of prejudice to or interference with pending court proceedings amounts to criminal contempt of court.[105] In 2013, a blogger put on the internet videos of interviews with two persons who claimed that police officers had assaulted them to get confessions. The videos were published while criminal proceedings were pending against those two persons. This led to a letter being issued by the Attorney-General's Chambers to the blogger warning her that she has committed contempt of court. It was deemed that a letter of warning was sufficient and no committal proceedings for contempt were instituted against her.[106]

Under guidelines contained in the *Code of Practice for the Conduct of Criminal Proceedings by the Prosecution and the Defence*, prosecutors and defence 'should avoid making public comments outside the courtroom including, inter alia, speaking to the media about the merits of particular cases or the details of the guilt

---

[101] *PP* v. *Mazlan bin Maidun* [1992] 3 SLR(R) 968.

[102] *Jaykumal* v. *PP* [1981-1982] SLR(R) 147; *Haw Tua Tau* v. *PP* [1981-1982] SLR(R) 13.

[103] An unauthorised recording of court proceedings amounts to an act of contempt of court under s. 5 of the Administration of Justice (Protection) Act 2016.

[104] *See* 'Parliamentary Debates Singapore: Official Report', vol. 49 (29 July 1987), especially at cols. 1441-1443, 1465-1466, 1474, 1491-1492, 1508.

[105] This common law offence was codified in 2016. It is now governed by s. 3(1)(b) of the Administration of Justice (Protection) Act 2016.

[106] *See* 'Film-maker warned over bus driver videos', *The Straits Times*, 15 June 2013; 'Contempt of court: AGC can decide over prosecution', *The Straits Times*, 24 June 2013.

or innocence of the accused person before judgment by the court, and making any public statements regarding the character, credibility, reputation, or record of an accused person.'[107] Further, they 'should not give any statement to the press or media that may amount to contempt of court or that is calculated to interfere with the fair trial of a case that has not been concluded.'[108]

3.2 *Public Interest in Miscarriages of Justice*

Occasionally, allegations of police abuse of suspects are reported in the press[109] and online fora,[110] and raised in Parliament. In all instances, the allegations were rejected by the government.

Noteworthy instances include one that occurred in 1994. The accused, a Thai construction worker, was prosecuted for murder. He alleged a series of ill-treatment at the hands of the investigating officers that included punching, kicking, hair-pulling, and hitting the sole of his feet with a cane. There was also evidence of a broken needle lodged in the accused's arm. The defence claimed that this resulted from the accused having been pricked with a sharp object when he used his arm to block an officer whom he thought was going for his eyes with the object. However, the accused's allegations were denied by the officers. After considering all the evidence, the trial judge excluded the statements because it 'appeared to [him] that the accused had been assaulted'.[111] The accused was acquitted and discharged without calling for his defence. This case drew public attention and the matter was raised and discussed in Parliament.[112] A year later, the accused was prosecuted and convicted for making up false evidence that the police were responsible for the needle in his arm.[113] It seems from the evidence adduced at the later trial that the accused had three other needles in his limbs. The needles, including the one that was

[107] Above note 16, guideline 52.

[108] *Ibid*, guideline 53.

[109] *See*, *eg*, 'Alleged Rioters file complaint claiming abuse by police; investigations into the veracity of the allegations are ongoing: Police spokesperson', *Today*, 9 January 2014. Alleged practices of mistreatment of persons detained for questioning by the Corrupt Practices Investigation Bureau were reported in 'Ways to make you talk…', *The Straits Times*, 8 April 2007 and 'Interrogation techniques designed to inflict mental and physical torture and break the toughest minds', *The Straits Times*, 22 April 2007.

[110] *See*, *eg*., 'SPF Internal Affairs Office initiated investigation on allegation of police violence', available online at <http://www.theonlinecitizen.com/2014/01/spf-internal-affairs-office-initiated-investigation-on-allegation-of-police-violence/>, accessed 31 October 2018.

[111] *PP* v. *Somporn Chinphakdee* [1994] SGHC 209. An appeal by the prosecution against the acquittal was dismissed by the Court of Appeal. *See* 'Thai worker jailed five years for making up false evidence', *The Straits Times*, 3 February 1995.

[112] 'Parliamentary Debates Singapore: Official Report', vol. 63 (25 August 1994) at col. 377-385; 'No black sheep allowed to tarnish integrity of ministry', *The Straits Times*, 26 August 1995.

[113] 'Thai worker jailed five years for making up false evidence', *The Straits Times*, 3 February 1995.

revealed at the first trial, were believed be 'charm needles' inserted long ago for superstitious purposes.

There have been a few well-publicized cases in which an accused person had his conviction subsequently overturned by the appellate court or had charges against him withdrawn. For example, in 1993, a murder charge was withdrawn against the accused after evidence emerged which indicated that he was out of the country at the time of the crime. The accused had been charged on the basis of a confession obtained by officers of the Criminal Investigation Department ('CID'). Questions were raised in Parliament[114] and in the press[115] about possible impropriety in the manner in which the confession was obtained. The Minister for Home Affairs said in Parliament that he was 'completely satisfied' that there was no impropriety.[116] When asked why he had confessed, the accused told the press: 'I was scared. It's easy for people to ask why but I am the one who suffered in the CID.' He declined to elaborate on how he suffered except to say: 'You never know what you are going to face in the CID.'[117]

A more recent example occurred in 2011. Mr. Ismil Kadar had his conviction for murder overturned by the Court of Appeal. By then he had already spent six years in prison.[118] In acquitting the accused, the Court of Appeal criticised the investigating officer for serious procedural lapses in the way he had taken statements from the accused and the prosecution for failing to make early disclosure of evidence to the defence.[119]

4 Incriminating Statements by the Accused: Relevant Rules of Evidence and Procedure

The prosecution does not have to produce any confession by the accused in order to secure a conviction. However, in most cases, the police are able to obtain a confession or other incriminating statements from the accused. It is very common for the prosecution to rely on evidence of such statements at a trial.[120] Confessions tend

[114]'Parliamentary Debates Singapore: Official Report', vol. 61 (12 April 1993) at cols. 14-15.

[115]*See, eg*, 'Some questions about Samat's case', *The Straits Times*, 24 March 1993; 'Prosecutor notified of alibi 23 months after Samat's arrest', *The Straits Times*, 30 March 1993. The acquittal received considerable press coverage. *See, eg*, 'Court frees innocent man after 2 ½ years' jail', *The Straits Times*, 18 March 1993 and 'Confession based on crimewatch', *The Straits Times*, 18 March 1993.

[116]'Parliamentary Debates Singapore: Official Report', vol. 61 (12 April 1993) at cols. 14-15.

[117]'Confession based on crimewatch', *The Straits Times*, 18 March 1993.

[118]'Man accused of murder freed after 6 years in jail', *The Straits Times*, 6 July 2011.

[119]*Muhammad bin Kadar* v. *PP* [2011] 3 SLR 1205.

[120]A distinction is drawn in s. 17 EA between a confession and a less incriminating statement known as an admission. But the courts have construed the meaning of 'confession' very broadly to include any statement that connects the accused in some way with the offence. *See, eg*, *Tong Chee Kong* v. *PP* [1998] 1 SLR(R) 591 at [18].

to be given a lot of weight. In the Court of Appeal case of *Lee Chez Kee v PP*,[121] V. K. Rajah JA attributed this to the fact that 'a confession is inculpatory in nature'; 'it is a statement made against the interest of its maker and hence inherently more reliable.' A person may be convicted on the basis of his pre-trial confession alone even if he retracts it at the trial, and no corroboration is required.[122] It is also possible to convict a person based solely on the confession of a co-accused provided 'that the evidence emanating from that confession satisfies the court beyond reasonable doubt of the accused's guilt.'[123]

It is because confession evidence is believed to be so highly probative of guilt that there is a reluctance to exclude it. This comes from the desire not to let the guilty go free. At the same time, it is also because the evidence can play such a decisive role in securing a conviction that its admissibility should be conditional on there being sufficient assurance of reliability and on its lawful and fair provenance. This springs from our interest in the accuracy and legitimacy of the conviction.

4.1 Rules on the Obtaining of Evidence

The police are legally constrained in seeking evidence. Certain methods of obtaining evidence are criminal or otherwise wrongful. For example, it is both a crime and a tort (a civil wrong) to extract a confession from a suspect by physically assaulting him.[124] The law that make this conduct criminal or tortious are general in the sense that it is not aimed specifically at regulating the process of obtaining evidence for a criminal prosecution. Some rules do have that specific aim. For example, the CPC requires the police to obtain a search warrant before they may conduct a search of premises for incriminating evidence and the court will grant the warrant only if certain conditions are satisfied.[125] Another example, one on which this chapter focuses, is the set of rules that regulate the obtaining of statements from the accused.

The police have the power under section 21 CPC to order anyone 'who appears to be acquainted with any of the facts and circumstances of the case' to attend before them. This includes the suspect. Section 22(1) empowers the police to question this person.[126] When questioned, the person must state truly what he

[121] *Lee Chez Kee* v. *PP* [2008] 3 SLR(R) 447 at [102].

[122] *See, eg, Ismail bin U K Abdul Rahman* v. *PP* [1974-1976] SLR(R) 91 at [84].

[123] *Chin Seow Noi* v. *PP* [1993] 3 SLR(R) 566, interpreting a former provision that now exists as s. 358(5) CPC. The soundness of this interpretation was questioned, in passing, by V K Rajah JA in *Lee Chez Kee* v. *PP* [2008] 3 SLR(R) 447 at [113] but was recently reaffirmed by the Court of Appeal in *Norasharee bin Gous* v. *PP* [2017] 1 SLR 820.

[124] *See* discussion on accountability of police officers above.

[125] s. 24 CPC. *See* generally Tan, 2007, vol. 1, ch. IV.

[126] This is only applicable to arrestable offences (formerly called seizable offences). *See Muhammad bin Kadar* v. *PP* [2011] 3 SLR 1205 at [42] (Court of Appeal).

knows of the facts and circumstances of the case. But this is qualified by the privilege against self-incrimination; he has the right not to make any statement that might 'have a tendency to expose him to a criminal charge or to a penalty or forfeiture.'[127] A statement taken from the accused under this section is popularly known as a 'long statement'. Section 22(3) requires the statement to be (a) in writing; (b) read over to the accused; (c) if he does not understand English, interpreted for him in a language that he understands; and, (d) signed by him.

When the police finally decides to charge or proceed against a person, they must follow the procedure set out in section 23. They must read out a notice to the person. The notice will set out the charge, invite the person to make a statement and contain the caution that if the person withholds any facts relevant to his defence and raises them only at the trial, the trial judge may be less likely to believe him. A statement recorded under this section is popularly known as the 'cautioned statement'. This statement, again, must be (a) in writing; (b) read over to him; (c) if he does not understand English, interpreted for him in a language that he understands; and, (d) signed by him.[128] The police may continue to question and take a 'long' statement from a person under section 22 even after he has been charged or proceeded against under section 23.[129]

4.2 The Privilege Against Self-incrimination and the Right of Silence

As noted, the suspect has the privilege against self-incrimination when questioned by the police. However, this privilege has been weakened in a number of ways. First, the police do not need to inform the suspect that he has this right.[130] That the suspect was not told, prior to making a statement, of his privilege against self-incrimination does not affect its admissibility.[131] Secondly, as already noted, the police may and often do deny the suspect access to a lawyer before the completion of investigation. As such, the suspect who is being interrogated, unless himself legally-trained, would

[127]s. 22(2) CPC. The legal position is different under the Prevention of Corruption Act, Cap. 241, 1993 rev. ed., s 27 of which gives investigating officers the power to require a person 'to give… information' relating to corruption cases. And s. 27 further provides that the person so questioned is 'legally bound to give that information'. In *Taw Cheng Kong* v. *PP*, the Singapore High Court held that a person who is being questioned under s. 27 is 'not entitled to refuse to answer incriminating questions'. (*See also* s. 75 of the Competition Act, Cap. 50B, 2006 rev. ed.).

[128]s. 23(3) CPC.

[129]s. 22(1). *See also Mohamed Bachu Miah* v. *PP* [1992] 2 SLR(R) 783 at [65].

[130]*PP* v. *Mazlan bin Maidun* [1992] 3 SLR(R) 968. In the past, the police had to inform the suspect of his right not to say anything before questioning him. This duty was set out in rules 3, 4 and 5 of Schedule E to the Criminal Procedure Code (Cap 113, 1970 rev. ed.). The Schedule was repealed in 1976. *See Mohamed Bachu Miah* v. *PP* [1992] 2 SLR(R) 783 at [43], [48].

[131]s. 258(3), Explanation 2(c), (d) CPC.

likely not know that he has the privilege against self-incrimination.[132] Thirdly, the judge may draw an adverse inference against the accused from his failure to disclose to the police facts he subsequently relies upon in his defence at the trial.[133] This adverse inference may be drawn not just from an omission to mention relevant fact in a cautioned statement obtained under section 23 but also from an omission to do so in a statement given under section 22 (at least those that were taken on occasions subsequent to the person having been cautioned under section 23).[134] Trial judges have not been reluctant to draw adverse inferences against accused persons for not disclosing material facts to the police.[135]

The risk of an adverse inference being drawn from silence provides strong inducement for the accused to speak. It may be argued that the section 23 notice and the power to draw adverse inferences from silence do not undermine the right against self-incrimination as they merely encourage the suspect to make early disclosure of *exculpatory* facts—which are facts supporting his defence as opposed to facts revealing his guilt.[136] But the practical reality is that the suspect is induced to incriminate himself. The suspect may not fully understand the notice. At this stage, he has no access to a lawyer and since the beginning of 2011, the police no longer have a legal duty to explain the notice to him.[137] He may form the mistaken impression that he is required to disclose everything that he knows about the case. Further, the 'exculpatory information may well be inextricably linked with self-incriminating information.'[138] It must also be remembered that some defences, such as provocation, works as a 'confession and avoidance'. To raise such a defence is already to confess to the elements of the offence. The suspect may not be aware that it is for the prosecution to prove the elements of the crime beyond reasonable doubt. The section 23 notice and the power to draw an adverse inference from the suspect's silence have the effect of weakening the right not to speak and the right to put the prosecution to proof at a trial.[139]

The current position has been defended by drawing on strands of crime control ideology. Singapore's political leaders have been praised for having 'the political will to enact an appropriate framework to achieve' 'a relatively safe and secure environment that is free from crime'. This includes the introduction of the power to

---

[132]*See* Ho, 2013.

[133]s. 261 CPC.

[134]The power to draw such adverse inferences 'as appear proper' is provided for in s. 261(1) CPC. It is controversial whether an adverse inference may be drawn from an omission to mention relevant facts in a statement taken by the police under s. 22 prior to action being taken against the accused under s. 23. *See* Ho, 2013; Pinsler, 2017 at 221–226.

[135]*See, eg*, Yeo, 1983; Tan, 1997.

[136]*Kwek Seow Hock* v. *PP* [2011] 3 SLR 157 at [18], [19].

[137]Prior to 2011, the police was required to explain the notice to the accused. On the practical difficulties that this created for the police, *see Tsang Yuk Chung* v. *PP* [1990] 2 SLR(R) 39 at [27], [28].

[138]Choo, 2013 at 102.

[139]*See* Philips, 1981 at [4.35], [4.37], [4.51], [4.52].

draw adverse inferences from silence.[140] The changes to the law show a shift from 'adherence to due process' towards 'crime control… values'.[141] It is also claimed that they have 'greatly assisted… law enforcement agencies in investigating offences, leading to many more factually guilty persons being convicted through guilty pleas or convictions at trial.'[142] This claim does not appear to be supported by the available empirical studies.[143]

4.3 Rules on Admissibility of Evidence

The legal rules on the admissibility of evidence are to be found mainly in the EA and the CPC. They are, broadly speaking, variations of rules that exist at common law. Thus, the admissibility of evidence is subject to the hearsay rule, character and similar facts rule, and so forth. Statements obtained from the accused by the police are admissible under section 258(1) CPC provided certain conditions are met. First, the statement must have been obtained by a police officer of the rank of sergeant and above.[144] Secondly, as discussed below, the statement must not have been obtained by applying undue pressure and the court has a limited discretion to exclude the statement on the ground of prejudice.

5 Exclusion of Evidence Obtained by Torture

5.1 Definition of Torture

There does not appear to be any domestic statute that defines torture.[145] The definition of torture in Article 1 of the *Convention against Torture, and Other Cruel, Inhuman, or Degrading Treatment or Punishment* (see also below, 'Effect of

[140]Chan, 2006 at 13.

[141]*Ibid* at 14.

[142]*Ibid* at 15. *See also* Chan, 1996 at 444.

[143]In one study published in 1986, the author concluded from an examination of crime statistics that the 1976 amendments were not 'perceived by potential offenders as sufficiently increasing their risk of detection to deter them from crime' and that 'there was no visible decrease in the crime rate after the amendments were introduced': Mohan, 1986 at xxxiv. An earlier study by Yeo, 1983 at 100–101, concluded that 'the amendments have not materially assisted the Singapore police force and prosecuting officers in their combat against crime'. It is noted by Tan, 1997 at 480, that '[e]mpirically, it is less than certain whether the existence of the silence provisions and the courts' invocation of these have truly resulted in accused persons speaking up more readily today than they would have done in the past.'

[144]s. 258(2) CPC.

[145]*Yong Vui Kong* v. *PP* [2015] 2 SLR 1129 at [77] (the Act cited by counsel for the appellant does not in fact contain any definition of torture).

International Law (Human Rights)) and decisions of international courts were considered by the Court of Appeal in *Yong Vui Kong v PP*.[146] (What fell for decision in this case was the constitutionality of caning as a form of criminal punishment which is not relevant for present purposes.) The Court of Appeal came to the conclusion 'that to determine whether particular conduct constitutes torture entails a fact-sensitive inquiry that requires a holistic analysis of the purpose of the conduct, the manner of its execution and its effect on the recipient.'[147]

5.2 Prohibition Against Torture and the Exclusion of Evidence Obtained by Torture

There is no express prohibition against torture in the Constitution and no provision explicitly requiring exclusion of evidence obtained by torture. However, article 9(1) of the Constitution protects against deprivation of 'life or personal liberty save in accordance with law'. In *Yong Vui Kong v PP*,[148] the appellant relied, among other things, on the common law prohibition against torture, citing in support the House of Lords judgment in *A v Secretary of State for the Home Department (No.2)*.[149] It was argued that this common law rule has constitutional force as a fundamental rule of natural justice included in the term 'law' in article 9(1). The Court of Appeal agreed 'that there is a common law prohibition against torture, and that this prohibition has been imported into domestic law pursuant to…Art 162 of the Constitution'.[150] However, 'the common law prohibition of torture does not prohibit caning or any other form of corporal punishment.'[151] It 'has a narrow and specific compass', is 'concerned with the practice of torturing suspects or witnesses for the purpose of extracting evidence and confessions' and does not 'cover the treatment of criminals after they were found guilty of their crimes.'[152] The Court of Appeal went on to state[153]:

> The fundamental rules of natural justice in the common law are … procedural rights aimed at securing a fair trial. Torture in its narrow sense (where it is used to extract evidence to be used as proof in judicial proceedings) would violate the fundamental rules of natural justice; to convict a person based on evidence procured by torture strikes at the very heart of a fair trial.

---

[146] *Yong Vui Kong* v. *PP* [2015] 2 SLR 1129 at [79] *et seq.*

[147] *Ibid* at [89].

[148] *Yong Vui Kong* v. *PP* [2015] 2 SLR 1129.

[149] *A* v. *Secretary of State for the Home Department (No.2)* [2006] 2 AC 221.

[150] *Yong Vui Kong* v. *PP* [2015] 2 SLR 1129 at [58]. Article 162 states that all existing laws shall continue in force on and after the commencement of the Constitution but they shall be construed in conformity with the Constitution. The common law rule on torture pre-dates the commencement of the Constitution.

[151] *Yong Vui Kong* v. *PP* [2015] 2 SLR 1129 at [60].

[152] *Ibid* at [59].

[153] *Ibid* at [64].

This passage suggests that the common law rule which renders evidence obtained by torture strictly inadmissible is part of Singapore law and has constitutional status. However, this was only an obiter dictum as the case itself was concerned with the constitutionality of caning.

This common law rule is of practical significance only in relation to evidence obtained from a third party by torture. This is because a statement obtained from the accused person by torture would be inadmissible anyway under the voluntariness rule or the oppression doctrine, both of which are examined in the next section.

6 Exclusion of Statements Obtained from the Accused by Undue Pressure[154]

That courts tend to give a lot of weight to confession evidence makes it all the more important for the police to obtain such evidence. The police might be tempted to go after a confession as a short-cut and at the expense of seeking out independent evidence.[155] It is necessary to have legal rules that protect against the risk of confessions being obtained by undue pressure. To those rules we now turn.

6.1 Voluntariness as a Condition of Admissibility

A statement obtained by the police from the accused is inadmissible if the prosecution is unable to satisfy the so-called 'voluntariness test' in section 258(3) CPC. This provision, which was previously in the EA, has been in existence since the passing of the EA in 1893; it is expressed in technical and archaic language. Under this test, the court must exclude a statement if the accused was caused to give it by any 'inducement, threat or promise' proceeding from a 'person in authority'. Where no inducement was in fact made, and the accused was labouring under a self-generated false impression of an inducement, this exclusionary rule would not apply.[156] The prototypical 'person in authority' is the law enforcement officer conducting the interrogation.[157] Another requirement is that the inducement, threat or promise must be sufficient to give the accused grounds which would appear to

---

[154]For greater details, *see* Ho, 2016.

[155]'Parliamentary Debates Singapore: Official Report', vol. 69 (1 June 1998) at col. 104 (Mr J B Jeyaretnam): 'the confession in many cases is the shortcut method[.] It spares the investigating officer from having to go and make minute, detailed investigations and to look for corroborative evidence. So he has an interest in, if it is possible, getting an accused person to admit to the offence.'

[156]*Lu Lai Heng* v. *PP* [1994] 1 SLR(R) 1037 (the inducement was 'self-perceived').

[157]Under certain circumstances, the interpreter assisting in the questioning is also a person in authority: *PP* v. *Lim Boon Hiong* [2010] 4 SLR 696.

him reasonable for supposing that he stands to gain an advantage if he makes the statement or suffer some 'evil' (that is, harm) if he does not give it.[158] (Read literally, the provision requires the inducement, threat or promise to have reference to the charge against the accused and the benefit to be gained or harm to be avoided must be in reference to the proceedings against him. But courts have not insisted on these requirements. Thus a statement obtained under a threat to forfeit property owned by relatives of the accused is also inadmissible.[159])

A statement is not rendered inadmissible merely by the fact that it was made 'under a promise of secrecy, or in consequence of a deception practised on the accused for the purpose of obtaining it'[160] or 'when the accused was intoxicated'.[161] In 2010, various MPs[162] and lawyers[163] objected to these provisions. The thrust of their argument was that a statement made under such circumstances cannot be said to be voluntary or reliable. But the government could not be persuaded to change the law.

6.2 *Doctrine of Oppression*

At one time, bad treatment of a suspect in the course of obtaining his statement—at least where it falls short of torture—was not considered capable, without a specific threat, inducement or promise, of rendering the statement inadmissible. Oppression came later to be accepted as a ground for exclusion. It was treated as having been 'subsumed' in the statutory voluntariness rule discussed in the preceding section.[164] English common law authorities on the definition of oppression were followed.[165]

---

[158]That the test of voluntariness was formulated in the late nineteenth century explains the archaic language of the section. There is a further requirement that the 'inducement, threat and promise', and the 'advantage' or 'evil', must have reference to the charge. But the courts have not insisted strictly on this requirement: *see Poh Kay Keong* v. *PP* [1995] 3 SLR(R) 887; *Chai Chien Wei Kelvin* v. *PP* [1998] 3 SLR(R) 619 at [55] (a promise to let the accused call his wife was held not to have 'reference to the charge').

[159]*Poh Kay Keong* v. *PP* [1995] 3 SLR(R) 887.

[160]s. 2583(3) Explanation 2(a) CPC.

[161]s. 2583(3) Explanation 2(b) CPC.

[162]*See* 'Parliamentary Debates Singapore: Official Report', vol. 87 (18 May 2010) (speeches of Mr K Shanmugam, Mr Alvin Yeo, Mr Michael Palmer, and Mr Hri Kumar Nair) and 'Parliamentary Debates Singapore: Official Report', vol. 87 (19 May 2010) (speeches of Mr Lim Biow Chuan and Mr K Shanmugam). Debates on this issue were extensively reported: *see, eg*, 'Can confession of a drunk person count as evidence', *The Straits Times*, 19 May 2010 and 'Intoxication issue gets another airing', *The Straits Times*, 20 May 2010.

[163]*See, eg*, views of Mr Subnas Anandan, president of the Association of Criminal Lawyers of Singapore, and Mr Edmond Pereira, a defence lawyer, as reported in 'Criminal lawyers concerned over clause in proposed criminal procedure code', *Today*, 17 May 2010.

[164]*Gulam bin Notan Mohd Shariff Jamalddin* v. *PP* [1999] 1 SLR(R) 498 at [53].

[165]*See, eg*, *Gulam bin Notan*, *ibid*; *Chai Chien Wei Kelvin* v. *PP* [1998] 3 SLR(R) 619 at [56]-[59].

According to that definition, oppression 'imports something which tends to sap, and has sapped, that free will which must exist before a confession is voluntary.'[166] In determining whether there was oppression, the court will look at the full circumstances, including length of time of questioning, period of rest, the provision of refreshment and the character of the person being questioned. In 2011, oppression as a ground for exclusion received explicit statutory recognition with the introduction of Explanation 1 to section 258(3) CPC.[167] Oppressive treatment will render the accused's statement inadmissible even in the absence of an "overt act from a person in authority such as a specific threat, inducement or promise".[168] However, bad treatment by the police must be very egregious for the doctrine of oppression to apply. This doctrine is seldom applied by the court.

Extremely taxing interrogation can amount to oppression. For example, in *Public Prosecutor v Lim Kian Tat*,[169] one of the statements was 'taken during an 18-hour interrogation with an hour's break. It was taken during the fourth night in a row in which the accused did not have any adequate sleep.' The High Court was 'satisfied that the accused had spoken, after the police had rejected his earlier versions, and had spoken when he would not have otherwise' and concluded that the statement was 'made in circumstances where there was oppression.'[170]

The failure to provide sustenance over a long period may also, depending on the circumstances, amount to oppression. In *Fung Yuk Shing v Public Prosecutor*,[171] the suspect had been deprived of food and drink for about 7 hours when his statement was taken. The trial judge held that this amounted to oppression. On appeal, the Court of Appeal expressed disagreement.[172] According to the Court of Appeal, whether deprivation of sustenance is sufficiently serious to justify exclusion of the evidence will depend on the circumstances of the case. The criminal bar has called for greater legal regulation of the recording process. For example, in his speech at the opening of the legal year in 2008, the President of the Singapore Law Society, Mr. Michael Hwang, reported 'a longstanding and widespread feeling at the Bar that legislation (or at least a protocol) is needed to prescribe how… statements… are recorded' by the police.[173] Similarly, Mr Sant Singh SC, a defence

---

[166] *R* v. *Priestley* (1967) 51 Cr App R 1 at 1; *R* v. *Prager* [1972] 1 WLR 260 at 266.

[167] *See* Chin, 2012 at 78–84.

[168] *Tey Tsun Hang* v. *PP* [2014] 2 SLR 1189 at [91].

[169] *Public Prosecutor* v. *Lim Kian Tat* [1990] 1 SLR(R) 273.

[170] *Ibid* at [29].

[171] *Fung Yuk Shing* v. *Public Prosecutor* [1993] 2 SLR(R) 92.

[172] *Fung Yuk Shing* v. *PP* [1993] 2 SLR(R) 771.

[173] 'Address of the President of the Law Society – Opening of the Legal Year 2008', 5 January 2008, at [9], available online at <https://www.supremecourt.gov.sg/news/speeches/opening-of-legal-year-2008—address-by-the-president-of-the-law-society-of-singapore>, accessed 31 October 2018. *See also* Hwang, 2010, which was reported in 'Set rules for police interrogation', *The Straits Times*, 25 June 2010.

lawyer who has considerable experience as a former police inspector and deputy public prosecutor, has urged that 'provisions… be enacted to put in place a protocol for the recording of statements from accused persons'.[174]

6.3 Burden of Proof

When admissibility is contested, it is for the prosecution to prove beyond reasonable doubt that the accused gave his statement voluntarily and without oppression.[175] The burden of proof is not as difficult to discharge as it may seem.[176] One reason for this might be judicial pragmatism. This can be detected, for instance, in judgment of the Court of Appeal in *Panya Martmontree v Public Prosecutor.*[177] While acknowledging that the accused need not do more than raise a reasonable doubt as to the voluntariness of his statement, the Court of Appeal added that this did not mean that 'the slightest suspicion of an inducement, threat or promise or of an assault [was] sufficient to rule out a statement'.[178] The Court of Appeal was sensitive to the fact that '[t]he police work in difficult circumstances. If they are required to remove all doubt of influence or fear, they would never be able to achieve anything.'[179] This message was reiterated in *Yeo See How v Public Prosecutor*[180] where the Court of Appeal took the position that 'there is no necessity… for interrogators to remove all discomfort. Some discomfort has to be expected—the issue is whether such discomfort is of such a great extent that it

[174]Interview published in *Inter Se*, January 2009 at 10, 11. A similar call was made by Judicial Commissioner Amarjeet Singh: 'Code of practice needed for police questioning—JC', *The Straits Times*, 5 November 1995. *See also*: Singh, 2006; 'Parliamentary Debates Singapore: Official Report', vol. 69 (1 June 1998) at cols. 78 and 104 (Mr J B Jeyaratnam); The Law Society of Singapore, 'Report of the Council of the Law Society on the Draft Criminal Procedure Code Bill 2009' (17 February 2009) at [3.7]-[3.9], available online at: <https://www.lawsociety.org.sg/Portals/0/MediaAndResourceCentre/FeedbackinPublicConsultations/ReportofCouncilLawSocietyDraftCPCBill2009.pdf>, accessed 31 October 2018.

[175]*PP* v. *Lim Boon Hiong* [2010] 4 SLR 696 at [36].

[176]*See* 'Parliamentary Debates Singapore: Official Report', vol. 69 (1 June 1998) at cols. 86, 87 ('[T]he courts admit almost all the statements. The courts find it difficult to believe that police officers would resort to the conduct [of ill-treating suspects for the purpose of extracting a confession].') Similarly, a different member of Parliament noted during the second reading of the *CPC* Bill on 19 May 2010 that when it comes to challenging the admissibility of his statement, it often boils down to the word of the accused against the word of the investigating officer. 'Unfortunately, the Courts would invariably believe the Investigating Officer. The odds are usually stacked against the accused person.' 'Parliamentary Debates Singapore: Official Report', vol. 87 (19 May 2010) at cols. 86, 87, 549.

[177]*Panya Martmontree* v. *Public Prosecutor* [1995] 2 SLR(R) 806.

[178]*Ibid* at [32].

[179]*Ibid* at [29].

[180]*Yeo See How* v. *Public Prosecutor* [1996] 2 SLR(R) 277 at [40]. *See also PP* v. *Ng Pen Tine* [2009] SGHC 230 at [20]; *Tey Tsun Hang* v. *PP* [2014] 2 SLR 1189 at [114].

causes the making of an involuntary statement'. The pragmatism discernible in these statements carries the risk of confusing the standard of proof (which goes to our knowledge of the disputed facts) and policy considerations that relate to the kinds or levels of pressure that should be judicially tolerated.

6.4 Discretion to Exclude Wrongfully Obtained Statements

There is a difference between inadmissibility as a matter of law and discretionary exclusion. A statement obtained by means of a threat, an inducement or a promise, or by oppression, is inadmissible under the legal rules discussed above. This means that the court must exclude it.[181] Even in the absence of any of these vitiating factors, and even when there is no rule of law that renders the statement strictly inadmissible, the court has discretion to exclude it in exceptional circumstances. There are three major groups of relevant cases.

One group involves entrapment. While it was previously acknowledged that there is some discretion to exclude evidence if it was obtained in an entrapment, this view has since been repudiated on the basis that such evidence will invariably be more probative than prejudicial.[182] Entrapment, it seems, cannot be a ground for discretionary exclusion.

Another group consists of cases where a statement was taken from the suspect while he was suffering from symptoms of drug withdrawal or suffering from the effects of drugs or medication. The scenario that arose in *Garnam Singh v PP* is a fairly typical one.[183] The accused was charged with drug trafficking. He gave incriminating statements to the investigating law enforcement officers. At the trial, he sought to have the statements excluded. The accused argued that his statements were not voluntarily given because he was a heavy user of drugs and at the time that he gave the statements, he was suffering from severe withdrawal symptoms. This argument was rejected by the Court of Appeal. It held that in order to justify exclusion, the suspect 'must be in a state of near delirium' such that 'his mind did not go with the statements he was making. Such, however, was not the case here.'[184] This test was found to be satisfied, and the affected statement excluded, in a subsequent case.[185] A distinguishing feature was that the statement was taken while the effect of drug was at its peak. The legal basis for exclusion in this kind of scenario is involuntariness of some sort and appears to be discretionary.

---

[181] *PP* v. *Ismil bin Kadar* [2009] SGHC 84 at [19].

[182] *See Cheng Swee Tiang* v. *PP* [1964] MLJ 291; *Law Society of Singapore* v. *Tan Guat Neo Phyllis* [2008] 2 SLR(R) 239.

[183] *Garnam Singh* v. *PP* [1994] 1 SLR(R) 1044.

[184] *Ibid* at [31].

[185] *PP* v. *Dahalan bin Ladaewa* [1995] 2 SLR(R) 124 at [74] (upheld by Court of Appeal in *PP* v. *Dahalan bin Ladaewa* [1995] SGCA 87).

The third group of cases involves failure to comply with the prescribed procedure in the taking of a statement. This will generally not have the consequence of rendering the statement strictly inadmissible.[186] The courts have not demanded strict adherence to the legally prescribed procedure as a condition of admissibility. For example, in *Panya Martmontree v Public Prosecutor*,[187] the Court of Appeal held that even though the disputed statement (which was taken by the police under the precursor of the current section 22 of the CPC) was not read back to the accused or signed by him, it remained admissible. Since 2011, this judicial approach of not allowing procedural lapses to result in strict inadmissibility has been statutorily endorsed.[188]

But this still leaves the possibility of discretionary exclusion in extreme cases of flagrant disregard of the applicable procedure. This discretion is a narrow one. In exercising the discretion, the judge has to weigh its likely prejudicial effect if it is admitted against the probative value of the evidence. The leading authority is *Muhammad bin Kadar v Public Prosecutor.*[189] Among other features that the court found disturbing, the statements were formally transcribed only hours after the questioning, and they were not read back or signed by the accused. No acceptable explanation was offered for these lapses. The Court of Appeal held that the statements should have been excluded by the trial judge in the exercise of his discretion.

The judgment contains a number of key rulings. First, it was held that the court has 'a common law discretion to exclude voluntary statements that would otherwise be admissible… where the prejudicial effect of the evidence exceeds its probative value'.[190] This discretion can be traced to the English (House of Lords') decision in *R v Sang.*[191]

Secondly, the court should not exclude a statement in the exercise of this discretion merely because of the manner in which it was obtained. It is proper to exercise this discretion only where the procedural breach results in the evidence being more prejudicial than probative. The Court of Appeal expressly disavowed any disciplinary function in the discretion. The exclusion of evidence is not to "discipline the wrongful behaviour of police officers… or the Prosecution."[192] Nevertheless, the exclusion of evidence may have the incidental effect of removing

[186] *See* s. 358(3), Explanation 2(e), CPC.

[187] *Panya Martmontree* v. *Public Prosecutor* [1995] 2 SLR(R) 806 at [6]. The Court of Appeal cited an earlier unreported judgment of the Court of Appeal in *Vasavan Sathiadew* v. *PP* [1992] SGCA 26. *See also Tsang Yuk Chung* v. *PP* [1990] 2 SLR(R) 39 at [13]-[17] (a statement obtained under the precursor of s. 23 CPC was held to be admissible even though the prescribed notice containing the charge was not explained to the accused).

[188] s. 258(3), Explanation 2(e), CPC.

[189] *Muhammad bin Kadar* v. *PP* [2011] 3 SLR 1205. On the evolution of the discretion, *see* Ho, 2012.

[190] *Ibid* at [53].

[191] *R* v. *Sang* [1980] AC 402.

[192] *Muhammad bin Kadar* v. *PP* [2011] 3 SLR 1205 at [68].

'the incentive for [future] non-compliance on the part of police officers.' This will help ensure that all evidence in the form of written statements coming before the court will be as reliable as possible.[193]

Thirdly, the governing procedures are important safeguards of reliability. A serious breach of the relevant rules may undermine the reliability of the recorded statement, resulting in the evidence having low probative value.[194] At the same time, the prejudicial effect of the evidence may be high in the sense that admitting the statement will expose the accused to the risk of the evidence being given more weight than it deserves. The risk comes from the general aura of reliability possessed by formal statements recorded by the police. This aura of reliability is misleading where the statement was not obtained, as it should have been done, 'under a set of strict procedures strictly observed by a trustworthy officer well-trained in investigative techniques.'[195]

Fourthly, if the prosecution seeks to admit in evidence a statement obtained by a police officer in violation of the relevant rules and procedure, the prosecution bears the burden of proving that the evidence is more probative than prejudicial. To show that the evidence is probative, the prosecution will have to offer some reasonable explanation for the procedural irregularity that is sufficient to re-establish confidence in the reliability of the statement.[196] The more deliberate or reckless the non-compliance, the more difficult it will be for the prosecution to offer a sufficiently cogent explanation.[197]

Applying these principles to the present case, the Court of Appeal doubted the bona fide of the investigating officer and the accuracy of the statements recorded by him. His procedural non-compliance was deliberate and not due to carelessness or operational necessity.[198] No plausible explanation was given for the 'manifest irregularities'.[199] The prosecution failed to show that the probative value of the statements outweighed their prejudicial effect. Hence, the trial judge ought to have excluded both statements in the exercise of his discretion.

One commentator reads this decision and other developments as heralding 'an impending spring' where we will see 'the use of broader and more abstract values like fairness to effect subtle changes in judicial attitudes'.[200] There is as yet no known judgment in which the court has cited *Muhammad bin Kadar* and exercised the discretion against the prosecution.

[193] *Ibid* at [68].
[194] *Ibid* at [56].
[195] *Ibid* at [58].
[196] *Ibid* at [61].
[197] *Ibid* at [62].
[198] *Ibid* at [140].
[199] *Ibid* at [147].
[200] Hor, 2013 at 849, 872.

7 Admissibility and Effect of Derivative Evidence

There is no 'fruit of the poisonous tree' doctrine in Singapore. A different doctrine exists. It is sometimes called the doctrine of 'confirmation by discovery of subsequent fact'. This doctrine is provided for in section 258(6)(c) CPC which states: 'when any fact or thing is discovered in consequence of information received from a person accused of any offence in the custody of any officer of a law enforcement agency, so much of such information as relates distinctly to the fact or thing thereby discovered may be proved.' This doctrine was applied in *PP v Chin Moi Moi*.[201] The accused, a saleswoman, was charged with theft of a gold bangle from a customer's flat. In her police statement, she stated, amongst other things, that she took the bangle and threw it out of the flat's window. But the accused claimed that she was forced to sign the statement and that she had been threatened, harassed and abused. The trial judge excluded the statement. On appeal, the prosecution relied on the fact that the statement had led the police to the field at the bottom of the flat where, after a search, they found the gold bangle. According to the High Court hearing the appeal, this meant that the prosecution should have been allowed to admit in evidence that part of her statement where she stated: 'Without much hesitation, I throw down… the gold bangle out of the kitchen window…' The truth of this part of her statement was, as it were 'confirmed', by the discovery of the gold bangle at the place where it was found. 'The rationale for the admissibility of that part of the statement which is subsequently confirmed by the discovery of a material fact is that it must be reliable'.[202]

8 Effect of International Law on Human Rights

8.1 International/Human Rights Law

Singapore has thus far ratified four international human rights treaties.[203] However, she is not a party to the International Covenant on Civil and Political

[201] *PP* v. *Chin Moi Moi* [1994] 3 SLR(R) 924. The court applied s. 27 EA which, until it was replaced by s. 258(6)(c) CPC in 2011, was where the doctrine was to be found.

[202] *PP* v. *Chin Moi Moi* [1994] 3 SLR(R) 924 at [22]. This doctrine is rejected by English common law as the exclusion of improperly obtained evidence is 'not dependent only upon possible unreliability but also upon the principle that a man cannot be compelled to incriminate himself and upon the importance that attaches in a civilised society to proper behaviour by the police towards those in their custody': *Lam Chi-Ming* v. *R* [1991] 2 AC 212 at 220.

[203] They are (with year of ratification within brackets): Convention on the Elimination of All Forms of Discrimination against Women (1995), Convention on the Rights of the Child (1995), Optional Protocol to CRC on the involvement of children in Armed Conflict (2008); and Convention on the Rights of Persons with Disabilities (2013).

Rights[204] or the Convention against Torture, and Other Cruel, Inhuman, or Degrading Treatment or Punishment (CAT).[205]

She is however a party to the ASEAN Human Rights Declaration,[206] article 14 of which states 'No person shall be subject to torture or to cruel, inhuman or degrading treatment or punishment'. Singapore is a member of the United Nations. The Universal Declaration of Human Rights (UDHR) was adopted by the United Nations in 1948.[207] Under Article 5 of the UDHR, 'No one shall be subjected to torture or to cruel, inhuman or degrading treatment or punishment.' Singapore has ratified the Convention on the Rights of Persons with Disabilities; article 15 of this Convention provides that 'No one shall be subjected to torture or to cruel, inhuman or degrading treatment or punishment.'

While the provisions in the above paragraph prohibit torture, they do not address the issue of the admissibility of evidence obtained by torture. In contrast, this issue is explicitly dealt with in article 15 of the CAT which prohibits the use as evidence of any statement obtained by torture. Although Singapore is not a party to the CAT, as noted earlier, evidence obtained by torture is likely to be treated as inadmissible.

8.2 Universal Periodic Review

Singapore has participated twice in the Universal Periodic Review (UPR). The UPR is conducted under the auspices of the United Nations' Human Rights Council for the purpose of reviewing the human records of member states. The first UPR of Singapore was conducted in 2011 and the second in 2016.

In the National Report submitted for the 2011 UPR, the government drew attention to the fact that the Singapore Constitution 'guarantees due process and fair trial, including prohibiting … evidence obtained by means of torture'.[208] It is an offence 'for anyone to cause hurt to or wrongfully confine a person for the purpose of extorting a confession or any information, which may lead to the detection of an offence'.[209] There is a need to subject 'individual rights…to legal limits in order to protect the rights of others, as well as to maintain public order and general welfare.'[210]

---

[204]Adopted and opened for signature, ratification and accession by the General Assembly resolution 2200A (XXI) of 16 December 1966, entry into force 23 March 1976, in accordance with Article 49. Article 7 of the ICCPR reads: 'No one shall be subjected to torture or to cruel, inhuman or degrading treatment or punishment.'

[205]Adopted and opened for signature, ratification and accession by General Assembly resolution 39/46 of 10 December 1984; entry into force 26 June 1987, in accordance with article 27(1).

[206]Adopted by the ASEAN Member States at Phnom Penh, Cambodia, on 18 November 2012.

[207]By General Assembly Resolution 217A on 10 December 1948.

[208]'National report submitted in accordance with paragraph 15 (a) of the annex to Human Rights Council resolution 5/1' (2 February 2011) at [23], available online at <http://www.ohchr.org/EN/HRBodies/UPR/Pages/SGindex.aspx>, accessed 31 October 2018.

[209]*Ibid* at [122].

[210]*Ibid* at [110].

The section of the Report on criminal justice stresses that 'it is a fundamental human right of all citizens to live in a safe environment, free from drugs, guns, random street violence and terrorism.'[211] The laws in Singapore 'are designed to protect the public against crimes, while ensuring that persons accused of alleged crimes have due process and fair trials. Singapore's crime rate is one of the lowest—684 per 100,000 population in 2008, with 111 violent crimes per 100,000 population—despite a relatively small police force.'[212]

Inputs from NGOs were sought as part of the UPR process. A Human Rights NGO (MURUAH Singapore) raised several features of Singapore's criminal process which they found to be troubling. These included the denial of access to counsel during police investigation and the permissibility of resting a criminal conviction solely on a confession recorded in the course of police interrogation. It noted that the defence often faced evidential difficulties in challenging the voluntariness of such confessions.[213] According to the 2011 Report of the Working Group on the Universal Periodic Review of Singapore,[214] Singapore did not support the recommendation by Canada to 'adopt new provisions to inform those detained of their right to counsel and guarantee their access to Counsel immediately upon arrest.'[215]

In the 2015 National Report for the second UPR,[216] the government reiterated that it considers 'the safety and security of the person to be a fundamental human right, without which other rights cannot genuinely be enjoyed.'[217] The priority of Singapore's criminal justice system is to 'deter crime and protect society against criminals.'[218] In its submission for the second UPR, MARUAH Singapore essentially repeated the observations and recommendations alluded to above.[219] The Report of the Working Group makes little mention of criminal justice issues save on the topic of the death penalty.[220]

---

[211] *Ibid* at [119].

[212] *Ibid* at [119].

[213] 'Universal Periodic Review – Singapore – Submission of MURUAH (Working Group for an ASEAN Human Rights Mechanism, Singapore)' (2011) at [6], available online at <http://www.ohchr.org/EN/HRBodies/UPR/Pages/UPRSGStakeholdersInfoS11.aspx>, accessed 31 October 2018.

[214] 'Report of the Working Group on the Universal Periodic Review – Singapore' (11 July 2011), available online at <http://www.ohchr.org/EN/HRBodies/UPR/Pages/SGindex.aspx>, accessed on 31 October 2018.

[215] *Ibid* at [97.11].

[216] 'National report submitted in accordance with paragraph 5 of the annex to Human Rights Council resolution 16/21' (28 October 2015), available online at <http://www.ohchr.org/EN/HRBodies/UPR/Pages/SGindex.aspx>, accessed 31 October 2018.

[217] *Ibid* at [100].

[218] *Ibid* at [101].

[219] 'MARUAH submission for Universal Periodic Review' (21 June 2015), available online at <http://www.ohchr.org/EN/HRBodies/UPR/Pages/UPRSGStakeholdersInfoS24.aspx>, accessed 31 October 2018.

[220] 'Report of the Working Group on the Universal Periodic Review – Singapore' (15 April 2016), available online at <http://www.ohchr.org/EN/HRBodies/UPR/Pages/SGindex.aspx>, accessed 31 October 2018.

9 Safeguards[221]

One way of safeguarding the voluntariness and accuracy of confessions is to allow the suspect access to legal advice before or during police interrogation. As we have seen, this safeguard is generally unavailable in Singapore as the right to counsel is a restrictive one.

In an effort to spread knowledge of rights in the course of a criminal investigation, search or prosecution, the Law Society of Singapore, working with the Attorney-General Chambers and with the support of the Ministry of Law, published a four-page pamphlet containing relevant information for distribution to police centres, police posts and community clubs and centres.[222] This pamphlet is available in the four official languages in Singapore.[223] However, follow-up checks revealed that "some Investigating Officers had never heard of [the pamphlets], they were unavailable in a number of land divisions, and not available in the lockups where they were most needed".[224]

An Appropriate Adult Scheme was introduced in 2015.[225] It allows a neutral third party who is a trained volunteer to be present during police questioning of a person with mental or intellectual disability.[226] Since April 2017, the scheme has been extended to minors.[227] This extension was made following the apparent suicide of a fourteen-year-old boy a few hours after his release by the police.[228] He had been picked up from his school and questioned alone at a police station.[229]

---

[221]*See* generally Singh, 2006.

[222]*See* 'Pick up "pamphlet of rights' to get it right', *The Straits Times*, 11 April 2015.

[223]They are Malay, Mandarin, Tamil and English. *See* art. 153A of the Constitution of Singapore.

[224]This was reported by the President of the Law Society: Thio, 2016.

[225]*See* 'Help for Suspects with Special Needs', *The Straits Times*, 1 April 2015. The launch was preceded by a pilot run in 2013.

[226]*See* 'Drug offenders with special needs to get support', *The Straits Times*, 18 January 2017.

[227]*See* 'Volunteers to offer minors support in police interviews', *The Straits Times*, 7 January 2017.

[228]*See* 'Parliamentary Debates Singapore: Official Report', vol. 94 (1 March 2016) (Minister for Home Affairs). *See also* 'Police to review the way youth are questioned', *The Straits Times*, 2 February 2016; 'Death of 14-year-old: Experts welcome police review on procedures for questioning youth', *The Straits Times*, 3 February 2016; 'Law Society sets up panel to study investigation protocols for young suspects', *The Straits Times*, 16 February 2016; 'Police review to consider three points', *The Straits Times*, 2 March 2016; 'Protecting minors suspected of crime', *The Straits Times*, 17 January 2017.

[229]The government strongly denied in Parliament that there was any police mistreatment: 'Parliamentary Debates Singapore: Official Report', vol. 94 (1 March 2016) (Minister for Home Affairs). *See also* 'No basis for hasty conclusion on boy's death: Shanmugam', *The Straits Times*, 2 March 2016.

The role of the appropriate adult is not to give legal advice but to prevent miscommunication and enhance accuracy in the recording of statements.[230] The scheme currently faces a shortage of volunteers.[231]

Another way to protect the voluntariness of statements is to have police interrogations video-recorded. The government had previously resisted repeated calls to implement a system of recording.[232] In July 2015, the government finally agreed to launch a pilot programme of video recording starting in the first quarter of 2016.[233] This pilot project was welcomed by the legal profession.[234] But it did not materialise due to a lack of 'appropriate legislative framework'.[235] Legislative reform to allow video-recording is currently underway.[236]

10 Statistics

It is difficult to find access to relevant statistics.[237] Below are some data obtained from indirect sources.

[230]The lawyer representing the suspect cannot serve as an Appropriate Adult under this scheme. *See* Lok, 2013.

[231]'More volunteers needed to help young suspects', *The Straits Times*, 23 May 2017. As of 30 March 2017, the scheme has a pool of 143 volunteers: '143 volunteers ready to help young suspects', *The Straits Times*, 30 March 2017.

[232]*See eg*, Singh, 2006.

[233]*See* 'Police to try out videotaping interviews with suspects', *The Straits Times*, 23 July 2015. The pilot project was also mentioned by the Attorney-General, Mr V K Rajah, SC, in his speech delivered at the Opening of the Legal Year 2016 (11 January 2016), available online at: <https://www.agc.gov.sg/docs/default-source/speeches/2016/ag's-oly-speech-2016-(as-delivered)-(4).pdf?sfvrsn=2>, accessed 31 October 2018.

[234]However, the exclusion from the programme of the Corruption Practices Investigation Bureau ('CPIB') was criticised: 'Lawyers want CPIB included in video-recording pilot programme', *The Business Times*, 20 August 2015.

[235]'Video recordings will help court assess statements', *The Straits Times*, 25 July 2017.

[236]Ministry of Law, 'Public Consultation on Proposed Amendments to the Criminal Procedure Code and Evidence Act' (24 July 2017), available online at: <https://www.mlaw.gov.sg/content/minlaw/en/news/public-consultations/public-consultation-on-proposed-amendments-to-the-criminal-proce.html>, accessed 31 October 2018.

[237]The lack of publicly accessible government information and data is a problem that has been raised by Singapore academics in various disciplines including economics and sociology. *See* 'Academics call for more detailed, regular data sharing', *The Straits Times*, 25 October 2011.

10.1 Statistics on Police Dismissals, Internal Investigations and Actions Against Officers

In a parliamentary speech delivered on 25 August 1994, the Parliamentary Secretary to the Minister for Home Affairs assured Parliament that allegations of Police abuse are not common. He revealed the following[238]:

> [In 1993], the [Internal Investigation Section, now called the Internal Affairs Office] investigated 94 complaints of Police abuse on suspects. This represents only 0.5% of the 18,000-19,000 suspects arrested each year. Of these, only 14 cases were substantiated. The 16 errant officers involved have all been dealt with departmentally or even prosecuted in court. This figure represents less than 0.2% of our Police Force which totals over 10,600 officers.

A member of Parliament sought clarifications on two points[239]: first, 'of the 14 cases that were substantiated, what kind of action was taken against the Police officers involved' and '[s]econdly, whether any confessions that were extracted in those circumstances were used in prosecutions against the offenders?' The Parliamentary Secretary did not answer the second question. In his answer to the first question, he revealed that '[o]ut of the 14 cases that were substantiated, one was prosecuted and charged in court. He was sentenced to one month imprisonment. The rest were departmentally dealt with.'[240]

The same minister reported in 1998 that the number of complaints against police abuse of suspects had dropped to 56 in 1994 which was 0.2% of the total number of suspects arrested in 1997. Only 10 cases involving 14 officers were found to be substantiated following internal investigation and they were 'dealt with departmentally or prosecuted in court'. This was said to represent less than 0.12% of the total number of officers in the police force.[241]

More recently, it is reported in a newspaper that in the first 10 months of 2011, 16 police officers were sacked. It is further stated that '[b]etween 2007 and [2010], 80 police officers were dismissed.'[242]

---

[238] 'Parliamentary Debates Singapore: Official Report', vol. 63 (25 August 1994) at col. 380 (Associate Professor Ho Peng Kee).

[239] 'Parliamentary Debates Singapore: Official Report', vol. 63 (25 August 1994) at cols. 383-384 (Associate Professor Walter Woon).

[240] 'Parliamentary Debates Singapore: Official Report', vol. 63 (25 August 1994) at cols. 383-384 (Associate Professor Ho Peng Kee).

[241] 'Parliamentary Debates Singapore: Official Report', vol. 69 (1 June 1998) at cols. 97-98 (Minister of State for Home Affairs, Assoc Prof Ho Peng Kee).

[242] 'New unit set up to police errant cop', *The Straits Times*, 21 October 2011. The figures of dismissal were derived from a count of dismissal notices posted in the Government Gazette.

10.2 Exclusion of Statements

It is uncommon for statements recorded by the police to be excluded.[243] However, full data is not easily available. In 1995, the Parliamentary Secretary to the Minister for Home Affairs reported in Parliament that from 1993 to April 1995, statements were ruled inadmissible in four out of 166 cases tried in the High Court. No data was available for cases decided in the Subordinate Court.[244] In 1998, the Minister of State for Home Affairs made the point in Parliament that the number of cases where a statement is challenged and excluded by the court is small. According to the Minister, that 'the police takes its work seriously; police knows that its work will be scrutinised by the courts'.

10.3 Conviction and Acquittal Rates

Anecdotally, the acquittal rate is low. There are no easily available statistics. It is reported that in 2011, '156 people were hauled to court as a result of [investigations by the Corrupt Practices Investigation Bureau ('CPIB')]. And in the last seven years, the conviction rate in such cases has hovered between 92 and 96%.'[245] A press release by the CPIB on 2 April 2015 showed that the 'conviction rates (excluding withdrawal) for cases charged by the CPIB for corruption offences and other related offences remained high for the past 3 years, well above 95% mark.'[246] It is unclear what inference is to be drawn from a high conviction rate. As one commentator observed, while one could argue that it reflects judicial reluctance to 'rule against the executive', it is equally 'consistent with a prosecutorial job so well done that only the obviously guilty are brought to court—even the most fair and independent minded judge would have little choice but to convict.'[247]

---

[243] *See PP* v. *Knight Glenn Jeyasingam* [1999] 1 SLR(R) 1165 at [17]: "[t]aking the example of confessions, the Prosecution submitted that such statements… are rarely excluded in Singapore courts unless the voluntariness of the statement had been disproved.".

[244] 'Parliamentary Debates Singapore: Official Report', vol. 64 (25 May 1995) at cols. 1109-1110.

[245] 'CPIB to mark 60 years of graft-busting', *The Straits Times*, 23 August 2012.

[246] Press Release by CPIB (2 April 2015) at [15]. Document available online at <https://www.cpib.gov.sg/sites/default/files/publication-documents/CPIB%20Corruption%20Statistics_0.pdf>, accessed 31 October 2018.

[247] Hor, 2002 at 507.

11 Conclusion

Official discourse on the criminal process in Singapore tends to draw on crime control ideology.[248] It is used for two main purposes. The first is to justify erosion or weak enforcement of rights, such as the right of silence and the right to counsel. The crime control ideology takes the suppression of crime as the dominant aim and is premised on an assumption about the impact of rights on crime control. To be strong on the suspect's rights, so the argument goes, is to be soft on crime, and, conversely, those rights needs to be weakened in order to be effective in crime control. The second is to justify judicial restraint from excessive interference with the work of the police. Judges should be mindful of the practical realities of criminal investigation when applying exclusionary rules.[249]

Rights of the accused are respected but they tend to be more narrowly construed or more weakly protected than in jurisdictions that are generally viewed as progressive. The approach taken in Singapore has been defended by pointing out how it has resulted in a low crime rate and by asserting the nation's right to set its own priorities and choose its own legal path. From time to time, concerns are aired about the criminal justice system and in connection with specific cases. These concerns have been raised in different fora—in Parliament, the press, online blogs, public speeches and professional and academic writings. Although there are reported instances of miscarriage of justice, none has generated sufficient controversy to be the catalyst for major reforms. Instead, change, when it comes about, tends come about slowly and incrementally. Singapore is concerned about its human rights image before the international community; how this will translate into legal reform in criminal justice is uncertain. International law thus far has had negligible impact in this area. There have been some welcome initiatives; especially welcome is the proposal to implement video-taping of police interviews. Certain changes have also alleviated previous perceptions of unfairness, such as the introduction of a new regime of pre-trial criminal disclosure. But there is still much that critics find to be unsatisfactory; particularly troubling is the difficulty the suspect faces in getting access to a lawyer at the police station.

---

[248]*See*, *eg*, Chan, 1996 at 438 ("If anything has been made clear in Singapore, it is that crime control has always been and is a high priority on the Government's action agenda"); Hor, 2001 at 28 ("official justifications of Singapore's criminal justice system appeal to Packer's 'crime control' model").

[249]*See*, *eg*, *Fung Yuk Shing* v. *PP* [1993] 2 SLR(R) 771 at [19]; *Seow Choon Meng* v. *PP* [1994] 2 SLR(R) 338 at [33]; *PP* v. *Sng Siew Ngoh* [1995] 3 SLR(R) 755 at [26]. *Cf Law Society of Singapore* v. *Tan Guat Neo Phyllis* [2008] 2 SLR(R) 239 at [143]: 'In Singapore, the Constitution establishes a form of parliamentary government (based on the Westminster model) based on the separation of the legislative, executive and judicial powers. Each arm of the government operates independently of the other and each should not interfere with the functions of the other.'

12 Addendum

A number of developments have occurred after the completion of writing of this chapter. The Criminal Justice Reform Act 2018 was passed on 19 March 2018 and assented to by the President on 11 April 2018. A number of provisions in this Act were brought into force in September and October 2018. Among other changes, a new regime of audiovisual recording of statements taken by law enforcement officers have been introduced. For the moment, this is a requirement only for rape cases. There is intention to extend this gradually to other types of offences. Another change is the removal of the committal hearing for cases to be tried in the High Court.

References

Books

Chan, Sek Keong, 'From Justice Model to Crime Control Model', address before the *International Conference on Criminal Justice Under Stress: Transnational Perspectives*, New Delhi, India (24 Nov 2006). [Chan, 2006]

Choo, Andrew L-T, *The Privilege against Self-incrimination and Criminal Justice*, Oxford 2013. [Choo, 2013]

Packer, Herbert, *The Limits of the Criminal Sanction*, Stanford 1968. [Packer, 1968]

Philips, Cyril (Chairman), *The Royal Commission on Criminal Procedure*, Cmnd 8092, 1981. [Philips, 1981]

Pinsler, Jeffrey, *Evidence and the Litigation Process* 6th edition, Singapore 2017. [Pinsler, 2017]

Tan, Yock Lin, *Criminal Procedure*, Singapore 2007. [Tan, 2007]

Thio Li-ann, *A Treatise on Singapore Constitutional Law*, Singapore 2012. [Thio, 2012]

Journal articles

Chan, Sek Keong, 'The Criminal Process – The Singapore Model', (1996) 17 *Singapore Law Review*, 433–503. [Chan, 1996]

Chin, Tet Yung, 'Criminal Procedure Code 2010: Confessions and Statements by Accused Persons Revisited', (2012) 24 *Singapore Academy of Law Journal*, 60–91. [Chin, 2012]

Chng, Melanie, 'Modernising the Criminal Justice Framework: The Criminal Procedure Code 2010', (2011) 23 *Singapore Academy of Law Journal*, 23–57. [Chng, 2011]

Chong, Steven, 'The Ethics of Criminal Practice', *Singapore Law Gazette*, April 2015, 12–22, available online at <http://v1.lawgazette.com.sg/2015-04/>, accessed 31 October 2018. [Chong, 2015]

Ho Hock Lai, 'On the Obtaining and Admissibility of Incriminating Statements', [2016] *Singapore Journal of Legal Studies*, 249–276. [Ho, 2016]

Ho Hock Lai, 'The Privilege against Self-incrimination and Right of Access to a Lawyer—A Comparative Assessment', (2013) 25 *Singapore Academy of Law Journal*, 826–846. [Ho, 2013]

Ho, Hock Lai, '"National Values on Law and Order" and the Discretion to Exclude Wrongfully Obtained Evidence', [2012] *Journal of Commonwealth Criminal Law,* 232–256. [Ho, 2012]

Hor, Michael 'Singapore's Innovations to Due Process', (2001) 12 *Criminal Law Forum*, 25–40. [Hor, 2001]

Hor, Michael, 'The Future of Singapore's Criminal Process', (2013) 25 *Singapore Academy of Law Journal*, 847–873. [Hor, 2013]

Hor, Michael, 'The Independence of the Criminal Justice System in Singapore', (2002) 2 *Singapore Journal of Legal Studies*, 497–513. [Hor, 2002]

Hwang, Michael, 'A Protocol for Police Interviews of Witnesses and Suspects?', *Singapore Law Gazette*, June 2010, 1–4, available online at <http://v1.lawgazette.com.sg/2010-06/>, accessed 31 October 2018. [Hwang, 2010].

Lok, Vi Ming SC, 'When the Incredible Lawyer isn't an Appropriate Adult', *Singapore Law Gazette*, March 2013, 1–4, available online at: <http://v1.lawgazette.com.sg/2013-03/>, accessed 31 October 2018. [Lok, 2013]

Mohan, Chandra, 'Police Interrogation and the Right of Silence in the Republic of Singapore' (1986) 2 *Malayan Law Journal*, xxviii–xxxix. [Mohan, 1986]

See, Kee Oon, 'Criminal Case Resolution', [2013] *Asian Journal on Mediation,* 76–81. [See, 2013]

Soh, Kessler, '"Criminal Case Resolution" in the Subordinate Courts of Singapore', [2011] *Journal of Commonwealth Criminal Law,* 209–225. [Soh, 2011]

Tan, Alan Khee-Jin, 'Adverse Inferences and the Right to Silence: Re-examining the Singapore Experience', [1997] *Criminal Law Review*, 471–481. [Tan, 1997]

Thio, Shen Yi, 'Vulnerable Suspects and Access to Counsel', *Law Gazette*, February 2016, 1–4, available online at: <http://v1.lawgazette.com.sg/2016-02/>, accessed 31 October 2018. [Thio, 2016]

Thio, Sheng Yi, President's Message, 'Enhanced CLAS Official Launch', *Singapore Law Gazette*, June 2015, 1–4, available online at <http://v1.lawgazette.com.sg/2015-06/>, accessed 31 October 2018. [Thio, 2015]

Wong, Denise Huiwen, 'Discovering the Right to Criminal Disclosure', (2013) 25 *Singapore Academy of Law Journal,* 548–579. [Wong, 2013]

Yeo, Stanley Meng Heong, 'Diminishing the Right to Silence: The Singapore Experience', [1983] *Criminal Law Review*, 88–101. [Yeo, 1983]

Contributions to Edited Volumes and Annotated Law

Singh, Sant, 'Treatment of Out-of-Court Statements in the Judicial Process', in: Teo Keang Sood (ed.), *Singapore Academy of Law Conference 2006 – Developments in Singapore law between 2001 and 2005*, Singapore 2006, 481–498. [Singh, 2006]

Hock Lai Ho is the Amaladass Professor of Criminal Justice at the NUS. He holds an LL.B. from NUS, a BCL from Oxford University and a Ph.D. from Cambridge University. He has published internationally in the fields of evidence, proof and aspects of the administration of criminal justice. His research ranges from doctrinal analysis of Singapore law to theoretical and comparative reflections on broader issues of the criminal trial.

Part II
Exclusionary Rules—Quo Vadis

The Purposes and Functions of Exclusionary Rules: A Comparative Overview

Jenia Iontcheva Turner and Thomas Weigend

Abstract The chapter analyzes the rationales for excluding relevant evidence with the aim of establishing the ideal type of exclusion system for each rationale. The authors then review to what extent individual legal systems have actually altered their legal rules in accordance with these ideal systems. An investigation into whether or not there are any consistent relationships between the ideal systems and proclaimed rationales is conducted. The structure of various exclusionary rules is also explored, as are other factors that may influence the law and practical application of such rules.

1 Introduction

The exclusion of relevant evidence from the trial interferes with one of the main goals of the criminal process, that is, the determination of all relevant facts ("the truth") as the basis of the verdict. For that reason, many criminal justice systems, both adversarial and inquisitorial, have long viewed rules demanding the exclusion of relevant evidence ("exclusionary rules") as an obstacle to the search for truth and therefore have greatly limited their application. Over the course of the twentieth century, however, the use of exclusionary rules has increased significantly. More

Portions of Jenia Turner's contributions to this chapter draw on her previous work in Turner, 2016; Turner, 2014.

J. I. Turner (✉)
SMU Dedman School of Law, Dallas, USA
e-mail: Jenia@mail.smu.edu

T. Weigend
Faculty of Law, University of Cologne, Cologne, Germany
e-mail: Thomas.Weigend@uni-koeln.de

S. Gless and T. Richter (eds.), *Do Exclusionary Rules Ensure a Fair Trial?*
Ius Gentium: Comparative Perspectives on Law and Justice 74,
https://doi.org/10.1007/978-3-030-12520-2_8

and more legal systems decided to use exclusion of evidence as a reaction to violations of rules concerning the acquisition of evidence.[1]

In adversarial systems, exclusion can be based on the logic that a party which obtains a piece of evidence illegally should not be allowed to benefit from the fruits of the violation. In inquisitorial systems, it is more difficult to rely on this rationale of exclusion because evidence is regarded as "belonging" to the court, not to one of the parties. Still, there are overriding concerns that may justify a court's decision to exclude a piece of evidence. Such concerns can be related to systemic interests (e.g., the appearance of fairness) or individual interests (e.g., vindication of the rights of the individual affected by the violation). Each of these interests may be so important as to outweigh the procedural interest in having the full range of relevant evidence available at the trial.

Every legal system recognizes exclusionary rules as a reaction to particularly serious violations. There is an almost universal rule that statements made as a result of torture must not be used in court.[2] But beyond this common core, the breadth and contents of exclusionary rules differ widely. In some jurisdictions, the law generally prohibits the admission of any evidence obtained illegally.[3] Other states are more reticent and recognize only a limited number of "absolute" exclusionary rules, leaving exclusion in other cases to the discretion of the court, or permitting the admission of illegally obtained evidence if the interest in making use of it for "finding the truth" outweighs the taint of its illegal acquisition.

At the same time, legal systems differ with respect to the purposes they proclaim to pursue by excluding illegally obtained evidence. In some systems, the integrity of fact-finding or of the judicial system as such is the most prominent concern that supports the exclusion of evidence. In other systems, deterrence of police misconduct is foremost. In yet others, the principal justification for exclusion rests on the protection of individual rights. The general tendency toward protecting human rights that has prevailed in the last few decades has given a boost to such considerations.

In this chapter, we will start out by analyzing the potential rationales for excluding relevant evidence (Sect. 2) and will then attempt to construe ideal types of exclusion systems based on each rationale (Sect. 3). We will then review to what extent individual legal systems have actually devised their legal rules in accordance with these ideal types (Sect. 4). By way of conclusion, we will ask whether there is any consistent relationship between the ideal types based on the proclaimed

---

[1]This chapter focuses on illegally obtained evidence and therefore does not discuss rules that some legal systems use to exclude evidence in order to "absolutely" protect specific interests, e.g., the core of the right to privacy, even in the absence of police misconduct.

[2]Art. 15 UN Convention against Torture (1984) ("Each State Party shall ensure that any statement which is established to have been made as a result of torture shall not be invoked as evidence in any proceedings, except against a person accused of torture as evidence that the statement was made.").

[3]Greece is an example of such an absolutist approach to exclusion. *See* Giannoulopoulos, 2007, p. 181.

rationales and the actual configuration of exclusionary rules, and what other factors may in fact influence the law and practice of excluding evidence (Sect. 5).

2 Rationales of Exclusionary Rules

In this chapter, we review the most common rationales used to support the exclusion of unlawfully obtained evidence. We will first deal with system-related considerations, such as promoting the search for truth and the integrity of the criminal justice system. We will then examine deterrence of police misconduct and protection of individual rights as justifications for excluding evidence.

2.1 Finding the Truth

In order to properly fulfil its functions, any procedural system, regardless of whether it is party-oriented or court-centered, must meet certain basic requirements: A functional procedural system needs to present courts as principally fair and oriented toward a just disposition of cases in accordance with the law; this includes an orientation of fact-finding toward the "truth", or more realistically, a renunciation of court decisions based on evident fiction. Courts are encouraged to pursue these basic goals through admitting and taking into consideration any evidence that appears to be factually relevant for the disposition of the case.

Yet in exceptional situations, the introduction of individual pieces of evidence may fatally undermine the integrity of the proceedings. For example, basing a conviction on a confession that the defendant made under torture not only conflicts with the ideal of judicial integrity but also raises doubts as to the court's truth-orientation, because torture tends to make the victim say anything that he thinks will put an end to the pain. Evidence may therefore be excluded if the methods used to obtain it have rendered it unreliable.[4] This rationale applies to the suppression of verbal statements obtained as a result of torture or, in some cases, deceit of the person questioned or the inability to confront key witnesses.[5]

The reliability-based rationale has a limited area of application, however. It rarely comes into play with regard to physical evidence. When drugs are seized illegally or a telephone conversation is taped without a necessary judicial warrant, the unlawful government action does not in any way reduce these items' probative value. Therefore, excluding such evidence would undermine the search for truth instead of advancing it.

[4]Jackson/Summers, 2012, at 154.

[5]Macula, 2019 at 3; *R* v. *Grant* [2009] 2 SCR 353, § 110 (Can.); *Chalmers* v. *H.M. Advocate* 1954 JC 66, 83 (Scot.); Israel Supreme Court, *Yissacharov v. Chief Military Prosecutor*, Judgment of 4 May 2006, CrimA 5121/98, § 71 (Justice Beinisch); Strafprozessordnung (Ger.) § 136a.

2.2 Upholding Judicial Integrity

A broader justification for the exclusion of illegally obtained evidence is the preservation of the integrity of the judicial system.[6] This rationale assumes that courts would taint their own reputation and dignity if they (routinely) base their decisions on evidence that has been obtained through gross violations of the law. Courts should therefore exclude tainted evidence in order to demonstrate to the public that they do not condone illegal acts of government agents and that they refuse to base their decisions on the results of such acts. By declining to become "accomplices in the willful disobedience of [the law] they are sworn to uphold"[7] and by renouncing the use of illegally obtained evidence, courts reaffirm the rule of law and buttress the legitimacy of criminal proceedings.[8]

To the extent the integrity rationale emphasizes the integrity of the individual judicial process, it tends to support robust, categorical approaches to exclusion. But in another variant of this rationale, also known as "systemic integrity," the focus is more broadly on "not bringing the administration of justice into disrepute."[9] This version of the integrity rationale recognizes that while exclusionary rules may contribute to the propriety of the criminal process, they can also undermine the acceptance of the criminal justice system if they lead to the non-prosecution or

---

[6] *See, e.g.*, ECtHR, *Gäfgen* v. *Germany,* case no. 22978/05, Judgment (Grand Chamber) of 1 June 2010, § 175 ("Indeed, there is also a vital public interest in preserving the integrity of the judicial process and thus the values of civilised societies founded upon the rule of law."). Like other courts and writers, the ECtHR here refers not only to "the integrity of the judicial process" but also to the "rule of law." The latter is a very basic value of any judicial system. However, exclusion of evidence does not specifically promote the "rule of law," because the law can provide for different ways of dealing with illegally obtained evidence. By contrast, "the integrity of the judicial process" (or, for short, "judicial integrity") describes the specific interest potentially violated by admitting tainted evidence.

[7] *Elkins* v. *United States*, 364 US 206, 223 (1960); *see also* Israel Supreme Court, *Yissacharov v. Chief Military Prosecutor*, Judgment of 4 May 2006, CrimA 5121/98 (Justice Beinisch), § 45 ("[T]he administration of justice is also based on the *way* in which the court reaches its decision in the circumstances of the case before it. Basing a conviction on evidence that was obtained in an illegal manner or by means of a substantial violation of a protected human right allows the investigation authorities to enjoy the fruits of their misdeed and it may create an incentive for improper acts of interrogation in the future. Admitting such evidence may be seen as the court giving approval to the aforesaid illegality and being an accessory, albeit after the event, to the improper conduct of the investigation authorities. Consequently, in certain circumstances admitting the evidence in court may prejudice the fairness and integrity of the judicial process.").

[8] This rationale has been particularly influential in countries emerging from authoritarian regimes and transitioning to liberal democracy. In those countries, the exclusionary rule has been valued for curtailing government abuse and for affirming that even government officials are subject to legal restraints. *See* Turner, 2014.

[9] Canadian Charter of Rights and Freedoms, Part I of the Constitutional Act, 1982, being Schedule B to the Canada Act, 1982, c. 24 (U.K.) ("[T]he evidence shall be excluded if it is established that, having regard to all the circumstances, the admission of it in the proceedings would bring the administration of justice into disrepute."); *R* v. *Grant* [2009] 2 SCR 353, §§ 68–70 (Can.).

acquittal of persons who are most likely to be guilty of serious crime. The public may lose faith in the proper functioning of the system if courts frequently exclude reliable evidence and consequently fail to convict because crucial evidence is then missing.

The systemic integrity approach therefore favors a balancing of factors reflecting these competing interests. On the one hand, courts should examine the seriousness of the official misconduct, including the culpability of the officers, the presence of a pattern of misconduct, and the significance of the right violated; on the other hand, to determine the costs of exclusion, courts should consider the gravity of the offense charged, the reliability of the evidence, and the centrality of the evidence to the case against the defendant.[10]

2.3 Deterring Police Misconduct

One aspect of promoting the integrity of the criminal process concerns the influence that exclusion of evidence may have on police conduct. In the great majority of procedural systems, most investigation work is performed by police officers, and it is often they who break the rules concerning the acquisition of evidence. The integrity aspect of criminal procedure is therefore most vulnerable on the police level.[11] Accordingly, one function of excluding illegally obtained evidence is to dissuade law enforcement officers from violating the law.[12]

Exclusion for "deterrence" purposes is based on the assumption that police officers, even if they are not at all times focused on respecting procedural safeguards, have a strong professional interest in seeing offenders convicted. By excluding evidence that the officer had acquired in violation of the law and thereby dramatically reducing the odds of conviction, courts hope to nudge police officers toward complying with the law in the future. It is not by chance that the notion of excluding evidence for the purpose of deterring unlawful police conduct has played a great role in the United States, following revelations of grave and systematic police violations of suspects' rights in the U.S. legal system in the 1960s.[13] Exclusion of evidence obtained through the use of illegal police methods was seen as an indispensable means for re-establishing the integrity and public acceptance of the criminal justice system.

---

[10] *See* Slobogin, 2016 at 287–291.

[11] In *Spano* v. *New York*, 360 US 315, 320 (1959), the U.S. Supreme Court explained its new emphasis on police illegality used to obtain the confession (rather than on the inherent untrustworthiness of coerced confessions): "[t]he abhorrence of society to the use of involuntary confessions does not turn alone on their inherent untrustworthiness. It also turns on the deep-rooted feeling that the police must obey the law while enforcing the law."

[12] *United States* v. *Leon*, 468 US 897, 918 (1984); *Hudson* v. *Michigan*, 547 US 586, 591 (2006); *Herring* v. *United States*, 555 US 135 (2009).

[13] Miller/Wright, 2007 at 521–522 (discussing the findings of the Wickersham Commission).

More recently, however, the U.S. Supreme Court has concluded that the social costs of exclusion may outweigh the benefits of deterrence.[14] As part of this cost-benefit analysis, the Court has taken into account the availability of alternative sanctions that may be able to discipline officers at a lesser cost to the administration of justice.[15] It has further limited the applicability of the deterrence rationale by declaring that deterrence can operate only where police officers violate procedural rules deliberately or recklessly.[16]

Although prominent in the United States, the deterrence approach has not gained much of a following elsewhere. To the extent deterrence of police misconduct is mentioned by European courts, it is typically used as a secondary consideration supporting other purposes of exclusion.[17] In Germany, a few authors have recognized deterrence of police misconduct as one purpose of excluding illegally obtained evidence[18]; but the majority have rejected that approach, arguing that this rationale does not fit the inquisitorial structure of the German criminal process and would interfere too much with the courts' mandate to search for the truth.[19]

The skepticism toward the idea of deterring police misconduct by excluding evidence from trial may be well-founded. There exists at best a tenuous psychological connection between excluding evidence of past misconduct and preventing future ones: the mechanism of "deterrence" can function only if: (a) offending police officers are informed of the forensic fate of the individual criminal process, and (b) they care about that fate. The empirical foundations of either precondition is doubtful, however.[20] Especially if police use torture or other unlawful means for purposes other than obtaining evidence to be used in criminal proceedings (e.g., because they wish to humiliate members of an ethnic group or because they are looking for information unrelated to criminal proceedings), the fact that statements obtained through their acts are inadmissible at trial will have little influence on their behavior.

---

[14]*United States* v. *Leon*, 468 US 897, 907 (1984); *Hudson* v. *Michigan*, 547 US 586, 591, 599 (2006); *Herring* v. *United States*, 555 US 135, 141 (2009).

[15]*Hudson* v. *Michigan*, 547 US 586, 591, 599 (2006).

[16]*Herring* v. *United States*, 555 US 135, 144 (2009).

[17]*See, e.g.*, Macula, 2019 at 3.1.1.

[18]*See* Grünwald, 1966 at 499–500; Spendel, 1966 at 1104–1105.

[19]Küpper, 1990 at 417; Jäger, 2003 at 69–71.

[20]Alschuler, 2008 at 1374 (reviewing U.S. studies of the exclusionary rule's deterrence effect and concluding that while the exclusionary rule does not have a direct and immediate deterrent effect on officers' behavior, it "works over the long term by allowing judges to give guidance to police officers who ultimately prove willing to receive it").

2.4 Human Rights Considerations

An alternative approach to justifying the exclusion of relevant evidence aims at the protection of human rights.[21] Exclusion, according to this rationale, is to provide the victims of human rights violations with an effective remedy. This rationale has been influential in several of the countries studied in this volume, including Germany, Switzerland, and Taiwan. The U.S. Supreme Court followed this approach in some of its earlier opinions on the exclusionary rule, explaining that without exclusion, provisions that protect fundamental rights would be reduced to "a form of words"[22] and would not have any meaningful legal effect.[23] Yet, the US Supreme Court has since abandoned this rationale and has switched to an emphasis on deterrence of police misconduct.[24]

Regional human rights courts, by contrast, have in recent years begun to prod states to provide for exclusion of evidence obtained through human rights violations. Human rights law requires states to ensure the protection of, *inter alia*, the right to a fair trial,[25] the right to be free from arbitrary searches and seizures,[26] the right to privacy,[27] and the right not to be compelled to testify against oneself.[28] The domestic implementation of provisions protecting human rights has made states aware of the need to adopt mechanisms that can effectively safeguard these rights. Human rights courts tend to leave questions of the admissibility of evidence to individual states and do not generally require that evidence be excluded if gathered in violation of one of these rights.[29] But they mandate exclusion of statements obtained through serious violations of fair trial such as entrapment of innocent citizens to commit crimes,[30] torture or degrading treatment,[31] and in the Inter-American human rights regime, even of statements obtained through lesser

---

[21]Israel Supreme Court, *Yissacharov v. Chief Military Prosecutor*, Judgment of 4 May 2006, CrimA 5121/98 (Justice Beinisch), § 61; Ashworth, 1977; Jackson/Summers, 2012, at 155.

[22]*Silverthorne Lumber Co.* v. *United States*, 251 US 385, 392 (1920).

[23]*Weeks v. United States*, 232 US 383, 393 (1914).

[24]*Id.*

[25]ICCPR art. 14(1); ECHR art. 6.

[26]ICCPR art. 17; ECHR art. 8.

[27]ICCPR art. 17; ECHR art. 8.

[28]ICCPR art. 14(3); ECHR art. 8.

[29]*See, e.g.*, ECtHR, *Khan* v. *United Kingdom*, case no. 35394/97, Judgment of 12 May 2000, (31 Eur. Ct. H.R. 45), § 34.

[30]*See, e.g.*, ECtHR, *Furcht* v. *Germany*, case no. 54648/09, Judgment of 23 October 2014, §§ 62–64.

[31]ECtHR, *Gäfgen* v. *Germany*, case no. 22978/05, Judgment (Grand Chamber) of 1 June 2010, §§ 166–168; *see* UN Convention Against Torture and Other Cruel, Inhuman or Degrading Treatment or Punishment, art. 15.

forms of coercion.[32] Human rights law has thus, directly as well as indirectly, contributed to the expansion of exclusionary rules designed to protect human rights.

However, the functional relationship between the exclusion of evidence and the protection of human rights is less than clear. One can conceive of exclusion as a mechanism for preventing future human rights violations; exclusion is to demonstrate to potential violators that it is not worthwhile to use torture or other prohibited methods because evidence obtained thereby will not be admissible in court. This is the logic of deterrence of police misconduct, which we have mentioned above (Sect. 2.3). But it is an open question whether (and why) the criminal justice system should be obliged to contribute to a better protection of human rights. Exclusion may have an indirect positive effect on reducing human rights violations, but its undeniable direct effect is a reduction of the factual basis on which the court's verdict can be based. It is thus the criminal justice system that has to pay the price for the possible improvement in human rights protection.

The main argument in favor of exclusion from a human rights perspective is, however, not systemic but individualistic: inadmissibility is to provide the victim of the violation with some kind of compensation. This argument, however, suffers from several flaws. First, compensation of this kind is provided only for a relatively small portion of victims of human rights violations, i.e., those who are subsequently subjected to a criminal trial. Second, exclusion can apply only if the human rights violation produced evidence relevant to a criminal case. Third, exclusion of evidence may give little satisfaction to the victim of a serious violation if the piece of evidence in question is of little significance to the outcome of the case and its exclusion does not preclude conviction.[33] In sum, exclusion of evidence affects only a very small, fortuitously composed portion of victims of human rights violations, and even for that group, its compensatory effect is dubious.

On the other hand, acquittal of a serious offender may be over-compensation for a minor violation of his procedural rights. For example, if an officer conducts a car search based on a good faith belief that she has sufficient cause to do so, but a court later disagrees and excludes a murder weapon seized in the search, so that the defendant is acquitted for lack of evidence, acquittal may be seen as an out-of-proportion reaction to the invasion of the defendant's privacy. And even if exclusion is not disproportionate—should the "criminal" go free because the constable has blundered? The fact that a police officer violated a defendant's rights does not in any way reduce the defendant's blameworthiness for the act he committed; and although he should be compensated for the violation of his rights, the exclusion of relevant evidence lacks an inherent nexus with the injury the defendant suffered.

[32] American Convention on Human Rights, art. 8(3) ("A confession of guilt by the accused shall be valid only if it is made without coercion of any kind.").

[33] For example, an intrusive bodily search of a suspect conducted by police without probable cause and without a warrant may produce evidence of drug-dealing (i.e., the drugs themselves) that is relevant but not crucial to the case against the suspect; its exclusion would hardly compensate the victim of the illegal search for the harm done to him.

The compensation rationale for the exclusion of evidence is, in sum, less than convincing. It might be useful, on the basis of the above considerations, to limit exclusion to instances in which the production of evidence in court would itself violate a person's human rights. This would be the case, for example, if the transcript of an illegally taped telephone conversation between the defendant and his wife would be read in open court, because disclosing this conversation to the public would be a new violation of the couple's right to marital intimacy. By contrast, the introduction of drugs discovered in the defendant's car through an illegal warrantless search would not, by itself, violate the defendant's human rights.

3 Ideal Types of Exclusionary Systems

In this section, we briefly sketch possible consequences of a system's decision to opt for one of the key exclusionary rule rationales discussed above: systemic integrity, deterrence, or protecting human rights. We do this by constructing ideal types of exclusionary regimes, that is, by postulating consequences from their underlying purposes without taking into account the individual factual and normative conditions and limitations of any specific legal system. In defining the ideal types, we cannot deal with all details and possible ramifications of exclusionary regimes; we will therefore focus on several key doctrinal questions that have the potential of differentiating between systems and also have significant practical effect. In this regard, we will highlight five aspects of the application of exclusionary rules: (a) whether there is a strict exclusionary rule or whether it is subject to balancing; (b) whether the decision to exclude depends on the specific right that has been violated; (c) whether the officer's good faith precludes exclusion; (d) whether evidence indirectly derived from the original violation is excluded; and (e) whether exclusion can be invoked by persons whose rights were not directly violated.

3.1 Ideal Type "System Integrity"

3.1.1 Balancing Interests

If the purpose behind excluding illegally obtained evidence is to preserve or restore the integrity of the judicial system, declaring inadmissible any evidence acquired in violation of a procedural rule might be counterproductive because exclusion itself can jeopardize the (perceived) integrity of the judicial process by leading to verdicts based on fiction rather than truth. Balancing between the interest in basing the judgment on the totality of available relevant evidence and disregarding items of evidence whose use would "shock the conscience" seems to be the optimal approach under this rationale.

3.1.2 Type of Right Violated

If the integrity of the criminal justice system is the purpose of exclusion, the type of right violated (e.g., privacy, bodily integrity, secrecy of telecommunications) should not play a decisive role, because all individual rights protected by applicable international or domestic law are part of the system and require equal respect. For the purpose of balancing, it is therefore irrelevant which individual right has been compromised[34]; it is only the intensity and scope of the violation that needs to be considered in the weighing process. Although the right to freedom and the right to bodily integrity both deserve protection under the "integrity" approach, a statement made by the defendant at the police station is more likely to be excluded if he was tortured than if police detained him for an hour longer than was permissible under the applicable law.

If, however, the finding of the "truth" is regarded as an important systemic interest, it matters whether the violation is likely to affect the reliability of the evidence in question. Accordingly, evidence derived from torture or coercion should be excluded, whereas violations of other important rights, such as the right to the privacy of telecommunication, should not necessarily lead to suppression.

Even if the type of right violated should not matter in a system promoting integrity, it can be argued that the sanction need not always be exclusion, but could instead vary based on the seriousness of the violation.

3.1.3 Good Faith Exception

The systemic integrity approach weighs the social costs of exclusion and demands exclusion only where the gravity of the violation outweighs the costs. If a law enforcement officer committed a procedural fault in good faith, for example, because he relied on a statute or a judicial decision later found to be unconstitutional, or on an innocent misconception of the relevant facts, the evidence obtained may be the result of a malfunctioning of the legal system as a whole, but the individual officer in question cannot be blamed with having violated the law. There is thus a lesser taint on the evidence in question, which should weigh in favor of admission especially if the evidence is needed in order to arrive at a factually correct judgment. The legal system might be expected to favor exclusion, however, if the misconduct is due to negligence. For example, where one officer relies on the actions of another officer, court administrator, or judge, a "system integrity" approach might base exclusion of evidence on the fact that at least one government agent acted against the law. If the officer knew that he violated the law or was reckless as to the legality of his acts, this fact shows a grave defect in the operation

[34]One might consider affording human dignity a special status; but given the vague contours of human dignity, a rule of absolute exclusion whenever human dignity had been infringed may lead to inappropriate results.

of the criminal justice system and should be a strong argument for exclusion.[35] For less serious breaches, courts following the systemic integrity approach might impose less drastic remedies, such as declaratory relief or sentence discounts after conviction.[36] For example, Dutch law provides several different remedies for violations of individual rights by government officials, ranging from a mere declaration of illegality to a sentence reduction and exclusion of the evidence.[37]

3.1.4 Exclusion of Derivative Evidence

The exclusion of evidence derived from results of an illegal investigatory act ("fruit of the poisoned tree") is ambivalent under the "integrity" rationale. On the one hand, one can argue that the evidence in question (e.g., drugs discovered as a result of an interrogation conducted without proper warnings) is not tainted by the illicit path that led to its discovery; therefore, admission of the item—which is of undiminished probative value—does not conflict with the ethical integrity of the system. Under an approach focusing on reliability, admitting evidence that was indirectly derived from the original violation also makes sense. Such derivative evidence is generally unlikely to be rendered less reliable on account of a preceding violation.[38]

On the other hand, it cannot be denied that the origin of the chain that leads to the acquisition of a piece of evidence can be so abhorrent that a system geared toward integrity should refrain from using it—for example, if the suspect had disclosed the place where drugs were hidden only after having been brutally tortured. A legal system that places great emphasis on the rule of law would therefore be inclined to exclude derivative evidence at least in cases of serious violations. A sensible solution to this dilemma may be to resort to balancing the interests involved: there should not be an absolute rule of admission or of exclusion, but the "taint" on the individual item of evidence stemming from the origin of its discovery should be weighed against its relevance for a just outcome of the process.

---

[35]*See, e.g.*, Evidence Act 1995 (Cth) s 138(3) (Austl.); Evidence Act 2006, § 30(3) (N.Z.); *R* v. *Grant* [2009] 2 SCR. 353, §§ 73–75 (Can.); *R* v. *Canale* [1990] 91 Cr. App. R. 1 (Eng.); Israel Supreme Court, *Yissacharov v. Chief Military Prosecutor*, Judgment of 4 May 2006, CrimA 5121/98, § 62 (Justice Beinisch).

[36]*See, e.g.*, *R* v. *Nasogaluak* [2007] 229 CCC (3d) 52 (Alta. C.A.); Butler/Butler, 2005 at 1037 § 29.6.5.

[37]Borgers/StevensLonneke in Thaman, 2013 at 183, 190.

[38]An exception to this presumption would be a second confession following an initial coerced confession. Studies of wrongful convictions have shown that, once a person has given a false confession under pressure from the police, the coercive influence of the first confession might lead to a second false confession, even when police are no longer applying deceptive or coercive tactics.

3.1.5 Standing of Persons Other Than the Victim of the Violation

If exclusion of evidence is designed to maintain the integrity of the judicial system, anybody should be entitled to raise the issue of exclusion. This means that a defendant should be able to demand exclusion even if only the rights of another person had allegedly been violated when the evidence was obtained. For example, a defendant would be able to claim that the search of a witness's home was illegal and that therefore contraband found in the home should not be introduced as evidence at the defendant's trial. Moreover, it would be consistent with this approach that the court could (and indeed, should) exclude illegally obtained evidence on its own motion, even if none of the parties requests exclusion.

3.1.6 Summary

A system justifying exclusion of evidence by the interest of maintaining the integrity of the judicial process would have these features: The interest in excluding illegally obtained evidence is weighed against the interest in having a complete array of relevant evidence available for the judgment.[39] There is hence no absolute rule of exclusion; the degree of the violation and the importance of the individual rights affected are parts of the balancing process, and so is the question of whether the item in question has been directly or indirectly obtained through an illegal method. Questions of standing do not play a role in the decision on exclusion: any participant in the trial (and indeed, the court) can trigger an examination of possible exclusion by claiming that a piece of evidence was obtained illegally.

3.2 *Ideal Type "Deterrence"*

3.2.1 Balancing Interests

If deterrence is the principal goal of exclusion, a categorical approach toward exclusion seems warranted. Deterrence will work only if law enforcement personnel are *certain* that their investigative efforts will be in vain if they resort to forbidden methods.

On the other hand, a judicial system may balance the interest in deterrence against other procedural interests, such as that of establishing the truth and of enforcing the criminal law, thereby carving out different categories of illegal conduct. If deterrence outweighs competing considerations (for example, in instances

[39]If the focus is on promoting the rule of law in systems that have recently moved to liberal democracy, perhaps there is a greater need for categorical rules because of concerns that a "balanced" exclusionary rule would be toothless.

of systemic or deliberate misconduct), evidence will invariably be excluded. If, on the other hand, deterrence benefits are marginal while social costs are significant (for example, where the officer has relied in good faith on an illegal warrant issued by a magistrate), evidence will be admitted.

3.2.2 Type of Right Violated

Under a deterrence approach, the type of right violated should not affect the decision whether to exclude evidence. The focus in this model is on encouraging police officers to abide by the law, not on the effect that the misconduct has on the individual. On the other hand, one could argue that if an officer is violating only a minor administrative regulation, deterrence is of lesser importance and exclusion of evidence would be an over-reaction. Other than in such extreme cases, however, courts focused on deterrence ought not to differentiate as to the type of the right that had been violated.

3.2.3 Good Faith Exception

How the deterrence model should view "good faith" violations of the law is a matter of continued debate. The dominant view is that if an officer has acted in "good faith," there is no room for deterrence. For example, if the officer relied on a statute or a judicial decision later found to be unconstitutional or on an innocent misconception of the relevant facts, he cannot be blamed for having violated the law, and there is no conduct from which he needs to be deterred. The need to "punish" a police officer for misconduct is therefore absent or at least strongly reduced if he acted without fault or was only slightly negligent in the course of investigating the crime.[40] If, on the other hand, the officer violated the law deliberately or recklessly, this is the type of misconduct that merits exclusion of the evidence, because the officer is to learn to abide by the legal norm in the future.[41]

Some scholars have contested this narrow view of deterrence as being too focused on individual officers rather than on police departments as a whole.[42] Commentators have further argued that negligent mistakes can and should be deterred and that exclusion therefore should not be limited to reckless or deliberate

---

[40] *United States* v. *Leon*, 468 US 897 (1984); *Illinois* v. *Krull*, 480 US 340, 347 (1987); *Arizona* v. *Evans*, 514 US 1, 11 (1995); *Herring* v. *United States*, 555 US 135, 141 (2009).

[41] *See, e.g.*, Evidence Act 1995 (Cth) s 138(3) (Austl.); Evidence Act 2006, § 30(3) (N.Z.); *R* v. *Grant* [2009] 2 SCR 353, §§ 73–75 (Can.); *R* v. *Canale* (1990) 91 Cr. App. R. 1 (Eng.); Israel Supreme Court, *Yissacharov v. Chief Military Prosecutor*, Judgment of 4 May 2006, CrimA 5121/98, § 62 (Justice Beinisch).

[42] Levine et al., 2016.

misconduct.[43] Under this view, the threat of exclusion would provide an incentive for police departments to conduct better training to minimize even negligent errors.

3.2.4 Exclusion of Derivative Evidence

Exclusion of derivative evidence should be favored under the deterrence paradigm, because police officers might be encouraged to employ forbidden methods if they know that derivative evidence can later be used in order to convict the suspect. If, however, the link between the violation and the evidence at issue is strongly attenuated, exclusion may not be warranted for deterring similar violations. For example, if the police arrest someone unlawfully, the person is subsequently released, and then returns to the police station to make a voluntary confession, this statement may be too distant from the unlawful arrest to warrant exclusion[44]: An officer in a similar situation would not expect that a person would voluntarily return to make a confession, and therefore is not likely to be deterred from misconduct by exclusion of the confession.

3.2.5 Standing of Persons Other Than the Victim of the Violation

If exclusion of evidence is designed to deter misconduct, anybody should be entitled to raise the issue of exclusion, just as under the judicial integrity approach.

3.2.6 Summary

A deterrence-based approach to the exclusion of evidence would have a relatively strict and categorical approach to exclusion in order to provide clear guidance to officers and minimize the likelihood of misconduct. The type of right violated and the question whether the item in question was directly or indirectly obtained through an illegal method would generally not be central to the question of exclusion, while the offending officer's culpability and the systemic nature of the misconduct would be. To maximize deterrence of misconduct, any participant in the trial should have standing to demand exclusion, even if his or her rights were not directly violated by the action that led to the acquisition of the evidence.

---

[43]*See, e.g.*, Lafave, 2009 at 768–70.

[44]*Wong Sun* v. *United States*, 371 US 471 (1963).

3.3 Ideal Type "Vindication of Individual Rights"

3.3.1 Balancing Interests

In a human rights centered ideal type, exclusion of evidence is a logical and unavoidable consequence of the violation of a procedural rule protecting the individual. There is no balancing against procedural interests; to the extent such interests are taken into consideration, they remain external to the rationale of exclusion. The only "internal" limit to exclusion would be its waiver by the affected individual: If the defendant does not object to the introduction of the tainted evidence, there is no reason for excluding it.

3.3.2 Type of Right Violated

Under this rationale, exclusion should ensue only if an individual right has been affected; a violation of general interests of the procedural system (e.g., the illegal exclusion of the public from the trial, or the unlawful disclosure of state secrets) cannot lead to the exclusion of relevant evidence. One could consider gradating human rights and attaching exclusion only to the violation of those rights deemed particularly important. But the admission of evidence obtained in violation of any human right protected by international law or domestic constitutional law would be difficult to reconcile with this rationale.

3.3.3 Good Faith Exception

From a human rights perspective, it makes little difference whether the officer conducting an unlawful search or interfering with a person's core privacy acted in good faith. What counts is the unlawful intrusion by a state agent into the protected sphere of an individual. A "good faith" exception would thus not be compatible with a human rights rationale.

3.3.4 Exclusion of Derivative Evidence

If exclusion of evidence is to reinstate the victim of a human rights violation to his or her prior status and to deprive the state of the fruits of the violation of human rights, exclusion should extend to the "fruits of the poisonous tree." Evidence derived from information obtained by a human rights violation thus should not be admitted if there exists a clear and direct causal connection between the violation and the acquisition of the evidence.

3.3.5 Standing of Persons Other Than the Victim of the Violation

Although rules on standing can be informed by various procedural considerations, the logic of the human rights rationale suggests limiting standing to the individual affected by the violation (or his survivors if he was killed).

3.3.6 Summary

In summary, the ideal type of an exclusion system based on a human rights rationale has these key features: Exclusion of evidence is an invariable consequence of any violation of an individual human right. Exclusion extends to violations that occurred unintentionally and also to evidence indirectly derived from the original violation. Only the individual affected has standing to demand exclusion; he or she may also waive exclusion, which is binding on the court.

4 Choice of Rationale and Its Consequences

Do real world systems reflect the ideal types described above? Can we detect any doctrinal patterns based on the rationale adopted? Legal systems do not tend to subscribe unconditionally to the ideal types as described here. In fact, many jurisdictions ground their exclusionary rules on more than one rationale. The mix of rationales—which the law often fails to spell out clearly—makes it difficult to predict the actual scope of exclusionary rules in any given legal system. Even where one rationale is dominant, courts and scholars often seek to accommodate subsidiary rationales as well. They may do so expressly by adopting a balancing test, or indirectly by carving out exceptions to categorical rules. In this section, we examine to what extent selected legal systems rely on one of the doctrinal bases identified above, and how that choice is reflected in the actual features of exclusion of illegally obtained evidence. For that purpose, we group legal systems along the three ideal types identified above, i.e., "system integrity," "deterrence," and "human rights," and then examine whether their choice of rationale bears on their position concerning the distinctive issues treated above (Sect. 3).

4.1 Legal Systems Based on the "System Integrity" Rationale

Canada and Israel are examples of legal systems that ground their exclusionary rule on a systemic integrity analysis.[45] Consistent with expectations, both systems apply a multi-factor, balancing test in deciding whether to exclude unlawfully obtained evidence. Empirical studies of rates of exclusion, however, suggest that the Canadian balancing test is more robust and more likely to produce exclusion than the Israeli approach.

Differentiation among various rights occurs in both Canada and Israel. Although the Canadian Supreme Court has abandoned a previous distinction between "conscripted" and "non-conscripted" evidence (under which courts were more likely to suppress evidence where the accused had been "compelled to participate in the creation or discovery of the evidence"),[46] courts still take the nature of the right violated into account when assessing the impact of police misconduct on the interests of the accused.[47] As the Canadian Supreme Court elaborated in *Grant*, "[t]he more serious the impact on the accused's interests, the greater the risk that admission of the evidence may signal to the public that *Charter* rights, however high-sounding, are of little actual avail to the citizen, breeding public cynicism and bringing the administration of justice into disrepute."[48] To determine the seriousness of the breach, Canadian courts look to the right violated: Thus "[a]n unreasonable search that intrudes on an area in which the individual reasonably enjoys a high expectation of privacy, or that demeans his or her dignity, is more serious than one that does not."[49] In Israel, courts likewise consider the type of right violated in deciding whether the breach is sufficiently serious to outweigh truth-seeking concerns. As the Israeli Supreme Court explained in a seminal case on the exclusionary rule, "[l]ogic dictates that a technical, negligible or inconsequential violation of the rules of proper investigation is not the same as a serious breach of these rules involving a significant violation of one of the main basic rights of the person under investigation."[50]

Both Canadian and Israeli courts, as expected, take the ***good faith*** of the individual police officer into consideration when deciding on the exclusion of evidence. As the Israeli Supreme Court noted, "When the investigation authorities have intentionally violated the provisions of law that bind them or they have knowingly

---

[45] *R* v. *Grant* [2009] SCC 32; Israel Supreme Court, *Yissacharov v. Chief Military Prosecutor*, Judgment of 4 May 2006, CrimA 5121/98, §§ 47, 68 (Justice Beinisch).

[46] Stuart, 2010 at 324.

[47] *R* v. *Grant* [2009] SCC 32, § 76; *R* v. *Harris* [2007] ONCA 574, § 63; *R. v. Bacchus* [2012] ONSC 5082, §§ 90–93.

[48] *R* v. *Grant* [2009] SCC 32, § 76.

[49] *Id.* § 78.

[50] Israel Supreme Court, *Yissacharov v. Chief Military Prosecutor*, Judgment of 4 May 2006, CrimA 5121/98, § 70 (Justice Beinisch).

violated a protected right of the person under investigation, this is capable of increasing the seriousness of the violation of the rules of proper investigation and the possible violation of due process if the evidence is admitted in the trial. Conduct that involves an intentional violation on the part of the investigation authorities may, therefore, be a circumstance of considerable weight for declaring the evidence inadmissible even when the defect is not serious."[51] In deciding how serious a breach is and what its effects are on systemic integrity, Canadian courts likewise consider it relevant to determine whether officers acted deliberately or recklessly, or conversely, in good faith.[52]

It is worth noting, however, that while culpability of the officers is relevant, good faith does not automatically make the resulting evidence admissible in either Canada or Israel.[53] As the Israeli Supreme Court explained, "for example, in circumstances where the defect that occurred in the manner of obtaining the evidence was serious and involved a substantial violation of the protected rights of the person under investigation, then the mere fact that the authority acted in good faith will not prevent the evidence being excluded."[54]

Canadian courts recognize the "fruit of the poisonous tree" doctrine, but limit it in situations where the evidence would have been obtained even if the violation had not occurred.[55] In Israel, by contrast, the courts have entirely rejected the doctrine.[56]

With regard to the issue of ***standing***, the Canadian Supreme Court has held that an accused may invoke the exclusionary rule only if the police misconduct affected his personal right.[57] Commentators have argued that this limitation of exclusion is more consistent with a compensatory, individual rights based approach, rather than the systemic integrity approach espoused by Canadian courts.[58]

---

[51]*Id.* § 70.

[52]*R* v. *Grant* [2009] 2 SCR 353, §§ 75, 214 (Can.); Stuart, 2010 at 314, 318; Porter/Kettles, 2012.

[53]*R* v. *Grant* [2009] 2 SCR 353, § 75 (Can.) ("[I]gnorance of [constitutional] standards must not be rewarded or encouraged and negligence or wilful blindness cannot be equated with good faith."); *R* v. *Wilson* [2003] CarswellOnt 9051 (citing unnamed case in which trial judge excluded evidence where officer relied on an invalid warrant in good faith); *R* v. *R (J.F.R.)* [1991] YJ No. 235 (Can. Yukon Terr. Ct.) (excluding evidence in a case of negligent police violation of the law).

[54]Israel Supreme Court, *Yissacharov v. Chief Military Prosecutor*, Judgment of 4 May 2006, CrimA 5121/98, § 70 (Justice Beinisch).

[55]*R* v. *Grant* [2009] 2 SCR 235 (Can.). Interestingly, the Canadian Court argued that the admission of evidence that would have been inevitably discovered has a lesser impact on the rights of the accused—a position criticized by some Canadian scholars; *see* Stuart, 2010 at 330.

[56]See, e.g., Israel Supreme Court, *Yissacharov v. Chief Military Prosecutor*, Judgment of 4 May 2006, CrimA 5121/98, § 71 (Justice Beinisch) (leaving exclusion of derivative evidence to case-by-case determination).

[57]*R* v. *Edwards* [1996] 1 SCR 128; *see also R* v. *Pasian* [2015] ONSC 1557.

[58]*See, e.g.*, Paciocco, 2011 at 32 ("If the repute of the administration of justice is indeed harmed by the admission of evidence it must be so whether or not the person whose rights have been violated complains. And if an objective is to vindicate Charter rights generally and not in the individual case it makes no sense for the framers of s. 24(2) to have linked the operation of the remedy to an application by the party whose rights have been violated.").

This short overview of two systems that both rely on an integrity approach to exclusion shows some similarities but also suggests that the same approach can yield different doctrinal paths. On some of the doctrinal touchstones, the two systems are in harmony and in line with our expectations, but in other regards both of them depart from the model of system integrity outlined above.

4.2 Legal Systems Based on the "Deterrence" Rationale

In the **United States**, the exclusionary rule is based on a deterrence-oriented analysis. Consistent with the expectation of the model, the U.S. approach is relatively ***rule-bound and categorical***, at least when compared with the more flexible balancing used in other jurisdictions.[59] If the police violate the Constitution, the exclusionary rule is presumed to apply, unless the prosecution can rely on a specific exception.

On the other hand, the U.S. Supreme Court has in recent years applied a cost-benefit analysis, weighing the deterrence benefits of exclusion against its social costs. This approach has led to the recognition of an increasing number of exceptions to the exclusionary rule[60] and is moving the U.S. away from a purely deterrence-oriented model toward the system integrity approach discussed in the previous section.

Concerning the possible ***differentiation among various rights***, the U.S. Supreme Court has not expressly acknowledged a differential treatment based on the right violated, yet its jurisprudence shows that mandatory exclusion is more likely to apply to coerced confessions, unlawful searches of a home, and particularly invasive body searches. By contrast, a cost-benefit analysis is more likely to result in admitting the tainted evidence when violations of seemingly less important rights—such as violations of the "prophylactic" *Miranda* regime—have occurred.[61] This gradation is not fully consistent with a purist deterrence model, which would generally not distinguish among rights violated.

The U.S. Supreme Court, following the narrow version of the deterrence approach, has taken the ***good faith*** of individual police officers into consideration when deciding on the exclusion of evidence. In *Herring v. United States*, the majority opinion explained:

> [P]olice conduct must be sufficiently deliberate that exclusion can meaningfully deter it, and sufficiently culpable that such deterrence is worth the price paid by the justice system. As laid out in our cases, the exclusionary rule serves to deter deliberate, reckless, or grossly negligent conduct, or in some circumstances recurring or systemic negligence.[62]

---

[59] *See* Levine et al., 2016.

[60] *See, e.g., Herring* v. *United States*, 555 US 135 (2009).

[61] Turner, 2019.

[62] *Herring* v. *United States*, 555 US 135, 144 (2009).

The Court has therefore rejected arguments that exclusion can be used more broadly to encourage police departments to adopt more rigorous training programs that help prevent even negligent mistakes by police officers.[63]

In line with its emphasis on deterring police misconduct, the U.S. Supreme Court has traditionally extended exclusion to "evidence obtained from or as a consequence of lawless official acts."[64] Yet the Court has gradually narrowed the ***fruit of the poisonous tree doctrine***, recognizing the competing interests at stake. For example, it has approved the admission of derivative evidence if the connection between the original violation and the evidence in question has been attenuated (e.g., if an event has broken the chain of causation between the original illegality and the derivative evidence).[65] The Court also declared derivative evidence admissible if the police would inevitably have discovered it in the course of its investigation. The Court justified these limitations on the exclusionary rule by pointing to the high costs of excluding probative evidence and the limited deterrent effect of excluding evidence that either has been or would have been discovered independently by lawful means.[66]

With regard to the issue of ***standing***, the United States Supreme Court has limited the right to invoke the exclusionary rule to individuals directly harmed by the misconduct.[67] This limitation cannot be easily squared with the Court's emphasis on deterrence. Yet the Court has refrained from extending standing to third parties, even in cases where it was clear that police intentionally conducted an unconstitutional search of a person who would not have standing in a criminal case to move for suppression of the evidence.[68]

The Supreme Court justified its narrow approach to standing by citing the significant costs of excluding evidence:

> Each time the exclusionary rule is applied it exacts a substantial social cost for the vindication of Fourth Amendment rights. Relevant and reliable evidence is kept from the trier of fact and the search for truth at trial is deflected [...]. Since our cases generally have held that one whose Fourth Amendment rights are violated may successfully suppress evidence obtained in the course of an illegal search and seizure, misgivings as to the benefit of enlarging the class of persons who may invoke that rule are properly considered when deciding whether to expand standing to assert Fourth Amendment violations.[69]

---

[63] *Id.* at 173–174 (Ginsburg, J., dissenting).

[64] *See Costello* v. *United States*, 365 US 265, 280 (1961).

[65] *Brown* v. *Illinois*, 422 US 590, 603–604 (1975); *Murray* v. *United States*, 487 US 533, 537 (1988).

[66] "If the prosecution can establish by a preponderance of the evidence that the information ultimately or inevitably would have been discovered by lawful means—here the volunteers' search—then the deterrence rationale has so little basis that the evidence should be received. The requirement that the prosecution must prove the absence of bad faith … wholly fails to take into account the enormous societal cost of excluding truth in the search for truth in the administration of justice." *Nix* v. *Williams*, 467 US 431, 444–445 (1984).

[67] *Rakas* v. *Illinois*, 439 US 128, 137–138 (1978); *Fisher* v. *United States*, 425 US 391, 397–398 (1976).

[68] *United States* v. *Payner*, 447 US 727 (1980).

[69] *Rakas* v. *Illinois*, 439 US 128, 137–138 (1978).

In this context, the Court seems to be mixing rationales, weighing the goal of truth-seeking, on the one hand, against the goal of deterring misconduct. We thus see that, like Canada and Israel, the United States is another example of a system that in practice departs in several respects from the exclusionary model it purports to follow.

4.3 Legal Systems Based on the Human Rights Rationale

Greece is an example of a legal system regarding exclusion of evidence as a means of vindicating fundamental individual rights.[70] Article 177 § 2 of the Greek Code of Criminal Procedure provides that evidence obtained through a criminal act must not be used in court, except in favor of the accused. More specifically, Article 19 § 3 of the Greek Constitution in its 2001 version strictly prohibits the use of evidence obtained through a violation of the secrecy of letters and telecommunication (Art. 19 § 1 Const.), a person's home or private life (Art. 9 § 1 Const.), or the protection of personal data (Art. 9A § 1 Const.). The courts have extended the application of this article to other serious violations of constitutional provisions, such as the use of torture in violation of Art. 7 § 2 of the Constitution.[71] The prohibition of "using" such illegally obtained evidence applies to: (1) all stages of criminal proceedings; (2) direct and derivative evidence; (3) evidence obtained by private actors and evidence obtained by state officials; and (4) cases in which a third party's rights, not the defendant's, were violated. The remarkable breadth of exclusion in Greece has been linked in part to the "bitter, and not-too-distant, experience of rule by military junta" and in part to the emphasis on fundamental rights.[72]

Although the Greek system comes close to the ideal type of a human rights based system, it does not fit the model in all respects. For example, courts have fashioned broad standing rules that allow third parties to invoke the exclusionary rule.[73] Under a strict individual-rights perspective, this is surprising (see Sects. 3.1.5, 3.2.5 and 3.3.5). But perhaps the broad Greek rule can be explained by the fact that Greece aims at making sure that no evidence based on human rights violations will be accepted by the courts, even when this may overcompensate individual litigants in some cases.

Furthermore, Greek courts have occasionally strayed from the broad rights-based approach to exclusion. With respect to unlawful wiretaps, for example, the Greek Supreme Court has held that they "may be used as evidence when they are the only means for proving innocence, or even guilt, in the case of a very serious crime."[74]

---

[70] Giannoulopoulos, 2007 at 192, 207–208; *see also* Kaissis, 2015 at 461–462.

[71] Spyropoulos/Fortsakis, 2009 at 229.

[72] Giannoulopoulos, 2007 at 208.

[73] *Id.* at 207.

[74] Triantafyllou, 2013 at 275.

In departing from the otherwise strict constitutional exclusionary rule, the court stressed the need for a balance between conflicting interests in the criminal process.[75]

Another example of a rights-based approach to exclusion is that of Ireland—at least, it was until 2015. Irish courts until recently justified exclusion based on the courts' duty: "to protect persons against the invasion of their constitutional rights; (ii) if invasion has occurred, to restore as far as possible the person so damaged to the position in which he would be if his rights had not been invaded."[76] Consistent with an approach based on vindicating individual rights, Irish courts used "one of the strictest exclusionary rules" in the world: "Where evidence is obtained in breach of the constitutional rights of a suspect it is subject to automatic exclusion at trial, unless there are in existence extraordinary excusing circumstances justifying its admission."[77] The exclusionary rule applied to inadvertent as well as deliberate violations of the law, and it extended to evidence derived from the original breach.[78] The Irish Supreme Court had rejected a good faith exception to the exclusionary rule on the ground of the "unambiguously expressed constitutional obligation as 'far as practicable to defend and vindicate the personal rights of the citizen.'"[79]

Yet after criticism of the broad Irish exclusionary rule by a number of judges and policymakers, the Irish Supreme Court in 2015 drastically reduced its scope, holding that an inadvertent breach of the law in the gathering of evidence would not lead to exclusion.[80] The new rule departs from the rights-based rationale of exclusion and appears to introduce a balancing approach more concerned with judicial integrity.[81]

The Greek and Irish systems of exclusion suggest that even seemingly absolute, rights-oriented approaches to exclusion at times give way to exceptions or balancing tests.[82] As the next section elaborates, the mixing of rationales is perhaps the most common approach to exclusion in practice.

---

[75] *Id.*

[76] *Trimbole* v. *Governor of Mountjoy Prison* [1985] IR 550, 573.

[77] Daly, 2011 at 199; *Director of Public Prosecutions* v. *JC* [2015] IESC 31, § 95 (noting that the previous rule called for "near absolute exclusion" and was "the most extreme" in the common law world).

[78] *Director of Public Prosecutions* v. *JC* [2015] IESC 31, § 95.

[79] *Director of Public Prosecutions* v. *Kenny* [1990] 2 IR 110, 134 (Ir.); Thaman, 2010 at 352.

[80] *Director of Public Prosecutions* v. *JC* [2015] IESC 31.

[81] *Id.* at § 97 ("When does the admission of that evidence itself bring the administration of justice in to disrepute? This analysis leads inevitably to a more nuanced position which would admit evidence by reason of a technical and excusable breach, but would exclude it where it was obtained as a result of a deliberate breach of the Constitution."); Leon/Ward, 2015 at 593.

[82] Slobogin, 2016 at 291 (reviewing countries that follow the rights vindication model and finding that they undermine the rule-as-vindication rationale in various ways).

4.4 Mixed Systems

Several legal systems have refrained from defining a single rationale for their exclusionary rules. Three of the countries discussed in this volume—Switzerland, Germany, and Taiwan—are examples of such hybrid systems.

The German and Swiss models have been grounded on the need to vindicate individual rights as well as to protect the rule of law. In Taiwan, the judiciary introduced an exclusionary rule in 1998, which was subsequently codified by the legislature as part of a broader effort to break with the legacy of a decade-long authoritarian regime. The rule "came about at a time that the new government was distancing itself from the previous government's perceived abuse of power …. [T] he post-martial-law government made a definitive statement that 'we are not them.'"[83]

The rationale for the Taiwanese exclusionary rules is to protect individual rights and safeguard the rule of law and judicial integrity.[84] While some specific exclusionary rules—for example, concerning confessions obtained through torture—are categorical and result in mandatory exclusion, others are flexible and applied on the basis of a balancing approach. The balancing takes into account a host of factors, but ultimately aims to weigh the protection of individual rights against the public interest in the enforcement of criminal law.[85]

The German and Swiss approaches to exclusion similarly follow a dual approach, with some rules, such as those pertaining to coerced confessions, resulting in mandatory exclusion, while others balance the public interest and individual rights.[86]

These systems share a tendency toward categorically excluding evidence if certain very important rights have been violated.[87] For example, statements obtained through torture are mandatorily excluded in most systems studied, and so are results of violations of a core sphere of privacy. On the other hand, physical evidence obtained through unlawful searches or seizures is less likely to be excluded; and the same is true with respect to violations of "administrative" or "technical" rules.[88]

Many "mixed" systems take the ***culpability of the officer*** into account when deciding on admissibility of evidence. In Taiwan, for example, one factor in the balancing analysis is "the subjective intentions of the official, i.e., whether the

---

[83]Lewis, 2011 at 648; *see also* Chen, 2011 at 719–720 (noting that the Taiwanese judiciary adopted the exclusionary rule in an effort to assert its independence and to gain legitimacy by protecting human rights).

[84]Lin et al., 2019 at 1.

[85]Lin et al., 2019.

[86]Macula, 2019.

[87]*See* Thaman, 2013 at 416–417 (discussing exclusionary rules in Spain, Colombia, Brazil, Portugal, Greece, and Germany); Macula, 2019; Lin et al., 2019.

[88]*See, e.g.*, Macula, 2019.

official knows his conduct is unlawful."[89] German courts are also more likely to exclude evidence where officers have purposefully or recklessly violated the law.[90] A similar inquiry into the officer's motivation and state of mind occurs with respect to indirect evidence in Spain.[91] It is possible that the consideration of the officer's state of mind in these systems is a nod to a subsidiary, competing rationale—to deter police misconduct or to safeguard the integrity of the criminal justice system.

We find a mixed pattern of solutions with regard to the "***fruits of the poisonous tree***" doctrine. In Taiwan, courts extend the exclusionary rule to derivative evidence[92] although "evidence acquired by an independent legitimate investigation shall not bc supressed."[93] Spanish,[94] German,[95] and Swiss[96] courts recognize the doctrine in a limited fashion. Spanish courts use a balancing test to determine whether to exclude evidence indirectly derived from a breach, and the officer's state of mind in committing the breach is an important factor.[97] In Switzerland and Germany, the fruit of the poisonous tree doctrine is used for some violations, but the courts recognize a "hypothetical clean path" exception, which is interpreted quite broadly.[98]

With regard to ***standing***, Germany pursues a strict approach, insisting that only the person whose rights were violated can invoke the exclusionary rule. For example, the Federal Court of Justice ruled that a defendant cannot demand the exclusion of the incriminating statement of a witness who had not been informed of his privilege against self-incrimination when interrogated by the police.[99]

---

[89]Lin et al., 2019 at 3.1.3.

[90]Bundesgerichtshof [BGH] [Federal Court of Justice] Judgment of 18 April 2007, 51 Entscheidungen des Bundesgerichtshofes in Strafsachen 285, 2007 (Ger.) (upholding exclusion where the police "intentionally circumvented the protective warrant requirement"); Bundesverfassungsgericht [Federal Constitutional Court], Judgment of 9 November 2011, [2011] Neue Juristische Wochenschrift 2417 (Ger.) (stating that evidence would be excluded "if there has been a grave, conscious, or arbitrary violation of procedural law which infringed upon the protection of an individual's fundamental rights in a planned or systematic fashion"). One of us has noted a trend toward exclusion in recent German decisions, "especially where important individual rights have been violated and the law enforcement officer acted without good faith."; Weigend, 2015 at 195.

[91]Bachmaier Winter, 2013 at 216–217.

[92]Lin et al., 2019 at 3.2.6.

[93]Lin et al., 2019 at 3.2.6.2 (quoting Supreme Court decision 102 taishangzih No. 4177 (最高法院102年度台上字第4177號判決)).

[94]Bachmaier Winter, 2013 at 232.

[95]Gless, 2013 at 128.

[96]Macula, 2019.

[97]Bachmaier Winter, 2013 at 232.

[98]Macula 2019; Weigend, 2019 (in this volume) German report at notes 98 et seq.

[99]BGH, Decision of 21 January 1958—GSSt 4/57 (11 Entscheidungen des Bundesgerichtshofes in Strafsachen 213, 215).

5 Conclusion: Aligning Doctrines with Rationales?

Looking at our findings from a comparative standpoint, the rationales that different systems rely upon do not fall into an expected pattern. No clear divide exists between adversarial and inquisitorial systems. A trend we do identify, however, is that for most systems, particularly those that have adopted exclusionary rules relatively recently, the dominant rationales for exclusionary rules are to protect individual rights and promote judicial integrity rather than to deter misconduct or promote the search for truth. This development can probably be attributed to the growing influence of international human rights law and to an emphasis on the rule of law in countries transitioning away from authoritarian regimes.

Not surprisingly, we have not encountered a legal system that exactly mirrors one of the ideal types construed in section 3. To begin with, virtually all the countries we examined pursue more than one goal when excluding evidence, even if one objective may be dominant; and the majority of systems rely on a mix of rationales to support their exclusionary rules.

But even where a legal system expresses a pronounced orientation toward a "human rights" or a "deterrence" rationale, such as Greece and the United States, respectively, the choice of rationale does not necessarily seem to determine the resolution of the key issues we have identified. Of course, quite a few of our findings comport with the ideal-typical models. The emphasis on protecting individual rights has led countries such as Greece, Ireland, and Russia to adopt—at least on paper—broad and categorical exclusionary rules; and "hybrid" systems such as Germany and Switzerland have embraced a broad balancing approach designed to make it possible to find compromise between conflicting interests in each case. Contrary to expectations, however, the United States—although oriented toward deterring police misconduct—limits standing to persons directly affected by the violation that led to the evidence, whereas Greece—although professing adherence to a "human rights" rationale—grants standing to individuals who were not personally affected by the human rights violation in question. On the other hand, adopting the same rationale does not necessarily lead to identical doctrines of exclusion, as can be seen from the examples of Israel and Canada. Instead, one and the same rationale can justify a variety of approaches to exclusion, from balancing to categorical exclusion and from relatively narrow to relatively broad rules.

These variations can easily be explained by the fact that even legal systems which emphasize a single basic rationale for exclusion reasonably take other considerations and interests into account when shaping rules on individual issues. Certain overriding considerations appear to influence exclusionary decision-making to a larger extent than adherence to basic rationales. For example, legal systems are most likely to use absolute exclusionary rules with respect to violations of certain fundamental rights, such as the right not to be subjected to torture. When rationales coincide, and especially when the truth-seeking rationale weighs on the side of exclusion, legal systems are most likely to exclude evidence.

Policy considerations can also be expected to have a great influence on the design of actual exclusionary rules. For example, legal systems that regard police misconduct as a serious problem—such as the United States in the 1960s and 1970s—can be expected to establish broad exclusionary rules but to limit them to bad-faith disregard of citizens' procedural rights; systems which have faith in police to obey the legal rules will see less need to shape their exclusionary rules in order to achieve deterrence.

In sum, we can say that a strict doctrinal adherence to particular rationales and purposes of exclusion of evidence plays a lesser role in the construction and application of exclusionary rules when compared to considerations of fairness, procedural expediency, and an interest in keeping a balance between the truth-orientation and the rights-orientation of the criminal process. The official purposes of excluding evidence are of course welcome arguments for supporting individual sub-rules and court decisions; but they are not determinative. Judges who shape and apply legal rules in difficult areas do not simply apply doctrines but take real life and basic notions of fairness into account. And that is probably how it should be.

References

Books

Butler, Andrew/Butler, Petra, *The New Zealand Bill of Rights Act: A Commentary*, Wellington NZ 2005. [Butler/Butler, 2005]

Jackson, John D./Summers, Sarah J., *The Internationalisation of Criminal Evidence: Beyond the Common Law and Civil Law Traditions*, Cambridge 2012. [Jackson/Summers, 2012]

Jäger, Christian, *Beweisverwertung und Beweisverwertungsverbote im Strafprozess*, Munich 2003. [Jäger, 2003]

Miller, Marc L./Wright, Ronald F., *Criminal Procedures: The Police*, New York 2007. [Miller/Wright, 2007]

Spyropoulos, Philippos/Fortsakis, Theodore P., *Constitutional Law in Greece*, Dordrecht 2009. [Spyropoulos/Fortsakis, 2009]

Journal Articles

Alschuler, Albert W., 'Studying the Exclusionary Rule: An Empirical Classic', (2008) 75 *University of Chicago Law Review*, 1365–1384. [Alschuler, 2008]

Ashworth, Andrew, 'Excluding Evidence as Protecting Rights', (1977) 3 *Criminal Law Review*, 723–735. [Ashworth, 1977]

Chen, Yu-Jie, 'One Problem, Two Paths: A Taiwanese Perspective on the Exclusionary Rule in China', (2011) 43 *NYU Journal of International Law and Politics* 713–728. [Chen, 2011]

Daly, Yvonne Marie, 'Judicial Oversight of Policing: Investigations, Evidence and the Exclusionary Rule', (2011) 55 *Crime, Law and Social Change*, 199–215. [Daly, 2011]

Giannoulopoulos, Dimitrios, 'The Exclusion of Improperly Obtained Evidence in Greece: Putting Constitutional Rights First', (2007) 11 *International Journal of Evidence and Proof* 181–212. [Giannoulopoulos, 2007]

Gless, Safine, 'Germany: Balancing Truth Against Protected Institutional Interests', (2013) 20 *IUS Gentium*, 113–142. [Gless, 2013]

Grünwald, Armin, 'Beweisverbote und Verwertungsverbote im Strafverfahren', (1966) 21 *Juristenzeitung*, 489–501. [Grünwald, 1966]

Kaissis, Athanassios, 'Exclusion of Illegally Obtained Evidence in Greek Civil and Criminal Proceeding—An Outline', (2015) 2 *Digesta OnLine Law Review*, 453–463. [Kaissis, 2015]

Küpper, Georg, 'Tagebücher, Tonbänder, Telefonate', (1990) 45 *Juristenzeitung*, 416–424. [Küpper, 1990]

Lafave, Wayne R., 'The Smell of Herring: A Critique of the Supreme Court's Latest Assault on the Exclusionary Rule', (2009) 99 *Journal of Criminal Law and Criminology*, 757–788. [Lafave, 2009]

Leon, Clare/Ward, Tony, 'The Irish Exclusionary Rule After DPP v JC', (2015) 35 *Legal Studies*, 590–593. [Leon/Ward, 2015]

Levine, Kay, et al., 'Evidence Laundering in a Post-Herring World', (2016) 106 *Journal of Criminal Law and Criminology*, 627–680. [Levine et al., 2016]

Lewis, Margaret K., 'Controlling Abuse To Maintain Control: The Exclusionary Rule in China', (2011) 43 *NYU Journal of International Law and Politics*, 629–697. [Lewis, 2011]

Paciocco, David M., 'Section 24(2): Lottery or Law—The Appreciable Limits of Purposive Reasoning', (2011) 58 *Criminal Law Quarterly*, 15–66. [Paciocco, 2011]

Spendel, Günter, 'Beweisverbote im Strafprozess', (1966) 19 *Neue Juristische Wochenschrift*, 1102–1108. [Spendel, 1966]

Stuart, Don, 'Welcome Flexibility and Better Criteria from the Supreme Court of Canada for Exclusion of Evidence Obtained in Violation of the Canadian Charter of Rights and Freedoms', (2010) 16 *Southwestern Journal of International Law*, 313–332. [Stuart, 2010]

Thaman, Stephen C., 'Fruits of the Poisonous Tree" in Comparative Law', (2010) 16 *Southwestern Journal of International Law* 333–384. [Thaman, 2010]

Turner, Jenia, 'The Exclusionary Rule as a Symbol of the Rule of Law', (2014) 67 *SMU Law Review*, 821–833. [Turner, 2014]

Contributions to Edited Volumes and Annotated Law

Bachmaier Winter, Lorena, 'Spain: The Constitutional Court's Move from Categorical Exclusion to Limited Balancing', in: Thaman, Stephen C., ed., *Exclusionary Rules in Comparative Law*, New York 2013, 209–234. [Bachmaier Winter, 2013]

Borgers, Matthias J./Stevens, Lonneke, 'The Netherlands: Statutory Balancing and a Choice of Remedies', in: Stephen C. Thaman ed., *Exclusionary Rules in Comparative Law*, New York 2013, 183–207. [Borgers/Stevens in Thaman, 2013]

Lin, Yu-Hsiung et al., 'The Potential to Secure a Fair Tiral Through Evidence Exclusion: A Taiwanese Perspective', in: Gless, Sabine/Richter, Thomas (eds.), *Do Exclusionary Rules Ensure a Fair Trial? A Comparative Perspective on Evidentiary Rules*, Cham 2019, 131–161. [Lin et al., 2019]

Macula, Laura, 'The Potential to Secure a Fair Tiral Through Evidence Exclusion: A Swiss Perspective', in: Gless, Sabine/Richter, Thomas (eds.), *Do Exclusionary Rules Ensure a Fair Trial? A Comparative Perspective on Evidentiary Rules*, Cham 2019, 15–60. [Macula, 2019]

Porter, David/Kettles, Brent, 'The Significance of Police Misconduct in the Analysis of s. 8 Charter Breaches and the Exclusion of Evidence Under s. 24(2) in R. v. Grant, R. v. Harrison and R. v. Morelli', (2012) 58 *Criminal Law Quarterly* 510–530. [Porter/Kettles, 2012]

Slobogin, Christopher, 'A Comparative Perspective on the Exclusionary Rule in Search and Seizure Cases', in: Ross, Jacqueline/Thaman, Stephen (eds.), *Comparative Criminal Procedure*, Cheltenham UK 2016, 280–307. [Slobogin, 2016]

Thaman, Stephen C., 'Balancing Truth Against Human Rights: A Theory of Modern Exclusionary Rules', in: Thaman, Stephen C., ed., *Exclusionary Rules in Comparative Law*, New York 2013, 403–446. [Thaman, 2013]

Triantafyllou, Georgios, 'Greece: From Statutory Nullities to A Categorical Statutory Exclusionary Rule', in: Thaman, Stephen C., ed., *Exclusionary Rules in Comparative Law*, New York 2013, 261–286. [Triantafyllou, 2013]

Turner, Jenia I., 'Regulating Interrogations and Excluding Confessions in the United States: Balancing Individual Rights and the Search for the Truth', in: Gless, Sabine/Richter, Thomas (eds.), *Do Exclusionary Rules Ensure a Fair Trial? A Comparative Perspective on Evidentiary Rules*, Cham 2019, 93–129. [Turner, 2019]

Turner, Jenia, 'Limits on the Search for Truth in Criminal Procedure: A Comparative View', in: Ross, Jacqueline/Thaman, Stephen (eds.), *Comparative Criminal Procedure*, Cheltenham UK 2016. [Turner, 2016]

Weigend, Thomas , 'The Potential to Secure a Fair Trial Through Evidence Exclusion: A German Perspective', in: Gless, Sabine/Richter, Thomas (eds.), *Do Exclusionary Rules Ensure a Fair Trial? A Comparative Perspective on Evidentiary Rules*, Cham 2019, 61–92. [Weigend, 2019]

Weigend, Thomas, 'Throw It All Out? Judicial Discretion in Dealing with Procedural Faults', in: Caianiello, Michele/Hodgson, Jacqueline S. (eds.), *Discretionary Criminal Justice in a Comparative Context*, Durham, NC 2015, 185–205. [Weigend, 2015]

Jenia Iontcheva Turner is the Amy Abboud Ware Centennial Professor in Criminal Law at SMU Dedman School of Law, where she teaches criminal procedure, comparative criminal procedure, international criminal law, and international law.

Thomas Weigend taught criminal law and criminal procedure at the University of Cologne (Germany). He also served as a visiting professor at Peking University and the University of Political Science and Law in Beijing. He retired from teaching in 2016. His research is primarily dedicated to comparative criminal procedure and international criminal law.

The Fair Trial Rationale for Excluding Wrongfully Obtained Evidence

Hock Lai Ho

Abstract Many rationales have been offered for the judicial power to exclude wrongfully obtained evidence. Each rationale shapes the scope of such power differently. This chapter selects for examination three legal systems in which the avowed rationale is to uphold the fairness of the trial. It explores the premises underlying, and the limitations of adopting, the fair trial rationale in these three jurisdictions. An examination of the case-law suggests that there is room for greater critical engagement on the meaning of a fair trial, clearer articulation of how fairness is undermined by allowing reliance on wrongfully obtained evidence, and deeper reflection on whether the fair trial rationale provides a sufficiently broad basis for exclusion.

1 Introduction

In most jurisdictions, the judge conducting a criminal trial has the power to exclude evidence obtained by unlawful or otherwise wrongful means. Legal systems have adopted different rationales for exclusion, resulting in variations in the scope of the exclusionary power.[1] This chapter engages in a study of three systems of law in which the avowed basis for exclusion is to uphold the fairness of the trial. Part II examines the jurisprudence of the European Court of Human Rights (ECtHR) on the right to a fair trial contained in article 6 of the European Convention on Human Rights ('the Convention'). Part III considers the common law and statutory rules

[1]*See* Ho, 2019; Turner/Weigend, 2019.

I am grateful to Sabine Gless and her team, Laura Macula, Thomas Richter and Peng Xinyun, for being wonderful hosts of the workshop at which I presented a version of this paper and to the participants for their valuable comments.

H. L. Ho (✉)
Faculty of Law, National University of Singapore (NUS), Singapore, Singapore
e-mail: lawhohl@nus.edu.sg

S. Gless and T. Richter (eds.), *Do Exclusionary Rules Ensure a Fair Trial?*
Ius Gentium: Comparative Perspectives on Law and Justice 74,
https://doi.org/10.1007/978-3-030-12520-2_9

relating to wrongfully obtained evidence in England. Part IV explores the admissibility and discretion to exclude such evidence under Singapore law.

These three case studies provide the contexts for probing the premises underlying, and the implications of adopting, the fair trial rationale for exclusion. This rationale raises a number of issues that deserve fuller attention by the courts. What is the point or purpose a trial? How should fairness be conceived? When would the admission of wrongfully obtained evidence undermine the fairness of the trial? The answers to these questions are contestable and bear on the scope of the exclusionary power. There is room for greater conceptual clarity in the law.

2 European Convention on Human Rights

2.1 Introduction

Member states of the Council of Europe are parties to the Convention. The Convention does not contain any provision that deals directly with the exclusion of wrongfully obtained evidence. However, article 6 of the Convention guarantees, as its title states, 'the right to a fair trial'. The ECtHR, which is an international court established to hear applications alleging violations of the Convention, has repeatedly held that article 6 'does not lay down any rules on the admissibility of evidence as such, which is therefore primarily a matter for regulation under national law.'[2] In determining whether there has been a violation of article 6, the ECtHR will consider 'whether the proceedings as a whole, including the way in which the evidence was obtained, were fair.'[3] The use or admission of unlawfully obtained evidence in a particular case may render the proceedings unfair as a whole.[4] It is in this indirect way—in the context of deciding whether, in the case at hand, there has been a breach of the right to a fair trial in article 6—that the issue of unlawfully obtained evidence has received attention by the ECtHR.[5]

---

[2]*Schenk* v. *Switzerland* (1991) 13 EHRR 242 at [46].

[3]*Jalloh* v. *Germany* (2007) 44 EHRR 32 at [95]. *See* also *X* v. *Belgium*, Application no. 8876/80, 16 Oct 1980: while art. 6(1) guarantee the right to a fair trial, it does not prescribe rules of evidence, in particular, rules of admissibility. For the purposes of art. 6(1), what has to be determined is 'whether evidence for and against the accused has been presented in such a manner and the proceedings in general have been conducted in such a way that he has had a fair trial'.

[4]*See* Summers, 2007 at 130, noting that the ECtHR has often emphasized the 'difficulties of separating the trial from the proceedings as a whole'. The fair trial requirements in art. 6 is not confined to the trial proceeding; they apply also to the investigative stage: *see*, *e.g.*, *Aleksandr Zaichenko* v. *Russia*, Application no. 39660/02, 18 February 2010 at [42].

[5]Jackson/Summers, 2012 at 163. See also *Ramanauskas* v. *Lithuania* (2010) 51 EHRR 11 at [52] ('In this context, the Court's task is not to determine whether certain items of evidence were obtained unlawfully, but rather to examine whether such "unlawfulness" resulted in the infringement of another right protected by the Convention.') Pattenden, 2009 at 61 (arguing, in the context of evidence obtained by torture or inhuman or degrading treatment, that the exclusionary rule should be read into Art. 3 itself and exclusion should not be based on Art. 6).

The method used in obtaining the evidence may be unlawful in a number of ways. It may have been in breach of domestic law or a Convention right other than article 6 (examples are given below) or a right implied in article 6 itself (such as the right of silence or privilege against self-incrimination).[6] The breach of a Convention right, or other law, that is committed in procuring evidence during criminal investigation is conceptually distinct from the breach of the right to a fair trial in article 6(1); the latter is occasioned by a separate event, namely, the use of the evidence at the trial. As Lord Hoffmann explained in the context of evidence obtained by torture in *Montgomery* v. *H. M. Advocate*[7]:

> Of course events before the trial may create the conditions for an unfair determination of the charge. For example, an accused who is convicted on evidence obtained from him by torture has not had a fair trial. But the breach of article 6(1) lies not in the use of torture (which is, separately, a breach of article 3) but in the reception of the evidence by the court for the purposes of determining the charge. If the evidence had been rejected, there would still have been a breach of article 3 but no breach of article 6(1).

2.2 *Approach to exclusion under article 6(1) of the Convention*

It is understandable why the ECtHR has repeatedly insisted that each member state is generally free to devise its own rules on the admissibility of evidence. This is in accord with the principle of subsidiarity and respect for the sovereignty of member states and with the reluctance of the ECtHR to act as a 'fourth instance' appeal.[8] At the same time, the right to a fair trial in article 6—being a human right—sets the basic and universally applicable standards that must be met for a trial in any member state to be considered fair.[9] In reality, and contrary to repeated disavowals by the ECtHR, article 6 does in effect require member states to adopt certain basic or minimal rules on admissibility (or, to use a broader term, 'useability') of evidence in the legal determination of guilt.

For instance, torture is prohibited by article 3, as is 'inhuman and degrading treatment'. In *Jalloh* v. *Germany*, the ECtHR took the view that 'incriminating evidence—whether in the form of a confession or real evidence—obtained as a result of …[torture]—should never be relied on as proof of the victim's guilt, irrespective of its probative value.'[10]. This principle was not applicable on the facts

[6] *See, e.g.*, *Saunders* v. *UK* (1997) 23 EHRR 313; *Allan* v. *UK* (2003) 36 EHRR 12 at [51] ('Whether the right to silence is undermined to such an extent as to give rise to a violation of Art. 6 of the Convention depends on all the circumstances of the individual case').

[7] (2003) 1 AC 641 at 649.

[8] Emmerson et al., 2012 at [2]–[114], [13]–[68].

[9] Ho, 2012a.

[10] *Jalloh* v. *Germany* (2007) 44 EHRR 32 at [105].

in *Jalloh* v. *Germany* as the treatment of the accused was found not to amount to torture. But the principle has been applied in later cases.[11] In effect, article 6(1) read with article 3 requires all member states to adopt the categorical rule that evidence obtained by torture is inadmissible and cannot be used as proof of guilt in legal proceedings. The same categorical approach applies also to evidence of a confession or statement obtained from the accused by inhuman or degrading treatment that falls short of torture.[12]

However, the ECtHR has not adopted a similar categorical rule of exclusion for other types of unlawfully obtained evidence such as real evidence obtained by inhuman or degrading treatment,[13] evidence derived from evidence obtained by torture or inhuman or degrading treatment ('fruits of the poisonous tree'),[14] and evidence obtained by means that contravene the right of privacy in article 8.[15] Use or admission of such evidence will not automatically render the trial unfair. The Strasbourg court will assess the fairness of the proceedings considered as a whole and engage in a balancing of countervailing considerations. In this connection, a number of factors have been treated as relevant in the overall assessment. They include[16]:

- the seriousness of the offence with which the accused is charged ('the weight of the public interest in the investigation and punishment of the offence in issue'[17]);
- 'whether the rights of the defence rights have been respected'[18];
- the opportunities afforded the accused to challenge the authenticity and oppose the use or admissibility of the evidence and whether the domestic court had the power to exclude the evidence if it were minded to do so[19];
- 'whether the circumstances in which [the evidence] was obtained cast doubts on its reliability or accuracy'[20]; and

[11]*Harutyunyan* v. *Armenia* (2009) 49 EHRR 9 at [63], [66]; *Levinta* v. *Moldova*, Application no. 17332/03, 16 December 2008.

[12]*Gafgen* v. *Germany* (2011) 52 EHRR 1 at [166], [173]; *see* also Pattenden, 2010 at 366, citing other earlier cases.

[13]*Jalloh* v. *Germany* (2007) 44 EHRR 32 at [107]: the 'general question whether the use of evidence obtained by an act qualified as inhuman and degrading treatment automatically renders the trial unfair can be left open'. It was held, taking into account the particular circumstances of the case, that use of the evidence of drugs obtained by forced administration of emetics rendered the trial unfair (*ibid.* at [108]).

[14]*See Gafgen* v. *Germany* (2011) 52 EHRR 1 at [147], [178] (it seems that there is a strong presumption in favour of exclusion).

[15]*See, e.g.*, *Khan* v. *UK* (2001) 31 EHRR 45; *PG and JH* v. *UK* [2002] *Criminal Law Review* 308; *Allan* v. *UK* (2003) 36 EHRR 12.

[16]*See* Choo, 2013 at 338.

[17]*Jalloh* v. *Germany* (2007) 44 EHRR 32 at [97].

[18]*Gafgen* v. *Germany* (2011) 52 EHRR 1 at [164].

[19]Emmerson et al., 2012 at [13]–[50].

[20]*Gafgen* v. *Germany* (2011) 52 EHRR 1 at [164].

- the role played by the wrongfully obtained evidence in supporting the guilty verdict (that is, whether the conviction was based on the evidence,[21] and if it was, whether it was the sole or decisive evidence or whether the guilty verdict was supported by other evidence).

To reiterate, under Strasbourg jurisprudence, the question raised by unlawfully obtained evidence is not whether the domestic court should have excluded it as such; it is whether, in the light of all relevant factors, the use or admission of the evidence in the domestic proceedings rendered it unfair as a whole and hence in contravention of article 6. How is this determination made? In particular, how can unlawfulness in the method used by investigators in obtaining evidence prior to the trial impact on the fairness of the trial?[22] And how are the factors mentioned above relevant to the fairness of the trial? It is difficult to extract clear and coherent principles from the Strasbourg jurisprudence.[23]

The relevance of the factors listed above and the adoption of a balancing approach (as opposed to categorical exclusion) have drawn criticisms from academics[24] and dissenting judges of the ECtHR.[25] One criticism that has been made is that a trial can never be fair if the accused was convicted on evidence obtained in violation of a Convention right. As Judge Spielmann pointed out in dissent in *Bykov* v. *Russia*,[26] 'the fairness required by article 6 of the Convention also entails a requirement of lawfulness. Fairness presupposes respect for lawfulness and thus also, *a fortiori*, respect for the rights guaranteed by the Convention'.[27] Now, one

---

[21]*Ibid.* at [164].

[22]Jackson/Summers, 2012 at 184 ('the ECtHR has been slow to elaborate on the relationship between the regulation of the investigation or pre-trial phase and the fairness of the trial').

[23]*See, e.g.*, Jackson/Summers, 2012 at 194 (noting that the ECtHR 'has not yet developed a deliberate and reasoned approach to determining why or under which circumstances evidence which has been improperly obtained during the pre-trial investigative phase will impact on the rights of the defence at trial'); Goss, 2014 at 58–62 (noting that the ECtHR's approach to the evidence law is marked by incoherence).

[24]*See, e.g.*, Ashworth, 2012. On balancing of rights and interests in the criminal process generally, *see, e.g.*, Maher, 1984 and Cottingham, 1984.

[25]*See, e.g.*, the dissenting judgments of Judge Bratza in *Jalloh* v. *Germany* (2007) 44 EHRR 32 at [0]–[I9] ('the fairness of the judicial proceeding is in my view irreparably damaged in any case where evidence is admitted which has been obtained by the authorities of the State concerned in violation of the prohibition of Article 3'); Judge Loucaides in *Khan* v. *UK* (2001) 31 EHRR 45 at [0]–[I4] ('I cannot accept that a trial can be "fair", as required by Article 6, if a person's guilt for any offence is established through evidence obtained in breach of the human rights guaranteed by the Convention'); and Judge Tulkens in *PG and JH* v. *UK*, Application no. 44787/98, 25 September 2001 at [1] ('I do not think that a trial can be described as "fair" where evidence obtained in breach of a fundamental right guaranteed by the Convention has been admitted during the trial').

[26]Judge Spielmann in *Bykov* v. *Russia*, Application no. 4378/02, 10 March 2009 at [7], joined by Judges Rozakis, Tulkens, Casadevall and Mijovic.

[27]Ashworth, 2012 at 159, reads this as an argument based on the rule of law and as a version of the integrity principle.

can accept that the fairness of a trial cannot only be about the reliability of the evidence on which the court acts and the accuracy of the verdict that it reaches. But it is not self-evident that 'fairness presupposes respect for lawfulness' and that a trial can never be fair if the accused is convicted on evidence obtained in violation of a Convention right. This further claim is in need of a supporting argument.

2.3 *Possible Theoretical Bases*

One argument that could be made is that it is unfair to allow the state to profit from its own wrongdoing.[28] In the situation where evidence has been obtained through a wrongful act on the part of an agent of the state (namely, the police), to allow the state (through the prosecution) to use the evidence against the accused is to allow the state to derive an advantage over the accused that it ought not to have in their adversarial contest. There are potential difficulties with this theory. Supporters of the so-called separation thesis would emphasize that it was the police who had committed the wrong in obtaining the evidence, and, insofar as there was no complicity by the prosecution in this wrong, the prosecution is arguably not benefiting from its own wrong in using the evidence at the trial. One way of getting around this difficulty is to treat the police and prosecution not as separate agents but as members of the collective agent that is the state.[29] If they are members of the same collective agent, the wrong of one qua member of the collective agent may be attributed to the other qua member of the same collective agent. This may dissolve the difficulty posed by the separation thesis to the no-profit principle.

A second possible argument has been advanced by Summers[30] together with Jackson.[31] As they explain, 'unlike the traditional legitimacy theories,... the focus [of their argument] is not on the moral reprehensibility of the state authorities' conduct, but rather on the effect of the conduct on the ability of the accused (and the defence) to present its case.'[32] The contention, in gist, is that the right to a fair trial is infringed by allowing the prosecution to use unlawfully obtained evidence at the trial where and insofar as this circumvents and irremediably undermines certain basic rights which the defence has at the trial, which rights are essential to uphold if the trial is to be considered fair.[33] In particular, for the trial to be considered fair, it

---

[28]*See, e.g.*, Duff/Farmer/Marshall/Tadros, 2007 at 107–8; Chau, 2016.

[29]*See* Ho, 2016a.

[30]Summers, 2007.

[31]Jackson/Summers, 2012 chapter 6 and especially at 169, 177. *See* also Jackson, 2009.

[32]Jackson/Summers, 2012 at 195.

[33]For a similar argument in Canadian jurisprudence, *see* Paciocco/Stuesser, 2015 at 406: earlier decisions of the Supreme Court of Canada adopted the reasoning that 'since a "fair trial" demands the Crown prove its case without calling the accused as a witness, a trial would become unfair if the Crown could indirectly co-opt the accused as a witness by presenting out-of-court statements obtained from the accused in violation of the [Canadian Charter of Rights and Freedoms]'.

is essential to uphold the general right of the accused person to have 'the opportunity to challenge the evidence levelled against [him or her] by the prosecution and to present [his or her] own evidence in adversarial proceedings, that is to say assisted by defence counsel in proceedings adjudicated by an independent and impartial judge.'[34] The admission of unlawfully obtained evidence may circumvent and irremediably undermine this general 'fair trial' right. Consider the situation where the accused was denied the assistance of a lawyer during police interrogation. The accused has a right to present his or her evidence assisted by a lawyer at the trial.[35] This right may be 'irretrievably prejudiced' if incriminating statements obtained from the accused during the interrogation and without prior access to legal advice are used—as pre-constituted or ready-made evidence—against him or her at the trial.[36]

However, this line of argument has not succeeded before the ECtHR for all breaches of Convention rights. As Jackson and Summers noted, the ECtHR displays a trial-centric bias. For instance, case-law on article 8 (right to privacy) violations 'suggests that provided that the applicant had the opportunity to raise the alleged impropriety at trial and that the trial court considered the applicant's argument and had the discretion to decide not to use the evidence, the fairness of the trial will not be compromised by the decision to make use of the evidence in convicting the accused.'[37] There is reluctance by the ECtHR to take a direct and more interventionistic stance in regulating the pre-trial investigative processes.[38] As such, the exclusionary rule, based as it is on the ECtHR's interpretation of the right to a fair trial, is of limited efficacy in regulating pre-trial evidence-gathering by law enforcement agencies.[39]

It is unclear how far this line of argument may be pushed. The resistance to regulating evidence-gathering at the investigation stage by the same set of norms as those that govern the trial stem in large part from the fear that this may hamper criminal investigation. For instance, it does not seem feasible to insist that police interrogation be conducted openly in the way trials are conducted openly. Is it any more feasible to insist that no statement obtained during any closed-door police interrogation should ever be admitted as evidence at the trial?[40]

---

[34] *Ibid.* at 195–6.

[35] Art. 6(3)(c).

[36] *See Salduz* v. *Turkey* (2008) 49 EHRR 19 at [55].

[37] Jackson/Summers, 2012 at 181. *See, e.g., Khan* v. *UK* (2001) 31 EHRR 45 at [38]–[40] and *Allan* v. *UK* (2003) 36 EHRR 12 at [48], *ibid.* at [52].

[38] Summers, 2007 at 163: 'it is insufficient and inconsistent continually to emphasise the importance of the adversarial trial and yet to neglect the ways in which this can be undermined.'

[39] *See* Jackson/Summers, 2012 at 186.

[40] Summers, 2007 at 131: criticizing the ECtHR for paying 'insufficient attention … to the type of regulation which is required in the investigation phase. The reluctance of the Strasbourg authorities to insist on the application of adversarial principles during the investigation stage gives rise to some serious tensions as to the theoretical ability of the provision to set out consistent principles for regulating fair trials…. If evidence is heard and challenged solely in a non-public forum which is not supervised by an impartial judge, it must be questioned to what extent the "trial rights" in Article 6(1) can still be said to have application and meaning.'

3 England

3.1 Common Law Approach to Wrongfully Obtained Evidence

At common law, the general rule is that the wrongfulness of the method by which the evidence was obtained does not affect its admissibility. In *R* v. *Leatham*,[41] a case before the Court of Queen's Bench, Justice Crompton famously stated: 'It doesn't matter how you get it; if you steal it even, it would be admissible.' There are exceptions to this rule. Involuntary confessions[42] and evidence obtained by torture[43] are inadmissible at common law.[44] The automatic exclusion of involuntary confessions has been rationalised in terms of reliability concerns, the privilege against self-incrimination and the legitimacy or integrity of the criminal process.[45] Of these three rationales, the last has been identified as the main reason for the strict inadmissibility of evidence obtained by torture.[46]

If the evidence is inadmissible, the judge must exclude it. No discretion is involved. If the evidence is admissible, the judge conducting a criminal trial may nevertheless exclude it under certain circumstances. Arguably, some support exists in a number of pre-1979 decisions for the view that the wrongfulness of the method by which the evidence was obtained can in itself justify the exercise of this exclusionary discretion. Dicta in cases such as *Kuruma* v. *R.*[47] (a decision of the

[41](1861) 8 Cox CC 498. *See* also *R* v. *Warickshall* (1738) 1 Leach 263.

[42]The confession must be voluntary 'in the sense that it has not been obtained … by fear of prejudice or hope of advantage or hope of advantage, exercised or held out by a person in authority, or by oppression': Mirfield, 1997 at 76 citing principle (e) of the Judges' Rules 1964 as a convenient statement of the common law rule.

[43]*A* v. *Secretary of State for the Home Department (No.2)* [2006] 2 AC 221.

[44]In addition to these common law exceptions, a categorical rule of exclusion also applies to intercepted communications to which the Regulation of Investigatory Powers Act 2000 applies: *see* Emmerson et al., 2012 at 651; Choo, 2013 at 331.

[45]As the Privy Council put it in *Lam Chi-Ming* v. *R* [1991] 2 AC 212 at 220 (decision on appeal from Hong Kong):

> [T]he rejection of an improperly obtained confession is not dependent only upon possible unreliability but also upon the principle that a man cannot be compelled to incriminate himself and upon the importance that attaches in a civilised society to proper behaviour by the police towards those in their custody. All three of these factors have combined to produce the rule of law applicable in Hong Kong as well as in England that a confession is not admissible in evidence unless the prosecution establish that it was voluntary.

See generally Mirfield, 1997, chapter 2.

[46]*A* v. *Secretary of State for the Home Department (No.2)* [2006] 2 AC 221 admitting evidence obtained by torture would 'compromise the integrity of the judicial process, dishonour the administration of justice' (*ibid.* at 280, per Lord Hoffmann), 'shock the conscience, abuse or degrade the proceedings and involve the state in moral defilement' (*ibid.* at 299, per Lord Carswell).

[47][1955] AC 197.

Privy Council hearing an appeal from Kenya) and *Callis* v. *Gunn*[48] (a judgment of the Queen's Bench Division of the English High Court)[49] suggest that the judge may exclude evidence where it was gained by 'a trick'[50] or by 'oppressive' means or 'by false representations,... by threats, by bribes, anything of that sort'.[51] However, in 1979, the scope of the common law discretion to exclude wrongfully gathered evidence was curtailed by the House of Lords in *R* v. *Sang*.[52] The House of Lords was asked to address a certified question of law on the scope of the exclusionary discretion. The following answer was given by Lord Diplock[53]:

> (1) A trial judge in a criminal trial has always a discretion to refuse to admit evidence if in his opinion its prejudicial effect outweighs its probative value.
> (2) Save with regard to admissions and confessions and generally with regard to evidence obtained from the accused after commission of the offence, he has no discretion to refuse to admit relevant admissible evidence on the ground that it was obtained by improper or unfair means.

Although all of the other law lords expressed agreement with this answer, there were significant differences in their views.[54] Of all the judgments, it is that of Lord Diplock that has had the greatest impact on later cases.[55] Glossing over differences in the judgments, the general effect of *Sang* was to confine within relatively narrow limits the scope of the discretion to exclude evidence on the ground of its wrongful provenance.

The discretion in limb (1) in the quotation above rests on a different ground. It allows the judge to exclude evidence where its prejudicial effect outweighs its probative value in the sense that the jury is likely to attach undue weight to the evidence.[56]

---

[48][1964] 1 QB 495.

[49]Other relevant cases include *Jeffrey* v. *Black* [1978] QB 490 at 498, *R* v. *Payne* [1963] 1 WLR 637 and *King* v. *R* [1969] 1 AC 304.

[50]*Kuruma* v. *R* [1955] AC 197 at 204.

[51]*Callis* v. *Gunn* [1964] 1 QB 495 at 502.

[52][1980] AC 402.

[53]*Ibid.* at 437.

[54]As one commentator put it, 'no single ratio clearly emerged from the case': Sharpe, 1998 at 52. Amongst the judges, Lord Diplock and Viscount Dilhorne gave the discretion the narrowest scope. The latter judge disagreed with the dicta found in earlier cases insofar as they suggested a wide discretion and he took the view that some of the earlier cases, such as *R* v. *Payne* [1963] 1 WLR 637 at 637 and *Jeffrey* v. *Black* [1978] QB 490, were wrongly decided: *R* v. *Sang* [1980] AC 402 at 440–441. Lord Scarman, on the other hand, explicitly declined to reject the earlier dicta: *ibid.* at 456.

[55]Mirfield, 1997 at 118, 119.

[56]*Scott* v. *R* [1989] 1 AC 1242 at 1256; *R* v. *Christie* [1914] 1 AC 545 at 559. *See* also Dennis, 2017 at 93: 'Evidence is unfairly prejudicial to the accused if its use at trial would tend to lead the factfinder to convict the accused for reasons other than the proper probative value of the evidence'. This is distinguishable from 'reasoning prejudice' and 'moral prejudice' which are more relevant in the context of evidence of the accused's bad character or previous misconduct: *see*, *ibid.* at 796–8.

The scope of the exclusionary discretion extends beyond this.[57] It also allows the judge to exclude evidence where admitting it 'will put the accused at an unfair advantage or deprive him of the ability to defend himself'.[58] Significantly, in all these instances, the focus is on the use of the evidence at the trial, in particular, on the impact of admitting the evidence on the reliability of the verdict or the fairness of the adversarial contest in court. The exclusion does not rest (at least, not directly) on any objection there might be to the manner in which the evidence was obtained prior to the trial.[59]

According to the answer given by Lord Diplock in *Sang*, the discretion to exclude evidence on the direct basis of its wrongful procurement is available only for the two categories of evidence stated in limb (2) above. Outside of these two categories, wrongfulness in the method of obtaining evidence does not on its own warrant its exclusion at common law. The first category consists of 'admissions and confessions'. For example, while a breach of the Judges' Rules in obtaining a confession does not make it inadmissible, the evidence may be excluded at the court's discretion.[60]

The second category is 'evidence obtained from the accused after commission of the offence'.[61] It is unclear what this category consists of. The only authority cited by Lord Diplock for this category was *R* v. *Payne*.[62] There the accused was charged with drunk-driving. The police obtained his agreement to undergo a medical examination to ascertain if he was suffering from any illness or disability. This was on the understanding that he would not be examined on his fitness to drive. In breach of this agreement, the doctor gave evidence at the trial of the accused's unfitness to drive. The English Court of Criminal Appeal held that the trial judge ought to have excluded the evidence, even though it was strictly speaking admissible, and quashed the conviction. In *Sang*, Lord Diplock interpreted *Payne* as a case which was 'analogous to unfairly inducing a defendant to confess to an

---

[57]*See R* v. *Sang* [1980] AC 402 at 445.

[58]*Grant* v. *R* [2007] 1 AC 1 at [21].

[59]However, the manner in which evidence was obtained may cast doubt on reliability of the evidence, and this in turn may cause its probative value to be outweighed by its prejudicial effect.

[60]The Judges' Rules were guidelines for police officers on interviewing suspects. As the Privy Council explained in *Peart* v. *R* [2006] 1 WLR 970 at [1]: 'Although classed formally as administrative directions…, they were afforded over time a higher status, and a general requirement became established that police officers had to observe them if confessions received were to be admitted in evidence. They have been replaced in England and Wales by the provisions of Code C made under the Police and Criminal Evidence Act 1984'.

[61]Lord Diplock confined this limb to cases where the evidence was 'tantamount to a self-incriminatory admission which was obtained from the defendant, after the offence had been committed, by means which would justify a judge in excluding an actual confession which had the like self-incriminating effect': *R v. Sang* [1980] AC 402 at 436. Other judges took broader views and were content to leave the discretion under limb (2) open-ended: Lord Salmon, *ibid.* at 445; Lord Fraser, *ibid.* at 450; Lord Scarman, *ibid.* at 456–7. Real and uncontroversial examples are difficult to find.

[62][1963] 1 WLR 637. Similarly, *see R* v. *Court* [1962] *Criminal Law Review* 697.

offence' and explained exclusion on the principle of the privilege against self-incrimination.[63] The accused was unfairly induced to submit to a medical examination which would and did expose his guilt. In effect, he was misled into condemning himself.

On Lord Diplock's statement of the common law, the discretion to exclude improperly or unfairly obtained evidence is of limited scope. If, say, the police were to enter illegally and steal real evidence from the premises of a third party,[64] this alone would not permit the judge to exclude it: the evidence falls outside of the second category since it is not of a confession or admission, and the police did not get it 'from the accused'. For the discretion to be available, not only must the evidence have been obtained from the accused, it must also have been obtained '*after* the commission of the crime'. Strictly speaking, this further requirement would not be satisfied where evidence was obtained *during* or *before* the commission of the crime such as 'evidence of an *agent provocateur*' or evidence procured 'by such means as illegal telephone tapping or bugging'.[65]

3.2 *Fair Trial Rationale and Its Limitations*

The common law exclusionary discretion is said to stem from 'a judge's duty in a criminal trial to ensure that a defendant receives a fair trial.'[66] Taking the central purpose of the trial as the search for the truth, the accused's right to a fair trial has come to be understood primarily as the right to have the truth in the criminal charge determined in a process that is accurate and reliable, and this right is subverted where the court relies on unreliable (and, hence, 'prejudicial') evidence in ascertaining the accused's guilt. This is a narrow reading of the concept of a fair trial.

Lord Diplock drew a firm line between fairness in the method of obtaining evidence in the course of criminal investigation and fairness in using the evidence at the trial. The use of wrongfully obtained evidence at a trial does not ipso facto render the trial unfair in the narrow sense. Where the reliability of the evidence is unaffected by its wrongful provenance, the interest in a fair trial does not call for its exclusion. The only exceptions where wrongful provenance alone justifies discretionary exclusion were, according to Lord Diplock, confession and analogous evidence; and he explained these exceptions as resting of the privilege against self-incrimination.

---

[63] *R* v. *Sang* [1980] AC 402 at 435.

[64] For Lord Fraser, the discretion applied not only to cases where the evidence was obtained from the accused but also to cases where the evidence was obtained from premises occupied by the accused: *ibid.* at 452.

[65] Pattenden, 1990 at 266.

[66] *Lobban* v. *The Queen* [1995] 1 WLR 877 at 886. *See* also *R* v. *Sang* [1980] AC 402 at 436–7, 445, 450, 454; *R* v. *Christie* [1914] 1 AC 545 at 559.

One serious limitation of the common law exclusionary discretion, as so interpreted, is that, leaving aside confession and analogous evidence, wrongfulness in the method by which the police had procured the evidence, however objectionable the method might be, would not alone allow the judge to exclude the evidence. For Lord Diplock, it is no part of the judicial function to exclude evidence for the reason that the judge dislike—and however much the judge may dislike—the way it was obtained.[67] This would appear to leave no room for the exclusionary discretion to serve any extra-epistemic purpose such as deterring the police from engaging in similar behaviour in the future or registering judicial disapproval of their conduct or protecting the integrity or legitimacy of the administration of criminal justice or upholding the rule of law.

3.3 *Position Under the Police and Criminal Evidence Act 1984 ('PACE 1984')*

Section 76(2) of PACE 1984 creates a new exclusionary rule that supplements the common law. Under this section, a confession obtained from the accused is inadmissible if it was obtained either (a) by oppression[68] or (b) 'in consequence of anything said or done which was likely, in the circumstances existing at the time, to render [the confession] unreliable'. In either of these situations, 'the court shall not allow the confession to be given in evidence against him except in so far as the prosecution proves to the court beyond reasonable doubt that the confession (*notwithstanding that it may be true*) was not obtained as aforesaid.' Emphasising the words in italics, Dennis contends, with the backing of authorities, that this section 'is concerned with the issue of the methods used to obtain the confession (the "legitimacy" issue) and not with the issue of the whether the actual confession itself is true or false (the "reliability" issue).'[69]

Section 76(2) concerns admissibility as a matter of law and is restricted to confession evidence. As noted, even where the (confession or other) evidence is admissible as a matter of law, the judge presiding over a criminal trial has some discretion at common law to exclude it in limited circumstances. The common law discretion is retained under section 82(3) of the Police and Criminal Evidence Act 1984. A new statutory discretion is created under section 78 of the same Act. Section 78(1) states (italics added):

> In any proceedings the court may refuse to allow evidence on which the prosecution proposes to rely to be given if it appears to the court that, *having regard to all the circumstances*, including the *circumstances in which the evidence was obtained*,

[67] *R* v. *Sang* [1980] AC 402 at 437.

[68] Section 76(8) PACE 1984 states that oppression 'includes torture, inhuman or degrading treatment, and the use of threat of violence (whether or not amounting to torture).'

[69] Dennis, 2017 at 239.

> the admission of the evidence would have such an *adverse effect on the fairness of the proceedings* that the court ought not to admit it.

'The precise scope of s. 78 and the extent to which it enlarges the exclusionary discretion at common law, is still not settled.'[70] Clarity is lacking in the drafting of the provision. One the one hand, it expressly instructs the judge, in exercising the discretion, to take into account the 'circumstances in which the evidence was obtained'. One might read this as a broadening of the common law discretion in the sense that the provision acknowledges the possibility of wrongfulness in the procurement of evidence being a sufficient ground for exclusion.[71] On the other hand, the provision also requires the court to consider all other relevant circumstances and the decisive factor is whether admitting the evidence would have an 'adverse effect on the fairness of the *proceedings*'.[72] If 'proceedings' is read narrowly to mean the 'trial', the discretion would seem no wider than at common law since the crucial consideration under this section, as at common law, would then be whether the use of the evidence at the trial will render the trial unfair,[73] and it is by no means obvious that 'what has gone on pre-trial is capable of adversely affecting the fairness of the trial itself'.[74]

3.4 *Reliability Interpretation of Fair Trial and Its Limitations*

The appellate courts have been reluctant to provide guidelines to trial judges on the exercise of the exclusionary discretion under section 78(1).[75] While it is difficult to discern 'a wholly coherent approach to this very wide discretion',[76] academic commentators have observed that the courts have 'wedded themselves…to the reliability principle'.[77] In exercising the discretion, 'evidential reliability is at the forefront of the…courts' thinking, the primary concern apparently being with

---

[70]Dennis, 2017 at 96.

[71]This reading was rejected by the Court of Appeal in *R* v. *Chalkley* [1998] 2 Cr App R 79 at 105.

[72]Bingham, 2000 at 48 ('It may be that the pendulum has swung too far towards exclusion upon breaches being shown, without adequate consideration of the effect on the fairness of the proceedings which the Act requires.')

[73]Dennis, 2017 at 104, 97–98 (making a compelling case for a broad interpretation of the section).

[74]Mirfield, 1997 at 131. On how fairness of the trial might be affected, *see ibid.* at 131–137.

[75]Choo, 2013 at 341, citing *R* v. *Samuel* [1988] QB 615 at 630.

[76]Bingham, 2000 at 47.

[77]Ormerod/Birch, 2004 at 779. Dennis, 2017 at 325, suggesting that the discretion is wide enough to achieve other goals.

the determination of the truth rather than with upholding due process.'[78] The fact that the evidence was obtained wrongfully is not enough to warrant exclusionary discretion; admitting the evidence must be shown to undermine the 'fairness of the proceedings'.[79] While the term 'proceedings' is potentially wider than 'trial', Lord Nicholls expressed the traditional view when he stated in *R* v. *Looseley*[80] that '"fairness of the proceedings" in section 78 is directed primarily at matters going to fairness in the actual conduct of the trial; for instance, the reliability of the evidence and the defendant's ability to test its reliability'. If the trial is considered in isolation from the pre-trial criminal process, the difficulty arises in explaining how wrongful evidence-gathering activities at the investigation stage can make the trial that occurs later unfair.[81] Sometimes, the courts are prepared to construe fairness more widely; most notably, there is judicial openness to using section 78(1) to exclude evidence obtained in an entrapment.[82] In *R* v. *Sultan Khan*,[83] Lord Nicholls stated that the approach to exclusion of wrongfully obtained evidence under article 6 of the ECHR and under section 78 of the PACE 1984 are essentially the same: both are directed at ensuring 'that those facing criminal charges receive a fair hearing'.

Founding the exclusionary discretion on a narrow conception of trial fairness, and having the reliability of the challenged evidence as the major preoccupation, will result in a restrictive—and critics would say, unduly restrictive—application of section 78. It will make the discretion narrower than an exclusionary rule that is based on the notion of integrity or legitimacy, such as a rule that requires evidence to be excluded where it would 'be detrimental to the administration of justice' (as in South Africa)[84] or would 'bring the administration of justice into disrepute' (as in Canada).[85] It is also narrower than an exclusionary rule that rests on broad public policy considerations (as in Australia[86]). As two authors have jointly argued[87]:

[78]Choo, 2013 at 352. Courts are content to restrict the focus of s. 78 on reliability concerns partly as a result of the expansion of the power to stay proceedings under the abuse of process doctrine, the latter being seen as an alternative judicial device for protecting rights in, and controlling, the criminal process: Ormerod/Birch, 2004 at 779.

[79]Emmerson et al., 2012 at 645.

[80]*R* v. *Looseley* [2001] 1 WLR 2060 at [12].

[81]*See* Mirfield, 1997 at 131 (noting the difficulty), 133–137 (discussing unusual situations in which the fairness of the trial might be affected).

[82]*R* v. *Smurthwaite and Gill* (1994) 98 Cr App Rep 437; *R* v. *Looseley* [2001] 1 WLR 2060 at [18], [42]–[44] (Lord Hoffmann thought that a stay of proceedings was the more appropriate remedy).

[83][1997] AC 558 at 583.

[84]Constitution of South Africa, s. 35(5).

[85]Canadian Charter of Rights and Freedoms, s. 24(2).

[86]Section 138 of the Uniform Evidence Act in Australia requires improperly or unlawfully evidence to be excluded 'unless the desirability of admitting the evidence outweighs the undesirability of admitting evidence that has been obtained in the way in which the evidence was obtained.'

[87]Ormerod/Birch, 2004 at 782. According to Dennis, 2017 at 325, the s. 78 discretion is in principle wide enough to allow exclusion to serve the other purposes mentioned above.

the trial is not merely about reliably convicting the guilty and ensuring the protection of the innocent from conviction; there is an important judicial responsibility to maintain the moral integrity of the process. To date, the courts have relinquished the opportunity to use s. 78 to establish and maintain this moral legitimacy.

4 Singapore[88]

4.1 Introduction

As Singapore was formerly a British colony, her law has been influenced by English common law. In Singapore, as at common law, wrongfully obtained evidence raises two separate issues. The first is the admissibility of such evidence as a matter of law. If the evidence is inadmissible as a matter of law, it must be excluded; the judge has no discretion not to do so. If the evidence is admissible as a matter of law, the party may seek to adduce it at the trial; but this does not mean that the court must admit the evidence. At this point, a second issue arises: the court may sometimes exclude wrongfully obtained evidence even though it is technically admissible. These two issues will be discussed in turn. We will consider, first, the extent to which wrongfulness in the means by which evidence was obtained affects its admissibility and, secondly, the discretion to exclude admissible evidence that has been wrongfully obtained.

4.2 Admissibility of Wrongfully Obtained Evidence

Evidence is rendered inadmissible by the wrongfulness of the means by which it was procured only in a small number of situations. The first set of situations involves statements obtained from the accused. As an exception to the hearsay rule, any statement made by the accused is generally admissible as evidence at his or her trial.[89] However, the statement would be inadmissible under the so-called voluntariness rule if the making of the statement was caused by any inducement, threat or promise proceeding from a person in authority.[90] Courts have founded this rule on the rationale of ensuring reliability of the statement[91] and, alternatively, deterring 'impropriety on the part of the interrogators'.[92] Complementing the voluntariness rule is the oppression doctrine. Under this doctrine, the statement would be

---

[88]*See* generally Ho, 2019.

[89]Section 258(1), Criminal Procedure Code, chapter 68, 2012 revised edition ('CPC').

[90]Section 258(3), CPC.

[91]*See, e.g.*, *Poh Kay Keong* v. *PP* [1995] 3 SLR(R) 887 at [42].

[92]*PP* v. *Sng Siew Ngoh* [1995] 3 SLR(R) 755 at [48].

inadmissible if it was obtained by means that tend to sap and have in fact sapped the free will of the accused.[93] It is rare to succeed in having a statement excluded under this doctrine as the threshold of oppression is pegged very high.[94] While the burden is on the prosecution to prove that the statement was made voluntarily and free of oppression,[95] the courts have stressed that the standard of proof must be consonant with investigative pragmatism. This attitude is reflected, for example, in judicial acknowledgement that the 'police work in difficult circumstances. If they are required to remove all doubt of influence or fear, they would never be able to achieve anything.'[96]

Neither the voluntariness rule nor the oppression doctrine is applicable if the wrongfully obtained evidence is not in the form of a statement by the accused. Thus, they would not apply where an incriminating blood sample was obtained from the accused without complying with the legal requirement of getting his or her prior consent.[97] Even if the evidence is of the form of a statement by the accused, the statement must have been obtained by the proscribed means for the voluntariness rule or the oppression doctrine to come into play. A statement taken by a police officer in flagrant disregard of the prescribed legal procedure but without any inducement, threat or promise, or oppression,[98] remains admissible as a matter of law. (Whether there is discretion to exclude admissible evidence is discussed below.)

While there is no direct authority on this point, it is likely that evidence obtained by torture will be treated as inadmissible in legal proceedings under article 9(1) of the Constitution of Singapore. This provision guarantees the right not to be deprived of one's life or personal liberty 'save in accordance with law'.[99] The term 'law' in this context has been interpreted to include fundamental rules of natural justice. In *Yong Vui Kong* v. *PP*,[100] a case involving an unsuccessful challenge to the constitutionality of caning as a form of punishment, the Court of Appeal noted in an obiter dictum that it 'would violate the fundamental rules of natural justice… to convict a person based on evidence procured by torture'. To do so would strike 'at the very heart of a fair trial.' While exclusion of evidence obtained by torture is explained with reference to the notion of a fair trial, the court did not explain how reliance on such evidence would render the trial unfair.

---

[93]Section 258(3), explanation 1, CPC.

[94]*See* Ho, 2016b at 256–260.

[95]*Panya Martmontree* v. *PP* [1995] 2 SLR(R) 806 at [26].

[96]*Ibid.* at [29].

[97]*See, e.g.*, *Ajmer Singh* v. *PP* [1985–1986] SLR(R) 1030.

[98]Section 258(3), explanation 2(e), CPC states that a statement will not be rendered inadmissible merely because it was obtained without full compliance with the prescribed procedure. Notwithstanding this, the court retains a discretion to exclude the statement where there was flagrant and serious irregularities as discussed below.

[99]*Ong Ah Chuan* v. *PP* [1979–1980] SLR(R) 710 at [26].

[100][2015] 2 SLR 1129 at [64]. *See* Ho, 2019.

4.3 *Discretion to Exclude Admissible Evidence to Ensure a Fair Trial*

Even where the wrongfully obtained evidence is not rendered inadmissible under any of the rules just mentioned, the court may in limited circumstances exclude the evidence at its discretion.[101] The availability and scope of this discretion was clarified in the leading case of *Muhammad bin Kadar* v. *PP*.[102] This case involved statements obtained by the police from an accused person in a highly irregular manner where the procedural rules set out in the Criminal Procedure Code ('CPC') and internal police rules (known as Police General Orders) were deliberately flouted. No reasonable explanation for the flagrant procedural deviations was given. The Court of Appeal held, following the House of Lords' decision in *R* v. *Sang*,[103] that the trial judge has the discretion to exclude evidence that is more prejudicial than probative and, in the case under appeal, the trial judge should have exercised the discretion to exclude the accused's statements.

Reversing the position arguably taken in earlier case-law,[104] the Court of Appeal stressed that 'courts…should refrain from excluding evidence based only on facts indicating unfairness in the way the evidence was obtained (as opposed to unfairness in the sense of contributing to a wrong outcome at trial).'[105] That the evidence was obtained unfairly prior to the trial cannot be used as the direct basis for exercising the discretion to exclude it at the trial. However, where the evidence was obtained in such a manner as to cast serious doubt on its reliability, its probative value would be very low; at the same time, the prejudicial effect of the evidence—in one sense of 'prejudice'—might be high. In *Muhammad bin Kadar* v. *PP*, there were serious doubts about the reliability of the statements given the highly suspicious manner in which the procedures were deliberately flouted. This undermined the probative value of the evidence. At the same time, the statements were prejudicial in the sense that the statements might attract more weight than they truly deserve, a risk that arises due to the 'aura of reliability' that formal statements obtained by the police tend to have.[106]

While exclusion serves the interest in a fair trial by ensuring the reliability of the evidence on which the court makes its findings of fact and the accuracy of those findings, other incidental benefits may also accrue at the broader or systemic level. The Court of Appeal noted that the exclusion of evidence obtained in flagrant

---

[101]The common law in this regard was held to be applicable via s. 2(2) of the Evidence Act, chapter 97, 1997 revised edition: *Muhammad bin Kadar* v. *PP* [2011] 3 SLR 1205 at [51].

[102]*Muhammad bin Kadar* v. *PP* [2011] 3 SLR 1205 at [68]. On the development of the law leading up to this case, *see* Ho, 2012b.

[103][1980] AC 402.

[104]*Cheng Swee Tiang* v. *PP* [1964] MLJ 291, approved by the Court of Appeal in *Chan Chi Pun* v. *PP* [1994] 1 SLR(R) 654 at [12].

[105]*Ibid.* at [68].

[106]*Ibid.* at [58].

disregard of the governing procedure would 'remove the incentive for such non-compliance on the part of police officers' in the future and that 'a vigilant emphasis on the procedural requirements...can have a positive effect on the quality of such evidence generally.'[107] However, this salutary consequence is not the point or purpose of exclusion; the avowed point or purpose is to maintain a fair trial, as narrowly construed.

4.4 Other Rationales

Other rationales have been considered in judicial decisions. However, they have either been rejected or assigned a marginal role. In *Muhammad bin Kadar* v. *PP*, the Court of Appeal rejected the disciplinary rationale; it cautioned that 'the court should be careful to avoid basing the exercise of the exclusionary discretion primarily on a desire to discipline the wrongful behaviour of police officers'.[108]

In *Wong Keng Leong Rayney* v. *Law Society of Singapore*,[109] Justice V. K. Rajah expressed provisional support for the judicial integrity rationale by stating, in an obiter dictum, that, if he 'were unfettered by any authority, [he] would be persuaded that there will be particularly egregious instances of misconduct where the courts should reject evidence that has been procured in a manner that might be inimically repellent to the integrity of the administration of justice.' However, in the later case of *Law Society of Singapore* v. *Tan Guat Neo Phyllis*,[110] the High Court, sitting as court of three judges, distanced itself from the view expressed by Justice Rajah by pointing out that the latter had expressed his views 'without the benefit of hearing arguments about the effect of the [Evidence Act] and the separation of powers'.[111] It appears that the judge has since abandoned the idea of using the principle of judicial integrity to widen the scope of the exclusionary discretion.[112]

---

[107] *Ibid.* at [68].

[108] *Ibid.* at [68]. *See* also *SM Summit Holdings Ltd* v. *PP* [1997] 3 SLR(R) 138 at [48] ('It is not the business of the court to discipline the police').

[109] [2006] 4 SLR 934 at [64]. Justice Rajah referred to Ashworth, 1999 at 307 and Ashworth, 2002 at 163.

[110] [2008] 2 SLR(R) 239 at [148].

[111] In the earlier case of *SM Summit Holdings Ltd* v. *PP* [1997] 3 SLR(R) 138 at [48], the High Court had noted that the integrity rationale is a double-edge sword: while 'the public would lose respect for the court as a dispenser of justice if it is seen to condone illegality', judicial integrity is equally undermined 'when the public perceives that factually-guilty people are getting away with serious crimes because of a trivial breach of legislation.'

[112] This is perhaps discernible from the later case of *Lee Chez Kee* v. *PP* [2008] 3 SLR(R) 447 at [106] where the judge endorsed the position adopted in *Law Society of Singapore* v. *Tan Guat Neo Phyllis* [2008] 2 SLR(R) 239. According to him, the court of three judges in the latter case had 'persuasively ruled that apart from the confines of the EA, there is no residual discretion to exclude evidence which is otherwise rendered legally relevant by the EA.'

In the civil context, the Court of Appeal has recently aired the tentative view that evidence obtained in violation of a person's rights or in an unlawful manner may justifiably be excluded in order to vindicate the rule of law. It is unclear whether the Court of Appeal would give this rationale equal force in the criminal context. According to the Court of Appeal, it 'may weigh against the court excluding the evidence' that it may deprive the prosecution of evidence needed to convict the accused.[113] Priority, it seems, was accorded to the social interests in crime control.

4.5 Evaluation

In summary, the criminal court in Singapore has discretion to exclude wrongfully obtained evidence. This discretion is available where the potential prejudicial effect of admitting the evidence outweighs its probative value. The reasoning is that admitting overly prejudicial evidence will undermine the fairness of the trial. To the extent that the fact-finder might give the prosecution's evidence more weight than it truly deserves, it exposes the accused to an unduly high risk of a miscarriage of justice. Thus, the notion of a fair trial is construed in terms of evidential reliability and accuracy in fact-finding in the case before the court.

Implicit in this approach are certain questionable premises. One of them, which has been encountered, is the separation thesis. On this thesis, unfairness in the method of obtaining evidence is distinct from, and does not taint, the fairness of the trial at which the evidence is sought to be used.[114] Another premise is the belief that exclusion of evidence as a direct response to police impropriety is tantamount to judicial activism inasmuch as it is an illegitimate judicial incursion into the executive sphere.[115]

There are limitations inherent in this approach. In theory, the judge would have no discretion to exclude evidence that is incontrovertibly and highly probative (as will often be the case with real evidence), however objectionable the method used in obtaining it.[116] In an entrapment where the accused was essentially caught red-handed, there is typically no dispute about the reliability of the evidence obtained in the operation.[117] It has been held, reversing an approach set out in an

---

[113] *ANB* v. *ANC* [2015] 5 SLR 522 at [29]. For a critique of this case, *see* Ho, 2016b at 274–275.

[114] *See, e.g.*, Ashworth, 2003. For a theoretical argument against the separation thesis, *see* Ho, 2016a.

[115] *See, e.g.*, *How Poh Sun* v. *PP* [1991] 2 SLR(R) 270 at [21]: 'It is not the province of the court to consider whether the [law enforcement officers] should have proceeded about its work in one way or the other. The court can only be concerned with the evidence before it.'

[116] Unless torture was applied, in which case the evidence is likely to be inadmissible as a matter of law as noted earlier.

[117] *See Law Society of Singapore* v. *Tan Guat Neo Phyllis* [2008] 2 SLR(R) 239 at [126] ('in the case of entrapment evidence…, by definition, the probative value of such evidence must be greater than its prejudicial value in proving the guilt of the accused').

earlier case,[118] that the fact that the evidence was obtained in an entrapment does not provide a basis for exercising the exclusionary discretion.[119] If the concept of 'prejudice' is limited to the notion that the evidence adduced by the prosecution might be given more weight than it objectively deserves, broader interests in protecting civil liberties,[120] or in upholding the rule of law[121] or the legitimacy of criminal convictions,[122] or in the integrity or repute of the administration of criminal justice[123] would apparently have to drop out of consideration entirely.

How the demands of a 'fair trial' are construed would depend on what we understand to be point of holding a trial. On a wider view, the trial is not only about getting the facts right; it is more broadly about securing the legitimacy of the verdict. On this argument, the aim is not simply to convict criminals; the aim is to ensure that no one is convicted unless and until guilt is proved by means that are fair and just. While society has an interest in convicting persons who are guilty of crimes, it also has a profound stake in the fairness and integrity of the criminal justice system, in holding officials who are tasked with enforcing the criminal law to the law. The police, perhaps more than ordinary citizens, have the duty to respect and uphold the law. Judges should not concern themselves only with the reliability of evidence and accuracy of the verdict. More fundamentally, they should see themselves as guardians of the legitimacy of criminal convictions and the rule of law. If this is accepted, an exclusionary discretion that is founded on the concept of a 'fair trial' would have to expand its scope beyond 'prejudice' in the narrow sense.

5 Conclusion

The three systems of law that we have examined endorse the fair trial rationale for excluding wrongfully obtained evidence. They share the conceptual premise that exclusion turns on whether reliance on the evidence in support of a criminal conviction would render the trial unfair. Under a system of separation of powers, there is an advantage in taking this trial-centric approach. It immunizes the judiciary from any accusation of judicial activism and of exceeding its legitimate remit. Maintaining the fairness of court proceedings is manifestly a judicial responsibility and, as some judges have felt the need to stress, the exclusion of evidence is not for the purpose of disciplining the police or telling them how to do their job.

---

[118]*Cheng Swee Tiang* v. *PP* [1964] MLJ 291.

[119]*Law Society of Singapore* v. *Tan Guat Neo Phyllis* [2008] 2 SLR(R) 239.

[120]*Cheng Swee Tiang* v. *PP* [1964] MLJ 291.

[121]*See, e.g.*, Ho, 2016a.

[122]*See, e.g.*, Dennis, 2017 at 52–59.

[123]*See, e.g.*, s. 24(2) of the Canadian Charter of Rights and Freedoms which requires the exclusion of evidence obtained in violation of a charter right or freedom if 'having regard to all the circumstances, the admission of it in the proceedings would bring the administration of justice into disrepute.'

The 'fair trial' rationalization faces a number of limitations. A common conception of a trial is as a fact-finding exercise. The principal aim is to ascertain the truth. There is a tendency to interpret 'fairness' purposively through the lens of reliability and accuracy. This promotes a narrow understanding of the right to a fair trial where, in the present context, it is not much more than the right to have the criminal charge determined by the court on reliable evidence and by an accurate process. On this narrow understanding of a fair trial, it is difficult to justify the exclusion of evidence that, despite its wrongful provenance, is reliable. Even the ECtHR, which frames the issue broadly as one involving the overall fairness of the trial and not merely as an evidentiary point, struggles to explain how the reception of wrongfully obtained evidence in determining the criminal charge can make the trial unfair, and the balancing approach applied by the ECtHR does not give clear guidance on when this will be the case.

Another limitation arises from viewing the trial in isolation from the criminal investigation that precedes it. On this view, the unfairness in obtaining the evidence in the course of criminal investigation and the fairness of using the evidence at the trial are separate matters. It does not follow from the fact that the evidence was obtained unfairly that it is unfair to use the evidence against the accused at the trial. As Justice Cardozo would ask: why should the criminal go free just because the constable has blundered?[124] Furthermore, any wrong committed by a law enforcement officer in getting the evidence is more appropriately addressed in a different forum or at a separate proceeding.[125] These arguments beg the question by denying the criminal court any role or responsibility beyond determining the criminal charge faced by the accused. This view is contestable and rejected in some legal systems. A foray into other rationales is beyond the scope of this chapter. It has only sought to question what it means to use fair trial as the basis for excluding evidence, the implications of doing so, and the suppositions that underpin the operation of this rationale.

References

Books

Dennis, Ian, *The Law of Evidence* 6th edn., London 2017. [Dennis, 2017]

Duff, Antony/Lindsay Farmer/Sandra Marshall/Victor Tadros, *The Trial on Trial: Towards a Normative Theory of the Criminal Trial*, Oxford 2007. [Duff/Farmer/Marshall/Tadros, 2007]

Emmerson, Ben et al., *Human Rights and Criminal Justice* 3rd edn., London 2012. [Emmerson et al., 2012]

Goss, Ryan, *Criminal Fair Trial Rights—Article 6 of the European Convention on Human Rights*, Oxford 2014. [Goss, 2014]

[124] *People* v. *Defore*, 242 N.Y. 13, 21 (1926) Court of Appeal of New York.

[125] On alternative ways of safeguarding the rights of an accused person, *see* Gless/Macula, 2019.

Jackson, John D./Sarah J. Summers, *The Internationalisation of Criminal Evidence—Beyond the Common Law and Civil Law Traditions*, Cambridge 2012. [Jackson/Summers, 2012]
Mirfield, Peter, *Silence, Confessions and Improperly Obtained Evidence*, Oxford 1997. [Mirfield, 1997]
Paciocco, David M./Lee Stuesser, *The Law of Evidence* 7th edn., Toronto 2015. [Paciocco/Stuesser, 2015]
Pattenden, Rosemary, *Judicial Discretion and Criminal Investigation*, Oxford 1990. [Pattenden, 1990]
Sharpe, Sybil, *Judicial Discretion and Criminal Investigation*, London 1998. [Sharpe, 1998]
Summers, Sarah J., *Fair Trials—The European Criminal Procedural Tradition and the European Court of Human Rights*, Oxford 2007. [Summers, 2007]

Journal Articles

Ashworth, Andrew, 'Re-drawing the Boundaries of Entrapment' [2002] *Criminal Law Review*, 161–179. [Ashworth, 2002]
Ashworth, Andrew, 'What is wrong with Entrapment?' [1999] *Singapore Journal of Legal Studies*, 293–317. [Ashworth, 1999]
Ho, Hock Lai, '"National Values on Law and Order" and the Discretion to Exclude Wrongfully Obtained Evidence' [2012] *Journal of Commonwealth Criminal Law*, 232–256. [Ho, 2012b]
Ho, Hock Lai, 'On the Obtaining and Admissibility of Incriminating Statements' (2016) *Singapore Journal of Legal Studies*, 249–276. [Ho, 2016b]
Ho, Hock Lai, 'The Criminal Trial, the Rule of Law and the Exclusion of Unlawfully Obtained Evidence' (2016) 10 *Criminal Law and Philosophy*, 109–131. [Ho, 2016a]
Jackson, John, 'Re-Conceptualizing the Right of Silence as an Effective Fair Trial Standard' (2009) 58 *International and Comparative Law Quarterly*, 835–861. [Jackson, 2009]
Ormerod, David/ Diane Birch, 'The Evolution of the Discretionary Exclusion of Evidence' [2004] *Criminal Law Review*, 767–788. [Ormerod/Birch, 2004]
Pattenden, Rosemary, 'Admissibility of Evidence Derived from the Interrogation of the Defendant by Methods Prohibited by Article 3—European Court of Human Rights' (2010) 14 *International Journal of Evidence and Proof*, 365–373. [Pattenden, 2010]
Pattenden, Rosemary, 'Evidence Obtained by Inhuman Treatment in Violation of Article 3—European Court of Human Rights' (2009) 13 *International Journal of Evidence and Proof*, 58-61. [Pattenden, 2009]

Contributions to Edited Volumes and Annotated Law

Ashworth, Andrew 'Exploring the Integrity Principle in Evidence and Procedure', in: P. Mirfield/R. Smith (eds.), *Essays for Colin Tapper*, London 2003, 107–125. [Ashworth, 2003]
Ashworth, Andrew, 'The Exclusion of Evidence Obtained by Violating a Fundamental Right: Pragmatism before Principle in the Strasbourg Jurisprudence', in: Paul Roberts/Jill Hunter (eds.), *Criminal Procedure and Human Rights—Reimagining Common Law and Procedural Traditions*, Oxford 2012, 145–161. [Ashworth, 2012]
Bingham, Tom, 'The Discretion of the Judge', in: Tom Bingham, *The Business of Judging—Selected Essays and Speeches*, Oxford 2000, 35–51. [Bingham, 2000]
Chau, Peter, 'Excluding Integrity? Revising Non-Consequentialist Justifications for Excluding Improperly Obtained Evidence in Criminal Trials', in: Jill Hunter/Paul Roberts/Simon N.M. Young/David Dixon (eds.), *The Integrity of Criminal Process: From Theory into Practice*, Oxford 2016, 267–279. [Chau, 2016]

Choo, Andrew L-T, 'England and Wales: Fair Trial Analysis and the Presumed Admissibility of Physical Evidence', in: Stephen C. Thaman (ed.), *Exclusionary Rules in Comparative Law*, Dordrecht 2013, 331–354. [Choo, 2013]

Cottingham, John, 'The Balancing Act—Weighing Rights and Interests in the Criminal Process', in: Antony Duff/Nigel Simmonds (eds.), *Philosophy and the Criminal Law*, Wiesbaden 1984, 109–115. [Cottingham, 1984]

Gless, Sabine/Macula, Laura, 'Exclusionary Rules—Is it Time for Change?', in: Gless, Sabine/Richter, Thomas (eds.), *Do Exclusionary Rules Ensure a Fair Trial? A Comparative Perspective on Evidentiary Rules*, Cham 2019, 349–380 [Gless/Macula, 2019]

Ho, Hock Lai, 'Criminal Justice and the Exclusion of Incriminating Statements in Singapore', in: Gless, Sabine/Richter, Thomas (eds.), *Do Exclusionary Rules Ensure a Fair Trial? A Comparative Perspective on Evidentiary Rules*, Cham 2019, 213–252. [Ho, 2019]

Ho, Hock Lai, 'Exclusion of Wrongfully Obtained Evidence: A Comparative Analysis', forthcoming in: Darryl Brown/Jenia I. Turner/Bettina Weißer (eds.), The Oxford Handbook of Criminal Process, Oxford, forthcoming. [Ho, forthcoming]

Ho, Hock Lai, 'The Presumption of Innocence as a Human Right', in: Roberts/Hunter (eds.), *Criminal Evidence and Human Rights—Reimagining Common Law Procedural Traditions*, Oxford 2012, 259-281. [Ho, 2012a]

Maher, Gerry, 'Balancing Rights and Interests in the Criminal Process', in: Antony Duff/Nigel Simmonds (eds.), *Philosophy and the Criminal Law*, Wiesbaden 1984, 99–108. [Maher, 1984]

Turner, Jenia I./Weigend, Thomas, 'The Purposes and Functions of Exclusionary Rules: A Comparative Overview', in: Gless, Sabine/Richter, Thomas (eds.), *Do Exclusionary Rules Ensure a Fair Trial? A Comparative Perspective on Evidentiary Rules*, Cham 2019, 255–282 [Turner/Weigend, 2019]

Hock Lai Ho is the Amaladass Professor of Criminal Justice at the NUS. He holds an LL.B. from NUS, a BCL from Oxford University and a Ph.D. from Cambridge University. He has published internationally in the fields of evidence, proof and aspects of the administration of criminal justice. His research ranges from doctrinal analysis of Singapore law to theoretical and comparative reflections on broader issues of the criminal trial.

Exclusionary Rule of Illegal Evidence in China: Observation from Historical and Empirical Perspectives

Weimin Zuo and Rongjie Lan

Abstract Although the use of torture and other illegal means to gather evidence was prohibited in China in 1979, legislators did not begin to embrace exclusionary rules until the turn of the 21st century. However, this legislative promise has yet to be fulfilled in practice as few defendants request that illegally obtained evidence be excluded and even fewer judges approve such requests. Even if such a request is granted by the court, it remains highly unlikely that the outcome of the case will change. Such discrepancies between legislative endeavors and judicial practice might suggest that torture and other illegal means of acquiring evidence are not routine practice in China, that the Chinese culture tends to trust the government and to prefer substantive truth over procedural fairness, and places public interest above individual interests. As a result, the future of China's exclusionary rules will depend upon transformation of China's legal culture in addition to practical application of the corresponding changes to the law.

As an effective measure to defer police wrongdoings, exclusion of illegal evidence in criminal procedure, ever since articulated by the United States Supreme Court in Mapp versus Ohio,[1] has emerged to be a core institution in any regime with genuine rule of law. The People's Republic of China (China), with the longest uninterrupted legal history in the world, has a legal legacy of obtaining evidence by coercive measures, and nowhere in its 2,000-year-plus documented history has seen the practice of excluding such evidence. After the Communist Party initiated the "Open-up and Reform" policy in late 1970s and endeavored to embrace universal principles and institutions of rule of law and human rights protection, legal academia

[1] *Mapp* v. *Ohio*, 367 US 643 (1961).

W. Zuo (✉)
Law School, Sichuan University, Chengdu, China
e-mail: zuowm@vip.163.com

R. Lan
Law School, Southwestern University of Finance and Economics, Chengdu, China
e-mail: lanrongjie@swufe.edu.cn

S. Gless and T. Richter (eds.), *Do Exclusionary Rules Ensure a Fair Trial?*
Ius Gentium: Comparative Perspectives on Law and Justice 74,
https://doi.org/10.1007/978-3-030-12520-2_10

and practitioners have since engaged in heated discussions of establishing exclusionary rules in China's Criminal Procedure Law (CPL). To better understand the status quo of China's exclusionary rules and their future, a careful observation of their history and an empirical analysis of their implementation is necessary.

1 The Evolution of China's Exclusionary Rules

1.1 *Budding Stage: 1979–1996*

Excluding illegally obtained evidence in China's criminal procedure is not a local tradition that can be traced back to China's long history. Despite the fact that the Communist Party has stated repeatedly in its policies that torture should not be allowed, the rules to exclude illegal evidence are still essentially a transplanted institution borrowed from the West, particularly the United States. That said, even compared with other transplanted legal institutions, such as presumption of innocence, right to counsel and right to public and speedy trial, exclusion of illegal evidence was also quite novel to most of China's legal practitioners and academia. But its roots can be traced back to the year of 1979, when China promulgated its first Criminal Procedure Law (CPL1979), 30 years after the Communist Party won national power from the Nationalists and established the People's Republic of China. Article 32 of CPL1979 prescribed, "torture, threat, inducement, deception and other forms of illegal methods of obtaining evidence are prohibited." The Criminal Code, which took effect in the year of 1980, also created the crime of torture in Article 136.[2] Nevertheless, whether such rules meant that evidence obtained through illegal methods would be excluded was unclear, not had there been any record showing any examples in which the court excluded evidence based upon findings that it had been obtained illegally.

One may argue that without excluding illegally obtained evidence, the practice of obtaining evidence with illegal methods can never be effectively deterred. Driven by desires to tackle crimes and put criminals behind bars, police officers, both good ones and abusive ones included, were sometimes inclined to use illegal but effective and productive methods to extract confessions or other evidence. Once the outcome proves correct, for instance, the true perpetrator being apprehended, the previous use of illegal methods may be completely ignored. After all, the public, and the authorities who pressured by public opinion, often prefer substantive correctness to procedural fairness. History has witnessed many of such examples.

[2]Art. 136 of the 1979 Criminal Code prescribed that "torture is strictly prohibited. Any state officer who extorts confession from a criminal by torture shall be sentenced to fixed-term imprisonment of not more than three years or criminal detention. If he causes injury or disability to the victim by using corporal punishment, he shall be convicted and given a heavier punishment in accordance with the provisions of the crime of assaulting."

This argument is doubtlessly true. The history after the effectuation of CPL1979 has witnessed some violations of Article 32 without consequences. Several widely published wrongful murder convictions, including the cases of Nie Shubin[3] and She Xianglin,[4] for instance, all involved police torturing the defendants during interrogation, and some police officers were awarded for solving such difficult cases, while none received punishment until the wrongful convictions were eventually revoked.

That said, Article 32 of CPL1979 was nevertheless a remarkable milestone in China's progress toward abolishment of torture and introduction of exclusionary rules into its criminal procedure. CPL1979 was promulgated in the wake of the Cultural Revolution, a 10-year catastrophe that destroyed all legal institutions and resulted in hundreds of thousands of torture actions and unknown numbers of wrongful convictions and even executions. The minister and all his eight deputies of the Ministry of Public Security (MPS), China's police force, for instance, were all jailed and some were subject to torture when the Cultural Revolution began. When the National People's Congress (NPC) were debating CPL1979 and the Criminal Code, some delegates from the police department actually were against the ban on torture, claiming it would hinder the police from effectively fulfilling its duty to combat crimes.[5] Indeed that by the time of 1979, Chinese police force was in tremendous shortage of financial, technical and personnel support, and quite many police officers in the rank and file mainly relied on interrogation, and sometimes even torture, to investigate crimes. It was under such circumstances that Article 32 of CPL1979 was introduced, banning police torture but saying nothing about excluding evidence from torture or other police wrongdoings. It might look more like a toothless manifesto, but it well served a troubled country that was healing from a 10-year long catastrophe and desperately needed effective policing from an unqualified police force. Moreover, Article 32 of CPL1979 was not always toothless, as it could be, and sometimes have been, effectuated with combination of

[3]Mr. Nie Shubin was charged of raping and strangling a female worker in the farm near his house. He was convicted and executed in 1995, after making over a dozen of inconsistent confessions to the police through suspicious interrogations. In 2005, a career murderer was accidentally arrested by the police and confessed to the raping and murder of which Mr. Nie previously was convicted. Mr. Nie was finally exonerated in 2016. No police officer took responsibility for Mr. Nie's wrongful conviction and execution.

[4]Mr. She Xianglin was charged of murdering his wife after a quarrel, and a body claimed by the police to be his wife was discovered one month later in a nearby water pond. After a sleepless 5-day interrogation with brutal torture, Mr. She confessed to the murder and was later sentenced to 15 years in imprisonment. After serving almost 11 years of his term, his wife mysteriously came back in 2005. One police officer involved in Mr. She's investigation committed suicide after the exoneration trial, while no other officers were punished.

[5]PENG Zhen, 1979 at 2.

Article 136 of the 1979 Criminal Code to punish certain forms of torture.[6] In other words, in addition to demonstrating the legislators' explicit ban of torture, Article 32 of CPL1979 might still have imposed some real deterrence effect upon police investigation, but largely by punishing or even convicting a few abusive police officers, instead of by excluding illegal evidence.

However, tolerating police wrongdoings in practice may become addictive, as some police officers stop taking Article 32 of CPL1979 seriously and hesitate to explore non-coercive ways of criminal investigation, without which the legislature may never be ready to really ban torture and other illegal but effective means of evidence collecting. That kind of addiction was witnessed in 1996, when the NPC amended CPL1979 for the first time. Although many clauses of CPL1979 were revised, Article 32 remained intact. In fact, from 1979 to the beginning of the 21st century, another 30 years have passed since China wrote into its national law to ban torture for the first time, no more provision regarding excluding illegally obtained evidence has been added to any national laws. Only the Supreme People's Court (SPC) and the Supreme People's Procuratorate (SPP) issued two separate judicial interpretations in 1998 and 1999 and prescribed that all confessions or witness testimony obtained through torture, threat, inducement or deception shall not be used when prosecuting or convicting the defendant.[7] Despite never adopted by national laws, the promises in these two judicial interpretations looked quite encouraging, in fact over-progressive even by today's standards, but neither the SPC nor the SPP further explained how such broad and ambiguous exclusionary rules should be implemented. Understandably, they would not, and largely could not be taken seriously in practice. Our research found no single case ended up in excluding illegal evidence under these two judicial interpretations. Not surprisingly, quite a few wrongful convictions still surfaced after 1996, including the cases of Zhao Zuohai[8] and Du Peiwu,[9] both of which involved obvious police brutality. In the Du Peiwu case, in particular, the defendant was in fact able to present a

[6]Although art. 136 of the 1979 Criminal Code seemed to criminalize all forms of torture, regardless severity or consequences, the SPP made it clear in a 1999 judicial interpretation that only those resulted in suicide or mental disorder of the victim, or causing wrongful convictions or other severe consequences should be prosecuted.

[7]*See* art. 61 of SPC's Interpretations regarding Multiple Issues in Applying Criminal Procedure Law (1998-23), and art. 265 of SPP's Rules of Criminal Procedure by the People's Procuratorates (1999-1).

[8]Very much similar to Mr. She's destiny, Mr. Zhao was charged of murdering one of his neighbors after a headless body was discovered and identified as Mr. Zhao's neighbor. He confessed to the police after a lengthy and coercive interrogation, and only regained his freedom 11 years later after the so-called victim came back alive.

[9]Mr. Du was a police officer and was charged of murdering his wife and her underground lover, both were also police officers and were shot in their car parking at a suburb park. Mr. Du confessed to the two murders after 11 days of torture, and was sentenced to death in the first instance trial. Several months after the appellate court commuted Mr. Du's sentence, the police arrested a serial killer by accident and the gun which was used to shoot the two victims was discovered in his possession.

bloodstained shirt to prove the torture to the judges, but the trial court only turned a blind eye and never bothered to mention the shirt in its verdict and sentenced Mr. Du to death.[10] The prohibition of illegal evidence in both CPL1979 and CPL1996, in this regard, seemed nothing more than a toothless manifesto and never meant to take effect in practice.

1.2 Development Stage: 2010 to Date

Despite CPL1996's inaction regarding excluding illegal evidence, quite many Chinese legal scholars and respected press kept pushing for legislative changes and calling for adoption of genuine exclusionary rules. The Internet has helped tremendously with enhancing such voice and spreading the idea of procedural fairness, as well as circulating scandals of police brutality. Quite surprisingly but understandably, after at least two decades of academic discussions and appeals, but almost suddenly from the year of 2010, probably due to the public outrage resulting from the surfacing of Mr. Zhao Zuohai's wrongful conviction and exoneration in that year, a flood of national legislations and policies regarding excluding illegally obtained evidence emerged in China and eventually pushed the practice into an unprecedented level.

(a) In 2010, the SPC, SPP, MPS, the Ministry of State Security (MSS) and the Ministry of Justice (MOJ) issued a joint regulation (JR2010) regarding excluding illegally obtained evidence in criminal procedure. This was the first time in the history of China's criminal procedure that the highest judicial authorities collectively proclaimed that illegally obtained evidence would be excluded from consideration of the court. Article 1 of JR2010 prescribed that "confessions of the suspect/defendant obtained by torture or other illegal means, as well as witness testimony or victim statements obtained by violence or threat are illegal testimonial evidence." No doubt that Article 1 alone looks similar to Article 32 of CPL1979, but Article 2 of JR2010 reads that "once such testimonial evidence has been confirmed illegal, it shall be excluded from being the foundation of judicial decisions." What makes JR2010 more important in legal history is the provision that once the defendant claims that his pretrial confessions were obtained illegally and successfully raises some doubt in the minds of the judges, the court shall order the prosecution to disprove that claim with sufficient evidence, otherwise the court shall exclude the confessions from consideration. In other words, when the legality of the procedure of obtaining pretrial confessions is under dispute, the burden of proof is on the prosecution side, although the defendant shall provide clues regarding

[10]The appellate court, citing "particular circumstances" of the case and "agreeable arguments" by the defense, commuted Mr. Du's death sentence to suspended death, indicating that the judges in fact believed the existence of torture during police investigation.

when, where, how and who violated his rights. Many observers argue that this joint regulation is a remarkable breakthrough in China's judicial history, as for the first time not only tortured confession will be excluded, but also the defendant will not have to prove the torture, which in most cases is beyond the capability of the defense.

(b) In 2012, the Criminal Procedure Law was once again thoroughly revised by the NPC. A total number of five articles regarding exclusion of illegal evidence were added to this CPL2012. In general, all major provisions in JR2010 were adopted by the NPC, and for the first time, Article 54 of CPL2012 stated that the exclusionary rules apply to both testimonial and tangible evidence. However, not all tangible evidence obtained in violation of law is automatically excludable; instead, the court shall first look into how serious the violation will damage "judicial fairness," and whether such violation can be corrected or reasonably explained. Only those disputed tangible evidence that damages judicial fairness to a great extent and is not correctable or explainable shall result in exclusion.

(c) Following the promulgating of CPL2012, a serial of interpretations was issued by the SPC, SPP and MPS in late 2012, all adding details as to how to define illegal evidence and how to exclude illegally obtained evidence in judicial practice. The SPC specifically defined torture as "corporal punishment or disguised corporal punishment," and "other illegal means" as "measures that result in severe physical or mental pain or suffering and forcing the defendant to confess involuntarily" (Article 95 of SPC interpretation2012). Similarly, the SPP defined torture as "corporal or disguised corporal punishment that inflict severe physical or mental pain or suffering on the suspect," and "other illegal means" as "any measure that violates the law or coerces the suspect to a degree equal to torture, violence or threat" (Article 65 of SPP interpretation2012). SPP also defines the phrase of "damaging judicial fairness" when the legality of tangible evidence is in dispute. It provides that if tangible evidence is obtained by blatant violation of prescribed procedure, and may severely damage the fairness of judicial process, it shall be excluded unless the procedural violation is immaterial, correctable or can be logically and reasonably explained.

(d) In 2013, the Central Political and Legal Committee (CPLC) of the Chinese Communist Party (CCP) issued a resolution tackling wrongful convictions, reiterating the principle of excluding illegally obtained testimonial evidence. Although the words read almost the same as CPL2012, the uniqueness of this resolution comes from its issuing body, the highest political apparatus within the CCP coordinating judicial affairs among the courts, procuratorates, police and lawyers. It reflects the will of the ruling party, not only that of the legislature or the judiciary, so that it would certainly be better implemented in practice. Similarly, when the fourth Plenary Session of the 18th CCP Central Committee stated similar requirement in its official report in 2014, the will of the Communist Party to tackle wrongful convictions through excluding illegal evidence became unprecedentedly obvious and straightforward.

(e) In 2016, the SPC, SPP, MPS, MSS, and MOJ promulgated a joint opinion to promote a trial-centered criminal procedure, requiring courts exclude evidence which was obtained in violation of existing laws. It appears that the central judicial authorities believe that only when the court is able to exclude illegally obtained evidence, even against protest of the prosecution or the police, that the trial can be considered the core of the criminal process.

(f) In April, 2017, the Central Task Force of Deepening Reforms (CTDR), the de facto highest decision-making body with President Xi Jingping as the head and a few top leaders as its members, unexpectedly issued a decree demanding strict exclusion of illegally obtained evidence in criminal procedure. This was encouraging for many of China's legal academia and practitioners, as very rarely the country's highest decision-making-body and top leaders have discussed criminal justice institutions, not mention such specific ones. Nevertheless, this unprecedented move by President Xi and his colleagues also indicated that exclusion of illegally obtained evidence is more difficult to carry out in practice than many have expected, therefore the direct involvement of the supreme leaders is warranted. Two months after the CTDR meeting, the SPC, SPP, MPS, MSS and MOJ promulgated another joint regulation (JR2017) emphasizing the exclusion of illegally obtained evidence. In this long-expected regulation, the five central judicial authorities stipulated that confessions obtained by threats of using violence or harming the suspect's or his families' lawful rights, as well as through illegal deprivation of the suspect's personal freedom shall all be excluded. In addition, once certain confession is deemed illegally obtained, any following confessions obtained under the influence of the previous illegal one shall also be excluded. Despite of these progresses, many observers were still disappointed by the fact that prolonged deprivation of sleep, as well as using of deception and inducement, are not explicitly considered illegal means of obtaining confessions by JR2017. That said, since JR2017 was only issued a few months ago and has yet been widely employed, it remains unclear how it would be implemented in practice.

1.3 Observations of the Development of Legislations

The development of China's legislations regarding exclusion of illegally obtained evidence from 1979 to 2017 results in the gradual institutionalization and localization of this important universal principle. CPL1979, emerging in wake of the catastrophic Cultural Revolution, illegalized torture and other coercive measures of obtaining evidence, but failed to clarify whether evidence obtained with such illegal measures should be excluded. As a result, although police wrongdoings were occasionally punished in accordance with CPL1979 and a corresponding article in the Criminal Code, no example of exclusion of illegally obtained evidence had been witnessed before the year of 2010, when the central judicial authorities issued the first joint regulation (JR2010) to tackle illegal evidence. Further legislations and policies, including the 2012 amendment to the CPL (CPL2012), the 2017 decree from the de facto highest decision-making-body, CTDR, as well as JR2017, all added details as to what evidence shall be considered illegal and how such evidence shall be excluded from criminal proceedings. In the end, the once empty promise of CPL1979 gradually gained practicability and enforceability.

Legal institutions do not grow by themselves. They are the result of the expansion of the general idea of rule of law and human rights protection, as well as the gradually increasing acceptance by the decision-makers and the public of procedural fairness, even with the cost of jeopardizing crime control. The accidental but inevitable emergence of wrongful convictions or even wrongful executions of innocent people in recent decades, combined with the exposure of police brutality and blatant violation of prescribed procedure, fueled by the powerful circulation of the Internet and social media, successfully sowed the seeds of human rights protection and procedural fairness in the minds of the public, and also forced the authorities, both judicial and political ones included, to tackle police wrongdoings in the criminal justice system. The concentration of legislations and policies after the year of 2010 regarding exclusion of illegally obtained evidence, was therefore a natural or even inevitable outcome of this combination of public opinion and government endeavors.

It is worth noting that China's legal scholars also contributed significantly to the introduction and development of exclusionary rules. Particularly in the wake of the 21st century, faced by repeated emergence of wrongful convictions and police brutality, many criminal procedure scholars have continuously argued for the legislation and implementation of exclusionary rules. Some also conduct pilot experiments to test how such rules shall be carried out in practice and whether the mission of tackling crime would be jeopardized as a cost of excluding illegally obtained evidence. Many journal articles and books on this matter have been published, and many scholars have spoken out in the press to promote exclusionary rules. It is fair to say that the academia has always been a major driving force, although not the decisive one, for the development of exclusionary rules in China.

2 Empirical Analysis of China's Exclusionary Rules: Are They Effectively Implemented in Practice?

Concerning the tortuous legislative history of China's exclusionary rules, one can almost be certain to predict that the implementation of such rules in practice is never a smooth task. On the one hand, almost every legal system, code law countries in particular, have repeatedly witnessed the wide gap between the law in books and the law in action. On the other hand, as China's exclusionary rules only started to take shape in the 21st century and was first written in the CPL as late as in 2012, it may be too soon to conclude how they are implemented in practice at this point.

That said, some general trends are ready for observation, which may help us evaluate the implementation of China's exclusionary rules, and predict how this universally important institution would develop in the future.

Empirical statistics regarding exclusion of illegal evidence are rare to see, due to both the short time since the emergence of the exclusionary rules and the government's reluctance to publish such information. The Supreme People's Court (SPC), however, did publish one set of simple numbers regarding how the exclusionary rules are implemented in practice. Earlier in 2017, with the purpose of promoting the use of big-data in the court system, one Associate Chief Justice of the SPC told the public that from 2014 to 2016, within 3 years, a total number of 2,765 cases involved exclusion of illegal evidence. This is not a very encouraging number, particularly if the total number of all criminal cases, over 3,238,000 during these 3 years, is taken into comparison. In fact, this number is only a little higher than the number of acquittals, which is, surprisingly but consistently, as few as 1,841 cases through all the 3 years. The statistics indicate that very likely the exclusionary rules are not effectively implemented all across China, at least not as satisfactorily as many have expected.

To better understand the implementation of exclusionary rules in China, we studied a pilot program in the western city of Chengdu from February 2015 to December 2016. The pilot program was designed under the broader reform called "trial-centered criminal procedure reform", aiming to reposition the trial as the core and decision-making stage of all criminal proceedings. Alternatively, this reform is also phrased as "substantializing criminal trial," indicating that previous trials are largely superficial. The titles also reflect that previous cases are often determined by police investigation, and the prosecution and the court are more like rubber stamps to confirm what the police claim, without imposing effective checks upon police wrongdoings. Such practice is popularly referred to as "investigation-centered criminal procedure," or "case-file-centered criminal procedure," as the prosecution and the court basically operate along with the case-file provided by the police, and in-court testifying of witnesses is rare to see in practice.[11] In this program, 454 criminal cases were selected as experiment samples to be tried in the "trial-centered" way or in a "substantialized trial," while 336 cases were selected as control samples to be tried in the traditional manner. None of the sample cases were tried in summary procedure, which means that these cases either involved material factual or legal disputes or carried potential sentence of life imprisonment or death penalty.[12] We also make use of another empirical study we conducted in 2013, one year after CPL2012 took effect. In that study, four courts in the same city of Chengdu were examined, including S Court at the provincial level, A Court at the

[11]ZUO Weimin, 2007 at 101.

[12]Art. 208 and 209 of CPL2012 provide that in basic courts, once a case involves no material factual disputes, nor it involves major social impact or mentally or physically retarded defendants, the court can try the case in a summary manner, which means the trial can be concluded in a few minutes.

intermediate level, B Court at the urban grassroots level and C Court at the rural grassroots level. In addition, we interviewed some judges in the sample courts to verify or supplement our data. Below are some of our findings.

2.1 *Overall Trend: From "Extremely Cold" to "Modestly Warm"*

An experienced observer may infer from the repetitive legislations regarding excluding illegal evidence that the rules are not implemented well in practice, otherwise the legislators do not have to promulgate new laws with similar provisions again and again. Statistics reveal that in the "substantialized trials," 97 (or 21.37%) out of all 454 experiment cases involved at least one defendant requesting exclusion of illegal evidence, while in the 336 control cases tried in traditional manner, only 15 cases (or 4.46%) encountered such application. No doubt that these numbers seem very high, or probably excessively high, particularly for the experiment group. One critical explanation is that the majority of all criminal cases were in fact excluded from this program, as they involved no material disputes and the defendants all confessed to the charged crime. If we count in those undisputed cases that were tried with summary procedure, the percentage of defendants applying for exclusion of illegal evidence immediately dropped drastically. Figure 1 and Table 1 show a previous empirical study we conducted back in 2013 in four courts of the same city.

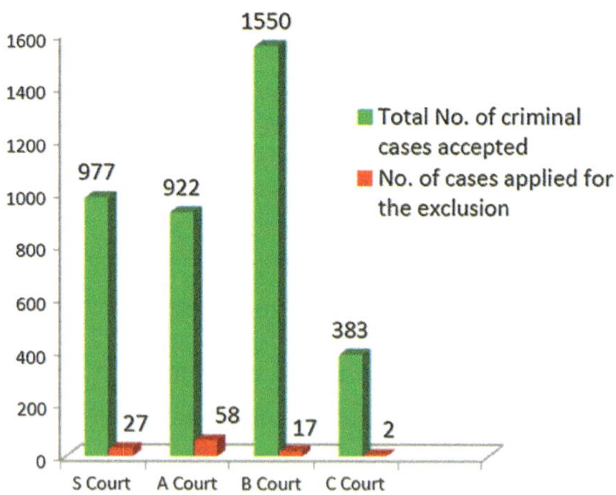

Fig. 1 Summary of cases with application by the defendant for exclusion of illegal evidence in the four sample courts (2013) (It should be noted that in Fig. 1, the number of cases in A Court was 468 in first instance of trial and 454 in second instance; while S Court did not handle criminal cases of first instance (n = 0), therefore, the number of cases handled in fact was the number of those in second instance)

Table 1 Radio of cases with application for exclusion of illegal evidence in the four sample courts (2013)

Content\court	S Court (%)	A Court (%)	B Court(%)	C Court(%)
% of cases without application for exclusion	97.2	93.7	98.9	99.5
% of cases with application for exclusion	2.8	6.3	1.1	0.50

Combining the two sets of statistics, we can conclude that although the overall numbers of cases involving application of exclusion of illegal evidence are still low, the exclusionary rules are taking up momentum in disputed cases, particularly in those selected by the court to test a new style of substantialized trial. Indeed, prior to the 2010 joint regulation of excluding illegal evidence, the environment for application for excluding illegal evidence was so cold that we barely witnessed any examples, but the introduction of new laws and policies have heated up the environment and more and more applications for excluding illegal evidence are emerging in practice. In other words, we can at least conclude that the atmosphere of excluding illegal evidence has progressed from "extremely cold" to "modestly warm".

One may ask why the substantialized trials saw much more applications of exclusion of illegal evidence. The answers are four-folded, although all rest on the fundamental objective that the trial itself, not the police investigation or the prosecution, shall be the core of the entire criminal procedure and the incubator of the final decision. First, the participation of defense lawyers, either hired by the defendant or appointed by the court, is required in all substantialized trials, which enables the defense to pinpoint illegal evidence and launch persuasive applications for exclusion. Second, a special mechanism is designed to accommodate filing motions for exclusion of illegal evidence in pretrial conferences and debating for suppression in a built-in hearing at the beginning of the trial. The implementation of exclusionary rules thus becomes a mini-trial within the regular trial, forcing the court and the prosecution to respond to claims of the defense regarding illegal evidence. Third, when debating the lawfulness of evidence gathering process, the prosecution is often required to present the audio/video recording of pretrial interrogations, and police officers conducting the investigations, including the interrogators, are all subject to summon by the court to testify in person, which may have given significant confidence and incentives to the defense for bringing about allegations of illegal evidence. Forth, a substantialized trial means that the collegial panel sitting on the bench is indeed the sole decision-making body of the case, and its decision often comes right after the conclusion of the trial and the completion of the deliberation among the members of the panel. As a result, the final verdict of the court is more likely to be shaped by the trial, and the defendant and his lawyer stand a better chance to influence the decision-makers through in-court activities, which encourages them to retract pretrial confessions on the ground of torture or other illegal means. In short, the reform of substantializing criminal trials paves way for exclusion of illegal evidence, and in return, the exclusion of illegal evidence by judges demonstrates that the trial is indeed a substantive incubator for court verdicts, not a rubber stamp to confirm what the police and prosecutors allege.

2.2 *Defendants Increasingly Apply for Exclusion of Illegal Evidence, and Chances of Success Are Low but Growing*

True that almost in all countries with exclusionary rules in their criminal procedure, defendants and defense lawyers apply for exclusion in quite many cases, but quite rarely the court grants suppression of illegally obtained evidence. In the 454 experiment cases of 2015 and 2016, 97 cases (21.37%) involved at least one defendant applying for exclusion of illegal evidence, among which 66 cases (68.04% of all applications, or 14.54% of all cases) ended up in refusal by the court, while only 12 cases (12.37% of all applications, or 2.64% of all cases) were accepted in entirety, and another 18 cases (18.56% of all applications, or 3.96% of all cases) received partial acceptance. In the control group, 8 of all the 15 applications (2.38% of the total number of sample cases) were rejected by the court, and the other 7 cases (or 2.08%) received partial acceptance. Similarly, as revealed by Table 2, in our 2013 study, only 9.6% of all applications of exclusion of illegal evidence succeeded, which counted 0.3% of all criminal cases heard by the sample courts.

It seems that in substantialized trials, the defense was not only more willing to apply for exclusion of illegal evidence, they also stand a relatively better chance (2.64% + 3.96% = 6.6%) than in a traditional trial (2.08%) to win a favorable decision from the court. Nevertheless, even excluding those substantialized trials, defendants in 2015 and 2016 had over 7 times more chances to exclude illegal evidence than those in 2013 (2.08% versus 0.3%). In other words, the exclusionary rules steadily gain popularity and effectiveness after it was written into CPL2012. Not only more defendants are inclined to utilize the rules, but also more courts are willing to realize their promise.

Table 2 Ratio of cases with exclusion of illegal evidence in the four sample courts (2013)

Courts	% of cases with exclusion in all criminal cases	% of applications for exclusion succeeded
S Court	0.2	7.4
A Court	0.7	12.1
B Court	0.06	41.2
C Court	0	0
Total	0.3	9.6

2.3 Courts Excluded Much More Testimonial Evidence Than Tangible Evidence

Among those 454 experiment cases tried in a substantialized manner, 30 cases (or 6.6%) resulted in exclusion of all or some of the disputed evidence. 5 exclusions involved tangible evidence, while all the rest only dealt with testimonial evidence, particularly confessions of the defendants. This disparity also exists in the applications for exclusions of illegal evidence. Among the 97 applications, 62 cases (or 63.92%) requested for exclusion of pretrial confessions by the defendants. 23 (or 23.71%) targeted pretrial witness testimony or victim statements. Only 12 applications (or 12.37%) asked the court to quash tangible evidence. Interestingly, no expert testimony was disputed to the extent warranting an exclusion application. In one word, both the parties and the court prefer challenging testimonial evidence, while tangible evidence is less frequently disputed.

As mentioned above, CPL2012 prescribed that when judicial fairness is severely jeopardized by violation of established procedure in the process of obtaining tangible evidence, and the damages are not correctable or reasonably explainable, the court shall suppress the evidence as well. In practice, however, not very often that the defense is able to launch such an application, and even less often that the court will grant exclusion. The main reason is two-folded: one is that Chinese police are widely permitted to conduct warrantless searches and seizures, and two is that China lacks a rigid requirement of chain of custody for tangible evidence. As a result, not very likely the obtaining of tangible evidence would fall into the gap of violating prescribed procedure and severely damaging judicial fairness. On the contrary, due to the lack of the right to silence and the right to counsel during interrogation, criminal suspects are routinely subject to police interrogation, sometimes coercive or even violent in nature, in almost all cases, and the majority confess to the police at very early stage. When their cases finally reach the court and face eminent conviction and punishment, some defendants are often desperate to plea for suppression of pretrial confessions, as this may be their last savior.

It is worth noting that compared with suppressing tangible evidence, judges are more comfortable with excluding confessions. After all, illegally obtained confessions often involve significant possibility of falseness, while tangible evidence collected in violation of prescribed procedure runs little risk of telling a lie. In addition, untrustworthy confessions are rectifiable, for instance, by questioning the defendant again in the open court, without using any coercion or threat, but obtaining tangible evidence is usually a one-shot game, bearing little likelihood of redoing. As a result, judges exclude more confessions than tangible evidence.

The most recent regulation regarding exclusion of illegal evidence, JR2017, issued by the five judicial authorities of the central government, prescribed that not only confessions obtained by torture, but also following confessions obtained under the influence of the previous tortured confession, shall both be excluded. In addition, threats of using violence or harming the suspect's or his families' lawful rights, as well as illegal deprivation of personal freedom, are all prohibited in police interrogation, and could also result in exclusion of the confessions so obtained. In this regard, one can easily predict that as JR2017 being implemented in practice, more applications for quashing testimonial evidence will emerge and the court will exclude more of such testimonial evidence.

2.4 Most Defendants Prefer Challenging Illegal Evidence Only at the Trial Stage

Although both CPL2012 and JR2017 state that not only the court, but also the police and prosecution are obliged to exclude illegal evidence, real exclusions seldom occur in the investigation and prosecution stages, and most exclusions are effectuated by the court. In fact, in our statistics no single evidence was excluded by the police or prosecutors. It is true that only the court publishes its opinions, thus even if some exclusions occur in earlier stages, there would be no official record available to the public. Our interview with prosecutors and police officers revealed that occasionally and increasingly, the prosecution also excludes illegal evidence, and sometimes such exclusion would result in the dismissal of criminal charges. Nevertheless, due to the fact that most defendants only hire their lawyers in the trial stage, and that most lawyers still prefer fighting the prosecutors in the courtroom (including pretrial conferences), implementation of the exclusionary rules in pre-trial stages is still rare.

2.5 Few but Increasing Numbers of Exclusions of Illegal Evidence Impact Case Outcomes

It is true that the life of exclusionary rules depends on its deterrence effect upon police wrongdoings, not on benefitting the accused. However, if exclusion of illegally obtained evidence only leads to taking away some evidence from the prosecution's case file, without significantly weakening or jeopardizing its case, very likely the police and prosecution may not feel deterred. In this regard, effective exclusionary rules often mean not only suppressing some evidence, but also forcing out some charges or even the entire case. Without the latter effect, the exclusionary rules are nothing more than a beautiful but useless show.

Among the 30 experiment cases tried in a substantialized manner and involved actual exclusion of prosecution evidence in 2015 and 2016, 4 cases (or 13.33%) were reported to have major impact upon conviction and sentencing, 17 cases (or 56.67%) left some impact, while 9 cases (or 30%) did not change anything about conviction or sentencing. However, the courts did not illustrate what constitutes major or minor impacts. One thing for sure is that no case resulted in acquittal, although some cases ended up in the prosecution's partial withdrew of charges.

Our fieldwork in 2013 collected 10 cases with actual exclusion of prosecution evidence, none of which changed the conviction. 8 of the 10 cases involved exclusion of the defendants' pretrial confessions, but the remaining confessions and other evidence still support a conviction. 2 of the 10 cases excluded expert opinions, and the prosecution simply provided another expert opinion to support the same conclusion.

The disparity between the numbers of excluding illegal evidence and the numbers of changing case outcomes indicates that when judges ponder over whether to exclude certain evidence, they often have the final verdict in mind. For instance, several judges frankly admitted in our interview that their decision of excluding illegal evidence mainly depends on "whether or not the exclusion will cause any effect on the conviction and sentencing."[13] In other words, whether the evidence is indeed illegally obtained is not the key factor dictating the application of the exclusionary rules. Judges care more about the final outcome of the case, particularly whether the defendant will still be convicted given the disputed evidence being excluded. One judge even stated to us in the interview that "we only decide to exclude certain illegal evidence on the condition that other evidence (especially repeated statements) can support the conviction and sentencing, while we will be very careful and generally will not exclude such illegal evidence when it may affect the case and cannot be regenerated in nature."

As mentioned above, more often pretrial confessions of the defendant are to be excluded in practice, usually on the basis of using torture or other means of coercive interrogations. As direct evidence to inculpate the defendant, pretrial confessions are often the key to convict the defendant. With such critical evidence being excluded, how does the prosecution rebuilt its case and secure a conviction? More importantly, if the court only intends to exclude the coerced confessions but determines to convict the defendant anyway, how does it justify its decisions in a written opinion that will be open to the public? One way is to rely on circumstantial evidence to build a "chain of evidence" capable of supporting a conviction, which is quite rare in practice. The other way is to rely on repeated confessions of the defendant, including both in-court ones and pretrial ones. JR2017 provides that repeated confessions obtained under the influence of previous tortured confession are inadmissible, but if the repeated confessions are obtained by different interrogators or at different stages, and the defendant has been informed of his rights and consequences of confessing, they shall be admissible. As a result, when judges decide to exclude certain pretrial confessions of the defendant, they can still rely on his later confessions made to different interrogators to convict him. The exclusion looks more like an empty check to the defendant, as it brings in nothing but false hope. What's worse, once the police learnt the trick, they may easily modify their interrogation tactics and change interrogators after torturing the suspect, so that later confessions of the suspect are still admissible and capable of ensuring a conviction in the court. In this regard, the effectiveness of the exclusionary rules depends on

[13]*See, e.g.*, interviews with Judge Q in S Court; Judge L in B Court; Judge Z in C Court.

the skillfulness of police wrongdoings and willingness of judges to look beyond the text of the rules into the true nature of police interrogations, which is, at least in most cases too demanding.

However, if the exclusion of illegal evidence has potential major impact on the conviction or sentencing, judges often prefer delaying the case for some time and request the prosecution to submit supplemental evidence to replace the excluded evidence. After all, acquitting a defendant usually means a slap in the face of the prosecution, which will not only result in the embarrassment of the prosecutor and his department, but also bring in fierce counter-attack from the prosecution in some cases. As comrades of the same battlefield to combat crimes, judges often feel reluctant to force fellow prosecutors into such a difficult position. Instead, if judges really believe that a defendant shall be acquitted as a result of excluding illegal evidence, they often will ask the prosecution to withdraw the case to avoid an acquittal. It is true that our research did not find any of such withdrawals arising from the exclusion of illegal evidence, but our experiences and observations tell us that this is often how the court and prosecution deal with substantively not-guilty cases.

3 What Causes the Gap Between Exclusionary Rules in the Books and in the Action?

Above empirical studies reveal a huge gap between legislation and practice of exclusion of illegal evidence. The legislature has been busy writing laws and policies to realize excluding illegally obtained evidence, but the judges move much slower, particularly before the reform of substantializing criminal trials. Lawyers are enthusiastic to utilize the exclusionary rules to vigorously defend their clients, while judges are reluctant to suppress the prosecution's evidence, not mention throwing out the charges. Generally speaking, despite being loudly promoted by the legislature, the academia and defense lawyers, exclusion of illegal evidence is still rare in practice, and no sign of drastic increase is seen in the near future. In other words, the gap between legislative promises and judicial practice will continue to exist for a long time, probably much longer than we have expected. Two questions worth asking are: what are the causes of such a gap? And what will be its future?

3.1 Police Wrongdoings Are Not Routine in China

The number one explanation for these surprising phenomena is that lawfully obtaining evidence is the main stream of China's criminal procedure, while torture, threat, deception or other illegal measures are indeed exceptions, although not entirely in absence. Specifically, critical evidence in most cases, such as the confession of the suspects, or the drug or gun in possession of the suspect, are often obtained in accordance with the law and related regulations. This trend becomes more obvious in recent years, as criminal investigation and evidence gathering become more institutionalized and standardized, and more technical and financial support is provided to assist police investigation. For instance, within the past few years, the Ministry of Public Security completed a historic task to install cameras and other recording equipment in all interrogation rooms of every police station within China, which, combined with the new provision in CPL2012 that all but exceptionally emergent interrogations shall only take place in such interrogation rooms, significantly reduced the number of tortures in the grass level, as stipulated by many practitioners and observers. In fact, allegations of police torture are in sharp decrease in the courtrooms, although many defendants still claim deprivation of sleep in police interrogations.

Comparative studies reveal that in all mainstream legal systems of the entire world, excluding illegally obtained evidence has always been exceptions, instead of routine practice. China may have lagged in the history, but after over two decades of reforms toward rule of law, it has improved its record in protecting human rights and gradually catching up with mainstream countries. The exclusionary rule is more of a weapon for deterrence, instead of for real punishment.[14] It matters as it exists and can be utilized if necessary, not as it takes effects in as many real cases as possible. In this regard, the gap between legislative promises and judicial practice regarding China's exclusionary rules is indeed quite normal, and shall persist in the foreseeable future as well.

3.2 *Discord Between Chinese Culture and Implanted Institutions*

Exclusionary rules are basically implanted institutions in China. Many legal implantations fail, largely due to the fact that translating the text of legal rules alone does not guarantee a successful implantation. Legal rules are embedded deeply in a given society, reflecting its history, culture, economy and power structure. Planting the same rules in another jurisdiction of different settings runs a considerable risk of collision and rejection. Certainly, the government can write certain foreign rules into local laws, but whether such rules can be effectively implemented in practice depends on the degree of compatibility between the translated rules and local conditions. As soon as exclusionary rules are concerned, despite the many similarities between China and the West, we have also seen quite a few discords, which may help explain the gap between legislative promises and judicial practice discussed above.

---

[14]*See, e.g.*, *United States* v. *Leon*, 468 US 897, 916 (1984) ("[T]he exclusionary rule is designed to deter police misconduct …"); *Elkins* v. *United States*, 364 US 206, 217 (1960) ("The rule is calculated to prevent, not to repair. Its purpose is to deter—to compel respect for the constitutional guaranty in the only effectively available way— by removing the incentive to disregard it.").

3.2.1 Trusting the Government Versus Guarding Against the Government

The logic of excluding illegal evidence is essentially a tradeoff between combatting crimes and tackling police wrongdoings. In the United States, for instance, where the exclusionary rules originated, a widely accepted idea is that compared to the crimes committed by individual citizens, the abuse of power by the government itself, particularly its armed apparatus, is way more dangerous and damaging, thus warrants more precautions. Accordingly, when a police officer violates the legal rights of a suspect and obtains sufficient evidence to convict him, it is more important to deter any further police wrongdoings than putting the criminal behind bars. It is upon such social, cultural and political consensus that the exclusion of illegally obtained evidence is acceptable, even if it means a true perpetrator who has been spotted and apprehended by the police must be set free.

The social consensus in China, however, is significantly different. The Chinese civilization has a long history of trusting the government, which is oftentimes referred to as the protector or guardian of the people, and government officials are sometimes called "parents-officials," meaning that they shall act for the best interest of the people, although sometimes it requires being tough. In some situations, as long as the government acts with right intention, even if what it does is indeed wrong, the people may nevertheless readily forgive it. Particularly, when it goes to the criminal justice system, average people are more willing to grant police officers as much flexibility and convenience as necessary to fight against criminals. Minor violation of laws and rights of the suspects are largely tolerated, if not awarded, as long as they catch the right person. In fact, many people believe that coercion and even violence is an indispensable component of criminal investigation and rehabilitation, just like a successful child often needs tough discipline of a "tiger mother." Excluding prosecution evidence due to police wrongdoings and consequently setting a known criminal free is hard to understand for many Chinese people. This explains, at least partially, why Chinese judges are reluctant to enforce the exclusionary rules and even if they do exclude some prosecution evidence as required by the law, very rarely they will acquit the defendant.

3.2.2 Substantive Truth Versus Procedural Fairness

Excluding illegally obtained evidence means that in some cases the substantive truth could be sacrificed, and a factually proven criminal could be set loose. As a trade-off, the integrity of the criminal procedure is preserved and enhanced. No surprise that the exclusionary rules were first articulated in the United States, where the principle of due process is the fundamental foundation of legal institutions and is widely accepted or even worshipped by the public. To some degree, due process of law has become an ideology of the United States, as well as in some other Western countries with mature rule of law. The public, the government and the judiciary often see no problem if the objective truth of an individual case must be compromised to maintain the fairness of judicial procedure. As Francis Bacon once said, "one foul sentence does more hurt than many foul examples. For these do but corrupt the stream;the other corrupt the fountain."[15]

The Chinese tradition, however, seems to value substantive truth more than procedural fairness. One widely circulated proverb reads "truth is beyond all." In Chinese legal history, as well as in contemporary legal fictions and movies, the best judges have always been those with exceptional skills to discover the truth while extending sympathy and kindness to those weak and suffering. Average Chinese people still believe that it is the responsibility of the court to probe into the confusing mist of evidence and ascertain the truth. In fact, back in the early 2000s, when the development of civil procedure required imposing the burden of proof on the parties, and judges began to refuse to conduct their own investigation outside of the courtroom and simply decide against the party who failed to fulfill his burden of proof, many people contended that the court was shifting its duty and was no longer a "People's court."

Understandably, the preference for substantive truth is often in conflict with the exclusionary rules. When tangible evidence is obtained in violation of law, for instance, it still possesses the same value of proving the case. A truth-minded tribunal may choose to admit the evidence and convict the defendant, while a fairness-minded tribunal is more likely to suppress the evidence and set the defendant free. Certainly, no system is that simple, and the exclusion of tangible evidence is often case-specific, requiring consideration of many conflicting values in each individual case. Nevertheless, the general preference of substantive truth or procedural fairness still makes huge difference.

3.2.3 Individual Rights Versus Public Interest

Excluding illegally obtained evidence means that in some cases public interest could be sacrificed to preserve personal rights. The deterrence effect of the exclusionary rules in fact rests on such a dilemma. Only when a police officer cares about failing to convict the suspect in the court, that he would choose to follow the rules and avoid violating the suspect's legal rights. Nevertheless, whenever a judge suppresses critical prosecution evidence and acquits a factually guilty defendant, he is also putting the public in danger. The logic seems to be that when a police officer makes mistakes, the public is paying for the costs. In a country where individual rights are upheld high, such a tradeoff may be acceptable. But in another jurisdiction that cherishes public security more than individual freedom, public resistance may become a major obstacle when introducing the exclusionary rules into the law.

The Chinese culture has a long history of preferring public interest to personal rights. Popular slogans of the Chinese society include "sacrifice personal interest and serve the many" and "collective interest out-values individual interest."

[15]Bacon, 1983 at 64.

In certain phrase of the history of the People's Republic of China, simply talking about personal interest was considered a shame. The transition from a planned economy to a market-oriented economy starting in the late 1970s drastically changed the social attitude, and pursuing of personal interest in current China is no longer a disgrace. Nevertheless, in public debates over major social policies, the traditional pro-public-interest discourse still returns frequently. Understandably, when it goes to whether a guilty criminal should be set free because of mistakes made by the police in gathering evidence, many would choose to protect public security and put the defendant in jail, probably with a lesser sentence.

4 The Future of China's Exclusionary Rules

4.1 Overall Assessment

Exclusion of illegally obtained evidence is basically new in China, particularly if China's 2,000+ years of legal history is taken into the calculation. Yet in only less than 40 years, China has inputted tremendous legislative efforts to implant and implement the rules of excluding illegal evidence, to the extent that even the de facto highest decision-making body and the most powerful state leaders of this mega country were directly involved in the legislative process. Certainly, progress in the books does not necessarily reflect the behavioral changes in the practice, but the continuous pushing from the legislators, academics and practicing lawyers, combined with the public outrage over surfaced wrongful convictions, will doubtlessly result in wider acceptance of the conception of excluding illegal evidence, and will eventually lead to better effectuation of the exclusionary rules. However, due to China's long history of prioritizing substantive truth and public interest against procedural fairness and individual rights, as well as the increasing crime rate China is facing, the exclusionary rules will not be as effective as expected.

That said, as China's legal culture and judicial practice transforms gradually, the exclusionary rules may become more prominent in the future. The last three decades have witnessed the growing acceptance of jeopardizing crime control to accommodate due process of law, not only within the academia and the legal circle, but also among the often more conservative general public and political circle. The Internet has played a remarkable role in this process, particularly by circulating scandals of wrongful convictions and stimulating discussions of procedural solutions. The introduction and rapid spreading of more advanced technologies of criminal investigation, including DNA testing and camera surveillance, have also helped reducing the demand for illegal means to obtain evidence. If we would to believe that exchange of information, especially that about scandalous government actions, will become freer and more convenient in the future, and that criminal investigation will more depend upon scientific and technical measures, we shall then believe that China's exclusionary rules will be better implemented in the future.

4.2 Short-Term and Long-Term Projections

In the short term, the development of China's exclusionary rules depends on the development of China's criminal procedure. For instance, earlier involvement of prosecutors in the process of criminal investigation will often improve the chance of convicting the suspect while deterring police wrongdoings. A trial-centered criminal procedure that produces a criminal verdict through an orally conducted trial is more likely to exclude previously transcribed confessions or witness testimony. Sending more lawyers to attend criminal trials and pushing for effective defense will generally result in more exclusions, too. Such procedural improvements can be largely accomplished by legislations at the national or local levels, and we can expect fast behavioral changes in the practice once such mechanisms are institutionalized.

In the long term, however, the future of China's exclusionary rules depends upon the transformation of China's legal culture. After all, exclusionary rules are basically a common law institution, and even in UK or US, they are not frequently applied in practice. Fewer applications can be found in continental countries in Europe. In this regard, the future of China's exclusionary rules eventually depends upon the degree of concord or discord between implanted institutions and local legal culture. Fortunately, the pursuits of procedural justice and personal rights in China have been rapidly growing for decades, and no sign has been confirmed that such pursuits would go into an end in the future. As a result, in the long run, public acceptance of exclusionary rules will be more satisfactory and implementation of such rules in practice will be easier and less costly.

References

Francis Bacon, 'Of Judicature', (1983) 9 *Litigation*, 64, 53–54 [Bacon, 1983].

彭真 (PENG Zhen): 在全国检察工作座谈会、全国高级人民法院和军事法院院长会议、第三次全国预审工作会议上的讲话 (Remarks at the National Conference of Prosecutorial Affairs, High Court Presidents, Military Court Presidents and the Third National Conference on Investigation Works), 人民司法 *(Renmin Sifa)*, 1979–10, 1–5 [PENG Zhen, 1979].

左卫民 (ZUO Weimin): 中国刑事案卷制度研究——以证据案卷为重心 (On the Criminal Dossiers System of China: Focusing on the Evidence Dossier),法学研究 *(Faxue Yanjiu)*, 2007–6, 94–114 [ZUO Weimin, 2007].

Weimin Zuo serves as the Dean of Sichuan University Law School and the Vice Chair of China Society of Criminal Procedure. He has published over 100 articles in major Chinese law journals, covering the topics of criminal procedure, judicial reform and dispute resolution. In recent years he has focused on empirical legal research and has led a number of projects investigating judicial practices in China.

Rongjie Lan received a Ph.D. in Law from Sichuan University in China and a SJD from Temple University in the USA. His research focuses on Chinese criminal procedure and evidence law, and he has published over two dozen articles and books in both Chinese and English. During his teaching, he also served as an adjunct judge and later an adjunct prosecutor.

Securing a Fair Trial Through Exclusionary Rules: Do Theory and Practice Form a Well-Balanced Whole?

Susanne Knickmeier

Abstract This chapter describes practitioners' understanding of excluding illegally obtained evidence. To gain deeper insight into the applicability of the exclusion of evidence obtained through illegal means and to evaluate regulations that have been implemented, fourteen experts from different legal professions (lawyers, judges, prosecutors) and countries (Germany, Singapore, Switzerland and Taiwan (ROC)) were interviewed about their experiences. All legal systems are faced with the use of illegally obtained evidence. Based on qualitatively analyzed data the frequency of the applicability of exclusionary rules, the types of cases in which they are seen, and experts' attitudes towards the function of exclusionary rules are described. Violations of rules around the gathering of evidence is a highly sensitive topic, particularly as the state (represented by police officers and prosecutors) plays a central and powerful role. To find out if exclusionary rules do indeed result in a more impartial trial or if further protective measures are required, factors influencing the procurement of evidence and the decision-making process around the legality of such procurement were evaluated. Subsequently, difficulties that law enforcement agencies and criminal courts are faced with were outlined, with an emphasis on the application of the law and the limitations in safeguarding criminal investigations and proceedings. Concluding remarks highlight best practices in securing a fair trial as well as ancillary measures (including unwritten techniques) that may be utilized to optimize the utility of exclusionary rules.

S. Knickmeier (✉)
Department of Criminology, Max Planck Institute for Foreign and International Criminal Law, Freiburg, Germany
e-mail: s.knickmeier@mpicc.de

S. Gless and T. Richter (eds.), *Do Exclusionary Rules Ensure a Fair Trial?*
Ius Gentium: Comparative Perspectives on Law and Justice 74,
https://doi.org/10.1007/978-3-030-12520-2_11

1 Theory and Practice

The project "Securing a fair trial through excluding evidence? A comparative perspective" fulfills the need to determine features of the criminal process that are conducive to enhancing respect for human rights in different legal and cultural environments. The legal situation is described in the country reports in the previous chapters. But how do exclusionary rules function in legal practice? Does practitioners' understanding of excluding illegally obtained evidences comply with the law? What are experts' experiences concerning the applicability and frequency of exclusionary rules in criminal proceedings? Are techniques of taking evidence that are forbidden really not used? How can violations be proved? Where do the experts identify gaps of protection, limitations of exclusionary rules and possible safeguards? Which potential alternatives and supplementary means of nudging law enforcement are identified? What ancillary measures (also not written ones) may be utilized to make exclusionary rules effective? To gain a deeper insight into the applicability of the exclusion of evidence obtained by illegal means and to evaluate implemented legal regulations, experts from different legal professions and countries were interviewed about their field experience.

2 Data Collection and Analysis

The aim of the interviews was mainly explorative and partly theoretical-based. Explorative interviews seek to get information about the research field, the experts' knowledge about their business as well as about their contextual knowledge.[1] Results from qualitative research based on a small number of interviews are not representative and do not allow for any generalization or statistical extrapolation.[2] Nevertheless, the results provide an insight into the application of exclusionary rules, the evaluation of existing measures, potential gaps of protection and alternative measures to secure a fair trial.

2.1 Collection of Data

The expert interviews were conducted using a qualitative interview guideline. Semi-structured interviews are appropriate to get open answers, to describe a problem and to access the implementation of legal regulations.[3] It is in the nature of things that for explorative aims, standardized questions could hardly be formulated.

[1]Bogner/Littig/Menz, 2014 at 23.

[2]Mayring, 2015 at 20.

[3]Mayring, 2015 at 23.

Guideline-based interviews enable the interviewer to encourage the expert to report complex issues and to cover different perspectives of the research question.[4] Therefore, the guideline included several questions to induce reporting, but also some hypothetical questions to explore the expert's attitude towards potential problems. The guideline also enabled the interviewer to follow a common thread of topics, which is important to analyze and compare the given information and perspectives.[5] The guideline also included some standardized detailed questions to ensure that certain questions were asked. If not discussed in the interview, these questions were then discussed at the end of the interview.

In the following study, fourteen interviews from Germany (5), Switzerland (2), Taiwan (ROC) (4) and Singapore (3) were included. The interviews were conducted in the years from 2015 to 2017. Depending on specific circumstances, interviews lasted between 27 and 80 min with an average duration of 48 min. The sample of experts covered all legal professions and included five judges, three prosecutors and three lawyers with long-term experience (at least five years) in the field of criminal law and criminal proceedings. (Police officers or police investigators were not questioned). Each professional group plays a special role within criminal proceedings and were able to describe the applicability of securing a fair trial from a different perspective. Several experts have worked in different legal professions, with professional experience as a prosecutor, judge or lawyer. The change of professional positions enabled the affected experts to obtain insights in different positions from different points of view, which made them valuable for explorative expert interviews. Experts were selected from European and Asian countries with different legal systems. Access to the sample of interviewees was possible due to personal contacts by the project team in Germany, Switzerland, Taiwan (ROC) and Singapore. The guideline-based interviews were conducted in German and English, the Taiwanese ones were partly discussed in Chinese and translated into English by a member of the project team familiar with the aims of the interviews. An extraordinary challenge occurred by conducting the interviews in different languages, particularly in interviews, in which neither the expert nor the interviewee were native speakers. To mitigate content-related problems due to language difficulties, the interviews were conducted by members of the project-team familiar with the legal situation in the expert's country and, if possible, with the expert's language.[6] The interviews were audio-recorded and transcribed. To ensure anonymity, interviews are cited by using the country and a number.

---

[4]Gläser/Laudel, 2010 at 116.

[5]Gläser/Laudel, 2010 at 116 and 145.

[6]Bogner/Littig/Menz, 2014 at 44 et seq.

2.2 Data Analysis

The collected data were analyzed by qualitative content analysis[7] with the aim to evaluate the legal implementation, to identify the legal reality and to examine motivations and best practices to secure a fair trial. A content analysis is a technique to analyze a document produced within a communication process through structuring and systematically analyzing the text on the basis of categories and adding explanations.[8] There are several approaches to conduct a qualitative content analysis, which cannot be discussed in this framework. Despite limitations, the qualitative content analysis was chosen as the method to analyze the interview data. It enables researchers to structure the interviews referring to the research questions, to structure the extracted data referring to an empirical and theoretical basis, to interpret them, but also to keep an open mind concerning information that was not expected before the data collection. After the content was structured on the basis of categories, the extracted text passages were either theory-based encoded and analysed or codes were developed on the basis of the extracted text passages. Categories included, for example: function of exclusionary rules, kinds of exclusionary rules, knowledge of illegally obtained evidence, awareness of exclusionary rules, motivation to obtain evidence legally and consequences for officers after the illegal obtainment of evidence. The categories and codes were developed on the basis of the theoretical framework (see below) and refer to the hypothesis that exclusionary rules secure a fair trial; this hypothesis was examined by several assumptions compiled from empirical and theoretical approaches. The leading questions were:

(1) The *function and role of exclusionary rules* within criminal proceedings: If exclusionary rules secure a fair trial, it is essential to get information about the frequency of their applicability, the kind of cases they cover and the experts' attitudes towards the function of exclusionary rules (Sect. 3.2).
(2) *Difficulties and limitations*: This part examines legal difficulties in applying exclusionary rules as well as limitations to obtaining evidence legally. To evaluate if exclusionary rules secure a fair trial or whether further protective measures are required, it was necessary to know which factors and decisions influence the procurement of admissible evidence (Sect. 3.3).
(3) *Compliance with rules to obtain evidence*: As norm compliance and prevention require awareness, the awareness for exclusionary rules in criminal proceedings was considered in a first step to evaluate compliance with exclusionary rules and rules to obtain evidence. Secondly, possible motivations for norm compliance in the field of obtaining evidence were discussed to examine which measures were suitable and effective to secure a fair trial, and whether,

---

[7]The German term "Inhaltsanalyse" was translated as "content analysis". It includes a qualitative text analysis without quantitative elements.

[8]Gläser/Laudel, 2010 at 197; Mayring, 2002 at 114 et seq.

for example, exclusionary rules could be strengthened through additional protective measures (Sect. 3.4).

3 Do Theory and Practice Form a Well-Balanced Whole?

In legal theory, exclusionary rules are implemented to secure a fair trial. But do theory and practice form a well-balanced whole? Do exclusionary rules secure a fair trial or is their applicability limited?

3.1 Theoretical Considerations

How can a fair trial be secured? In other words: which strategies can be applied to ensure evidence is obtained legally? In order to regulate criminal proceedings and to secure human rights within proceedings, governments establish laws and rules, for example exclusionary rules, which should be observed by police, prosecutors and judges. The rationale behind exclusionary rules is the expectation that law enforcement officers will refrain from employing prohibited evidence-gathering methods if they know that physical and testimonial evidence obtained by illegal methods will be excluded. It is assumed that they will realize that using such methods will not contribute to convicting the suspect and are therefore useless.

But how can compliance with the law be achieved? Which factors motivate people to comply with rules? Referring to social psychological theories, people can be intrinsically or extrinsically motivated to comply with existing rules. People's compliance with the law can be obtained through deterrence strategies (so-called instrumental strategies), which means that individuals are afraid of punishment (referring to the idea of general prevention), for example consequences under criminal or labor law. As an action theory, the rational-choice-theory is inter alia based on the assumption that people balance advantages and disadvantages before deciding how they react. Referring to the rational-choice-theory, potential offenders are deterred from violating rules, if the costs of criminal offences are higher than the advantages.[9] Based on this idea, the situational crime prevention theory proposed measures that reduce the opportunity for crime and increase the risk of detection, for example through control measures or surveillance (e.g., audio- or video-recording of interrogations, interrogations conducted by at least two officers or physical examination of an arrested person).[10] Yet, it is assumed that besides rational choice, normative considerations also play an equally important role in the

[9]Becker, 1968 at 207 et seq.

[10]Clarke, 1997 at 4 et seq.

willingness of people to comply with the law.[11] Enforcement of legal rules is linked to people's attitudes towards trust in justice, legitimacy, but also to the acceptance of a rule, which in the case of exclusionary rules is the legal taking of evidence respecting the suspect's rights. The acceptance of a rule is, therewith, one key precondition for norm compliance.[12] In this context, Tyler pointed out: "*If people view compliance with the law as appropriate because of their attitudes about how they should behave they will voluntarily assume the obligation to follow legal rules*".[13] Following this approach, the acceptance of rules depends on the individual's attitudes and conviction that a rule is morally legitimized.[14] To achieve the acceptance of legal rules, people have to be convinced of their moral alignment with the rule, for example through training measures, educational work and communication between all actors concerned. While instrumental compliance includes external factors and people's self-interest not to be detected and punished, normative compliance focuses on the acceptance of a legal rule and its legitimacy, even if norm compliance is not to their own advantage.[15] Referring to these theoretical ideas, the following section examines the hypothesis that exclusionary rules as an instrumental strategy secure a fair trial.

3.2 Legal Rules in Practice

The following chapter includes the function of exclusionary rules according to practitioners, the frequency of exclusionary rules in criminal proceedings, kinds of exclusionary rules in the daily work of practitioners as well as controversially discussed topics in practice. The results have to be considered in light of national legal rules and legal cultures. For example, the relationship between police and the prosecution service differs in the surveyed countries. In Germany, the prosecution service is responsible for preliminary proceedings and police officers are auxiliary officers of the prosecutor's office, while in Singapore the police and prosecution are different organizational entities.[16]

3.2.1 Function of Exclusionary Rules

One of the core questions concerns the function of exclusionary rules in criminal proceedings from the experts' perspective. The function of exclusionary rules is still

---

[11] *See* Tyler, 1990; Lind/Tyler, 1988.
[12] Tyler, 2003 at 284.
[13] Tyler, 1990 at 3.
[14] Tyler, 1990 at 4.
[15] Bottoms, 2001 at 90; Jackson et al., 2012 at 1053.
[16] Sing_02, 00:12:04.

discussed between scholars and lawyers.[17] Should they (a) discipline police or the prosecution service, (b) protect the legal system, human rights or the integrity of court proceedings, (c) maintain legal certainty or justice or (d) ensure that the trial court does not consider inherently unreliable evidence? Criminal proceedings contain a natural conflict between the retrieval of information and substantive truth. For this reason, criminal proceedings consist of difficult challenges to verify whether a piece of information was gained lawfully and if it is valid and reliable.[18]

Despite some differences between the legal systems in the surveyed countries, there are no controversial opinions in the analyzed interviews. According to the experts, exclusionary rules protect the rights of the accused person and ensure a fair trial.[19] Even if it is not the primary objective and maybe not suitable, the exclusion of illegally obtained evidence could help to discipline police officers and to demonstrate to investigative officers that information obtained illegally is useless.[20] One expert added to the latter argument that exclusionary rules have a disciplining effect, as police are usually interested in excellent work.[21] Additionally, exclusionary rules uphold the rule of law, the principle of a fair trial, the integrity of the proceeding and the accused's rights.[22] Nevertheless, conflicts can occur between the protection of the accused's rights and the protection of obtaining evidence to get valid information.[23] In this context, a German expert pointed out that a judge or prosecutor never knows if the accused really committed the crime and needs to prove the accused's guilt in a fair trial using lawfully obtained evidence.[24]

3.2.2 Frequency of Exclusionary Rules in Practice

Next, the experts were asked about their experiences with illegally obtained evidence. All experts emphasized that cases concerning the exclusion of illegally obtained evidences are rare. The Taiwanese interviewees pointed out that their safeguards to obtain evidence legally have been improved in the last thirty years, particularly after the legal reform in 2003.[25] Nowadays the system works and the number of cases in which evidences have to be excluded are only a few.[26]

[17]Jugl, 2017 at 53.

[18]Germ_03, 01:16:01, 01:17:16.

[19]Ch_01, Sec. 4; Germ_02, 01:05:00; Germ_03, 01:16:01; Sing_02, 01:03:51; Taiw_02, 00:41:37.

[20]Ch_01, Sec. 4; Germ_02, 01:06:13; Germ_03, 01:24:06; Sing_03, 00:33:51, 00:37:42; Taiw_02, 00:41:16; Taiw_03, 01:10:37.

[21]Germ_05, 00:12:01.

[22]Germ_02, 01:05:00; Germ_03, 01:16:01; Germ_05, 00:13:11; Sing_02, 01:03:51; Taiw_02, 00:41:37.

[23]Germ_03, 01:16:01.

[24]Germ_03, 01:37:20.

[25]Taiw_04, 00:03:42.

[26]Taiw_02, 00:14:18.

According to the experts, the estimated number of cases dealing with exclusionary rules is usually far below 10% of their cases. Some practitioners pointed out that they are only discussed in exceptional cases, for example: in 5 out of 1500 cases or less than 10 cases in the last five years.[27] Depending on the area of responsibility, the problem of exclusionary rules can be discussed more regularly. One judge dealing with serious cases in a Grand Criminal Chamber of a regional court guessed that exclusionary rules were discussed in three out of 15 cases (20%). This number can be explained partly via the extent of cases concerning serious criminal offences like murder and manslaughter. Torture exists only in very exceptional cases and no expert has ever dealt with such a case or with other coercive measures in hearings. German experts pointed out that cases of torture or the threat of torture are hardly conceivable,[28] except the well-known Gäfgen-case in 2003.[29] In this context, one German expert emphasized that torture is absolutely prohibited. Any possible exception must not be discussed, even if the exception includes, like in the Gäfgen-case, saving the life of a person. Exemptions on the ban of torture would lead to a dangerous slippery slope and open the discussion of when and which kind of torture should be possible.[30] All experts agreed that the number of illegally obtained confessions is significantly smaller than the number of cases concerning other pieces of unlawfully obtained evidence, for example unlawful surveillance of telecommunication.[31]

3.2.3 Kind of Exclusionary Rules in Practice

Errors leading to exclusionary rules occur particularly in connection with unlawful searches, defective warrants, instructions, telecommunication surveillances or undercover investigations.[32] In cases involving searches in Taiwan (ROC), the use of a voluntary agreement from the accused can be questioned. Police do not always point out that the agreement is voluntary and the affected person is allowed to deny the signature.[33] Sometimes police officers misjudge the legal preconditions of warrants or other measures of taking evidence. For example: a situation of imminent danger is assumed by police, while the prosecutor a posteriori denied it.[34] Next to legal misjudgement, necessary decisions under time pressure, lack of time and

[27]Ch_01, Sec. 8; Ch_02, 00:02:33; Germ_01, 00:01:14; Sing_02, 00:04:11; Taiw_04, 00:03:06.

[28]Germ_01, 00:08:41; Germ_02, 00:56:49; Germ_04, 00:04:42.

[29]*See* Weigend, National Report Germany.

[30]Germ_04, 00:51:15.

[31]Ch_01, Sec. 6; Germ_04, 00:04:42; Germ_05, 00:18:56.

[32]Germ_01, 00:02:21, 00:44:57; Germ_03, 00:03:15; Germ_04, 00:04:42, 00:05:53; Germ_05, 00:05:24, 00:10:09; Taiw_02, 00:14:18, 00:23:33; Taiw_03, 00:29:48, 00:43:22.

[33]Taiw_03, 00:43:22 et seq.

[34]Germ_04, 00:04:42; Taiw_04, 00:11:25.

overload of police or prosecutors are mentioned as potential reasons for illegally obtained evidence.[35] In Switzerland, the right to participate in interrogations is a typical problem.[36] Referring to Art. 147 Swiss Code of Criminal Procedure,[37] the parties involved in the criminal proceedings have the right to attend measures of taking evidence by the prosecution service. In cases with several accused parties, every accused person has to be informed about hearings of his accomplices. Sometimes accomplices are interrogated independently without giving notice.[38] In Germany, in turn, the instruction of offenders and particularly of their relatives are error-prone, as the legal situation in cases of instructing relatives can be very difficult.[39]

The consequences of exclusionary rules for the criminal proceeding are difficult to evaluate. In as far as it is not the only or main evidence that is being excluded, the exclusion of illegally obtained evidence has no significant impact on the criminal proceedings, as there is usually corroborative evidence that can be gathered. Experts pointed out that the investigation process and judgement are usually based on several pieces of evidence. It is really unusual to rely on only one piece of evidence which might be unreliable, or on the accused's statement which the accused could deny in court.[40]

3.3 *Difficulties and Limitations to Secure a Fair Trial Through Exclusionary Rules*

The following chapter describes challenges that law enforcement agencies and criminal courts are faced with, particularly concerning difficulties in applying the law and limitations of safeguarding criminal investigations and proceedings.

3.3.1 Difficulties in Applying the Law

One difficulty concerns the incorrect application of the law to legally difficult questions. Where is the borderline between protecting core fundamental rights and the need to use procedures to get a rational suspect to confess?[41] Could a consistent interrogation of twelve hours or an uncomfortable interrogation room result in

[35]Germ_01, 00:04:31; Taiw_03, 00:26:53.

[36]Ch_02, 00:02:33.

[37]Schweizerische Strafprozessordnung vom 05.Oktober 2007 (Stand am 01. Januar 2018) (SR 312.0).

[38]Ch_02, 00:04:34.

[39]Germ_01, 00:44:57; Germ_05, 00:10:09.

[40]Germ_04, 00:18:14; Germ_05, 00:18:56; Sing_01, 00:22:48; Sing_03, 00:18:31.

[41]Germ_04, 00:09:13; Sing_02, 00:58:44.

illegally obtained evidence?[42] Does the deliberate provocation of an offence by state officials result in the reduction of sentence, the exclusion of thereby collected evidence, or in a procedural impediment? The jurisdiction of the European Court of Human Rights has found that all evidence must be excluded and that measures short of excluding are insufficient to secure a fair trial (in this case, in Germany).[43] Further problems concern new technical developments that require new techniques to investigate them as well as new possibilities to gain evidence, for example, in the area of telecommunications surveillance including text messages and the analysis of radio cells.[44] However, in some cases it depends on the legal culture, whether the tactic of questioning can still be certified as legal. In Germany, for example, a tactic that is sometimes used to get a suspect to talk is to say that their accomplice has made a statement.[45] It must be concluded that such legal grey-zones are open to misuse. Before evidence can be excluded, a claim of such has to be made by the suspect. One expert made reference to his experience with the assertion of claims after evidence was obtained illegally. The injured party, who is the accused, could be too afraid to press charges against police officers, particularly if they are foreigners who are not familiar with the legal system.[46]

3.3.2 Limitations of Safeguarding a Fair Trial

Next to the abovementioned difficulties of the legal applicability, exclusionary rules are faced with several limitations.

3.3.2.1 Subjective Assessments and Balancing Process

Some limitations, particularly an assumed dependence on subjective assessment by courts, judges, prosecutors or police officers, are inherent in the legal system. They particularly appear in cases of balancing competing interests: the guarantee of valid information on one hand and inalienable rights of the suspect on the other hand.[47] Despite the legal need for an extensive balancing of arguments, information and evidence, experts from all countries pointed out the imponderability of a balancing procedure.[48] During the criminal proceeding, the careful balancing of exclusionary

[42]Sing_02, 00:58:44.

[43]European Court of Human Rights (ECtHR), *Frucht* v. *Germany*, case no. 54648/09, Judgement (5.Chamber) of 23 October 2014 at § 68.

[44]Germ_04, 00:30:11.

[45]Germ_04, 00:25:46.

[46]Sing_03, 00:43:04, 00:43:09.

[47]Germ_03, 01:16:01.

[48]Germ_02, 01:08:54; Germ_03, 01:35:15; Sing_01, 00:22:48; Taiw_03, 00:52:20.

rules includes risks of wrong decisions being made.[49] For example: where does the effect of coercion end? Where is the line between legal and illegal influence through tactical interrogation by police officers or prosecutors?[50] Which information collected by police officers is comprised in a case file? Generally, police officers preselect the information included in the file.[51] It is not predictable, how evidence is evaluated by the judge or prosecutor[52] and to which extent a prosecutor, police officer or judge is influenced by the impression of a suspect, when the credibility of an accused person has to be examined.

3.3.2.2 Credibility and Proof of Violations of Rules

The credibility of a claim pertaining to illegally obtained evidence is another imponderability. It is questionable, how a suspect can prove threats, inducements, promises, pressure or use of force to gain a statement, confession or evidence. If the suspect claimed to be beaten by police or exposed to undue coercion, he has to state the circumstances and sometimes prove them.[53] During the investigation process, prosecutors or (pretrial) judges evaluate the claim and possible evidence. How can the deprivation of sleep or food and drinks be proved? In Taiwan (ROC) the person concerned has, in some cases, to sign a form which voluntarily allows for the police to conduct a search.[54] How can the affected person prove that he/she felt under pressure to sign? Such cases of controversial provability and credibility can also include serious accusations against police officers, for example the suspect made a confession immediately after an unexpected and undue arrest by special police forces.[55] Did the suspect confess voluntarily or under the maintenance of pressure? How reliable is a confession after an extended time-period of interrogation? In the end, it is a matter of who to believe: the police or the accused. Crucial factors that determine the credibility of claimed illegally obtained evidence are the plausibility of the assertion, inside-knowledge about involved policemen (are they known as quick-tempered or calm characters?), but also possible motives of the suspect to claim, for example the crown witness programme.[56] However, the uncertainty will clearly remain about the veracity of the confession.[57]

---

[49] Germ_05, 00:20:57.

[50] Germ_04, 00:04:42.

[51] Germ_04, 00:10:50.

[52] Sing_01, 00:22:48.

[53] Ch_02, 00:39:25; Germ_05, 00:15:22, 00:15:53.

[54] Taiw_03, 00:46:01.

[55] Germ_05, 00:15:22.

[56] Germ_04, 00:27:02.

[57] Taiw_04, 00:55:46.

3.3.2.3 Extend of Protection

The question of the extent to which a suspect can and should be protected is closely connected to the provability of inducement and/or threat. Situations where a suspect is questioned without being informed of his/her rights could occur, for example, when he/she waits in the police station and smokes with officers or when he/she is driven to be taken into custody in another city.[58] One expert recounted a case in which a bound suspect (hand and foot cuffs) was not properly fastened in the car so that he lost his balance.[59] Who is responsible and takes care in such a situation? Could such a situation be misused by officers to maintain inducement? In the mentioned case, the judge responsible for the pretrial detention investigated the assertion, spoke to the involved officers and discussed solutions.[60] But the judge had to trust the officer and could not control whether something else happened during the ride. Threats or inducements were not claimed, but could be easily expressed or maintained in nearly all situations (for example the abovementioned arrest through special police forces).

3.3.2.4 Knowledge of the Excluded Evidence

Another limitation exists in countries where the same judge decides about the admissibility of the evidence and the case. Even if the illegally obtained evidence is excluded, the court knows about it and could be influenced in decision-making or try to evade the undesired outcome.[61] Referring to German law (§ 257 Criminal Procedure Code), the accused and his defense counsel have the opportunity to make a statement after evidence has been taken. If no statement is given, the tainted evidence could be used. If an accused is not represented by a lawyer, he may not know the legal possibilities, which leads to a legal limitation.[62] A German prosecutor mentioned that it is sometimes difficult to know more information about an accused if that information is not admissible in the criminal proceeding. However, it has to be taken into consideration that the judge, who does not know these information, remains impartial.[63]

---

[58] Germ_04, 00:43:11; Germ_04, 00:44:55.

[59] Germ_02, 00:56:49.

[60] Germ_02, 00:56:49.

[61] Ch_01, Sec.12; Taiw_04, 00:31:49.

[62] Germ_01, 00:07:31.

[63] Germ_04, 00:25:05.

3.3.2.5 Responsibilities and Control

Further protection gaps concern the control of police. Contrary to the situation in Germany or Switzerland, in Singapore, police forces are independent from the prosecution service.[64] Prosecutors cannot instruct police and control their daily work. In Taiwan (ROC), control of the police is often lacking due to a work overload of prosecutors.[65] Nevertheless, it is questionable whether informal control options, or independent investigations, lead to more control and pressure to obtain evidence legally. A limitation here is the allocation of responsibilities that depends on the personality of the responsible judge or prosecutor. If the judge/prosecutor is responsible, the prosecutor/judge will maybe remain silent if a defendant with a black eye arrives, arguing he/she is not responsible in this part of the process.[66]

The described limitations take place at a human level that can be influenced and standardized, but lawyers, courts and prosecutors should be aware of limitations. Challenges referring to provability and the extent of protection could be solved by legal rules or using new techniques like video or audio taping, physical examinations after arresting someone or control measures.[67] Others limitations are dependent on balancing and the attitudes of the people deciding.

3.4 *Compliance with Rules to Obtain Evidence*

All legal systems are faced with deviance. Deviations from norms ultimately enhance for social cohesion and justify the legitimacy of the criminal law and state-run institutions like prosecutions service and criminal courts.[68] As a matter of fact, use of illegally obtained evidence is possible in each and every legal system. Violations of rules to obtain evidence are a highly sensitive area, as the state, represented by police officers and the prosecution service, has an overpowering role. The following chapter deals with awareness for exclusionary rules, possibilities of contributing to norm compliance and the discussion of measures suitable to safeguard proper evidence procedures.

---

[64]Sing_02, 00:16:11.

[65]Taiw_03, 00:22:55.

[66]Ch_02, 00:11:05; Germ_01, 00:14:25.

[67]*See below*: Section 3.4.1.

[68]Lamnek, 2007 at 44 et seq.

3.4.1 Motivation of Norm Compliance and Awareness of Illegally Obtained Evidence

Based on their long-time professional experience with criminal investigations and criminal proceedings, the questioned experts agreed, as previously mentioned, that torture and undue coercion are an exceptional phenomenon. Although the exclusion of evidence is not an important issue in the experts' daily work, and exclusion is regularly focused on particularly serious crimes, investigation officers obtain evidence daily and this should be gathered legally. The system relies on legally obtained evidence. Which factors motivate officers to gain evidence legally, even if it is maybe easier to gain it illegally? Are they deterred by deterrence strategies or do normative considerations play a role? Understanding people's motives is an important step in identifying measures of prevention. What motivates police officers and prosecutors to comply with legal regulations: (1) fear of criminal liability, (2) fear of consequences under employment law, (3) fear of being detected, (4) acceptance of the necessity of exclusionary rules and (5) fear of wasting time if evidence has to be excluded due to illegal methods? While the first three points are based on the idea of rational choice, the fourth and fifth issues are focused on normative considerations. Experts pointed out that police officers are generally motivated to do excellent work, to avoid mistakes and to prepare, as far as possible, police operations to be conducted legally.[69] This motivation includes the fear to waste time, if an evidence has to be excluded after spending weeks or months for investigation.[70] One expert is convinced that the rationale behind prohibited measures of interrogation is convincing in a constitutional state and is usually internalized by every police officer.[71] It is assumed that legal consequences have a preventive effect on investigation officers, if they witness that their colleague is punished, suspended and maybe loses their future pension.[72]

Norm compliance and prevention also require awareness. If society tolerates deviant behaviour, deviant behaviour can be normalised.[73] To analyze their awareness of illegal measures to obtain evidence, the example of a suspect with a black eye was raised with the experts. The presumed case included a suspect with a black eye brought by police to court. The suspect later withdrew his confession due to undue coercion. Asked what they would think in such a situation, some experts were surprised and convinced that such things won't happen. One expert assumed that the accused was involved in a fight in jail.[74] Depending on their personality and position, a judge or prosecutor feels or does not feel responsible to investigate the

[69]Germ_01, 00:20:07; Germ_05, 00:12:01.

[70]Ch_02, 00:52:51, Germ_03, 01:25:37.

[71]Germ_01, 00:18:57.

[72]Germ_03, 01:27:19; Sing_01, 00:26:13.

[73]Wagner, 2010 at 88.

[74]Germ_01, 00:15:13.

case and to ask the accused person what has happened.[75] One expert pointed out the specific duty of care for persons concerned by enforcement measures like pretrial detention.[76] If it is necessary, an investigation of the case has to be started.[77]

3.4.2 Protective Measure to Safeguard the Legal Obtainment of Evidence

Finally, the experts were asked about consequences after evidence was illegally obtained and possible incentives to stop public officials from illegally obtaining evidence. Are exclusionary rules sufficient safeguards or are further safeguards during criminal proceedings necessary?

3.4.2.1 Legal Consequences for Police Officers

The experts agreed that police misconduct is taken seriously, in order to safeguard a fair trial. It is, depending on the credibility of the accusation, regularly investigated if it is mentioned by the affected person.[78] If misconduct by civil servants can be proved, there will be consequences under employment law, civil liability, disciplinary action and ultimately criminal liability.[79] As described above, experts assumed that legal consequences have a preventive effect on investigation officers. It was noted that the necessity of serious personal legal consequences should be dependent on the seriousness of the infringement.[80] One expert added that the mere violation of procedural rules should not be prosecutable, if no crime is committed.[81]

3.4.2.2 Legal Consequences for the Affected Person

In addition to the exclusion of illegally obtained evidence, the affected person can claim compensation for personal suffering as well as damages.[82] In general, people must be aware of their rights.[83] A reduction of the sentence was evaluated as

---

[75]Ch_02, 00:10:22, 00:11:05; Germ_01, 00:15:30; Germ_02, 00:52:44; Germ_04, 00:11:48; Taiw_01, 00:54:11.

[76]Germ_02, 00:52:44.

[77]Ch_02, 00:10:52; Germ_02, 00:51:43.

[78]Germ_03, 00:16:49; Sing_01, 00:34:08.

[79]Germ_02, 00:52:44; Germ_03, 00:21:54; Ch_02, 00:59:48, 00:59:51; Sing_01, 00:14:54, 00:45:34; Sing_03, 00:45:02; Taiw_03, 00:55:27, 00:56:43; Taiw_02, 00:23:33.

[80]Sing_02, 01:08:26.

[81]Germ_01, 00:28:41.

[82]Ch_02, 01:00:53; Germ_04, 00:59:50; Sing_03, 00:45:02; Taiw_01, 00:58:32.

[83]Sing_02, 01:10:43.

controversial. Mainly the experts agreed not to reduce the sentence, but it was remarked that in Germany the illegal obtainment of evidence could be taken into account.[84] As discussed, controversial evidence is of little value, and judges tend to exclude this evidence if there are any doubts that a confession could be unlawful. Usually, the judgement is based on several pieces of evidence.[85]

3.4.2.3 Control Measures: Physical Examinations, Recording of Interrogations, Participation of Lawyers

Control measures have a twofold purpose: on the one hand they increase detection of undue coercion, on the other hand they enable illegal behavior to be proved. The audio and or video recording of police interrogations and hearings, implemented in different degrees in Taiwan (ROC) and Singapore,[86] is used to provide proof of potential misconduct to prevent investigation officers from using coercion.[87] Experts evaluate the recording of hearings as positive. Nevertheless, loopholes are possible, for example, before the recording starts or on the way to the hearing.[88] In the abovementioned example of an accused with a black eye, Taiwanese experts mentioned their mechanism to mitigate such possible misconducts. Accused are physically examined at their arrest and have to be brought before an investigation magistrate within 24 h of being arrested. If the person has injuries that are not documented at the time of arrest, the injuries must have happened while he/she was in pretrial custody.[89] One expert recommended the participation of a lawyer in hearings to safeguard the accused's rights.[90]

3.4.2.4 Practical Measures and Incentives

In Germany, the responsibilities of police officers working in larger police departments are usually divided. While (special) forces are responsible for arrest, officers from criminal investigation departments are responsible for conducting interrogations. The division of responsibilities is described as positive to enhance an

[84] Ch_02, 01:02:53; Germ_04, 01:04:18; Sing_01, 00:47:53; Sing_02, 01:15:55; Sing_03, 00:47:01; Taiw_01, 01:04:13.

[85] Germ_04, 00:18:14, 00:47:14; Germ_05, 00:13:11.

[86] In Singapore, the audio- and video-recording was implemented as a pilot project.

[87] Taiw_02, 00:36:13; Taiw_01, 00:36:09, Taiw_04, 00:50:05, Sing_02, 00:48:31, Sing_03, 00:11:48.

[88] Sing_01, 00:20:03, Sing_02, 00:48:31, 00:49:44, Sing_03, 00:11:48.

[89] Taiw_01, 00:40:41.

[90] Ch_01, Sec. 16.

internal control system and social control.[91] As the legal obtainment of evidence and a fair trial should be the rule, incentives for lawful conduct are not necessary.[92]

3.4.2.5 Training of Police Officers and Communication

The experts agreed that police officers are well-educated and endeavor to comply with the law, but legal regulations are sometimes confusing and their application in stressful situations can be difficult.[93] Problems particularly occur if small local police stations are responsible for everything.[94] Some police headquarters offer internal trainings for difficult issues arising in criminal proceedings.[95] Legal training of police officers and communication with police officers were seen as important measures, not only to educate police, raise awareness for exclusionary rules and provide a fair trial, but also to reduce prejudices against judges and prosecutors, to develop an understanding for their (ex post) decisions, to demonstrate social control and to reduce the officer's potential frustration by explaining the reasons for a decision.[96] Communication and education cannot replace exclusionary rules, but enhanced attitudes could influence the acceptance of norms, procedural justice and norm compliance.

4 Conclusion

Do theory and practice form a well-balance whole and are practitioners concerned about possible limitations and difficulties related to exclusionary rules? The interviewed experts agreed that the use of illegally obtained evidence before courts is rare and that torture and other undue coercion are an exceptional phenomenon. In particular, the German experts pointed out the police officers have usually internalized the principles of the rule of law. Despite all safeguards, every system is nevertheless aware that a suspect's rights may be violated, for example through undue coercion on the way from a police station to court or jail. When accusations of illegally obtained evidence are raised, judges have to balance the competing interests and arguments of both sides. Compliance with the law depends on control measures and the threat of legal consequences, but also on attitudes and awareness of investigating officers. Therefore, proper training and the use of internal incentives amongst police and investigating officers are considered more useful than

[91]Germ_04, 00:14:02.

[92]Germ_04, 00:58:47.

[93]Germ_02, 00:50:23, Germ_04, 00:30:11.

[94]Germ_04, 00:27:59.

[95]Germ_01, 00:32:42.

[96]Germ_03, 01:24:15; Germ_04, 01:09:37.

more detailed and complex exclusionary rules. On the other hand, measures like audio and video recording as well as physical examinations and the participation of lawyers can help control officers and enable accused persons to prove claimed illegal behavior. In conclusion, it can be said that despite the existence of some loopholes, exclusionary rules—when accompanied by protective, deterrent and educational measures—do provide the basis for a fair trial.

References

Books

Bogner, Alexander/Littig, Beate/Menz, Wolfgang, *Interviews mit Experten*, Wiesbaden 2014. [Bogner/Littig/Menz, 2014]
Gläser, Jochen/Laudel, Grit, *Experteninterviews und qualitative Inhaltsanalyse*, Wiesbaden 2010. [Gläser/Laudel, 2010]
Jugl, Benedikt, *Fair Trial als Grundlage der Beweiserhebung und Beweisverwertung im Strafverfahren*, Baden-Baden 2017. [Jugl, 2017]
Lamnek, Siegfried, *Theorien abweichenden Verhaltens*, München 2007. [Lamnek, 2007]
Lind, Edgar/Tyler, Tom R., *The Social Psychology of Procedural Justice*, New York 1988. [Lind/Tyler, 1988]
Mayring, Philipp, *Einführung in die qualitative Sozialforschung*, Weinheim, Basel 2002. [Mayring, 2002]
Mayring, Philipp, *Qualitative Inhaltsanalyse*, Weinheim, Basel 2015. [Mayring, 2015]
Tyler, Tom R., *Why people obey the law?*, New Haven 1990. [Tyler, 1990]

Journal articles

Becker, Gary S., 'Crime and punishment: an economic approach', (1968) *78 Journal of Political Economy*, 169–217. [Becker, 1968]
Jackson, Jonathan/Bradford, Ben/Hough, Mike/Myhil, Andy/Quinton, Paul/Tyler, Tom. R., 'Why people obey the law? Legitimacy and the Influence of Legal Institutions', (2012) *52 British Journal of Criminology*, 1051–1071. [Jackson et al., 2012]
Tyler, Tom R., 'Procedural Justice, Legitimacy, and the Effective Rule of Law', (2003) *30 Crime and Justice*, 283–357. [Tyler, 2003]

Contributions to Edited Volumes and Annotated Law

Bottoms, Anthony E.,'Compliance and community penalties', in: A. Bottoms (ed.), *Community penalties change and challenges*, Cullompton 2001, 87–116. [Bottoms, 2001]
Clarke, Ronald V., 'Introduction', in: R. Clarke (ed.), *Situational Crime Prevention. Successful Case Studies*, New York 1997, 1–44. [Clarke, 1997]
Wagner, Matthias, 'Die moralische Ökonomie des Schmuggels', in: M. Wagner/W. Łukowski (eds.), *Alltag im Grenzland*, Wiesbaden 2010, 73–89. [Wagner, 2010]

Interviews

Germany: interview conducted in German.
Germ_01: Judge, District Court. Conducted by Gless, Sabine in November 2015.
Germ_02: Judge, Federal Court. Conducted by Gless, Sabine in November 2015.
Germ_03: Judge, Federal Court. Conducted by Gless, Sabine in November 2015.
Germ_04: Prosecutor. Conducted by Knickmeier, Susanne/ Richter, Thomas in February 2016.
Germ_05: Judge, District Court. Conducted by Gless, Sabine in November 2015.
Singapore: interview conducted in English.
Sing_01: Lawyer. Conducted by Gless, Sabine in February 2016.
Sing_02: Lawyer. Conducted by Gless, Sabine in February 2016.
Sing_03: Lawyer. Conducted by Gless, Sabine in February 2016.
Switzerland: interview conducted in German.
Ch_01: Lawyer. Conducted by Gless, Sabine in February 2016.
Ch_02: Prosecutor. Conducted by Macula, Laura in April 2016.
Taiwan (ROC): interview conducted in Chinese, translated to German.
Taiw_01: Judge. Conducted by Richter, Thomas in March 2016.
Taiwan (ROC): interview conducted in German.
Taiw_03: Lawyer, former prosecutor. Conducted by Richter, Thomas in March 2016.
Taiwan (ROC): interview conducted in English.
Taiw_02: Prosecutor. Conducted by Richter, Thomas in March 2016.
Taiwan (ROC): interview conducted in Chinese, translated to English.
Taiw_04: Lawyer. Conducted by Richter, Thomas in March 2016.

Susanne Knickmeier is a German lawyer who also holds a master's degree in criminology. She is a researcher at the Max Planck Institute for Foreign and International Criminal Law in Freiburg, Germany. Her research focuses on organized crime, economic and industrial espionage, as well as trust in the justice system and European criminal and security policy, with a particular focus on migration, human rights, and border security.

Exclusionary Rules—Is It Time for Change?

Sabine Gless and Laura Macula

Abstract This chapter explores whether exclusionary rules serve as efficient tools to streamline criminal procedure in a way that safeguards the rights of an accused or whether they exist merely as law on the books with limited actual utility. Relevant benchmarks for the evaluation of exclusionary rules are discussed, in addition to their structure. The question of which characteristics of exclusionary rules optimize the protection of procedural rights is analyzed along with other options to prevent violations. Possible alternatives to exclusionary rules are suggested to help answer the question: Is it time for a change?

1 Exclusionary Rules—Efficient Tools or Illusory Giants (紙老虎)?

Exclusionary rules have long been a topic of interest for legal scholars and the subject of comprehensive study in law journals and textbooks.[1] The concept originated in common law and was later adopted by civil law and so-called mixed systems and, most recently, in China.[2] In the Western world, exclusionary rules are featured in flashy criminal cases, detective novels, and movies. However, in ordinary legal practice, in most countries, the exclusion of evidence by courts appears to

[1]Wohlers, 2016 at 427.
[2]For an overview Ho, 2019a *passim*; Macula, 2019 *passim*; Jiang, 2019 *passim*; Turner, 2019 *passim*; Lin et al., 2019 *passim*, Weigend, 2019 *passim*.

S. Gless (✉)
Chair for Criminal Law and Criminal Procedure at the Faculty of Law, University of Basel, Basel, Switzerland
e-mail: Sabine.Gless@unibas.ch

L. Macula
Faculty of Law, University of Basel, Basel, Switzerland
e-mail: Laura.Macula@unibas.ch

S. Gless and T. Richter (eds.), *Do Exclusionary Rules Ensure a Fair Trial?*
Ius Gentium: Comparative Perspectives on Law and Justice 74,
https://doi.org/10.1007/978-3-030-12520-2_12

be the exception rather than the rule.[3] Anecdotal evidence depicts evidentiary rules as toothless tigers or illusory giants (紙老虎), and likens them to empty threats made by fictional characters in children's books. Mr Tur Tur appears as a giant when seen from afar, but shrinks to normal size as soon as one approaches him.[4] A closer look at exclusionary rules reveals that while they are lauded as indispensable in legal literature, their practical impact is more akin to the fictional characters described above, which raises doubts about their raison d'être, or reason for existence.

This chapter explores whether exclusionary rules serve as efficient tools to streamline criminal procedure in a way that safeguards the rights of an accused[5] or whether they exist merely as law on the books with little utility in practice.[6] For this purpose, standards for the evaluation of exclusionary rules are discussed, as is the structure of exclusionary rules with particular detail paid to the question of what characteristics appear to optimize the protection of procedural rights. Thereafter, existing alternatives to prevent violations of procedural rights are examined alongside alternatives to exclusionary rules. Finally, the question is posed, is it time for a change?[7]

1.1 Standards for the Evaluation of Exclusionary Rules

The first question in the assessment of the impact of exclusionary rules is, what are the expectations of such rules and what goals they are intended to achieve? This question is difficult to answer as it varies throughout different criminal justice systems. As pointed out by *Jenia Turner*, *Thomas Weigend* and *Ho Hock Lai*, exclusionary rules can serve a multitude of purposes, including safeguarding individual rights, protecting the integrity of procedures, achieving reliable fact-finding, and deterring police misconduct.[8]

---

[3]Calabresi, 2003 at 112 et seq.; Caldwell/Chase, 1994 at 65; Geller, 1975 at 671; Ho, 2019a at 4 et seq. and 10; Macula, 2019 at 3.1.3, 3.2.4.2, 3.2.5.2 and 4; Jiang, 2019 at 3.2.3.2, 3.2.5.2, 3.3.2.2, 3.3.4.2 and 4; Slobogin, 2013 at 341 et seq.; Starr, 2009 at 1514 et seq.; Turner, 2019 at 4 and 5; Lin et al., 2019 at 4, Weigend, 2019 at 3.1.1.1 et seq., 3.2.6, 3.3.2 and 5; Wohlers/Bläsi, 2015 at 167 et seq., all with further references.

[4]*See* Michael Ende, Jim Knopf und Lukas der Lokomotivführer, 1960.

[5]Giannoulopoulos, 2007 at 181; Ormerod/Birch, 2004 at 141; Pakter, 1985 at 56; Pattenden, 2006 at 13; Roberts/Hunter, 2013 at 176 et seq.; see also arguments provided by the Association for the Prevention of Torture <http://www.apt.ch/en/evidence-obtained-through-torture> accessed 21 November 2018.

[6]Gless, 2018 at 159 et seq.

[7]*See* for that discussion e.g. US Supreme Courts in *Hudson* v. *Michigan*, 547 US 586, 591, 599 (2006); Greco, 2018, 485, 512.

[8]Turner/Weigend, 2019 at 2. Regarding the fair trial rationale, *see* Ho, 2019b, at 1 et seq.; regarding the judicial integrity rationale, *see* Ho, 2014 at 112; Taslitz, 2013 at 419 et seq.

Legal goals vary from jurisdiction to jurisdiction, and most systems have several rationales behind the creation of a law. What follows are vast differences in the degree of protection of individual rights and the exclusionary rules themselves.[9] Often, exclusionary rules serve different purposes in different situations.[10] Excluding evidence may potentially hinder the pursuit of truth (e.g., excluding illegally taped communications) or promote valid fact-finding (e.g., excluding confessions elicited through torture).

It is often assumed that authorities will refrain from violating individual rights during criminal investigations if the consequence is the exclusion of the evidence obtained.[11] Naturally, the effectiveness of exclusionary rules in deterring misconduct will depend on a variety of factors that differ across jurisdictions, but important aspects are (1) the likelihood that tainted evidence is identified and exclusionary rules are applied in a timely manner, and (2) whether or not the costs of implementing such a procedure are unduly burdensome on law enforcement and prosecutors. Additionally, if the goal of developing exclusionary rules is to deter misconduct during investigations, such rules must be designed in a way that prohibits any gain from illegally obtained evidence. Or phrased differently, exclusionary rules must be created in a way that the risks of engaging in misconduct outweigh the potential benefits.[12] This notion is the rationale behind the common law *fruit of the poisonous tree* doctrine.

The aforementioned concepts beg the question of whether or not the impact of exclusionary rules as a deterrent could potentially be quantified by counting the number of cases in which tainted evidence has successfully been contested and excluded from trial.[13] Unfortunately, not only do we lack the necessary empirical data (not to mention it is unlikely it will ever exist in a representative and consolidated form),[14] but any such pursuit would only tell half the story. It would be impossible to measure the full impact of such a deterrent given the difficulty of identifying cases in which the impending exclusion of evidence might actually have prevented misconduct in the first place. The rare exclusion of evidence in case law,

---

[9]Turner/Weigend, 2019 at 1 et seq.

[10]Starr, 2009 at 1566.

[11]Turner/Weigend, 2019 at 3.2.

[12]In detail Starr, 2009 at 1522 with further references. For a behavioural theory approach to deterrence, *see* Slobogin, 1999 at 373 et seq.

[13]Shereshevsky, 2015 at 92 et seq.

[14]Caldwell/Chase, 1994 at 50; Ho, 2019a at 10.; Macula, 2019 at 4; Jiang, 2019 at 4; Lin et al., 2019 at 4, Weigend, 2019 at 3.1.1.1 et 4. Some empirical studies have been made, however, for the US Oaks, 1970 at 665 et seq.; Orfield, 1987 at 1016 et seq., for China Zuo/Lan, 2019. Also the evaluation of expert interviews made during this project in Knickmeier, 2019. A further problem is that strongly conflicting conclusions can be drawn based on the few empirical data available, Jacobi, 2011 at 110 et seq., pointing out that empirical data produced conflicting conclusions on exclusionary rules due to the selection bias, for instance. Also Slobogin, 1999 at 368 et seq.

which, at first glance, might be discouraging, likely only represents a fraction of the overall effectiveness of exclusionary rules as a deterrent, not to mention other goals.

Aside from the lack of empirical data, the anecdotal evidence gathered during our project overwhelmingly indicates that courts are quite reluctant to apply exclusionary rules due to a hesitancy to reject otherwise relevant evidence in the pursuit of the truth.[15] The disparity between the attention paid in the literature to the various theories behind exclusionary rules and the few actual cases of evidentiary exclusion is striking. However, even though one finds little analytical reflection in most textbooks and standard legal publications often just assume exclusionary rules are a critical foundation of legal institutions and ensure fairness in criminal proceedings without delving into the doubts, a closer look at their practical application reveals certain weaknesses of exclusionary rules.

1.2 Structural Inefficiency in Exclusionary Rules

A cursory glance indicates that exclusionary rules cost substantial time and money in what are generally overburdened criminal justice systems.[16] These apparent expenses seem justified only if exclusionary rules can in fact safeguard procedural rights.

1.2.1 Limited Scope: Are Only the Guilty Protected?

However, several aspects have been pointed out over the years that might raise doubts whether resources allocated to exclusionary rules are a wise investment, among them: Exclusionary rules do not trigger a consequence for violating procedural rules unless potentially excludable evidence is obtained in the first place. If there is no evidence to exclude, perhaps because a suspect does not confess or is eventually exonerated, the investigators violating the law suffer no consequences.[17] It is for this reason that some scholars argue exclusionary rules only protect the guilty.[18]

A similar argument can be made in the case of the illegal procurement of irrelevant evidence. Such evidence usually is not presented to the court and, therefore, cannot be excluded.[19] On the other hand, the application of exclusionary rules might even prove disadvantageous for a defendant if the illegally obtained

---

[15]*See* above at 1, footnote 2.

[16]Caldwell/Chase, 1994 at 52; Geller, 1975 at 679 et seq. with further references; Kafka, 2001 at 1926; Starr, 2009 at 1520; Wilkey, 1982 at 532 and 534 et seq. with further objections.

[17]Webster, 1982 at 703 and 713.

[18]Kafka, 2001 at 1922; Wilkey, 1982 at 532.

[19]Geller, 1975 at 669 with further references.

evidence is exonerating.[20] Nevertheless, none of these issues would impact the deterrent effect of an exclusionary rule because law enforcement personnel are not privy to evidence before it is uncovered.[21]

1.2.2 Between a Rock and a Hard Place

If evidence has been obtained illegally, courts are faced with the decision to either exclude relevant evidence or use tainted information. They either allow a potentially guilty defendant walk free or fail to provide a remedy for violations of procedural rules and a defendant's rights.[22]

The possibility of setting a guilty defendant free by excluding relevant and reliable evidence seems to be viewed by courts as particularly undesirable.[23] It interferes with a deeply-rooted sense of justice and responsibility towards victims and the public.[24] These notions are also captured in sentencing goals, including retribution, deterrence, incapacitation, rehabilitation, and condemnation of wrongdoing.[25] In both adversarial and inquisitorial systems the public expects reliable evidence to be used to establish the truth. Accordingly, prosecutors are under considerable pressure and, while the public may support the hypothetical use of exclusionary rules, both parties may feel differently when a court excludes seemingly reliable and crucial evidence.[26] In systems where judges are elected they may fear making such unpopular decisions could result in their not being re-elected.[27] However, it should be noted that any of the above concerns do not apply in cases where the violation of procedural rights affected the reliability of the evidence as in the case where torture or coercion are utilized.[28] Furthermore, this idea that the public may have, that individuals who commit murder are able to walk free as a result of exclusionary rules is hardly conform with reality.[29] In the US, for example, exclusionary rules are more often applied in cases of minor offenses like drug

[20]In detail on this controversy Erb, 2017 at 113 et seq.

[21]Geller, 1975 at 669; Thaman, 2013 at 408.

[22]Geller, 1975 at 675 et seq. with further references; Shereshevsky, 2015 at 85; Starr, 2009 at 1510 et seq. and 1538. Also Wilkey, 1982 at 533 criticizing that the exclusionary rule is not proportional to the crime of the accused and the misconduct of the officer.

[23]Calabresi, 2003 at 111 et seq.; Orfield 1992, at 119; Wilkey 1982 at 532 et seq.

[24]Caldwell/Chase, 1994 at 50 et seq.; Estreicher/Weick, 2010 at 951 and 966; Kafka, 2001 at 1925 et seq.; Wilkey, 1982 at 534.

[25]Starr, 2009 at 1543 and 1547.

[26]Geller, 1975 at 674 et seq. and 678 with further references; Starr, 2009 at 1529; Thommen/Samadi, 2016 at 84; Vetterli, 2012 at 450.

[27]Geller, 1975 at 676 et seq. with further references; Jacobi, 2011 at 169; Rychlak, 2010 at 241; Starr, 2009 at 1516; Wilkey, 1982 at 534.

[28]Calabresi, 2003 at 111; Shereshevsky, 2015 at 73 and 86.

[29]Taslitz, 2013 at 467 et seq., however, argues that some studies suggest that the informed public supports exclusionary rules because of its importance for judicial integrity.

possession.[30] Even if this were not the case, as one legal scholar pointed out, "rather than take advantage of public 'lack of understanding,' our courts should fulfil their great educative role by explaining the importance of safeguarding fundamental rights."[31]

The conclusion that can be drawn from both practical reports and this project's research is that courts all over the world are reluctant to exclude evidence[32]: Perhaps this is due to the fact that "when faced with all-or-nothing remedial choices, courts tend to choose nothing,"[33] which is particularly the case for serious offenses like murder.[34] Courts even tend to interpret the underpinning rights restrictively to narrow down the scope of an exclusionary rule and be able to admit evidence.[35] Naturally, if the exclusion of evidence is rarely granted, it cannot adequately protect the underlying individual rights.[36] Furthermore, the inconsistent narrowing of the law in order to avoid the exclusion of evidence leads to legal uncertainty, which in turn renders compliance even more difficult.[37]

This concern of letting the guilty walk free is emblematic of the underlying difficulties faced by legal systems seeking to ensure the substantive rights of defendants and is beyond the scope of exclusionary rules.[38] The question then becomes whether or not law enforcement and the public at large can change their mindset about exclusionary rules. The problems faced in a criminal investigation, the significance of a defendant's rights, and the potential for such rights to be violated must be explained to the broader public. Everyone should understand that if misconduct by law enforcement rises to the level for which the legislature established an exclusionary rule, it must be respected in practice, and doing so is in the public's interest. The segregation of society from an accused impedes the effectiveness of exclusionary rules.[39] Defendants should be seen for who they are: members of society under suspicion of committing a crime. A defendant's individual rights should not be taken lightly.

---

[30]Regarding some US states Geller, 1975 at 676 et seq. and Kamisar, 2003 at 131 et seq. with explanations and further references; Slobogin, 2013 with further references; regarding the jurisprudence of the ECtHR Oberholzer, 2012 at no. 700 et seq. Dissenting Jacobi, 2011 at 170; Kafka, 2001 at 1927; Orfield, 1992 at 117 et seq.; Wilkey, 1982 at 536 et seq. with further references states that "the multitude of criminals who go free because of the exclusionary rule are those who have committed such hateful crimes as murder, rape, and drug trafficking."

[31]Geller, 1975 at 678.

[32]*See* above at 1, footnote 2.

[33]Starr, 2009 at 1517.

[34]Kamisar, 2003at 132 with further references; Oberholzer, 2012 at no. 700 et seq.

[35]Calabresi, 2003 at 112 et seq.; Caldwell/Chase, 1994 at 53 et seq.; Estreicher/Weick, 2010 at 951 with further references; Geller, 1975 at 682 et seq. with further references; Jacobi, 2011 at 168 et seq.; Starr, 2009 at 1515, 1518 and 1563.

[36]Starr 2009 at 1511, 1532, 1537 et seq. and 1565.

[37]Jacobi, 2011 at 171.

[38]Kamisar, 2003 at 134 with further references.

[39]Geller, 1975 at 681 with further references.

1.2.3 Empty Threats? Exclusionary Rules as Deterrents

The efficacy of exclusionary rules as deterrents is questionable on a practical level,[40] particularly in cases where the police do not expect a prosecution[41] and are not anticipating going in front of a judge and explaining the techniques by which they obtained evidence. It is very difficult to assess how law enforcement officials respond to exclusionary rules[42] and past studies have asserted that empirical data has been unable to substantiate or refute a deterrent effect.[43] Nevertheless, some presumptions can be made. First, scholars point out that, with the exception of a potential blow to the ego, the exclusion of evidence imposes no personal cost on police officers engaging in misconduct.[44] Second, if police officers are more concerned with arrests rather than convictions, they are not likely to be deterred in the heat of the moment with the threat of an exclusionary rule that may or may not be used in the distant future.[45] In situations ripe for abuse obtaining admissible evidence may not even be the primary objective.[46] In cases where the authorities need informants rather than information[47] or are looking to scare potential suspects,[48] exclusionary rules may not prevent the use of illegal force. In other situations, police may be prone to taking liberty with individual rights to show they are tough on crime.[49] In many criminal justice systems, officials who violate an exclusionary rule never learn whether or not the evidence they obtained is excluded.[50] Some scholars have gone one step further and claim that the exclusionary rule incentivizes the police to perjure themselves in denying misconduct rather than deterring the misconduct itself.[51]

[40]*See*, for instance, Slobogin, 1999 at 368 et seq. For an attempt to empirically evaluate the deterrent effect of the exclusionary rule, *see* Oaks, 1970 at 672 et seq.

[41]Sklansky, 2008 at 581 et seq. with further references.

[42]Wilkey, 1982 at 533; *see* above at 1.1.

[43]Geller, 1975 at 651 et seq. with further references. These studies, however, were later interpreted to disprove the deterrent effect of the rule, *see* Geller, 1975 at 662 et seq. with further references.

[44]Caldwell/Chase, 1994 at 56; Geller, 1975 at 665 et seq. with further references; Jacobi, 2011 at 114 et seq.; Slobogin, 1999 at 372.

[45]Jacobi, 2011 at 119; Kafka, 2001 at 1923 et seq. with further references.

[46]Caldwell/Chase, 1994 at 55 et seq. with further references.

[47]In detail Geller, 1975 at 667 et seq. with further references.

[48]Jacobi, 2011 at 119 et seq.

[49]Calabresi, 2003 at 117; Kafka, 2001 at 1922 et seq. with further references.

[50]Caldwell/Chase, 1994 at 53 with further references.

[51]Jacobi, 2011 at 121 et seq. and 170 with further references.

1.3 To Replace or Enhance Exclusionary Rules?

In response to the above critiques of exclusionary rules, one could ask if they should be modified or replaced altogether. These positions are intertwined and trigger additional questions: What types of legal frameworks can actually safeguard individual rights at risk during criminal fact-finding? How must exclusionary rules be written to enhance respect for the rights of defendants and witnesses? These positions are not mutually exclusive and existing criminal justice systems illustrate that a combination of enhancement and alternatives may be the best option.

2 Are Exclusionary Rules Inherently Disadvantaged?

Based upon the hypothesis that exclusionary rules are essentially a means to safeguard individual rights in criminal proceedings but with little practical impact, the question arises: What kind of institutional, procedural, and factual conditions are required to optimize the effectiveness of exclusionary rules?

2.1 Institutional Framework

A certain degree of institutional structure is necessary to successfully enforce procedural rules, the first and foremost of which is respect for the rule of law. Only where all people and institutions are subject to the law and held accountable can the threat of an exclusionary evidentiary rule have an impact.[52] Furthermore, a general commitment to human rights,[53] including those of the accused standing trial, is a necessary prerequisite for the acceptance of exclusionary rules.[54]

In addition to the statutory structure, the organizational structure of a criminal justice system is crucial to the effectiveness of exclusionary rules. The division of power and finances both play a role, as does the education of law enforcement personnel[55] and the salaries of police officers, prosecutors, and judges.[56] Most criminal justice systems have developed specific frameworks in which checks and balances are created in an effort to prevent abuse. Clear administrative hierarchies

---

[52]Exclusionary rules and the acceptance of the rule of law seem closely connected in various criminal justice systems, for Germany *see*: Gless in Löwe/Rosenberg, 2007 at § 136a note 1; for China *see* Jiang, 2019 at 1 and 3.2.2 with further references.; for the US *see* Turner, 2014 at 101 et seq.

[53]Regarding the connection of human rights and exclusionary rules, *see* Gless, 2018 at 163 et seq.

[54]Summers/Jackson, 2012 at 77 et seq., 151 et seq.

[55]*See* below at 3.2.1 et seq.

[56]For example, Solomon, 2010 at 357; Thelle, 2006 at 272.

can foster a culture that does not tolerate abuse, especially where police and prosecutors are integrated into a common chain of command and the requirements of evidence gathering can be supervised throughout the various phases of a criminal investigation.[57]

Beyond statutory law, the ethical attitudes of authorities directly involved in evidence gathering are of great importance. The culture of the workplace and the example set by superiors is more likely to shape the behavior of investigators than the rare condemnation by a judge. An exclusionary rule will be of little value as a deterrent if the (unspoken) departmental policy condones illegal methods of obtaining evidence, due, for example, to the enormous public pressure to prosecute.[58]

2.2 *Pitfalls Across Legal Systems*

2.2.1 In Pursuit of the Truth

The inquisitorial and adversarial models of criminal justice are often distinguished with regard to their commitments to finding the truth. A firm commitment to discerning the truth is said to be paramount to inquisitorial systems, whereas in adversarial models it might be superseded.[59] This position dates back to the traditions of the respective jurisdictions. German and Swiss textbooks, for instance, still emphasize determination of the "substantive truth" as the basis for a just and fair outcome in any criminal case.[60] However, in the everyday of today's inquisitorial systems, legal practice has shifted to use of various plea-bargaining techniques with an emphasis on confessions, thereby prioritizing the closing of cases over finding the truth. In 2009, a variation of plea-bargaining was introduced into the German Code of Criminal Procedure (§ 257c German CCP).[61] Meanwhile, in Switzerland today more than 95% of criminal cases end with a "Strafbefehl," or summary penalty order, rather than prosecution.[62]

Ultimately, in all criminal justice systems there is a gap between theory and practice when it comes to evidentiary exclusion rules. In all jurisdictions there is a strong interest in determining the truth because that is the foundation upon which

---

57 Geller, 1975 at 721 et seq.; Thaman, 2013 at 408.

58 Geller, 1975 at 669 et seq. with further references.

59 Eser, 2014 at 22 et seq.

60 *See* for Germany: Kühne, 2015 at 206 et seq.; Roxin/Schünemann, 2017 at 87 et seq.; for Switzerland: Macula, 2019 at 2.1.1.1.

61 According to that practice, the trial judges and the defense can negotiate a lenient sentence in exchange for the defendant making a confession, in open court, to the crime charged. For further information, *see* German Country report; regarding similar procedures in Switzerland *see* Macula, 2019 at 2.1.1.3 with further references.

62 Macula, 2019 at 2.1.1.3 with further references.

judgments of guilt or innocence ought to be made. To that end, authorities strive for comprehensive fact-finding and exclusionary rules are perceived as undesirable hurdles.[63] Additionally, courts rarely address the beneficial effects of exclusionary rules in their opinions.[64] Further, at least in the US, the argument has been made that exclusionary rules can fuel police and prosecutorial misconduct due to a win-at-all-costs mentality which may simultaneously encourage defense attorneys to challenge even minor missteps by police.[65]

2.2.2 Record Keeping and the Role of the Prosecution

For inquisitorial systems, well-kept files are the foundation for valid and transparent fact-finding. Each step taken by the police or prosecution must be recorded, with a document placed in a single case file accessible to the defense. The file is eventually sent to the court for a decision. This form of record keeping is basically different from the adversarial system, which has separate files for the prosecution and defense, and which involves specific disclosure proceedings of prosecution material to the defense. The difference accounts for one of the most important characteristics regarding the success of exclusionary rules: In the adversarial system certain evidence may never even reach a jury due to the fact that any (potentially tainted) evidence must first be ruled admissible by a judge following prosecution and defense submissions. When potentially tainted evidence never even reaches a jury, it is more effectively kept out of trials by exclusionary rules. The inquisitorial system, on the other hand, involves a continual fact-finding process, beginning with the prosecution's collection and evaluation of *all* evidence—both incriminating and exonerating—and subsequent presentation to the court. Notably, the sequencing of events is based upon the narrative of the case file, one consequence of which is the availability of tainted evidence to the bench prior to its being ruled upon.[66] It seems obvious that the effectiveness of exclusionary rules is in part due to the withholding of tainted evidence from the adjudicator, as is the case in a jury trial.[67] Within inquisitorial systems this could be achieved by the removal of tainted evidence from the file as early as practically possible.[68]

---

[63]In detail above at 1.2.2. Although in certain situations, exclusionary rules aim at protecting valid fact-finding like in the case of torture evidence.

[64]For more information on the function of exclusionary rules, *see* Turner/Weigend, 2019 at 2 et seq.

[65]Slobogin, 2013 at 354 with further references.

[66]In fact, in Germany the court will explain in its verdict why tainted evidence cannot be included for fact-finding, *see,* for example, BGH, Judgement of 6 October 2016 - 2 StR 46/15; AG Kehl, Decision of 29 April 2016 - 2 Cs 303 Js 19062/15.

[67]In detail Wohlers, 2016 at 430 et seq.; also Wohlers/Bläsi, 2015 at 169 et seq.

[68]Wohlers, 2016 at 433 et seq., describing, however, also the practical problems that may arise due to such removal.

2.2.3 Checks and Balances: Supervision of Evidence Gathering

Another procedural aspect important for the functioning of exclusionary rules is a system of checks and balances that triggers exclusionary rules during the criminal investigation, not just at trial. Such a system of control and accountability could be shaped in a number of ways. One option could be to involve an outsider, such as a defense representative or an NGO, who could supervise and monitor the evidence gathering process in real time. Evidence obtained without the supervision of this external party would then be excluded and prosecutors and defense attorneys would also be obliged to report police misconduct.[69] A monitoring regime could also be set-up with technical devices, such as videotapes[70] or bodycams. This type of a system could have a preventative effect and, in the case of misconduct, help a defendant assert his or her rights under the exclusionary rule while also providing reliable evidence.[71]

2.2.4 Procedural Protections for Defendants

The effectiveness of exclusionary rules is also predicated upon certain rights granted to a defendant, namely, access to publicly funded and adequately trained defense counsel. The need for effective assistance of counsel is central to the adversarial criminal justice system and this belief is also shared by most European countries.[72] In Germany, for instance, the right to consult with a lawyer before being questioned by the police or other law enforcement personnel is an important procedural right that safeguards against potential abuses of power and is the foundation of the right to remain silent.[73] Similarly, in Switzerland, the right to have a defense lawyer present at the time of the first interview by police personnel is defined in Art. 159 of the Swiss Criminal Procedure Code, which was adopted following several European Court of Human Rights (ECHR) decisions.

---

[69]Hilton, 2008 at 80 et seq.

[70]For Taiwan: Lin et al., 2019 at 2.1.1.2. et seq. and 3.2.4; for Singapore: Ho, 2019a at 6; for the US: Turner, 2019 at 3.4.2; Kamisar, 2003 at 127, with further references; for Germany: the new § 136 (4) of the German Code of Criminal Procedure explicitly regulating the optional videotaping of the interrogation of the accused. In Switzerland, recent reform efforts plan to amend the CPC by adding a new art. 78a CPC on the recording of interviews with technical devices; *see* art. 78a of the preliminary draft regarding a reform of the CPC submitted by the Swiss Federal Council in December 2017, available online at <https://www.bj.admin.ch/dam/data/bj/sicherheit/gesetzgebung/aenderungstpo/vorentw-d.pdf>, accessed 22 November 2018.

[71]Summers/Studer, 2016 at 63.

[72]Art. 6 (3) c) ECtHR; Summers/Jackson, 2012 at 80 et seq. It is likely that this rule will change in light of the case law of the ECtHR since *Salduz* v. *Turkey,* case no. 36391/02, Judgment of 27 November 2008.

[73]BGH, Judgement of 22 November 2001 - 1 StR 220/01 (=BGHSt 47, 172).

2.2.5 Effective Remedies

Clearly, an efficient remedy is crucial for the functioning of exclusionary rules, i.e. that information obtained through a violation of individual rights can actually be blocked from fact-finding. Without adequate remedies those whose rights have been infringed upon cannot benefit from the procedural protections granted by the law and officials who are inclined to violate procedural rules are not deterred.

Remedies for violations of procedural rules designed to guarantee a fair trial should actually benefit the defendant, otherwise, as a Swiss trial observation study found,[74] they will not be invoked. Ideally, effective use of exclusionary rules becomes integrated within general practice so that the role of procedural rights does not deteriorate into a theoretical remedy, potentially available by law, but not used due to a restrictive "customary procedure."[75] To this point, the exclusion of evidence is not an effective remedy if it is circumvented by plea-bargaining or if procedural requirements, such as time limitations and prerequisites for standing, are too onerous. Additionally, a defendant should be able to make a motion to exclude evidence for the entirety of the criminal trial.[76] He or she should also be granted the opportunity to prohibit tainted evidence from entering the fact-finding process very early in the proceeding. Where, as is often the case in Germany and Switzerland, the admissibility of evidence cannot be challenged separately, but only on appeal following a final judgement, the appellate authority who decides whether or not the evidence should have been admissible also adjudicates guilt or innocence.[77] In these cases, exclusionary rules run a risk to prove futile.

2.3 *Legislative Techniques to Promote Efficient Exclusionary Rules*

2.3.1 Improving Statutory Structure

The design and content of exclusionary rules vary widely across jurisdictions, particularly with regard to their clarity and comprehensiveness. It is also the case that certain statutory schemes are more effective than others. An important aspect to start with, is a clear statutory regime featuring a systematic set of exclusionary rules that is well-integrated into the corresponding procedural code.[78] Instead, in most jurisdictions, exclusionary rules are shaped by case law in a certain number of cases

[74]Summers/Studer, 2016 at 63.
[75]Summers/Studer, 2016 at 64.
[76]Macula, 2019 at 3.1.4.
[77]For Germany, *see* Weigend, 2019 at 3.1.1; for Switzerland, *see* Macula, 2019 at 3.1.4.
[78]Vetterli, 2012 at 458 et seq.

and are difficult to access.[79] Without a clear statutory basis for excluding evidence, motions to exclude it become difficult to substantiate in practice. It is also true that more flexible legal solutions, like the balancing approach used by some courts, risks paving the way for arbitrary decisions.[80] With vague and discretionary exclusionary rules, individual rights may not receive the weight they are due. That said, the mere adoption of a statutory exclusionary provision is not the end-all be-all either. If courts find exclusionary rules too inflexible, they might use their decision-making authority to circumnavigate them,[81] for instance, by narrowly defining the underlying rights.[82] On the other hand, vague rules may end up promoting misconduct because of a lack of clear rules for police.[83] Regardless of the model, there remains the risk that tainted evidence will be admitted without a remedy. It is for this reason that the initial drafting of exclusionary rules is optimized by the creation of a law that strives to prevent unforeseeable results and deters investigative authorities from misconduct.[84] Severe consequences such as mandatory exclusion of evidence obtained through substantial procedural violations (e.g. torture) are better suited to deter such behavior.

2.3.2 Exclusion of Fruit of the Poisonous Tree

Throughout this project it became clear that the exclusion of indirect evidence, or fruit of the poisonous tree, has become a sort of litmus test for the effectiveness of exclusionary rules. The importance of this concept is highlighted in cases where particularly disturbing means, such as torture, were used to obtain evidence. In such cases it is not sufficient to simply exclude evidence that was gleaned through torture of the suspect. Rather, only the exclusion of all evidence gained as a consequence of the physical abuse, including derivative or indirect evidence, is apt to deter torture. For example, if a defendant confesses to a murder while being tortured and reveals the location of a dead body, all indirect evidence, such as DNA on the body, should be excluded along with the confession in order to deter state agents from engaging in such behavior. Therefore, the assessment of any legal framework to exclude illegally obtained evidence must be based not only on its capacity to

---

[79]A commendable exception is Switzerland, *see* Macula, 2019 at 3.1.2, with its comprehensive provision in Art. 141 CH-CCP, that can nevertheless not avoid surprises completely, *see* Gless/Martin, 2015 at 178 et seq. In Singapore, as well as in the US or Germany, exclusionary rules involve considerable legal uncertainty, Ho, 2019a at 4 et seq.; Turner, 2019 at 4; Weigend, 2019 at 3.

[80]Macula, 2019 at 3.1.3 with further references. For a comparative overview on the balancing approach *see* Thaman, 2003 at 403 et seq.

[81]Gless/Martin, 2015 at 178 et seq. and *see* above at 1.2.2.

[82]Starr 2009 at 1515, 1518 and 1563; also Gless/Martin, 2015 at 178 et seq.; Macula, 2019 at 3.1.3 and 3.2.5.2.

[83]Kafka, 2001 at 1924 et seq.

[84]Geller, 1975 at 666 et seq. with further references; Jacobi, 2011 at 115 et seq.

prohibit coerced confessions from entering criminal proceedings, but the availability to also exclude fruit of the poisonous tree.[85]

2.4 Interim Conclusion

Whether exclusionary rules are deemed illusory giants depends on a number of factors, all of which are contingent upon the interaction of key stakeholders, institutions, and the procedural code of each criminal justice system. Independent of culture-specific characteristics, it appears plausible that where a system of checks and balances is in place and where a defendant has standing to challenge tainted evidence, an exclusionary rule can successfully achieve the goal of protecting individual rights. However, the criminal justice system in which the rule is created must also be committed to protecting these rights even where it may result in a guilty defendant walking free. This requires the commitment of all stakeholders involved in order to be effective and such an investment can be difficult to achieve. As such, the question of potential alternatives to exclusionary rules remains.

3 Alternatives to Exclusionary Rules

Aside from ways to enhance exclusionary rules discussed in the previous section, potential alternatives must also be addressed. Where courts are unwilling to exclude any information from the fact-finding process as a deterrent to procedural violations during criminal investigations, lawmakers must search for other ways to achieve the same goal.[86] They can go about this in vastly different ways, such as decriminalization, which would reduce the risk of governmental transgression via global changes to a jurisdiction's criminal code. Preventative measures against police misconduct, enhancement of remedies where law enforcement authorities are held accountable, or other compensation schemes, including sentence reductions or complete dismissals are also possibilities. In order to be effective, such alternatives must be created to incentivize prosecutors and impose real costs on transgressors.[87] Furthermore, alternative remedies must be more likely to be granted by courts than exclusionary rules—otherwise they do not amount to a viable alternative.[88]

---

[85]Gless, 2018 at 159 et seq.

[86]Kamisar, 2003 at 126 et seq. with further references.

[87]*See* above at 1.1.

[88]*See* above at 1.2.1. et seq.

3.1 *Decriminalization*

Decriminalization as an alternative to exclusionary rules involves a number of considerations. First, decriminalization offers the potential benefits of saving resources and prioritizing quality criminal investigation of the remaining crimes. Decriminalization could also act as a means of preventing infringements on individual rights in minor offenses that maybe more prone to abuse by the authorities. In fact, studies have shown that based on a higher number of motions to exclude evidence in such cases, police are particularly tempted to use illegal techniques when investigating crimes sometimes depicted as "victimless," such as illegal drug use and gambling.[89] However, these findings can be interpreted in a number of ways. Courts may be more inclined to exclude evidence in "victimless" cases as the prospect of allowing a guilty defendant to walk free is more palatable where there is little impact on a victim's interests.[90] On the other hand, the rarity of evidence exclusion in cases with larger victim impacts may be the result of more diligent and specialized investigations with fewer mistakes or, more realistically, the immense public pressure on courts to admit evidence in such cases, even where it should be excluded.[91] Given such difficulties, the decriminalization of certain "victimless" offences might be worth considering[92] as a legitimate means of decreasing violations of human rights by the police. Additionally, the extent to which the threat of punishment offers any social benefit, particularly with regard to such offences, is unclear. Alternatively, if a jurisdiction sought to handle such cases differently, it could implement mandatory exclusion of illegally obtained evidence without judicial discretion and potentially achieve the same goal.

3.2 *Preventative Measures: Establishing Incentives and Reducing Barriers to Procedural Compliance*

Some scholars argue that jurisdictions should focus on *promoting* constitutional rights in criminal proceedings by preventative measures rather than *deterring* abuse.[93]

---

[89]Geller, 1975 at 625 with further references; Kamisar, 2003 at 131 et seq. with further references; Oaks, 1970 at 724.

[90]Oberholzer, 2012 at no. 700 et seq., pointing out that the ECtHR has been more reluctant to exclude evidence in a murder case than in a victimless drug offence. Oberholzer compared the two cases of ECtHR (GC), *Gäfgen* v. *Germany*, case no. 22978/05, Judgment of 1 June 2010 and ECtHR (GC), *Jalloh* v. *Germany*, case no. 54810/00, Judgment of 11 July 2006.

[91]Kamisar, 2003 at 132.

[92]Geller, 1975 at 624 et seq.

[93]Estreicher/Weick, 2010 at 960.

3.2.1 Improved Law Enforcement Training

One way of shaping police behavior proactively is to improve law enforcement training by focusing on developing an understanding of the value of civil liberties and individual rights.[94] Police officers should be well-informed about criminal procedure and the consequences of rule violations to realize the personal impact.[95] The same training should specifically focus on developing an awareness among law enforcement personnel that the rights granted to suspects are not without good reason.[96] An emphasis on ethics is also important,[97] as are clear and concise evidence gathering guidelines.[98] Law enforcement training should also provide officers with problem solving strategies that can easily be applied in real-life situations.[99] In cases of misconduct, educational measures should be implemented: the offending officer (and perhaps his agency) must be informed of his misconduct and he or she should then be required to attend training (preferably during off hours) to remedy the misconduct and to guide future behavior.[100] Another important aspect of improved law enforcement training is the diligent selection of instructors. If training personnel display a cynical attitude towards the role of police officers and the rights of accused, this will often be adopted by their students.[101]

Training police officers, by itself, may not be enough to deter misconduct. To optimize results, it should be supplemented with incentives for compliance with the law.[102]

3.2.2 Stress Management Programs

Police misconduct does not occur in a vacuum. Thus, a preventative approach should also consider the psyche and wellbeing of law enforcement personnel. Studies in the US classify police officers as part of an occupational group that is particularly likely to experience a high level of stress and are far more likely to commit suicide compared to the general population. Stress at work or home can increase the risk that an officer will engage in misconduct.[103] Accordingly, law enforcement agencies should provide peer support programs, professional

[94]On the inadequacy of present law enforcement training in the US, *see* Hilton, 2008 at 71 et seq.

[95]Estreicher/Weick, 2010 at 961; Hilton, 2008 at 75; critical Slobogin, 1999 at 393 et seq.

[96]Geller, 1975 at 721; *see also* Hilton, 2008 at 75.

[97]Hilton, 2008 at 75.

[98]Estreicher/Weick, 2010 at 961.

[99]Hilton, 2008 at 75.

[100]Caldwell/Chase, 1994 at 68 et seq. and 74 et seq.; also Hilton, 2008 at 79.

[101]Hilton, 2008 at 76.

[102]Calabresi, 2003 at 114.

[103]Hilton, 2008 at 74.

counselors, and training that includes practical stress management skills to help address the source of a police misconduct.[104]

3.2.3 Incentive Systems

Another promising strategy might be to replace or supplement deterrence-based models with a reward model and reporting system that keeps track of misconduct. For example, police officers could receive nominal monetary compensation each time evidence they collected legally was later used in court. An advantage of this solution is its direct and seemingly positive effect on the officials gathering the evidence (the same people who are at risk of violating the rules in the first place).[105] This option could be successful, especially in countries where torture and mistreatment by authorities remains a major problem. That said, this type of system would increase the time and monetary demands placed upon the administration and could significantly alter the working environment within police departments. Furthermore, such incentive systems may be susceptible to exploitation as police would be encouraged to prioritize the prosecution of certain arrests.[106] But, for some criminal justice systems, where these risks could be considered sufficiently marginal, such a structure could achieve higher compliance with procedural rules and thus fairer trials for defendants. As with exclusionary rules, these rules and structural changes would only apply to police conduct related to securing evidence for prosecution.[107] Unfortunately, it would not have an impact upon other misconduct—that which may have no particular purpose or that is motivated by inherent aggression.

One other idea for an incentive system could be to establish standard promotions of officials after a certain period of lawful work. If an official violates important procedural rules during evidence collection, the promotion would be refused and he or she may even be demoted. Promotions could also depend on satisfactory testing results in training courses.[108]

3.2.4 Elimination of Quotas

Quota systems pressuring officials to meet a certain number of arrests and summons are inherently flawed. Instead of increasing efficiency within a police department, experts warn that this may lead to cynicism and disillusionment. Officers often experience such quotas as unfair and arbitrarily enforced; they also tend to feel

[104]Hilton, 2008 at 74 et seq.

[105]Geller, 1975 at 720.

[106]Geller, 1975 at 721.

[107]Geller, 1975 at 721.

[108]Estreicher/Weick, 2010 at 961.

pressured to falsify evidence in order to meet the requirements.[109] Consequently, such systems should be abandoned to avoid provoking rather than preventing police misconduct.

3.2.5 Monitoring Evidence Gathering

The aforementioned measures to monitor evidence gathering, including defense participation and the use of recording protocols,[110] could also be viewed as an alternative to exclusionary rules due to the potential deterrent effect on prosecutors. Additionally, in order to achieve transparency, law enforcement agencies could be required to maintain a public and regularly updated registry of certain evidence gathering processes such as searches, property seizure, and arrests, as well as complaints stemming from those actions.[111] This does not, however, represent a viable surrogate to exclusionary rules because not every evidence gathering action can be monitored, nor does monitoring result in consequences for violations of procedural rules that might still occur.

3.2.6 Injunctive Relief

In cases of systematic illegal searches and seizures[112] an injunction to forbid, and thus prevent, any further illegal searches might be a helpful measure to supplement (but not replace) the exclusion of evidence, although courts might be reluctant to grant such a remedy.[113]

3.2.7 Interim Conclusion

All of the preventive measures discussed in this section could potentially enhance compliance with procedural rules but they do not stipulate consequences for procedural violations. Thus, a defendant whose rights have been violated will nevertheless be prosecuted using tainted evidence. Therefore, these measures do not constitute adequate replacements for exclusionary rules but could be promising supplementary means.

---

[109] Hilton, 2008 at 70 et seq. and 76.

[110] *See* above at 2.2.3. et seq.; for internal monitoring measures *see* Hilton, 2008 at 68.

[111] Estreicher/Weick, 2010 at 953 and 961.

[112] This requirement might make injunctions ineffective, Jacobi, 2001 at 164 et seq.

[113] Geller, 1975 at 715 et seq. with further references; Hilton, 2008 at 61; Sklansky, 2008 at 574.

3.3 *Other Means of Holding Law Enforcement Accountable*

3.3.1 Claims Under Tort Law

It has been argued that a modified remedy under tort law, where monetary compensation and damages were awarded, would be superior to exclusionary rules.[114] As an alternative, it could also act as a supplementary measure in a comprehensive system.[115] Such a remedy could include both compensatory and punitive damages.[116] The advantage to this option is that it does not interfere with the primary sentencing goals of punishing the wrongdoer and providing a remedy to the victim/claimant.[117] It also follows the idea that where nonpecuniary damages cannot be undone, monetary compensation comes the closest to compensating the damaged party.[118] Despite this fact, tort actions would face similar and maybe even more issues around efficiency than exclusionary rules,[119] for instance because public authorities may often be immune to such actions[120] and a defendant may not have standing to sue while incarcerated.[121] Additionally, law enforcement officials are likely to be given more credence than criminal defendants and it may be difficult for defendants to prove police misconduct or actual damages.[122] The typical defendant would also probably lack the resources, energy, time, and knowledge to raise such claims against the authorities,[123] although these problems could be mitigated by reducing or eliminating certain rules[124] such as sovereign immunity in the case of significant violations.[125]

---

[114]Especially regarding search and seizure exclusionary rules, *see*, for instance, Amar, 1994 at 800 et seq.; Kafka, 2001 at 1934 et seq.; Oaks, 1970 at 756 et seq.; Slobogin, 1999 at 384 et seq.; Wilkey, 1982 at 538. For Germany: Greco, 2018, at 512.

[115]Estreicher/Weick, 2010 at 962 et seq.

[116]Amar, 1994 at 812 et seq.; Kafka, 2001 at 1938.

[117]Shereshevsky, 2015 at 90 et seq.

[118]Shereshevsky, 2015 at 91 et seq.

[119]Sklansky, 2008 at 580 et seq.

[120]Estreicher/Weick, 2010 at 949; Starr, 2009 at 1518.

[121]In detail to the problems and to proposals for modifying the tort action Geller, 1975 at 690 et seq. with further references.

[122]Calabresi, 2003 at 114 et seq.; Estreicher/Weick, 2010 at 949; Geller, 1975 at 671 and 692 et seq. with further references; Kamisar, 2003 at 135.

[123]Geller, 1975 at 655 et seq. with further references.

[124]Kafka, 2001 at 1937 with further references.

[125]Amar, 1994 at 812 et seq.; Estreicher/Weick, 2010 at 963 who suggest a waiver of immunity for jurisdictions that want to replace the exclusionary rule with efficient alternatives.

3.3.2 Official Apologies

Social science research has found that just the fear of condemnation and the inherent social disapproval of wrongdoing do have a deterrent effect, but only if certain requirements are met.[126] The wrongdoer must first possess fear around the risk of being discovered and, if misconduct has been identified, the individual must be informed and (optimally) experience a direct negative consequence to achieve the greatest impact on future behavior.[127] Accordingly, an official announcement of misconduct and/or an official apology by the responsible party could be a good supportive measure. Oversight from the media, citizen review boards, and elected officials[128] might also have similar effects. However, such sanctions alone, which primary affect the person's reputation, may be limited in their deterrent effect if not combined with concrete consequences to mitigate the impact of the actual misconduct.[129]

3.3.3 Criminal Prosecution

Another alternative to the exclusion of evidence could be criminal prosecution of the officials responsible for the violation of the defendant's rights. Of course, this sanction is quite severe and would need to be proportionate to the misconduct.[130]

Criminal prosecution of police officers is rare in most countries[131] and, given the controversy around whether it serves its purposes of providing justice and deterring unlawful conduct, it is disputable if such an alternative remedy to exclusionary rules is effective at all. Criminal prosecution of law enforcement comes with many of the same problems as tort actions: a defendant whose rights have been violated often lacks the resources to file such a claim and officials,[132] even though they may not always be entirely truthful, are generally given more credence than criminal defendants.[133] Furthermore, the burden of proof is particularly high in criminal prosecutions and would be very difficult to meet.[134] In reaction to such hurdles it has been proposed that the violation of important procedural rules should, by themselves, constitute contempt of court.[135] This would mean that the court could

---

[126]Starr, 2009 at 1535 et seq. with further references.

[127]Caldwell/Chase, 1994 at 54 et seq.

[128]Hilton, 2008 at 69.

[129]Shereshevsky, 2015 at 86 and Starr, 2009 at 1527 et seq. and 1536 et seq. both with further references.

[130]Caldwell/Chase, 1994 at 75 et seq.

[131]For the US, Hilton, 2008 at 63 et seq.

[132]Hilton, 2008 at 72 et seq. and Kamisar, 2003 at 130 et seq. with further references.

[133]*See* above 3.3.1.

[134]Geller, 1975 at 715.

[135]*See* Rychlak, 2010 at 241 et seq. and 249 et seq. regarding illegal searches and seizures.

take the initiative without the prosecution and the matter would be dealt with in summary proceedings.[136] Another idea is the establishment of a separate office for such claims to guarantee an independent assessment of the case.[137] An ombudsman system[138] could also be established. The ombudsman, as an independent official, could be entitled to take penal action against the wrongdoer or attempt to shape police behavior through public relations.[139]

3.3.4 Other Sanctions

In cases of impropriety detected in the context of administrative supervision, executive or supervisory bodies should be able to directly impose disciplinary measures.[140] They could offer counseling to officers and, at least in cases of repeated or intentional violations, impose disciplinary sanctions such as mandatory training, reassignment to less desirable duties,[141] a prohibition on carrying a weapon,[142] forfeiture of promotion, removal from duty,[143] or suspension without pay[144]—depending on the nature of the misconduct.[145] The disciplinary sanctions that apply should be communicated clearly and in writing to both the officer and the public in order to reinforce the importance of defendants' rights and to increase trust in law enforcement.[146]

3.3.5 Interim Conclusion

Any instrument imposing direct sanctions on law enforcement will face significant barriers to enforcement. Perjury is likely to be encountered regularly[147] and such means are very difficult to implement from a legislative and enforcement standpoint because of public pressure to convict criminals. There is also strong political

[136]Geller, 1975 at 717 with further references; also Rychlak, 2010 at 241 et seq. and 249 et seq. regarding illegal searches and seizures.

[137]This exists, for example, in parts of Switzerland, *see* Macula, 2019 at 2.1.3.3.

[138]Estreicher/Weick, 2010 at 962. This exists, for example, in parts of Switzerland, *see* Macula, 2019 at 2.1.3.3.

[139]Geller 1975 at 717 et seq. with further references.

[140]Wilkey, 1982 at 537 et seq.; Slobogin, 1999 at 422 et seq. considers a pure administrative sanction model with administrative law judges and agency-based litigators as superior to any other remedy.

[141]Caldwell/Chase, 1994 at 69 et seq. and 76.

[142]Hilton, 2008 at 79.

[143]Estreicher/Weick, 2010 at 961; Geller, 1975 at 718 et seq.

[144]Caldwell/Chase, 1994 at 69 and 76; Estreicher/Weick, 2010 at 961; Kamisar, 2003 at 129.

[145]Caldwell/Chase, 1994 at 69.

[146]Hilton, 2008 at 76 et seq.

[147]Kamisar, 2003 at 131.

opposition to restricting police behavior.[148] Furthermore, separate accountability measures cannot completely replace exclusionary rules or similar measures in cases of severe procedural violations or in cases where the reliability of the evidence may be negatively affected by the way in which it was obtained: The UN Convention Against Torture, for instance, explicitly indicates that statements "made as a result of torture shall not be invoked as evidence in any proceedings"[149] and prescribes an "enforceable right to fair and adequate compensation, including the means for as full rehabilitation as possible."[150] In a case from 2014, also the ECHR[151] held that in cases of police incitement in breach of art. 6 § 1 ECHR "all evidence obtained [...] must be excluded or a procedure with similar consequences must apply."[152]

3.4 Sentence Reductions

When tainted evidence is used to convict a defendant, the issue of sentence reduction as a remedy arises. According to this approach, tainted evidence is still admitted but the resulting sentence is reduced (potentially considerably).[153] Some scholars have argued for a combined system of sentence reduction to create an incentive to raising claims in the first place and direct sanctions against the police as a means of deterrence.[154] Naturally, a defendant might find such an option to be satisfactory compensation for violations of procedural rights—especially if the alternative is not to have any efficient remedy at all.

---

[148]Kamisar, 2003 at 127 et seq. and 137 et seq. with further references.

[149]Except against a person accused of torture as evidence that the statement was made, art. 15 CAT.

[150]Art. 14 (1) CAT.

[151]The ECtHR sets absolute limits to evidence taking in cases of torture, but it is less severe in cases of inhuman treatment, indirect evidence or violations of other fair trial rights, for example, ECtHR (GC), *Gäfgen* v. *Germany*, case no. 22978/05, Judgment of 1 June 2010 at § 131 et seq., § 169 et seq. and 167; ECtHR (GC), *Jalloh* v. *Germany*, case no. 54810/00, Judgment of 11 July 2006 at § 83 and 103 et seq.; Gless in Niggli et al. 2014 at art. 141 no. 14 and 22; Thommen/Samadi, 2016 at 76 et seq.

[152]ECtHR, *Furcht* v. *Germany*, case no. 54648/09, Judgment of 23 October 2014 at § 64 and 68.

[153]For instance, it is explicitly mentioned in section 359a of the Dutch Code of Criminal Procedure. According to this provision, the court may "determine that the length of the sentence shall be reduced in proportion to the gravity of the non-compliance with procedural requirements, if the harm or prejudice caused can be compensated in this manner". However, it is the court's prerogative to choose this solution. Alternatively, the court may exclude the tainted evidence or even dismiss the case by baring the prosecution. Sentence reduction is also practised in Canada, *see* Bick, 2006 at 199 et seq. For information on further models: Starr, 2009 at 1511.

[154]Calabresi, 2003 at 116 et seq.; Caldwell/Chase, 1994 at 68 et seq.; critical: Kamisar, 2003 at 136 et seq. and Starr, 2009 at 1512 et seq. and 1521.

3.4.1 Advantages

As we have seen above, courts tend to reject remedies akin to evidence exclusion.[155] Sentence reduction, by contrast, represents what has been termed an "intermediate remedy"[156] because it can be tailored in response to the particular procedural violation and the resulting harm. Given this flexibility, it could also offer an attractive alternative to the "all-or-nothing" nature of exclusionary rules.[157] Courts would not be required to let a guilty defendant walk free but could also compensate the defendant in the form of sentence reduction, with the discretionary means to limit its scope in order to avoid controversy.[158] These types of sentence reductions might be more likely to be granted by courts and eventually more effective in safeguarding a defendant's rights than exclusionary rules that remain unapplied.[159] Although sentence reduction is not as strong a remedy as evidence exclusion (and thus may be more appealing to the public), it can be argued that sentence reduction is a corrective and expressive remedy that publicly embarrasses the wrongdoer (thus deterring further misconduct), while simultaneously recognizing the defendant's rights and dignity.[160] In addition, it offers the defendant a proportional measure of compensation in the form of years or months of freedom.[161] Furthermore, it is a simple and practical remedy that can easily be implemented in current legal systems[162] and could provide a strong incentive to defendants to report misconduct due to the potential for a reduced sentence.[163]

3.4.2 Shortcomings

The concept of sentence reduction would likely face many objections. First, sentence reduction is not an option in cases where the misconduct rendered a fair trial impossible.[164] The option to reduce a sentence in such cases would conflict with international case law and treaties prescribing the exclusion of evidence in severe cases.[165] Furthermore, although the ECHR has accepted sentence reduction as a

---

[155]*See* above 1.2.2.

[156]Starr, 2009 at 1511; for a detailed presentation of the pros and cons of sentence reduction *see* Starr, 2009 at 1520 et seq., 1539 et seq. and 1562 et seq.

[157]Kafka, 2001 at 1928 with further references. *See* above 1.2.2.

[158]Starr, 2009 at 1520 et seq. and 1539 et seq.

[159]Starr, 2009 at 1513, 1519, 1522, 1539 and 1565 et seq. Bick, 2006 at 221, however, doubts the deterrent effect of sentence reduction.

[160]Starr, 2009 at 1513, 1537 and 1539 et seq.

[161]Starr, 2009 at 1513, 1541 and 1566.

[162]Starr, 2009 at 1566.

[163]Calabresi, 2003 at 115.

[164]*Also* Starr, 2009 at 1523, 1564 and 1566.

[165]*See also* above 3.3.5.

remedy in cases of excessive pre-trial detention, violations of the right to a speedy trial, and unlawful detention conditions,[166] it also held that in cases of police incitement in breach of art. 6 § 1 ECHR, a sentence reduction (even if considerable) does not amount to a "procedure with similar consequences" to an exclusionary rule. It is thus not a sufficient remedy and is not appropriate where evidence has erroneously been admitted.[167] Similarly, a lack of judicial expediency is not comparable to a violation of the right against self-incrimination, and certainly not to the use of torture as a means of obtaining evidence. That said, the ECHR has remained silent as to what might be equivalent, admissible alternatives to exclusionary rules.

Sentence reduction is also not an appropriate solution in cases where the violation of procedural rules could have also affected the reliability of the evidence.[168] Since misconduct is often committed deliberately with the aim of increasing the chance of a conviction, sentence reduction may not deter authorities from misconduct where such misconduct improves the likelihood of a conviction.[169] For example, the reliability of evidence obtained in breach of the right against self-incrimination (particularly in cases of torture) is dubious at best.[170] Sentence reduction may also encounter the rather serious problem of commodification; law enforcement may get the impression that they can violate suspects' rights in pursuit of a conviction so as long as they are aware of the "price" of the sentence reduction. Such beliefs, if accepted by others, would reduce the stigma associated with procedural misconduct and also reduce any deterrent effect.[171] Some scholars have gone one step further, arguing that police are primarily interested in convictions and accord less thought to sentencing[172] in a balancing act of whether or not the misconduct "paid off."[173] Consequently, sentence reduction might not effectively deter police misconduct. It may, however, be effective against prosecutorial misconduct given the numerous incentives they have to pursue longer sentences.[174]

---

[166] *Chraidi* v. *Germany*, case no. 65655/01, Judgement of 26 October 2006 at §§ 24–25; *Scordino* v. *Italy*, case no. 36813/97, Judgement of 29 March 2006 at §§ 185–186; *Mathew* v. *Netherlands*, case no. 24919/03, Judgement of 29 September 2005 at §§148–149.

[167] ECtHR, *Furcht* v. *Germany*, case no. 54648/09, Judgment of 23 October 2014 at § 69.

[168] Starr, 2009 at 1519, 1523, 1564, 1566. Accordingly, Starr proposes sentence reduction only as a remedy for speedy trial violations, race discrimination in jury selection and misconduct that is presently deemed "harmless" in the US and currently does not trigger any remedy, *see* Starr, 2009 at 1548 et seq.

[169] Starr, 2009 at 1523.

[170] Schlauri, 2003 at 100 et seq. with further references. Ruckstuhl, 2006 at 20, however, claims that all influence exerted during the taking of evidence might change the content of the evidence.

[171] Starr, 2009 at 1539 with further references.

[172] Estreicher/Weick, 2010 at 966.

[173] Kamisar, 2003 at 136 with further references.

[174] E.g. political pressure, efficiency efforts, office policy and culture, career interests, the incentive to win and ideologies of justice or crime deterrence, *see* Starr, 2009 at 1513 and in detail at 1522 et seq and 1531 et seq.

Other arguments against sentence reduction are around the issue of enforcement. These include the difficulty in quantifying the harm caused by the procedural violation in terms of a specific reduction in the sentence,[175] particularly where formal sentencing guidelines are absent.[176] This flexibility could potentially add a new source of arbitrariness in sentencing[177] and tempt judges to raise the minimum sentence of crimes to circumvent the remedy entirely.[178] The ECHR has also held that where an exact reduction in a sentence is not quantified in a judgment it cannot be deemed measurable.[179]

3.5 Amnesty and Pardons

Where authorities have failed to grant a remedy in cases of illegally obtained evidence, and the mistake is eventually realized, they might resort to the delayed remedies of amnesty or pardons. This was the case in Virginia where four sailors who were bullied into confessing to rape and murder were pardoned nearly 20 years after their conviction.[180] In such cases, amnesty is a delayed, albeit corrective measure, to compensate for the earlier denial of more appropriate remedies, such as evidence exclusion. Certainly, it is better that a remedy be granted late than not at all, though it poses problems similar to those of sentence reductions. If the conviction is based on evidence rendered unreliable due to misconduct, it offers no alternative to remedies granted prior to conviction and, therefore, does not prevent miscarriages of justice. Furthermore, it is not compatible with international case law where torture or severe breaches of a right to a fair trial have occurred. In cases where a defendant was guilty, it also leads to problems of commodification and enforcement, and interferes with sentencing goals.[181]

3.6 Case Dismissals

If a violation of procedure is severe, for instance in a case where torture has been used to gather information, the question arises as to whether such an abuse vitiates a

[175] I.e. the problem of incommensurability, *see* Starr, 2009 at 1539 et seq. with counter arguments, inter alia that "liberty is the currency of the criminal law".

[176] Estreicher/Weick, 2010 at 965.

[177] Starr, 2009 at 1542 with counter arguments, inter alia the proposal of fixing sentence reduction in statutory law.

[178] Caldwell/Chase, 1994 at 72; Starr, 2009 at 1562 with further references.

[179] ECtHR, *Furcht* v. *Germany*, case no. 54648/09, Judgment of 23 October 2014 at § 70.

[180] <https://www.nytimes.com/2017/03/21/us/norfolk-four-sailors-rape-murder-mcauliffe.html>, accessed 21 November 2018.

[181] *See* above 3.4.2.

criminal proceeding in such a way that it must be dismissed.[182] German courts have rejected this proposition, arguing that a dismissal of the case infringes upon the protection of third parties. Moreover, dismissal and the failure to allocate satisfactory sentences jeopardize the important constitutional interest in prosecuting, convicting, and punishing criminal offenders.[183]

3.7 Interim Conclusion

There are no alternatives to exclusionary rules that are free from shortcomings. However, until the alternatives are tested in practice and data on their impact is available, it is impossible to definitively predict their outcome.[184] It may be worthwhile to experiment with some alternatives to determine whether they are better at ensuring compliance with procedural laws and protecting overriding interests, especially individual rights. The most effective way to find this out would be to suspend the operation of exclusionary rules and to replace them with various alternatives in randomly selected jurisdictions. However, it seems more appropriate to experiment with different alternatives as mere *supplements* to the exclusionary rule and to see how they work in practice.[185] Another suggestion might be to allow law enforcement agencies to operate free of the exclusionary rule in certain areas (e.g., illegal searches and seizures) under the condition that they implement a set of alternatives to deter police misconduct that are regularly reviewed by the courts.[186] Notably, some measures discussed in section C do not require the admission of evidence. Such measures can and should be *combined* with exclusionary rules (or an alternative) in order to achieve the best possible degree of prevention and compensation.

Real alternatives offering consequences other than the exclusion of evidence, such as sentence reductions, might be particularly helpful as supplementary measures. This could be the case where evidence exclusion does not apply, for example, because the police misconduct is minimal, the defendant is innocent, or the obtained evidence was not crucial for the conviction. It is important that such misconduct

---

[182]For an overview and discussion, *see* Julius/Schmidt in Gercke et al., 2019 at § 206a notes 8 et seq.

[183]The Federal Constitutional Court has held this interest to be part of the principle of *Rechtsstaatlichkeit* (a state based on the rule of law); *see* e.g. BVerfG, Decision of 15 January 2009 - 2 BvR 2044/07 (= BVerfGE 122, 248, 273); BVerfG, Judgement of 19 March 2013 – 2 BvR 2628/10, 2 BvR 2883/10, 2 BvR 2155/11 (=BVerfGE 133, 168, 200–201); BVerfG, Decision of 18 December 2014 - 2 BvR 209/14, 2 BvR 240/14, 2 BvR 262/14 (=StV 2015, 413, 415) as well as BGH, Judgement of 18 November 1999 - 1 StR 221/99 (=BGHSt 45, 321, 333–334); BGH, Judgement of 11 December 2013 - 5 StR 240/13 (=NStZ 2014, 277, 280).

[184]Geller, 1975 at 665.

[185]Geller, 1975 at 689 et seq. and 722; Kamisar, 2003 at 139 et seq.

[186]Estreicher/Weick, 2010 at 951 et seq. and 960 et seq.; similar proposal in: Wilkey, 1982 at 538 et seq.

does not go without consequence. Such a complementary system appears to be the best possible deterrent for misconduct without generally leading to the acquittal of guilty defendants.

4 Conclusion

Exclusionary rules have been invoked to solve the dilemma of how the law can address infringements upon procedural rights in criminal investigations, even if at the expense of comprehensive investigation. The various contributions to this volume have shown that exclusionary rules can be designed in a way that helps safeguard individual rights in all systems. However, the goal of protecting individual rights with such rules appears to be achieved best in adversarial systems compared to inquisitorial models outside the Western world.

Ultimately, one of the findings of this research project is that there is no "one size fits all" toolkit for all jurisdictions as the measures must be tailored to fit into each respective system. The exclusion of certain information, for instance, has to be administered differently in adversarial proceedings than it would be in an inquisitorial system. Furthermore, in all systems problems arise that are inherent to evidence exclusion, namely that a court must decide and explain why it will exclude a certain piece of evidence and, thereby restrict the relevant information under its consideration. Due to these problems, some scholars have abandoned the idea of exclusionary rules as an efficient remedy and are in search of alternatives.[187] A thorough analysis of these alternatives reveals some potentially severe downsides. A single "ideal" alternative has not be found, likely in part due to the fact that exclusionary rules have many purposes, some of which are conflicting.[188] However, the inefficiency and other imperfections of exclusionary rules should not take away from their advantages. A rule with imperfections and gaps, but also clear advantages, should be supplemented rather than abandoned.[189] In this context, the solution might be a comprehensive system of (1) several possibilities (including well-drafted exclusionary rules) and (2) a set of complementary measures to enhance the achievement of the various purposes of exclusionary rules. Courts could be empowered to choose the consequence for violations of procedural rules that fits best, as it is already the case in the Netherlands.[190]

Finally, it should be realized that the function of exclusionary rules might simply be to serve as illusionary giants or "paper tigers" (徒负虚名 [tu fu xu ming]), something that motivates law enforcement to play by the rules because of the

[187]For instance, the detailed and manifold considerations in Geller, 1975 at 689 et seq.; Greco, 2018 at 507.

[188]*See* above 1.1.

[189]Geller, 1975 at 669.

[190]Section 359a of the Dutch Code of Criminal Procedure; *see* above 3.4. in footnote 156.

potential threat of serious consequences. Such rules, even if they remain somewhat obscure, retain the vital practical function of deterring legal authorities from abusing their power.

References

Books

Kühne, Hans-Heiner, *Strafprozessrecht* 9th ed., Heidelberg 2015. [Kühne, 2015]

Oberholzer, Niklaus, *Grundzüge des Strafprozessrechts* 3rd ed., Bern 2012. [Oberholzer, 2012]

Roxin/Schünemann, *Strafverfahrensrecht* 29th ed., München 2017. [Roxin/Schünemann, 2017]

Schlauri, Regula, *Das Verbot des Selbstbelastungszwangs im Strafverfahren: Konkretisierung eines Grundrechts durch Rechtsvergleichung*, Zürich 2003. [Schlauri, 2003]

Summers/Jackson, *The Internationalisation of Criminal Evidence: Beyond the Common Law and Civil Law Traditions*, Cambridge 2012. [Summers/Jackson, 2012]

Journal Articles

Amar, Akhil Reed, 'Fourth Amendment First Principles', (1994) 107 *Harvard Law Review*, 757–819. [Amar, 1994]

Bick, Oren, 'Remedial Sentence Reduction: A Restrictive Rule for an Effective Charter Remedy', (2006) 51 *Criminal Law Quarterly*, 199–237. [Bick, 2006]

Calabresi, Guido, The Exclusionary Rule, (2003) 26 *Harvard Journal of Law & Public Policy*, 111–118. [Calabresi, 2003]

Caldwell, Harry M./Chase, Carol A., 'The Unruly Exclusionary Rule: Heeding Justice Blackmun's Call to Examine the Rule in Light of Changing Judicial Understanding about Its Effects outside the Courtroom', (1994) 78 *Marquette Law Review*, 45–78. [Caldwell/Chase, 1994]

Erb, Volker, 'Beweisverwertungsverbote zum Nachteil des Beschuldigten? Bemerkungen zu einem rechtsstaatlich gefährlichen Irrweg', (2017) 164 *Goltdammer's Archiv für Strafrecht*, 114–129. [Erb, 2017]

Estreicher, Samuel/Weick, Daniel, 'Opting for a Legislative Alternative to the Fourth Amendment Exclusionary Rule', (2010) 78 *University of Missouri-Kansas City Law Review*, 949–966. [Estreicher/Weick, 2010]

Geller, William, 'Enforcing the Fourth Amendment: The Exclusionary Rule and Its Alternatives', (1975) 3 *Washington University Law Review*, 623–722. [Geller, 1975]

Giannoulopoulos, Dimitrios, 'The Exclusion of Improperly Obtained Evidence in Greece: Putting Constitutional Rights First', (2007) 11 *International Journal of Evidence & Proof*, 181–212. [Giannoulopoulos, 2007]

Greco, Luís, 'Warum gerade Beweisverbot? Ketzerische Bemerkungen zur Figur des Beweisverwertungsverbots', in: Ulrich Stein et al. (eds.), Systematik in Strafrechtswissenschaft und Gesetzgebung. Festschrift für Klaus Rogall zum 70. Geburtstag, 585–515. [Greco, 2018]

Hilton, Alicia M., 'Alternatives to the Exclusionary Rule after Hudson v. Michigan: Preventing and Remedying Police Misconduct', (2008) 53 *Villanova Law Review*, 47–82. [Hilton, 2008]

Ho, Hock Lai, 'The Criminal Trial, the Rule of Law and the Exclusion of Unlawfully Obtained Evidence', (2014) 10 *Criminal Law and Philosophy*, 109–131. [Ho, 2014]

Jacobi, Tonja, 'The Law and Economics of the Exclusionary Rule', (2011) 87 *Notre Dame Law Review*, 101–186. [Jacobi, 2011]

Kafka, Michael T., 'The Exclusionary Rule: An Alternative Perspective', (2001) 27 *William Mitchell Law Review*, 1895–1939 [Kafka, 2001]

Kamisar, Yale, 'In Defense of the Search and Seizure Exclusionary Rule (Law and Truth – The Twenty-First Annual National Student Federalist Society Symposium on Law and Public Policy – 2002)', (2003) 26 *Harvard Jounal of Law & Public Policy*, 119–140. [Kamisar, 2003]

Oaks, Dallin H., 'Studying the Exclusionary Rule in Search and Seizure', (1970) 37 *University of Chicago Law Review*, 665–757. [Oaks, 1970]

Orfield, Jr., Myron W./Orfield, Jyron W., 'The Exclusionary Rule and Deterrence: An Empirical Study of Chicago Police Narcotics Officers', (1987) 54 *University of Chicago Law Review*, 1016–1069. [Orfield, 1987]

Orfield, Myron W., 'Deterrence, Perjury, and the Heater Factor: An Exclusioanry Rule in the Chicago Criminal Courts', (1992) 63 *University of Colorado Law Review*, 75–162. [Orfield, 1992]

Ormerod, David/Birch, Diane, 'The Evolution of the Discretionary Exclusion of Evidence', (2004) Supp *Criminal Law Review* (50th Anniversary Edition), 138–159. [Ormerod/Birch, 2004]

Pakter, Walter, 'Exclusionary Rules in France, Germany, and Italy', (1985) 9 *Hastings International and Comparative Law Review*, 1–58. [Pakter, 1985]

Pattenden, Rosemary, 'Admissibility in Criminal Proceedings of Third Party and Real Evidence Obtained by Methods Prohibited by UNCAT', (2006) 10 *International Journal of Evidence & Proof*, 1–41. [Pattenden, 2006]

Roberts, Paul/Hunter, Jill, 'Criminal Evidence and Human Rights: Reimaging Common Law Procedural Traditions', (2013) 2 *Criminal Law Review*, 176–179. [Roberts/Hunter, 2013]

Ruckstuhl, Niklaus, 'Rechtswidrige Beweise erlaubt', (2006) 23 *plädoyer*, 15–22. [Ruckstuhl, 2006]

Rychlak, Ronald J., 'Replacing the Exclusionary Rule: Fourth Amendment Violations as Direct Criminal Contempt', (2010) 85 *Chicago-Kent Law Review*, 241–254. [Rychlak, 2010]

Shereshevsky, Yahli, 'Monetary Compensation as a Remedy for Fair Trial Violations Under International Criminal Law', (2015) 18 *New Criminal Law Review*, 71–99. [Shereshevsky, 2015]

Sklansky, David Alan, 'Is the Exclusionary Rule Obsolete?', (2008) 5 *Ohio State Journal of Criminal Law*, 567–584. [Sklansky, 2008]

Slobogin, Christopher, 'The Exclusionary Rule: Is It on Its Way Out? Should It Be?', (2013) *10 Ohio State Journal of Criminal Law*, 341–355. [Slobogin, 2013]

Slobogin, Christopher, 'Why Liberals Should Chuck the Exclusionary Rule', (1999) 1999 *University of Illinois Law Review*, 363–446. [Slobogin, 1999]

Solomon Jr, Peter H., 'Authoritarian Legality and Informal Practices: Judges, Lawyers and the State in Russia and China', (2010) 43 *Communist and Post-Communist Studies*, 351–362. [Solomon, 2010]

Starr, Sonja B., 'Sentence Reduction as a Remedy for Prosecutorial Misconduct', (2009) 97 *The Georgetown Law Journal*, 1509–1566. [Starr, 2009]

Summers, Sarah/Studer, David, 'Fairness im Strafverfahren? Eine empirische Untersuchung', (2016) 134 *Schweizerische Zeitschrift für Strafrecht*, 45–72. [Summers/Studer, 2016]

Taslitz, Andrew E., 'Hypocrisy, Corruption, and Illegitimacy: Why Judicial Integrity Justifies the Exclusionary Rule', (2013) 10 *Ohio State Journal of Criminal Law*, 419–474 [Taslitz, 2013]

Thelle, Hatla, 'Torture in China', (2006) 16 *Torture*, 268–275. [Thelle, 2006]

Thommen, Marc/Samadi, Mojan, 'The Bigger the Crime, the Smaller the Chance of a Fair Trial? Evidence Exclusion in Serious Crime Cases Under Swiss, Dutch and European Human Rights Law', (2016) 24 *European Journal of Crime, Criminal Law and Criminal Justice*, 65–86. [Thommen/Samadi, 2016]

Turner, Jenia Iontcheva, 'The Exclusionary Rule as a Symbol of the Rule of Law', (2014) 67 *SMU Law Review*, 101–126. [Turner, 2014]

Vetterli, Luzia, 'Kehrtwende in der bundesgerichtlichen Praxis zu den Verwertungsverboten', (2012) 130 *Schweizerische Zeitschrift für Strafrecht*, 447–70. [Vetterli, 2012]

Webster, Aloysius T., 'Protecting Society's Rights while Preserving Forth Amendment Protections: an Alternative to the Exclusionary Rule', (1982) 23 *South Texas Law Journal*, 693–718. [Webster, 1982]

Wilkey, Malcolm R., 'Constitutional Alternatives to the Exclusionary Rule', (1982) 23 *South Texas Law Journal*, 531–557. [Wilkey, 1982]

Wohlers, Wolfgang/Bläsi, Linda, 'Dogmatik und praktische Relevanz der Beweisverwertungsverbote im Strafprozessrecht der Schweiz' (2015) 134 *recht*, 158–75. [Wohlers/Bläsi, 2015]

Contributions to Edited Volumes and Annotated Law

Eser, Albin, 'Adversatorische und inquisitorische Verfahrensmodelle. Ein kritischer Vergleich mit Strukturalternativen', in: Schroeder, Friedrich-Christian, Kudtratov, Manuchehr (eds.): *Die strafprozessuale Hauptverhandlung zwischen inquisitorischem und adversatorischem Modell: eine rechtsvergleichende Analyse am Beispiel des deutschen und des zentralasiatischen Strafprozessrechts*, Frankfurt am Main, 2014, 11–29. [Eser, 2014]

Gercke, Björn/Julius, Karl-Peter/Temming, Dieter/Zöller, Mark A. (eds.), *Strafprozessordnung. Heidelberger Kommentar* 6th ed., Heidelberg 2019. [Julius/Schmidt in Gercke et al., 2012]

Gless, Sabine/Martin, Jeannine, 'Water Always Finds its Way - Discretion and the Concept of Exclusionary Rules in the Swiss Criminal Procedure Code', in: Hodgson, Jackie/Caianiello, Michele (eds.), *Discretionary Criminal Justice in a Comparative Context*, Durham 2015, 159–184. [Gless/Martin, 2015]

Gless, Sabine, 'Protecting Human Rights through Exclusionary Rules? – Highlights on a Conflict in Criminal Proceedings from a Comparative Perspective', in: Böse/Bohlander/Klip/Lagodny (eds.), *Justice without Borders. Essays in the Honour of Wolfgang Schomburg*, Leiden 2018, 159–179. [Gless, 2018]

Ho, Hock Lai, 'Criminal Justice and the Exclusion of Incriminating Statements in Singapore', in: Gless, Sabine/Richter, Thomas (eds.), *Do Exclusionary Rules Ensure a Fair Trial? A Comparative Perspective on Evidentiary Rules*, Cham 2019, 213–252. [Ho, 2019a]

Ho, Hock Lai, 'The Fair Trial Rationale for Excluding Wrongfully Obtained Evidence', in: Gless, Sabine/Richter, Thomas (eds.), *Do Exclusionary Rules Ensure a Fair Trial? A Comparative Perspective on Evidentiary Rules*, Cham 2019, 283–305. [Ho, 2019b]

Jiang, Na , 'The Potential to Secure a Fair Trial Through Evidence Exclusion: A Chinese Perspective', in: Gless, Sabine/Richter, Thomas (eds.), *Do Exclusionary Rules Ensure a Fair Trial? A Comparative Perspective on Evidentiary Rules*, Cham 2019, 163–211. [Jiang, 2019]

Knickmeier, Susanne, 'Securing a Fair Trial Through Exclusionary Rules: Do Theory and Practice Form a Well-Balanced Whole?', in: Gless, Sabine/Richter, Thomas (eds.), *Do Exclusionary Rules Ensure a Fair Trial? A Comparative Perspective on Evidentiary Rules*, Cham 2019, 329–347 [Knickmeier, 2019]

Lin, Yu-Hsiung et al., 'The Potential to Secure a Fair Tiral Through Evidence Exclusion: A Taiwanese Perspective', in: Gless, Sabine/Richter, Thomas (eds.), *Do Exclusionary Rules Ensure a Fair Trial? A Comparative Perspective on Evidentiary Rules*, Cham 2019, 131–161. [Lin et al., 2019]

Löwe, Ewald/Rosenberg, Werner (eds.), *Die Strafprozessordnung und das Gerichtsverfassungsgesetz: StPO Band 4: §§ 112–150* 26th ed., Berlin 2007. [Gless in Löwe/Rosenberg, 2007]

Macula, Laura, 'The Potential to Secure a Fair Tiral Through Evidence Exclusion: A Swiss Perspective', in: Gless, Sabine/Richter, Thomas (eds.), *Do Exclusionary Rules Ensure a Fair Trial? A Comparative Perspective on Evidentiary Rules*, Cham 2019, 15–60. [Macula, 2019]

Niggli, Marcel Alexander/Heer, Marianne/Wiprächtiger, Hans (eds.), *Basler Kommentar. Schweizerische Strafprozessordnung/Jugendstrafprozessordnung (StPO/JStPO)* 2nd ed., Basel 2014. [Gless in Niggli et al., 2014]

Thaman, Stephen C., 'Chapter 17. Balancing Truth Against Human Rights: A Theory of Modern Exclusionary Rules', in: Thaman, Stephen C. (ed.), *Exclusionary Rules in Comparative Law, Ius Gentium: Comparative Perspectives on Law and Justice, vol. 20*, Dordrecht 2013, 403–446. [Thaman, 2013]

Turner, Jenia I./Weigend, Thomas, 'The Purposes and Functions of Exclusionary Rules: A Comparative Overview', in: Gless, Sabine/Richter, Thomas (eds.), *Do Exclusionary Rules Ensure a Fair Trial? A Comparative Perspective on Evidentiary Rules*, Cham 2019, 255–282 [Turner/Weigend, 2019]

Turner, Jenia I., 'Regulating Interrogations and Excluding Confessions in the United States: Balancing Individual Rights and the Search for the Truth', in: Gless, Sabine/Richter, Thomas (eds.), *Do Exclusionary Rules Ensure a Fair Trial? A Comparative Perspective on Evidentiary Rules*, Cham 2019, 93–129. [Turner, 2019]

Weigend, Thomas , 'The Potential to Secure a Fair Trial Through Evidence Exclusion: A German Perspective', in: Gless, Sabine/Richter, Thomas (eds.), *Do Exclusionary Rules Ensure a Fair Trial? A Comparative Perspective on Evidentiary Rules*, Cham 2019, 61–92. [Weigend, 2019]

Wohlers, Wolfgang, 'Verwertungs-, Verwendungs- und/oder Belastungsverbote – die Rechtsfolgenseite der Lehre von den Beweisverwertungsverboten', in: Herzog, Felix/ Schlothauer, Reinhold/Wohlers, Wolfgang (eds.), *Rechtsstaatlicher Strafprozess und Bürgerrechte. Gedächtnisschrift für Edda Weßlau*, Berlin 2016, 427–444. [Wohlers, 2016]

Zuo, Weimin/Lan, Rongjie, 'Exclusionary Rule of Illegal Evidence in China: Observation from Historical and Empirical Perspectives', in: Gless, Sabine/Richter, Thomas (eds.), *Do Exclusionary Rules Ensure a Fair Trial? A Comparative Perspective on Evidentiary Rules*, Cham 2019, 307–328. [Zuo/Lan, 2019]

Sabine Gless teaches criminal law, criminal procedure, and international criminal law at the University of Basel, Switzerland. Her research includes comparative work in evidence law and international cooperation with a focus on human rights issues and exclusionary rules.

Laura Macula holds a Master's degree in law (summa cum laude). Her master's thesis discusses possible conflicts between the right against self-incrimination and information duties under the Swiss financial market regulation. It was published in 2016. Her doctoral theses analyzes exclusionary rules from a comparative perspective with a particular focus on the exclusion of exonerating evidence.

The manufacturer's authorised representative in the EU is Springer Nature Customer Service Centre GmbH, Europaplatz 3, 69115 Heidelberg, Germany. If you have any concerns regarding our products, please contact ProductSafety@springernature.com

Printed and bound by CPI Group (UK) Ltd, Croydon, CR0 4YY
22/09/2026
02221048-0003